Soldiers and Civilians

The BCSIA Studies in International Security book series is edited at the Belfer Center for Science and International Affairs at Harvard University's John F. Kennedy School of Government and published by The MIT Press. The series presents books on contemporary issues in international security policy, as well as their conceptual and historical foundations. Topics of particular interest to the series include the spread of weapons of mass destruction, internal conflict, the international effects of democracy and democratization, and U.S. defense policy.

A complete list of BCSIA Studies appears at the back of this volume.

Soldiers and Civilians

The Civil-Military Gap and American National Security

Peter D. Feaver and Richard H. Kohn, editors

BCSIA Studies in International Security

Triangle Institute for Security Studies

MIT Press
Cambridge, Massachusetts
London, England

Library of Congress Cataloging-in-Publication Data

Soldiers and civilians : the civil-military gap and American national security
/ edited by Peter D. Feaver and Richard H. Kohn.
p.   cm. — (BCSIA studies in international security)
Includes bibliographical references and index.
ISBN 0-262-06223-2 (hc. : alk. paper) — ISBN 0-262-56142-5 (pbk. : alk. paper)
1. Civil-military relations — United States. 2. National security — United
States. 3. Militarism — United States. 4. Public opinion — United States.
5. Sociology, Military — United States. I. Feaver, Peter. II. Kohn, Richard H.
III. Series.
UA23 .S5269   2001
306.2'7'0973 — dc21   2001042558

Cover graphic designed by Jared Bishop. Cover photographs clockwise from
upper left: "Drill Sergeant Reprimanding a Navy Recruit,"
© www.corbis.com. "President Bill Clinton Shakes Hands with Soldiers at
the Tuzla Air Field, Bosnia-Herzegovina," Department of Defense photo by
Spc. Richard L. Branham, U.S. Army. "Franklin D. Roosevelt, General
Marshall, and General Patton in Casablanca," courtesy of the Franklin D.
Roosevelt Library Digital Archives. "Drop Acid Not Bombs," © Robert
Altman, used with permission. "President Abraham Lincoln with Allan
Pinkerton and Major General John A. McClernand at Antietam," Library of
Congress, Prints and Photographs Division, LC-B8171-7949 DLC.

Printed in the United States of America

Contents

Acknowledgments

Any work of this magnitude incurs debts that can never be repaid, to a large and varied group of people without whom the work would not have succeeded. First we owe our appreciation to the Smith Richardson Foundation, in particular Marin Strmecki and Nadia Schadlow, for their encouragement and support, and to the Board of the Foundation for expressing such interest in our work. The Robert R. McCormick Tribune Foundation and the National Strategy Forum, especially Richard Behrenhausen and Richard Friedman, also supported our efforts at a crucial point. Michael Noonan ably edited the conference proceedings which contributed to our outreach effort.

Our two universities, Duke and the University of North Carolina at Chapel Hill, provided grant support and office space and in innumerable ways eased our work. Keith Lawrence of the Duke News Service and David Williamson of UNC's News Services Office advised us on press relations and helped craft a strategy to maximize the dissemination of our results.

The staffs of the Project on the Gap Between the Military and Civilian Society and of the Triangle Institute for Security Studies were indispensable to the collection and interpretation of our data, to outreach, and to the management of the studies—indeed to all the myriad details involved in a sprawling team effort. We thank Lindsay Cohn, Catherine Hart, Carrie Liken, Anna Levinsohn, Ruby Potts, Kuba Stolarski, and Christine Young, and hope that in future projects we will always have staff as creative and hardworking as they have been.

Carolyn Pumphrey, TISS's Coordinator, organized our conferences, collected survey responses, and in many other ways aided our efforts. Jackie Gorman, of the Curriculum in Peace, War, and Defense of the University of North Carolina at Chapel Hill, ably oversaw TISS finances and connected the two universities' often disparate accounting systems. Rye

Barcott helped immeasurably by assisting in the preparations for the authors' conference in July 1999 and then reporting on it.

We are very grateful to Ole Holsti, who served as TISS Survey Director. We relied heavily on his 25 years of experience conducting surveys. The project simply could not have been done without his guidance, administration, and willingness to push the survey forward. We also depended greatly upon Janet Newcity, our survey coordinator, who saved the day more times than we can count. We are very much in her debt.

We are grateful we have had the opportunity to work with such a splendid, cooperative, and intelligent group of authors as those whose work appears in this book and related publications of the project. Each of these busy scholars produced first-rate scholarship and prepared their results for publication with good cheer, and a willingness to meet exacting deadlines. Many of these authors are featured in this book, but we want to acknowledge those whose work for our project is published not in this book but elsewhere: Cori Dauber, Christopher Gelpi, Howard Harper, Felisa Lewis, David Paletz, Robert A. Priest, Don M. Snider, Judith Stiehm, and Krista Wiegand.

We thank our Advisory Panel: Robert Art, Deborah Avant, Andrew C. Bacevich, Archie Barrett, Richard Betts, Stephen Biddle, John Brehm, Charles F. Brower, Alexander S. Cochran, Charles J. Dunlap, Robert L. Goldich, John Hillen, Samuel P. Huntington, Charles Moskos, Allan R. Millett, Williamson Murray, Thomas E. Ricks, Alex Roland, Scott Silliman, Glenn Snyder, Bernard Trainor, Walter F. Ulmer, and the late Adam Yarmolinsky. They rendered indispensable service: they participated in our conferences to critique our work, debated the issues with us, helped us formulate our questionnaire, and helped us think through the basic concepts of the project. We owe a special debt in this regard to Joseph Collins and Walter Ulmer of the Center for Strategic and International Studies who, in connection with their related project, "American Military Culture in the 21st Century," shared results, critiqued our work, attended numerous meetings and conferences, and supported our efforts even when they did not agree with our interpretations. We also thank Hein Goemans, Catherine Lutz, Madeline Morris, Thad Moyseowicz, Mark Padgett, James Seaton, Rob Sikorski, and Russell Van Wyk for participating in our framing conference in February 1998; Milton H. Hamilton, James Lindsay, Bruce Jentleson, and Macubin Owens, who participated in our July 1999 conference; and Charles Boyd, Joseph Collins, Stephen M. Duncan, Senator Gary Hart, Thomas Keaney, James Kitfield, Steve Komarov, Edward C. Meyer, Stephen Lee Myers, Rick Newman, Michael Noonan, John Sirek, William D. Smith, Richard Sobel, Jim Sutherland, and George Wilson for participating in the "Conference on the Military and Civilian Society" held at Cantigny in Wheaton, Illinois, in October 1999 and offering their critiques of the papers.

We also thank Department of Defense and Armed Forces people who helped formulate our questionnaire, advised us on access to our officer sample, and permitted us to survey their students. We owe a debt of gratitude in that regard to the Presidents and Commandants of the Army and Naval War Colleges, the Command and General Staff College at Fort Leavenworth, the Chief of Naval Education and Training, and the Commander of U.S. Army Cadet Command. Special mention is due Lieutenant General Richard Chilcoat, former president of the National Defense University, for supporting our effort and permitting us to survey his students, and Colonel Bryant Shaw, director of academic affairs at NDU. We thank Lieutenant General Tad J. Oelstrom, then Superintendent of the Air Force Academy, who early in the project permitted us to survey the senior class, which aided greatly in our efforts to secure the agreement of other school commandants and presidents. Lieutenant General Joseph J. Redden of the Air University was also supportive. We are extremely grateful to other heads of schools and their staffs who facilitated our work: the United States Military Academy, West Point; Captain James Boyer of Rice University; Captain Patrick Casey of Notre Dame; Captain Daniel Gabriel of the University of Virginia; Captain Marc Goldberg of Pennsylvania State University; Captain Douglas B. Guthe of the University of North Carolina at Chapel Hill, Duke University, and North Carolina State University; Captain Michael J. Kehoe of Cornell University; Captain George Schaeffer of the University of Kansas; Captain Joel Weber of Purdue University; Lieutenant Colonel Charles Lynch of the University of Connecticut and Yale University; Lieutenant Colonel Kevin L. Kelly of the University of Massachusetts; Lieutenant Colonel John C. Dean of the University of Virginia; Lieutenant Colonel Julie A. Hermann of the University of Houston and Rice University; Lieutenant Colonel John M. Keefe of Cornell University; Lieutenant Colonel Robert W. Wolfenden of Lehigh University; Lieutenant Colonel Donald Denmark of the University of Kansas; Lieutenant Colonel Michael C. Berendt of Purdue; Lieutenant Colonel Wallace Thompson of Tulane University; Lieutenant Colonel Harold Burns of Washington University; Lieutenant Colonel Raymond M. Lambert of Xavier University; Lieutenant Colonel Anthony Rojek of the Rose Hulman Institute of Technology; Lieutenant Colonel Michael Edwards of Notre Dame; Lieutenant Colonel Jerry R. Bolzak, Jr., of Princeton University; Lieutenant Colonel Paul R. Plemmons of Duke University; Lieutenant Colonel James B. Rhoads of the University of North Carolina at Chapel Hill; Lieutenant Colonel David Cannon of North Carolina State University; Lieutenant Colonel Arnold L. Leonard, Jr., of the College of William and Mary; and Lieutenant Colonel William E. Haner, Jr., of Pennsylvania State University.

We are especially grateful to Eliot Cohen, Thomas Keaney, and Courtney Mata of the Paul H. Nitze School of Advanced International Studies, Johns Hopkins University, for hosting our outreach effort in Washington in early 2000. Their care and attention to detail, and their effectiveness in promoting the results of our work, were most helpful. We very much appreciate the candid responses of those who attended the sessions, and the private briefings for busy officials, scholars, and national security experts who made the effort to hear our results and to give us the benefit of their wise counsel. We especially thank Representative Ike Skelton and Representative Steve Buyer, Admiral William Crowe, Deputy Secretary of Defense Rudy DeLeon, Undersecretary of Defense Bernard Rostker, Secretary of the Air Force F. Whitten Peters, General Richard B. Myers, General Eric Shinseki, General James Jones, and Assistant Secretary of State Morton Halperin.

We are grateful to our editor, Sean Lynn-Jones, and the publishing team of the Belfer Center for Science and International Affairs. We also thank our consulting editor, Teresa Lawson, who improved our work and that of our authors, and harmonized the disparate styles of so many contributors. We are also grateful to Karen Motley for shepherding the manuscript through the final stages and ensuring that we met our deadlines. And we thank Ole Holsti for shouldering the herculean task of doing the index for the book under extraordinarily tight time constraints.

Last, and perhaps most important, we thank the numerous officers and civilians who took the time and care to respond to our survey and thus help us understand the nature and extent of the gap.

Peter D. Feaver
Durham, N.C.

Richard H. Kohn
Chapel Hill, N.C.

Introduction

The Gap Between Military and Civilian in the United States in Perspective

Peter D. Feaver
Richard H. Kohn
Lindsay P. Cohn

In a 1997 speech at Yale University, Secretary of Defense William Cohen raised the possibility of "a chasm . . . developing between the military and civilian worlds, where the civilian world doesn't fully grasp the mission of the military, and the military doesn't understand why the memories of our citizens and civilian policy-makers are so short, or why the criticism is so quick and so unrelenting" (Cohen 1997).

Cohen voiced an age-old concern about America's relations with its military, one that has been renewed recently by many observers and policymakers. They express the fear that, without a manifestly urgent threat to the nation's security, a democratic society will not nurture and support an adequate military, or that the military might diminish in its loyalty to democratic values and to its civilian bosses.

The issue has been framed as "cultural." The concern is that a "gap" in values or attitudes between people in uniform and civilian society may have become so wide that it threatens the effectiveness of the armed forces and civil-military cooperation.

Differences between civilian and military are, of course, necessary and desirable: even in a society based on civil liberty, personal autonomy, and democratic governance, military institutions must subordinate the individual to the group, and personal well-being to mission accomplishment. Members of the military must risk their lives and give up many personal freedoms in order to succeed in battle. But some scholars and commentators have argued that the typical differences are changing into something more ominous. This concern is fueled by anecdotal reports of military contempt for civilian culture, accounts of civilian hostility to the traditional martial values, and evidence from the inexorable demographic trends showing fewer and fewer personal connections with the military as it contracts.

Concerns about a troublesome "gap" are hardly new, as several chapters in this book explain.[1] The framers of the Constitution divided control over the military between the three branches of government and preserved a separate citizen-soldier militia to insure the civilian control of the military necessary for liberty, and to avoid reliance on a professional military which they knew to be different from, and a threat to, society. Since World War II, there have been at least three distinct waves of literature addressing the nature of the gap, the factors that shape it, the significance for public policy, and the policies necessary to keep civil-military differences from harming national security.

The first wave, which started soon after World War II and ran through the end of conscription in 1973, was marked by a classic debate between Samuel P. Huntington and Morris Janowitz. Huntington's 1957 book, *The Soldier and the State,* explicitly attempted to reconcile American society's traditional hostility to the military and Cold War America's need for a massive standing military establishment to deter the Soviet Union (Huntington 1957). Huntington argued that the civil-military gap was an ideological divide between a generally conservative officer corps and a liberal and individualistic civilian society. The size of the gap would change in response to fluctuations in the level of the external threat to the nation (and so the need for a large standing army). It would also be affected by civilian leaders' efforts to remake the military in a civilian image; such "fusionist" efforts would be disastrous for military effectiveness, Huntington argued, and he urged that the gap must instead be managed by civilian society tolerating, if not embracing, the conservative values that animate military culture. Others in Huntington's camp argued that military officers ought to be trained to integrate political concerns into their strategic advice and, reciprocally, that civilian officials ought to be better educated about military culture and technical matters in order to make more appropriate policy decisions.

The sociologist Morris Janowitz accepted some of Huntington's characterization of the nature of the divide, but disagreed with Huntington's assessment of its impact on military effectiveness. Janowitz's 1960 book, *The Professional Soldier,* argued that in a democracy, military culture must

---

1. For a discussion of the literature, see Lindsay Cohn, "The Evolution of the Civil-Military 'Gap' Debate," TISS Project paper, available at <www.poli.duke.edu/civmil>. See also Chapter 5 in this volume by Russell Weigley, "The American Civil-Military Cultural Gap: A Historical Perspective, Colonial Times to the Present."

adapt to changes in civilian society and to the technology of war: the gap is narrowed as the military adjusts to the needs and dictates of its civilian masters (Janowitz 1960). If the gap were allowed to remain too large, Janowitz argued, the military would become unresponsive to civilian control, and civilians would therefore stop providing the support needed to maintain an adequate or effective military posture. Many who agreed with Janowitz's analysis also argued that the civilian government would be unlikely or unable to trust the advice and reporting of a military whose value-system was so markedly different from the civilian mainstream.

The trauma of the Vietnam War renewed public attention to civil-military relations, and a second wave of literature addressed the nature of the gap. Animosity between the military and civilian elites had been aroused by the Vietnam experience. At the same time, service in the military was becoming more like a civilian office job and less like a calling, a development hailed by some and lamented by others. The divisions caused by the war and then the end of the draft were causing demographic changes in the military: it became a self-selecting organization, more divergent from society. The military was forced to compete for "employees" like any other employer. The results that were feared, however, hardly differed from those of the earlier period: that civilian society would be ignorant of and unsympathetic to the military's needs; that the U.S. public would not elect officials with military savvy who could make prudent decisions; that the effectiveness of the military would suffer; and that an isolated military might neglect its obligations to society and turn hostile. Greater funding figured large in many proffered solutions. Others proposed allowing lateral entry into the higher ranks for specialists, emphasizing the study of civics in the military academies, and drawing a greater proportion of officers from the Reserve Officers Training Corps (ROTC) at the nation's colleges and universities, all aimed at ensuring that military officers were less likely to have authoritarian or militaristic leanings. The feminist movement of this period also contributed to the debate, but offered diametrically opposed solutions: either boycott the military altogether, or integrate women fully into every corner of the organization.

The end of the Cold War and the extraordinary changes in U.S. foreign and defense policy in the mid-1990s have given fresh life to the "gap" debate, with distinct echoes of the earlier literature. An influential book by prominent defense correspondent Thomas Ricks (Ricks 1997c) framed the issue as a product of broader culture wars in America. Ricks wrote about the experience of a group of young recruits as they left civilian society, underwent Marine boot camp, and then returned to their homes for a visit. According to Ricks, the new Marines seemed to have developed a strong sense of alienation from civilian society, and Ricks warned that this sense was not merely a boot-camp phenomenon but rather reflected a similar alienation at more influential levels of the officer corps. Ricks's concerns augmented the arguments of other civil-military observers, who wrote of the growing and perhaps overreaching influence of the Joint Chiefs of Staff within policymaking circles (Weigley 1993; Kohn 1994).

Collectively these widely quoted voices revived the old Huntington-Janowitz debate. The intellectual heirs of Janowitz see the all-volunteer military drifting too far away from civilian society, thereby posing problems for civilian control. They make four principal assertions. First, the military has grown increasingly out of step ideologically with the civilian mainstream: it is disproportionately hard-core right-wing politically, and also much more religious (and fundamentalist or evangelical), with a predominant association with the Republican Party (Bacevich and Kohn 1997; Holsti 1998). Second, the military has become more alienated from, disgusted with, and even hostile to civilian society (McIsaac and Verdugo 1995; Ricks 1997d; Maslowski 1990). Third, the military has resisted change, particularly the integration of women and homosexuals and the constabulary missions that have dominated post–Cold War operations (Hutcheson 1996; Kier 1998). Fourth, civilian control and military effectiveness will suffer if the military, by seeking to expand its autonomy and avoid civilian oversight, and by getting out of step with civilian society, loses the respect and support of that society (Danzig 1999).

The heirs of Huntington, in contrast, argue that an unraveling civilian culture has strayed so far from traditional values that it seeks to eradicate healthy and functional civil-military differences, particularly in the areas of gender, sexual orientation, and discipline. They also make four key claims. First, they assert that the military is mainstream, and that its values diverge, rather, from those of a political and cultural elite that is itself not representative of the general public (Webb 1997; 1998; 2000; Hillen 1998a).

Second, they believe that the governing political and social elite are ignorant, uncaring, and hostile to the military. Civilian leaders are eager to use it as a laboratory for social change, even at the cost of crippling the military's ability to win in combat, by attacking the military's "warrior" behaviors and culture (Kitfield 2000; Hillen 1999; Murchison 1999). Third, they discount problems with civilian control in the United States because they see a military so thoroughly inculcated with the principle of subordination that its leaders are excessively deferential to civilian control: micro-management and political correctness stifle the military's ability to function effectively (Sarkesian 1998; Webb 1999). Fourth, because support for the military among the general public is rock-solid, any "values gap" is inconsequential, and the problem is with the governing elite: its Vietnam-era prejudices against the military and its relativist values contrast with the opinions of the general public, which holds the military in high esteem (Maynes 1998). Thus, these scholars and observers draw a sharp contrast between the nature of the gap between the military and elite civilian society on the one hand, and the nature of the gap between the military and mass civilian society on the other.

The debate has been lively (and inside the Beltway sometimes quite acrimonious), but it has heretofore rested on very thin evidence: on dueling anecdotes, assertions, and counter-claims about the nature of civilian and military attitudes. More systematic data was needed on the actual opinions, values, perspectives, and attitudes of the military compared with the civilian elite and the general public. Analysts first turned to existing studies of civilian and military attitudes. For example, the Foreign Policy Leadership Project (FPLP) directed by Ole Holsti and James Rosenau has analyzed opinion data from quadrennial surveys of elites over two decades (1976–96). However, while the FPLP did include a small sub-sample of military officers, the sample was too small to explore differences within the military, and the survey itself was not designed to address the full range of issues raised in the civil-military culture gap debate. No survey of the military had been conducted in parallel with a survey of the civilian population that focused on issues pertinent to an assessment of the "gap." Civilian and military surveys have not asked important questions regarding the civil-military relationship itself, nor has data been gathered that would allow us to explore the attitudes of each group toward the other.

Therefore, the editors of this book organized the "Project on the Gap Between the Military and Civilian Society." The project was sponsored by the Triangle Institute for Security Studies (TISS), a consortium of faculty at Duke University, the University of North Carolina at Chapel Hill, and North Carolina State University who are interested in national and international security broadly defined.

A significant part of the Project was to gather data to help answer four questions. What is the nature or character of the civil-military gap today?[2] What factors shape it? Does the gap matter for military effective-

---

2. Although we adopted the "gap" language because of its popular currency, we never assumed a gap is by nature negative; we expected to find differences across (and within) the groups, largely because of the nature of military institutions and the special demands of the military profession. We did not assume that every difference

ness and civil-military cooperation? What, if anything, can and should policymakers do about the gap? To answer these questions, the TISS project undertook a comprehensive comparison of civilian and military values, opinions, and perspectives. To explore attitudes across a wide segment of civilian and military elites and the mass public, the project completed a broad, in-depth survey of some 4,891 respondents representing three key groups: the general public, influential civilian leaders, and up-and-coming military officers.[3]

The project's survey instrument was designed to generate data that would be comparable to data obtained by earlier surveys of attitudes about foreign and domestic policy.[4] The survey sought responses to some 250 questions covering a range of issues: from the respondent's social and religious values to views on national security policy, and from military professionalism to the civil-military relationship itself. (The survey instrument is presented in the Technical Appendix to this book.) Between fall 1998 and spring 1999, the survey instrument was mailed to civilian leaders and administered to military officers.

To reach the group that our studies refer to as "civilian elite" or "civilian leaders," we followed procedures developed by Ole Holsti and James Rosenau in the Foreign Policy Leadership Project (FPLP) (Holsti 1996, 129–190). To achieve a broad, comprehensive sample, eight subsamples were chosen to receive the survey.[5] Our elite civilian sample generated 989 responses out of 3,435 requested.

We sought to reach a comparable group of military officers, which we refer to as "military elite," "up-and-coming military officers," or "military leaders." We defined this group as "officers whose promise for advancement has been recognized by assignment to attend in residence the professional military education course appropriate for their rank." Thus, our military sample of 2,901 respondents (out of 5,889 surveys sent out) is not meant to be a sample of the entire military, which would include both

---

would cause problems, nor every convergence be beneficial for civil-military cooperation and for military effectiveness.

3. The methods employed in conducting these surveys as well as reports on sub-sample response and sub-sample characteristics are described in greater detail in Janet Newcity (1999) and available at the project website, www.poli.duke.edu/civmil.

4. In addition to drawing on earlier FPLP instruments, our questionnaire also included items that were featured in Vietnam-era analyses of civil-military relations, as reported in Segal (1975), Segal and Blair (1976), and Clotfelter (1969).

5. The eight subsamples are drawn from lists such as "Who's Who in America," and other directories of prominent Americans in the categories of "Clergy," "Women," "American Politics," "State Department," "Media," "Foreign Affairs," and "Labor."

officers and enlisted, nor even of the entire officer corps. The elite military sample is drawn just from among officers who are likely to emerge as leaders and are likely to be promoted. These officers come from the pool of those military leaders that shape the military profession in America and function as the custodians of military culture over time.[6] The sample covers the active and reserve officer corps of the Army, Navy, Air Force, and Marines, at four stages of advancement.[7] For the first category, that of officer candidates before commissioning, we administered the survey at the U.S. Military Academy, the Naval Academy, the Air Force Academy, and at a sample of Army and Navy ROTC units across the country. To reach the staff college level (officers roughly a decade plus into their careers), we surveyed students in the resident courses at the U.S. Army Command and General Staff College and the Naval War College (junior class). For the war college level (officers roughly 17 years into their careers), we surveyed students in the resident courses at the Army War College, the Naval War College, the National War College, and the Industrial College of the Armed Forces. For generals, the so-called "baby flags," or officers at roughly the twenty-five year mark who have been selected for promotion to brigadier general or rear admiral, we surveyed current attendees and recent graduates of the Capstone course at the National Defense University.[8] We also surveyed Army, Navy, Air Force, and Marine Reservists who were at comparable stages of their military ca-

---

6. While the rank and file is somewhat less central to civil-military controversies, it is by no means of trivial concern and has, in fact, received close scrutiny in a parallel study by the Center for Strategic and International Studies, "American Military Culture in the 21st Century" (Washington, D.C.: CSIS, January 2000). See also the discussion in Chapter 4 of this volume by David Segal, et al., which relies upon data drawn from the Monitoring the Future Project, rather than the TISS survey.

7. The TISS sample is somewhat skewed compared to the distribution among the four principal services of the officer corps as a whole. The TISS sample is slightly over-represented with Navy (34 percent of the TISS sample vs. 25 percent of the officer corps) and Army officers (39 percent of the TISS sample vs. 35 percent of the officer corps), and under-represented with Air Force officers (17 percent of the TISS sample vs. 32 percent of the officer corps). This is due to the fact that the Air Force did not allow us to survey Air University students. Neither were we allowed to survey Marine Corps University students; however, our sample of Marine officers corresponds to their numbers in the military establishment (9 percent of the TISS sample, 8 percent of the officer corps). Our Marine and Air Force samples were drawn, instead, from students attending either Army and Navy Staff and War Colleges, or the National Defense University. We have no reason to believe that this feature of the TISS military sample influenced the findings of the project.

8. Capstone is an orientation course of several weeks for new active-duty flag officers and is conducted under the auspices of the National Defense University in Washington, D.C.

reers and who took courses by correspondence from the Army War College, the Naval War College, and the National Defense University.

A shortened version of the survey instrument was also administered by telephone to a representative random national sample of 1,001 members of the general public during September and October 1998.

We broke down our basic questions—what is the nature of the gap, what factors shape it, and what does it matter—into nearly two dozen research questions. For instance, we asked, "How does the civil-military gap affect the management of the military during the use of force?" We commissioned a series of 21 original studies investigating those questions from a variety of disciplinary perspectives, marshaling the efforts of some two dozen experts. They draw upon both the original data generated by the TISS survey and other sources.[9]

In this book, we present twelve of those studies; five others, which address specific factors that shape civil-military relations, have been published separately.[10] Yet another stream of research resulting from the TISS project is being developed into a separate book-length project: a series of analyses by Peter D. Feaver and Christopher Gelpi of the implications of U.S. civil-military opinion gaps for the actual use of force.

The studies presented in this book cluster into three groups of four chapters each. In the first section, we present four comparative analyses of civilian and military opinion, three of which are based primarily on the TISS survey data. The second cluster comprises studies exploring changes in various civil-military gaps over time. The third explores the implications of these gaps for military effectiveness and civil-military cooperation.

Chapter 1 by Ole Holsti introduces the survey data in more detail, and compares the two "elite" groups, military and civilian, across a wide range of issues. This chapter also compares the findings of the 1999 TISS

---

9. Of necessity, we had to narrow the scope of the project in several ways. We focused our investigation on relations between the officer corps and civilian society, and within the officer corps on the four categories described. Other important questions, such as the role of the Reserves in bridging any gap between civilian and military, could only be treated briefly. On many issues, we have collected extensive data that have yet to be analyzed, opening the way to future research and discoveries.

10. See the special issue of *Armed Forces & Society* (Winter 2001): Cori Dauber, "Image as Argument: the Impact of Mogadishu on U.S. Military Intervention"; Howard Harper, "The Military and Society: Reaching and Reflecting Audiences in Fiction and Film"; Don M. Snider, Robert F. Priest, and Felisa Lewis, "The Civilian-Military Gap and Professional Military Education at the Precommissioning Level"; Judith Hicks Stiehm, "Civil-Military Relations in War College Curricula"; and Krista E. Wiegand and David L. Paletz, "The Elite Media and the Military-Civilian Culture Gap."

survey to the results of the earlier quadrennial FPLP studies to assess whether civil-military differences have changed over time.

Chapter 2 by James Davis uses the TISS data, as well as other survey data including the annual General Social Survey by the National Opinion Research Center, to compare the military with civilians in the general public.

Chapter 3 by Paul Gronke and Peter Feaver examines whether high levels of professed public confidence in the military are a reliable indicator that there is no alienation in the relationship, using TISS project and other data.

Chapter 4, by David Segal, Peter Freedman-Doan, Jerald Bachman, and Patrick O'Malley, uses data collected for a project called "Monitoring the Future" to compare prospective and junior members of the enlisted military with their corresponding cohort in the general public.[11] This chapter adds an important dimension because it is the only one that looks at the enlisted ranks, and its findings differ from those of some of the analyses of relations between officers and society.

The second group of chapters puts the issue into historical perspective and examines civil-military relations along dimensions other than the attitude and value gaps addressed in the first section. In Chapter 5, Russell Weigley compares the civil-military friction of the 1990s with the historical pattern, finding that periods of tension and conflict have characterized relations between the military and executive branch throughout American history. Generally wars and external threats forced cooperation, explaining in part why the end of the Cold War brought increased antagonism, which Weigley believes will increase in the future.

In Chapter 6, James Burk shows that in the last half-century, the military's moral and material presence in society has been immense, and that while military institutions do differ in practice from others in democracies, the military has successfully adjusted to the great social changes of the era such as racial integration, expanded roles for women, and the increased civil and personal rights of individuals.

In Chapter 7, William Bianco and Jamie Markham demonstrate that the gap between the population and the military has increased in the last quarter-century as indicated by the number of veterans in Congress. Up

---

11. Monitoring the Future is an ongoing study of American youth conducted by the Institute for Social Research at the University of Michigan under a series of grants from the National Institute of Drug Abuse (Bachman, Johnston and O'Malley, 1996). The Monitoring the Future project surveys approximately 17,000 high school seniors on a wide variety of social and political questions in the spring of each year. Follow-up surveys are mailed every two years to sub-samples from each cohort to assess how attitudes change over time.

until 1995, there were always higher percentages of veterans in the Congress than in corresponding age and educational cohorts in the population; this over-representation began to shrink in 1975, and after 1995 there have been fewer veterans as a percentage in the political leadership than in the population as a whole.

In Chapter 8, Michael Desch evaluates alternative explanations for the changing nature of the civil-military gap. Desch argues that among the many causes of the growing civil-military political gap have been: the decline of the mass army; the introduction of the all-volunteer force; the chasm opened in American society by the Vietnam War; and the dramatic shift in the political landscape of the American South.

The Desch chapter relies heavily on TISS and FPLP survey data. The other three chapters rely on other sources: Weigley evaluates the primary and secondary literature in American military history; Burk analyzes a wide range of sociological and economic data about the salience of military institutions in American society; and Bianco and Markham developed their own data on the percentage of military veterans in the U.S. Congress and use U.S. government data on the percentage of military veterans in the population as a whole.

The third cluster of chapters explores implications of the civil-military gap for public policy. In Chapter 9, Benjamin Fordham analyzes whether the civil-military opinion gaps described in earlier chapters have affected defense outlays and support for defense spending over time. He concludes that the impact so far has been minimal when compared with other factors that explain defense support, such as external threat or the party and ideological balances in Congress.

In Chapter 10, Laura Miller and John Allen Williams examine the politically sensitive issue of gender and sexual orientation in the military: whether respondents inside and outside the military believe there is a civil-military gap in this area and, if so, whether and how it influences military effectiveness. They confirm that military service is correlated with more conservative policies on military personnel, while civilian leaders are more likely to believe that the civil rights concerns of women and homosexuals are not at odds with military effectiveness. This chapter also finds compelling evidence on both sides of the debate about whether diversity harms unit cohesion and thus combat effectiveness: although little existing research is actually based on service members serving under the unique circumstances of combat, the social science literature agrees that social integration rarely proceeds without conflict.

In Chapter 11, Peter Roman and David Tarr assess the gap in light of their research into civil-military relations at the highest policymaking levels. They draw on the results of their not-for-attribution interviews with more than 130 of the most senior civilian and military leaders of the past decade and a half. They argue that the gap is minimal at the highest levels of civilian and military interaction. Both sides strive to cooperate and often end up in a sort of fusion, with the military sometimes assuming civilian functions of policy advocacy and decision-making but without the necessary background or experience that would best prepare them for such roles.

In Chapter 12, Eliot Cohen explores civil-military cooperation and military effectiveness in the crucial arena of the management of the military during the actual use of force. He finds that only by close questioning, careful oversight, and on occasion actual intervention by civilians into the technical matters of military affairs can a democratic government wage war effectively.

The TISS project led us to conclude that there are many "gaps," only some of which are troubling. Although it should not be exaggerated, concern is justified: numerous schisms and trends have undermined civil-military cooperation and in some circumstances harmed military effectiveness; they will, if not addressed, continue to do so and with worsening consequences. Therefore, in our conclusion we offer some recommendations to eliminate or mitigate the most troubling problems uncovered by our study.

With several dozen authors and advisors, the project did not produce a single consensus report, and none of the authors can be presumed to endorse every finding. From the perspective of the project as a whole and in the context of all the findings, the project directors do not always agree with every interpretation of the authors, and on some occasions we interpret the authors' data and analyses somewhat differently than do the authors themselves. Collectively, however, some consensus emerged: at present the gap between the military and society in values, attitudes, opinions, and perspectives presents no compelling need to act to avert an immediate emergency. However, there are problems that, if left unaddressed, will undermine civil-military cooperation and hamper military effectiveness. The result might well harm the national security of the United States.

Part I
The Growing Gap

Chapter 1

Of Chasms and Convergences: Attitudes and Beliefs of Civilians and Military Elites at the Start of a New Millennium

Ole R. Holsti

Relations between the military and civilian society have long been a central concern of political scientists, sociologists, and historians, as well as of statesmen, reformers, and many others. As with many other issues of governance, attention to civil military relations has waxed and waned in the United States. The end of conscription a generation ago; the end of the Cold War a decade ago; the emergence of leaders in major political parties who have had no military experience; widespread publicity about sex scandals involving the president, Republican congressional leaders, and high-ranking military officers; and the nature of post–Cold War conflicts are among the developments that have drawn a good deal of attention to relations between the military and American society in recent years. Charges that the Kosovo bombing campaign was initiated by a president who hoped that the public would thereby be induced to forget his sordid sexual behavior added fuel to what has at times been an incendiary debate.

In the July 1997 issue of *Atlantic Monthly* magazine, an article by Thomas E. Ricks on "The Widening Gap Between the Military and Soci-

Although they are absolved from all deficiencies, it is appropriate to acknowledge and thank the following: The Smith-Richardson Foundation for financial support; Paul Gronke for many fruitful discussions about analyzing the TISS data; Deborah Avant, Barbara Bardes, John Brehm, James Lindsay, and Tom Ricks for thoughtful comments on an earlier draft; Janet Newcity for assistance on many aspects of sampling and preparing the data for analysis; Catherine Hart, Ruby Potts, and Anna Levinsohn for general assistance on all phases of the project; Rita Dowling and Anne Marie Boyd for typing (including all the tables) as well as many other kinds of assistance; Carrie Liken, Christy A. Hamilton, and Eddy Malesky for programming assistance; and all those who took the time to complete the TISS survey.

ety" presented some disturbing observations about a growing estrangement between the post–Cold War military and the society that it is trained and pledged to defend (Ricks 1997d). These themes were more fully developed in a book published some month later (Ricks 1997c). Ricks was certainly not the first or only recent critic of the post–Cold War military, but his stature as the distinguished defense reporter for the country's most conservative national newspaper—*The Wall Street Journal*—meant that his observations could not be dismissed. Although the Ricks thesis is not universally accepted—in part because his evidence is largely anecdotal and because it was mostly drawn from a single branch of the service, the Marine Corps—it has served as an important catalyst for the most recent deliberations on the state of civil-military relations, framing the terms of debate on at least one important cluster of issues in recent discussions of the military in the post–Cold War era. It serves as the springboard for the analyses to be undertaken in this chapter.[1]

Debates about the role of the military in American society have a venerable provenance, having engaged the Founding Fathers and many others at various times during the more than two centuries since then.[2] A brief discussion of some important themes emerging from the debates since World War II may be helpful for placing the "gap thesis" in a broader context.[3]

Until 1945 the favorable geographic position of the United States permitted it to demobilize rapidly after each war. The onset of the Cold War almost before the guns of World War II had cooled ensured that the United States would maintain a large military establishment. The unprecedented threats arising from the Cold War and the inception of nuclear weapons heightened concerns about relations between the military and civilian society. They also triggered a flurry of important studies on civilian-military relations, as well as a warning from retiring President Dwight D. Eisenhower on the potential dangers to democratic society of a permanent "military-industrial complex" (Smith 1951; Ekirch 1956; Huntington 1957; Janowitz 1960; Eisenhower 1961). Two major schools of thought about coping with the civilian-military gap emerged from these studies. According to one perspective, associated most closely with Sam-

---

1. After the Ricks publications, *Orbis* devoted much of the Winter 1999 issue to essays on the gap thesis by John Hillen, Williamson Murray, and Don Snider. It has also been discussed in various issues of the *Marine Corps Gazette* by Robert Bracknall, John Coonradt, George Flynn, and James B. Woulfe.

2. See, for example, *Federalist Papers*, numbers 8, 24, 25, 26, and 28 by Alexander Hamilton, and numbers 42 and 46 by James Madison.

3. In addition to books and articles cited below, the journal *Armed Forces & Society* is an indispensable source of relevant studies.

uel Huntington, because military values and ways of thinking were more appropriate for dealing with the external threats of the Cold War, the gap would best be closed by American society moving toward the more conservative values of the military. Military sociologist Morris Janowitz presented an alternative perspective, arguing that the technological requirements of modern warfare should lead toward civilizing the military.[4]

Controversies surrounding the Vietnam War provided the impetus for renewed consideration of the relationship between the military and civilian society. The flood of postmortems on the causes of U.S. failure in Vietnam has only slightly abated, more than a quarter-century after the last evacuation of Americans from Saigon. The wide range of explanations includes some that lay the blame on the civilian leadership for incompetence—or worse—and undue meddling in the conduct of war, as well as others that indict the military leadership for a variety of serious shortcomings (for example, McMaster 1997; Buzzanco 1997).

The end of conscription in 1973 and the disintegration of the Soviet Union in 1991 have given rise to a "third wave" of questions about civilian-military relations. The United States has reverted to an older tradition of an all-volunteer military, but barring some wholly unforeseen and implausible developments, it will remain far larger than it was in previous periods of peace. Other issues have further roiled civil-military relations, including the efforts to avoid military service during the Vietnam War by top political and opinion leaders in Washington such as former President Bill Clinton, former House Speaker Newt Gingrich, Senate Majority Leader Trent Lott, and columnists George Will and Patrick Buchanan; the treatment of women in uniform; a host of widely publicized sex scandals involving both civilian and military leaders;[5] incidents of mutual disrespect between the military and members of the Clinton administration, and policies toward gays and lesbians in uniform.[6]

---

4. For a discussion of the Huntington and Janowitz schools on civil-military relations, see Feaver (1996).

5. The controversy surrounding military sex scandals has not been so much the illicit behavior itself as the widely divergent punishment meted out to enlisted personnel, junior officers, and senior officers. Some enlisted service members were sent to prison for sexual harassment, whereas flag rank officers who engaged in similar conduct received little more than a slap on the wrist. For example, Lieutenant Kelly Flinn was cashiered from the Air Force for having an affair with an enlisted man. In contrast, Major General David Hale had affairs with the wives of four subordinates, all of which resulted in divorces, and was also found guilty of lying about his affairs; he not only escaped prison, he was not even reduced in rank to private E-1. Thus, although Hale lost one star, he continues to enjoy the generous retirement pay and benefits of a brigadier general.

6. See, for example, Rabil (1998), Sellers (1998), and Radatz (1999).

Still another source of controversy centers on potential use of the armed forces to cope with a plethora of domestic problems.[7] The military were deployed to cope with the Los Angeles riots following the Rodney King verdict, in which four white police officers were found not guilty of beating a black motorist, and there have been proposals for using the armed forces to cope with domestic terrorism, drug interdiction, immigration control, and other problems. The role of the military was among the controversies over the 1993 siege of the Branch Davidian compound in Waco, Texas, and the assault that brought the standoff to an end at the cost of some eighty lives. Some recent articles in military journals have even suggested that it may be necessary for the armed forces to cope with domestic "chaos" and to arrest a societal decline into decadence. According to one author, "We must be willing to realize that our real enemy is as likely to appear within our own border as without" (quoted in Ricks 1997d, 294).[8]

In short, the 1990s witnessed many developments that have generated a vigorous debate centering on an important question: Is there a crisis in civil-military relations?[9] The Ricks article and book are but two of the important contributions to the ongoing discussions of the issue. Ricks's diagnosis of the issue cited three sources for the widening gap between the military and civilian society: civilian ignorance about military affairs arising from a decline in the number of persons with any experience in the armed forces during the post-conscription era; politicization of the military, accompanied by a growing estrangement from the values of civilian society, or "a private loathing for public America"; and the post–Cold War security environment, which lacks the kind of unifying threat that the Soviet Union had posed during the previous four decades (Ricks 1997d, 66).

A study that drew upon six Foreign Policy Leadership Project (FPLP) surveys of American opinion leaders, covering the period 1976–96, found

---

7. Federal military forces have been used to deal with civil disturbances, racial disorders, labor unrest, and other domestic problems since the early days of the republic. For excellent summaries and analyses of these episodes, see Coakley (1989) and Laurie and Cole (1997).

8. In response to an earlier study on these issues, a military officer wrote me, "I find myself reciting internally my obligation to defend this country against all enemies foreign and domestic, and lamenting that there are more domestic enemies than foreign now in the United States." After citing the Oklahoma City and World Trade Center bombers, he went on to include those who are undermining the core values of American society.

9. Other contributions to these debates may be found in Kohn (1994), Powell et al. (1994), Desch (1999), and Feaver (2001).

considerable support for Ricks's thesis, but also uncovered evidence that called into question some of his conclusions (Holsti 1998–99).[10] However, that study was far from a conclusive answer to the questions posed by Ricks, because the FPLP surveys had been designed for purposes other than an analysis of civil-military relations. Thus, they could not address some central concerns such as the alleged contempt among the military for civilian culture, values, and institutions. Moreover, because the FPLP samples were largely drawn from senior officers at the Pentagon and the National War College, they were less than ideal for addressing one of the central aspects of the Ricks thesis: that the youngest cohorts of military personnel are the most deeply alienated from contemporary civilian society.

Although Ricks has presented a provocative and disturbing thesis, neither his analyses nor the FPLP study provided definitive answers about the existence, size, scope, and trends in the alleged civil-military "gap." This very brief background serves in part to explain the rationale for the Triangle Institute Security Studies (TISS) surveys described in this book. The TISS project was designed to provide additional systematic evidence, if not necessarily conclusive answers, to the important questions posed by Ricks and others who have pondered the "gap" issue.

The TISS Surveys

The research instrument for the TISS survey of military and civilian leaders was a 24-page questionnaire of 81 questions, many of which included multiple items.[11] For example, the first question asked respondents to rate the importance of ten possible foreign policy goals for the United States; the next one requested an assessment of thirteen controversial propositions about the conduct of foreign and defense policy. The questionnaire also asked respondents to provide some standard background information, including age, gender, occupation, military service, educa-

---

10. The Foreign Policy Leadership Project (FPLP) was initiated by the author and James Rosenau in order to conduct nationwide surveys on the post-Vietnam foreign policy attitudes and beliefs of American opinion leaders, including senior military officers at the Pentagon and National War College. Responses to the six surveys, conducted at four-year intervals between 1976 and 1996, ranged from 2,141 to 2,515, resulting in a data set of almost fourteen thousand completed questionnaires. Findings of the FPLP surveys are described in Holsti and Rosenau (1984), Holsti (1996), and three dozen articles and chapters. Some comparisons of civilian and military leaders are reported in Holsti (1998–99).

11. For a complete copy of the questionnaire, see the Technical Appendix.

tion, race/ethnicity, region, education of parents, religious affiliation, party affiliation, and ideology.

The sampling design was intended to reach elite members of the military in all branches of the service at various stages in their careers, including pre-commission personnel at three service academies and in Reserve Officer Training Corps (ROTC) units; mid-career and senior active-duty officers at various service schools; and members of the active reserves and National Guard. However, the Air Force and Marine Corps denied permission for their officers to take part in the TISS survey, and thus the sample includes only a small number of Air Force and Marine officers: students at the National Defense University, the Army and Naval War Colleges, and the Army's Command and General Staff College. Specifically, the "elite military" sample includes 723 officers at the Naval War College (334), Army War College (72), Command and Staff College (93), National Defense University (156), and the Capstone course (68).[12] These up-and-coming officers are identified as "military leaders" throughout the tables in this chapter. The 420 "active reservists" who were part of the leadership group in the TISS surveys were drawn from the Army War College Reserves (210), Army National Guard (62), National War College Reserves (57), and National Defense University Reserves (91). Forty-six foreign military officers attending U.S. service schools also completed questionnaires, but these were excluded from this analysis.

The sample of 935 civilian leaders was drawn from people listed in *Who's Who in America* and other directories for leadership groups, including State Department and Foreign Service Officers, foreign policy experts, media leaders, and labor leaders. In order to provide some basis of comparison with the pre-commission students at the military academies and the ROTC programs, a small sample of senior students at Duke University were also asked to complete the questionnaire.[13] For purpose of the analyses that follow, the civilian leaders are sub-divided into two groups: those who indicated that they had served in the military ("civilian veterans") and those who had no military experience ("civilian non-veterans"). A search through the sub-sample derived from *Who's Who* revealed that it included a very small number of professional military officers, who were transferred to the "elite military" category.

The overall return rate for the TISS elite survey was 43 percent, but it

---

12. The Capstone Course is a shorter-than-year-long course for officers who have been selected for flag rank (generals and admirals) in their services.

13. Responses from cadets at the service academies, ROTC, and civilian students, not included in the totals listed above, are being analyzed separately by Snider, Priest, and Lewis (2001).

varied widely by sub-samples. It was highest when the questionnaire was administered on site at the service schools. The return rate was 49 percent among military personnel compared to 32 percent for civilian opinion leaders.

In order to provide additional comparisons, the TISS project also included a parallel telephone survey of 1,001 randomly-selected members of the general public, conducted by Princeton Research Associates in October 1998. The TISS/PRA survey asked six questions about respondents' backgrounds and fifty-two substantive items about policy issues that are reflected in some of the tables and analyses that follow. The economics of telephone surveys and, more importantly, the limits of respondents' patience, precluded asking all of the questions that appeared in the questionnaire administered to the military and civilian leaders.

Findings

The analyses are grouped into seven sections below. The first six include tables summarizing responses to relevant items in the TISS questionnaire. All of the tables in this chapter identify responses by the four leadership groups identified above: *military leaders, active reserve leaders, civilian veteran leaders*, and *civilian non-veteran leaders*; respondents taking part in the survey of the *general public* are classified as *veterans* or *non-veterans*. The first section describes the socio-demographic attributes—gender, age, etc.—of these six categories of respondents. Because party affiliation and ideology played an especially important role in the analyses by Thomas Ricks (1997c; 1997d), these attributes receive special attention. The section that follows next focuses on views of foreign and defense policy issues, including foreign policy goals, propositions that should guide the conduct of foreign affairs, national security threats and how best to cope with them, uses of the military, and assessments of the 1998 air strikes against suspected terrorist sites in Sudan and Afghanistan. Several of the questions on these issues also appeared in the FPLP surveys, providing the basis for some comparisons with earlier studies of opinion leaders. The third data section turns to a number of controversial domestic policy issues, including some questions that also appeared in the FPLP surveys. The fourth data section presents responses to several clusters of items that focus on general assessments of civilian culture, military culture, and confidence in American institutions, as well as more specific questions about politicians, the media, and the military. These are useful in examining one of the central features of the Ricks thesis: the alleged contempt of many military personnel for American culture and values. The fifth section centers on several facets of relations between the military, civilian authorities, and civilian society, including attention to and knowledge about military issues, the perceiv?d values of some important leadership groups, the role of the media, sources of information about the military, opinions about the military, constraints on military effectiveness, and the proper role of senior military leaders in decisions to commit U.S. forces abroad. The sixth and final data section deals with religious beliefs and practices, including beliefs about life after death, the nature of the Bible, and the role of religion in daily life, and frequency of attendance at religious services. It also includes two questions on trust and child-rearing. Because data from the survey of the general public are much scantier, their analysis here is not as detailed as the comparison of military and civilian leaders. However, the penultimate section of this chapter presents an overview of the differences and convergences among the leadership groups and the members of the general public. The conclusion highlights some major themes and implications of the findings.

SOCIO-DEMOGRAPHIC ATTRIBUTES OF THE RESPONDENTS
The TISS/PRA survey of the general public was designed to reflect as accurately as possible the demographic attributes of adult Americans. Details may be found in the Appendix of this volume. The military and civilian elite samples vary from those of the general public and from each other in a number of respects, including gender, age, race and ethnicity, religion, region, and education. Because of their importance to the current debate about a civil-military gap, variations in partisanship and ideology are examined in particular detail.

Although women have come to play a more significant role in the military since the end of conscription in 1973, men still dominate the elite military, active reserve, and civilian-veteran sub-samples: women constitute fewer than ten percent of these three groups. Among veterans in the general public, the preponderance of men is almost as high (89 percent). Women constitute a much higher proportion of non-veteran civilian leaders (41 percent), an indication of the increasing professional opportunities for women in recent years. Women make up well over half (61 percent) of those in the general public who have not served in the military.

The military respondents, both active-duty officers and, to a lesser extent, those in the active reserves, are by far the youngest groups among those in the leadership sample. Reflecting the requirement that almost all military officers must retire after thirty-five years of service or at age fifty-nine, whichever comes first, well over 90 percent of those in both military groups are under the age of fifty-five. In contrast, very substantial numbers of respondents among civilian leaders and the general public are older than fifty-five; almost 70 percent of veterans among civilian leaders have reached that milestone, and the comparable figure among veterans in the general public approaches 50 percent. The age differences among civilians also reflects the end of conscription, as relatively few of those who came of military age during the intervening years have volunteered for military service.

Nor is it very surprising that more than 90 percent of respondents in the four leadership groups are Caucasians, but it is worth noting that, compared to the civilian elites, both the active and reserve military groups include higher proportions of minorities, including African-Americans, Hispanics, and, to a lesser extent, Asian-Americans. These results appear to reflect the frequently stated thesis that, compared to the private sector in American economic life, the military services have proven to be attractive and effective avenues of social mobility for minorities. Nevertheless, the proportion of African-American (4.2 percent) and Hispanic (2.6 percent) officers among the active-duty military leadership group still lags far behind the percentages of minorities in the military enlisted ranks or in the population as a whole.

Those taking part in the TISS surveys were asked to "be specific" in responding to an open-ended item on religious affiliation. The resulting answers were then aggregated into eight groups according to a classification scheme developed by Kellestedt, Green, Guth, and Smidt (1997): Evangelical Protestants, mainline Protestants, Catholics, other Christians, Jewish, non-Judeo-Christian, agnostic/atheist, and refused/none (see Table 1.1). Several points emerge from the responses. First, among the leaders, both military and civilians, there are relatively small differences with respect to the two clusters of Protestants, who constitute very close to half of each of the four leadership groups, with ratio of about three members of "mainline" churches for each of the "evangelical" Protestants. In contrast, respondents in the survey of the general public, both veteran and non-veteran, included a higher percentage of Protestants, with a significantly higher proportion of evangelicals. The figures for the general public are very similar to the 58 percent of all Americans who identify themselves as Protestants (*Statistical Abstract of the United States 1998*, Table 60). Conversely, the data reveal that, compared to the civilian leaders and the general public, the elite military (37 percent) and active reservists (34 percent) groups include a much higher proportion of Catholics and fewer members of the Jewish faith; well under one percent in either group identified themselves as Jews. Figures on the religious preferences of the entire American population indicate that 26 percent are Catholic and 2 percent are Jewish (*Statistical Abstract of the United States 1998*, Table 60). Thus, Catholics are substantially over-represented and Jews under-represented among those in the elite military and reservist

Table 1.1. Religious Affiliation of Respondents in the 1998–99 TISS Survey.

	Military leaders	Active reserve leaders	Civilian veteran leaders	Civilian non-veteran leaders	General public veterans	General public non-veterans
	Percent					
Mainline Protestant	37.4	36.6	38.4	37.3	33.7	34.9
Catholic	37.2	33.5	22.1	20.3	22.4	21.1
Evangelical Protestant	13.2	16.2	12.0	13.4	23.9	21.8
Other Christian	2.6	1.5	5.3	4.4	1.0	1.8
Non Judeo-Christian	0.6	0.8	0.8	1.3	8.3	9.4
Agnostic/atheist	0.6	0.0	0.3	0.9	0.0	0.0
Jewish	0.3	0.8	8.4	7.1	1.5	2.3
Refused/none	8.0	10.6	12.6	15.4	9.3	8.8

NOTE: Differences between groups significant at the .001 level.

sub-samples. Also under-represented are the non-Judeo-Christians, who accounted for about 9 percent of respondents among the general public, but only about 1 percent of the leadership sample. Not even 1 percent of respondents in any of the sub-samples identified themselves as atheists or agnostics.

The conventional wisdom is that the American South is an especially fertile area for military recruiting, in part because the states of the old Confederacy are said to have a greater appreciation for the martial virtues. That generalization may well be especially valid for enlisted personnel, a group that is excluded from the TISS samples, but it appears to receive only modest support from the TISS and overall population figures reported in Table 1.2. These figures indicate that the military and active reservists include a significant over-representation of those who grew up in New England and a concomitant under-representation from the Pacific coast.[14] It is important to note that the survey responses reflect past experiences of as many as several decades ago, whereas the figures in the right-hand column report the current distribution of the population. More generally, the data mirror the migration of Americans from the Northeast to the South and Pacific coast. The increasing mobility of Americans and the growth of national electronic and print media that have largely supplanted local newspapers as the primary sources of information also may have tended to erode some of the distinctive regional attributes of an earlier era.

The level of educational attainment by leaders taking part in the TISS surveys far exceeds the national average. Specifically, well over half of each sub-sample have earned a graduate degree—elite military (72 percent), active reservists (69 percent), civilian veterans (71 percent), and civilian non-veterans (68 percent)—and significant proportions of the remainder have had at least some graduate work. No one in the first three groups had failed to experience at least some college, and only 1 percent of the civilian non-veteran leaders had ended their education at the high school level. Although there is ample evidence that education is strongly correlated to attitudes about foreign affairs, the highly skewed nature of the TISS leadership samples significantly reduces the probability that education will prove to be a powerful variable in explaining differences among the groups of respondents.

Those taking part in the TISS leadership surveys were also asked about the educational attainments of their parents. Their responses provide strong evidence of upward mobility from one generation to the next.

---

14.   For a further assessment of the impact of region on civil-military relations, see Chapter 8 by Michael Desch in this volume.

Table 1.2. Region of Origin Responses in the 1998–99 TISS Survey.

Where did you live most of the time when you were growing up?

	Military leaders	Active reserve leaders	Civilian veteran leaders	Civilian non-veteran leaders	General public veterans	General public non-veterans	U.S. Population*
				Percent checking each option			
Midwest	21.6	25.1	26.5	30.8	31.5	29.7	24.7
South	20.3	22.0	18.0	15.7	22.5	21.2	17.0
Mid-Atlantic	20.3	19.9	27.3	24.5	13.5	14.1	22.5
New England	10.8	11.3	10.9	9.2	11.0	9.2	5.0
Pacific Coast	10.6	7.6	6.3	8.8	9.5	10.9	16.1
Southwest	6.9	5.0	5.5	4.5	5.5	6.7	11.6
Mountain States	2.9	3.1	3.0	2.0	4.5	3.6	3.2
Other/moved around	6.5	6.1	2.5	4.6	2.0	4.6	—

SOURCE: *Statistical Abstract of the United States* (Washington: U.S. Government Printing Office, 1999), Table 26.

The modal level of education among both fathers and mothers of the elite respondents was a high school diploma. Although parents of the military leaders were somewhat more likely to been college graduates—45 percent of fathers and 30 percent of mothers had earned a college degree—the differences between the leadership groups in this respect are not dramatic.

PARTISANSHIP AND IDEOLOGY

A key feature of the Ricks thesis is that members of the military are not only becoming more politicized in the sense that they are less likely to think of themselves as "independent," but also that they increasingly identify with the Republican Party. Analyses of the six FPLP surveys revealed very strong support for Ricks's thesis. Each of the surveys found increasing military identification with the Republican Party, rising from 33 percent in 1976 and reaching to 67 percent in 1996, and a concomitant decline in support for the Democratic Party, just 7 percent in the most recent survey. Among civilian leaders, identification with the Republican Party also increased by 9 percentage points (from 25 percent to 34 percent) during the period of two decades of the FPLP surveys, but the increase was almost wholly at the expense of independents; preference for the Democratic Party held steady at about 40 percent throughout the period (Holsti 1998 99, Table 1). This evidence provided little support for the frequently advanced argument that military preference for the Republican Party was a short-term phenomenon arising from military distaste for President Clinton: the trend toward increasing Republican partisanship among the military officers taking part in the FPLP surveys was established long before Clinton entered the White House.

Table 1.3 summarizes the party preferences of respondents in the TISS survey. They are fully consistent with the Ricks thesis as well as the results of the six FPLP surveys. Among those in both the elite military and active reserve groups, Republicans outnumber Democrats by margins of approximately 8 to 1 and 6 to 1, respectively. In contrast, the civilian leaders were more evenly divided, with a strong plurality of the veterans preferring the Republicans, and a somewhat weaker plurality of the civilian non-veteran leaders identifying themselves as Democrats. Respondents in the survey of the general public were divided almost equally between Republicans, Democrats, and independents.

The data do not, however, provide a great deal of support for the thesis that the youngest cohorts of the two military groups are even more strongly wedded to the Republican Party. Multivariate analyses revealed that among the elite military, younger officers are only slightly more Republican than their seniors. This effect is contrary to the finding that

Table 1.3. Party Identification in the 1998–99 TISS Survey.

	Military leaders	Active reserve leaders	Civilian veteran leaders	Civilian non-veteran leaders	General public veterans	General public non-veterans
			Percent checking each option			
Republicans	63.9	62.5	46.2	30.3	36.9	29.1
Democrats	8.1	10.5	22.1	43.1	31.0	33.0
Independents	16.7	18.4	25.7	20.1	27.6	32.9
Other & None	11.3	8.7	6.0	6.5	4.4	4.9

NOTE: Differences between groups significant at the .001 level.

younger Americans in general are *less* Republican. Although the ratio of Republicans to Democrats was higher among the younger reservists, many identified themselves as independents rather than as members of either major party. Responses of the civilian leadership groups revealed a strong preference—but not a majority—for Republicans among veterans of all age groups, with less allegiance to the Democrats and increasing self-identification as "independents" by the younger respondents. Among the non-veterans, a plurality of all except the oldest age group described themselves as Democrats. Responses to the survey of the general public revealed that the oldest veterans preferred the Republican Party by a margin of 46 percent to 25 percent, whereas the figures were almost reversed for non-veterans (45 percent to 27 percent). The younger respondents favored the Democratic Party by a very slight margin.

Some observers have questioned these results on several grounds, the first of which is that they merely reflect the rising electoral fortunes of the Republican Party in recent decades. In a long-term project on the sociology of military careers, David Segal has noted that the partisan preferences of American youth prior to joining the military have closely tracked those of the overall population. Thus, the proportions of Republicans among both the general population and those who selected a military career rose during the Reagan years, but declined somewhat during the 1990s. Segal's data are, however, drawn largely from those entering the enlisted ranks, whereas the FPLP and TISS surveys focused on officers. Moreover, although the pattern of party preferences among the general population has indeed fluctuated during the quarter-century covered by these surveys, including Segal's, at no time has the Republican Party been the party of choice among a majority of Americans, much less enjoyed margins over the Democratic Party of the magnitude revealed in the FPLP and TISS surveys of 6 to 1 or higher. This point is underscored by the partisan preferences of respondents to the TISS survey of the general public, as well as a *New York Times*/CBS News Poll showing that 31 percent of the public is Democratic, while 29 percent identify with the Republican Party (Clymer 1999, A15).

A second and related objection emerged during an October 1999 discussion of the TISS survey results. Professional pollster Andrew Kohut dismissed the significance of a strong Republicanism among the military because his own surveys found that, among the U.S. population as a whole, white male Christians under age 65 with high educational attainments and better-than-average incomes are generally Republicans (47 percent), rather than Democrats (20 percent) or independents (31 percent). Certainly most active-duty military respondents in the TISS leadership sample fit that demographic profile, but the distribution in Kohut's study of 47 percent Republican and 20 percent Democrat falls far short of the 64 percent-vs.-8 percent gap revealed in the TISS survey.

Kohut also asserted that the TISS study greatly overstates the civil-ian-military gap because *Who's Who in America*—a prime source of the TISS civilian elite sample—vastly over-represents liberals in the enter-tainment/sports industry and retirees "who have nothing better to do with their time than to fill in questionnaires." In fact, however, the TISS sampling design explicitly excluded *all* entertainers and athletes, as well as most if not all of those over the age of seventy.[15] Moreover, it included a substantial number of business executives who, as Kohut has rightly observed, are predominantly associated with the Republican Party; busi-ness leaders constituted approximately one-eighth (12.4 percent) of the TISS sample, and Republicans among them outnumbered Democrats by a margin of 56 percent-to-16 percent.

A third objection focuses not on the TISS samples, but on the inter-pretation to be assigned to findings. The argument is that members of the military are not so much biased toward a single party as reflecting a rea-soned preference based on a careful appraisal of the policies, experiences, and values of current leadership in the two major political parties. Ac-cording to that view, just as a vast majority of African-Americans support the party and candidates most closely identified with the civil rights movement of the past several decades, the military support the Republi-cans because that party and its leaders are seen as better at espousing ex-periences, policies, and values such as service in the military, high de-fense spending, family values, and religiosity.

The theory could well explain "easy" cases such as the military pref-erences for George Bush and Bob Dole—both of whom had sterling World War II records—in their presidential campaigns against Bill Clinton in 1992 and 1996. In contrast, Clinton was regarded as a Vietnam draft dodger. Moreover, although Dole had been divorced, both he and Bush were regarded as having good family records, whereas even in 1992 Clinton's fidelity to family values was questioned. But this reasoning is undercut by the overwhelming military preferences in the 1980 presiden-tial election: whereas Jimmy Carter was an Annapolis graduate who had served with distinction in the U.S. Navy, Ronald Reagan could charitably be described as a shirker who sat out World War II in Hollywood, albeit in uniform. Carter was widely respected as a devout Christian and de-voted husband and father. In contrast, prior to Reagan's political career

---

15. Some sampling sources did not list date of birth. For example, the "foreign pol-icy expert" category included authors of recent articles in *Foreign Affairs, Foreign Policy,* and *International Security,* some of whom may have been older than seventy.

with its obligatory appearances at Sunday services, there is little indication that religion or religious values played a central role in Reagan's life. Moreover, Reagan's family life fell far short as a model. Leaving aside his divorce, his relations with his children during their early years were notoriously poor; indeed his daughter wrote a book about his parental neglect.

Some might argue that the military experiences and family values of the candidates take a back seat to self-interested appraisals of the candidates' policy stances. Ronald Reagan had indeed called for a large increase in spending for the military, but his record as governor of California had demonstrated a consistent inability to translate his core campaign promises—the most important of which was to reduce the size of the government in Sacramento—into policies. In contrast, President Carter had actually started a major military build-up in the wake of the Soviet invasion of Afghanistan. On this score, then, the choice was between the promises of one candidate and the deeds of the other.

In short, if the experiences, values, and policies of leaders in the two major political parties had been the driving force behind partisan choices, then Jimmy Carter should have been the overwhelming favorite of the military in 1980. In fact, however, he received fewer than one vote in eight among military officers.[16] Meanwhile, the FPLP surveys indicated that the margin of preference for the Republicans over the Democrats among the military jumped from less than 3:1 in 1976 to almost 5:1 in 1980.

The 2000 presidential election offered still further evidence that a vast majority of military personnel support the Republicans irrespective of the candidates' military records. Al Gore volunteered for and served in the Army after graduating from Harvard. In contrast, George W. Bush was able to join the Texas Air National Guard, ensuring that he would escape serving in Vietnam, despite a score of just 25 percent on the flight aptitude examination. He did not fulfill all his Guard obligations; he transferred from his unit in Texas to take part in a senatorial campaign in Alabama, failed to report to his newly assigned unit in Alabama, and never flew again. Bush was nevertheless the overwhelming favorite of officers in the Pentagon. Gore's Vietnam service as an enlisted military journalist was dismissed by one of them as "public relations puke" (Myers, 2000b, A1). The argument that military officers were merely expressing their self-interest does not seem especially persuasive in this case, as the major post–Cold War cutbacks in the military were planned and approved by

16.   Thomas Ricks, presentation to Triangle Institute of Security Studies, North Carolina State University, November 1997.

Republican vice presidential candidate Dick Cheney while he served as Secretary of Defense under President George Bush.

A fourth response to the FPLP and TISS findings of a huge partisan gap between civilians as the military is easily summarized as "So what?" What differences do these finding make? This point is considered in more detail in the conclusion.

Ricks also argued that the military are becoming increasingly conservative; as he put it, they are increasingly comfortable with the "Rush Limbaugh variant" of Republican conservatism. Analyses of the FPLP data uncovered strong support for Ricks's thesis: a rising proportion of military officers identified themselves as conservatives, reaching 73 percent in 1996, while those who admitted to being liberals of any variety declined almost to the vanishing point. However, the data did not reveal a comparable increase in the most conservative categories. The growth was in the "somewhat conservative" category.

In contrast, civilian leaders were evenly divided between liberals and conservatives at 36 percent each in 1996, with the remaining 28 percent describing themselves as "moderates" (Holsti 1998–99, Table 2).

Ideological self-identifications of those taking part in the TISS survey are summarized in Table 1.4. Respondents in all groups other than the "civilian non-veteran leaders" are, on balance, tilted somewhat to the conservative side of the scale.[17] Nevertheless, there are quite significant differences between the military and civilian respondents, with the former expressing substantially stronger affinity for conservatism. Indeed, as was the case in the six FPLP surveys, liberals appear to be an endangered species among both the military and active reserves. There are also significant differences among the two groups of civilian leaders; compared to civilian veterans, the non-veterans in the leadership group were considerably more likely to identify themselves as liberals. Multivariate analyses including age as a variable provided moderate support for the Ricks thesis that younger members of the military are the most conservative. For example, more than 70 percent of the younger age group identified themselves as conservatives, and about one-fifth (14.7 percent) stated that they were in the most conservative group—either "very conservative" or "far right." The comparable figures for older members of the elite military were 62.0 percent and 9.9 percent, respectively. In contrast, the younger members of the active reserve were significantly more

---

17.   The questionnaire included a standard seven-point ideology scale, with "far left" and "far right" categories. Because few respondents checked these options, they have been grouped with those in the "very liberal" and "very conservative" categories, respectively.

Table 1.4. Ideological Self-Identification in the 1998–99 TISS Survey.

	Military leaders	Active reserve leaders	Civilian veteran leaders	Civilian non-veteran leaders	General public veterans	General public non-veterans
			Percent checking each option			
Very liberal	0.5	0.5	3.0	12.6	7.8	7.4
Somewhat liberal	4.7	6.0	15.3	24.9	13.2	21.1
Moderate	28.4	27.5	28.1	28.4	24.4	27.3
Somewhat conservative	53.8	50.1	40.4	23.3	31.7	26.9
Very conservative	12.3	14.3	11.2	8.2	18.5	11.5
Other/no response	0.7	1.6	1.9	2.5	4.4	5.7

NOTE: Differences between groups significant at the .001 level.

likely to describe themselves as "moderates." Responses of neither civilian leaders nor members of the general public gave rise to striking ideological differences across age groups.

In summary, the Ricks thesis that partisan and ideological preferences among the military have moved toward the Republican Party and conservatism receives significant support from those participating in the TISS survey, as it did in the earlier FPLP studies. Although the sampling designs of the FPLP and TISS surveys of leaders differed somewhat—notably because the latter included military officers from institutions encompassing a much wider range of ages and ranks—the partisan and ideological gaps emerging from the two sets of studies are remarkably similar. Whether these gaps have any broader policy implications is explored in the conclusion.

FOREIGN AND DEFENSE POLICY ISSUES

The FPLP analyses revealed that the partisan and ideological differences between military and civilian leaders carried over to opinions on many aspects of domestic and foreign policy, but they also showed that gaps did not exist on all issues, were not uniformly large, and have increased on some issues and actually decreased on others since the end of the Cold War. For example, by 1996 there were virtually no differences on such once-controversial issues as validity of the "domino theory" or the nature of Russian foreign policy goals.

The first item on the TISS questionnaire asked respondents to rate the importance of several possible foreign policy goals for the United States. This cluster of questions also appeared in all six FPLP studies, as well as in seven quadrennial surveys conducted by the Chicago Council on Foreign Relations (Reilly 1975–1999).[18] The results summarized in Table 1.5 reveal areas of widespread agreement and others of substantial dissensus. Respondents in all four groups attributed considerable importance both to preventing nuclear proliferation and to the related goal of worldwide arms control. Although there were statistically significant differences in responses to the former item, the more impressive point is that all four groups ranked these goals among the three most important. With the single exception of the civilian non-veterans, there was also wide-

---

18.   The Chicago Council on Foreign Relations (CCFR) surveys, conducted by the Gallup Organization, included random national samples of approximately 1,500 members of the general public and much smaller samples of about 375 leaders. Although the CCFR surveys are a useful source of questionnaire items, the absence of military officers in either CCFR sample limited their use as a source of data for the TISS study.

Table 1.5. Assessments of Foreign Policy Goals: Responses in the 1998–99 TISS Survey.

Here is a list of possible foreign policy goals that the United States might have. Please indicate how much importance you think should be attached to each goal.

	Percent "Very important"			
	Military leaders	Active reserve leaders	Civilian veteran leaders	Civilian non-veteran leaders
A. Helping to improve the standard of living in less developed countries	8.4	12.7	25.0	36.0
B. Worldwide arms control	72.0	69.8	63.9	68.2
C. Combating world hunger	14.6	20.2	35.7	46.9
D. Strengthening the United Nations	18.7	20.5	23.4	28.8
E. Fostering international cooperation to solve common problems, such as food, inflation, and energy	41.7	45.9	52.2	60.0
F. Containing communism	16.1	14.5	17.6	14.8
G. Preventing the spread of nuclear weapons	89.5	93.0	85.2	82.4
H. Promoting and defending human rights in other countries	13.4	12.1	21.4	33.9
I. Helping to bring a democratic form of government to other nations	19.6	24.0	16.7	16.0
J. Maintaining superior military power worldwide	74.4	78.5	64.5	47.4

NOTES: Differences between groups significant at the .001 level for all items except B, where the level was .06. These questions were not included in the survey of the general public.

spread agreement that "maintaining superior military power world-wide" is a very important goal.[19]

At the other end of the scale, respondents in none of the leadership groups expressed much enthusiasm for the pre-eminent Cold War goal of containing communism, for strengthening the United Nations, or for "helping to bring a democratic form of government to other nations." Although the expansion of democracy abroad has been given a high priority by the Reagan, Bush, and Clinton administrations, at least at the level of doctrine and rhetoric, it appears to have engendered relatively little support among those taking part in the TISS survey as a possible core foreign policy concept.[20]

The data also revealed very substantial differences between the military and civilian sub-samples on several goals relating to less developed countries, including helping to improve the standard of living in these countries, combating world hunger, and promoting human rights abroad. These goals, which are often supported by liberals and have been dismissed by some realist critics as "international social work" or "globaloney," elicited very little support from the military or active reserve groups when compared to ratings of the two civilian groups (Mandelbaum 1996).

Table 1.6 presents a summary of responses to a series of propositions that have at times been put forward as lessons about foreign and defense policy that the United States should draw from past experience. They represent a wide range of perspectives rather than a unified doctrine on the conduct of foreign affairs. In light of the very low priority assigned to "strengthening the United Nations" as a foreign policy goal (Table 1.5), the exceptionally high level of agreement within all groups for the proposition that "it is vital to enlist the cooperation of the UN in settling international disputes" may appear rather anomalous. Indeed, this was only one of two items among the thirteen in Table 1.6 that gained agreement of more than seventy percent of both military and civilian respondents. One possible explanation for the strong agreement that the United Nations should be involved in settling international disputes draws upon other surveys that have revealed widespread support for multilateralism—sharing the costs and risks with other countries—rather than

---

19. Table 1.5 reports only "very important" responses; to report all the others would make the table unwieldy. However, statistical analyses for this and all other tables in this chapter included the data for all response options.

20. For a fuller analysis of democracy-promotion as a foreign policy goal, drawing on surveys of both opinion leaders and the general public, see Holsti, 2000.

unilateralism in coping with any situations that may involve American intervention abroad (Kull and Destler 1999).

Although there were statistically significant differences across groups, an additional four items were supported by majorities in all four: the validity of the "domino theory," the need to use force to prevent aggression by any expansionist power, a preference for using force quickly and massively rather than by gradual escalation, and the belief that "the American public will rarely tolerate large numbers of U.S. casualties in military operations."

The proposition that the U.S. public is casualty-averse has become such an entrenched part of the post–Cold War conventional wisdom that it was hard to find a single commentary on the recently-concluded air war against Yugoslavia that did not describe it as virtually an "iron law" of American politics. Surveys undertaken before and during the Kosovo campaign in 1999 do not sustain the view that the public was overwhelmingly opposed to the use of American ground forces against Yugoslavia, an option that certainly would have entailed some casualties (Jentleson, 2000). Thus, there are reasons to suspect that this may represent another case of elites "misreading the public" (Kull and Destler 1999). Indeed, the "body bag syndrome" appears to have become part of the unquestioned dogma in other NATO countries as well. In this respect, it may be useful to ponder the recent observation of a Dutch public opinion analyst:

"In this connection one is struck by the facile way in which the body bag argument was used by politicians and the media. There is a tendency to parrot one another and to anticipate on situations, which may indeed be caused by such talk. Frequent statements of politicians and observers about the expected body bag effects on public support may turn out to be a self-fulfilling prophecy" (Everts, 2000, 192).

It is worth considering whether this supposed "iron law" has become a convenient scapegoat for military and political leaders who seek to legitimate their own unwillingness to contemplate certain policy options.[21]

There are also very substantial differences between the military and civilians on about half of the items in Table 1.6, including the use of the CIA to undermine hostile governments, aid to poor countries, the use of force only for the goal of total victory, permitting military rather than political goals to determine the use of force, the relative importance of eco-

---

21. For a detailed analysis of other TISS survey questions on casualties, see Feaver and Gelpi (forthcoming).

Table 1.6. Assessment of Foreign and Defense Policy Propositions by Respondents in the 1998–99 TISS Survey.

This question asks you to indicate your position on certain propositions that are sometimes described as lessons that the United States should have learned from past experiences abroad. Please indicate how strongly you agree or disagree with each statement.

	Percent "Agree strongly" or "Agree somewhat"			
	Military leaders	Active reserve leaders	Civilian veteran leaders	Civilian non-veteran leaders
A. There is considerable validity in the "domino theory" that when one nation falls to aggressor nations, others nearby will soon follow a similar path	52.1	56.7	59.3	52.8
B. It is vital to enlist the cooperation of the UN in settling international disputes	79.6	77.5	72.7	78.7
C. Russia is generally expansionist rather than defensive in its foreign policy goals	27.2	35.1	36.4	27.0
D. There is nothing wrong with using the CIA to try to undermine hostile governments	64.5	64.7	53.9	43.8
E. The U.S. should take all steps including the use of force to prevent aggression by any expansionist power	76.9	75.4	67.1	59.5
F. The U.S. should give economic aid to poorer countries even if it means higher prices at home	33.5	33.6	44.2	52.2
G. Any Chinese victory is a defeat for America's national interest	23.7	32.6	23.6	19.0
H. We shouldn't think so much in international terms but concentrate more on our own national problems	21.1	23.2	31.0	28.2

Table 1.6. Continued.

This question asks you to indicate your position on certain propositions that are sometimes described as lessons that the United States should have learned from past experiences abroad. Please indicate how strongly you agree or disagree with each statement.

	Percent "Agree strongly" or "Agree somewhat"			
	Military leaders	Active reserve leaders	Civilian veteran leaders	Civilian non-veteran leaders
I. Military force should be used only in pursuit of the goal of total victory	41.7	56.9	47.7	36.8
J. Use of force in foreign interventions should be applied quickly and massively rather than by gradual escalation	79.4	80.9	71.3	57.1
K. When force is used, military rather than political goals should determine its application	26.8	36.2	48.4	40.7
L. The American public will rarely tolerate large numbers of U.S. casualties in military operations	77.9	77.2	76.3	78.5
M. American national security depends more on international trade and a strong domestic economy than on our military strength	37.0	42.5	49.2	59.5

NOTES: Differences between groups significant at the .001 level for all items except L. These questions were not included in the survey of the general public.

nomic and military power as elements of national security, and an isolationist preference for concentrating on domestic rather than international problems. The pattern of responses is reasonably predictable on most of these items, but it appears to contradict the conventional wisdom on one of them. The military and active reserve respondents were *less* rather than more likely than the civilians to agree that, "when force is used, military rather than political goals should determine its application."

Finally, appraisals of the foreign policies of Russia and China, the only plausible rivals to the United States for the near future, are quite benign. By quite substantial majorities, respondents in all four groups rejected the propositions that Russian foreign policy goals are expansionist or that relations between Beijing and Washington can be described as a zero-sum game in which gains for one of them must entail comparable losses for the other.

Most of the surveys of the World War II and early Cold War periods measured foreign policy attitudes on a single isolationist-to-internationalist scale, but more recent studies have shown that views of both opinion leaders and the general public are better described in multi-dimensional terms (Wittkopf 1990; Hinckley 1992; Holsti and Rosenau 1993; Chittick, Billingsley, and Travis 1995; Holsti 1996; Chittick and Billingsley 1999; Richman, Nolle, and Malone 1999). Studies by Eugene Wittkopf, replicated by others, have identified "two faces of internationalism": militant internationalism (MI) and cooperative internationalism (CI). Crossing these two dimensions yields four types of belief systems: *hard-liners* (support MI, oppose CI), *accommodationists* (oppose MI, support CI), *internationalists* (support both MI and CI), and *isolationists* (oppose both MI and CI).[22]

Seven items that appeared in Table 1.5 and Table 1.6 were used to develop the militant internationalism (MI) scale: containment (Table 5, item F), maintaining military superiority (5-J), the "domino theory" (6-A), Russian foreign policy goals (6-C), the CIA (6-D), using force to prevent aggression (6-E), and China's gains (6-G). Many of these items also formed the MI scale in the six FPLP studies, but some had to be changed in later FPLP studies to reflect changing international realities such as disintegration of the Soviet Union.

---

22. A number of studies have shown that a third dimension—unilateralism-multilateralism—is often also important in defining foreign policy orientations (Hinckley 1992; Chittick, Billingsley, and Travis 1995; Holsti 1997). However, the TISS surveys were designed to meet the data needs of more than a half-dozen investigators and, thus, competition for space on an already overly-long questionnaire made it impossible to add further clusters of items that might have been used to create a unilateralism-multilateralism scale.

Seven items served to define the cooperative internationalism (CI) scale: helping to improve living standards in less developed countries (Table 5, item A), combating world hunger (5-C), strengthening the UN (5-D), fostering international cooperation (5-E), promoting human rights (5-H), gaining UN cooperation in international disputes (6-B), and economic aid to poorer countries (6-F). These elements appeared in both the TISS and FPLP surveys. One additional TISS question that did not appear in the CI scale of the FPLP surveys was added: human rights. When those taking part in the TISS survey were classified according to this scheme, respondents in the four groups were distributed into the four categories. Several generalizations emerge from the results shown in Table 1.7.

Consistent with almost all other surveys, persons in the leadership groups are more internationalist than the general public. Compared to similar data from the 1976–96 FPLP studies, the TISS survey reveals that there has been some overall increase in the number of leaders in the *isolationist* category: about one-sixth of the military elites are in that group, almost exactly the same proportion as in the 1996 FPLP survey. In the previous FPLP surveys, fewer than 10 percent of military officers were found in the isolationist quadrant. However, these results provide modest support, at best, for the thesis put forward by the historian and former presidential adviser, Arthur Schlesinger (1995), that both American leaders and the general public are abandoning internationalism in favor of a "return to the womb." The euphoria over the end of the Cold War and the quick victory in the Gulf War, still strong in 1992, may have worn off, though not nearly to the extent nor with the consequences suggested by Schlesinger.

Overall, these results are fairly consistent with the FPLP survey findings on differences between military officers and civilian leaders. The active reserves are strongest in the *hard-liner* category, where civilian non-veterans are the smallest group. A plurality of military elites is found in the *internationalist* category, followed very closely by the *accommodationist* quadrant, and they also constitute the largest group in the *isolationist* category. In contrast, a plurality of the civilian veterans and a strong majority of the civilian non-veterans are *accommodationists*.

The specific policy preferences that have the most effect on the distribution in Table 1.7 arise from variation in responses to items in the cooperative internationalism scale that involve policies toward the less developed countries. Members of the military samples were less likely to express support for foreign aid and related undertakings directed at improving the lot of Third World countries.

Those taking part in the TISS survey were also asked to rate the seriousness of a dozen possible threats to American national security. The re-

Table 1.7. Foreign Policy Orientations Among Respondents to the 1998–99 TISS Survey.

		Cooperative Internationalism (CI)			
		Oppose		Support	
		Hard-liners		*Internationalists*	
	Support	MIL	15.4%	MIL	34.0%
		AR	21.2	AR	33.9
		CV	17.3	CV	27.0
Militant		CNV	11.0	CNV	22.8
Internationalism (MI)		*Isolationists*		*Accommodationists*	
	Oppose	MIL	16.9%	MIL	33.9%
		AR	14.5	AR	30.4
		CV	13.9	CV	41.8
		CNV	10.3	CNV	55.9

KEY: MIL = Military leaders; AR = Active reserve leaders; CV = Civilian veteran leaders; CNV = Civilian non-veteran leaders.
NOTES: Differences between groups are significant at the .001 level. Questions for these scales were not included in the survey of the general public.

sults, summarized in Table 1.8, reveal statistically significant differences across the leadership groups for all but one of the twelve items. But if we examine the columns, group by group, rather than the rows, issue by issue, a pattern of considerable agreement across groups emerges: despite differences in emphasis, the rank orderings of potential threats are rather similar. For example, respondents in all four leadership groups ranked the following among the top three threats: proliferation of weapons of mass destruction to Third World countries, international terrorism, and terrorist attacks upon the United States. At the other end of the threat spectrum, relatively few civilian or military respondents expressed concern about threats arising from immigration or foreign economic competition.

Other potential threats gave rise to quite substantial variations among the groups, including the emergence of China as a military power, the decline of standards and morals in American society, international drug trafficking, environmental problems, and Islamic fundamentalism. The military regarded rising Chinese military power and declining standards in American society as a greater threat than did their civilian counterparts. The latter concern is a central element in the Ricks "gap" thesis,

Table 1.8. Assessments of Threats to American National Security: Responses in the 1998–99 TISS Survey.

This question asks you to evaluate the seriousness of the following threats to American national security.

			Civilian			
	Military leaders	Active reserve leaders	Civilian veteran leaders	Civilian non-veteran leaders	General public veterans	General public non-veterans
A. The emergence of China as a great military power	33.1	39.5	30.9	28.0	42.4	29.7
B. The proliferation of weapons of mass destruction to less-developed countries	80.9	83.5	78.8	72.4	—	—
C. American interventions in conflicts that are none of our business	12.5	14.5	19.9	18.2	—	—
D. Large number of immigrants and refugees coming to the U.S.	7.8	16.5	15.9	12.5	35.1	32.0
E. International terrorism	58.8	65.2	65.1	62.0	—	—
F. The decline of standards and morals in American society	42.0	41.6	40.2	32.0	60.5	61.3
G. International drug trafficking	30.0	41.3	38.3	33.7	—	—
H. Economic competition from abroad	5.8	8.5	6.4	8.8	30.2	26.9
I. Environmental problems such as air pollution and water contamination	9.9	11.9	17.8	29.0	—	—
J. Expansion of Islamic fundamentalism	8.9	19.4	19.0	21.0	—	—
K. Terrorist attacks on the United States	56.5	59.5	55.0	55.3	67.8	62.1
L. Attacks on American computer networks	43.1	50.1	39.6	42.5	—	—

Percent "Very serious"

NOTE: Differences between groups significant at the .001 level for all items except E.

Table 1.9. The Effectiveness of Military and Non-Military Tools in Coping
With Threats to National Security: Responses in the 1998–99 TISS Survey.

Reviewing some of the earlier lists of possible threats to national security, how effective is the use of military tools compared to non-military tools for coping with them?

	Percent Military Tools "Much more" or "Somewhat more" effective			
	Military leaders	Active reserve leaders	Civilian veteran leaders	Civilian non-veteran leaders
A. The emergence of China as a great military power	32.6	31.4	31.7	27.3
B. The proliferation of weapons of mass destruction to less-developed countries	49.2	62.1	51.6	46.0
C. Large numbers of immigrants and refugees coming to the U.S.	3.4	7.5	10.2	8.0
D. International terrorism	52.8	63.1	58.3	54.0
E. International drug trafficking	28.6	42.5	43.5	36.3
F. Expansion of Islamic fundamentalism	11.2	15.5	21.5	17.9
G. Attacks on American computer networks	14.8	15.5	17.6	17.2

NOTES: Differences between groups significant at the .001 level for all items. These questions were not included in the survey of the general public.

and we revisit it below in connection with the discussion of American culture, values, and institutions.

Five of these items were also included in the survey of the general public, and their responses diverged sharply from both military and civilian leaders on four issues: immigration, moral decline, economic competition from abroad, and terrorist attacks on the United States. Members of the general public, whether veterans or not, rated each of these potential threats as significantly more serious. These results are consistent with other surveys showing that public concern over immigration and imports far outstrips that of leaders (Holsti 1996, 89; Rielly 1999, 15).

After having rated the various dangers to American national security, respondents were then asked to assess the relative effectiveness of military and non-military tools for coping with seven of the threats. Once again the statistically significant differences across rows in Table 1.9 mask some areas of agreement. Moderate majorities in all groups felt that military tools would be more effective for dealing with international terror-ism, and all but the civilian non-veterans came to the same conclusion about coping with proliferation of weapons of mass destruction. Con-versely, few military or civilian leaders rated military instruments as more effective for dealing with immigration, Islamic fundamentalism, or attacks on American computer networks. Interestingly, only slightly more respondents judged military tools as relatively more effective for re-sponding to any threat arising from China's growing military capabili-ties. Finally, the effectiveness of using the military to cope with interna-tional drug trafficking was the most divisive issue, but the cleavages were not between the military on one side and the civilians on the other.

Still another cluster of items focused on a wide range of possible uses for the military, from the most traditional one of fighting and winning wars to dealing with domestic disorders within the United States (Table 1.10). The former function gained a "very important" rating from virtu-ally all respondents in the four leadership groups. Although use of the military for dealing with domestic disturbances has a long history, going back to putting down Shays's rebellion and earlier, it is also one of the more contentious issues in current debates about civil-military relations. In his discussion of the "gap," Ricks cites some intemperate comments by Marine officers about using the military to deal with enemies at home. However, of the TISS survey respondents, members of the elite military and active reserve groups were the *least* likely to express support for this mission. Two possible uses of the military received virtually no support from any of the four leadership groups: to redress historical discrimina-tion and to intervene in civil wars abroad. That only 1 percent of the elite military assigned a "very important" rating to such interventions abroad is interesting in light of the post–Cold War interventions in Kosovo, Gre-nada, Panama, Somalia, Haiti, and Bosnia. Two other possible missions gained only modestly higher support: dealing with humanitarian needs abroad and combating drug trafficking. Although disaster relief has been a traditional mission of the reserves and National Guard—that role has also been given a high degree of prominence in radio ads for the Guard—it failed to elicit very much support from the active reserves, and it was assigned only a slightly higher priority by respondents in the other three leadership groups. The possible use of the military that most dis-tinctly divided the TISS respondents along military-civilian lines was, "As an instrument of foreign policy, even if that means in operations other than war." The military have traditionally been used for a variety of such purposes—actions short of war against non-state actors such as pi-rates, and sending a signal of resolve to both allies and enemies, are two of the more venerable and prominent roles for military power—but only

Table 1.10. Uses of the Military: Responses in the 1998–99 TISS Survey.

The following are some possible uses of the military. Please indicate how important you consider each potential role for the military.

	Percent "Very important"			
	Military leaders	Active reserve leaders	Civilian veteran leaders	Civilian non-veteran leaders
A. As an instrument of foreign policy, even if that means engaging in operations other than war	52.9	55.4	33.7	32.4
B. To fight and win our country's wars	99.0	99.2	96.7	90.0
C. To redress historical discrimination, for instance against African-Americans and women	0.8	1.8	4.9	7.4
D. To provide disaster relief within the U.S.	26.4	26.4	26.9	36.8
E. To address humanitarian needs abroad	4.8	5.7	10.2	18.4
F. To deal with domestic disorder within the U.S.	9.0	14.5	19.2	20.9
G. To intervene in civil wars abroad	1.0	1.8	1.9	2.2
H. To combat drug trafficking	10.6	25.8	19.5	20.5

NOTES: Differences between groups significant at the .001 level for all items except G. These questions were not included in the survey of the general public.

a bare majority of the elite military and active reserves assigned that a "very important" rating, and strong majorities in the civilian leadership groups gave it a lower priority.

On balance, the level of agreement exhibited in Table 1.10 is at least as impressive as the extent of dissensus. It seems clear that substantial majorities among the respondents were generally comfortable with the most traditional use of the military—fighting and winning wars—while also expressing very limited support for using the military to redress social and economic problems, whether at home or abroad.[23]

The final foreign policy item in the TISS survey asked whether the 1998 U.S. bombing raids on suspected terrorist sites in Afghanistan and Sudan were a legitimate response to the bombing of American embassies in Kenya and Tanzania. Majorities of respondents in all four leadership groups agreed on the legitimacy of the retaliation, but there were nevertheless quite striking inter-group differences; among the leaders, the elite military (78 percent) and active reserves (79 percent) expressed greater support for the raids than did the civilian veterans (72 percent) and civilian non-veterans (67 percent). The differences between the military and civilians were even larger in the extreme response options, "agree strongly" and "disagree strongly."

Although there are strong partisan and ideological differences between military and civilian leaders taking part in the TISS survey, divisions on defense and foreign policy issues were often more muted and subtle, and they did not consistently follow any single or simple pattern. The military leaders followed "realist" reasoning on many issues, assigning a relatively low priority to goals and instruments often favored by liberal internationalists, whereas civilians were more inclined to give higher priority to the latter. But in many respects, the areas of agreement that are displayed on Tables 1.5 through 1.10 were almost as striking as those of dissensus

DOMESTIC ISSUES

The first cluster of domestic issues presented respondents with some of the more controversial economic and social issues of the past few decades. Many of these items also appeared in the four most recent FPLP surveys. Table 1.11 summarizes responses of the military and civilian leaders taking part in the TISS survey.

Several of the questions yielded very strong majorities across all

---

23. Jentleson (1992) and Jentleson and Britton (1998) have shown that a "pretty prudent public" supports interventions abroad to prevent or redress international aggression, but not to deal with civil wars.

Table 1.11. Positions on Selected Domestic Issues: Responses in the 1998–99 TISS Survey.

This question asks you to indicate your position on certain domestic issues.

| | | | Percent "Agree strongly" or "Agree somewhat" | | | |
	Military leaders	Active reserve leaders	Civilian veteran leaders	Civilian non-veteran leaders	General public veterans	General public non-veterans
A. Busing children in order to achieve school in-tegration	21.9	16.6	21.5	37.9	—	—
B. Using any budget surpluses to reduce the na-tional debt rather than to reduce taxes	84.6	79.6	75.3	76.4	—	—
C. Relaxing environmental regulations to stimu-late economic growth	19.2	29.5	30.5	20.8	—	—
D. Providing tuition tax credits to parents who send children to private or parochial schools	52.5	55.3	50.0	43.2	—	—
E. Leaving abortion decisions to women and their doctors	64.9	67.6	76.8	77.9	—	—
F. Encouraging mothers to stay at home with their children rather than working outside the home	51.1	46.8	57.7	41.0	—	—
G. Permitting prayer in public schools	73.8	73.3	53.6	46.6	80.0	74.6
H. Reducing the defense budget in order to in-crease the federal education budget	14.0	11.1	33.7	51.4	—	—

Table 1.11. *Continued.*

This question asks you to indicate your position on certain domestic issues.

				Percent "Agree strongly" or "Agree somewhat"			
	Military leaders	Active reserve leaders	Civilian veteran leaders	Civilian non-veteran leaders	General public veterans	General public non-veterans
I. Barring homosexuals from teaching in public schools	44.4	41.6	29.0	18.1	—	—
J. Easing restrictions on the construction of nuclear power plants	31.9	35.5	44.1	28.7	—	—
K. Redistributing income from the wealthy to the poor through taxation and subsidies	23.5	17.1	31.8	45.6	44.9	53.7
L. Banning the death penalty	10.4	7.8	24.3	37.3	—	—
M. Placing stringent controls on the sale of handguns	69.2	54.1	68.1	79.3	—	—

NOTE: Differences between groups significant at the .001 level for all items.

groups. These included an issue that generated a good deal of debate in the long run-up to the 2000 presidential election: whether to use budget surpluses to reduce the national debt or to reduce taxes. The former option won strong support from all groups of respondents taking part in the TISS survey of leaders.[24] Somewhat smaller majorities in all groups favored keeping the government out of abortion decisions, but there were quite substantial differences between the military and civilian sub-samples, with the civilian leaders expressing greater support for leaving such decisions to women and their doctors. Stringent controls on the sale of handguns were also favored by a large segment in all groups, but there was more variation here than for abortion rights. All four groups of respondents were strongly opposed to "relaxing environmental regulations to stimulate economic growth."

There were quite substantial differences on a large number of the domestic issues, and supporters and opponents tended to divide along civilian-military lines. Six issues gave rise to inter-group gaps exceeding 20 percent, including four that centered on educational institutions: school busing, school prayer, homosexual teachers in public schools, and the federal education budget. Military respondents were least enthusiastic about school busing and, not surprisingly, about reallocating some defense budget funds for education. They were also by far the strongest supporters of school prayer and banning gay teachers from public schools. Two other issues that tended to divide respondents along civilian-military lines were income redistribution and banning the death penalty. Neither proposal won a majority of support from any group, but the military expressed the strongest opposition. Two issues yielded rather divided results among all four leadership groups: encouraging mothers to stay at home with their children, and tuition tax credits for parents who send their children to private or parochial school.

The TISS survey of the general public included only two of these domestic policy issues. School prayer has stronger support in the general public than among either the military or civilian leaders. In contrast, public agreement and disagreement were almost evenly balanced on the issue of income distribution. Even this more modest level of approval for

---

24. According to a *Washington Post*–ABC survey, the general public also prefers that surpluses be used to cope with the future Social Security shortfalls (43 percent) and reduction of the national debt (24 percent), rather than for tax cuts (20 percent) (Stevenson 1999, A1). This finding seems more consistent with the "rational public" thesis, which holds that even a poorly informed public can express preferences that reflect broad national values rather than merely narrow, short-sighted, and self-interested ones. Popkin (1991) has described this ability as "low information rationality."

such a proposal nevertheless far outstripped the level of support expressed by the elite military, active reservists, and civilian veterans.

Responses to twelve of these items—six economic and six social issues—were used to create two scales to classify respondents into four groups. A single liberal-to-conservative dimension did not seem adequate, because policy preferences on economic issues do not necessarily correspond ideologically to those on social issues. Therefore, it may be useful to distinguish between them.

For purposes of creating a domestic issue typology, on economic issues liberals were assumed to *favor*: an active role for government in regulating the economy and activities that may threaten the environment; and taxation for purposes of income redistribution, while opposing tax policies that provide benefits mainly for the more affluent. On social issues, liberals were assumed to *support*: an active role for government in promoting the interests of those who have traditionally been at a disadvantage owing to race, class, gender, or other attributes, and a ban on the death penalty, at least in part because it has been inflicted disproportionately upon members of some disadvantaged groups.

Conservatives were assumed to *favor* the following positions on economic issues: removal or reduction of governmental restrictions on economic activity, including environmental regulations; reduction in taxes; and a large defense budget to ensure a strong national defense. On social issues conservatives were assumed to *oppose*: an active role for government in attempting to legislate equality between classes, sexes, races, or other groups; and an active role for government in support of those who challenge "traditional values," including advocates for gay rights or a pro-choice position on abortion.

These premises provided a set of guidelines to score responses to twelve of the items in Table 1.11. A response of "agree strongly" with a conservative position as described above was scored as 2, "agree somewhat" as 1, "no opinion" as 0, "disagree somewhat" as -1, and "disagree strongly" as -2. Each respondent was assigned two summary scores, the first based on responses to six economic issues: allocation of budget surpluses (Table 11, item B), relaxing environmental restriction (11-C), tuition tax credit (11-D), the defense budget (11-H), nuclear power (11-J), and income redistribution (11-K). The second score was derived from answers to six social issues: school busing (11-A), abortion (11-E), where mothers should work (11-F), school prayer (11-G), gay teachers (11-I), and the death penalty (11-L). The two scores were then used to classify each respondent as belonging to one of four groups: *liberals* (liberal on both scales), *conservatives* (conservative on both scales), *populists* (liberal on

Table 1.12. Domestic Policy Orientations Among Respondents to the 1998–99 TISS Survey.

		Economic Issues		
		Liberal		Conservative
		Liberals		Libertarians
		MIL	14.4%	MIL	8.2%
	Liberal	AR	14.5	AR	8.0
		CV	31.1	CV	10.5
Social Issues		CNV	49.8	CNV	9.9
		Populists		Conservatives
		MIL	36.4%	MIL	40.9%
	Conservative	AR	27.2	AR	50.3
		CV	18.7	CV	39.7
		CNV	17.2	CNV	23.1

KEY: MIL = Military leaders; AR = Active reserve leaders; CV = Civilian veteran leaders; CNV = Civilian non-veteran leaders.
NOTE: Most of the questions for these scales were not included in the survey of the general public, thereby eliminating the possibility of classifying these respondents.

economic issues, conservative on social ones), and *libertarians* (conservative on economic issues, liberal on social ones).

Table 1.12 reveals the distribution of the four groups of respondents in the domestic issue classification scheme. The results are very much in line with those of the earlier FPLP studies, which employed the same scoring scheme. Members of the military groups dominate the two quadrants defined by social conservatism. They are largely *conservatives*—an absolute majority of the active reserves are in that category—but many are also *populists*, perhaps in part because many aspects of military life involve a very active economic role by government, including services that range from medical care to retail outlets and recreational facilities. In contrast, a plurality of the civilian veterans are in the *conservative* quadrant, followed by *liberals*, *populists*, and *libertarians* in that order. The civilian non-veterans constitute by far the most *liberal* group: almost half of them are in that category. Fewer than one in ten of those taking part in the TISS survey were classified as *libertarians*—those favoring a liberal stance on social issues and a conservative one on economics—with only a very modestly higher proportion of civilian respondents.

Another cluster of questions asked both leaders and the general public to assess the importance of several domestic issues on a scale of 1 to 100. As revealed in Table 1.13, wide gaps between the military and civilians emerged on all items with the exception of the illegal drug problem, which ranked at or near the middle for all the leadership groups. Although the growing gap between rich and poor Americans ranked last in importance among all groups except the civilian non-veterans, there were wide disparities among them, with very few among the two military sub-samples expressing great concern for the issue.

Civilians attributed greater importance to environmental protection by fairly substantial margins, and those in the military sub-samples rated "the decline in integrity among public officials" as more important than did their civilian counterparts, some of whom are themselves public officials (elected officeholders, State Department personnel, Foreign Service Officers, etc.). Indeed, the latter issue ranked first among the elite military and reservists, but well behind the stability of Social Security among civilians.

Compared to those of the military leaders, more of the general public expressed concern over these five issues, notably with respect to Social Security, illegal drugs, the environment, and the rich-poor gap, and to a lesser extent the integrity of public officials. For members of the general public, Social Security payments are likely to constitute a higher proportion of their pensions than is the case for elites, whether military or civilians. There was also a significant gap between the public and civilian leaders, most strikingly on the drug issue. These results parallel responses on the threat question—summarized in Table 1.8 above—wherein the general public expressed greater apprehension about many possible threats to the national security.

Still another cluster of items asked those taking part in the TISS survey to express their views on a half-dozen questions about social values (Table 1.14). Two-thirds or more of the four leadership groups, as well as the general public, agreed that "the decline of traditional values is contributing to the breakdown of our society," but a considerable gap between the military and civilians emerged on the question of whether definitions of right and wrong need to be adjusted in light of a changing world; relatively few agreed with that proposition, but civilians were significantly more likely to do so. Two of the items in Table 1.14 focus on one of the themes in the Ricks "gap" thesis: the possible role of the military in redeeming American society. Well over two-thirds of those in the military sub-samples agreed that, by its example, "the military could help American society become more moral," and approximately similar proportions accepted the proposition that "civilian society would be better off it if adopted more of the military's values and customs." Neither of

Table 1.13. Assessments of Selected Issues: Responses in the 1998–99 TISS Survey.

Please tell us how important the following issues are to you. Please rate them from 100 (most important) to 1 (least important).

	Military leaders	Active reserve leaders	Civilian veteran leaders	Civilian non-veteran leaders	General public veterans	General public non-veterans
			Percent giving a rating of 80 or more			
Financial stability of Social Security	47.6	52.0	65.5	65.0	77.0	69.2
The illegal drug problem in the U.S.	41.4	50.3	45.7	40.6	75.4	64.8
Protection of the environment	35.3	38.0	43.6	52.9	61.8	69.3
The growing gap between rich and poor Americans	16.2	15.2	31.9	40.7	30.4	38.8
The decline in integrity among public officials	64.6	58.9	56.3	45.5	63.4	61.1

NOTE: Differences between groups significant at the .001 level for all items.

Table 1.14. Positions on Social Issues: Responses in the 1998–99 TISS Survey.

This question asks you to indicate your position on a variety of social issues.

	Percent "Agree strongly" or "Agree somewhat"					
	Military leaders	Active reserve leaders	Civilian veteran leaders	Civilian non-veteran leaders	General public veterans	General public non-veterans
A. The decline of traditional values is contributing to the breakdown of our society	88.6	88.5	78.3	67.0	83.4	81.5
B. Through leading by example, the military could help American society become more moral	70.3	72.1	56.6	37.4	—	—
C. The world is changing and we should adjust our view of what is moral and immoral behavior to fit these changes	10.1	19.3	24.5	33.6	—	—
D. Civilian society would be better off if it adopted more of the military's values and customs	77.0	72.9	44.5	25.0	47.8	33.5
E. American society would have fewer problems if people took God's will more seriously	60.6	62.3	54.6	48.0	79.5	81.7
F. All Americans should be willing to give up their lives to defend our country	80.2	84.0	77.2	60.0	72.7	67.9

NOTE: Differences between groups significant at the .001 level for all items.

those prescriptions for redeeming American society gained powerful support among civilians, although the veterans were far more favorably inclined than non-veterans to accept them. The final two items also yielded discernible differences from the civilian and military groups. All but the civilian non-veterans agreed, although by less than overwhelming margins, that society would benefit from taking "God's will" (not further defined) more seriously. This prescription received especially strong support from the general public. The proposition that all Americans should be prepared to give up their lives in defense of the country gained strong support from the elite military, active reserves, civilian veterans, and the general public, rather less (but still a majority) from the non-veterans.

The final cluster of domestic policy questions centered on censorship and the willingness of respondents to have their local public libraries remove books by a communist, by an author attacking religion, or by a writer defending homosexuality. None of these items yielded statistically significant differences: censorship has few proponents among either civilians or the military. Retention of books favoring homosexuality received slightly less support—in the range of 82–86 percent—compared to 89–94 percent in the other two hypothetical situations. Assuming that these responses express genuine views, it seems clear that book burning is not highly regarded by either military or civilian leaders.

The previous section revealed evidence of both disagreement and convergence between military and civilian leaders on defense and foreign policy issues. To a somewhat greater extent the domestic issues discussed in this section gave rise to cleavages, but once again the evidence points toward some areas of consensus as well as those of dissensus. For example, what might broadly be called social or value issues such as school prayer, gay rights, or the death penalty were generally more divisive than those that revolved around economics.

CULTURE, VALUES, AND INSTITUTIONS

The Ricks thesis that there is a growing gap between the military and civilian society assigns a central role to the alleged contempt of the military for civilian culture, values, and institutions.[25] Both in his depiction of young Marines who have returned to their homes after the rigors of boot camp and in recounting the views of some younger officers in the Corps, he revealed that many Marines regard civilian culture as fundamentally

---

25.   These issues are explored in greater length by Gronke and Feaver in Chapter 3.

lacking in such values as self-discipline, hard work, honesty, and loyalty. The perceived materialism, hedonism, and selfishness of civilians has, according to Ricks, bred a growing contempt among those in uniform for the society that they are trained and pledged to defend.

Because the FPLP surveys were short on questions that might put this central element of the Ricks thesis to a rigorous test, the TISS questionnaire included several clusters of items that might be used to compare the ways in which military and civilian leaders appraise contemporary American culture and institutions. The first of these asked respondents to make a judgment about twelve terms, some favorable and others not, as appropriate descriptors of civilian and military cultures.

Table 1.15 summarizes the manner in which members of the four leadership groups judged civilian society. Based on these responses, it appears that neither the elite military nor active reservists hold contemporary civilian culture in very high regard. They are willing to concede that Americans work hard, are creative, and are not overly cautious, and to deny that they are intolerant or rigid. With respect to the latter, it is not wholly clear whether these respondents thought of "rigid" as an unfavorable trait (as in knowing only a single way to tackle a wide range of complex problems), or a favorable one (as in an unwillingness to compromise one's core values and beliefs for personal gain). Military responses to the remaining items suggest a very dismal picture indeed: civilian culture is viewed as materialistic, self-indulgent, undisciplined, and dishonest, on balance ungenerous, and worst of all, from the perspective of core military values, disloyal. Large minorities of the elite military and active reserves describe civilian culture as corrupt.[26] Because the term "culture" may be somewhat ambiguous, it is possible that not all respondents defined it in precisely the same way. For example, for some it might refer to modal beliefs and behavior patterns of the society as a whole, whereas others may have been thinking, somewhat more narrowly, about such ar-

---

26. Although public comments on the FPLP study by active and retired military personnel have tended to be dismissive (for example, Collins 1999), virtually all of the many e-mails about the study from members of the military have indicated that, if anything, the findings have understated rather than overstated the magnitude and consequences of the civilian-military gap. For example, an active-duty officer at the Army's Command and General Staff College wrote: "I am sorry to say that you would not believe the fierce Republican partisanship of what seems to me to be the preponderance of my fellow officers, especially when confronted with President Clinton's ongoing crisis. What troubles me most about my fellow officers is the general contempt that they hold for civilian society. You slightly hedge on this issue in your essay but I can tell you from my experience here at Leavenworth most mid-career officers do believe that civilian society is generally without values or moral direction."

Table 1.15. Judgments About Civilian Culture: Responses in the 1998–99 TISS Survey.

This question asks you to make some judgments about civilian culture in this country. Please indicate all terms that you believe apply to civilian culture.

	Military leaders	Active reserve leaders	Civilian veteran leaders	Civilian non-veteran leaders	General public veterans	General public non-veterans
			Percent checking each description			
Honest	38.4	40.8	44.4	40.3	—	—
Intolerant*	21.7	32.6	32.1	37.5	55.1	50.0
Materialistic	92.9	91.3	88.8	91.9	—	—
Corrupt	34.5	38.4	31.2	33.8	—	—
Generous	42.4	46.3	51.3	42.7	—	—
Self-indulgent	76.7	74.7	73.6	74.7	82.0	83.2
Hard-working	64.5	63.2	64.2	63.8	74.6	76.4
Rigid	5.3	5.8	6.3	8.2	—	—
Disciplined	3.4	5.8	9.5	6.9	—	—
Creative*	78.5	80.3	77.7	69.3	—	—
Loyal*	12.5	14.2	23.2	21.8	—	—
Overly cautious	15.6	21.3	20.9	22.1	—	—

NOTE: Differences between groups significant at the .001 level only for items marked with an asterisk.

tifacts of popular culture as music, art, literature, movies, television, theater, and the like.

While this evidence might immediately lead one to conclude that Ricks had accurately located the source of the civilian-military gap, a glance at the responses of the civilian leaders—and of the general public on three of the items—suggest that in fact the highly critical views of the military about American culture are more widely shared. There are, to be sure, statistically significant differences among groups on several of the twelve traits, but the much more striking pattern that emerges from Table 1.15 is that U.S. civilian leaders also have a very jaundiced view of contemporary American culture; not even a quarter of them are willing to describe it as "loyal."

The corresponding appraisals of military culture are presented in Table 1.16. In comparison to the dismal report card on civilian culture, that of the military comes off rather better. The elite military respondents rate their own culture in exceptionally favorable terms. It is honest, disciplined, loyal, and free of materialism, corruption, or self-indulgent tendencies, according to more than 90 percent of the surveyed officers; and only somewhat fewer rate it as tolerant, generous, and appropriately cautious. Only on creativity and rigidity do a majority of the military seem to harbor some doubts but, as noted earlier, it is not clear that the term "rigid" is a term of opprobrium in this context. The active reserves offered appraisal that deviated only in minor ways from those of their active-duty counterparts. The civilian leaders and the general public on balance held military culture in higher esteem than civilian culture, although they nevertheless expressed somewhat less enthusiastic judgments than did their military counterparts. For example, they offered a significantly less favorable assessment of military culture on such traits as honesty, tolerance, generosity, corruption, hard work, rigidity, and creativity. These points aside, it is clear that most American leaders view military culture in more favorable terms than civilian culture.

To gain a somewhat more specific perspective on appraisals of American society, those taking part in the TISS survey were also asked to rate their levels of confidence in seventeen major institutions. The data shown in Table 1.17 tend to reinforce the view that most American leaders have a rather dismal view of contemporary society, and to confirm that the data in Table 1.15 reflect actual judgments of the country's culture. Only the Supreme Court gained a "great deal of confidence" rating from a majority among each of the four leadership groups. The other political institutions, including the presidency, the executive branch, and Congress, received abysmal assessments; not even a quarter of respondents in any group expressed a high degree of confidence in any of them. But as bad as these

Table 1.16. Judgments About Military Culture: Responses in the 1998–99 TISS Survey.

This question asks you to make some judgments about military culture in this country. Please indicate all terms that you believe apply to military culture.

			Percent checking each description			
	Military leaders	Active reserve leaders	Civilian veteran leaders	Civilian non-veteran leaders	General public veterans	General public non-veterans
Honest*	94.4	87.9	75.1	58.0	—	—
Intolerant*	30.2	29.7	36.7	49.9	44.9	60.8
Materialistic*	9.2	7.4	14.6	15.7	—	—
Corrupt*	2.6	3.4	6.3	15.4	—	—
Generous*	52.7	47.6	35.2	26.8	—	—
Self-indulgent*	8.7	11.8	15.2	16.7	34.6	36.5
Hard-working*	96.4	94.5	80.5	77.5	85.4	87.6
Rigid*	51.5	54.2	69.1	78.6	—	—
Disciplined	97.5	96.6	94.8	93.9	—	—
Creative*	43.5	37.4	22.9	15.6	—	—
Loyal*	96.7	95.3	90.3	84.4	—	—
Overly cautious	30.7	32.4	28.9	26.1	—	—

NOTE: Differences between groups significant at the .001 level only for items marked with an asterisk.

Table 1.17. Confidence in American Institutions: Responses in the 1998–99 TISS Survey.

The following is a list of some institutions in this country. As far as these institutions are concerned, would you say you have a great deal of confidence, only some confidence, or hardly any confidence in them?

Percent "Great deal" of confidence

	Military leaders	Active reserve leaders	Civilian veteran leaders	Civilian non-veteran leaders	General public veterans	General public non-veterans
Organized religion	39.6	36.2	26.3	24.5	—	—
Presidency	16.9	17.6	21.1	20.3	27.8	29.1
The press	3.9	4.6	10.3	10.4	6.8	7.1
U.S. Supreme Court	72.1	58.0	58.1	52.5	50.2	41.9
Congress	12.5	9.8	7.2	6.3	15.1	16.0
Major companies	11.6	10.9	10.8	7.7	21.5	15.9
Primary and secondary education*	16.5	15.2	17.3	18.1	—	—
The executive branch of the federal government	14.7	11.1	13.9	15.3	24.9	18.0
Universities	33.7	33.8	38.2	45.3	—	—
Law enforcement agencies	49.9	42.7	26.7	25.2	—	—
Labor unions	1.6	1.6	3.6	7.7	—	—
The legal profession	1.9	4.9	8.7	6.5	—	—
Organized political parties (such as the Republican and Democratic parties)*	1.4	1.5	3.6	2.7	—	—
The military	86.3	79.8	51.8	34.9	65.4	50.8
The medical profession	58.4	54.1	50.4	41.1	—	—
Voluntary organizations*	43.9	42.6	39.9	47.3	—	—
Television	1.0	1.3	2.5	2.4	9.8	7.2

NOTE: Differences between groups significant at the .001 level for all items except those marked with an asterisk.

scores are, they are better than those assigned to other American institutions, such as the press, labor unions, the legal profession, political parties, and television. Not even 5 percent of the two military groups expressed strong confidence in them, and civilian ratings of them were only slightly better. Institutions that, on balance, received middling ratings include law enforcement agencies, the medical profession, voluntary organizations, and universities, while major companies, organized religion, and primary and secondary education were rated only slightly more favorably than the pariahs.

Although there were significant differences among the four leadership groups in their ratings of all but three institutions listed in Table 1.17, the degree of agreement, especially on the least esteemed of them, is also impressive. The largest gap between the military and civilian respondents emerged on assessment of the military as an institution. Not surprisingly, the elite military and active reservists overwhelmingly expressed a "great deal" of confidence in their own institution, a level of enthusiasm less widely shared by the civilians; a bare majority of the veterans gave the military that rating, but only a little more than a third of the non-veterans did so. Consequently, the range of appraisals of the military across the four groups spanned an exceptionally wide range, exceeding 50 percent.[27]

Appraisals by the general public of these institutions were on balance more generous than those expressed by leaders, although assessments of the military and Supreme Court fell well short of those expressed by members of military and active reserve. The general public was asked to rate few of the institutions that generated the strongest disdain from the military and civilian leaders.

Tables 1.15, 1.16, and 1.17 indicate that most aspects of military culture and the military as an institution received a rather strong report card from both leaders and the general public. Favorable public ratings notwithstanding, however, it appears that many members of the military feel inadequately appreciated. Those taking part in the TISS leadership survey were asked about the level of respect accorded to the military by most Americans. A majority among the elite military (51 percent), active reservists (64 percent), and civilian veterans (51 percent) replied that the military gets "less respect than it deserves," whereas a plurality (49 percent) of civilian non-veterans judged that the armed forces get "about as much respect" as they deserve. Although differences among the four groups of leaders were significant, very few respondents in any of the

---

27. For a further and more detailed summary of public confidence in the military, see King and Karabell (1999).

groups felt that the military is accorded "more respect than it deserves" by most Americans.

Table 1.17 indicated that public education is not a revered institution among most American leaders, and such issues as school busing, school prayer, and school vouchers have engendered contentious local, state, and national debates in recent years. In light of this background, the TISS questionnaire included a question about the precollegiate schooling that respondents' children had received. Notwithstanding the controversies surrounding public schools in many areas, substantial majorities of those with children among the elite military (82 percent), active reservists (79 percent), civilian veterans (78 percent), and civilian non-veterans (74 percent) sent them to public schools. Nevertheless, some interesting differences did emerge from the data: home schooling was used by an infinitesimally small fraction of reservists and civilians, but it was selected by a larger number of the military: more than 3 percent of those with children. Of those with children, more than a quarter of the civilian non-veterans and about a fifth of the civilian veteran and active reserve leaders opted to send their children to private or parochial schools, whereas fewer than 15 percent of the military leaders selected those schools for their children.

MILITARY AND RELATIONS WITH CIVILIAN SOCIETY
The TISS survey asked both the four leadership groups and the general public how closely they follow military issues. Not surprisingly, members of the military and active reserves were by far the most attentive to questions involving their profession; more than 70 percent of them reported that they pay "a great deal" of attention to questions such as weapons systems, military deployments abroad, and the capabilities of the armed forces (Table 1.18). Among civilians, both opinion leaders and members of the general public, veterans were much more inclined to be attentive to military issues than those who had not served on active duty. On the whole, the reported attentiveness of those in the general public sample appears very high, as 48 percent of the veterans and 17 percent of the non-veterans stated that they paid "a great deal" of attention to military subjects; most other surveys have found that public attention to domestic issues such as education, crime, drugs, the economy, and the like rank far ahead of foreign and defense policy.

Upon what sources do members of the four leadership groups rely for information about the military? The TISS survey asked each respondent to indicate their top three sources. The results, displayed in Table 1.19, reveal very wide disparities between the military and civilian groups. The military leaders and active reservists relied far less on news-

Table 1.18. Attention to Military Issues by Respondents to the 1998–99 TISS Survey.

Please indicate how closely you tend to follow issues involving the military, such as weapons systems, military deployment abroad, the capabilities of the armed forces, and so on. Would you say that you pay a great deal of attention to military issues, some attention, a little attention, or almost no attention?

	Military leaders	Active reserve leaders	Civilian veteran leaders	Civilian non-veteran leaders	General public veterans	General public non-veterans
			Percent "Great deal" of attention			
A great deal	75.4%	72.4%	38.9%	22.3%	48.0%	17.0%
Some	22.2	25.1	48.7	49.0	42.2	49.0
Little	1.9	2.6	10.3	22.2	6.4	24.0
Almost none	0.5	0.0	3.1	6.4	3.4	10.1

NOTE: Differences between groups significant at the .001 level.

Table 1.19. Sources of Information About the Military of Respondents to the 1998–99 TISS Survey.

This question asks you about the information you obtain from the media about the military. Please circle your top three sources of information about the military.

	Percent checking each option			
	Military leaders	Active reserve leaders	Civilian veteran leaders	Civilian non-veteran leaders
Newspapers	66.9	57.8	89.2	88.5
Television network news	55.3	46.6	65.3	69.4
Television local news	3.4	3.6	6.9	12.7
Television talk shows	1.6	1.3	1.9	5.4
Radio news	5.5	5.4	15.0	23.6
Radio talk shows	0.5	0.6	0.7	1.9
General news magazines * (e.g., *Time, U.S. News and World Report*)	6.6	4.8	8.2	15.0
Special news magazines (e.g., *Congressional Quarterly*)	0.8	1.3	0.9	2.2
Opinion magazines (e.g., *New Republic, National Review*)	3.2	3.9	9.2	12.2
Movies	1.3	1.3	1.1	4.9
Fiction books*	1.1	1.3	1.1	2.1
Nonfiction books*	3.1	2.6	2.3	4.3
Military trade/professional publications	56.5	72.5	19.7	6.3
Army/Navy/Air Force Times	54.6	44.8	9.4	1.3
Internet newsgroups	7.4	6.7	1.7	1.9
Other*	5.8	8.0	9.4	7.4

NOTES: Differences between groups significant at the .001 level except for items marked with an asterisk. This question was not included in the survey of the general public.

paper, and somewhat less on television, radio, news magazines, and opinion magazines; these two groups made far greater use of military trade and professional publications, as well as of newspapers published by their branches of the service. The military and reservists also relied on Internet news groups to a much greater extent than their civilian counterparts. These results are revisited in the conclusion as part of an analysis of the military and the media.

Still another question asked those taking part in the TISS survey to assess how the mass media depict the military. As revealed in Table 1.20, quite significant differences emerge from responses of the four groups. Only a small minority of civilians believes that the media depict the military in a hostile manner, whereas a much large proportion of the military believes that to be the case. Fewer than half of the elite military believe that the media have been even "somewhat supportive," much less "very supportive." Whether or not these judgments reflect accurately the performance of the media, they may help to explain in part the very negative military assessments of the media, as revealed in several places above.

The TISS survey also included more specific questions about several major American institutions. Three of them asked respondents whether political leaders, journalists, and military leaders "share the same values as the American people." Presumably deviations from those values might be regarded as somehow undesirable, but in light of the very dismal appraisals of American culture summarized above, that premise is not necessarily beyond doubt. In any case, the results presented in Table 1.21 tend to confirm the previous judgments about political leaders and journalists. Within none of the four leadership groups did a majority believe that either political leaders or journalists share the values of the American people. Once again, opinions about journalists are even less flattering than those of political leaders. In contrast to the rather uniformly negative view of those two groups, quite substantial differences emerged on the perceived concordance between values of military leaders and those of the general public; the elite military and active reservists generally answered in the affirmative, as did a majority of the civilian veterans, whereas the civilian non-veterans were less sure on that score. It is worth pointing again to a possible ambiguity in responses to this item: a "no" answer on this question might reflect a belief on the part of the military that they do not share the values of the American people because theirs are in fact superior.

Respondents in the four leadership groups were given a further opportunity to assess the country's civilian leadership with a question that asked, "How knowledgeable do you think our political leaders are about the modern military?" The responses of the military officers and active

Table 1.20. Depictions of the Military in the Mass Media, According to Respondents to the 1998–99 TISS Survey.

In general, mass media depictions of the military are:

| | Percent checking each option | | | |
	Military leaders	Active reserve leaders	Civilian veteran leaders	Civilian non-veteran leaders
very supportive	3.4	1.8	8.9	13.9
somewhat supportive	44.7	51.9	50.3	51.1
neutral	16.5	10.9	12.3	12.8
somewhat hostile	32.1	29.5	23.5	16.0
very hostile	1.8	4.4	1.7	1.5
no opinion	1.5	1.6	3.4	4.6

NOTES: Differences between groups significant at the .001 level. This question was not included in the survey of the general public.

Table 1.21. Perceived Values of Political Leaders, Journalists, and Military Leaders: Responses to the 1998–99 TISS Survey.

Do you think our political leaders, in general, share the same values as the American people?

| | | Percent checking each option | | |
	Military leaders	Active reserve leaders	Civilian veteran leaders	Civilian non-veteran leaders
yes	40.6	36.2	37.9	35.9
no	35.4	35.4	37.3	36.7
not sure	22.9	26.6	26.0	24.7
no opinion	1.1	1.8	1.0	2.0

Do you think journalists, in general, share the same values as the American people?

| | | Percent checking each option | | |
	Military leaders	Active reserve leaders	Civilian veteran leaders	Civilian non-veteran leaders
yes	31.1	21.4	27.2	31.0
no	46.7	56.6	51.4	44.9
not sure	20.7	20.7	20.0	21.3
no opinion	1.4	1.3	1.4	2.8

Table 1.21. *Continued.*

Do you think military leaders, in general, share the same values as the American people?

| | Percent checking each option | | | |
	Military leaders	Active reserve leaders	Civilian reserve leaders	Civilian non-veteran leaders
yes	60.3	69.8	55.0	38.5
no	25.9	14.9	21.4	29.9
not sure	13.2	14.2	22.2	29.0
no opinion	C.6	1.0	1.4	2.7

NOTES: Differences between groups significant at the .001 level for only the third item. These questions were not included in the survey of the general public.

reservists are a stunning indictment of political leaders in Washington: well over 60 percent of both groups describe them as either "somewhat ignorant" or "very ignorant" (Table 1.22). President Clinton's lack of military experience no doubt lay behind some of these responses, but this assessment of civilian ignorance is also rooted in a more general trend. As Bianco and Markham reveal in Chapter 7, the percentage of members of Congress with any military service has declined steadily during recent decades. Civilian leaders, whether veterans or not, were significantly more generous in their appraisal of the knowledge levels of political leaders.

A cluster of eleven items asked respondents a number of questions about the military and its place in American society. The results summarized in Table 1.23 reveal near-consensus on several items, including pride in the military; confidence in the ability of the military to perform well in war, to maintain the standards required by national security, and to remain the best military in the world through the next decade; and an absence of disappointment should the respondent's child join the military. Each of these items gave rise to statistically significant differences across the leadership groups, but only on the latter did the range of responses exceed 12 percent; the civilian non-veterans were considerably less enthusiastic than leaders in the other groups about having a child in the military, but even at that, those who expressed disappointment constituted a distinct minority of about one in five.

Much larger gaps emerged on the other six items. In many respects the most interesting and puzzling gap concerns responses to the first item: "Most members of the military have a great deal of respect for civilian society." Almost 90 percent of the elite military and active reservists agreed, whereas civilian leaders and the general public were less sure. Recall the results cited above, especially in Tables 1.15 and 1.17, wherein most military officers disparaged civilian culture and expressed little confidence in most major American institutions. In light of such consistently negative judgments, it is not wholly clear why such an overwhelming majority of the military also believe that the military's members respect civilian society. Perhaps cognitive dissonance provides at least a partial explanation for this seeming anomaly: although many in the military are clearly critical of *specific aspects* of American society, it may be much harder for them also to state that they have no respect for a society that they are sworn to defend.

A comparable item on civilian respect for the military yielded rather strong support. Questions about obligatory national service for males and females gave rise to sharp differences approaching 30 percent in both cases, with military respondents expressing stronger agreement. Wide

Table 1.22. Knowledge About the Military Attributed to Political Leaders by Respondents to the 1998–99 TISS Survey.

How knowledgeable do you think our political leaders are about the modern military?

	Military leaders	Active reserve leaders	Civilian veteran leaders	Civilian non-veteran leaders
			Percent checking each option	
Very knowledgeable	1.0	0.5	8.1	10.2
Somewhat knowledgeable	33.0	35.9	53.8	58.0
Somewhat ignorant	52.3	49.6	30.4	25.7
Very ignorant	13.5	13.4	7.0	3.9
No opinion	0.3	0.5	0.8	2.2

NOTES: Differences between groups significant at the .001 level. This question was not included in the survey of the general public.

Table 1.23. Opinions About the U.S. Military: Responses in the 1998–99 TISS Survey.

Here are some statements people have made about the U.S. military. For each, please indicate whether you strongly agree, somewhat agree, somewhat disagree or strongly disagree.

			Percent "Agree strongly" or "Agree somewhat"			
	Military leaders	Active reserve leaders	Civilian veteran leaders	Civilian non-veteran leaders	General public veterans	General public non-veterans
A. Most members of the military have a great deal of respect for civilian society	85.5	89.7	78.5	65.5	83.0	76.0
B. Most members of civilian society have a great deal of respect for the military	76.9	63.4	67.6	69.6	63.4	75.6
C. All *male* citizens should be required to do some national service	81.7	84.1	74.6	52.2	—	—
D. All *female* citizens should be required to do some national service	65.3	71.0	55.6	42.5	—	—
E. I am proud of the men and women who serve in the military	99.6	99.8	98.4	93.7	—	—
F. I have confidence in the ability of our military to perform well in wartime	98.2	96.9	94.9	93.0	89.8	92.6
G. The U.S. Armed Forces are attracting high-quality, motivated recruits	76.8	78.9	59.9	47.4	—	—

Table 1.23. Continued.

Here are some statements people have made about the U.S. military. For each, please indicate whether you strongly agree, somewhat agree, somewhat disagree or strongly disagree.

	Percent "Agree strongly" or "Agree somewhat"					
	Military leaders	Active reserve leaders	Civilian veteran leaders	Civilian non-veteran leaders	General public veterans	General public non-veterans
H. Even if civilian society did not always appreciate the essential military values of commitment and unselfishness, our armed forces could still maintain required national standards	85.6	83.6	78.5	69.7	—	—
I. The American people understand the sacrifices made by the people who serve in the U.S. military	36.2	37.2	49.5	54.4	—	—
J. I expect that ten years from now America will still have the best military in the world	89.1	86.7	85.8	82.0	82.0	83.9
K. I would be disappointed if a child of mine joined the military	6.3	4.4	6.7	20.6	15.2	21.5

NOTE: Differences between groups significant at the .001 level for all items.

gaps dividing the military from civilian groups also emerged on the other two issues: the ability of the armed forces to recruit well-qualified personnel and the level of public understanding of the sacrifices entailed in a military career. The military sub-samples expressed much stronger agreement with the former proposition, and they disagreed sharply with the latter; only about a third of those in the military and reserves agreed that public understanding of their sacrifices is adequate. In this as in many other respects, it seems quite clear that many in the military feel a sense of disappointment, if not alienation, about aspects of American society.

Responses of the general public to five of these questions are very much in line with those of the civilian leaders, with one exception. Compared to civilian veterans in the leadership survey, general public respondents with military experience expressed a greater sense of disappointment should one of their children join the military.

Still another cluster of ten questions asked respondents to address certain specific features of military organization and culture (Table 1.24). Three of the items elicited nearly unanimous agreement: the need for a clear chain of command, the vital role of symbols and traditions to maintain morale and loyalty, and the importance of physical strength and courage even in a high-tech era. The latter two items also gained overwhelming approval from both veterans and non-veterans in the general public. Another half-dozen propositions gained the support of all four leadership groups, but with significant variations across them: the military has earned high marks for dealing with racial discrimination; the bonds of loyalty in the military differ from those in the business world; military leaders care more for their subordinates than do their civilian counterparts; good military pensions at an early age are important, as are the wide range of services and facilities at military bases; and joint training and doctrine have improved the performance of the military. Although majorities in each group agreed with these six propositions, civilian support tended to be somewhat lower. It may be worth noting that whereas the military did not assign a very high priority to stability of the Social Security system (Table 1.13), a very strong majority of civilians agreed that early retirement with a good pension is vital for the military. The item in Table 1.24 that generated the least agreement centered on the role of women: "Even though women can serve in the military, the military should remain basically masculine, dominated by male values and characteristics." The elite military and reservists, as well as the civilian veterans and members of the general public were almost evenly divided on the questions, with levels of agreement ranging between 42 percent and 52 percent. In contrast, only a third of the civilian non-veterans agreed.

A cluster of twelve items asked respondents to assess a number of factors that might constrain military effectiveness during times of war (Table 1.25). Although there were statistically significant differences among the four leadership groups on all of them, their rank orderings revealed some areas of agreement. A poor system of promotions was, for all groups, among the three most frequently cited factors that would "greatly hurt" effectiveness. Inaccurate reporting by the media appeared high in the rankings of the two military groups, and it was also among the top factors mentioned by the civilians. The military groups and the civilian veterans also saw a high risk from "Americans' lack of trust in the uniformed leaders of the military," but civilian non-veterans saw that as less of a problem. The obverse factor, "the military's lack of confidence in our political leadership" also ranked fairly high among all four groups. An issue that has received a good deal of public scrutiny in recent years—sexual harassment in the military—was also widely cited as a source of ineffectiveness, especially by the civilian non-veterans. Approximately one-fifth of the respondents in each group felt that military involvement in non-military affairs would also be a constraint on effectiveness. It is not altogether clear, however, whether all respondents had the same "non-military affairs" in mind. Was it a reference to interventions in civil wars? Delivery of humanitarian supplies? Interdictions of drug trafficking? Partisan political activity at home? Dealing with disorders within the United States?

Several of the items in Table 1.25 refer to cultural factors, including women entering the workplace, diminished male dominance, a ban on camaraderie-inducing language and behavior, old-fashioned views of morality, and differences between military and civilian cultures. None of these were very frequently identified as a potential constraint on effectiveness but, compared to the civilians, the military were somewhat less likely to do so. Strong majorities among the military clearly believe that most features of military culture are consistent with the effective performance of their duties. These judgments are also consistent with those encountered above in Tables 1.16, 1.17, 1.23, and 1.24, indicating that the military have a very favorable opinion of and take great pride in the culture of their own organization.

Only four of these questions were posed in the TISS/PRA survey of the general public: those on declining male domination of the military, a ban on certain language and behavior, maintenance of old-fashioned views of morality, and the nature of military culture. Compared to military and civilian leaders, in each instance both veterans and non-veterans among the general public expressed significantly greater concern that

Table 1.24. Statements About the U.S. Military: Responses in the 1998–99 TISS Survey.

Here are some statements people have made about the American military.

	Percent "Agree strongly" or "Agree somewhat"					
	Military leaders	Active reserve leaders	Civilian veteran leaders	Civilian non-veteran leaders	General public veterans	General public non-veterans
A. An effective military depends on a very structured organization with a clear chain of command	98.4	98.2	98.3	96.5	—	—
B. Military symbols—like uniforms and medals—and military traditions—like ceremonies and parades—are necessary to build morale, loyalty, and camaraderie in the military	97.1	99.0	95.8	91.3	96.1	94.1
C. Even though women can serve in the military, the military should remain basically masculine, dominated by male values and characteristics	41.2	45.1	51.8	33.6	53.6	49.8
D. The U.S. military has done a much better job of eliminating racial discrimination within the military than American society in general	95.6	94.0	87.6	66.1	—	—
E. Even in a high-tech era, people in the military have to have characteristics like strength, toughness, physical courage, and the willingness to make sacrifices	99.0	99.3	96.0	94.0	96.6	94.9

Table 1.24. *Continued.*

Here are some statements people have made about the American military.

	Percent "Agree strongly" or "Agree somewhat"					
	Military leaders	Active reserve leaders	Civilian veteran leaders	Civilian non-veteran leaders	General public veterans	General public non-veterans
F. The bonds and sense of loyalty that keep a military unit together under the stress of combat are fundamentally different than the bonds and loyalty that organizations try to develop in the business world	87.7	79.5	73.0	63.9	—	—
G. Since military life is a young person's profession, the chance to retire with a good pension at a young age is very important to the military	87.0	81.6	81.7	68.6	—	—
H. On most military bases there are company stores, childcare centers, and recreational facilities right on the base. It is very important to keep these things on military bases in order to keep a sense of identity in the military community	78.7	83.9	80.3	67.6	—	—
I. Military leaders care more about the people under their command than leaders in the non-military world care about the people under them	88.2	85.2	70.2	60.7	—	—
J. The new emphasis on joint education, training, and doctrine across branches of the military has improved the effectiveness of the Armed Forces	90.3	92.5	70.9	58.0	—	—

NOTE: Differences between groups significant at the .001 level for all items except A.

Table 1.25. Constraints on Military Effectiveness: Responses to the 1998-99 TISS Survey.

There are many different things that people say might keep the military from being effective during times of war. For each of the following, please indicate if it might greatly hurt military effectiveness, somewhat hurt military effectiveness, has no effect on military effectiveness, or it is not happening at all in the U.S. military.

	Percent "Greatly hurts"					
	Military leaders	Active reserve leaders	Civilian veteran leaders	Civilian non-veteran leaders	General public veterans	General public non-veterans
A. Americans' lack of trust in the uniformed leaders of the military	33.0	33.3	28.9	21.5	—	—
B. The tensions created when women enter a new workplace	3.2	5.5	7.1	6.5	—	—
C. The military becoming less male-dominated	5.3	6.8	7.1	6.0	26.3	13.3
D. The military getting too involved in non-military affairs	19.4	22.1	20.8	18.4	—	—
E. A ban on language and behavior that encourage camaraderie among soldiers	9.8	14.6	13.6	9.9	25.9	18.0
F. A system for promotions and advancement in the military that does not work well	37.9	48.3	44.4	35.2	—	—
G. Non-military people getting too involved in military affairs	23.0	28.9	24.1	15.8	—	—
H. Sexual harassment in the military	27.2	28.8	25.2	39.8	—	—
I. The military trying to hold on to old-fashioned views of morality	1.8	3.7	6.2	11.5	15.1	12.7

Table 1.25. *Continued.*

There are many different things that people say might keep the military from being effective during times of war. For each of the following, please indicate if it might greatly hurt military effectiveness, somewhat hurt military effectiveness, has no effect on military effectiveness, or it is not happening at all in the U.S. military.

	Percent "Greatly hurts"					
	Military leaders	Active reserve leaders	Civilian veteran leaders	Civilian non-veteran leaders	General public veterans	General public non-veterans
J. A military culture and way of life that is very different from the culture and way of life of those who are not in the military	3.9	5.5	6.8	8.7	11.7	9.5
K. The military's lack of confidence in our political leadership	23.0	29.4	24.0	29.7	—	—
L. Inaccurate reporting about the military and military affairs by the news media	29.0	36.9	28.5	27.6	—	—

NOTE: Differences between groups significant at the .001 level for all items except B.

these features of the contemporary military could "greatly hurt" effectiveness of the armed forces.

A related set of items focused on one of the key aspects of the Ricks thesis: the proper role of the military in relations with civilian society. The results for these questions are summarized in Table 1.26. They reveal widespread support, especially among the elite military and active reservists, for the propositions that members of the military should not publicly criticize senior civilians in the government nor American society. The third item, the obverse of the first two, found members of the military sub-samples somewhat less likely to accept the view that they "should be allowed to publicly express their political views just like any other citizen"; only the civilian non-veterans expressed strong support for that proposition.

Two items in Table 1.26 focus on the appropriate role of the military in publicly explaining and advocating policies of U.S. government. Although there have been no recurrences of episodes such as General Douglas MacArthur's public attacks on the Korean War policies of the Truman administration, some high-ranking uniformed officers, including General Colin Powell, have taken an active and public role in debates about post–Cold War U.S. foreign and defense policies (Powell 1992a; 1992b). The "explain and defend" item found moderate agreement among all groups, but the civilian leaders were significantly more inclined than military leaders to believe that it was indeed proper for the military to undertake such actions. The question about policy advocacy is worded rather differently—the phrase "in the best interests of the United States" gives it a somewhat positive bias. Thus, responses are not directly comparable to the previous item. It yielded quite strong agreement from all four groups, with the civilians very slightly more supportive of the advocate role for the military.

Members of the general public consistently took the most permissive view of appropriate actions by the military. Whether or not they had served in the armed forces, they were the least inclined to restrict military criticism of senior civilian officials. They also agreed by overwhelming margins that members of the military should be permitted to express their political views and even to advocate policies publicly.

A related cluster of items posed a series of seven questions about one of the more contentious issues in the current debates about civil-military relations: the appropriate relationship between the military and senior civilian leaders. This venerable issue often surfaces in time of war; for example, the Lincoln-McClellan confrontations during the Civil War and the Korean War dispute between Truman and MacArthur. Many recent manifestations of tensions between senior military and civilian officials

Table 1.26. The Military Role in Civilian Society: Responses to the 1998–99 TISS Survey.

This question asks for your opinion on a number of statements concerning the military's role in civilian society.

	Percent "Agree strongly" or "Agree somewhat"					
	Military leaders	Active reserve leaders	Civilian veteran leaders	Civilian non-veteran leaders	General public veterans	General public non-veterans
A. Members of the military should not publicly criticize a senior member of the civilian branch of the government	88.6	85.9	81.5	73.0	62.4	64.9
B. Members of the military should not publicly criticize American society	63.5	63.3	61.1	55.4	—	—
C. Members of the military should be allowed to publicly express their political views just like any other citizen	34.9	44.4	53.8	61.7	76.6	83.8
D. It is proper for the military to explain and defend in public the policies of the government	50.8	52.3	65.4	61.7	—	—
E. It is proper for the military to advocate publicly the military policies it believes are in the best interests of the United States	64.6	66.8	73.7	69.6	84.4	83.6

NOTE: Differences between groups significant at the .001 level for all items.

predate the Clinton era. Responses to TISS surveys of both leaders and the general public are summarized in Table 1.27. More than 90 percent of the elite military and active reservists agreed that civilian officials rather than military officers should have the "final say on *whether or not* to use military force," and that "civilian control of the military is absolutely safe and secure in the United States." Fewer civilian leaders, but still a majority, agreed with both propositions. The related question of who should have the final say on *what type* of force to use gave rise to rather wide differences between the military and civilian leaders, as only about one-quarter of the military respondents were willing to leave that decision to the civilian leadership. Members of the general public were almost evenly divided on the first two questions. Only slight majorities among both veterans and non-veterans subscribed to the principle of civilian control of decisions to use force. In light of that permissive attitude, it is perhaps not surprising that they also harbored substantial doubts about whether the core constitutional principle of civilian control of the military is absolutely safe and secure. The thesis that military leaders do not have enough influence in foreign policy received only modest support from respondents in the four leadership groups. The issue of who should be in charge during wartime found all but the civilian non-veterans willing to let the military take over running the war, and even a stronger majority of the general public accepted this proposition.

The other two items in Table 1.27 appear to have special relevance for the persistent tensions between the Pentagon and the Clinton White House. The four leadership groups were almost evenly divided, with agreement ranging between 49 percent and 56 percent, on the proposition that domestic politics rather than national security requirements tend to drive civilian decision-making on military issues; strong majorities among the general public agreed that this was the case. The other item with Clintonesque overtones stated, "To be respected as Commander-in-Chief, the President should have served in uniform." The elite military, active reservists, and civilian veterans were almost evenly divided in their responses, whereas fewer than one in five civilian non-veterans agreed. Because the pool of political leaders with any military experience has been steadily shrinking during the post-conscription era—in 2000, only John McCain and Al Gore of the presidential contenders had seen any active duty—responses of the military leaders on this question point to a possible time bomb in future civil-military relations. By the 2008 or 2012 elections, it is very possible that none of the candidates will have served in the military. The prospect that a future occupant of the White House, and commander-in-chief, might not have the full respect of the military is disturbing.

Table 1.27. Assessments of Proper Relations Between the Military and Senior Civilian Leaders: Responses to the 1998-99 TISS Survey.

This question asks for your opinion on a number of statements concerning relations between the military and senior civilian leaders.

	Percent "Agree strongly" or "Agree somewhat"					
	Military leaders	Active reserve leaders	Civilian veteran leaders	Civilian non-veteran leaders	General public veterans	General public non-veterans
A. In general, high-ranking civilian officials rather than high-ranking military officers should have the final say on *whether or not to* use military force	90.7	92.4	89.2	78.4	54.2	52.8
B. In general, high-ranking civilian officials rather than high-ranking military officers should have the final say on *what type of* military force to use	26.1	23.0	38.4	39.0	36.6	40.0
C. When civilians tell the military what to do, domestic partisan politics rather than national security requirements are often the primary motivation	48.9	53.9	56.3	51.2	70.2	65.8
D. In wartime, civilian government leaders should let the military take over running the war	53.4	61.2	55.9	46.6	76.1	65.4
E. To be respected as Commander-in-Chief, the President should have served in uniform	42.3	52.3	46.7	19.4	—	—
F. Civilian control of the military is absolutely safe and secure in the United States	92.7	90.4	79.9	58.6	52.7	45.7
G. Military leaders do not have enough influence in deciding our policy with other countries	27.4	37.5	26.5	22.1	—	—

NOTE: Differences between groups significant at the .001 level for all items.

Decisions to commit American forces abroad have been contentious almost from the beginning of the republic. During the War of 1812 some doubted that the right of self-defense justified sending U.S. units into Canada. As a young Whig Congressman, Abraham Lincoln mercilessly hectored the Polk administration with "spot resolutions," demanding that the White House reveal precisely where Mexico had committed the aggression that allegedly justified the U.S. decision to go to war with its southern neighbor. Decisions to declare war on Spain in 1898 and Germany in 1917 came only after protracted debates in the Congress. Commitments of American forces abroad in the absence of declarations of war have been equally controversial, especially during the post-Vietnam era.

The TISS survey of military and civilian leaders included a cluster of items focusing on the proper role of senior military leadership in such decisions. It asked whether the military leaders should be neutral, advise, advocate, or insist on having their way in seven elements of the decision process: deciding whether to intervene; setting the rules of engagement; ensuring that clear political and military goals exist; deciding on what the goals or policy should be; generating political support for the intervention; developing an "exit strategy"; and deciding what kinds of military units will be used to accomplish all tasks. Several generalizations emerge from the responses summarized in Tables 1.28. First, a majority of military officers prefer the advisory role on whether to intervene and on the goals of the intervention, but they would insist on having their way on ensuring that clear political and military goals exist, developing an exit strategy, and selecting the types of military units to be employed. A plurality would also insist on setting the rules of engagement. Only on the task of generating public support for the intervention did the military officers prefer to remain neutral. Responses of the active reserves are very much in line with those of the elite military. Although some previously-cited issues revealed that civilians were somewhat more permissive about the appropriate role of the military, they tended to favor a less vigorous military role on several elements of decisions to deploy American forces abroad, including setting the rules of engagement, ensuring that clear political and military goals exist, developing an exit strategy, and selecting military units. Only relatively minor differences between veterans and non-veterans characterized the responses of civilian leaders on these issues.

RELIGION AND VALUES

As noted at several points, those who identify a "gap" between the military and civilian society often focus on differences of culture and core values. Previous sections have touched upon questions of ethics and values, and also discussed presented data on the religious affiliations of those taking part in the TISS survey. Except for the larger proportion of Roman Catholics and a smaller proportion of Jews and non-Judeo-Christians, the military religious identification was approximately the same as that of the American population. Several additional items probed more deeply into these questions.

One of these questions asked respondents to reveal their views on "life after death" (Table 1.29). The data reveal quite significant differences that tend to fall along military-civilian lines. More than half of those in the two military groups reported that "I am sure there is life after death," well in excess of the civilians who gave the same answer. Conversely, civilians were far more likely (12 percent, compared to 4 percent military) to express certainty that there is *no* life after death. Between 39 percent and 46 percent of respondents in each of the four groups stated that they had doubts and uncertainties on this question.

A somewhat related question asked those taking part in the TISS survey to describe their feelings about the Bible (Table 1.30). The military are more likely than civilian elites to agree that "the Bible is the inspired word of God, true, and to be taken word for word" (18 percent vs. 11 percent); more likely to agree that "the Bible is the inspired word of God, true, but not to be taken word for word" (48 percent vs. 34 percent); and less likely to agree that "the Bible is a book of myths and legends" (3 percent vs. 7 percent). These differences, while statistically significant, are not strikingly large, and they more or less mirror those on the question about life and death.

The final set of questions on religion centered on behavior rather than beliefs. Compared to the items on beliefs about life after death and the Bible, these generally gave rise to somewhat smaller differences among the four groups.[28] The military officers we surveyed are more "religious" than civilian elites, but not as dramatically as some have claimed. If "religious" is measured by the frequency of engaging in religious activity, the difference is slight. The difference is somewhat greater if "religious" is measured by the degree of guidance respondents claim religion provides for their daily living and the specific content of those beliefs. For instance, roughly comparable percentages of officers and civilian elites report that

---

28.   As shown in Table 1.1, religious affiliations of the four groups of leaders varied somewhat, notably in the over-representation of Catholics and under-representation of Jews in the military. But the leadership groups differed little with respect to the "non-Judeo-Christian" and "agnostic/atheist" categories; very few military or civilian respondents checked either of these options. Thus, variations reported in Tables 1.28 and 1.29 largely reflect differences among respondents who identify themselves with the Judeo-Christian tradition.

Table 1.28. The Proper Role of Senior Military Leadership in Decisions to Commit U.S. Armed Forces Abroad: Responses to the 1998–99 TISS Survey.

This question asks you to specify the proper role of the senior military leadership in decisions to commit U.S. Armed Forces abroad. The following are typical elements of the decision the President must make. Please specify the proper role of the military for each element.

	Percent checking each option			
	Military leaders	Active reserve leaders	Civilian veteran leaders	Civilian non-veteran leaders
A. Deciding whether to intervene				
Be neutral	3.4	7.8	5.4	7.8
Advise	83.4	78.6	77.3	74.1
Advocate	9.8	9.4	15.3	13.6
Insist	3.4	4.2	1.4	2.0
No opinion	0.0	0.0	0.6	2.4

B. Setting rules of engagement

	Percent checking each option			
Be neutral	0.0	0.3	1.1	2.0
Advise	16.7	20.6	26.9	29.6
Advocate	33.6	37.6	44.8	44.8
Insist	49.7	41.5	26.6	21.1
No opinion	0.0	0.0	0.6	2.4

C. Ensuring that clear political and military goals exist

	Percent checking each option			
Be neutral	0.2	1.0	2.3	3.5
Advise	12.0	11.5	23.1	26.7
Advocate	21.3	22.2	32.1	27.2
Insist	66.5	65.3	41.7	40.1
No opinion	0.0	0.0	0.8	2.4

D. Deciding what the goals or policy should be

Be neutral	7.3	11.0	15.8	15.6
Advise	66.0	60.3	56.3	52.6
Advocate	22.1	23.8	20.3	21.4
Insist	4.4	4.4	6.5	8.1
No opinion	0.2	0.5	1.1	2.3

Table 1.28. *Continued.*

This question asks you to specify the proper role of the senior military leadership in decisions to commit U.S. Armed Forces abroad. The following are typical elements of the decision the President must make. Please specify the proper role of the military for each element.

	Percent checking each option			
	Military leaders	Active reserve leaders	Civilian veteran leaders	Civilian non-veteran leaders
E. Generating political support for the interventions				
Be neutral	48.5	55.4	52.8	47.4
Advise	24.3	20.4	26.8	27.0
Advocate	20.8	15.7	14.7	18.7
Insist	5.1	7.8	3.4	2.6
No opinion	1.3	0.8	2.3	4.4

F. Developing an "exit strategy"

	Percent checking each option			
Be neutral	1.0	0.8	2.0	1.6
Advise	19.0	19.5	28.5	32.0
Advocate	27.8	23.4	36.2	25.7
Insist	51.9	55.8	32.2	38.1
No opinion	0.3	0.5	1.1	2.7

G. Deciding what kinds of military units (air vs. naval, heavy vs. light) will be used to accomplish all tasks

	Percent checking each option			
Be neutral	0.0	0.8	0.8	1.3
Advise	11.4	15.2	17.2	21.2
Advocate	25.6	21.5	32.7	29.7
Insist	63.0	62.5	48.7	45.8
No opinion	0.0	0.0	0.6	2.0

NOTES: Differences between groups significant at the .001 level. This question was not included in the survey of the general public.

Table 1.29. Beliefs About Life After Death: Responses to the 1998–99 TISS Survey.

Which of the following comes closest to your views on life after death?

			Percent checking each option		
	Military leaders	Active reserve leaders	Civilian veteran leaders	Civilian non-veteran leaders
1. I am sure there is life after death	50.5	52.6	38.8	38.9
2. I believe in life after death but have some doubts	25.4	22.5	16.8	17.9
3. I am uncertain about life after death	16.2	16.0	28.1	27.6
4. I am certain there is no life after death	4.4	5.2	13.2	11.6
5. No opinion	3.6	3.7	3.0	4.1

NOTES: Differences between groups significant at the .001 level. This question was not included in the survey of the general public

Table 1.30. Feelings About the Bible: Responses to the 1998–99 TISS Survey.

Which of these statements comes closest to describing your feelings about the Bible?

	Military leaders	Active reserve leaders	Civilian veteran leaders	Civilian non-veteran leaders
			Percent checking each option	
1. The Bible is the inspired word of God, true, and to be taken word for word	18.0	13.9	9.2	11.6
2. The Bible is the inspired word of God, true, but not to be taken word for word.	47.5	47.6	35.6	32.4
3. The Bible is the inspired word of God, true for religion, but with some errors	8.3	8.2	10.8	8.9
4. The Bible is a great book of wisdom and history	19.1	24.5	36.7	36.6
5. The Bible is a book of myths and legends	2.8	2.4	5.6	7.8
6. No opinion	4.2	3.4	2.2	2.7

NOTES: Differences between groups significant at the .001 level. This question was not included in the survey of the general public.

they pray several times a day (18 percent vs. 22 percent), once a day (24 percent vs. 18 percent), a few times a week (24 percent vs. 18 percent), or once a week (23 percent vs. 20 percent), although only half as many officers say they never pray (12 percent vs. 22 percent). In summary, differences in religious behavior appear more muted than those on beliefs about the Bible and life after death.

The final items pertaining to values are a pair of questions that have often been included in the General Social Survey (GSS) conducted annually by the National Opinion Research Center at the University of Chicago.[29] The first of these, on trust of others, has been widely used in the extensive literature on "social capital" (for example, Brehm and Rahn 1997; Rahn and Transue 1998). The results, summarized in Table 1.31, indicate that the military, active reservists, and civilian veterans responded almost identically, with just fewer than two-thirds of them expressing the view that "most people can be trusted." Although civilian non-veterans did not check the less-trusting response more frequently, many more of them were uncertain. By far the most striking pattern on this question is the wide gap between respondents in the four leadership groups and the general public. Strong majorities among the general public, whether veterans or non-veterans, asserted that "you can't be too careful in dealing with people."

The second question in Table 1.31 asked those taking part in the TISS survey whether it is more important to prepare children to be "obedient" or to "think for themselves." This item has often been used in studies of authoritarianism. Respondents in all groups expressed a strong preference for teaching children to think for themselves, but the military officers were somewhat more inclined to emphasize obedience.

Conclusion

A number of conclusions may be adduced from the preceding tables and analyses. This summary focuses on some of the major divergences and convergences in responses to the TISS surveys by military leaders, civilian leaders, and the general public.

The data provide strong support for the Ricks thesis that members of the military are becoming increasingly partisan, and that they are also significantly more Republican than civilians in comparable leadership positions. Military respondents, including the active reserves, identified

---

29.   The GSS studies encompass a wide range of questions on the opinions and behavior of Americans. A summary of results from some 300 questions posed during the 1972–89 period may be found in Wood (1990).

Table 1.31. Trust and Child-rearing Values Among Respondents to the 1998-99 TISS Survey.

Generally speaking, would you say that most people can be trusted or that you can't be too careful in dealing with people?

	Military leaders	Active reserve leaders	Civilian veteran leaders	Civilian non-veteran leaders	General public veterans	General public non-veterans
				Percent checking each point		
Can be trusted	65.2	66.5	63.0	58.1	36.6	34.5
Can't be too careful	26.5	25.7	28.7	28.6	59.0	63.7
Uncertain	8.3	7.8	8.3	13.3	4.4	1.8

Which of these would you say is more important in preparing children for life?

				Percent checking each option		
To be obedient	13.1	9.9	9.7	7.7	—	—
To think for themselves	79.9	82.5	84.8	85.3	—	—
Can't choose	7.0	7.6	5.5	7.0	—	—

NOTE: Differences between groups significant at the .001 level for the first item only.

overwhelmingly with the Republican Party by margins of 6:1 or higher. In contrast, although the civilian leadership sample included strong representation from groups that have traditionally been aligned with the Republican Party, such as business executives, and excluded persons in the entertainment industry, who are generally identified with the Democratic party, the civilian elites are much more evenly divided in their political loyalties. These results are fully consistent with the previous findings that the civilian-military gap in partisan identifications had widened during the 1976–96 period covered by the FPLP surveys (Holsti 1998–99, Table 1). The partisan gap between the military and the general public is even wider: party preferences among the latter group of respondents reflect rather accurately the results of other recent surveys showing that the general public is fairly evenly divided among Republicans, Democrats, and independents. In the absence of comparable data from earlier eras in American history, it is impossible to assert with confidence whether these gaps are unique. Evidence presented in Huntington's classic study (1957) and by others suggests that the military in these earlier periods was indeed marked by low levels of political participation and partisanship. It is beyond dispute, however, that American armed forces are far larger than during any previous peacetime period and there appears little likelihood that they will shrink to levels that were typical between wars in the nineteenth or first part of the twentieth centuries. These points lend a good deal of support for the concerns expressed by Ricks about the "gap" and its implications.

The TISS data do not, however, provide much support for the hypothesis that the youngest military officers are even more firmly wedded to the Republican Party. Overwhelming preferences for the Republican Party pervaded all age groups among military elites.

The evidence also supports the Ricks thesis of a wide ideological gap between the military and civilian leaders. As in the earlier FPLP surveys, fewer than one officer in twenty in the elite military sample used even the "somewhat liberal" self-identification, and the figures for the active reserves were not substantially different. Although responses by both civilian leaders and the general public surveys revealed a slight tilt toward the conservative end of the ideological spectrum, the widest gaps found civilians on one side and the military on the other. The civilian leaders were more liberal than their counterparts in the general public, but by only a very slight margin.

As in the earlier FPLP study, the TISS survey also revealed that partisan and ideological differences did not necessarily spill over into the full range of domestic and foreign policy issues. Responses to a broad spectrum of foreign policy questions revealed significant evidence of both similarities and differences among the various military and civilian groups taking part in the TISS surveys. For example, questions relating to the domino theory, arms control, and nuclear proliferation gave rise to very similar responses. The widest gaps emerged on such issues as humanitarian interventions abroad and questions concerning the appropriate level of U.S. concern for and responses to problems in less developed countries.

Still other foreign policy issues found that the leaders—both military and civilian—adopted a more internationalist stance than did respondents among the general public. This pattern of differences between leaders and the general public is consistent with virtually every other survey.[30] Trade and concern about inflows of goods and immigrants from abroad are among the currently controversial questions that conformed to such a pattern. Appraisals of the level of threat posed by China and terrorist attacks on the United States also tended to create sharper divisions between leaders and the general public than between military and civilian leaders.

The question of trust—can most people be trusted?—gave rise to one of the very deepest chasms between leaders and the general public. Strong majorities among military and civilian leaders answered the question in the affirmative, whereas equally strong majorities among the general public believed that "you can't be too careful." This finding is consistent with the propensity of the general public to perceive a more threatening environment than do their elite counterparts.

Responses to domestic issues also yielded a mixed pattern of responses. Such social-value issues as school prayer, gay rights, and the death penalty revealed wide gaps between the military and civilian leaders, whereas some of the other controversial questions, including a pro-choice position on abortion rights and strict control of handgun sales, found strong majorities among both military and civilian leaders on the same side. Economic issues were generally less divisive, although anything suggesting income redistribution, either domestically or internationally, found far less favor among the military. Members of the general public were closer to the military on school prayer, but their responses resembled those of their civilian counterparts on income redistribution.

The gap between civilian and military leaders tends to be wider and more pervasive in the realm of ideas and values than on more specific policy issues. Ideological self-identifications (Table 1.4) and appraisals of

---

30. See, for example, the Chicago Council of Foreign Relations surveys conducted between 1974 and 1998, as reported in seven monographs by John Reilly (1975–99); and Holsti (1996).

the breakdown of traditional values, the role that the military could play in the moral redemption of American society, definitions of morality, and adherence to "God's will" (Table 1.14) provide a few illustrations of this observation. Responses to several of the items on religion appear to give rise to a somewhat related conclusion: the gap seems wider on core religious beliefs than on behavior, such as on church attendance.

Huge majorities of military respondents—both active-duty officers and reservists—expressed considerable distaste for many features of contemporary American culture and institutions. Expressions of disapproval clearly went far beyond the White House and its occupant at the time of the surveys. The evidence revealed, however, that civilian leaders and the general public are also very critical of American society and its culture. Most branches of government, political parties, the press, labor unions, television, and the legal profession are among the institutions that appear to have few friends among any of the groups taking part in the TISS surveys. These results generally mirror recent public assessments of American institutions in the annual General Social Survey conducted by the National Opinion Research Center.

The military as an institution received very positive evaluations from all groups of respondents, above all from the elite military and active reservists. Civilian respondents were only moderately less laudatory about most major aspects of the military. However, although military culture also received high marks from civilians, neither civilian leaders nor members of the general public expressed very strong enthusiasm for redeeming the faults of society by adopting the military's values and customs.

Evidence of high civilian regard and support for the military was clearly reflected in responses to the TISS surveys, but many military leaders nevertheless expressed disappointment at the level of public respect for their institution. Moreover, it appears that they have identified at least two culprits for this state of affairs: political leaders and the media are regarded as espousing different values than the American people and as fundamentally ignorant about military issues. These appraisals are not merely a response to the real and perceived deficiencies of the Clinton administration: according to one military officer, "We were taught at [a senior military educational institution] that our three main enemies are the Soviets, the Congress, and the media."[31]

The hostility of the military to the media is one of the dominant themes that emerges from the TISS survey. Clearly few respondents in any of the surveyed groups held television in high regard. Moreover, as-

---

31. Private conversation, Atlanta, Georgia, September 3, 1999.

sessments of the press have declined a long way since the days, more than a quarter-century ago, when investigative reporting of the Watergate break-in by Carl Bernstein and Robert Woodward led to record numbers of applications to schools of journalism. Yesterday's heroes are now widely perceived to have feet—and perhaps heads—of clay. But even given these broader social currents, the persistent hostility of the military seems to warrant further investigation. A recent book suggests that the lack of technical competence of American journalists lies at the root of the problem (Kennedy 1993). Perhaps that is the explanation, but maybe it is just a bit too facile to locate but a single source for a problem that is both complex and crucial to the defining the appropriate relationship between two of the most crucial institutions in any democracy.

A companion TISS study shows that the press in fact treat the military quite favorably, but in a somewhat less laudatory manner than professional military publications which, like similar publications for other occupations, tend to serve as cheerleaders (Weigand and Paletz, 2001). If members of the military regard the latter as the appropriate standard against which to assess coverage by other media sources, then it may well be a reason why other publications are perceived as less adequate or fair.

Military preferences on some key issues are very respectful of the tradition of civilian control. For example, military respondents agreed overwhelmingly that civilian leaders should have the final word on when to use force, and that they should not be the targets of public criticism by senior uniformed personnel. On both of these questions, civilian respondents were less inclined to place restrictions on the military. Once a decision to use force or to intervene abroad has been made, however, most members of the military expect to have a strong voice—perhaps even to insist on their views—on such questions as setting the rules of engagement, ensuring that clear political and military goals are established, developing an "exit" strategy, and deciding what types of units should be used. Civilian preferences on questions about relations between senior civilian and military leaders were somewhat mixed, in some instances favoring a strong military voice, and in others taking the opposite view. The civilians were also much less certain that civilian control of the military is absolutely assured.

SO WHAT?

Every profession espouses norms, values, and expectations that distinguish it, to a greater or lesser degree, from the rest of society; indeed this is what distinguishes a "profession" from a "job." We would hardly trust a physician, attorney, accountant, teacher, or member of the clergy who did not adhere to the norms and standards of those professions. Moreover, we are rarely shocked when professional associations take action to protect those norms and the interests of its members. In this sense, some "gap" between the military and civilian society is inevitable, probably desirable, and certainly neither surprising nor necessarily a cause for concern. To dismiss the Ricks thesis and evidence of some significant civilian-military gaps, however, on the grounds that other occupations may also have opinions and beliefs that vary from those of society at large is to assume that the military constitute just another interest group.[32] But the military are not just another profession or interest group: as an active-duty military officer noted at a recent conference on civil-military relations, "We are trained to kill people and to break things." More broadly, the frequency of military coups in Latin America, Asia, Africa, and elsewhere underscores the unique position of the military in every society. Although there is little threat of a military coup in the United States, the possible implication of a gap between civilians and the military are rather different from gaps with other professions.[33] At this point diverse voices emerge.

In a critique of the "gap" thesis, retired Army Colonel Joseph Collins questions whether the partisan, ideological, or other gaps identified by Ricks (1997c; 1997d), and discussed in my analysis (Holsti 1998–99) of the FPLP data on American opinion leaders, have any relevance for the conduct of foreign and defense policy. He asserts, "I was not able to recognize the professional military that I had been part of for nearly three decades" from the Ricks article or the FPLP data. "If we cannot correlate or otherwise connect the growth in the number of officers who describe themselves as moderately conservative or Republican with significant political activity or fractious differences on policy issues, we will have to redefine our terms or move the analysis of the 'gap' to another plane" (Collins 1999).

The data adduced above are clearly insufficient to provide a definitive response to Colonel Collins's points. Moreover, evidence and speculation about the policy consequences of any "gap" from other sources is mixed. Leading students of civil-military relations who more or less share Colonel Collins's views include Powell et al. (1994), Roman and Tarr (Chapter 11 in this volume), and Davis (1999). The latter has

---

32.   For example, some critics have asserted that media shortcomings can be traced to the alleged domination of liberal Democrats among media personnel. The TISS sample of media leaders found that 40 percent are Democrats, 27 percent Republicans, and 33 percent independents or others.

33.   For a discussion of the policy implications of the civilian-military gap and several prescriptions, see Holsti (1998–99).

flatly denied that there is a policy-relevant "gap." Others with equally impressive credentials as students of civilian-military relations are less inclined to dismiss evidence of a gap as a tempest in an academic teapot that has no bearing on the real world of policymaking (Dunlop 1992–93; 1994; Kohn 1994; Luttwak 1994; Foster 1997; Bacevich and Kohn 1997). In a recent study, Desch (1999) found systematic evidence of changes and strains in contemporary civilian-military relations in an analysis of seventy-five policy disagreements between civilian and military authorities spanning a period of more than six decades ending in 1997. Prior to the end of the Cold War, civilian preferences prevailed in well over 90 percent of the cases (fifty-nine of sixty-three), whereas during the post–Cold War period they did so in fewer than half (five of twelve).[34] The studies commissioned by the TISS project found strong policy consequences in some areas but only nominal effects in others.

Perhaps the different diagnoses arise at least in part from definitions as to what constitutes "significant political activity" or, more importantly, inappropriate activities. The case of General MacArthur's egregious conduct in 1950–51 seems unambiguous, but some recent episodes are much less so. In response to a charge of being a political general, Colin Powell pointed out that, "there isn't a general in Washington who isn't political, not if he's going to be successful" (quoted in Johnson and Metz 1994, 203). If being "political" means competing for roles, missions, resources, and the like, then that does not represent a recent or especially worrisome change, although questions might be raised about the propriety of the military using Congress, such interest groups as defense contractors or veterans organizations, the media, and the public to gain leverage. More generally, we can see two trends that have an important bearing on relations between the military and civilian authorities, and the principle of control of the former by the latter: through changes in professional education, the military are becoming more politically sophisticated and adept, while the number of political leaders in the executive and legislative branches with military experience is declining.[35]

The evidence adduced above highlights another dimension of the issue: the dividing line between "political" (as defined above) and being partisan. Military elites are clearly abandoning non-partisanship; whereas in the 1976 FPLP survey, 55 percent identified their party affiliations as "independents," "other," or "none," the comparable figure

---

34. For other discussions of the gap thesis and the other aspects of civil-military relations, see Johnson and Metz (1994), and Towell (1999).

35. Further evidence on the latter point is presented by Bianco and Markham in Chapter 7 below.

in the TISS survey was only 28 percent for the elite military and 27 percent for active reservists. Moreover, there appear to be fewer self-imposed restraints on public expressions of partisan sentiments by active-duty personnel. In these circumstances, sensing the opportunity to garner votes in the 2000 elections, the Republican National Committee took out a large ad in the *Air Force Times* attacking the Democratic leaders by name and concluding with the message, "Congressional Republicans: Supporting America's Military" (December 13, 1999, 57). In the same spirit, although some officers expressed doubts about the propriety of do-ing so, the four branches of the military spent more than a half million dollars to put on a show of its weapons for delegates to the 2000 Republi-can convention in Philadelphia. According to one military officer, "to say that this is not a partisan event is borderline absurdity" (Myers, 2000a).

In his critique, Colonel Collins asks, "does the Chairman of the Joint Chiefs writing an op-ed piece supporting administration policy on Bosnia constitute a political act because it took place in an election year?" (He might also have noted that General Powell [1992–93] wrote an article defending administration policy for the prestigious journal of the Council on Foreign Relations, *Foreign Affairs*). As Bosnia was a major campaign issue in 1992, the answer seems quite clear, just as retired Admiral Wil-liam Crowe's public support of Democratic presidential nominee William Clinton, or the speeches General Powell and General H. Norman Schwarzkopf gave at the 2000 Republican convention were "significant political acts." The crucial distinction is that the latter instances were par-tisan acts by retired officers rather than active-duty personnel. Once such behavior is deemed acceptable for active-duty officers, where does one draw the line? Would a critique of the foreign policies or credentials of a presidential challenger be equally acceptable? Consider also some hypo-thetical situations. During the 1952 presidential primaries, would it have been appropriate for a member of the Joint Chiefs to endorse the views of Dwight Eisenhower and to question those of Senator Robert Taft on the North Atlantic Treaty Organization? What about an op-ed article on de-fense policy during the 1980 election, mentioning that Annapolis gradu-ate Jimmy Carter had had a distinguished career in the U.S. Navy, whereas Republican presidential nominee Ronald Reagan had sat out World War II in Hollywood? Is it wholly utopian to hope that the self-ab-negating standard of General George Marshall—who demonstrated his support for the military tradition of nonpartisanship by refusing to vote—has not gone the way of muskets and horse-mounted cavalry?

Military leaders might gain some short-term benefits by becoming more active politically, perhaps even by identifying more closely with one of the political parties. But over the longer haul, it cannot be in the interest of the military itself to become perceived as a political and partisan institution. Two decades ago, S.L.A. Marshall offered a succinct reminder of this point: "Paradoxically, it is only when the Army has a truly military posture that its political position becomes invulnerable" (Marshall 1980, 112).[36] It does not seem wholly fortuitous that the highest levels of public confidence in governmental organizations are bestowed upon three institutions that are, at least in theory, intended to be free of political activity and partisanship: the military, the Supreme Court, and law enforcement agencies. In contrast, public confidence in the avowedly and legitimately political and partisan institutions—Congress, the presidency, and the major political parties—can only be described as abysmal (Table 1.17). Moreover, given the likelihood that the military will face difficult budgetary and recruitment problems during the next several decades, a reputation for political activity, especially of the kind that has a strong partisan tenor, is not likely be an asset in the absence of permanent conservative Republican domination of the White House and Congress.

---

36.   I am grateful to Tom Ricks for bringing this quotation to my attention.

Chapter 2

Attitudes and Opinions Among Senior Military Officers and a U.S. Cross-Section, 1998–99

James A. Davis

The Bridging the Gap project asks not just whether military officers are different from typical Americans, but whether there is a distinctive culture (attitudes, opinions, values) that distinguishes military leaders from civilians and that creates animosity and potentially threatens military effectiveness or civil-military cooperation.

The best publicized statement of the "gap problem" is a 1997 article by Thomas E. Ricks (1997d):

New Marines seemed to experience a moment of private loathing for public America. . . . [They] were experiencing in a very personal way the widening gap between today's military and civilian America. . . . Officers are beginning to feel that they are special, better than the society they serve. . . . Open identification with the Republican Party is becoming the norm. . . . These isolating attitudes, while most extreme in the Marines, are also found in varying degrees elsewhere in the military. . . . [Two Marine reservists wrote that,] "we have thrown away the values, morals, and standards that define traditional culture. . . . The next real war we fight is likely to be on American soil."

Troubling if true, but is it true? The Project's surveys were designed to assess this, by posing a common battery of questions to a national cross section of U.S. adults—hereafter, the "Mass"; samples of high-ranking Army and Navy officers—hereafter the "Brass"; samples of cadets at the three service academies; and samples of civilian elites.

In this chapter I compare results in the Brass and Mass samples to see whether the differences in their attitudes and opinions justify the "gap" image. The Mass sample comprises 1,001 respondents in a September–

October 1998 telephone survey of U.S. households carried out by Princeton Survey Research Associates. The Brass sample comprises 1,028 Army and Navy officers from the sample of 1,105 "military elite," from which are excluded a handful of foreign officers and a handful under the rank of major or lieutenant commander.[1] Within the brass, the ranks were as follows: 6.5 percent generals or admirals; 23.8 percent colonels or captains; 43.8 percent lieutenant colonels or commanders; and 26.4 percent majors or lieutenant commanders.

According to *The Statistical Abstract of the United States*, these ranks comprised 39 percent of the officers on active duty in 1996 (the rest were lower ranks). Since the surveyed Brass were mostly sampled in advanced schools where young officers are groomed for promotion, they are probably more influential or potentially influential than their ranks suggest. Table 2.1 shows the makeup of the Brass sample in terms of service and appointment.

Note that the Mass and civilian elite samples differ substantially in their compositions, as well as their attitudes and opinions. In this chapter, the word "civilian" refers to the sample of all U.S. adult householders 18 years of age and older, rather than to the civilian leaders surveyed and discussed in other chapters.

The Gap Described

To assess the gap, I chose the 55 items that appeared in both the military and mass questionnaires and which had a pro-con or favor-oppose content.[2] To make them comparable I combined the answer categories of each item to give two categories with equal frequencies (or as equal as possible), and assigned "plus" to the category that received a higher per-

---

1.   As reporting tables without N's (total cases) or significance tests is usually a sin in surveys, my practice here merits explanation. First, consider the samples: while the mass survey is a probability sample of telephoned households, the data set I used is weighted to compensate for the common biases of telephone surveys. Thus, the "true N" is a complicated matter. Although the military samples are unweighted, they are not probability samples but a collection of sub-samples chosen to catch high-ranking officers (the vast majority in the lieutenant commander/captain or major/colonel range). Therefore, conventional "significance" tests are unwarranted. Second, with few exceptions all the percentages reported here are based on total sample cases. Where N's are not reported, the percentage is based on at least 850 "mass" cases and 888 "brass" cases. In lieu of "significance tests," I discuss only differences of .05 (five percentage points) or more, and treat differences in the 5–10 point range as small.

2.   Some of the questions I excluded are evaluated in companion studies associated with this project. See Chapter 3 by Paul Gronke and Peter Feaver, Chapter 10 by Laura Miller and John Allen Williams, and studies by Peter Feaver and Christopher Gelpi.

Table 2.1. Composition of Brass Samples (number of respondents).

Service	Active	Reserves	National Guard	Total
Army	309	79	160	548
Navy	214	39		253
Air Force	117	20	17	154
Marines	82	20		102
Coast Guard	16	4		20
Totals	738	162	177	1077
			No Answer	28
			Total	1105

centage among the brass. Thus for Question 8f, "All Americans should be willing to give up their lives to defend our country" the split was: "Agree strongly" and "Agree somewhat" versus "Disagree somewhat" and "Disagree strongly." Both samples responded more on the "agree" side of the split, but among the Brass, the "Agree" percentage was 83.2, while among the Mass it was 72.0. The difference—the gap—was 11.2 points.

Maximum	43.0
Upper quartile	26.7
Mean	17.2
Median	13.5
Lower quartile	7.7
Minimum	0.0

Over the 55 items, the gaps distributed as follows:

Thus the item with the largest gap showed a 43 percentage point difference between Mass and Brass; the average (mean) difference was 17.2 points; and only a quarter of the differences were 7.7 points or less.

As public opinion surveys go, 15-point differences are not routine. Compared to predictors of attitudes such as age or region or marital status, these differences are impressive. In national surveys, 40 points is a typical maximum; it is found, for example, in cross-tabulations of race and questions about race relations. Occupational differences may also tend to correlate with distinctive attitudes, but this does not mean that, say, tree surgeons, police officers, or kindergarten teachers are estranged from the larger society. Nevertheless, because the role and function of the military is unique, even "normal" gaps may be consequential for civil-military relations.

FINDING #1: OVER 55 ATTITUDE ITEMS, THE GAP BETWEEN ELITE OFFICERS AND THE MASS PUBLIC AVERAGES A SUBSTANTIAL 15 PERCENTAGE POINTS. Averages as always conceal variation by summarizing. To understand the gap (or gaps) we must look at specific questions, but 55 distinct "gaplets" go to the other extreme of confusing detail. As a compromise, I begin by looking at the classic measures of generalized ideology: political party identification and self-rated liberalism–conservatism. Then I divide the specific attitudes into three groups: (1) civilian matters: salient issues in contemporary society with no particular reference to the military, such as free speech, immigration, religion; (2) military matters: salient issues about policy within the armed forces, such as women in combat or foreign threats; and (3) civil-military matters: issues regarding civilian control and the gap itself.

PARTY AND IDEOLOGY

Virtually all discussions of the "gap" issue begin by noting the officers' predominant preference for the Republican Party. Our surveys are no exception, as shown in Table 2.2. Almost two-thirds of the Brass describe themselves as Republicans, while just 28.8 percent among the Mass do so. This is a 26-point gap, placing it in the top quarter of the item gaps. Among the Brass, 10 percent identify themselves as Democrats, in contrast to 35 percent of the Mass.

That is a lot of Republicans, but is it out of line with what one would expect, given the demographic characteristics of the Brass? Table 2.3 gives one clue. The NORC General Social Survey samples the same population as the Mass survey.[3] From it, we can distinguish the characteristics of the most pro-Republican subgroups in contemporary America. They are: non-African-American, college graduates, in moderate or liberal Protestant denominations, who rate their income as "above average."

Save perhaps for religion, these variables support the popular political stereotypes that African-Americans and lower socio-economic groups lean Democratic rather than Republican. The popular impression is also that Catholics, Jews, and people who profess no particular religion are more likely to identify themselves as Democratic; what is less well known, but is well documented, is that fundamentalist Protestants are *not* especially Republican at the mass level.

---

3. The National Opinion Research Center (NORC) is a not-for-profit research institute affiliated with the University of Chicago. Its General Social Survey (GSS) is a periodic monitoring of American adults' opinions and social characteristics. Twenty-two such samplings were carried out between 1972 and 1988. GSS results are often used as a yardstick to assess results in other studies.

While college graduates who are not African-American and not fundamentalist Protestant and who have high incomes are clearly more Republican than the generality (49.4 - 28.8 = 20.6), the elite officers are still more Republican than that (61.7 - 49.4 = 12.3). No doubt one could find even more extreme subgroups with even more pronounced numbers of Republican adherents (multi-millionaire businessmen, for example), but it is clear that the party preferences of the military elite are unrepresentative of even the Republican-inclined subgroups of U.S. society.

The implications may become clearer if we look at another overall measure, that of self-rated political position (Question 75: "How would you describe your views on political matters?"). Table 2.2b shows the two distributions: two-thirds of the Brass say that they are conservative, while 7 percent identify themselves as liberal, compared with the more even split in the Mass of 39 percent conservative, 28 percent liberal. But there is a quirk: most of the officers who identify themselves as conservative (half of all of the officers) chose the category "Somewhat conservative," while virtually none chose "Very conservative" or "Far right." In contrast, just 26 percent of the Mass sample chose the "somewhat conservative" category: almost all of the ideological gap of 25 points comes from that single category.

In each sub-table in Table 2.2c, the nine combinations sum to 100 percent. For example, the 19 in the upper right corner of Table 2.2c.1 (mass sample) says that 19 percent of the Mass sample characterized themselves as conservative *and* Republican. The third table, Table 2.2c.3, shows the difference between the Mass and Brass cells. The +31 in its upper right-hand corner says that the combination of conservative and Republican is 31 points more common in the sample of officers.

Tables 2.2c.1, 2.2c.2, and 2.2c.3 combine the Party and Ideology questions. The main result is simple: half the Brass are conservative Republicans, compared to 19 percent for the Mass, a gap of 31 points. These tables also show that three-quarters (2 + 13 + 50 + 11 + 1 = 77 percent) of the Brass are either conservative or Republican or both, compared to 48 percent for the Mass, a gap of 25 points.

Putting the same numbers another way: a good third of the mass public (13 + 13 + 12 = 38 percent) is neither Republican nor conservative, but this point of view turns up in just ten percent (5 + 3 + 2) of the elite officers.

How do these abstract preferences translate into specifics? Our frame comes from a distinction made forty years ago by Seymour Martin Lipset:

It is necessary to distinguish between so-called economic liberalism (issues concerned with the distribution of wealth and power) and non-economic lib-

Table 2.2. Party Identification and Self-Rated Ideology by Sample (comparison of officers and civilian cross-section).

2.2a. "Generally speaking do you consider yourself as a . . ."

	Brass	Mass	Gap
Republican	61.7	28.8	32.9
Independent	18.0	30.8	−12.8
No Preference	8.7	4.9	3.8
Other	1.7	0.1	1.6
	28.4	35.4	−7.4
Democrat	9.9	35.4	−25.5
Total	100.0	100.0	
N	(1086)	(973)	

2.2b. "How would you describe you views on political matters?"

	Brass	Mass	Gap
Far Right	0.3%	2.1	−1.8
Very Conservative	13.1	10.6	2.5
Somewhat Conservative	51.1	26.0	25.1
	64.5	38.7	25.8
Moderate	27.5	26.6	0.9
Other	0.5	0.1	0.4
No Opinion	0.6	7.2	−6.6
	28.6	33.9	−5.3
Somewhat Liberal	6.2	19.9	−13.7
Very Liberal	0.6	6.6	−6.0
Far Left	0.6	1.0	−1.0
	6.8	27.5	−20.7
Total	99.9%	100.1%	
N	(1090)	(1001)	

Table 2.2. Continued.

2.2.c.1. Mass sample*

	Democrat	Other	Republican	Total
Conservative	10	10	19	39
Other	13	14	6	33
Liberal	13	12	3	28
Total	36	36	28	100% (N=973)

2.2.c.2. Brass sample*

	Democrat	Other	Republican	Total
Conservative	2	13	50	65
Other	5	13	11	29
Liberal	3	2	1	6
Total	10	28	62	100% (N=1083)

2.2.c.3. Gap (cell entry in Table 2.2.c.2 minus entry in table 2.2.c.1)

	Democrat	Other	Republican	Total
Conservative	−8	+3	+31	+28
Other	−8	−1	15	−4
Liberal	−10	−10	−2	−22
Total	−26	−8	+34	+2

NOTE: * the nine cell percentages sum to 100 percent.

eralism (issues concerned with civil liberties, race relations and foreign affairs). The fundamental factor in non-economic liberalism is not actually class, but education, general sophistication, and probably to a certain extent psychic security. But since these factors are strongly correlated with class, non-economic liberalism is positively associated with social status (the wealthier are more tolerant), while economic liberalism is inversely correlated with social status (the poor are more leftist on such issues) (Lipset 1981, 318; Olson 1997, 237–258).

The two dimensions—economic liberalism (laissez-faire economics or hostility to the welfare state) and social liberalism (indifference or tolerance toward other people's reading materials, chastity, piety, etc.)—are, perhaps surprisingly, uncorrelated in the mass public. Thus we can specify four types or clusters of characteristics:

		Economic	
Social		*Liberal*	*Conservative*
Liberal		Social and Economic Liberals, or "New-Dealers"	Social Liberals/ Economic Conservatives, or **"Libertarians"**
	Conservative	Social Conservatives/ Economic Liberals, or "Populists"	Social and Economic Conservatives, or **"Gingrich-ites"**

Our questionnaires enable us to develop measures of both dimensions. For example, the economic aspect is measured by responses to Question 5k, "Redistributing income from the wealthy to the poor through taxation and subsidies" (agree or disagree). The social dimension is addressed by a number of questions, including Question 8a: "The decline of traditional values is contributing to the breakdown of our society" (agree strongly, agree somewhat, disagree somewhat, or disagree strongly). Question 8e asks: "American society would have fewer problems if people took God's will more seriously" (agree strongly, agree somewhat, disagree somewhat, or disagree strongly). Question 3f asks respondents to evaluate the seriousness of "the decline of standards and morals in American society" (very, moderately, slightly, or not at all serious). Question 5g asks respondents to indicate their position on "permit-

Table 2.3. Party Preferences: Brass Sample, Most Republican Subgroup in NORC General Social Survey (1993–98), and Mass Sample.

Sample	Democrat	Independent	Republican	Total	(N)
BRASS	9.9	28.4	61.7	100.0%	(1086)
CIVILIAN:					
Most Republican subgroup	23.3	27.4	49.4	100.0%	(318)
Cross section:					
Total mass sample	35.4	35.8	28.8	100.0%	(973)
Total GSS (1993–98)	34.4	36.8	28.8	100.0%	(9504)

NOTE: "Most Republican sub-group" has the following characteristics: Race = not African-American; education = college graduate; self-classified income = above average; religious denomination = moderate or liberal (non-fundamentalist) Protestant. In General Social Survey, 1993–98.

ting prayer in public schools" (agree strongly, agree somewhat, disagree somewhat, or disagree strongly).

The four social items hang together statistically,[4] which justifies a simple index: the sum of "liberal" answers from 0 to 4. I split the index in half, dubbing the three or four conservative choices "Conservative" and the zero to two choices "Liberal." As expected, the two are completely uncorrelated statistically. Persons high or low on the one scale fall anywhere on the other (r = .015).

That done, we can lay out a graph (Figure 2.1), with two axes: from left to right the degree of economic conservatism, and from low to high the degree of social liberalism. Answers to the two indices determine placement in the graph. For example, consider a group where 75 percent scored high on social conservatism and 75 percent high on economic conservatism. Their point would lie in the upper right quadrant.

The graph is centered on the Mass, who are close to an even split on both measures (because I constructed the indices that way): in absolute terms, however, the Mass is quite conservative on the social items (75 to 83 percent on the "Agree" side of each item).

The results on the global items, party and ideology, are as one would expect. Liberals and Democrats appear in the lower left "New Deal" quadrant, while Republicans and conservatives appear in the upper right "Gingrich-ite" quadrant.

The Brass fall below and to the right, in the heart of the Libertarian quadrant, some distance from their "moderately conservative Republican" self-designation. That is, the Brass are as liberal as Liberals and Democrats on social matters, and as conservative as Republicans and the Very Conservative on economic matters. This leads to the second major finding of this study.

FINDING #2: ALTHOUGH THE ELITE OFFICERS OVERWHELMINGLY DESCRIBE THEMSELVES AS REPUBLICANS AND CONSERVATIVES, THEIR GENERAL STANCE, COMPARED TO THE MASS PUBLIC, IS "LIBERTARIAN" — LIBERAL ON SOCIAL ISSUES, CONSERVATIVE ON ECONOMIC ISSUES.

Having described our two samples in these "global" terms, we turn to a comparison of their specific attitudes on civilian matters.

CIVILIAN MATTERS

Twenty-two items treated civilian issues with no obvious connection to military matters. I divided them into four groups: economic issues, "authoritarianism," religion, and confidence in institutions. See Table 2.4.

---

4. For the four dichotomized social items, coefficient alpha is .680 and each has a .40 or higher item to total correlation.

Figure 2.1. An Ideological Map.

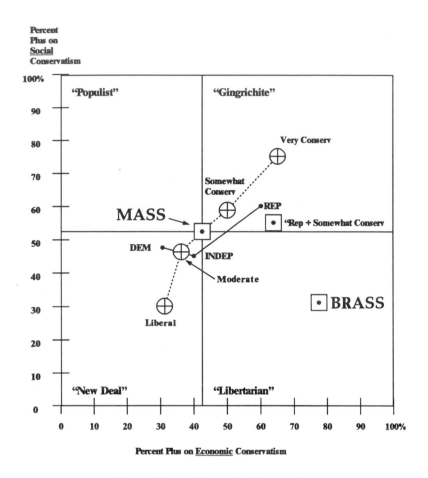

Percent Rate on <u>Economic</u> Conservatism

	Social	Economic
BRASS	32%	78%
MASS	52	42
Rep + Somewhat Conserv	58	62
Republican	63	61
Other	45	40
Democratic	48	31
Very Conserv + Far Right	74	67
Somewhat Conserv	61	50
Moderate	46	37
Liberal	35	34

Table 2.4. Gaps: Civilian Matters.

Question	Topic	"Plus" Response	Gap
Economics			
5k	Should redistribute income	Disagree (3,4)	35.1
3h	How serious—foreign competition	Slight (3,4)	29.5
3d	How serious—many immigrants	Slight (3,4)	27.0
		Average	30.5
Authoritarianism			
9	Can most people be trusted	Yes (1)	39.1
12	Remove communist's book from library	Not remove (2)	27.3
11	Remove atheist's book from library	Not remove (2)	22.7
3f	How serious "decline of standards and morals"	Not (1=Very serious)	19.1
10	More important for children: be obedient, or think for themselves	Think for selves (2)	18.9
13	Remove book advocating homosexuality from library	Not remove (2)	13.5
8a	Decline of traditional values leading to social breakdown	Not (1=Agree strongly)	8.9
		Average	21.3
Religion			
8e	American society (should) take God's will more seriously	Not (1=Agree strongly)	31.1
5g	Permit prayer in public schools	Not (1=Agree strongly)	15.8
14	Bible	Not (1 = inspired word of God, to be taken verbatim)	14.6
18	Frequency of church attendance	(monthly or more)	9.4
		Average	17.7

Confidence in Institutions

"As far as these institutions are concerned, would you say you have a great deal of confidence, only some confidence, or hardly any confidence in them?" (Percent great deal+only some)

Question	Topic		Gap
32q	Television		−12.4
32d	U.S. Supreme Court		9.5
32b	Presidency		−6.7
32f	Major companies		6.0
32n	The military		5.4
32e	Congress		4.8
32h	The executive branch of the federal government		3.7
32c	The press		−0.1
		Average	1.3
		Absolute Average	6.1

KEY: Question = question number in military questionnaire.
   Topic = question (paraphrased).
   "Plus" Response = answer categories coded plus.
   Gap = difference between Brass and Mass.

In the table, *Question* refers to the item number in the military version of the questionnaire. *Topic* is a paraphrase of the question content, not necessarily the exact wording. The positive pole was given to the answer that was more frequent among the military (except for confidence in institutions, where skipping back and forth from pro to anti would be confusing). This is referred to as the *Plus response*. *Raw gap* identifies the percentage difference between Brass and Mass. Save for "institutions," all gaps are necessarily positive.[5] To take an example from the table, in the first row under "Authoritarianism," the item is Question 9, which asks whether the respondent believes most people can be trusted. "Yes," coded number 1, is the positive answer. The raw gap is 38.7 points: the Brass are that much more likely to claim to be trusting.

The first three clusters do not tell us much that is new, since many of these items were used in creating the Libertarianism clusters. However, it emphasizes that, by comparison with representative U.S. adults, elite military officers are unambiguously on the tolerant side for the three free-speech items (Questions 11–13); less upset about "declining morals" and the "decline of traditional values"; and more likely to favor "think for themselves" than "obedience" as a value that should be imparted to children.

On religious matters, the Brass are distinctly (15 to 30 points) less likely than the general public to opt for the "religious right" positions, although they are hardly un-religious: they are more likely (by 9 points) to attend religious services weekly.

So far, the examples add little new to the view that, relative to the general public, elite officers are more socially liberal and more economically conservative. The word "relative" is important here. Consider, for example, the question on declining morals (Question 3f). The Brass are 19.1 points more liberal than the Mass; still, 42 percent of the officers consider that declining morals do pose a "very serious threat to American national security," less than the 60 percent of the Mass who made that choice but still a large proportion. Since the absolute levels of agreement in survey items are easily influenced by the wording, relative group differences are more persuasive. These results can be summed up in the next finding.

FINDING #3: RELATIVE TO THE GENERAL POPULATION, THE MILITARY ELITE ARE MORE LIBERAL ON SOCIAL ISSUES SUCH AS FREE SPEECH, "MORAL DECLINE," AUTHORITARIAN VALUES, AND RIGHT-WING RELIGION. Turning

---

5. In Tables 2.1 through 2.3, the gaps were obtained from percentage tables. Starting with Table 2.4, all tables obtain the gaps by regression analysis of the "dummy variables." The numbers come out almost exactly the same.

to the question of "Confidence in Institutions," however, the results are different.[6] The Gap hypothesis in its extreme form would cause one to expect the officers to be alienated from the basic institutions. Table 2.4 shows, on the contrary, that the gaps are small, averaging just one point; that five of the nine gaps are positive, with officers less alienated and less likely to choose "hardly any confidence"; and that the only sizeable difference (near the median for all gaps) is -12.4 for television, which is hardly a fundamental institution (it is among the lowest rated institutions in survey after survey of a variety of segments of U.S. society).

The only other negative value is a -6.7 for the Presidency, which might suggest that military officers were disenchanted with the then-current occupant of the White House. These results lead to the fourth finding.

FINDING #4: ELITE MILITARY OFFICERS ARE ABOUT AS SUPPORTIVE OF BASIC INSTITUTIONS AS THE MASS PUBLIC.

MILITARY MATTERS

Four items can be loosely grouped as touching upon general support for the military, as shown in the top of Table 2.5.

For three of the four items, the Brass are more pro-military than the civilians, even though in absolute terms the Mass views range from 69 percent (Question 8f) to 92 percent (Question 33f) on the favorable side. The other item (Question 33j) reveals trivially small differences.[7]

The only two "strategic" items in both questionnaires do not reveal much about the gap.[8] Concerns about China and terrorist attacks produce small gaps (average of 7.2 points). The elite military are more worried than the general public about China, but less worried about terrorists. However, an un-measured gap is not a non-gap: the military questionnaire contains many questions on high-level strategy (such as whether the military should do international social work or stick to casualty-free combat), but the civilian questionnaire does not, so such issues are not compared here.

Eight questions grouped under "reforms" deal with gender issues broadly defined. It is useful here to divide them into what the military *has*

---

6. Recall that, unlike the rest of the tables, the plus and minus categories here are not adjusted to make all gaps positive.

7. I consider differences of less than 5 points trivially small, differences of 5 to 9 points "small," and differences of 10 or more points "clear-cut."

8. The three questions on acceptable battle deaths (Question 38) receive detailed analysis elsewhere in this volume.

Table 2.5. Gaps: Military Matters.

Question	Topic	"Plus" Response	Gap
General Support			
33k	Disappointed if child joined military	Disagree Strongly	22.0
8f	Americans should be willing to give lives for country	Agree (1,2)	11.7
33f	Confident military will perform well in war-time	Agree Strongly (10)	9.2
33j	Expect US will still have best military ten years from now	Not "Agree Strongly:" (2-3-4)	1.2
		Average	11.0
Threats			
3a	Threat to security: China as a great military power	Moderately/very serious (1,2)	8.1
3k	Threat to security: terrorist attacks on the United States	Not "Agree serious" (2–3–4)	6.4
		Average	7.2
Reforms			
59	Gays and lesbians should be allowed to serve openly	No (2)	39.4
41i	Hurt military effectiveness: trying to hold on to "old fashioned views of morality"	"Isn't happening," "No effect" (3,4)	24.4
41c	Hurt military effectiveness: military becoming less male dominated	"Isn't happening," "No effect" (3,4)	22.2
50	Should women be allowed to serve in all combat jobs	No (2)	17.9
41e	Hurt military effectiveness: ban on language and behavior that encourage camaraderie	"Isn't happening," "No effect" (3,4)	14.5
42c	Military should retain basically masculine values	Disagree (3,4)	8.3
42b	Uniforms, medals, military traditions are necessary	Not Agree (2,4)	8.0
42e	Military must have strength, toughness, physical courage	Agree Strongly (1)	6.1
		Average	17.1

KEY: Question = question number in military questionnaire.
   Topic = question (paraphrased).
   "Plus" Response = answer categories coded plus.
   Gap = difference between Brass and Mass.

done and what the military *might do.*[9] What it has done is to integrate women into non-combat roles and tone down overt sexism. The first two items ask whether these changes, if they have occurred, have affected military effectiveness:

- Question 41c: The military becoming less male-dominated;
- Question 41e: A ban on language and behavior that encourage camaraderie among soldiers;
- Question 42c: Although women can serve in the military, should it remain basically masculine, dominated by male values and characteristics?
- Question 42b: Are military symbols such as uniforms, medals, and ceremonies necessary?
- Question 42e: In a high-tech era, do people in the military still need characteristics such as strength, toughness, courage, and the willingness to sacrifice?

These issues produce gaps between military and civilian views of 6 to 20 points. In all but the smallest difference (the last question quoted), the officers are on the socially liberal side.

One question (Question 41i) is ambiguous, and therefore I did not include it in the "reform" cluster. Responding to the statement "The military trying to hold on to old-fashioned views of morality," more officers chose "isn't happening" or "no effect" rather than "greatly hurts" or "somewhat hurts" military effectiveness. If they considered traditional sex roles to be part of "old fashioned morality," this would create an apparent contradiction, but it is not clear that they do. While the four "gender reform" items hang together statistically, Question 41i isn't much related to any of them.

These results, then, suggest that elite military officers are less nostalgic for the bygone macho military culture than are mass civilians in general. But the results are reversed when we turn to what the military might do: elite officers are much more opposed to "allowing gays and lesbians to serve openly in the military" (39.4 point gap), and to allowing women "to serve in all combat jobs" (17.9 points). Table 2.6 shows the absolute percentages, subdivided by gender (the Brass sample included 61 female officers).

Roughly two-thirds of civilian women favor both proposals, with slightly more supporting service by gays than a combat role for women.

---

9. Deborah Avant suggested this useful distinction.

Table 2.6. Responses on Gays in Military (Q59) and Women in Combat (Q50) by Sample and Sex.

| Sex | Sample | (Percentage Favorable) | | (N) | Diff. |
		Gays	Women		
Male	Brass	16.3	30.4	(884)	+14.1
	Male	51.4	49.4	(459)	−2.0
	Diff.	−34.4	−12.7		
Female	Brass	47.5	70.4	(61)	+22.9
	Mass	69.5	58.6	(460)	−10.9
	Diff.	−22.0	−11.8		

Civilian males are less progressive; about half (51 and 49 percent) back both reforms. Putting them together gives a small majority of civilians favoring both changes.

Female officers are *more* supportive of women in combat than civilian females (70.4 vs. 59.6), while male officers are *less* supportive than civilian males (30.4 vs. 49.4). The consequence is a 40-point gender gap *within* the military, considerably larger than the Brass/Mass differences.

For the issue of whether homosexuals should be allowed to serve openly in the military, differences reach 53 points between civilian women and male officers. Just 16.3 percent of male Brass favor gays and lesbians "serving openly," while nearly 70 percent of civilian women do. Thus we derive the next two findings.

FINDING #5: ELITE MILITARY OFFICERS ARE MORE SUPPORTIVE OF GENDER EQUALITY IN THE SERVICES THAN ARE MASS CIVILIANS, UP TO, BUT NOT INCLUDING, WOMEN IN COMBAT.

FINDING #6: MALE ELITE OFFICERS ARE LESS FAVORABLE TO WOMEN IN COMBAT THAN ARE MASS CIVILIANS; ELITE OFFICERS, ESPECIALLY MALES, ARE OVERWHELMINGLY OPPOSED TO "GAYS AND LESBIANS SERVING OPENLY"; MASS CIVILIANS ARE DIVIDED ON BOTH ISSUES.

MILITARY/CIVILIAN MATTERS

Finally, we consider perceptions of the gap itself, asking, as it were, if there is a gap in perceptions of the gap.[10] We consider first military culture versus civilian culture, and then a fundamental policy issue: civilian control of the military. Table 2.7 lays these issues out item by item.

10. This issue is explored in greater detail in Chapter 3 by Paul Gronke and Peter Feaver.

Table 2.7. Gaps: Military/Civilian Matters.

Question	Topic	"Plus" Response	Gap
Military v. Civilian Culture			
8kk	Civilian society (should adopt) military's values and customs	Not disagree strongly (1–3)	28.4
39b2	(Does this term) apply to military culture . . . Intolerant	Not circled (2)	26.7
39f2f	(Does this term) apply to military culture . . . Self-indulgent	Not circled (2)	25.5
39b1	(Does this term) apply to civilian culture . . . Intolerant	Not circled (2)	24.8
39g1	(Does this term) apply to civilian culture . . . Hard-working	Not circled (2)	13.8
33a	Most members of military have a great deal of respect for civilian society	Agree strongly (1)	9.0
39g2	(Does this term) apply to military culture . . . Hard working	Yes (1)	8.3
41j	Hurt military effectiveness: Military culture very different from (civilians)	"Isn't happening," "No effect"	8.2
39f1	(Does this term) apply to civilian culture . . . Self-indulgent	Not circled (2)	6.4
33b	Most (civilians) have a great deal of respect for the military	Disagree (3,4)	3.5
		Average	15.5
Civilian Control			
47c	Military should be allowed to express political views	Not Agree Strongly (3,4)	43.0
49	Military leaders will avoid carrying out civilian orders they oppose	Rarely, Never (4,5)	42.2
48f	Civilian control is absolutely safe and secure	Agree (1–2)	40.7
48a	Civilians should have final say on *whether* to use force	Agree (1–2)	35.5
47a	Military should not publicly criticize senior civilians	Agree (1,2)	20.0
47e	Proper for military to advocate publicly military policies	No Agree Strongly (2–4)	19.2
48b	Civilians should have final say on *what type* of military force to use	Disagree (3,4)	18.5
48c	Partisan politics often motivate civilian (orders to military)	Disagree (3,4)	17.2
48d	In wartime civilians should let military take over running the war	Disagree (3,4)	12.8
		Average	27.7

KEY: Question = question number in military questionnaire.
   Topic = question (paraphrased).
   "Plus" Response = answer categories coded plus.
   Gap = difference between Brass and Mass.

Table 2.8. Responses to Questions 33a and 33b by Sample (Percent "Agree").

Military Respects Civilians Q33a	Civilians Respect Military Q33b	Brass	Mass	Brass-Mass
Yes	Yes	63.6	63.0	0.6
Yes	No	23.5	17.1	6.4
No	Yes	6.0	11.2	−5.2
No	No	6.9	8.9	−2.0
	Total		100.0%	100.2%
	N		(1033)	(962)

The greatest difference is one of 28.4 points in the item "Civilian society would be better off if it adopted more of the military's values and customs." Three-quarters of the officers (77.6 percent) agreed, far more than the 41.0 percent of the Mass who agreed.

Making sense of this finding requires a look at some of the more specific items, bearing in mind that tree surgeons, police officers, and primary school teachers would also probably disproportionately agree that society would be better off if it adopted their values. However, the roles and functions of the armed forces are unique and so crucial that what is unproblematic in other cohesive organizations might be highly problematic in the military.

Questions 33a and 33b ask whether members of the military have a great deal of respect for civilian society and vice versa. Table 2.8 displays the results side by side.

The top line gives a reassuring 63 percent in both columns: clear majorities among elite officers and the civilian cross-section see mutual respect. The other three rows indicate tensions that have not been treated separately in other discussions. The rarest is at the bottom: less than 10 percent of either group sees mutual disrespect. The second from the bottom comes closest to the Ricks characterization: the belief that the military does not respect civilians but that civilians do respect the military. In fact, however, only 6.0 percent of the officers agree with this view. Combining the two categories yields a total of just 12.9 percent of the military who see lack of respect from their side. (Happily, this is a low number, but this is what is known in the survey business as an easy question: it is hard to imagine a lot of military officers claiming that the military do *not* respect society unless relations were in an extreme crisis.) The last combination and the most common tension comes where it is believed that military respect is not reciprocated by civilians. Almost a quarter (23.5 per-

Table 2.9. Percent Checking the Characteristic (Questions 39b1, 39b2, 39f1, 39f2, 39g1, 39g2) by Sample.

Trait	Target	Brass	Mass
	Civilians	75.4	81.7
Self-indulgent	Military	10.5	37.4
	Difference	64.9	44.3
	Civilians	36.0	22.7
Lazy (not "hard working")	Military	4.4	12.1
	Difference	31.6	10.6
	Civilians	26.2	51.3
Intolerant	Military	31.8	58.3
	Difference	−5.6	−7.2
N		(1079)	(994)

cent) of the Brass fall in this group and 17.1 percent of the civilians agree. The suggestion here is not of military disdain for a decadent civilian society, but rather the military's unrequited positive feelings. Again, comparisons with other occupations would be necessary before drawing firm conclusions.

Question 39 tempted both samples to engage in name-calling by asking them to judge whether civilian and military cultures are "intolerant," "self-indulgent," and "hard working." Table 2.7 shows gaps ranging from 29.5 to 4.8 on various items. Table 2.9 shows the absolute values.

The top two sub-tables of Table 2.9 come closer to supporting the Ricks quotations than anything else in this chapter. They say that vast majorities rate civilians as self-indulgent, while much smaller proportions believe this to be true of the military. Furthermore, the contrast is greater for the Brass (a difference of 64.9 points) than the Mass (44.3 points). Thus both samples claim that civilians are more self-indulgent, but even more of the Brass believe this than do the Mass. For the characteristic "lazy" (not "hard working"), all the absolute figures are low, but the same pattern appears. Civilians are judged lazier, especially by the Brass (31.6 minus 10.6 equals 21.0). Judgments of the third characteristic, "intolerant," follow a different pattern. Both samples rate the military as relatively more intolerant, but the difference is about the same in both samples. These results lead to the next finding.

FINDING #7: THE ELITE MILITARY CLAIM NOT TO DISDAIN CIVILIAN SOCIETY BUT RATHER CLAIM TO GIVE IT UNREQUITED RESPECT. THEY ARE MORE LIKELY THAN CIVILIANS TO EMPHASIZE SOME OF ITS NEGATIVE FACETS.

Nine items about civilian control of the military (see Table 2.7) show

Table 2.10. Civilian Control Items by Sample.

Item	Topic	Percent "Agree"		Gap
		Brass	Mass	
48b	Military should have final say on type of force*	70.7	58.7	+12.0
48d	In wartime civilians should let military run war	56.6	69.7	−13.1
47e	Proper for officers to advocate military policies	67.9	86.2	−18.3
47a	OK for military to criticize senior civilians*	12.4	33.7	−21.3
48a	Military should have final say on whether to use force*	7.9	44.4	−36.5
47c	Proper for officers to express political views	39.7	83.8	−43.9

* Item slightly paraphrased here to make pro and con consistent for all items.

significant gaps, about the largest in this chapter, ranging from 12.8 to 43.0 points, but the results definitely favor *civilian* control of the military. The substantive pattern is revealed by the absolute values displayed in Table 2.10, where a reversal of the signs of some items means that a greater percentage always indicates a looser civilian rein on the military.

In Table 2.10, the civilian control items are presented in order of gap size. Just half the officers agree that civilians should let the military run the war, and 83.3 percent of civilians agree that it is proper for officers to express their political views. These views are quite contrary to accepted principles of civilian control of the military and as such might make one's hair stand on end. But there is at least some good news in the right-hand column: with one exception, more military officers than the mass public express support for assertive civilian control. Moreover, the exception (Question 48b) is actually consistent with accepted principles that "civilians decide whether, the military decides how."[11]

This gap may have has a simple explanation. Civilian control is a fairly sophisticated doctrine, while common sense suggests that important decisions should be made by people who are best informed. Americans think highly of their military, as shown here and in many other studies. In the absence of formal indoctrination, and given cynicism about civilian politics, perhaps it is not surprising for civilian respondents to give the "wrong" answer. The principle of civilian control of the military may not be much emphasized in American schools, but it certainly is in

11.   Needless to say, the boundary is ambiguous in practice, as in the choice of bombing targets.

military training: the military are formally indoctrinated with the correct line, and those who become visibly out of line suffer for it.[12]

FINDING #8: AMONG THE MASS PUBLIC, THERE IS EVIDENCE OF AN "UNDERSTANDING GAP" CONCERNING ISSUES OF CIVILIAN CONTROL OF THE MILITARY, AND IN SOME RESPECTS, THE MASS PUBLIC SEEMS MORE WILLING TO GIVE THE MILITARY MORE LEEWAY THAN THE ELITE MILITARY CLAIM FOR THEMSELVES.

SUMMARY

The attitude and opinion gaps between the average American and the military elite are substantial, but their content does not fit the stereotype. On civilian social issues, the Brass are clearly more liberal, although they are more conservative on economic matters. There is some evidence that they lack respect for civilian society, but that evidence is ambiguous. On military matters they are more supportive of the inclusion of women in the military, and accompanying changes, than civilians are. On other military matters, elite officers are predictably more "pro-military" than even the highly pro-military civilian mass public. On civilian control matters, the military elite are more aware of civilian control principles than are the generality of U.S. adults. On two sensitive issues—women in combat and gays and lesbians serving openly in the military—there is a clear-cut "non-libertarian" gap that contradicts the officers' general ideologies.

The Demographics

Demography is not destiny, but it is often the best clue surveys can provide when trying to understand the sources of attitude differences. In this section I compare the Brass and the Mass in terms of education, military experience, age, gender, religion, race, class background, and region.

The most striking characteristic of the military samples is their high level of formal education. Virtually all military officers are college graduates, and the officers in this sample go beyond that: 71 percent hold a graduate degree and almost all, 93 percent, have done graduate work. By comparison, only 10.8 percent of the Mass sample report study beyond the bachelor's degree.[13] The level of the respondent's "Mother's Educa-

---

12.   This topic is explored in greater detail in Chapter 3 by Paul Gronke and Peter Feaver.

13.   Since the military sends many officers to graduate school, one might view education as an consequence of service, not a prior characteristic. However, a bachelor's degree is an almost universal requirement for an officer's commission, and only 29.8 percent of the Mass sample obtained one.

tion" sheds light on whether these numbers reflect privileged backgrounds, as it is an indicator of parental social class. Officers differ little from the cross-section in maternal schooling. While they are clearly an educational elite themselves, there is no evidence that they are much different from the general public in their origins.

By definition, 100 percent of the Brass have military experience; this is true of only 18.4 percent of the Mass, producing an 81.6 point gap. On about half of the items, veterans in the Mass sample differ from non-veterans; thus, lack of military experience on the civilian side tends to correlate with greater gaps. This would be a fruitful topic to pursue, because it would give clues as to what to expect as the percentage of veterans in the mass public declines in the coming years.

Today's military elite is still preponderantly male (93 percent). The age gap is built into the survey design: elite officers are concentrated in the 35–54 bracket, while the Mass sample ranges from 18 to over 100 years of age, producing a 53.6 point difference. Artificial as it may be, the age pattern guarantees that the gaps are not because officers are from the "older generation."

Three demographic characteristics—religious preference, race/ethnicity, and region in which the respondent grew up—show relatively small differences, and two of these defy stereotypes. Officers are, as expected, disproportionately white (91.5 percent, compared to 78.5 percent for the Mass sample), but the difference is not a good candidate for explaining gaps because both Mass and Brass are overwhelmingly majority. Any presumed Southern or Protestant domination of the military is not reflected in the demographics: in fact, officers (and cadets as well) show numbers of Roman Catholics and Middle Atlantic hometowns that are disproportionately high compared to the general population. Thus military leaders, these at least, are hardly the "southern gentlemen" or John Wayne cowboys of many stereotypes. Given these data without an occupational label, one could guess they were CPAs, civil engineers, or even Wall Street traders.

FINDING #9: ELITE OFFICERS ARE DISPROPORTIONATELY HIGHLY EDUCATED, MIDDLE-AGED, AND MALE. THEY ARE ALSO SOMEWHAT MORE LIKELY THAN THE GENERAL POPULATION TO BE WHITE AND CATHOLIC, BUT DIFFER LITTLE FROM IT IN CLASS OR REGIONAL ORIGINS.

THE IMPACTS OF DEMOGRAPHIC DIFFERENCES

We have seen that the elite military are predominantly college-educated, male, middle-aged, economically conservative, Republican, and socially liberal. We now ask how far these characteristics go in accounting for specific attitude and opinion gaps—whether their attitudes are essentially what one would expect among similar civilians, or whether there is additional variation due to military life.[14]

I proceeded as follows. The goal is to estimate what the Brass attitudes would be if the officers had the same demographic and ideological characteristics as the Mass—for instance, if they were 49 percent male rather than 93 percent male. That is, I want three numbers for each item: the actual Mass mean, the actual Brass mean, and the estimated mean in a population with the same demographics and ideology as the Brass.

I ran a series of statistical regressions in which the dependent variable was an attitude in the survey and the six predictor variables were: (1) college graduate vs. less education; (2) high vs. low on social liberalism index; (3) party preference Republican vs. independent and Democrat; (4) male vs. female; (5) high vs. low on economic conservatism index; (6) age 35–54 vs. older and younger. These were the demographics and ideological measures where Mass and Brass differ most.

This produced 44 regression equations (the eleven other items were either included in the ideological indices or were drawn from the NORC General Social Survey). Regression equations consist of a constant term and a coefficient (multiplier) for each predictor. If one multiplies each coefficient by the mean of its variable, sums these products, and adds the constant term, one gets the overall mean. I entered the means from the Brass sample into each equation, multiplied, and summed. This gives a predicted mean in a hypothetical population identical to the Brass in attitudes and demography.

Consider, for example, Question 48c: "Partisan politics often motivates civilian orders to the military" (disagree). In the Mass sample, 29.8 percent disagree, in the Brass 47.0, giving a gap of 17.2 points (as shown in Table 2.7). In the modeled data, the percentage is 42.2. This allows us to divide the original gap into two parts: 42.2 - 29.8 = 12.4 and 47.0 - 42.2 = 4.8. This says that 12.4 points of the gap are accounted for by ideology and demography, while 4.8 points come from something about the Brass not accounted for by ideology and demography. We can call the differences between Brass and modeled estimate "residuals."

For a global measure of success I ran the correlation (Pearson) between the actual gap and the gap predicted using the six demographics. The coefficient turned out to be +.702. In statistical terms about half the typical gap (.702 * .702 = .4928) can be explained by the officer's distinctive social characteristics and basic ideology.

---

14. Military life might have its effects due to socializing experiences during a military career, or by the extensive winnowing out as some rise in the ranks and others leave service. There is no way to distinguish the two with these data.

The residuals indirectly support the demographic approach. They can be either positive or negative. Since the original gaps are constructed to be positive, a positive residual means the elite military's opinions are more pronounced than would be accounted for by their demography and ideology. Of the 44 residuals, 38 are positive, 31 are five points or more, 18 ten points or more. Only six are negative, and none of these exceed nine points. On the vast majority of issues, therefore, we can say that military experience tends to accentuate the "natural" bent of an officer's opinions. Putting it another way, the officers usually differ from the Mass the way their civilian demographic twins do—but more so.

FINDING #10: THE DEMOGRAPHIC CHARACTERISTICS AND BASIC IDEOLOGY OF THE ELITE OFFICERS TYPICALLY EXPLAIN ABOUT HALF OF THEIR ATTITUDE GAPS, AND THE REMAINDER IS USUALLY AN ACCENTUATION OF THESE DIF-FERENCES. Table 2.12 shows the independent contribution of each of the six predictors.[15] For example, over the 44 items, whether one is a college graduate or not produces 15 gaps of five points or more, seven of three or four points, 13 of one or two points, and so on. Of these 44 small gaps, 35 were positive (the disproportionately high number of college graduates in the elite military adds to the total gap), and eight were negative (the excess of college graduates lowers the gap, because the better educated were less likely to agree with the item).

I draw two conclusions from Table 2.12. First, the six factors are fairly similar in their effects. One may claim that education is the most power-ful and social liberalism the least, but the difference is not overwhelm-ing.[16] Thus, one should be wary of drawing strong conclusions from par-ticular imbalances. Although the officers are overwhelmingly Republican (compared to the Mass) and their party preference contributes to 28 of 44 gaps, it is just one of six variables showing independent effects, and it is not outstanding in its impacts on other attitudes.

Second, Table 2.12 tells us that 56 of 264 gaps (21 percent) are nega-tive; in other words, a given variable counteracts the others, slightly re-ducing the total gap. Table 2.13 shows this; its cases are coefficients, not people. For example, the figure of +.463 for Social Liberal and College Graduate means that social liberalism and college graduation tend to have similar correlations with the 44 gap items. (Correlations can range from -1 to +1. Positive values mean that the two variables tend to line up

---

15. To get the numbers, one multiplies each variable's coefficient by the difference between Brass and Mass (the Brass-Mass numbers in Table 2.11). The six products will sum to the regression prediction of the total gap.

16. These are, of course, net or independent effects. Education's contribution would loom even larger if we also assessed its influence on the two ideological indices.

Table 2.11. Demographic Characteristics of the Two Samples.

Item	Category	Brass	Mass	Brass-Mass
65	Education			
	Graduate work or degree	92.6%	10.8	+81.8
	College Degree	7.4	19.0	−11.6
	Part College	0.0	28.0	−28.0
	High School or Less	0.0	42.2	−42.2
		100.0%	100.0%	
		(993)	(1041)	
68	Military Experience			
	Yes	100.0%	18.4%	+81.6
64	Age			
	55	3.3	30.1	−26.8
	35–54	92.4	38.8	+53.6
	18–34	4.3	31.2	−26.9
		100.0%	101.0%	
		(1001)	(1082)	
63	Gender			
	Male	93.1%	49.3%	+43.8
		(1045)	(1001)	
19	Religious Preference			
	Protestant	54.6	57.8	−3.2
	Catholic	37.7	21.2	+16.5
	None	5.9	9.6	−3.7
	Other	1.3	9.2	−7.9
	Jewish	0.5	2.1	−1.6
		100.0%	99.9%	
		(1011)	(1001)	
80	Race/Ethnicity			
	White	91.5	78.5	+13.0
	Black	3.9	9.8	−5.9
	Hispanic	2.0	7.4	−5.4
	Asian	0.9	2.1	−1.2
	Other	1.8	2.1	−0.3
		100.1%	99.9%	
		(1031)	(996)	

Table 2.11. *Continued.*

Item	Category	Brass	Mass		Brass-Mass
78	Mother's Education (Mass and from NORC General Social Survey)				
	College Graduate	26.2	21.7	26.5*	+4.5
	Part College	22.7	18.9	19.9	+3.8
	High School Graduate	41.8	40.9	39.0	+0.9
	Less than High	9.2	18.4	14.6	−9.2
		99.9%	99.9%		100.0%
		(1092)	(2396)		
79	Region When Growing Up				
	New England	10.8	9.8		+1.0
	South	20.3	20.9		−0.6
	Mountain	2.7	3.9		−1.2
	Pacific	9.4	11.3		−1.9
	Mid-Atlantic	20.9	13.9		+7.0
	Midwest	23.6	28.8		−5.2
	Southwest	6.0	7.0		−1.0
	Other	6.2	4.4		−2.0
		99.9%	100.0%		
		(1091)	(983)		

*NORC General Social Survey (1996–98), college graduates 35–54.

together.) Table 2.13 reveals two clear clusters: social liberalism, college graduation, and age of 35–54 tend to have similar effects on these attitudes; so do being male, economically conservative, and having a Republican affiliation. These two clusters show positive internal correlations and mostly negative cross-cluster ones. That is, economically conservative male Republicans tend to disagree with socially liberal middle-aged college graduates. Since the elite military have huge surpluses in both clusters, and all six items contribute to Brass/Mass differences, the social structure of attitudes tends to diminish aggregate attitude gaps between the military elites and the civilian sample.

FINDING #11: THE DEMOGRAPHIC AND IDEOLOGICAL PECULIARITIES OF THE ELITE MILITARY DO NOT HAVE A CUMULATIVE IMPACT ON ATTITUDE GAPS BECAUSE THEY OFTEN PUSH IN OPPOSITE DIRECTIONS. Question 59 on gays serving in the military is an important example of this pattern. The raw gap is a very large 39.4 but only 2.0 points comes from the six predictors, because the six work in opposite directions. Here, a positive number

College graduate	8.7
Social liberal	2.5
Economic conservative	0.2
Age 35–54	0.0
Republican	–4.5
Male	–8.5
Total	**2.0**
Residual	37.4
Raw gap	39.4

means that the variable contributes to the gap in an anti-gay direction, while a minus means it tends reduce the gap. The results are:

Although four of the six factors contribute to the gap, they cancel each other out. The elite officers "should" have about the same opinion as the Mass, but in fact the difference is an enormous 37.4 points, almost none of which can be explained by the demographic or ideological characteristics of the officers.

Conclusion

The major findings of this analysis are, first, that there are many large differences between Mass and Brass opinions, but that many of them are in a surprising "liberal" direction. However, on the major civilian/military issue of the day, whether homosexuals should be allowed to serve openly

Table 2.12. Contribution to Gap by Individual Variable.

Points	Social Liberal	35–54	GOP	Econ. Conserv.	Male	College Graduate	Total
5+	0	2	2	0	5	15	24
3–4	5	2	7	9	10	7	40
1–2	15	17	18	19	13	13	95
	20	21	27	28	28	35	159
0	11	12	8	9	8	1	49
–1–2	11	10	7	4	6	2	40
–3–4	2	1	2	3	1	2	11
–5 or more	0	0	0	0	1	4	5
	13	11	9	7	8	8	56
Total	44	44	44	44	44	44	264

Table 2.13. Inter-correlations (Pearson r) of Coefficients over 44 Dependent Variables.

	Social Liberal	College Grad.	Age 35–54	Male	Economic Conserv.	GOP
Social Liberal		.463	.357	−.207	−.289	−.581
College Grad	.463		.089	.130	.175	−.221
Age 35–54	.357	.089		−.184	−.561	−.263
Male	−.207	.130	−.184		.261	.289
Econ. Conserv.	−.289	.175	−.561	.261		.420
Conserv. GOP	−.581	−.221	−.263	.289	.420	

in the military, elite military opinion is very far from civilian opinion even after allowing for demographics and ideology. Although the military are overwhelmingly Republican, male, middle-aged, and economically conservative, they are also extremely well educated and socially liberal. Demography and ideology tend to separate the Brass from the Mass, but the effects often move in opposite directions and thus cancel each other out.

Chapter 3

Uncertain Confidence: Civilian and Military Attitudes about Civil-Military Relations

Paul Gronke
Peter D. Feaver

Americans regularly profess a great deal of confidence in the military. From one perspective, this is not terribly surprising. The U.S. armed forces are the premier military institution in the world: the best-trained, best-equipped, most capable fighting force in history. Moreover, the proud tradition of military professionalism is reflected in a record of more than 200 years of democratic rule and acceptance across all ranks and branches of the military of principle of civilian control.

From another perspective, however, public confidence in the military is remarkable because it cuts against a historical distrust of the military that is part of America's liberal democratic tradition. Fears of a standing army and an overly powerful military have been part of American political culture since before the Revolution, and had a profound influence in shaping the Constitution, the system of checks and balances, and the Bill of Rights. Continued confidence in the military over the past two decades stands against a backdrop of declining trust in the government more generally, and dwindling respect for other governmental and public institutions. It is all the more curious at a time when fewer Americans have a direct connection with the military, either through prior service or through friends and relatives with military experience.

The empirical results, while perhaps surprising, are incontrovertible. Confidence in the military is widely established via extensive polling and has become part of the conventional wisdom regarding public opinion

We thank Christy Hamilton, Carrie Liken, and Damon Coletta for research assistance; and Deborah Avant, James Burk, John Brehm, Timothy Cook, Michael Desch, John Hibbing, James Lindsay, and Charles Stevenson for comments on earlier drafts.

about American institutions (King 1999; Nye 1997; Lipset and Schneider 1987). It is regularly cited as an indication that the American military has not lost its connection with American society, even after 25 years as an all-volunteer force (AVF) and in a time of radical downsizing. If the military is one of the most revered institutions in American society, one might argue that there can be no crisis in civil-military relations.

This chapter assesses the basis for the claim that, since Americans profess great confidence in the military, there is no danger of alienation between the military and civilian society. Even senior policymakers have expressed concerns about a growing gulf between civilian society and the military, as Secretary of Defense William Cohen's remarks in a May 10, 1998, speech at Ohio Wesleyan University attest:

Regrettably, [military service] is a privilege which too few Americans enjoy today, and it's somewhat understandable. With a smaller military and all volunteer force, there are fewer Americans who have fathers and mothers or brothers and sisters who are wearing a uniform. . . . Perhaps because we live in largely peaceful time, most Americans tend not to think about those who endure the risks and trials so that we can enjoy this tranquillity. And so one of the challenges that we have in peacetime is to prevent any kind of a gap from developing between the military and civilian worlds.

As explained in the introductory chapter to this book, these concerns are often referred to as the "gap" or "culture gap" thesis.

The premise of Cohen's concern is that support for the military is partly a function of association or at least familiarity with the military. As fewer Americans enjoy such associations or familiarity—a consequence of the passing of the conscript generations and the downsizing of the AVF in the post–Cold War era—will support for the military and confidence in the military institution decline? The opposite dynamic is at least logically possible: perhaps familiarity breeds contempt, so that support for the military actually grows as people lose any personal awareness of how alien military culture is to the classical liberal American way of life. Or perhaps social distance from the military permits shallow and superficial support, the kind that results in affirmative answers to easy questions but masks a deeper alienation that could quickly come to the fore if favorable security conditions change. This could even work for both sides of the relationship: perhaps social distance creates a superficial respect among military officers for civilian society that is fragile and unlikely to withstand the vicissitudes of fiscally constrained defense spending, a high rate of deployments on missions the military considers secondary, and the like.

We frame these questions in the following way: does strong public confidence in the military institution mask latent alienation and distrust that suggest the existence of deeper ideological and attitudinal divides between the military and the public it serves, and thus a fundamental divide in civil-military relations? Such alienation, we hypothesize, would be present if one of the following conditions were present: first, as Secretary Cohen and others posit, if public professions of confidence are merely a function of a personal connection to the military so that, as these connections decline with the downsizing of the force, so too would confidence in the military; second, if confidence were not undergirded with strong measures of support as expressed in other attitudes about the military; third, if either group sensed alienation, for instance, if civilians believed the military did not respect civilian society or vice versa; fourth, if public professions of respect and confidence were modified by entrenched views based on negative stereotypes of the opposite group; or fifth, if there were wide dissensus on a variety of core issues concerning the relationship itself, such as the extent to which military culture should be distinctively different from civilian culture, the extent to which a distinctive culture is necessary for military effectiveness, or the practical working of civilian control and military professionalism.[1]

To explore these issues, we analyze results from the TISS set of surveys described in the Introduction, in Chapter 1 by Ole Holsti, and in Newcity (1999). The project polled officers at various stages of military careers and used an identical instrument to survey what may be called a foreign policy elite (Holsti 1996), specialists in foreign policy, and a larger sample of opinion leaders. A shorter version was administered to a representative sample of the general public.

We adopt a two-stage approach. First, we look to our data to replicate the findings of other studies, showing that expressed confidence in the military is indeed very high. Besides providing baseline estimates of confidence in the military, these figures supply an external validity check on our survey. We then explore the determinants of these attitudes, showing that mutual respect, while high, is not uniform across the population. Rather, these attitudes correlate, at least in part, with contact or experience with the military.

Next, we unpack the concept of "confidence" into four component issues to explore possible underlying disaffection in the civil-military relationship:

---

1. This is not an exhaustive list of possible forms of latent alienation. Other companion studies from this project consider alternative forms (see particularly Chapter 1 by Ole Holsti, Chapter 2 by James Davis, and Chapter 9 by Benjamin Fordham).

- Do civilians and the military say that they themselves are alienated, in response to direct questions asking about how each group is perceived by the other?
- Is there latent alienation in the form of wide disagreements over how different military culture should be from civilian culture, and the relative merits of the respective cultures?
- Is there consensus on how best to preserve the military's ability to perform its core missions, expressed as agreement on the determinants of military effectiveness?
- Beyond the lip-service paid to the principle of civilian control, is there a consensus on the practical workings of the principle and what it means in the day-to-day context of policymaking?

We find that the conventional wisdom that there is widespread public support for the military is misleading, and that in fact there is real cause for concern about an undercurrent of alienation in the relationship. Specifically, we find that, beneath superficial responses to an institutional trust item, public faith and confidence in the military is less certain. In some ways, the civilian and military elites agree upon the proper role for the military, the relevance of military symbols, and the expected future quality of our armed forces, but in other ways, distrust is quite apparent. The less an individual has contact with military culture, either through friends and acquaintances, or through military service, the less inclined is that person to support important aspects of military culture.

Americans' High Confidence in the Military

It is commonplace in the study of American politics to bemoan the decline in social capital (Putnam 1995a; 1995b; Brehm and Rahn 1997). Declines in social trust are particularly worrisome because they have been accompanied by a long decline in faith and confidence in governmental institutions (Hibbing and Theiss-Morse 1995). Fewer and fewer Americans join the institutions that bind society together, while more and more express low levels of trust in the public institutions and procedures that are thought to be essential for a healthy democracy. Declining levels of participation in democratic political activities have been caused in part by declines perceived in political efficacy (a sense that an individual can make a difference in politics), trust in others (fostered by social involvement), and trust in government.

Public attitudes towards the military provide a striking counterexample, so much so that some have pointed to the military as illustrating a revival of faith and trust in civilian society. Thus, a *Parade* magazine excerpt of a book about how the rigorous Marine boot camp experience forges upstanding citizens out of slacker teenagers was titled, "What We Can Learn From Them" (Ricks 1997b). While confidence in the executive and legislative branches has languished since Vietnam and Watergate, confidence in the military has soared (see the top panel of Figure 3.1).[2] The military likewise fares very well in public esteem compared to non-governmental institutions such as the media and public schools (see the bottom panel of Figure 3.1). Only religion and such hallowed public institutions as the Supreme Court receive the strong expressions of support that the American public gives the military. During an era when Americans show great skepticism about most of the institutions that make up American society, the general support for the military is a powerful counter-trend.

Previous research has demonstrated that confidence in political institutions is a product of two separate factors: *process*, a sense that the institution operates fairly, and *policy*, an evaluation of the products or behavior of the institution (Hibbing and Theiss-Morse 1995). If it is valid to think of the military in this way, then on both process and policy grounds the last fifteen years have been an almost unbroken series of successes. After the Vietnam debacle, the military began again to earn the respect of the American public and, with the arms build-up begun in 1979, reshaped itself into the premier fighting force in American history. Along the way, the military addressed, more successfully than any other institution, two crucial scourges that plagued American society, drug abuse and racism, although the sexual harassment scandals of Tailhook and Aberdeen were serious blots on the escutcheon. An impressive record of battlefield successes is reflected in the upticks in poll responses at the time of the 1990–91 Persian Gulf War and the 1999 Kosovo conflict, both military victories at remarkably low costs. They support the impression that Americans have confidence in the military because the military can get the job done. Thus, the most obvious explanation for the high level of confidence is probably the correct one: the military is respected because it *is* competent and, beginning since the mid-1980s, has demonstrated success at what it does.

Support for the military remained strong even though the military

---

2. The Gallup and Harris organizations and the General Social Survey, among others, have surveyed Americans' attitudes toward a variety of public institutions for several decades. The Gallup data, reported in Figure 3.1, show that confidence in most institutions has declined since the early 1970s. A few institutions, including the military, have countered the trend. See Lipset and Schneider (1983) for an extensive account of these items, their use by different polling organizations, and trends over time.

Figure 3.1. Confidence in the Military Compared to Confidence in Governmental Institutions and other Public Institutions

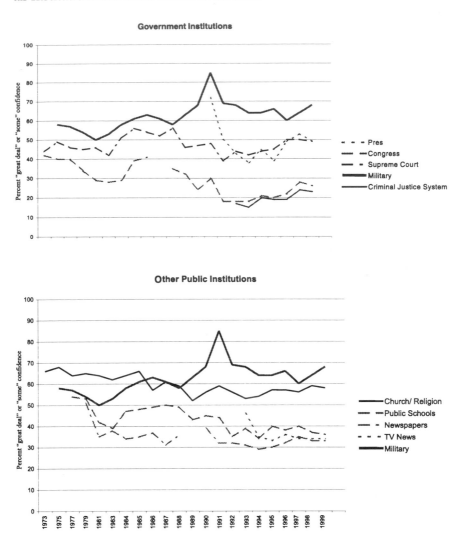

Source: Gallup Survey from the Roper Center; see <http:pollingreport.cominstitut.htm>.

moved from a conscription-based force to an all-volunteer force and so lost some of its avenues of connection to civilian society (King 1999). Among the general public, a direct connection to the military in the form of prior or expected military service was apparently not needed to keep confidence in the institution high. Arguably, the end of the draft made room for even more support for the military, as fear of involuntary service no longer cast a shadow over public perceptions of the institution. Thus, King (1999) finds that support for the military is very high even among the so-called Generations X and Y (those born since 1961), the same ones who are least likely to join the military or have family members who served in the military.

Still, one cannot discount the concerns expressed by prominent leaders of the military and civilian establishment as well as informed academic observers of the civilian-military relationship. The problem with the conventional wisdom is that it has never been subjected to a careful analysis using data tailored to understanding the civil-military gap. For example, up to now there has not been a survey of the *military* conducted in parallel with a survey of the *civilian* population focusing on these issues. Civilian and military surveys have not asked important questions regarding the civil-military relationship itself, nor aimed extensive batteries of questions to explore the attitudes of each group towards the other. More than just confidence in the military as an institution needs to be examined. We need to understand the images that civilians possess about the military, how the military views civilian society, and whether gaps, if they exist at all, have any implications for civil-military cooperation.

Data and Measurement

The TISS survey data explicitly redresses weaknesses in other public opinion surveys by polling all three relevant groups—up-and-coming officers, civilian elites, and the general public—using the same battery of questions.[3] The instrument that TISS used to survey the general public was shorter and did not include every question of interest to this chapter. We note in the text where we do have relevant data on the mass public.

As discussed elsewhere (Gronke 1999), there are numerous ways of measuring a "gap": comparing mean responses to individual questions or scales, comparing the distributions of responses (standard deviations, slopes of distribution, etc.), or comparing the correlations of attitudes and the underlying demographics of the respondents. In this chapter, we do all of these kinds of analyses, using what we call a "relative gap" measure, defined as the absolute value of the difference between the individual's score on a set of opinions and the average military or civilian score on those same opinions.

In Figure 3.2, we present an idealized example of how we calculate our gap measure. A large value (positive or negative) on one "military

---

3. Due to cost, a parallel survey of the rank-and-file military was not conducted.

Figure 3.2. Illustrating the Civilian-Military "Gap" Measure.

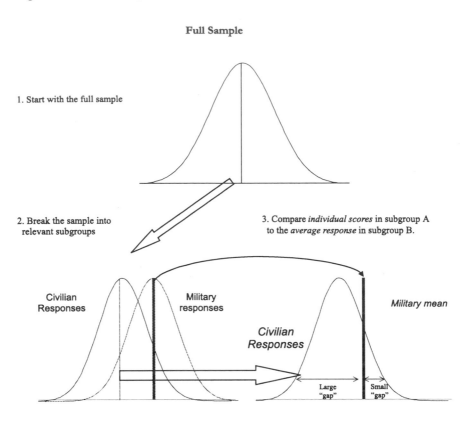

gap" variable indicates that the average civilian gave a response that differed substantially from the average military response. With this measure in hand, we can include other variables (age, veteran status, education, ideology) to test explanations for why a respondent may be more similar to or different from the "average" military respondent. There is no reason that this analysis cannot be conducted for both military and civilian samples: for example, we might ask whether young military officers deviate significantly from the "average" military response, or whether the variables that help us explain this deviation are the same for the civilian and for the military sample. For now, however, we limit the studies to cross-sample comparisons. In this chapter, we examine descriptively the "military gap" and "civilian gap" on a variety of opinions about the military (see Gronke 1999 for regression analyses).

DECONSTRUCTING THE GAP

The TISS surveys permit a more extensive and direct examination of the determinants of public confidence in the military, in particular exploring possible elite-mass and veteran-civilian differences, than are possible using just the Gallup data. Among the items in the survey, respondents were asked to indicate their level of agreement to a variety of statements that touch upon public confidence in the military: "I am proud of the men and women who serve in the military" (Question 33e); "I have confidence in the ability of our military to perform well in wartime" (Question 33f); "The U.S. Armed Forces are attracting high-quality, motivated recruits" (Question 33g); and "I expect that ten years from now America will still have the best military in the world" (Question 33j). The survey also asked the Gallup question on confidence in public institutions: "The following is a list of some institutions in this country. As far as these institutions are concerned, would you say you have a great deal of confidence, only some confidence, or hardly any confidence in them" (Question 32).

The conventional wisdom that support for the military is generally high leads to an expectation that the active-duty military elite should show the strongest support, and that there should be no meaningful difference in the confidence in the military expressed by the other sub-groups. The gap hypothesis, on the other hand, would predict, for example, decreased support as the connection to the military became more distant. Active-duty elite officers would express the highest level of support, with active elite Reserve and National Guard officers next. Civilian veterans (elite and mass) should differ significantly from non-veterans, with non-veterans (elite and mass) expressing the lowest level of support. Within the non-veteran groups, contacts with the military should have some explanatory effect on attitudes, so that respondents with more social connections such as friends or relatives in the military would also have higher confidence.

Viewed through this lens, even the simple "confidence" measure reveals a complex picture. In Figure 3.3, we plot the levels of confidence in major American political and social institutions expressed by the elite military, Guard and Reserve, elite civilian veteran, elite civilian non-veteran samples, and mass public (veteran and non-veteran) in major American political and social institutions. First, we note that the TISS numbers are similar to the figures reported in Gallup surveys. In June 1998, for example, just over 50 percent of the Gallup respondents expressed a "great deal" or "quite a lot" of confidence in the presidency, and 28 percent expressed confidence in Congress. The comparable TISS figures, collected later in 1998, are lower (29 percent and 18 percent, re-

Figure 3.3. Confidence in Institutions (TISS Survey).

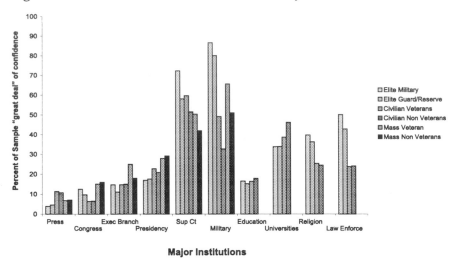

spectively), but this figure includes just those respondents who expressed a "great deal" of confidence.[4] More importantly, the relative ranking of the institutions, except for the lower ratings given to the presidency which may be due to a particular scandal, are identical across the Gallup study and the TISS study. This provides an important external validity check on the TISS study.

The relative levels of confidence, especially for democratic institutions, are disturbing. It is cold comfort that military elite and civilian elite respondents (and mass public) express similar levels of confidence in our political institutions, when the confidence levels are so low. Nor is there any clear pattern that we can discern between the elite military, elite civilian, and mass samples. It is not the case, at least as reflected in these measures, that the military elites stand "in the middle" between a skeptical civilian elite and a trusting mass populace. The largest difference among the groups—15 percent more mass non-veterans express confidence in the presidency than do elite military respondents—may only reveal that military respondents at this time were especially sensitive to scandals involving superior-subordinate sexual relations, given the series of similar events that have rocked the military establishment in recent years.

The contrast between the elite military and civilian responses is made more stark when we compare institutions that have an air of stability and

---

4. The two items did not have identical response categories.

permanency, such as the Supreme Court, organized religion, and law enforcement as well as the military itself, with institutions that engage in the hurly-burly of politics, such as the press, Congress, or the presidency. All of the former institutions are held in higher esteem by elite military respondents than elite civilian respondents. In contrast, civilian elites express higher levels of confidence in the "political" institutions than do military elites. Neither group expresses much confidence in the educational establishment, although the civilian elites do express somewhat higher confidence in universities.

However, looking across all institutions, one conclusion stands out: civilian elites have less confidence than the military in all major American institutions, save the press, universities, and the president. In this respect, then, the gap in confidence in the military is not simply a result of a self-identification or a cohesive institution (military elites disproportionately approving of their own organization and implicitly themselves), but rather may reveal a deeper gap in trust and confidence.

This conclusion becomes even clearer when other dimensions of confidence in the military are explored. A simple cross-tabulation, reported in Table 3.1, shows that there is some difference in attitudes across the various sub-groups. While majorities in each of the groups give responses indicating confidence in the military, there is a marked drop-off from category to category of respondents. The percentage of civilian elites with no military experience, for example, who agree strongly with the statement, "I am proud of the men and women who serve in the military," is a relatively low 56 percent, 15 percent below elite civilians with military experience, and 35 to 40 points below the elite military responses. This is a significant gap, and is a cause of concern among military advocates, as well as others who wonder how civil-military relations will change with the emergence of a new generation of leaders inexperienced in military affairs (Feaver and Gelpi 1999b). Of further concern is the position of the mass public. The elite military expresses the most confidence in the military (not surprisingly), followed by the mass public (with veteran status making little difference), followed by the civilian elites (where veteran status makes a large difference on at least the first item). Generally, the gap between the military and civilian elites, while perhaps not as extreme as doomsayers view it, strengthens our conclusion that, at least among civilian elites, there is a real and measurable gap in confidence and trust in the military.

The cross-tabulation provides a ready indication of differences, but it does not convey much direct information about the "shape" of the gap. To capture this, we turn to our "relative gap" measure, which allows us to ask how much more "pro-military" are the responses of elite military

Table 3.1. Dimensions of Confidence in the Military.

	I am proud of the men and women who served in the military	I have confidence in the ability of our military to perform well in wartime	The U.S. Armed Forces are attracting high-quality, motivated recruits	I expect that ten years from now American will still have the best military in the world
Active-duty Military Elite	91.6	83.3	25.2	55.9
Elite Guard and Reserves	95.1	76.5	24.2	50.7
Civilian Elite Veterans	71.8	64.3	8.4	42.8
Civilian Elite Non Veterans	56.2	57.2	7.5	43.0
Mass Veterans	n/a	72.2	n/a	56.6
Mass Non-Veterans	n/a	70.3	n/a	53.6

NOTE: Cell entries are the percentage of the subsample that responded "agree strongly."

Figure 3.4. Gap in Responses (from Overall Mean).

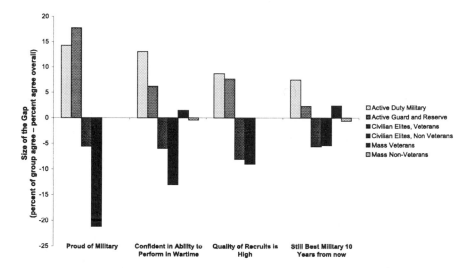

respondents compared to the average respondent, or, alternatively, how much more "pro-military" are elite military respondents compared to the average *civilian* respondent. Figure 3.4 provides one illustration of the relative gap in public confidence for the military, as measured by the percentage above or below the average sample response.[5] Figure 3.4 shows a systematic pattern. The more the military experience, the greater the confidence in the military; elite civilians without any military experience show consistently lower levels of support, by as much as 38 percent. This is, moreover, a conservative estimate: we plot in Figure 3.5 the deviations from the *sample mean*, whereas if we plotted the civilian non-veteran deviations from the *military mean*, the differences would be even larger.

To summarize, we have demonstrated that there is a military and civilian gap, at least when we compare higher-ranking elite military officers and civilian elites. On some measures, elite military officers appear far more similar to the mass public in their pattern of confidence in major American institutions than do the presumed leaders of those institutions, the civilian elites. This should alert us to subtleties underlying confidence in the military. In the rest of this chapter, we provide some ex-

---

5.   For the elite respondents (military and civilian), we subtract the group mean from the overall elite mean (since all these respondents filled out the same survey instrument). For the mass public, we subtract the veteran and non-veteran means from the overall mass sample mean.

Figure 3.5. A Moral Crisis in Civilian Society? Elite Military, Elite Civilian, and Mass Public Responses.

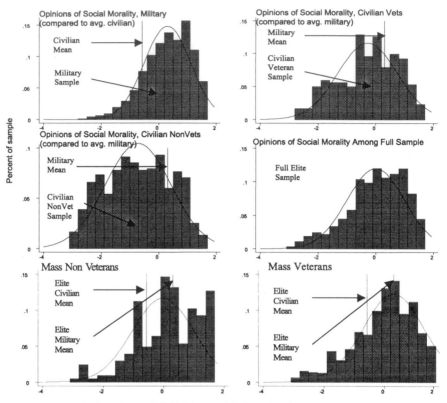

Difference between Individual Scores and the Comparison Group Mean (see text and Figure 3.2)
Positive values = Individual feels there is more of a moral crisis than comparison group

ploratory examinations of how the notions of "confidence" may be profitably unpacked.

The analysis thus far suggests that confidence in the military may not be as solid and stable as the commonly reported Gallup results imply. People who have little or no contact with the military express lower levels of confidence in the military. The effect is sharpest at the elite level, where an absence of contact with the military can have a large impact on expressed confidence. Nevertheless, majorities even among the least pro-military groups express confidence in the military. Thus, to a certain extent, the conventional wisdom is correct: American civil-military relations are blessed by the remarkable degree of confidence the military enjoys from the mass and elite public. But does this confidence extend beyond a mere appreciation that the military is capable of doing what it is asked to do? Is there an underlying sense of alienation between the groups, acknowledged or latent? Is there a consensus on how civil-military relations affects military effectiveness or on the day-to-day workings of civilian control? To answer these questions, we analyze civilian and military opinion across a broader range of topics.

DO CIVILIANS OR THE MILITARY SENSE ANY ALIENATION IN THE RELATIONSHIP?

The TISS survey asked respondents to assess the level of alienation the military feels from civilian society and that civilian society feels from the military. Respondents were asked to indicate their level of agreement to the following statements: "Most members of the military have a great deal of respect for civilian society" (Question 33a); "Most members of civilian society have a great deal of respect for the military" (Question 33b); and "The American people understand the sacrifices made by the people who serve in the U.S. military" (Question 33i). The survey also asked respondents, "Do you think military leaders, in general, share the same values as the American people?" (Question 27); and "Thinking about the way most Americans view the military, would you say the military gets more respect than it deserves, less respect than it deserve, or about as much respect as it deserves?"(Question 31). Tables 3.2 and 3.3 report the responses to these questions by military status.

The most obvious inference from these data is that there is something approaching a consensus among respondents. Large majorities in all categories believe that there is no alienation between civilian and military sectors. There are differences: the elite military is far more certain that the military respects civilian society than are elite civilian non-veterans; more importantly, while a majority of elite civilian non-veterans agree that the American people understand the sacrifices made by the military, barely one-third of the elite military officers do. But in context these differences do not appear to be consequential. To be sure, the absence of a military connection is associated with higher levels of distrust, but the general impression surely is one of consensus, colored with a dose of skepticism. Civilians are confident that civilians respect the military, and the elite military is confident that the military respects civilian society; each group, however, doubts to some degree whether the respect is reciprocated.

These results are not inconsistent with those from a separate study that looked at the mass military, although the mass military reports perhaps a bit more awareness of alienation. The "Study on Military Culture in the 21st Century," conducted by the Center for Strategic and International Studies, surveyed enlisted personnel and junior officers in the field

Table 3.2. General Perceptions of Military Culture.

	Most members of the military respect civilian society	Most members of civilian society respect the military	The American people understand the sacrifice made by the people who serve in the U.S. military
Active Military Elite	85.5	76.9	36.2
Elite Guard and Reserves	89.7	63.4	37.2
Elite Civilian Veterans	78.2	69.4	53.4
Elite Civilian Non Veterans	65.3	69.1	55.1
Mass Veterans	83.0	63.4	n/a
Mass Non-Veterans	76.0	75.6	n/a

NOTE: Cell entries are the percentage of the subsample that responded "agree strongly" or "agree somewhat."

Table 3.3. Degree of Respect for the Military.

Do you think military leaders, in general, share the same values as the American people? (% yes)

Active-duty Military Elite	Elite Guard and Reserves	Elite Civilian Veterans	Elite Civilian Non Veterans
60.3	69.8	54.2	38.2

Thinking about the way most Americans view the military, would you say the military gets more respect than it deserves, less respect than it deserves, or about as much respect as it deserves?

	Active Military Elite	Elite Guard and Reserves	Elite Civilian Veterans	Elite Civilian Non Veterans
More than deserves	0.6	1.3	3.7	8.3
Less than deserves	50.5	63.5	48.5	40.5
As much as deserves	47.9	33.7	47.1	48.0
No Opinion	1.0	1.6	0.7	3.2

and found that these respondents generally report that the military respects civilian society and that their respect is (more or less) reciprocated.[6] Asked whether "most members of the armed forces have a great deal of respect for American civilian society," the mass military reported at least some sense of alienation: fully 26 percent of respondents showed some disagreement ("strongly disagree" plus "disagree" plus "disagree somewhat"), and only 43 percent "agreed" or "strongly agreed" (another 28 percent "agreed somewhat"). Asked to gauge civilian society's views about the military, a strong majority of Army personnel indicated agreement with the statement, "people in my hometown have high regard for America's armed forces." Fully 75 percent of Army personnel reported agreement with that statement ("strongly agree," plus "agree," plus "slightly agree") although a not-inconsiderable 21 percent report disagreement (although half of those only "slightly disagree"). There was a bit more doubt expressed about whether "most civilians have a great deal of respect for the armed forces"; only 61 percent show agreement (of which 26 percent only "slightly agree"), while 38 percent disagree to some extent. The only question that showed an unambiguous *absence* of alienation was the least diagnostic one: "Whenever I have the opportunity I socialize with civilians as well as with military friends." Here fully 86 percent of the Army respondents showed agreement and only 11 percent showed disagreement, but this is hardly a conclusive rebuttal to concern about alienation, since only extremely alienated individuals would disagree with such a benign statement.

On balance, given the overall positive responses, we conclude that there is at most only modest self-conscious alienation in the elite military and barely more in the mass military, except over whether the American people understand the sacrifices the military must make. On that one issue, the military does show alienation, but we are hesitant to make much of this: probably many professionals believe that the public does not fully understand or appreciate their group. Like the more superficial measure of "confidence in the institution," and perhaps reflecting the conventional wisdom that the military is highly respected, military and civilian respondents report little direct concern about the degree of alienation between the groups.

---

6. The CSIS sample primarily drew from the Army and Coast Guard but also from other services at joint commands. In this chapter, we only report results from the Army, by far the largest sub-group in the CSIS data. Data proprietary to the Study on Military Culture in the 21ˢᵗ Century at the Center for Strategic and International Studies; used by permission.

Is There Latent Alienation Across the Civilian and Military Groups?

The results thus far do not provide strong support for the culture gap hypothesis, but they do not pose much of a challenge to it either. These questions are what public opinion scholars call "easy issues": survey items on which the socially desirable response is well known. Survey results showed, instead, that high percentages of officers believe that the American public does not support them or that high percentages of elite officers believe that the military does not respect civilian society would constitute real evidence of alienation. But it would be very premature to conclude on the basis of the indicators shown thus far that there is no alienation in the civil-military relationship. Alienation may indeed be present beneath the surface expressions of socially desirable responses, discoverable in opinions and attitudes that each group has about the nature and quality of the other. The culture gap hypothesis predicts such underlying clusters of attitudes, reflecting a larger gulf between the military and civilian society than the conventional wisdom implies.

The culture gap hypothesis claims, first, that the military is especially critical of a perceived moral decay in civilian society and that it is, at the same time, especially certain that the military is morally superior to the civilian society it is protecting. Secretary Cohen described it in a speech at Yale University:

Not long ago there were a number of prominent journalists, students of military matters, who were wondering if the armed forces were too good for America. They wanted to know whether the standards were too high, too rigid; whether we were out of touch with contemporary mores; whether perhaps the military is becoming too elitist, that a separate cult as such was developing; whether this group of highly educated, highly motivated, highly disciplined individuals might be looking down their noses with contempt upon contemporary society whose standards were not quite as high or rigid or moral.

Second, the culture gap thesis predicts that civilians, or at least influential civilians, are skeptical about military culture, in particular skeptical about those distinctive elements that make the military so unlike other institutions in a liberal democracy: emphasis on hierarchy and teamwork over egalitarianism and individualism. Thus, John Hillen writes that the general public recognizes "that the unique values and attributes of military culture are an occupational necessity," but he goes on to worry that members of the civilian elite, drawn from "the counterculture, all grown up and gone to work in Washington, New York, and Los Angeles, are the ones offended by military values" (Hillen 1998a). In short, the culture gap thesis predicts that public statements of support and respect belie underlying negative stereotypes held by civilians, especially elite civilians with no military experience, about the military and by the military about civilians.

Third, the culture gap thesis predicts that the elite military are alienated from the key political institutions of American democracy: that the military would show considerable doubt about the trustworthiness and responsibility of the very institutions it is pledged to defend. Here the issue is not so much whether elite military attitudes diverge from others, but rather the specific content of the elite military attitudes themselves.

The TISS survey was designed explicitly to uncover whether such latent alienation exists. The survey asked respondents to indicate their level of agreement with a variety of statements that would reflect a negative view of society's moral health and a belief that the military is morally superior: "The decline of traditional values is contributing to the breakdown of our society" (Question 8a); and "The world is changing and we should adjust our view of what is moral and immoral behavior to fit these changes" (Question 8c). Other statements addressed the issue of whether the military is morally superior: "Through leading by example, the military could help American society become more moral," (Question 8b); and "Civilian society would be better off if it adopted more of the military's values and customs" (Question 8d). We combined these items into a single scale, which we call the moral crisis scale, and analyzed civilian and military responses.[7] Figure 3.5 depicts the scale values for the different sub-groups to facilitate comparisons of the means as well as the distributions underlying the means. This approach helps bring to light attitudinal features such as whether the responses of a certain group are tightly clustered or widely scattered around a mean. The reader should interpret the figures by comparing the vertical stacks of figures; for instance, the three figures on the left allow a comparison of elite military attitudes relative to the average elite civilian (upper left) with the attitudes of elite civilian non-veterans relative to the average elite military officer (center left) and mass non-veterans relative to the average military and civilian elite (lower left). For each figure, the mean of the focus sample is represented by the peak of the curve, while the mean of the referent sample is represented by the vertical line; thus, in the upper left, the mean

---

7. The scale is an additive index of survey items Question 8a through Question 8e. The weights were determined via exploratory factor analysis, using principal components. The number of factors was restricted to one.

elite military response is above zero (the peak of the curve) while the mean elite civilian response is below zero (the vertical line).

Consistent with the culture gap hypothesis, indications of alienation emerge. Figure 3.5 shows that elite military officers evaluate civilian society far more negatively than do elite civilians (positive numbers indicate more agreement with a series of negative statements about a moral crisis in civilian society). The average elite military response on the scale is −.309, compared to a score of −.577 among elite civilians, almost a full standard deviation apart (the scale is centered on zero, with a unit standard deviation). Moreover, few of the elite military officers agreed with any positive statements about civilian society at all; the elite military's negative assessment of the moral state of civilian society is widely shared, at least among the respondents to our survey.[8] Elite civilians, by contrast, show a wide range of attitudes toward civilian society. The majority is quite optimistic about the moral health of American civilian society (though note, once again, the important contrast between veteran and non-veteran elite civilian respondents).

These results are supported by multivariate analysis, detailed in Gronke and Feaver (2000). The greater the degree of military contact, the more likely the respondent is to hold views that civilian society is in moral crisis and that the military can help in this regard. Elite civilians with no military contact whatsoever are less likely to believe that civilian society is in a moral crisis and substantially less likely to believe that the military can help.

The survey also addressed the issue of military's traditional culture, which is so distinctive from liberal civilian society, and whether such traditional distinctiveness is desirable in light of the military's special function. Specifically, the survey asked for the respondents' level of agreement with the following statements: "An effective military depends on a very structured organization with a clear chain of command" (Question 42a); "Military symbols—like uniforms and medals—and military traditions—like ceremonies and parades—are necessary to build morale, loyalty, and camaraderie in the military" (Question 42b); "Even though women can serve in the military, the military should remain basically masculine, dominated by male values and characteristics" (Question 42c); "Even in a high-tech era, people in the military have to have charac-

8. CSIS's survey of the mass military found somewhat the same attitude prevalent among Army enlisted personnel and junior officers. It asked only one of the questions on our scale: "civilian society would be better off if it adopted more of the military values and customs"—and 64 percent of respondents showed agreement, although a sizable minority, nearly one-third, disagreed to some extent.

Figure 3.6. Elite Military and Civilian Endorsements of Principles of Military Traditionalism.

Difference between Individual Scores and the comparison Group Mean (see text and Figure 3.2)
Positive values = Individual is more in favor of a traditional military than comparison group

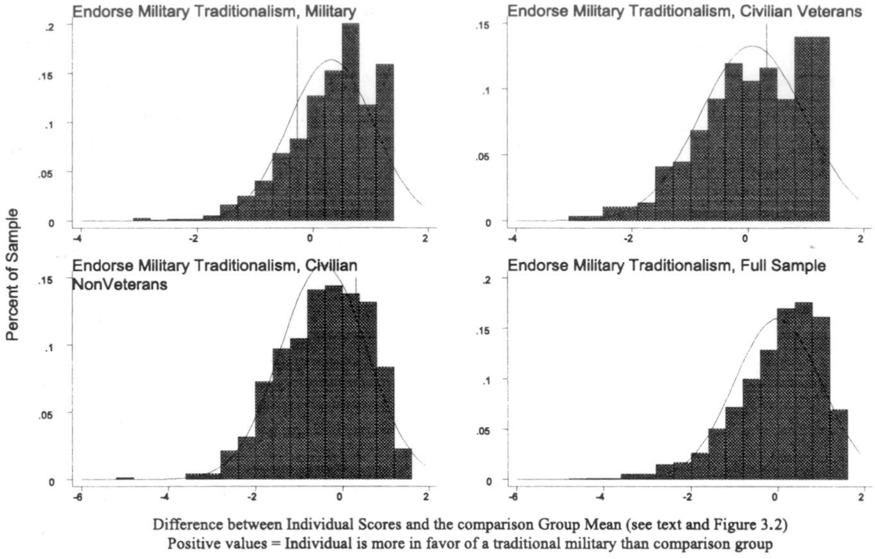

teristics like strength, toughness, physical courage, and the willingness to make sacrifices" (Question 42e); "The bonds and sense of loyalty that keep a military unit together under the stress of combat are fundamentally different than the bonds and loyalty that organizations try to develop in the business world" (Question 42f); and "Military leaders care more about the people under their command than leaders in the non-military world care about people under them" (Question 42g).

These questions tap into an underlying set of attitudes that we call military traditionalism. As the culture gap thesis predicts and as Figure 3.6 shows, civilians and the elite military disagree on the value of military traditionalism. The gap is quite large, as the different civilian and military means make evident (illustrated by the vertical lines in each graph). Likewise, as we report elsewhere (Gronke and Feaver 2000), military status and connection with the military are the most significant contributors to views on military traditionalism.

Our results are supported by Holsti's analysis in this volume (Chapter 1) of a different survey question, in which respondents were asked to indicate whether particular traits such as "honest," "intolerant," "corrupt," and so on, applied to civilians and/or to the military. The traits were selected because they fit negative and positive general stereotypes about both cultures. As the culture gap thesis would predict, stereotypes followed a distinctive pattern, with a consistent civil-military gap. If alienation can be said to exist not only when groups say they feel estranged but also when their attitudes and opinions about the other groups reflect division and hostility, then the TISS data support the conclusion that there is considerable latent alienation between the military elite and elite civilians.

Elite military responses to direct questions about the leaders of key democratic institutions corroborate these findings. When asked to gauge how knowledgeable political leaders are about military affairs, two-thirds of the elite military said leaders are "somewhat ignorant" or "very ignorant." Elite military opinion was about evenly split (40 percent yes, 35 percent no) on whether "political leaders, in general, share the same values as the American people." Since the elite military also hold somewhat negative views about the values of the American people, this question might cut both ways; is it that political leaders are "out of step" with the American people or "in synch" with a morally corrupt American society? Since fully 60 percent of elite military believe that "military leaders, in general, share the same values as the American people," the former interpretation is more likely. In neither case, however, can the elite military attitudes be construed as showing great trust in key democratic institutions.

Is There a Consensus on How Distinctive the Military Needs to Be to Preserve Military Effectiveness?

The general consensus on how capable the U.S. military is at doing what civilian society asks of it could also mask disagreements about what sorts of problems could erode that effectiveness. The culture gap thesis suggests that one way a civil-military gulf might threaten national security would be if the military and civilians hold sharply divergent opinions on what hurts military effectiveness and therefore, by implication, endorse sharply different policies for preserving the combat effectiveness of the armed forces. Indeed, John Hillen has argued that "If [the military] goes too far in pleasing the social mores of contemporary society, it may lose the culture needed for success in war" (Hillen 1998a).

The TISS survey asked respondents to indicate whether they believed civil-military alienation would erode military effectiveness and then whether they believed certain conditions, such as "Americans' lack of trust in the uniformed leaders" or "a ban on language and behavior that encourage camaraderie among soldiers," were in fact occurring and if so, whether they would hurt military effectiveness. If there is a civil-military consensus on these issues, military effectiveness might still be a matter for concern, but any problems would not be exacerbated by a civil-military culture gap. Dissensus, however, would be evidence that a gulf between civilians and the military threatened core values that at least some influential groups believe to be essential to the military's ability to be effective in combat.

As Figure 3.7 shows, elite military officers and elite civilians, particularly elite civilians with no military experience, gave differing responses to the statement, "Even if civilian society did not always appreciate the essential military values of commitment and unselfishness, our armed forces could still maintain required traditional standards" (Question 33h). Somewhat contrary to conventional wisdom, it is the elite military that has the more optimistic view, and it is the elite non-veteran civilians who express the greatest level of concern about the gap—even though it is their attitudes that comprise the largest gap with the military.

By contrast, a clear consensus emerges when we look at a series of responses concerning potential threats to military effectiveness.[9] Elite civilians and the elite military officers generally agree on whether a particular problem is happening in the military today. What differences of opinion do appear are subtle and marginal, far more so than one would expect given the ambiguity inherent in the topic: even experts have trouble agreeing on what is necessary for military effectiveness. After a first cut, this uncertainty does not appear in the TISS survey. We cannot say conclusively what this means, but it does suggest the optimistic finding that military effectiveness may be an issue on which there is a healthy civil-military consensus.

Is There a Consensus on the Practical Workings of Civilian Control?

Other studies in the TISS project have addressed how civilians and the military interact in the decisions about the use of force (Feaver and Gelpi

---

9. The question asked for what amounted to a two-stage judgment from the respondent: is the alleged problem happening and, if so, how much does it hurt military effectiveness. In only four cases was there a gap of more than 5 percent between civilian and military judgments about whether a problem was even happening: "A system for promotions and advancement in the military that does not work well," "Non-military people getting too involved in military affairs," "Inaccurate reporting about the military and military affairs by the news media," and "The military getting too involved in non-military affairs." In no case, including these four, was the perceived level of the severity of the problem more than a third of a point on a three-point scale. In most cases, the difference was less than .10.

Figure 3.7. Endorsement of Military Standards and Effectiveness.

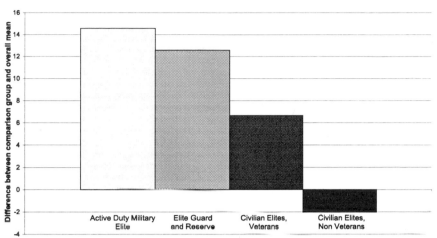

Even if civilian society did not always appreciate the essential military values of commitment and unselfishness, our armed forces could still maintain required traditional standards

1999b; Cohen, Chapter 12 in this volume). They found, consistent with the case-study literature on Cold War crises, that civilians and military elites agree that civilian leaders should have the final say on whether to use force, but disagree more sharply on who should have the final say on operational decisions concerning how to use force. Elite military officers are far more likely to hold the opinion that the military should make operational decisions, while substantial numbers of elite civilians believe civilians should retain decision-making control; elite veterans, as the culture gap thesis expects, give intermediate responses that are closer to the military profile. Here we analyze attitudes on other civilian control issues, specifically, on whether civilian control is assured in the United States today, and on the day-to-day workings of civilian control such as the appropriate circumstances under which civilian orders may be challenged.

The conventional wisdom is that civilian control is safe and secure in the United States. The unbroken record of civilian democratic rule bears out this view, as does the centrality given to military subordination in the professionalization and socialization of the officer corps. To be sure, concern has been voiced in influential circles that civilian control, at least at the margins, is less stable in recent years than it was during the Cold War (Dunlap 1992; Weigley 1993; Dunlap 1994; Kohn 1994; Luttwak 1994; Feaver 1998a; Desch 1998). These authors argue that as civilians ask the military to do things it prefers not to do, increasingly the military may show a reluctance bordering on (and perhaps crossing over into) outright resistance. Moreover, the culture gap thesis explicitly states that a growing gulf between civilians and the military is worrisome because it could complicate civil-military cooperation. Accordingly, we examined the extent to which concern about civilian control is reflected in the opinions and attitudes of military officers, elite civilians, and the mass public.

Three questions directly explored respondents' opinions on the health of this aspect of American civil-military relations. Respondents were asked to indicate their level of agreement with the following questions: "To be respected as Commander-in-Chief, the president should have served in uniform" (Question 48e); and "Civilian control of the military is absolutely safe and secure in the United States" (Question 48f). The survey also asked respondents to indicate how often civilian control is flouted: "If civilian leaders order the military to do something that it opposes, military leaders will seek ways to avoid carrying out the order: all the time, most of the time, some of the time, rarely, never, or no opinion" (Question 49). Of course, *opinions* about the stability of civilian control should not be confused with the objective stability of civilian control; the public opinion literature is replete with examples of viewpoints that are quite at odds with objective reality. Nevertheless, the survey results on these questions are particularly interesting, even disturbing, for what they say about the mindset of key elements of the public.

Table 3.4 reports the cross-tabulations for opinions on the current status of command and control in the United States, and whether the president should have served in uniform. A significant portion of elite military officers and a surprisingly high (but smaller) percentage of elite civilians believe that the president should have served in uniform to earn the respect of the military. There is a gap in opinion—more military believe this than civilians—but the gap is not as important as the fact that in both camps there is a significant plurality that adopt this view, which is strikingly at odds with a classical civilian control perspective.

Since the period of the survey overlapped with the scandal-ridden Clinton tenure, and more particularly with the impeachment proceedings, these opinions might be dismissed as reflecting either a partisan spirit or a personal animus toward President Clinton. A multivariate analysis, detailed in Gronke and Feaver (2000), provides little insight to confirm or disconfirm this hypothesis. Veteran status seems to have been important in shaping this viewpoint. Conservatives are no more likely to hold this view than liberals, nor do many of our contact measures help us discriminate among respondents.

Nevertheless, the Clinton factor may explain the responses to the question of whether civilian control is absolutely safe and secure, as re-

Table 3.4. Perceptions of Current Control and Respect for the Commander-in-Chief.

	Active-duty Military Elite	Elite Guard and Reserve	Elite Civilian Veterans	Elite Civilian Non Veterans	Mass Veterans	Mass Non-Veterans
Civilian control of the military is absolutely safe and secure in the United States.	74.2	90.4	78.5	56.1	52.7	45.7
To be respected as Commander-in-Chief, the President should have served in uniform.	18.5	52.3	47	29.8	—	—

ported in the top panel of Table 3.4. Consistent with the conventional wisdom, the elite military, elite Reserve and Guard, and elite veterans overwhelmingly agree with this statement. A slim majority of mass public veterans agree and a comparable percentage of elite civilian non-veterans agree. The fascinating figures, however, are the large number of elite civilian non-veterans who disagree. Even more fascinating is the still larger number of mass public non-veterans who disagree; indeed, more mass non-veterans apparently think civilian control is *not* safe and secure than believe it is (47 percent disagree, 46 percent agree). Without focus groups, we cannot be confident about how respondents interpreted this question. Perhaps the absolute nature of the question disturbed people who have less familiarity with the military and so chose to hedge their bets.

In any case, the results suggest that there is, at a minimum, something of a crisis in *understanding* about civilian control even if there is not a crisis in civilian control as such. While it is not implausible that the extensive attention paid to President Clinton's troubled relationship with the military took hold in the public mind and gave root to a view that future presidents ought to be veterans, this hypothesis needs further study. It will be important to conduct similar polls during the next administration to see whether the view outlasts the Clinton years.

In one respect, however, the doubters of the stability of civilian control may have legitimate grounds for worry. A remarkable number of our respondents, both in the mass and elite survey, believe that if civilian leaders order the military to do something that the military opposes, then the military will seek ways to avoid doing it, at least some of the time. The correct textbook answer, given the principle of civilian supremacy and the record of democratic control, is "never." Respondents with a long historical memory who could balance the conventional wisdom against such clashes as those between Lincoln and McClellan, Truman and MacArthur and, more recently, over gays in the military, might answer "rarely." Indeed, over two-thirds of the elite military officers give the "correct" answer of "rarely or never." But nearly one-fifth of elite military officers expect the military to try to avoid orders from civilians some of the time, and a not-insignificant 5 percent think the military will do so most or all of the time. Veterans are even more cynical about military obedience, with fully 40 percent of elite veterans expecting military resistance. The non-veteran elites show the greatest doubt of all. Nearly half of the elite non-veterans expect what amounts to military insubordination at least some of the time.

Again, opinions about insubordination are not the same as evidence of insubordination, although it bears emphasis that a surprising number of elite officers, who presumably are in a better position to know, believe the military tries to avoid unpopular orders from civilian leaders at least some of the time. Perhaps these numbers reflect different interpretations of "orders" and "avoid carrying out" or even "some of the time." But just as we worry about survey results that report high expectations that others are cheating in schools, so too should we worry about survey results that report high expectations that the military "cheats" in its constitutional obligation to submit to civilian orders. At a minimum, the numbers indicate a fair degree of alienation or lack of trust of the military, contrary to what the high-confidence polling results would suggest.

This picture of civilian control becomes even more ambiguous and troubling when respondents were asked to prescribe proper behavior in a variety of hypothetical situations. Respondents were asked what military responses would be appropriate when the military is asked to do something "unethical but legal," and then when the military is asked to do something "unwise." The list of possible responses ranged from "carry out the order anyway," through a variety of "internal" resistance measures (attempts to persuade superiors to change their minds, appeal up the chain of command, seek bureaucratic allies), to a variety of dramatic "external" forms of resistance (retiring in protest, facing a court-martial, leaking the matter to the press).[10] Obviously, this is a wide-ranging set of options, some having severe career consequences for the military officer, calling for behavior that would be considered at best questionable and at worst mutinous or treasonous.

Respondents were not asked about illegal orders because it is widely accepted ever since Nuremburg, reinforced by My Lai, that officers must resist when ordered to do something illegal. The "unethical but legal" scenario was meant to capture more of a gray zone, and the "unwise" scenario a zone more murky still. An example of unethical but legal orders might be instructions to stonewall a congressional or White House request for information, perhaps by some form of misrepresentation. An example of unwise orders might be excessively strict rules of engagement that put soldiers' lives at unnecessary risk. What we found is that the

---

10. Respondents indicated whether the steps were appropriate, not appropriate, or no opinion. The list of steps includes: (1) carry out the order anyway; (2) attempt to persuade the civilian or military leader to change his/her mind but, failing that, carry out the order anyway; (3) attempt to change the civilian or military leader's mind by informing other civilian or military officials who might disagree with this policy; (4) retire or leave the service in protest; (5) refuse to carry out the order even if it means facing a court-martial; (6) appeal the matter to higher authority, even if it means leaping the chain of command; (7) report the matter to an Inspector General or Judge Advocate General office or officer; (8) leak the matter to the press and alert others to this problem.

Figure 3.8. Military and Civilian Gap: Appeal Unethical and Unwise Orders.

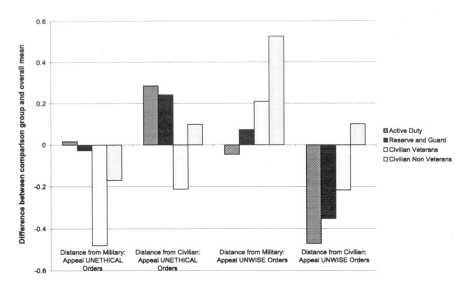

word "unethical" must surely mean different things to the military and civilian audiences, for the responses varied in striking and unexpected ways.

We constructed a scale of these responses, distinguishing between the two broad categories of options: carrying out the order, either immediately or after a modest effort at persuading the superior to change his or her mind, and not carrying out the order via any of a number of methods. The results, as captured in the relative gap measure, are reported in Figure 3.8.

Elite military officers are far more likely to say that an officer should look for some avenue of appeal to an unethical order. Civilian elites, however, are far more likely to assert that the officer should carry out the order, regardless of its ethics. These patterns suggest that several decades of post–My Lai training on ethics have perhaps erased the distinction in the minds of officers between "illegal" and "unethical but legal." While the distinction may have meaning in the civilian world, perhaps officers are prone to perceive "unethical" as tantamount to "illegal."

Surprisingly, the opposite phenomenon crops up in analyzing opinions about unwise orders. Figure 3.8 shows the relative gap between civilian and military elites on whether military officers should appeal unwise orders.

Here it is the elite military who endorse the "salute and obey" response, while it is elite civilians who are far more likely than the average elite military respondent to say that an appeal of an unwise order is acceptable. Why elite civilians are more willing, compared to the average elite military, to tolerate appeals of "unwise" orders more than of "unethical" ones is not clear and probably not discernible from the data. It is clear, however, that the parties to the civil-military relationship have different understandings of what problematic orders are and how the military should respond to those problematic orders.

The now familiar pattern of confusion over what military obedience involves is replicated in the responses to still another battery of questions concerning the military's role in civilian society. The questions asked respondents to indicate their level of agreement with five different statements: "Members of the military should not publicly criticize a senior member of the civilian branch of the government" (Question 47a); "Members of the military should not publicly criticize American society" (Question 47b); "Members of the military should be allowed to publicly express their political views just like any other citizen" (Question 47c); "It is proper for the military to explain and defend in public the policies of the government" (Question 47d); and "It is proper for the military to advocate publicly the military policies it believes are in the best interests of the United States" (Question 47e). The items scale onto a single "military activism" index ranging from silent subservience to public advocacy. As Figure 3.9 indicates, responses vary in a predictable direction as one moves from the pure civilian to the pure military elite sample. Elite civilian non-veterans are the most strict about restricting the military's voice in society, while elite military officers are the most strict about preserving that voice.

It is not altogether clear what all these results mean, except that there is no consensus among civilians (elite and mass) and the military elite on some of the most important and basic questions of military professionalism and civilian control. The absence of consensus implies that beneath the surface of civil-military harmony and mutual respect lies considerable confusion and uncertainty on how the relationship is functioning and ought to function on a day-to-day basis, with the potential for turmoil in actual civil-military cooperation.

Conclusion and Implications

Our analysis shows that public expressions of confidence in the military, however laudable and reassuring, should not be taken as conclusive evidence that the military is not alienated from civilian society. To be sure, the alienation would be worse if the public expressed *low* levels of confidence in the military. Even the consensus belief among all groups

Figure 3.9. Military and Civilian Gap: Military Free to Involve Selves in Civilian Society?

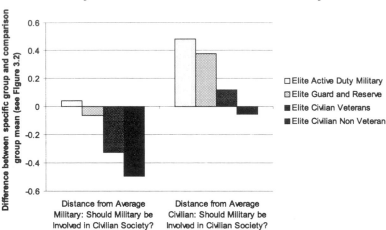

Figure 3-9. Military and Civilian Gap:
Military Free to Involve Selves in Civilian Society?

that the military by and large respects civilian society and that civilians by and large respect the military is misleading. When the matter is probed further, several distinctive patterns emerge.

First, viewpoints track fairly consistently according to the military status of the respondents: elite active-duty military officers have the most confidence in the military, elite Reserve and Guard the next most, veterans somewhat less so, and non-veterans the least confidence of all. This finding is not shocking. One would expect members of a profession to think differently from non-members, and association with the profession to have some lingering attitudinal effects. But given downsizing of the military and the changing character of the political elite, this finding suggests that the gaps we have uncovered will grow because there will be fewer veterans (and possibly fewer Reserve and Guard) over time. The middle ground may be disappearing, while among and between the groups that remain there may be increasingly sharp and deep cleavages.

Second, and more worrisome, specific indications of latent alienation emerge from an analysis of elite civilian and military opinion. Elite military officers, far more than elite civilians, are prone to view civilian society as troubled and in need of reform. Elite military officers, far more than elite civilians, are prone to think that civilian society could be repaired if military values were more widely accepted. On the other hand, elite civilians, far more than their elite military counterparts, think that a traditional military culture—one embracing distinct and even alien values in the liberal American context—is not essential. When it comes to the practical workings of civil-military relations, confusion abounds. Elite civilians and elite military officers disagree sharply over what counts as military obedience and what counts as insubordination. Despite a conventional wisdom that treats civilian control as assured and unproblematic, we found a surprising amount of skepticism, especially among elite civilians, about whether the military normally obeys civilian orders it opposes. In short, public confidence in the military masks latent distrust and a deeper divide in civil-military relations.

In one case, however, we did find a deeper consensus to match the surface confidence. Elite civilians and the military agree about the determinants of military effectiveness and what kinds of problems could degrade the military's ability to perform its mission. Whether this consensus is solid, our analysis cannot show. The apparent agreement, however, is reassuring and suggests that civilian and military elites find common ground in meeting challenges to the effectiveness of the military that lie rooted in attempts to erode a distinct military culture.

In sum, these findings confirm the existence of more alienation between the military and elite civilians than is commonly understood. While our findings do not suggest any civil-military "crisis" or an unbridgeable gap in these issue areas, they do suggest that the concern expressed by Secretary Cohen and other senior national security policymakers is justified. There is reason to worry about the differences in opinion and belief between civilian society and the military and to be vigilant about finding ways to manage it. Our research suggests that a good place to start is a healthy public dialogue and professional discussion within the military and national security community, involving both civilians and the military, about what civilian control of the military truly entails. Support for the principle is reassuringly solid. Understanding about what it means in practice is distressingly lacking.

Chapter 4

Attitudes of Entry-Level Enlisted Personnel: Pro-Military and Politically Mainstreamed

David R. Segal, Peter Freedman-Doan, Jerald G. Bachman, and Patrick M. O'Malley

The culture gap argument has sought to make comparisons between civilian and military segments of American society in the absence of data that are broadly representative of either military or comparable civilian populations. This chapter reviews theories of why differences might be expected among young men who follow different trajectories after graduating from high school. We then present data from the Monitoring the Future project—an annual survey of about 17,000 high school seniors, sub-samples of which are tracked after graduation—to compare the political attitudes of young men who enlist in the armed forces with their peers who either enter the civilian labor force or go to college. We find that, contrary to "gap" theories, those going into the military are not the most Republican, the most conservative, or the least trustful of civilian government among these post–high school trajectories.

Analyses of American civil-military relations in the early years of the Cold War focused in part on the attitudes of American military personnel and civilians. Huntington (1957, 89–94) saw an incompatibility between the professional ideology of the military and societal liberalism, with its emphasis on individualism, hostility to standing armies, and denial of the importance of power. He viewed the ethic of military professionalism as more compatible with conservative ideologies, and believed that the

This research was supported in part by the Army Research Institute under Contracts No. DASW 01–95-K005 and 01–00-K-0016, and MDA 903-D-0032. Data were collected under Grant Number DA01411 from the National Institutes of Drug Abuse. The views expressed in this paper are those of the authors and not necessarily of the Army Research Institute, the Department of the Army, or the Department of Defense. We are indebted to Deborah Avant, James Lindsay, and John Brehm for insightful comments on an earlier draft of this paper.

armed forces must be insulated from liberal trends in society to remain effective. Studies in the early years of the volunteer force echoed this concern. Hauser (1973), for example, argued that in order to maintain the traditional military structure of authority, hierarchy, discipline, and austerity of combat formations in the context of increasing civilian social permissiveness, the combat arms of the services would have to be insulated by their support branches from social issues and processes in the civilian world such as racial tension, drug use, and lack of discipline.

Janowitz (1960) proposed an alternative model of civil-military relations. Recognizing that informal social networks are more important constraints on behavior than are formal mechanisms of social control, he proposed that, in a democratic state, civilian control of the military would best be achieved when the military was woven into the fabric of society. He envisaged a military some of whose personnel identified first as citizens, then as soldiers, some of whose officers attended civilian colleges and universities, and some of whom lived with their families in civilian communities. He acknowledged that the professional military would have a unique organizational culture, much as many civilian occupational and professional groups and many work organizations have their own cultures. However, he felt that citizen-soldiers and structural linkages would help coordinate this culture with American society.

The citizen-soldiers in the conscription era included draftees as well as members of reserve components, but with the advent of the volunteer force, the mix of short-term and career-oriented military personnel changed markedly. Early in the volunteer force years, Janowitz (1975) suggested that the military was increasingly emphasizing distinctive military values; that its linkages to society had become attenuated and tied to limited segments of the social structure; that changes in the recruitment base were making the officer corps and the enlisted force less representative of society; and that such processes might create an "ideological caste" in the military and be a source of political cleavage from civilian society. The military culture might, as a result, become decoupled from its civilian culture. What Huntington viewed as important for military effectiveness, Janowitz viewed as problematic for civil-military relations.

The change in the composition of the military was not wholly a result of the end of conscription and the advent of the volunteer force. One can imagine a volunteer military whose soldiers spend a brief period fulfilling a responsibility of citizenship by serving in the military, and then return to civilian life, as with, for example, the U.S. Marine Corps, whose enlisted personnel have been predominantly volunteers who leave the Corps after a single tour. However, the Marine Corps gets much of its technical support from the Navy, and thus can focus on traditional military skills. Changes in the technology of warfare have, over time, had a marked impact on the distribution of skills, and on the occupational structure of the armed forces more broadly. These changes have moved the American military in the direction of becoming a more career-oriented and professionalized force, with less "leavening" by citizen-soldiers.

At the time of the Civil War, over 90 percent of enlisted military personnel needed only general military skills (including combat skills), and less than one-half of one percent could be regarded as technicians. By World War II, just one-third of U.S. military personnel possessed only general military skills, and more than 10 percent were technicians. By the Vietnam War, fewer than 15 percent of enlisted personnel had only general military skills, and almost a quarter were technicians. During the all-volunteer force era, the percentage of technicians has varied between 25 and 30 percent, and fewer than 20 percent of enlisted personnel required only general military skills (Eitelberg 1988).

The costs involved in recruiting the personnel required for more technical specialties, and the increased time required to train them, have required the services to increase the proportion of the force that remains on active duty beyond their obligated period of conscription or first enlistment, changing the mix of first-term versus career personnel. In 1969, almost 80 percent of the enlisted force had served five years or less on active duty. In 1979, during the first decade of the volunteer force, this figure was still almost 60 percent. Today, however, it is closer to 50 percent. If we regard the percentage of the force that has served for more than five years as career-oriented, then during this thirty-year period, the career-oriented enlisted force increased from about 20 percent to about 50 percent.

The transition to a more career-oriented force, according to Moskos (1977), has transformed the military from a "calling" to an "occupation." This has implications for civil-military relations. Rather than increasing the distance between military and civilian cultures, it suggests that the military might develop an occupational culture that is more similar to those of other occupations. One of the issues we consider below is the degree to which the military has been able to maintain an emphasis on traditional military values in a recruiting environment that stresses the same incentives to serve that are found in the civilian labor force.

Sociological theory and research suggest that there are linkages between occupations and the values and attitudes held by those who practice them, and that these linkages transcend the distinction between military and civilian employment. Rosenberg (1957), for example, suggests that people aspiring to employment in different occupations tend to differ in attitudes and values in ways that are compatible with differences in the characteristics of the occupations they seek to enter. The research of Kohn and Schooler (1983) supports this hypothesis. From this perspective, members of an occupational group go through a period of anticipatory socialization that leads them to their jobs. Thus, the transition to a more career-oriented military force, regardless of the degree to which it reflects the end of conscription or the evolution of military technology, would be expected to produce a more attitudinally distinct military. However, the important question for civil-military relations is not the existence of these occupational attitudes, but their compatibility with the attitudes and structure of civilian society.

These changes in retention and career orientation have also changed the nature of the military profession, with potential consequences for the attitudes of military personnel. When Huntington and Janowitz first discussed the military profession in America, they were writing about a career-oriented officer corps. As the military has become increasingly dependent on a technically trained corps of senior non-commissioned officers, however, those NCOs have also become a part of the profession.

With the increasing professionalization of the military, it was reasonable to expect that through processes of self-selection and professional socialization, military personnel, while not becoming ideologically homogeneous, would increasingly take on a common professional orientation that differentiated them to some degree from those outside the profession. Abrahamsson (1972) identified the components of the military orientation as nationalism, pessimism about human nature, pessimistic estimates of the probability of war, political conservatism, and authoritarianism. Military personnel would not be of a single mind on these dimensions, nor would the beliefs that characterized the military be absent from the civilian population. However, on average, the distributions on these dimensions among the military would be different than among civilians.

The development of a common and to some degree self-serving orientation as a facet of professionalism is not unique to the military. It has been common among other occupations that, because of the expertise they possess and the important social functions that they fulfill, are afforded the socially privileged and relatively autonomous status of being regarded as professions. In the 1950s and 1960s, professions such as medicine, law, and the clergy, which also developed common orientations that differentiated practitioners from non-practitioners, were highly regarded, and interpretations of them focused on their contribution to society and their service ethic. Subsequent analyses have become more critical of them, and their differentiation from other occupations has come to be regarded as sometimes problematic (Segal and Lengermann 1980). Thus, concerns about the potential isolation of the military from society reflect, in part, changes in the internal occupational structure of the armed forces, and also in the occupational structure of society, as increasing numbers of occupations seek to claim the mantle of "profession." From this perspective, just as medicine and the law have to some degree become estranged and criticized for being self-serving and resisting accountability, the military could be expected to be increasingly estranged and criticized as well.

Attitudinal differences based on the end of conscription, the increasingly career-oriented force, and the increasing professionalization of the military came to be regarded in some quarters as problematic for American civil-military relations in the 1990s. Initially, a gap was seen emerging between senior military leaders and the civilians who exert constitutional control over the armed forces (see, for example, Kohn 1994). Holsti (1998) then identified it as a gap between military and civilian elites generally. He presented data to document changes over time, drawing on surveys of opinion leaders from 1976 to 1996; reported a growth in the proportion of military officers who regard themselves as Republicans; suggested that they overwhelmingly regarded themselves as conservative in political orientation; and provided tentative support for a hypothesis, which he attributes to Ricks (1997d), that "younger members of the military are even more pronounced in their embrace of hard-core Republican conservatism." However, he acknowledged that his officer samples "are not adequately representative of the military [and] . . . did not include junior officers . . . or personnel in the enlisted ranks." Our analysis tries to address this lack by providing data on the youths who entered the enlisted force since the 1970s. Holsti's (1999) subsequent analysis of data from 1998-99 continued to find a gap between military personnel and civilians in terms of political partisanship and ideological leaning, with the military being more Republican and more conservative than civilians.

Recently, the gap has been seen as a broader cultural divide between the American armed forces, including enlisted personnel, and the civilian society they defend. In particular, analysts who see the "culture gap" as problematic view the military as becoming increasingly conservative ideologically, strongly Republican in political party preference, and distrustful and disrespectful of the civilian government. Ricks (1997d), for example, suggests that "U.S. military personnel of all ranks are feeling increasingly alienated from their own country, and are becoming both more conservative and more politically active than ever before." Kitfield (1998) agrees, suggesting that "soldiers [are] increasingly estranged from society, and vice-versa."

The increasingly technical nature of military service, and the increasing professionalization and career orientation of the military, may portend differences in job-related attitudes between military personnel and civilians. However, this does not necessarily reflect a broader commitment to political conservatism or a "culture gap" separating most military personnel from their civilian counterparts. Any tendencies toward such a gap are likely to be minimized by recruitment appeals that emphasize the degree to which military service provides skills that can later be used in the civilian labor force, and offers resources to attend civilian institutions of higher education. The evidence presented thus far provides no basis for generalizing to all ranks, and other than Holsti's data on military officers and leaders of civilian institutions, no basis for measuring change over time. Our analysis therefore focuses primarily on young enlisted personnel, and covers most of the period of the all-volunteer military force.

Research in the early years of the volunteer force addressed both the socio-demographic and ideological representativeness of the force. These two domains are not independent: people's ideologies, attitudes, and values are influenced by their locus in the social structure. The emergence of a "military caste" is not simply a matter of ideology, but more importantly of structural isolation. To the extent that the military remains broadly representative of society in structural terms, the emergence among military personnel of attitudes compatible with the conditions of military life, and beliefs that the military is performing a necessary and important social function, should be no more problematic than would be similar attitudes in any legitimate occupational community.

It may well be that the attitudes of civilian and military leaders are diverging with regard to military matters, since a declining proportion of civilian leaders has served in the military. This is a function of the aging of the World War II and Korean War cohorts, which experienced high rates of wartime mobilization (Bianco and Markham, Chapter 7). However, it is a large inferential leap from available data on the attitudes of military elites to claims about the culture of an organization as large and complex as the armed services, and an even greater leap to infer American culture from the attitudes of civilian elites. Even if a substantial body of evidence suggested that military and civilian leaders held disparate views on military policy, that would not constitute evidence of a crisis in civil-military relations. The culture of the military may be influenced by the attitudes of the current officer corps, but officers comprise only about 15 percent of military personnel. American military culture is determined more by the history of the military, which defines and shapes the role expectations of its current members, and by the views of the other 85 percent of current military personnel, particularly the non-commissioned officers, who are the transmitters of culture. Observation of enlisted personnel in any of the services would disabuse the observer of the notion that the culture of the soldier is solely a reflection of the attitudes of the officer corps (see, for example, Moskos 1970, especially chapter 3, "The Enlisted Culture"; and Ingraham 1984).

Regardless of how one views the issues of "culture" and "culture gaps," if American military personnel were to experience widespread political alienation and estrangement and to increase their level of activity in the political system significantly, civil-military relations might be altered in potentially problematic ways. Since Kitfield and others attribute the "culture gap" largely to the end of the draft, and because the empirical research in the field has largely focused attention on the officer corps, we focus on the young men who have replaced the draftees: the male rank-and-file recruits into America's all-volunteer force. Young volunteers are the people who represent American society within the armed forces. Our analysis focuses on men both because the draftees replaced by contemporary volunteers were all male, and because the representation in our data base of women who served in the military is too small to allow reliable estimates of the variables with which we are concerned.

Socio-Demographic Representativeness

One of the criticisms of the end of conscription was that voluntarism would produce an underclass military (e.g., Marmion 1971). Segal et al. (1998b) analyzed the high school class of 1972—the last class to graduate before the advent of the all-volunteer force—to study the dynamics of recruiting in the early years of the volunteer force. The analysis of who volunteered among the young men in the class of 1972 disproved the underclass thesis. There were not sufficient numbers of women who entered the military from the class of 1972 to sustain analysis. Indeed, one of the major consequences of the shift from conscription to a volunteer military force was to increase the representation of women, as well as of African-Americans, in the armed forces. These are changes that were not anticipated by the architects of the volunteer force.

African-American men were over-represented in the volunteer force from the class of 1972, and particularly in the enlisted ranks (they were largely absent from the officer corps); it is also true that enlistees tended to come from lower socio-economic backgrounds than those who did not serve. Nevertheless, the lowest socio-economic quartile was over-represented only by about 6 percent, and the highest quartile under-represented by an equal amount. Middle America, in socio-economic terms, was over-represented. Similarly, those who served had lower high school grade point averages than those who did not, but the difference of means was small. The force recruited those with mid-range academic achievements. Young men from the South were more likely to serve than were those from other regions. Among those who served in this first volunteer force cohort, officers on average had higher high school grades than did enlisted personnel, came from higher socio-economic status backgrounds, and were more likely to have been in academically-oriented high school programs. This was not surprising, since receipt of an officer's commission has virtually required a baccalaureate degree. All of these patterns were continuations of, rather than departures from, the socio-demographic composition of the military in the last years of conscription, and did not suggest that structural isolation of the military would increase. To the extent that marginal differences did exist from the broader social structure, they did not portend a shift to a primarily Republican military caste that is distrustful of government: such a shift is not likely to occur in an occupational population that over-represents the American working class in general, and African-Americans in particular.

More recently, Bachman et al. (1998a) have studied the correlates of enlistment among both male and female high school graduates in the classes of 1976 to 1991. Graduating classes were aggregated into two sets (i.e., time intervals) to accumulate sufficient numbers of alumni who joined the military. Among men in the classes of 1976 to 1983 who joined the military within two years of high school graduation, whites were under-represented, as were men from intact two-parent households, men whose parents had achieved high levels of education, men who lived outside the South, men who planned to go to college, men who had been in college-preparatory high school programs, and men whose high school grades had averaged B or better. The same pattern held for men in the high school classes of 1984 to 1991, who joined the military by 1993.

Similarly, among women in both the classes of 1976 to 1983 and the classes of 1984 to 1991, whites were under-represented, as were women from intact two-parent families, those whose parents achieved high levels of education, those who planned to go to college or were in academically-oriented high school programs, and those with high grades in high school.

In the decade of the 1990s, the enlisted ranks of the armed forces were attracting high school graduates, both men and women, disproportionately from minority racial and ethnic groups, from single-parent working-class families, who were less academically oriented on average than their peers who did not serve. However, the differences between those who did and those who did not serve for the most part reflected statistically significant but proportionately small deviations, making the enlisted population of the military resemble what one might find in other elements of the American working class. Most importantly, while both the very highest and the very lowest strata of society tend to be excluded on the basis of self-selection and educational, physical, and legal requirements for service, the picture of the military population that emerges is not one that is structurally isolated from the rest of society.

Representativeness of Attitudes

In the early years of the volunteer force, Bachman, Blair, and Segal (1977) compared the attitudes of American civilians with the attitudes of the Army and Navy personnel. The analysis focused on attitudes regarding military organization, the use of force, and civil-military relations. Within both the military and civilian samples, there was diversity of attitudes. Among civilians, attitudes varied based on age, education, and military experience. Young non-military college graduates were generally critical of the use of force, and of virtually all aspects of military organization and civil-military relations; this was the kind of societal stance about which Huntington and Abrahamsson had been concerned. Older non-graduates were generally more pro-military, though still critical of the use of military force, levels of military spending, and fairness of treatment in the military. There were few major differences in the civilian sample between veterans and non-veterans.

Among military personnel there was also a great deal of diversity, with major variation due to career orientation. Career military men were pro-military concerning all aspects of military life, military organization, and military missions.[1] Non-career personnel were more diverse, and significantly different from their career-oriented counterparts. Thus, the trend toward higher proportions of career-oriented personnel during the volunteer force years would be expected to produce an aggregate shift in attitudes.

Career military men were not only more pro-military than non-career personnel, but also more pro-military than their civilian counterparts.

---

1. Pro-military responses included feeling that the armed services have too little influence in the way the country is run; that they should have more influence; that the United States spends too little on defense; that there are good job opportunities for people in the military; that people in the military can expect fair treatment; that military leaders are smart and trustworthy; and that military intervention is appropriate.

Attitudes of non-career personnel were not as distinct from those of civilians. Moreover, career personnel were more homogeneous in their attitudes than were either civilians or non-career personnel, with career officers being more homogeneous than career enlisted personnel. Thus, in the early years of the volunteer force, there was an attitudinal difference between the career military, on the one hand, and civilians and citizen-soldiers, on the other. It was a difference that probably existed to an even greater degree during the years of military conscription, and could have been anticipated on the basis of the trend toward a more career-oriented force and the tendency of people to manifest attitudes favorable toward the occupations they have chosen to enter. There was also a difference among career-oriented military personnel between what they perceived to be the actual role of the military in the policy process and what they thought that role should be. While both civilians and non-career military personnel thought that the military was influential in the development of policies dealing with military affairs, and that the level of influence was about right, career-oriented personnel thought that military influence on policy was low, and strongly preferred that it be greater.

Subsequently, Bachman, Sigelman, and Diamond (1987) studied how expectations for military service and the military career plans of high school seniors in the classes of 1976–85 were related to their attitudes about military job opportunities and fairness of treatment in the military, military spending, influence, intervention, supremacy, and discipline. This was not a direct comparison between American youth in the military and their civilian peers, but we know that among high school senior men who definitely intend to join the military, about 70 percent do join within six years of high school graduation (Bachman, Segal, Freedman-Doan, and O'Malley 1998b). Thus, this was a comparison between future military personnel and civilians.

Both general expectations of serving in the military and specific expectations of pursuing a military career made contributions to pro-military attitudes. The seniors who said both that they definitely expected to serve and that they expected to pursue a military career had the most positive views of military opportunities and fair treatment, the greatest desires for increased military spending and influence, the greatest support for military intervention and supremacy, and the strongest endorsement of unquestioning military obedience. The link between military plans and military attitudes was not as strong for women as for men. Among those students who did not expect to serve, women were more pro-military on these items than men, while among those who expected to have military careers, the women were less pro-military than the men. Perhaps most interestingly, while there were significant relation-ships with propensity to serve and career expectations, no groups that were examined were very far from the midpoint on the military attitude scales. If we take the data on the seniors who were oriented toward a mil-itary career to reflect the attitudes of new military recruits, we could ex-pect that a difference between military personnel and civilians would exist, but it would be fairly small, and it would be attributable to self-selection for military service rather than the inculcation of pro-military attitudes once in service.

Most recently, Bachman et al. (2000a) extended this analysis, studying high school seniors in the graduating classes of 1984 to 1991, and a sub-sample followed up one or two years after graduation. Among se-niors, with regard to attitudes toward the military as an occupation, con-trolling for social background factors, "high-propensity" men and women—those most likely to join the military—were significantly more likely than their low-propensity peers, male and female, to feel that the military does a good job for the country as a whole, that the military should have more influence than it does in society, that the United States spends too little on the armed forces, and that soldiers should always fol-low orders. High-propensity senior men, but not women, were less likely to agree that the United States should only go to war to defend against an attack on the U.S. homeland. Seniors inclined to serve in the military tended to evaluate the military favorably, feel that it should have more public support, value obedience, and support the use of force.

With regard to evaluations of the military as a workplace, high-propensity men and women were more likely than their low-propensity peers to say that they would find the military an acceptable place to work, that opportunities and treatment in the military were favorable, that it was not important for them to have a job that allowed them to put down roots in the community without moving, and that it was not im portant to them to have a job that left them free from supervision by oth-ers. That is, their attitudes were favorable, but they acknowledged the re-ality that military service required both geographical mobility and hierarchical authority.

Among the graduates surveyed two years after high school regarding attitudes toward the military as an institution, the men who went into the armed forces, more than their peers who did not, continued to feel that the military did a good job for the country, that the military should have more influence on society than it does, that the United States spends too little on the armed forces, that the use of force should not be limited to continental or homeland defense, and that soldiers should always follow orders. Women who joined the military differed significantly from their peers who did not serve only in feeling that the military should have more influence in society than it does.

The Political Attitudes of Soldiers and Civilians

That people who choose to serve in the armed forces believe they will have good job opportunities and receive fair treatment, that people in the military should be highly disciplined, and that the military should get more money and have more influence in society is not surprising. Parallel attitudes could be found in most occupations. Neither is it surprising that people who choose to serve believe in American military supremacy and feel that the military should be used as an instrument of foreign policy. These views are held by many civilians as well, and people in many professions see importance in the jobs they do. The question is whether the occupational attitudes of military personnel distance them from the host society which they serve, and which exerts constitutional control over them.

We analyze the political attitudes of young Americans entering the military with data from the Monitoring the Future project, conducted by the Survey Research Center at the University of Michigan. Monitoring the Future is an ongoing cohort-sequential study in which questionnaires are administered to groups of nationally representative samples of approximately 17,000 high school seniors in the spring of each year, starting in 1975. Seven follow-up surveys are mailed to sub-samples of 2,400 students from each senior class, with the first mailed one or two years after graduation, and continuing through the final follow-up, thirteen or fourteen years after graduation. Our analysis focuses on men in the senior classes of 1976–95 (Freedman-Doan et al. 2000). (The class of 1975 is omitted because instrumentation and design changes took place after the 1975 survey.) We end most analyses with the class of 1995 to allow us to include data from follow-up surveys conducted one or two years after graduation, during which time most of the seniors who will ever join the military as enlisted personnel will already have done so (Bachman et al. 1998b). Women were not included in the analysis because too few women joined from these classes to allow reliable estimation of the political attitudes of those who served. If a culture gap were emerging between the military and civilian sectors of society, it is not likely that it could be attributed to the increasing presence of women in the military; indeed, some analysts have attributed a declining warrior culture in the military to increasing gender integration of the armed forces, making them increasingly resemble civilian culture (e.g., Webb 1997). Our analysis is

based on 13,695 men in the senior classes of 1976–95 who returned follow-up questionnaires one or two years after graduation, or about 73 percent of those who had been surveyed as seniors.

The political attitudes and reported behaviors of these men are compared with regard to which of three post–high school trajectories they followed: entering the military; going to college full-time and not working
full-time; all other men (some of whom are in college but less than
full-time). Comparisons were also made over time to allow us to analyze
change. We pooled the senior classes of 1976–85, and similarly those of
1986–95: we pooled ten senior classes to produce samples that included
sufficient military entrants to produce reliable estimates of attitudes.
These pools were followed up in the years 1977–87 and 1987–97 respectively. We are concerned with political attitudes expressed during the
senior year in high school, those expressed one or two years after graduation, and changes between the two.

POLITICAL PARTISANSHIP

One of the concerns in the debate on military culture has been whether
the military was becoming disproportionately Republican. Political partisanship has been regarded as a long-lasting identification, rooted in one's
location in the social structure (e.g., Janowitz and Segal 1967). We include
in the denominator all men who responded to the party identification
question, including "Strongly Democratic," "Mildly Democratic," "Independent," "Other," and "No Preference," and we focus on the proportion
of respondents who identified themselves as Republican (combining
"Strongly Republican" and "Mildly Republican" responses). This convention corresponds for purposes of comparison to other recent studies
(e.g., Holsti 1998).

As Figure 4.1 shows, the percentage of high school senior men who
considered themselves Republican has increased during the past two decades, but with wide fluctuations. Republicans outnumbered Democrats
(not shown in figure) in this age group in every year since 1984. Republican identification rose from 24 percent in 1976 to 34 percent in 1981, declined slightly during the first years of the Reagan administration, and
then rose again, to 42 percent, in 1985 and 1986. In 1989, 45 percent
identified as Republicans. This fell to 27 percent by 1993, and with the exception of 1995, has stayed below 27 percent, but has not declined to the
level of the late 1970s.

In this context, we would expect an increase in the proportion of men
going into the military who regard themselves as Republicans as a function of trends in youth partisanship. Table 4.1 presents the proportion of
Republican identifiers in their senior year, and one to two years after

Figure 4.1. Comparison of Trends in Republican Party Identification and Self-Identified Conservative Ideology among High School Seniors: Males, 1976–99.

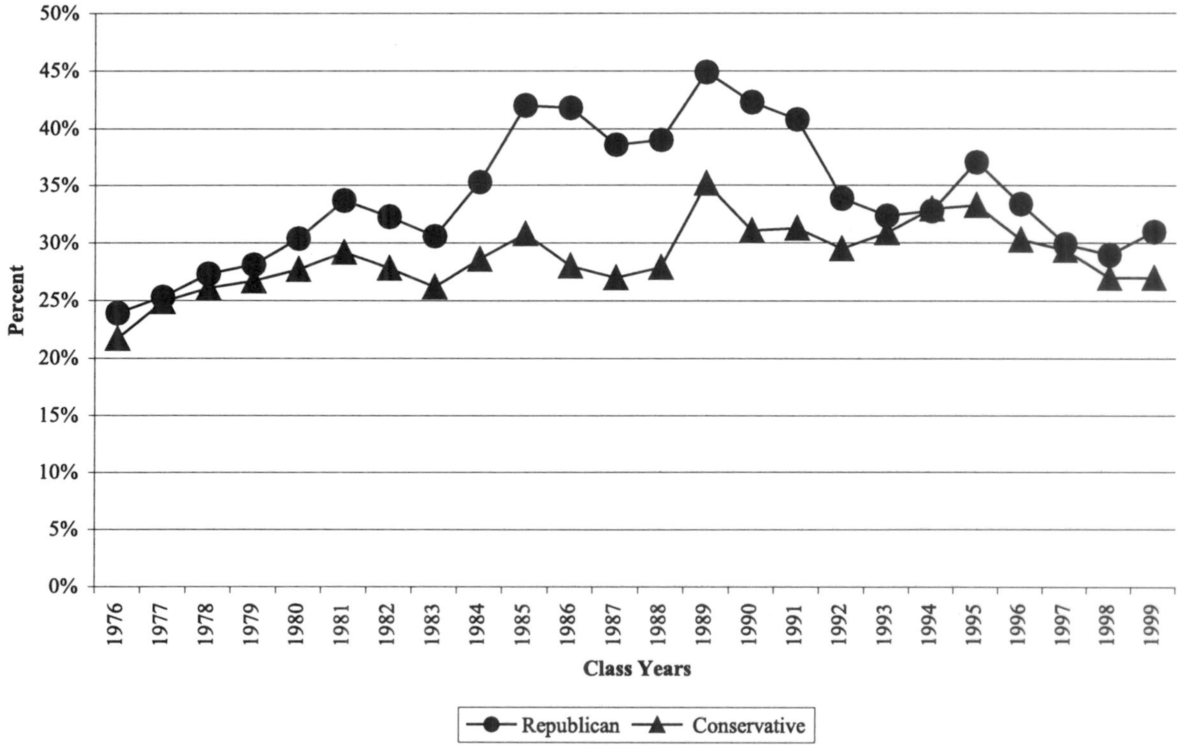

graduation, by post–high school environment, for the two pools of male high school graduates.

Republicans were not a majority in any group. For both time periods, in the senior year of high school, the men going on to college full time were significantly more likely to be Republican than those going into the military or following other pursuits. In neither time periods were those going into the military significantly different in Republican party affiliation from those who were to do things other than military service or full-time college. The percentage of Republicans increased in all three groups between the two time periods.

Earlier studies have focused on the party preference of military officers; our data reflect primarily enlisted personnel. More officers would tend to be Republican based on education level and social status. We switch our focus briefly from panel data to the cross-sectional data obtained from seniors, examining those with high propensity to serve. The senior data include a question to those likely to serve about whether they expect to be officers. Using this information from all seniors permits us to examine larger numbers and to include men whose military service might be delayed until after college. Moreover, using cross-sectional data from seniors permits us to bring time-series data up through 1999, which turns out to be an important addition to our analysis. Figure 4.2 presents the percentages of Republican identifiers among high-propensity high school seniors who expected to serve in the military as officers, compared to (a) those who expected to serve, but not as officers, and (b) those who were uncertain about whether they would be officers.

Those who expected to be officers were 5 to 15 percent more likely to be Republican than those who did not, except in the early 1990s, when the Republican percentage among them declined. However, it never reached as high as the level of Republican preference of the officers studied by Holsti (1999), nor did the level of Republican preference reported among Holsti's officers decline in the 1990s. Among the seniors, those who were uncertain about officership were 5 to 15 percent less likely to be Republican than those who were certain. The level of Republican affiliation increased in all three groups between 1976 and 1991, reflecting the general trend and supporting the assertion that younger men were more likely to be Republicans than older ones. However, the highest percentage of Republicans, which was among those expecting to be officers in the classes of 1988–91, occurred at the same time as the peak for the whole sample. For officers entering service from the late 1970s through the 1980s, who may constitute most of the officers analyzed by Holsti, younger officers would be more likely to be Republican than those just ahead of them. However, after 1991, percentages of Republicans de-

Table 4.1. Comparisons of Proportions of Republican Party Identifiers[a] during Senior Year and 1 to 2 years after High School, by Post–High School Occupational Group.

Males: 1976–85	Proportion Senior Year	Proportion 1–2 Years after High School	Proportion Change	N
Military	0.23	0.26	0.02	439
Full-Time College Students	0.30	0.33	0.03H	3,054
Other Civilian Young People	0.21	0.21	0.00	2,671
Total	0.26	0.27	0.02	6,164
Standard Deviation (Total Sample)	0.44	0.45	0.41	
Difference between Military and Full-Time College Students	−0.07*	−0.08*	−0.01	
Difference between Military and Other Civilian Young People	0.03	0.05	0.02	

Table 4.1. Continued.

Males: 1986–95	Proportion Senior Year	Proportion 1–2 Years after High School	Proportion Change	N
Military	0.27	0.32	0.04H	415
Full-Time College Students	0.37	0.35	-0.01	3,808
Other Civilian Young People	0.26	0.25	-0.01	2,397
Total	0.32	0.32	-0.01	6,620
Standard Deviation (Total Sample)	0.47	0.47	0.42	
Difference between Military and Full-Time College Students	-0.09*	-0.04	0.05*	
Difference between Military and Other Civilian Young People	0.01	0.06*	0.05*	

NOTES: [a]Based on responses to the survey question, "How would you describe your political preference?" "Strongly Republican" and "Mildly Republican" are combined in this table.

*Mann-Whitney tests were performed to test for significant mean differences between the sub-groups "Military" and "Other Civilian Young People" and "Military" and "Full-Time College Students." The * indicates significant mean differences at the .05 level, two-tailed.

HWilcoxon ranked sign tests were performed to test for significant changes in within sub-group means. The H indicates significant mean changes at the .05 level, two-tailed.

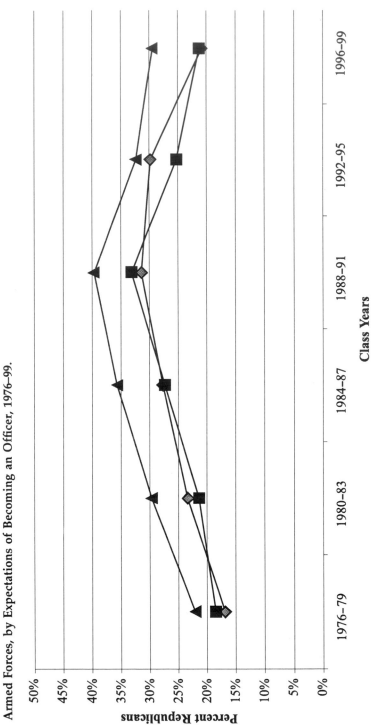

Figure 4.2. Comparison of Trends in Republican Party Identification among Male High School Seniors Who Intend to Enter the Armed Forces, by Expectations of Becoming an Officer, 1976–99.

creased, continuing to reflect the general trend, and suggesting that among these respondents, younger officers would be less Republican than their immediate superiors.

A similar pattern emerged when we examined the partisanship of high-propensity seniors who expected a military career. Republican preference increased in this group from 24 percent in the 1976–79 period to 46 percent in the 1988–91 period, but then decreased to 33 percent in 1996–97. High-propensity youth who expected to serve but not to make the service a career were more Republican than the career-oriented men in the 1976–87 period, but since 1988, the career-oriented men have been more Republican than those who expected to serve but not pursue a military career.

Returning to the data displayed in Table 4.1, we can see that one or two years after high school graduation, the full-time college students were still the most Republican, and that all three groups were proportionally more Republican in 1987–97 than they had been in 1977–87. In the earlier time period, college students were significantly more likely to be Republican than were those who went into the military or other pursuits. In the later time period, the difference between college students and those in the military was not significant. For the classes of 1976–85, the college-bound men increased slightly, but significantly, in percentage Republican. There were no significant changes in Republican affiliation among those who went into the military or those who went into other pursuits. For the classes of 1986 to 1995, however, while there were no significant changes in Republican affiliation among the college students or other non-military men, there was a significant increase among those who went into the military, showing a change after entering service. For this group there may have been partisan socialization within the military.

Since political party identification can continue to change through the course of life, and since restricting our analysis to people one or two years out of high school would omit military officers from the analysis, Figures 4.3 and 4.4 present additional analyses of party identification of young men who responded to three post–high school follow-up surveys, conducted within five or six years after graduation. Because there are several forms of the follow-up survey questionnaire and party identification appears on all of them, this was the only attitude variable for which we had sufficient data for reliable estimates up to six years after graduation. Analysis of these data allows us to evaluate whether partisan differences among the three post–high school trajectories continue beyond the first two years, and whether amount of time spent in the military has an effect on Republican party affiliation.

Figures 4.3 and 4.4 classify high school graduates according to mili-

Figure 4.3. Comparison of Republican Party Identification by Post-High School Occupation Group: Males, Class Years 1976–83.

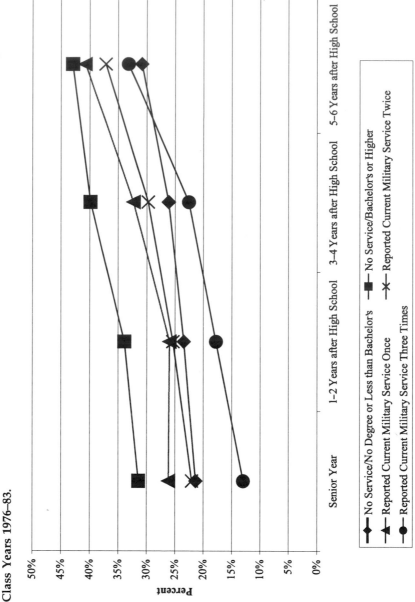

Figure 4.4. Comparison of Republican Party Identification by Post-High School Occupation Group: Males, Class Years 1984–91.

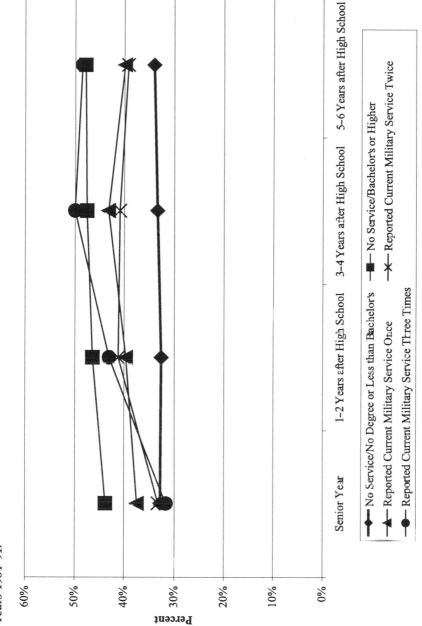

tary service and completion of a bachelor's degree, and show the percentages of Republicans at four times: their last high school semester, the first follow-up survey one or two years later, the second follow-up three or four years after graduation, and the third follow-up five or six years after graduation. We have again aggregated two groups of high school seniors—the classes of 1976–83 and 1984–91—so that we would have sufficient numbers of men who went into the military to provide reliable estimates, and at the same time allow us to make comparisons over time. We ended with the class of 1991 because the third follow-up survey of this class was not completed until 1997.

Not surprisingly, the earlier group was less Republican in their senior year than the later group for all three post–high school trajectories. Those who completed bachelor's degrees (but did not serve in the military) were the most likely to call themselves Republicans. Among those who went into the military, for both time periods, the more frequently respondents reported current military service in the follow-up surveys, the less likely they were to have been Republicans in their senior year. Men who served in the military from the classes of 1976 to 1983 became more Republican with each follow-up, but the inverse relationship between years of military service and Republicanism seemed to hold: at each survey wave, the more total waves in which they reported current military service, the less likely they were to be Republicans (see Figure 4.3). However, none of these differences was statistically significant. For this cohort, by the time they had been out of high school for six years, the highest percentage of Republican identification was among those who had earned bachelor's degrees (43 percent), and the lowest was among men who had not gone into the military and had not earned bachelor's degrees (31 percent). This difference was significant.

For the men in the classes of 1984–91, by contrast, the pattern differed (see Figure 4.4). Although as seniors they had been slightly less Republican than their peers who neither served in the military nor earned bachelor's degrees, and had been significantly less Republican than their peers who were to earn bachelor's degrees, young men in these classes who had served in the military for six years by the time of the third follow-up survey were significantly more Republican than non-servers who did not earn bachelor's degrees, and about as likely as their peers who did complete college (about 50 percent Republican). In addition to the trend toward higher percentages of Republican affiliation among young men, it appears that for classes that graduated at the high points of Republican identification among seniors, those who went into military service after graduation became even more Republican, and this effect was stronger the longer they served in the military. These data also support the contention that, at least until the turn of the decade, younger people going into the military were more likely to be Republican than those who had preceded them. These people would now be approaching the middle of their military careers. However, the most Republican of these groups never accounted for more than half of their cohorts, and were never significantly more Republican than their peers who went to college. Interestingly, the college-bound students were somewhat more Republican than the civilian opinion leaders studied by Holsti, suggesting that the socialization effects of reaching political awareness during the Reagan era might have been more powerful than the maturational effects that tend to make birth cohorts more Republican as they age.

We considered whether the racial demographics of the military (the over-representation of African-Americans, who are unlikely to be Republican, in the enlisted ranks) might mask a shift toward Republicanism among whites by reducing the total Republican percentage. However, when we repeated the analysis controlling for race, the same patterns appeared. Although white men were consistently and significantly more Republican than non-white men, the more frequently the members of this group in the classes of 1976-83, both white and non-white, reported military service in the first three follow-up surveys, the less Republican they were. From high school to three to four years thereafter, the white men who went to college were significantly more likely to be Republicans than the other groups. Five to six years after high school, there were no significant differences among these groups. Among non-whites, there were no significant differences across post–high school trajectories at any point in time. Race was the dominant determinant of their party preference.

Both white and non-white men in the classes of 1984–91 were more Republican than their older counterparts, but whites were consistently more Republican. The pattern of comparisons was different from that of the earlier group. In high school, the college-bound were the most Republican, and differed significantly from the others. After high school, however, those white men who entered the military converged in their partisanship with those who went to college, while those who neither joined the armed forces nor completed a bachelor's degree were significantly less Republican. Although those who served in the military, like those in the other two groups, increased in Republicanism the longer they were out of high school, the change over time within the military groups was not statistically significant, while the increases in Republicanism within the college group and the non-military non-college group were statistically significant. Among non-whites in these classes, the college-bound tended to be the most Republican, but there were no significant differences among groups.

CONSERVATISM

One of the long-standing controversies about the social-psychological effects of military experience cross-nationally has focused on the relationship between military service and conservatism or authoritarianism. While authoritarian personalities have been shown to have preferences for the military (Roghmann 1966), and military members have been shown to be relatively conservative (Abrahamsson 1970), it is not clear whether this relationship has been due to self-selection or to military service itself. Research has shown a variety of results on authoritarianism as a function of military service: no change (e.g., French and Ernest 1955); increase (Christie 1952); and decrease (Campbell and McCormack 1957). Research on a panel of recruits in the German army from 1966 to 1968 found a decrease in authoritarianism (Roghmann and Sodeur 1972). While there has been debate on the interpretation of these findings (Stinchcombe 1973; Roghmann and Sodeur 1973), the direction of change has not been questioned, and past research provides no strong basis for asserting that military service changes attitudes in a conservative direction. Data on the ideological orientation of the American public reflect a statistically significant but proportionally very small shift in the direction of conservative self-identification since the 1950s (Robinson and Fleishman 1988). Thus, a small shift in conservative identification in the military might be a reflection of national ideological drift, rather than divergence between military and civilian cultures.

The Monitoring the Future data can be used to revisit whether, during the current volunteer-force era, young Americans with conservative inclinations are more likely to select military service as their preferred post–high school environment. Figure 4.1 shows an upward trend in conservatism among all male high school seniors from 1976 to 1999. Table 4.2 presents the proportions of young men in the high school classes of 1976–95 by post-graduation trajectory who identified themselves as "Conservative" or "Very Conservative," among all men who responded to a political ideology question (including those who called themselves Moderates, Liberals, or Radicals). This convention corresponds to other studies. Again, data are presented from the senior year survey and the first post-graduation follow-up survey, for men in the graduating classes of 1976–85, and of 1986–95. No sub-group is dominated by conservatives. Similar to the political party identification data, the most conservative group of young men, both in their senior year and one to two years after graduation, are the college-bound. Those going into the military appear less likely to be conservative than the college-bound, and contrary to the party identification data, the percentage of conservatives seems to decrease from the earlier group to the later. However, most of these differences are not significant. What is significant is that these young men entering the military as enlisted personnel are only about a third as likely to consider themselves "Conservative" as the military officers in Holsti's sample. Beyond the fact of self-identified conservatives constituting a minority (even among the college-bound), what most characterizes these data is the general lack of significant differences of proportions of conservatives between groups at both points in time, and the general stability of proportions within groups across time.

Two significant differences are notable, however, because the patterns are different for the two pooled groups. For the earlier classes, those going into the military were significantly more conservative than their non-college non-military peers at both points in time and did not differ significantly from those going to college. Since the difference existed in the senior year, it seems to be due to self-selection. For the more recent classes, on the other hand, those who entered the military were significantly less likely than their college-bound peers to consider themselves conservative and did not differ from the non-military non-college group when surveyed after graduation. We do not see the proportion of self-described conservatives increasing over time the way the proportion of self-identified Republicans did in these data.

TRUST IN GOVERNMENT

The fear on the part of those concerned with the gap between military and civilian culture that the military has become mistrustful of the civilian government is not a new one. Critics of the Vietnam War argued that service in that conflict produced hostility toward the government, alienation, and disorientation among its veterans (e.g., Helmer 1974; Lifton 1973). However, research has suggested that Vietnam veterans were, on the whole, less cynical than their non-veteran peers (Jennings and Markus 1974a), that they were more similar to than different from non-veterans (Bachman and Jennings 1975), and that with regard to trust in government, there was no difference between veterans and non-veterans (Segal and Segal 1976).

In the American population generally, trust in government declined in the mid-1960s and never recovered (Lipset and Schneider 1983). For the Congress in particular, public confidence hit an all-time low in March and April of 1992, with only 17 percent of the population approving of the way the Congress did its job (Patterson and Magleby 1992).

Table 4.2. Comparisons of Proportions of Self-Identified Conservatives[a] during Senior Year and 1 to 2 Years after High School, by Post–High School Occupational Group.

Males: 1976–85	Proportion Senior Year	Proportion 1–2 Years after High School	Proportion Change	N
Military	0.23	0.25	0.02	407
Full-Time College Students	0.24	0.25	0.02H	2,890
Other Civilian Young People	0.19	0.19	0.00	2,492
Total	0.22	0.22	0.01	5,789
Standard Deviation (Total Sample)	0.41	0.42	0.47	
Difference between Military and Full-Time College Students	-0.01	-0.01	0.01	
Difference between Military and Other Civilian Young People	0.04*	0.06*	0.02	

ATTITUDES OF ENTRY-LEVEL ENLISTED PERSONNEL | 189

Table 4.2. Continued.

Males: 1986–95	Proportion Senior Year	Proportion 1–2 Years after High School	Proportion Change	N
Military	0.22	0.21	−0.01	376
Full-Time College Students	0.26	0.27	0.00	3,613
Other Civilian Young People	0.19	0.20	0.01	2,333
Total	0.24	0.24	0.00	6,221
Standard Deviation (Total Sample)	0.42	0.43	0.45	
Difference between Military and Full-Time College Students	−0.04	−0.05*	−0.02	
Difference between Military and Other Civilian Young People	0.03	0.01	−0.02	

NOTES: [a] Based on responses to the survey question, "How would you describe your political beliefs?" "Very Conservative" and "Conservative" are combined in this table.

*Mann-Whitney tests were performed to test for significant mean differences between the sub-groups "Military" and "Other Civilian Young People" and "Military" and "Full-Time College Students." The * indicates significant mean differences at the .05 level, two-tailed.

[H]Wilcoxon ranked sign tests were performed to test for significant changes in within sub-group means. The [H] indicates significant mean changes at the .05 level, two-tailed.

Monitoring the Future surveys asked respondents to reply to five items dealing with trust in government.[2] As Figure 4.5 shows, among high school seniors, trust in government actually remained fairly stable between 1976 and 1989. However, it declined through the 1990s.

Table 4.3 presents the mean levels of trust in government across these five items during the senior year in high school and two years thereafter for men who graduated in both time periods. As with our analyses in Tables 4.1 and 4.2, data are presented for those who went into the military after graduation, those who became full-time students, and those who went on to other pursuits. Levels of trust in government were relatively high among those who went into the military.

In their high school senior year, men who planned to go into the military were statistically indistinguishable with regard to trust in government from those who were to go on to college, for both groups of classes. For men in the classes of 1986 to 1995 (but not for the earlier classes), the military-bound were significantly higher in trust in government than their non-military non-college-bound peers. Two years after high school, those in the military appear to have the highest levels of trust in government, and the non-military non-college group the lowest levels. However, for both sets of classes, the differences are significant only between those two groups, not between the military and college groups. The only group to increase significantly in trust in government between senior year and two years later was the military group in the classes of 1976 to 1985. Neither the college students nor the other group in these classes changed significantly during this period. By contrast, for the classes of 1986 to 1995, trust in government decreased between senior year and two years later, reflecting the general decline of the 1990s. The declines were fairly similar in magnitude for all three groups, but did not reach statisti-

2.   The items were: Do you think some of the people running the government are crooked or dishonest? (Responses ranged from 1 = Most of them are crooked or dishonest, to 5 = None at all are crooked or dishonest); Do you think the government wastes much of the money we pay in taxes? (Responses ranged from 1 = Nearly all tax money is wasted, to 5 = No tax money is wasted); Do you feel that the people running the government are smart people who usually know what they are doing? (Responses ranged from 1 = They always know what they are doing, to 5 = They seldom know what they are doing [this item was reverse-coded for scale construction]); How much of the time do you think you can trust the government in Washington to do the right thing? (Responses ranged from 1 = Almost always, to 5 = Almost never [this item was reversed for scale construction]); Would you say the government is pretty much run for a few big interests looking out for themselves, or is it run for the benefit of all of the people? (Responses ranged from 1 = Nearly always run for a few big interests, to 5 = Nearly always run for the benefit of all of the people).

Figure 4.5. Comparison of Trends in Mean Trust in Government and Mean Interest in Government among High School Seniors: Males, 1976–99.

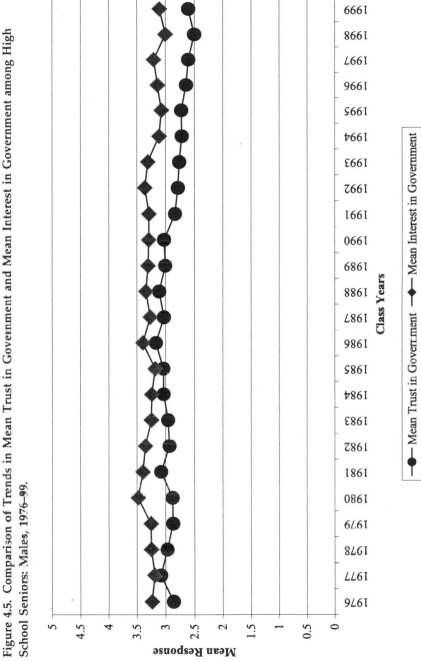

Table 4.3. Comparisons of Mean Levels of Trust in Government and Governmental Actors (index) [a] Senior Year and 1 to 2 Years after High School, by Post–High School Occupational Group.

Males: 1976–85	Mean Senior Year	Mean 1–2 Years after High School	Mean Change	N
Military	2.97	3.11	0.14H	85
Full-Time College Students	3.05	3.04	−0.01	620
Other Civilian Young People	2.90	2.89	−0.01	548
Total	2.98	2.98	0.00	1,252
Standard Deviation (Total Sample)	0.56	0.54	0.55	
Difference between Military and Full-Time College Students	−0.07	0.07	0.14*	

Table 4.3. *Continued.*

Males: 1986–95	Mean Senior Year	Mean 1–2 Years after High School	Mean Change	N
Military	3.05	2.93	−0.12	71
Full-Time College Students	2.96	2.86	−0.10H	647
Other Civilian Young People	2.89	2.75	−0.14H	388
Total	2.94	2.83	−0.11	1,106
Standard Deviation (Total Sample)	0.60	0.57	0.58	
Difference between Military and Full-Time College Students	0.09	0.07	−0.02	
Difference between Military and Other Civilian Young People	0.16*	0.18*	0.02	

NOTES: [a]Based on an index of 5 items. Higher score indicates more trust in government and government actors.
*Mann-Whitney tests were performed to test for significant mean differences between the sub-groups "Military" and "Other Civilian Young People" and "Military" and "Full-Time College Students." The * indicates significant mean differences at the .05 level, two-tailed.
HWilcoxon ranked sign tests were performed to test for significant changes within sub-group means. The H indicates significant mean changes at the .05 level, two-tailed.

cal significance for those in military service because of the relatively small number of respondents in this group.

INTEREST IN GOVERNMENT AND CURRENT EVENTS

Another measure of whether men who go into the military are more politically alienated than those going to other environments is the degree to which they are interested in government and current events. Level of interest in government is presumed to result from early political socialization processes (see Jennings and Niemi 1974b; Segal 1967), and to be positively related to family education (Nie, Petrocik, and Verba 1980). Since young men going into the military have lower levels of educational attainment, on average, than those going to college, but higher levels of educational performance than those directly entering the civilian labor force (because of military entrance standards), we might expect the level of political interest of the military-bound to lie between that of these two other groups.

Respondents in the Monitoring the Future surveys were asked how much interest they take in government and current events. As Figure 4.5 shows, there was general stability in interest in government among seniors from 1976 to 1997. Table 4.4 presents the mean scores for respondents in their senior years and the first follow-up across the three post-graduation trajectories. As expected, for both the 1976–85 and the 1986–95 senior classes, men who entered the military were significantly more interested in government in their senior year than were those who pursued non-military and non-college activities, and in the earlier period they were significantly less politically interested than those going to college. By the later period, this latter difference had disappeared.

Young men from the college sub-group confirmed our expectations for the stability of interest in government and current events over a long period. In both time periods, interest in government among the college sub-group did not change substantially between high school and the first year or two after high school. Men who entered the civilian job market after high school exhibited a significant increase in interest in government in the first time period, but not in the second time period. However, two years after graduation, those in the military confounded both our expectations for stability over the life span and our notions of the relationship between interest in government and educational level. In both time periods, men in the military increased their level of interest in government in the first year or two after high school, and their level of interest in government was higher than that of their peers in college.

Table 4.4. Comparisons of Mean Levels of Interest in Government and Current Events[a] Senior Year and 1 to 2 Years after High School, by Post–High School Occupational Group.

Males: 1976–85	Mean Senior Year	Mean 1–2 Years after High School	Mean Change	N
Military	3.31	3.66	0.36H	300
Full-Time College Students	3.50	3.54	0.04	2,198
Other Civilian Young People	3.11	3.22	0.11H	1,904
Total	3.32	3.41	0.09	4,403
Standard Deviation (Total Sample)	0.97	0.92	0.91	
Difference between Military and Full-Time College Students	−0.19*	0.13*	0.32*	

Table 4.4. Continued.

Males: 1986–95	Mean Senior Year	Mean 1–2 Years after High School	Mean Change	N
Military	3.45	3.65	0.20ᴴ	214
Full-Time College Students	3.47	3.43	-0.04	1,912
Other Civilian Young People	3.10	3.13	0.03	1,231
Total	3.34	3.34	0.00	3,357
Standard Deviation (Total Sample)	0.98	0.95	0.93	
Difference between Military and Full-Time College Students	-0.02	0.21*	0.29*	
Difference between Military and Other Civilian Young People	0.35*	0.52*	0.17*	

NOTES: [a] Based on responses to the survey question, "How much of an interest do you take in government and current events?" Response scale 1 to 5, where 1 = No interest at all; 5 = A very great interest.

*Mann-Whitney tests were performed to test for significant mean differences between the sub-groups "Military" and "Other Civilian Young People" and "Military" and "Full-Time College Students." The * indicates significant mean differences at the .05 level, two-tailed.

ᴴWilcoxon ranked sign tests were performed to test for significant changes in within sub-group means. The ᴴ indicates significant mean changes at the .05 level, two-tailed.

INTENTION TO VOTE

Political involvement has behavioral as well as attitudinal dimensions. Democratic political cultures define actual participation in party and electoral processes as virtues. There has long been a strong positive correlation between education and voting (Nie, Petrocik, and Verba 1980), and since some of the men we are studying intended to continue their education in college while others were going to enter the civilian labor force after twelve years of education, we expected to find differences in voting participation between these groups. Those men going into the military in the year or two after high school are educationally equivalent to those entering the civilian labor force, and this might suggest that their voting turnout would be similar to their non-college-bound peers. However, we have seen above that in terms of political interest, those entering the military seemed more like the college-bound than like those who entered civilian jobs after high school. If behavior reflects attitudes and interests, it would not be surprising to find differences in voting behavior between these two latter groups.

The high school seniors were asked about their voting behavior. Since many of the respondents had not been old enough to vote in their senior year, we aggregated two response categories on our voting question, "have already voted" and "probably will vote." We recognized that this would give us an overestimate of voting turnout, but we did not want our results to be biased by eligibility. For consistency, we maintained the same coding in the follow-up surveys. Table 4.5 presents voting intention data for our respondents in their senior years and one to two years after graduation, by the post-graduation trajectory they followed.

For men in the graduating classes of 1976–85, senior year voting intention was highest among those intending to go to college, and their difference from the other groups was significant. Those who planned to enter the military did not differ significantly from those entering other civilian pursuits. For men in the classes of 1986–95, their voting intentions were generally higher than for the 1976–85 group, and those going into the military did not differ significantly from either of the other groups.

For the men in the classes of 1976–85 who went into the military, there was a slight and insignificant increase in voting intention two years after graduation. There was not a significant difference between men in this group and in either of the other two groups at this point, and no group changed significantly during this two-year period. For the men in the classes of 1986–95, however, while neither the college-bound nor the military-bound changed significantly in their intention to vote, the other

Table 4.5. Comparisons of Plans for Voting[a] Senior Year and 1 to 2 Years after High School, by Post–High School Occupational Group.

Males: 1976–85	Mean Senior Year	Mean 1–2 Years after High School	Mean Change	N
Military	2.83	2.86	0.03	85
Full-Time College Students	2.95	2.94	-0.01	621
Other Civilian Young People	2.79	2.80	0.01	559
Total	2.87	2.87	0.00	1,265
Standard Deviation (Total Sample)	0.43	0.42	0.49	
Difference between Military and Full-Time College Students	-0.12*	-0.07	0.05	

Table 4.5. Continued.

Males: 1986–95	Mean Senior Year	Mean 1–2 Years after High School	Mean Change	N
Military	2.91	2.92	0.00	73
Full-Time College Students	2.92	2.92	0.00	656
Other Civilian Young People	2.81	2.75	-0.06H	398
Total	2.88	2.86	-0.02	1,127
Standard Deviation (Total Sample)	0.40	0.44	0.39	
Difference between Military and Full-Time College Students	-0.01	-0.01	0.00	
Difference between Military and Other Civilian Young People	0.10	0.16*	0.06	

NOTES: [a] Based on responses to the survey question, "Have you ever, or do you plan to vote in a public election?" 1 = Probably won't, 2 = Don't know, 3 = Probably will or already have voted.

*Mann-Whitney tests were performed to test for significant mean differences between the sub-groups "Military" and "Other Civilian Young People" and "Military" and "Full-Time College Students." The * indicates significant mean differences at the .05 level, two-tailed.

HWilcoxon ranked sign tests were performed to test for significant changes in within sub-group means. The H indicates significant mean changes at the .05 level, two-tailed.

civilian young men declined significantly in their voting intention, so that those entering the military, while not significantly different from those who went to college, had significantly higher intentions to vote than civilians who did not go to college.

OTHER POLITICAL ACTIVITY

Voting is not the only way that people express themselves politically. The men in the Monitoring the Future samples were asked about writing to political officials, contributing to campaigns, and working in campaigns. Table 4.6 presents scores on an index that aggregates these three forms of behavior for respondents who followed each of the post–high school trajectories, both in their senior year, and one or two years thereafter.

For both sets of senior classes, men going to college had higher levels of political involvement than their peers, both while still in school and thereafter. Those in non-military and non-educational pursuits had the lowest involvement. For men in the classes of 1976–85, those going into the military were not significantly different from those going to college, and were significantly higher in their political involvement than those in other pursuits, both while they were still in high school and thereafter. For men in the classes of 1985–96, however, those entering the military had lower levels of involvement than those going to college, and did not differ significantly from their non-college peers. For both groups of classes, the full-time college students increased their levels of political participation significantly between their senior year and one or two years later. Neither of the other groups changed significantly. All differences are small.

DEFENSE POLICY ISSUES

Holsti's analysis (1998–99 and Chapter 1) compared military and civilian samples on a range of foreign and domestic policy issues in the domains of militant and cooperative internationalism and of defense and social policy. We do not have as wide a range of questions in Monitoring the Future, but we have addressed some of the dimensions considered by Holsti (Bachman et al. 2000b).

MILITANT INTERNATIONALISM. Holsti built on Wittkopf's distinction (1990) between militant and cooperative internationalism. The former emphasizes a world of conflict, and the necessity to be prepared and willing to use force to address it. The latter stresses cooperation, international organizations, humanitarianism, foreign aid, and arms control. We do not have data to address this latter face of internationalism, but we can explore attitudes toward militant internationalism.

Holsti (1998) found that military officers were more supportive of militant internationalism than were their civilian counterparts, but that the difference had tended to narrow rather than widen over time, primarily reflecting increased militancy among civilians. The difference was consistent with earlier findings. When Bachman et al. (1977) compared the attitudes of soldiers, sailors, and civilians in the early years of the all-volunteer force, they found career enlisted personnel in the army and navy to be significantly more militant with regard to support for military intervention, preference for U.S. military supremacy, and support for U.S. military actions in Vietnam than were non-career personnel, and career officers in both services to be more militant than non-career navy officers (but not non-career army officers). Non-career personnel tended to be similar to their civilian counterparts, while career personnel tended to be more militant than their civilian counterparts. Given the increasing presence of career personnel in the force, we might expect the mean difference between military personnel and civilians to increase. However, when Bachman, Sigelman, and Diamond (1987) revisited these attitudes a decade later, they found that support for intervention among American youth increased with intention to serve and expectation of a military career, but did not change very much over a ten-year period.

We combined two items from Monitoring the Future into an index of support for U.S. military supremacy, which we offer as a surrogate for militant internationalism (Bachman et al. 2000b). The items were: "The U.S. ought to have much more military power than any other nation in the world," and "The U.S. does not need greater military power than the Soviet Union [later: Russia]." (The latter item was reverse-coded.)

Table 4.7 presents the scores on this index of the men in the two sets of graduating classes in their senior year and the first follow-up, as they relate to post–high school trajectory. For both groups of classes, men who were to enter the military were significantly more supportive of U.S. military supremacy than were those who were to go to college, and this difference was sustained two years after graduation. The military sample did not differ significantly from the non-college, non-military youth in the senior high school year for either set of classes, but was significantly more supportive two years after graduation for the classes of 1986–95. The men who went into the military did not change significantly in level of support for military supremacy between the two survey waves, but for both groups of senior classes, both the college-bound and the non-college, non-military youth significantly decreased their levels of support for U.S. military supremacy. These findings are consistent both with the patterns observed by Bachman et al. (1977) in the early years of the volunteer force, and with the differences that Holsti has observed more recently between senior leaders of the military and civilian institutions.

Table 4.6. Comparisons of Mean Levels of Traditional Political Activity (index) [a] Senior Year and 1 to 2 Years after High School, by Post–High School Occupational Group.

Males: 1976–85	Mean Senior Year	Mean 1–2 Years after High School	Mean Change	N
Military	2.00	2.11	0.12	84
Full-Time College Students	2.14	2.20	0.06H	616
Other Civilian Young People	1.81	1.84	0.03	549
Total	1.99	2.04	0.05	1,249
Standard Deviation (Total Sample)	0.69	0.75	0.65	
Difference between Military and Full-Time College Students	−0.14	−0.09	0.05	
Difference between Military and Other Civilian Young People	0.18*	0.26*	0.09	

Table 4.6. Continued.

Males: 1986–95	Mean Senior Year	Mean 1–2 Years after High School	Mean Change	N
Military	1.83	1.90	0.06	72
Full-Time College Students	1.98	2.11	0.13[H]	654
Other Civilian Young People	1.78	1.83	0.05	396
Total	1.90	2.00	0.10	1,122
Standard Deviation (Total Sample)	0.63	0.73	0.62	
Difference between Military and Full-Time College Students	–0.15*	–0.21*	–0.04	
Difference between Military and Other Civilian Young People	0.05	0.07	0.02	

NOTES: [a]Mean index of three measures of political activity: writing to officials, contributing to a campaign, and working in a campaign. Higher scores indicate more activity.

*Mann-Whitney tests were performed to test for significant mean differences between the sub-groups "Military" and "Other Civilian Young People" and "Military" and "Full-Time College Students." The * indicates significant mean differences at the .05 level, two-tailed.

[H]Wilcoxon ranked sign tests were performed to test for significant changes in within sub-group means. The [H] indicates significant mean changes at the .05 level, two-tailed.

Table 4.7. Comparisons of Mean Levels of Support for U.S. Military Supremacy (index)[a] during Senior Year and 1 to 2 Years after High School, by Post–High School Occupational Group.

Males: 1976–85	Mean Senior Year	Mean 1–2 Years after High School	Mean Change	N
Military	3.78	3.89	0.11	84
Full-Time College Students	3.40	3.23	−0.17H	614
Other Civilian Young People	3.66	3.54	−0.12H	546
Total	3.54	3.41	−0.13	1,244
Standard Deviation (Total Sample)	1.15	1.17	1.21	
Difference between Military and Full-Time College Students	0.38*	0.65*	0.28*	
Difference between Military and Other Civilian Young People	0.12	0.34	0.23*	

Table 4.7. Continued.

Males: 1986–95	Mean Senior Year	Mean 1–2 Years after High School	Mean Change	N
Military	3.46	3.63	0.17	72
Full-Time College Students	3.17	3.05	-0.12H	643
Other Civilian Young People	3.42	3.27	-0.15H	391
Total	3.28	3.16	-0.11	1,105
Standard Deviation (Total Sample)	1.21	1.20	1.19	
Difference between Military and Full-Time College Students	0.29*	0.53*	0.29	
Difference between Military and Other Civilian Young People	0.04	0.35	0.32*	

NOTES: aMean index of two items: "The U.S. does not need greater military power than Russia" (item reverse-coded); "The U.S. ought to have much more military power than any other nation in the world" (1 = Disagree, 3 = Neither, 5 = Agree).

*Mann-Whitney tests were performed to test for significant mean differences between the sub-groups "Military" and "Other Civilian Young People" and "Military" and "Full-Time College Students." The * indicates significant mean differences at the .05 level, two-tailed.

HWilcoxon ranked sign tests were performed to test for significant changes in within sub-group means. The H indicates significant mean changes at the .05 level, two-tailed.

SOURCE: These data are taken from J.G. Bachman, P. Freedman-Doan, D.R. Segal, P.M. and O'Malley, "Distinctive Military Values Among U.S. Enlistees, 1976–1997: Self-Selection Versus Socialization." (2000).

SUPPORT FOR MILITARY SPENDING. One of the issues explored by Holsti (1998) was opinion on reducing the defense budget in order to increase the federal education budget. Senior military officers were significantly less willing to agree with such an action than were leaders of civilian institutions. The Monitoring the Future surveys did not ask respondents to choose between these forms of social expenditure, but they did ask for views about the adequacy of military spending. As noted, in the early years of the volunteer force, Bachman et al. (1977) found that military personnel had a significantly higher preference for increased military spending than did civilians. More recently, Bachman et al. (2000b) found that for the high school classes of 1976–85 and 1986–95, men going into the military had a significantly greater preference for increased military spending than did those going to college or to the civilian work force, and these differences persisted two years after graduation. For both of these groups of seniors, preferences for greater military spending increased significantly during the first two years after graduation among those going into the military, while they decreased significantly among those going to college. There was no significant change among those entering the civilian work force. This is consistent with the findings from the first years of the volunteer force, and, while the items differ, is consistent with the patterns observed by Holsti. The data are presented in Table 4.8.

The patterns observed for militant internationalism and support for defense spending are generally consistent with the observed patterns of other military attitudes (Bachman et al. 2000b). Seniors going into the military tend to have more pro-military attitudes than those going to college or the civilian labor force. This indicates occupational self-selection, and holds across the realms of preferences for U.S. military spending and supremacy, views on acceptable conditions for U.S. military intervention, and views about unquestioning obedience by servicemen. In addition to these self-selection effects, there was evidence of occupational socialization for some items. For example, while more recent military recruits indicated less support for military funding than earlier recruits, reflecting a general trend toward reduced support for military spending, in both groups support for military spending increased during the first two years out of high school. Some changes, however, were in what might be regarded as a less militaristic direction. For example, while seniors who were going into the military were more likely than their non-military counterparts to endorse unquestioning obedience to orders on the part of military personnel, they were less likely to take this position after two years of service. And while differences between groups increased in some instances, it was more often because the men who entered college became significantly less pro-military than because those in the military became more so.

While some analysts fear a gap between military and civilian culture, possibly contributing to problems in civil-military relations, others warn of a closing of the gap—a "civilianization" of the military—contributing to a decline in military effectiveness. One variant is a concern with a decreasing "masculine" culture in the military. A more general statement is Moskos's occupational model of the military (1977). Moskos argued that with the end of conscription in America, and with the adoption of labor-market dynamics to recruit military personnel, the military would lose the commitment to national symbols, values, and purposes that characterized the conscription-era military institution and the citizen-soldier for whom service was a calling. Military service would become just another job in the labor force.

Interestingly, this theme was not a new one, although the attribution of the change to the end of conscription was new. Stein (1960, 177), discussing the conscripts of World War II, had described them as viewing their service as a form of impersonal corporate employment, rather than a calling, and Janowitz (1960, 117), writing about professional soldiers of the conscription era, had noted that "those who see the military as a calling or a unique profession are outnumbered by the greater concentration for whom the military is just another job." The conscription-era institutional soldier celebrated by Moskos may be a romantic idealization, representing a minority of personnel, rather than the norm of that period. If soldierly values were to be found less than universal in the personnel of the volunteer-force era, this would not necessarily indicate a break from the past.

Research conducted on the issue raised by Moskos showed the persistence of normative values, even in a volunteer force recruited through labor market processes emphasizing pay and benefits (Segal 1986). One might expect that recruitment appeals that emphasize individualistic self-interest would be unlikely to produce a force concerned with serving the country or making the world a better place, but these values appear in studies of contemporary military personnel. As one example, in late 1998, the Army surveyed almost 9,000 recent recruits at six training centers. Among the things they were asked were how important were job characteristics such as pay, benefits, steady employment, serving the country, and making the world a better place. The attributes that are emphasized in recruiting appeals—those applicable to civilian jobs as well—were given the highest importance ratings: 80 percent cited the im-

Table 4.8. Comparisons of Mean Level Preferences for More Military Spending[a] during Senior Year and 1 to 2 Years after High School, by Post–High School Occupational Group.

Males: 1976–85	Mean Senior Year	Mean 1–2 Years after High School	Mean Change	N
Military	3.51	3.82	0.31H	91
Full-Time College Students	3.15	2.94	-0.20H	572
Other Civilian Young People	3.16	3.14	-0.02H	542
Total	3.18	3.10	-0.08	1,205
Standard Deviation (Total Sample)	1.08	1.08	1.09	
Difference between Military and Full-Time College Students	0.36*	0.88*	0.52*	
Difference between Military and Other Civilian Young People	0.35*	0.68*	0.33*	

Table 4.8. Continued.

Males: 1986–95	Mean Senior Year	Mean 1–2 Years after High School	Mean Change	N
Military	3.02	3.76	0.74H	66
Full-Time College Students	2.56	2.47	−0.09H	617
Other Civilian Young People	2.60	2.66	0.05	431
Total	2.60	2.62	0.02	1,114
Standard Deviation (Total Sample)	0.99	1.02	1.02	
Difference between Military and Full-Time College Students	0.46*	1.29*	0.83*	
Difference between Military and Other Civilian Young People	0.41*	1.10*	0.69*	

NOTES: [a] Based on responses to the survey question, "Do you think the U.S. spends too much or too little on the armed services?" (1 = Far too much, 3 = About right, 5 = Far too little).

*Mann-Whitney tests were performed to test for significant mean differences between the sub-groups "Military" and "Other Civilian Young People" and "Military" and "Full-Time College Students." The * indicates significant mean differences at the .05 level, two-tailed.

HWilcoxon ranked sign tests were performed to test for significant changes in within sub-group means. The H indicates significant mean changes at the .05 level, two-tailed.

SOURCE: These data are taken from Bachman, J. G., Freedman-Doan, P., Segal, D.R. and O'Malley, P.M. "Distinctive Military Values Among U.S. Enlistees, 1976–1997: Self-Selection Versus Socialization" (2000).

portance of good benefits, 78 percent indicated good pay, and 72 percent noted steady job. However, half of the recruits also assigned importance to the more traditional, less individualistic values of serving the nation and the world. These data do not allow us to compare these soldiers either to their civilian peers or to soldiers of the past, but they do indicate that those elements that may have contributed to some people's views of military service as a calling in the past have not completely dissipated.

Discussion

Like many other occupations, professions, and work organizations, the military has a culture. The attitudes associated with it include views that the military as a workplace has attributes that are seen as desirable, or at least acceptable, by some people; that the military performs useful functions for society; and that the military should perhaps have more influence than it does in the society it protects, as well as a larger share of the budget. These attitudes are compatible with both Janowitz's and Huntington's views of the military, are probably functional for the operation of the military institution (Hillen 1999), and pose no obvious threat to the nation. They are held most clearly by career military personnel, and the shift toward a more career-oriented force may have made these views more pervasive in the armed forces.

To the extent that the emergence of a more career-oriented force has been driven by the end of conscription, we might argue that the culture has been influenced by the changes in processes of military recruitment. However, this change has been at the margins: we have not replaced a force wholly composed of citizen-soldiers with a force wholly composed of professional soldiers; rather, we have changed the mix. This change would have occurred without a change in accession processes, because of the increasing need to keep people with technical military specialties under arms for longer service due to the length and expense of required training.

One element of the culture of the military that may have changed is its politicization. The American military has been politically neutral (although some victorious generals have later been elected president and others have had political aspirations), and participation in electoral politics has been low among active-duty American military personnel. In the current era, our data suggest that people going into the armed forces as enlisted personnel are politically engaged. Again, this is not surprising. The American military, as it has become increasingly career-oriented, has also become increasingly professionalized. One aspect of professionalization is political mobilization in pursuit of collective interests.

The nature of this mobilization, however, is not what some critics have feared. Ricks (1997d), for example, suggested that "U.S. military personnel of all ranks are feeling increasingly alienated from their own country, and are becoming more conservative and more politically active than ever before." Our data on voting and other forms of traditional political behavior suggest that he might be correct with regard to political activity. However, our data on trust in government and interest in government suggest a very high level of engagement rather than alienation. Indeed, military service seems to engender both trust and interest in government.

While there has been an increase in Republican identifiers among young men entering the military, these men are primarily reflective of their generation, as a group are predominantly not Republican, and are less Republican than their peers who go to college. Indeed, for men who graduated in the high school classes of 1976–83 and entered the military, it appears that the longer they served, the less they preferred the Republican Party, although this pattern changed for the classes of 1984–91. While the men who entered the military were more likely to characterize themselves as conservative than were their peers who entered the civilian labor force after high school, they tended to lag behind their college-bound peers in their conservatism. Rather than alienation or disproportionate conservatism, what the data seem to suggest is a political mainstreaming and *embourgeoisment* of American military personnel.

With regard to the impact of the advent of a volunteer force on motivation to serve, it is to be expected that a career-oriented force is going to be more concerned with pay and benefits than was a conscripted force. In this area, military personnel may be increasingly similar to, rather than different from, their civilian peers. At the same time, the materialism associated with professional career-oriented military service does not seem to preclude a concern with serving the country or making the world a better place. This confluence of concerns with public service and economic comfort might be regarded as pragmatic professionalism. With an increase in economic concerns, there may have been a decrease over time in the normative values that Moskos identifies as the underpinnings of the more institutional conscription-based force. However, nothing in the volunteer force precludes service out of a sense of calling, and it is possible that, as Stein and Janowitz suggest, the majority of American military personnel never had the institutional orientation that Moskos ascribes to them, and that there has been less historical change in the normative basis for military service than Moskos's formulation implies.

As we look at the generation entering the American labor force during the volunteer force era, we do not find those who chose the armed

forces as their post–high school trajectory to be very different in their political attitudes from their peers who entered the civilian labor force or
who continued their education. Where differences occur, they are compatible both with the historic relative conservatism of the military, and
with more general conceptualizations of organizational culture. These
differences seem primarily to be results of self-selection into the military,
rather than of attitude changes that take place after entering service.
The differences are sufficiently small to suggest that the culture of the
American military is well embedded into the broader culture of American society.

Part II
Changes in Civil-Military Gaps Over Time

Chapter 5

The American Civil-Military Cultural Gap: A Historical Perspective, Colonial Times to the Present

Russell F. Weigley

The current American civil-military gap, described and assessed in the other chapters of this book, extends deep into the American past, as this chapter will show. It began with the stationing of British regular troops in North America in sizeable numbers beginning during the colonial era in 1755, and the emergence of proto-professional U.S. military forces in the form of the Continental Army of the War for Independence and the embryonic Regular Army of the United States in the early Republic. From the beginning, career soldiers perceived themselves as occupying a somewhat hostile environment, distrusted by American civilians—which indeed they were, because American civilian culture had absorbed an English tradition inimical to standing armies even before any such armies appeared in the colonies that were to become the United States. The soldiers reciprocated civilian distrust with ill-feeling of their own, often fortified by their sense that they themselves represented an ethos of discipline and manly virtue superior to the easygoing values of civilian society—a military attitude still familiar today. When a professional military officer corps emerged during the middle years of the nineteenth century, the military culture became, and its members felt themselves to be, more separate from civilian society and values, yet more representative of a distinctive kind of discipline, virtue, and responsibility.

After the founding of the United States, however, the cultural gap became obscured by the growth of an American military tradition that accepted the constitutional principle of civilian control of the military. Through the early years of the Republic and throughout the nineteenth century, military forces were too small and too peripheral to American politics and to society at large to be anything but compliant with civilian control, except possibly during the Civil War. By the time of that conflict, the tradition of acceptance had become too deeply ingrained to be set aside readily, and when truly professional officers rose to head the Army for the first time during the Civil War, they confirmed the constitutional tradition in the course of the war. The culture gap has never been so wide, however, as to prevent soldiers from remembering that they are Americans first, and respecting the Constitution of the United States accordingly. A deeper than ordinary loyalty to the nation and its governing traditions is, after all, part of the military's self-perception of what sets its ethos apart.

Still, the return to civilian neglect of the military after the Civil War encouraged a rebirth of military distrust in civilian America. The Army was largely relegated to the Indian frontier, out of sight and out of mind, its manpower and other resources disproportionately small in contrast to the huge territory it had to police. The Navy was long denied modern steam warships. Military resentment of neglect grew so severe as to include a certain diminution of respect for the Constitution itself, and for American democracy. While the outward military acceptance of civilian control remained for the most part exemplary, the distrust between the two cultures that had existed from the beginning continued to fester and to some degree worsen, at least on the military side; most civilians were too indifferent to care much.

The emergence of the United States as a world power from the 1890s onward, accelerating in the early twentieth century, blurred the cultural gap. The Navy, especially, enjoyed so rapid a growth that the attitudes of its officers toward civilians could hardly help but grow more benign as the civilians dispensed generous largesse. The Army, while treated less generously, at least emerged from obscurity and indifference to undergo civilian-sponsored reforms to prepare it for international missions. Then the World Wars brought about an unprecedented expansion of the armed forces, albeit interrupted for twenty years between the wars, that saw something of a military reversion to post–Civil War attitudes. Moreover, the existence of severe external threats to the national interest, both civilian and military, tends to force civil-military cooperation, and both World Wars certainly had that effect.

So, in slightly lesser degree, did the Cold War, although a brief crisis flared in the form of the 1951 affray between President Harry S. Truman and General of the Army Douglas MacArthur. In retrospect, moreover, the latter event can be perceived as a harbinger of the deeper and longer-term deterioration of civil-military relations during and after the Vietnam War. The Civil War and the World Wars had blurred the culture gap not only because they created pressures for civil-military harmony in defense of common national interests, but also because the civilian government had bestowed on the military resources sufficient to win overwhelming victories. From those experiences had come a military conception of overwhelming force mobilized for the complete submission of the enemy as the classic and characteristic American way of war. When in Vietnam the civilians denied the military the instrument of overwhelming force, the disgruntled military were no longer so willing to patch over the culture gap.

When the close of the Cold War at the beginning of the 1990s removed the pressure for civil-military unity posed by a major external threat, conditions were ripe for the civil-military culture gap to open, and for American civil-military relations to become more evidently strained and more of a threat to coherent national policymaking than ever before. Civil-military distrust and an awareness of differing values on both sides had existed throughout American history. But previously, either the military had been too peripheral to policymaking and to society at large for the culture gap to have much impact, or the pressures posed by the Civil War, World Wars, and Cold War had led both parties to feel obliged to work together despite their differences. Since 1990, however, the end of the Cold War notwithstanding, external threats to United States national interests have persisted, on a scale not large enough to demand a closing of civil-military ranks, but troublesome enough to require maintaining military forces much larger than in any previous period when no full-scale military rivalry was afoot. So, unlike most of the nineteenth century, the military is not merely peripheral and irrelevant to the concerns of most Americans and of the civilian government. The military must continue to be central players in foreign and domestic affairs, in Bosnia, in Haiti, and in Kosovo, while in numerous other places and roles (even homeland defense), American military intervention will persist as a possibility.

The civil-military relations of the end of the twentieth century are no doubt more difficult still because of shorter-range aggravating factors. The Vietnam War created special sources of civil-military suspicions that will tend to widen the culture gap as long as those who remember the war are making policy. The end of selective service increasingly deprives the military of large numbers of civilians who have first-hand understanding of the military derived from a tour in uniform. Since 1993 the presidents of the United States have been without a record of military service for the first time since Franklin D. Roosevelt. President William Jefferson Clinton further widened the culture gap in the eyes of the military because he had participated in the anti–Vietnam War movement of the 1960s. A lack of a military background is almost certain to become the rule rather than the exception, among other civilian officeholders as well as presidents.

Such aggravating circumstances specific to the late twentieth century notwithstanding, the larger issue is that historically American soldiers and civilians have always represented two different cultures. The former stand for discipline, the submergence of the individual into the group, and sacrifice of self for larger responsibilities. The latter stand for the liberation of the individual, in pursuit of a democratic society but also of economic gain and material gratification. Either the peripheral position of the military or overriding national crises have prevented the culture gap from posing severe political and social problems in the past, but neither of these redemptive conditions applies today. While the constitutional tradition of civilian control of the military is deeply entrenched, and the republic will probably survive the dangers posed by these unprecedented circumstances, the path of survival will probably not be smooth.[1]

This essay explores the history of civilian control in the United States, the reasons for the general success of the constitutional tradition, the tensions that have nevertheless underlain such success and the recent and current circumstances that have brought those tensions closer to the surface of civil-military affairs than ever before.

Anti-Military Ideology and Practical Military Strength

Civil-military tensions have always been present in American history, ready to grow more acute should any circumstances exacerbating them arise. In the separation of thirteen of Great Britain's North American colonies from the British Empire and the consequent creation of the United States, the American colonists' fear of a British military despotism was probably as important a source of the Revolution as any, including the controversy over direct taxation of the colonies by the British Parliament. The decision of the British Ministry to maintain a permanent military garrison in North America following the close of the French and Indian War in 1763 was the principal precipitant of the decision to tax the colonies, in order that the colonists should pay their share for the expensive pillar of empire that the garrison represented. At the same time, the garrison

---

1.   I have addressed the history of American civil-military relations in two earlier articles: "The American Military and the Principle of Civilian Control from McClellan to Powell" (Weigley 1993, 27–58) emphasizes the military's acceptance of civilian control; "The Soldier, the Statesman, and the Military Historian: The First Annual George C. Marshall Lecture in Military History" (Weigley 1999, 807–822) emphasizes the underlying distrust.

awoke among the Americans deep-seated fears of military forces as inherent agents of tyranny, fears to which the Americans were all the more susceptible because the extinction of New France removed from the scene the most obvious reason for maintaining military force (Shy 1965).

In such conditions, the colonists asked themselves, what could be the purpose of the garrison other than to enforce unpopular British edicts and laws and to undermine colonial self-government? The military dictatorship of the Lord Protector Oliver Cromwell was not a remote memory for English people in either the New World or the Old, for they were closer in time to the autocracy of Cromwell and his army than we are to the American Civil War. Moreover, once the Stuart kings, Charles II and James II, returned to the English throne, the English Whigs perceived them as moving toward the establishment of a new autocracy of their own based upon the muskets of the newly created English regular army of permanent regiments. The consequent Whig fears did much to precipitate the Glorious Revolution of 1688, exiling James II and prompting Parliament to legislate on behalf of its own in place of the monarch's control of the military. In reaction to Cromwell and the Stuarts, however, there emerged an English national tradition of suspicion of the military as an intrinsic threat to civilian self-government and liberties. The American colonists fully accepted the Whig antimilitary tradition and indeed integrated it into American political culture (Schwoerer 1974; Robbins 1959, 115–125, 413–414; Cress 1982, 15–33, 34–50, 181–188; Cress 1979, 43–60).

Therefore, when the government of King George III created its garrison in the colonies, the Americans reacted as if George III were going to become another James II in his intended use of military force for domestic repression. The British government obtusely played into colonial fears with the "Intolerable Acts" of 1774, particularly with the Massachusetts Government Act that not only limited self-government but implicitly asserted that the British Parliament could alter all colonial governments at will. London also heavily reinforced its troops in Boston to assure compliance with the offensive legislation. The province responded by reinvigorating its own militia system to offset the strength of the redcoats. With two armed forces hostile to each other operating within the narrow boundaries of the Bay Colony, it is not surprising that they clashed with each other in Lexington and Concord on April 19, 1775, and so American suspicion of British military power helped to bring about revolutionary war (Higginbotham 1971, 46; Phillips 1999, 90–91).

To fight a war against the British army in America, the colonists— and, from July 4, 1776, the newborn United States—needed a similar military force. Thus, on the foundations provided by the militia of citizen-soldiers that each colony possessed, the rebels erected the Continental

Army—reluctantly, doubting that any military organization, even one of their own, could resist the tendencies of armies to impose tyranny. The Continental Congress supervised the Continental Army with irrational distrust of it, and with irrational apprehension that Congress's own military commander-in-chief, General George Washington, would turn into another Oliver Cromwell.

Far from fulfilling such fears, General Washington proved scrupulous to a fault in his acceptance of civilian control. He was extremely meticulous in consulting with the Continental Congress and, following March 1, 1781, the Confederation Congress and all their committees concerned with the war effort. He resigned his command on December 28, 1783, promptly following the close of hostilities (Cunliffe 1958; Boatner 1974, 264–274; Heitman 1903, 1, 17, 1004–1007).

On the whole, the army waged the War of Independence without raising Cromwellian threats to civilian authority, the chronic weakness of that authority notwithstanding. Various mutinies, particularly of the Massachusetts, Connecticut, Pennsylvania, and New Jersey lines, were responses to grievances brought on by the inability of Congress to pay for and administer the war adequately, but were directed almost as much at the military as the civil authorities. On June 21, 1783, Pennsylvania soldiers for a time held Congress hostage in the Pennsylvania State House at Philadelphia demanding settlement of questions over pay, but this mutiny quickly fizzled when the soldiers found strong drink and became distracted—or besotted—enough simply to let the Congressmen walk away (Boatner 1974, 757–759, 759–769; Van Doren 1943; Brunhouse 1971, 135–140, 271–273).

More serious as a civil-military crisis was the officers' conspiracy, in concert with conservative members of Congress, that issued the Newburgh Addresses of March 10 and 12, 1783. The officers threatened action by the army unless demands for half-pay for life were met, and some in Congress hoped to turn military discontent into an instrument for strengthening the central government. Not only, however, did Washington quickly report on the conspiracy to the whole Congress, but on March 15, in his appearance before his assembled officers at the cantonment near Newburgh at New Windsor, New York, he eloquently shamed them into silencing the conspirators. The Newburgh conspiracy might have set the American military on a path toward lasting involvement in civilian politics had it not been for Washington's intervention. Nevertheless, it is probably fair to say that this and other disturbing affairs of the latter part of the Revolution reinvigorated Whig anti-militarism more than their actual potential for danger warranted (Kohn 1975, 17–39, 309–319; 1970, 187–220; Nelson 1972, 143–157; Kohn 1972a, 151–158;

Skeen 1974, 273–290; Kohn 1972b, 290–298). They contributed to the decision of Congress to disband the Continental Army almost completely on June 2, 1784, and, beginning the next day, to raise only a minimal replacement establishment, the First American Regiment of 700 men, in spite of evident dangers on the "Indian frontier" (Kohn 1975, 60).

For all of that, when the weaknesses of the Confederation against the Native Americans and in commercial and diplomatic dealings with the European powers, along with the threat of internal chaos represented by Daniel Shays's Rebellion in 1786, led to the Constitutional Convention of 1787 and the creation of a much stronger central government, the military clauses of the consequent Federal Constitution proved most notable not for their distrust of military forces but for their strengths. The new Congress received categorical authority to raise and support armies, the only limitation being that Army appropriations were not to run for more than two years (Killian and Costello 1996, 8, 9).[2]

Federal military power was subjected, however, to the Constitution-makers' favorite device of checks and balances. While it was the legislature that raised and supported armies and navies, the executive was to be commander-in-chief (Killian and Costello 1996, 14).[3] Federal military power was to be checked further by the retention of the militia systems of the states, most explicitly under the Second Amendment (Killian and Costello 1996, 14, 26).[4] At the time, the state militias could be regarded as a realistic check upon federal military power because an army

---

2.   Article I, Section 8, Paragraph 1, "The Congress shall have Power . . . (Paragraph 12) To raise and support Armies, but no Appropriation of Money to that Use, shall be for a longer term than two years." See also Paragraph 11, giving Congress power "to declare War, grant Letters of Marque and Reprisal, and make Rules concerning Captures on Land and Water"; Paragraph 12, "to provide and maintain a Navy"; and Paragraph 14, "to make Rules for the Government and Regulation of the land and naval Forces."

3.   Article II, Section 2, Paragraph 1 states that "The President shall be Commander in Chief of the Army and Navy of the United States, and of the Militia of the several States, when called into the actual Service of the United States."

4.   Amendment II says: "A well-regulated Militia being necessary to the security of a free State, the right of the people to keep and bear Arms shall not be infringed." For the militia in the original Constitution, see Article II, Section 2, paragraph quoted in note 3 above; also Article I, Section 8, enumerating the powers of Congress, including Paragraph 15, "to provide for calling forth the Militia to execute the Laws of the Union, suppress Insurrections and repel Invasions;" and Paragraph 16, "To provide for organizing, arming and disciplining the Militia, and for governing such Part of them as may be employed in the Service of the United States, reserving to the States respectively the Appointment of the Officers, and the Authority of training the Militia according to the discipline prescribed by Congress."

built upon them had so recently defeated the British Army. More-over, more than half a century later, the Civil War would demonstrate that with their militia systems, the states retained sufficient sovereignty in a military sense to wage a large-scale war against the federal government.

The Constitution created a skeletal structure capable of supporting impressive military strength, as the history of the United States as a world power in the twentieth century would confirm. When the new federal government was inaugurated on April 30, 1789, nevertheless it remained to be seen how much and how soon the bones could be fleshed out, against the ongoing heritage of Whig distrust of armies. The George Washington administration eventually made impressive beginnings, with a modestly sized Army of 5,120 officers and men, along with a commanding general and his staff. By 1794 it became a highly disciplined and effective regular force in the form of Major-General Anthony Wayne's Legion of the United States (Jacobs 1947, 124–152; Kohn 1975, 91–127, 139–157, 333–350, 353–360). In addition, the administration secured the Uniform Militia Act of May 8, 1792, which, despite weaknesses, signified the adoption by the United States from the colonial militia tradition of the principle of universal compulsory military service, in this instance by white males aged eighteen to forty-five (Mahon 1983, 52–53; Cress 1982, 120–121).

In the second Federalist administration, that of President John Adams, the further fleshing out of the constitutional military skeleton was marred by the fact that substantial authorized increases in both regular forces and various kinds of provisional federal forces—authorizations complete or provisional for over 50,000 men in response to the quasi-war with France of 1798–1800—embodied partisan political more than national security motives (Kohn 1975, 229n). The extreme Federalists, largely led by Alexander Hamilton, who was commissioned major-general and Inspector-General of the Army, intended the large land force not so much to fight the French, an extremely unlikely prospect, as to enforce the suppression of Jeffersonian Republicanism that was implicit in the Alien and Sedition Acts (Kohn 1975, 214–273, 386–408; Kurtz 1957, 316–317, 323, 354–356).

To the extent that it was actually a war, the quasi-war was a maritime conflict, for which Secretary of the Navy Benjamin Stoddert efficiently oversaw the birth of a small but effective navy (Palmer 1987). The Army enlargements included a Federalists-only expansion of the officer corps and carried the risk of creating a politically partisan military. Fortunately for the continuation of both civilian supremacy and an apolitical military, the effort to use the army as a partisan instrument backfired. Recruitment of the rank and file was minimal, and the Federalists' military program helped bring about Thomas Jefferson's 1800 presidential victory over John Adams, who had recognized the danger of what the Hamiltonians were up to and had negotiated an end to the war as soon as he could, too late to save his re-election (Kohn 1975, 248–249, 270–271; Kurtz 1957, 336–345, 352–365, 376, 378–379, 389–402).

The latter events confirmed among Jefferson's Republicans their already strong commitment to the Whig anti-military tradition. Jefferson initially secured reduction of the Regular Army and elimination of the wartime federal volunteers, indicating his conviction that the military reliance of the nation ought to be upon the citizens' militia. On the other hand, during Jefferson's administration and that of his chosen successor, James Madison, America's entanglement in the rival British and French commercial regulations of the Napoleonic Wars increased, culminating in the new war against Great Britain in 1812–15. Against the resulting foreign threats, both Jefferson and Madison acquiesced in the most practical means of military defense: they sponsored re-enlargement of the Regular Army and the Navy. Jefferson also somewhat surprisingly fostered the founding of the United States Military Academy at West Point in 1802, motivated probably by a combination of recognition of the nation-building potential of officers educated in engineering and mapping, the prospect that educated officers could in time be dispersed throughout the militia, and the desirability of diluting the Federalist partisanship he found among most officers when he took office (Cress 1982, 150–171, 212–215; Crackel 1987; Ambrose 1966, 22).

In the military policies of Jefferson and Madison lay a key to understanding the beginnings of civil-military relations in the United States. Ideologically, they and their Republican Party were committed to the English Whig legacy of distrust of the military and particularly of opposition to standing armies. Ideology nevertheless did not prevent them from turning to regular military forces when required for national defense. Their stance reflected that of the nation at large, except for certain conservative Federalists. In ideology, the American people remained suspicious of permanent military forces as inherent threats to liberty. Antimilitary rhetoric reflecting that ideology remained a staple of American political discourse through the Jacksonian era and beyond. In terms of practical policy, nevertheless, the electorate and the government were ready to support a small regular army and a navy strong enough to meet the peacetime requirements of national security but to rely on reinforced regulars, including federalized military—in short, citizen-soldiers—for wartime forces. The result was the remarkably strong military provisions of the Constitution of the United States.

Professional Officership and Civilian Control

Fear of military power based on the inheritance of Whig ideology nourished a deep American commitment to the principle of civilian control. While the Constitution created the possibility of strong military forces, at the core of its military clauses lay an emphasis on civilian control, shared among Congress, the president, and the states. If anti-military ideology must sometimes be sacrificed to the expediencies of national security, civilian control offers a means for at least partially reconciling the disjuncture. Civilian control of the military is an American constitutional imperative.

The problem of maintaining civilian control has changed greatly, however, since the founding of the Republic. Only gradually, from the American Revolution to the Civil War, did an American profession of military officership evolve to articulate military interests and values distinct from those of American civilians. The rise of professional military officership in the United States before the Civil War should not be minimized. In educational qualifications expected for the advancement of Army officers, in Army officers' self-consciousness as a corporate body, and in their corporate sense of responsibility to serve the entire society, American Army officers' professionalism may well have been exceeded only by the Prussian officer corps. The American Navy lagged only slightly behind the Army.

Nevertheless, no graduate of the United States Military Academy became Commanding General of the Army until Major-General George B. McClellan on November 1, 1861, during the Civil War.[5] In the meantime, the soldiers who reached the summit of the Army were not so distinctively military professionals that the entry of several of them into partisan politics posed serious issues of military subordination to civil authority: they were still essentially civilians in uniform.

Andrew Jackson was a political leader before he became a major-general and was of course soon to be a political leader again. When his military activities in Spanish Florida exceeded the instructions of Secretary of War John C. Calhoun, he was acting less in any distinctively military interest than on behalf of his political convictions about American

---

5. Skelton (1992) argues persuasively that an American professional officer corps was established well before the Civil War, contrary to the argument of Samuel P. Huntington (1957) that before the Civil War American officers were at best technologists, not professionals; but see Huntington, pp. 11–18, 469–470 for the educational, corporate, and responsibility qualifications defining a profession. See also McKee (1991) and, despite Karsten's somewhat jaundiced view of naval officers, Karsten (1972), as well as Heitman (1903).

expansionism at a time when the line between his political and military capacities was not as well defined as it would have been by the era of the Civil War. He also had the support of Secretary of State John Quincy Adams when chains of command were not as well defined as today (Remini 1977, 240–243, 351–392, 415–416, 418–419; 1981; 1984; Bemis 1950, 326).

Major-General Zachary Taylor began his pursuit of the presidency in 1848 while still in uniform, but he represented Whig Party political expediency—the appeal of a general for the voters—more than any military interest, for he had no strong views on policy, either political or military. Major-General Winfield Scott (from March 29, 1847, Brevet Lieutenant-General) was sufficiently self-educated in military literature to be the closest approximation of a professional officer to have headed the Army to that time. While General-in-Chief (1841–61), he also was the unsuccessful Whig presidential candidate in 1852 (Hamilton 1941; 1951; Eisenhower 1997; Elliott 1937; Heitman 1903, 870). In pre–Civil War America, the military was not separated clearly enough from civil life for such dual military-civil careers to cause most Americans much concern, notwithstanding the persistence of the English Whig antimilitary tradition.

It was only with the rise of West Point military professionals to the command of the Army that professional military interests, attitudes, and values became both well enough defined and influential enough within the military to create the beginnings of the modern issue of civilian control, which entails assuring that the military will not be able to use its bureaucratic influence and its claim to special expertise to bend larger national policy to the service of military institutional desires. The founders had feared a more blatant, less subtle kind of threat, a military *coup d'etat* somewhat on the model of Cromwell's seizure of authority, as some feared the Newburgh Conspiracy had intended. The founders had feared, too, that an ambitious chief executive might employ the military as his instrument to establish an autocracy, as James II was suspected of intending before the Glorious Revolution, or George III in establishing a permanent garrison in North America. By the Civil War, however, the United States military had become too long conditioned to a habit of obedience and to loyalty to the Constitution, whatever the occasional political adventures of certain officers, for a military *coup d'etat* of any sort to be at all likely. Henceforth, with the swelling of the armed forces to wage the Civil War, and again with their further expansion in the World Wars and the Cold War, the danger to civil control was not of anything so unsubtle as a coup, but rather that of a disproportionate military influence on policymaking, conditioned by an increasingly distinct (because professional) military interest.

On the whole, the conduct of professional officers in the highest positions of military authority was from the beginning also a testimony to the long conditioning in obedience to civil authority and in fidelity to the Constitution that had occurred between 1789 and 1861. General McClellan, General-in-Chief from November 1, 1861, to March 11, 1862, while also commanding general of the principal field army of the United States (usually styled the Army of the Potomac) from July 25, 1861, to November 9, 1862, set a pattern for subordination of the West Point–educated military professional to the civil authority (Heitman 1903, 656; Boatner 1991, 664). Privately McClellan did grumble about both the politics of the Lincoln administration and its conduct of the Civil War, especially in letters to his wife and even to opposition Democratic Party leaders with whom he consorted. He believed the Republican administration denied him some of the appropriate means to conduct the war, and he despised the drift of Lincoln's policy toward emancipation. His discussions with and advice to President Lincoln often blurred policy with military strategy. Nevertheless, McClellan's professional conduct was properly subordinate. While he loathed the official declaration of anti-slavery policy in the Preliminary Emancipation Proclamation of September 22, 1862, he did nothing to resist it. His 1864 run for the presidency occurred after he was no longer on active duty (Sears 1989; McClellan 1989). The precedents set by McClellan persisted deep into the twentieth century and past the World Wars in a remarkably consistent military adherence to civilian control. By World War II, exemplary military acceptance of civilian dominance in the making of military policy and even of strategy appeared to be a fixed star in the American constellation.

The external perils posed by the World Wars probably helped perpetuate this civil-military harmony.[6] With the nation manifestly in danger, the avoidance of discord held a high value. The Cold War following the World Wars similarly represented perils demanding civil-military harmony, if not quite so acutely as the hot wars had done. The first major public resistance to civilian policy and strategy in the history of American professional military command came in 1951 with the dispute between General of the Army Douglas MacArthur and President Harry S. Truman over the conduct of the Korean War. Still, as long as the Cold War lasted, and even though the Vietnam War imposed strains on military acceptance of civilian decisions in policy and strategy that were unprecedented in their severity, there was no repetition of the Truman-MacArthur crisis.

---

6.   Michael C. Desch (1998) suggests, among other complex conclusions, that a high external threat environment tends to enhance civilian control. See also the further development of his thesis in Desch's 1999 book, *Civilian Control of the Military.*

Only when the Cold War ended and the external imperative for civil-military concord lost much of its urgency did any public military challenges to civilian supremacy occur again. Even so, there has been nothing so dramatic as the MacArthur affair. However, there have been enough tensions and open debate between civil and military leadership to warrant a fear that civil-military difficulties are at hand; these tensions might even justify the word crisis, perhaps to describe the immediate civil-military relations of the post–Cold War 1990s, or to warn against possible developments of the near future. This essay will return to the condition of civil-military relations in the 1990s. In the meantime, it is necessary to consider why, if the emergence of professional military leadership during the Civil War gave the United States a history of exemplary military acceptance of civilian control, such constitutional stability could give way to an apparent crisis in the final years of the twentieth century.

The Distrustful Military

The many decades of apparent civil-military harmony have a misleading quality. From 1861 through 1945 and beyond, Army and Navy leaders acted faithfully in accord with their constitutional duty to respect civilian control, especially when World Wars and threats of them made civil-military harmony seem essential. But adherence to a constitutional duty was never quite the same as mutual trust between soldiers and civilians in each other's good judgment. Instead, the legacy of the Whig anti-military tradition among American civilian leaders, and the military chieftains' awareness that they were viewed with a certain suspicion, combined with their consequent reciprocal suspicion, made for a continuing climate of distrust. Military leaders quietly obeyed civilian commands, but rarely did they and their civilian superiors feel sufficient confidence in each other's good will and each other's understanding of particularly military or particularly civilian problems to be able to discuss the reasons behind civilian command with complete candor. The anti-military attitudes of civilian Americans, and the military's resistance to them, meant that apparent civil-military accord rested on a precarious foundation of incomplete understanding and even of distrust.

Faithful military acceptance of civilian control is a major desideratum of the U.S. constitutional system. Better yet, however, is faithful obedience based on candid civil-military discussions and on mutual understanding and trust. That kind of civil-military relations has much less frequently been achieved in the United States. Without it, the potential has always existed for a breakdown of the salutary pattern that our civil-military relations displayed through the World Wars and much of the

Cold War, especially once an external threat no longer produced acute pressures for civil-military unity.

Civil-military distrust was present despite the appearance of harmony from the beginning of professional military command. Various particular issues occasioned various, albeit subdued, displays of it, with the anti-military legacy from England always in the background. General McClellan would not discuss military issues candidly with the president, in part because he did not trust Lincoln to keep secrets. Worse than that, when Lincoln refused to accept McClellan's strategic and operational projects without demur, and particularly when the administration refused to send all the reinforcements McClellan thought he needed for his Peninsula Campaign in the spring of 1862, the general's distrust of his civilian superiors reached the extreme of a belief that they deliberately sought his failure.

After McClellan's removal as General-in-Chief on March 11, 1862, President Lincoln and Secretary of War Edwin M. Stanton attempted to fill that role themselves. They did not perform badly but, aware of their professional deficiencies and unable to give all their attention to military strategy and operations, they installed Major-General Henry Wager Halleck as General-in-Chief. Halleck lacked McClellan's irrational degree of suspiciousness, but his communication with Lincoln and Stanton was not ideal. Halleck was the country's pre-eminent military scholar and intellectual; not wearing his professional attainments lightly, he could not bring himself to be altogether forthright on military matters with his civilian superiors, whose professional ignorance would in his view have prevented their fully understanding anyway (Halleck 1846; 1862; Heitman 1903, 491; Williams 1950–1959, 187–213, 409–413; Hattaway and Jones 1983, 209–211, 237–242, 285–289, 291–295, 333–337).That shortcoming on Halleck's part, along with a paradoxical unwillingness to accept responsibility for military decisions, helped bring about the eventual importation of yet another leader from the West: Lieutenant-General Ulysses S. Grant rose from the Military Division of the Mississippi to become General-in-Chief in place of Halleck on March 9, 1864. Grant brought a more substantial record of strategic, operational, and tactical achievement in the field—as distinguished from military scholarship. Grant also brought a new attitude toward the civilian leadership, but unfortunately one that has proven almost unique to him. His achievements were grounded in sound practical sense combined with just enough professional knowledge derived from his West Point education and from experience. Unlike the book-nourished Halleck, Grant was utterly without pretensions, did not feel superior to President Lincoln, and brought to the office of General-in-Chief the friendly candor toward the commander-in-chief that embodies the ideal. With President Andrew Johnson, Grant's relations were not quite so representative of the ideal model, but that was for complex political rather than military reasons, and the fault lay mainly with Johnson (Heitman 1903, 470; Catton 1960; 1969; McFeely 1981, 238–242, 246–260, 266–271).

Even his closest wartime friend did not follow Grant's example. General William Tecumseh Sherman, General-in-Chief from March 8, 1869, to November 1, 1883, possessed a high-strung, irascible temperament and a certain contempt for politicians. His relationship with President Grant's Secretary of War, William W. Belknap, lacked candid communication; it fell apart altogether when Sherman betook himself and the headquarters of the Army to St. Louis in October 1874, to be as much as possible out of contact with Belknap. Not until March 1876 did Belknap's successor, Alphonso Taft, persuade Sherman to return to Washington. But Sherman could never bring himself to be more than remote and formal with the civilian leadership of the War Department (Heitman 1903, 882; Marszalek 1993, 385–388; Lewis 1932, 615, 622).

Sherman's problem with the Secretary of War was in part institutional, representing a special difficulty of civil-military relations until the early twentieth century. His absence from the War Department in Washington followed the example of Winfield Scott, who had his headquarters in New York City from just after the March 4, 1853, inauguration of his presidential election rival Franklin Pierce, until December 11, 1860, when the Civil War was about to erupt. Scott had done so partly to avoid Pierce, but more because of his distaste for Pierce's and James Buchanan's Secretaries of War, Jefferson Davis and John B. Floyd (Elliott 1937, 649, 649n, 679). Friction between personalities was aggravated by a flaw in the civilian-to-military chain of command: constitutional authority over the military presumably flowed from the civilian commander-in-chief—the president—through his civilian deputy for military affairs—the Secretary of War—to the Army. The General-in-Chief, or Commanding General, nevertheless tended to perceive his office as literally fulfilling the second of those titles, leaving little room for command by the civilian Secretary of War. In practice, consequently, the Secretary of War commanded the administrative and logistical staff bureaus of the War Department, while the General-in-Chief commanded the Army. The units in the field, however, could not function without the administrative and logistical support of the War Department bureaucracy, while the activities of the War Department had little purpose apart from the troops in the field. Moreover, if the General-in-Chief in fact commanded the Army, to the point that twice while occupying the office he virtually removed himself from contact with the president's civilian deputy, there was little left of civilian control. (Huntington 1957, 208–211; Millett and Maslowski 1994, 127, 327)

Early in the twentieth century, Secretary of War Elihu Root went far toward correcting this problem by sponsoring the General Staff Act of February 14, 1903. This statute abolished the position of General-in-Chief or Commanding General and gave to the professional head of the Army instead the post of Chief of Staff. The Chief of Staff directed the newly created War Department General Staff, a collective brain for the Army that was eventually to distinguish itself especially for its work in contingency war planning. In addition, the Chief of Staff of the Army became principal military advisor to the Secretary of War, so that the chain of command henceforth ran from the civilian commander-in-chief through his civilian secretary, the latter advised by the professional Chief of Staff. Abolishing the title of Commanding General undermined the pretensions of the professional head of the Army to an unconstitutional level of command (Hammond 1961, 10–24; Huntington 1957, 251–254; Bernardo and Bacon 1957, 290–296). Ideally, the Secretary of War and the Chief of Staff would enter into a symbiotic relationship of intimate contact and mutual trust, such as that of Secretary of War Henry L. Stimson and General George C. Marshall, men of similar character and values, during World War II. But even the relationship between Stimson and Marshall, probably closest to Root's vision, was not altogether harmonious. The movement toward some form of inter-service unity particularly threatened it, because Stimson felt obliged to forward the process, while Marshall, though certainly not opposed, was under pressure from his service to guard its particular interests (Pogue 1963–1987).

The Navy never established a Chief of Staff. Until March 3, 1915, the Secretary of the Navy supervised his service through its administrative bureaus, a system that awarded disproportionate weight to logistical and administrative functions at the expense of the combat fleet and its operations. Thereafter, establishment of a professional Chief of Naval Operations somewhat redressed the balance, but in the process the emphasis on professional command of operations tended to create implicitly the same sort of strain between civilian and professional control that had existed in the War Department and the Army until 1903 (Hammond 1961, 49–61; Huntington 1957, 247–257; Hagan 1991, 250).

As for the Army, Elihu Root's structural reform, constructive as it was, could not remedy all the difficulties of civil-military relations. Indeed, in another way one of Secretary Root's contributions aggravated the problems: he sponsored the publication of *The Military Policy of the United States* by Colonel, Fourth Artillery, and Brevet Major-General

Emory Upton in 1904. He did so presumably because the book was the first systematic military history of the United States, and also perhaps because it called in a provocative way for reassessment of almost every aspect of American military policy. Root had been appointed Secretary of War on August 1, 1899, after the Army's less than effective prosecution of the War with Spain of 1898, and had aimed to reform the Army so that it might better contribute to the new role of the United States as a world power. Demonstrating that the methods and institutions of the past were inadequate might well contribute to that goal. By disseminating Upton's ideas, however, Root was poisoning the well of civil-military relations, worsening the professional soldiers' distrust of civilian leadership, and thus assuring increased difficulty in candid communication from the civilian side as well. Upton opposed a reliance on citizen soldiers, urging the military to battle against every aspect of the American system of civilian control, and ultimately to reject democracy itself (Upton 1904; Heitman 1903, 16–17; Ganoe 1964, 531–532).

Upton, a West Pointer with an outstanding Civil War record, had tried during and after the war to reform tactics in order to cope with the devastating fire power of rifled weapons. He came to the attention of General-in-Chief Sherman (whose patronage of Upton is more evidence of his own dubious record in matters of civil-military harmony). Sherman arranged for Upton to visit armies around the globe in search of ways to improve the U.S. Army. From the tour came Upton's first book, *The Armies of Asia and Europe*, which described foreign military systems and also began Upton's published attacks on the American pattern of civil control. Upton observed the German Army when it was fresh from its rapid victories in the Wars of National Unification against Denmark in 1864, Austria-Hungary in 1866, and France in 1870–71. In contrast, as Upton saw it, the Union war effort against the Confederacy had been unduly prolonged, bumbling, and shamefully wasteful of lives and resources. Thus, he argued, the United States had much to learn from Germany in military affairs: emulating its practices held the key to American military improvement (Upton 1878, 317–323; Heitman 1903, 978–979; Ambrose 1964, 75–77, 87; Marszalek 1993, 442).

In his second book, Upton concluded that the real roots of Prussian-German military superiority over the United States lay not in issues of military organizational detail but rather in the American system of civilian control. In the German Empire, Upton argued, all essential military decisions were left to the professionals. Although the Reichstag and Bundestag had enough financial authority that they could delay military appropriations, they were not likely to do so, and they and other civilian authorities did not tamper with military details.

In the United States, in contrast, militarily ignorant presidents and Congresses injected themselves into every aspect of military decision-making, causing excessive loss of life and treasure and undue prolongation even of wars that were won. The root of excessive civilian control lay, said Upton, in democratic politics. The implication was that the United States could never compete militarily with such a power as Prussia-Germany unless it abandoned its system of civilian control, left decision-making to the military professionals (discarding the citizens' militia to transfer military power altogether to the professionals of the regular forces), and rejected democracy in favor of German-style autocracy in military decisions (Upton 1878, 317–323; Upton 1904, xii, 97–135, 256–261, 287–293). Naturally, Upton met only frustration when he prescribed such nostrums in the United States. The isolated, militarily secure nation of the 1870s rejected even his minor prescription for the three-battalion regiment. With his second book unfinished, and in ill health, Upton resigned his commission and, on March 15, 1881, shot himself in the head (Ambrose 1964, 148; Heitman 1903, 979). His service friend and executor, Captain, Fifth Artillery, and Brevet Lieutenant-Colonel Henry A. du Pont, saw to the circulation of Upton's unfinished manuscript, which carried the history of the Army to 1862. Almost all well-informed Army officers were aware of its arguments by the turn of the century. In the neglected Regular Army of the last years of the Indian Wars, with the duties of a frontier constabulary dying and after 1890 virtually dead, and with the Army having no clear mission for most of the rest of the decade, Upton's thinking found a responsive audience, and by the late 1890s had saturated the Army's professional opinion. The Navy, similarly neglected until the 1880s, had an officer corps similarly receptive to the conviction that the American civilian superiors of the military could never properly comprehend military problems. Emory Upton's influence confirmed the distrust of civilian government that already underlay the country's civil-military relations. When Elihu Root granted a kind of imprimatur by publishing Upton's *Military Policy of the United States*, this completed the entrenching of Upton's views (Ambrose 1964, 141–159, 174–175; Heitman 1903, 390; Lane 1978, 150–152, 173–174, 228; Michie 1885; Fitzpatrick 1997).

The Spanish-American-Cuban War of 1898 restored to the Army a sense of mission as an instrument of world power, and confirmed that mission for the Navy, whose preparation for its new destiny had begun a decade before. Yet for the Army particularly, the new role could not override Uptonian attitudes. The Army believed it was thrown into Cuba in 1898 with inadequate preparation and equipment, and then punished with excessively critical public appraisals of its campaign there. The Filipino Insurrection reinforced these reactions, especially as anti-imperialists seized upon excesses of repression against the insurgents.

In the early phases of the history of America as a world power, the relationship between the military and the civilian leadership remained well short of mutual understanding and trust. On the eve of World War I, the persistence of Emory Upton's influence surfaced in the efforts of the Army to exploit the preparedness movement in order to substitute for the successors to the state militias, the National Guard, a first line reserve much more directly under the control of the federal government and the Regular Army. The professionals persuaded President Woodrow Wilson's first Secretary of War, Lindley M. Garrison, to accept the essentials of their plan in his Continental Army proposal, which predictably failed to win acceptance in Congress (Mahon 1983, 147; Derthick 1965, 33–44). Harmony at the top continued to be personality-driven. General-in-Chief (1888–95) John M. Schofield anticipated Elihu Root's solution to the rivalry between the Commanding General and the Secretary of War by acting as de-facto chief of staff (Heitman 1903, 865; Millett and Maslowski 1994, 279–280). But his successor, Nelson A. Miles, strenuously resisted Secretary Root's efforts toward permanent reform of the command system, and when Miles stepped down as General-in-Chief on August 8, 1903, the office became extinct (Millett and Maslowski 1994, 280; Hammond 1961, 11; Heitman 1903, 708–709). The early Chiefs of Staff were distracted from any departure from acquiescence in civil authority that they might otherwise have essayed by the burdens of winning acceptance within the Army for their own authority and that of the War Department General Staff against a rearguard action by the administrative and logistical bureaus to retain their autonomy from the leadership of the field Army. The most dynamic of the early Chiefs, Major General Leonard Wood (1910–14), found his tenure almost consumed by Adjutant General Fred C. Ainsworth's effort to keep day-to-day control of the Army away from the Chief of Staff. Though Wood had the backing of Secretary of War Henry L. Stimson, a Root protégé, and to some degree of President William Howard Taft, the ascendancy of the Chief of Staff was not yet fully assured when the United States entered World War II (Lane 1978, 156–167, 294–295; Deutrich 1962, 105–122, 151–154).

The World Wars

World War I further complicated the Root-Stimson institutional reform of civil-military relations by creating another rival to the Chief of Staff within the Army. The Wilson administration granted so much autonomy to the commanding general of the American Expeditionary Forces (AEF) that the occupant of that lofty position, General John J. Pershing, was able to treat the Chief of Staff was little more than his representative in Washington. General Peyton C. March, Chief of Staff during the latter part of the war, had the backbone to stand up to Pershing, no small accomplishment and the source of a famous resentment between them. But Pershing commanded the AEF with so much autonomy that the civilian and military leaders of the Associated Powers had to deal with him almost as if he constituted a sovereign power in his own right. At the bottom of this situation lay President Wilson's acute distaste for all things military. Not far from being a pacifist and a Jeffersonian Democrat as well, who inherited many of the third president's prejudices on matters of the military and war, Wilson experienced severe qualms of conscience over feeling obliged to lead the country into war. His sense of guilt evidently could be assuaged only by transforming the struggle into one to end all wars and to safeguard democracy everywhere. Meanwhile Wilson also placated his uneasiness by having as little as possible to do with the military conduct of the war. His near abdication of his role as commander-in-chief could only weaken the principle of civilian control. Fortunately for the principle, its active exercise in the manner of Abraham Lincoln was to be reasserted by the next wartime commander-in-chief, Franklin D. Roosevelt (Trask 1993, 11–13; Smythe 1986, 6–7, 9–10; Coffman 1966; Ganoe 1964, 533; Link and Chambers 1991, 317–375).

Thus it was fortunate also that Wilson had chosen Pershing to head the AEF, largely because of his admirable record of accepting subordination to the civil power when he was a brigadier and then major general commanding the Punitive Expedition of 1916–17 into Mexico. During this enterprise, diplomatic constraints prevented Pershing from fulfilling what appeared to the public to be the purpose of the expedition, the capture of General Francisco "Pancho" Villa after the latter's incursion across the international border to Columbus, New Mexico on March 8, 1916. Pershing therefore tended to look like a failure through no fault of his own, but he uttered no word of public complaint, and he generally maintained this attitude toward the civilian leadership throughout his command in Europe (Smythe 1973, 217, 220–282, 320–329; Vandiver 1977, 604, 606–668, 790; Smythe 1986, 56).

This did not mean, however, that Pershing trusted the judgments of the president. The record of American command in World War I continued to be one of exemplary military acceptance of civil control, but its subtext was an absence of understanding and communication, aggravated by Wilson's anti-military phobia. Even the well-disciplined Pershing nearly kicked over the traces of military subordination near the end of the war. With Wilson leading the Entente Powers in the process of negotiating an armistice, Pershing declared to the Allied Supreme War Council that he favored no prompt cessation of hostilities but rather a continuation of them so that the Allied and Associated Armies could march deep into Germany, arguing that otherwise Germany would be insufficiently convinced that it had lost the war and would have to be fought again. Wilson cared deeply, however, about an early restoration of peace, and Pershing was thus guilty of trying actively to undermine national policy, to the point that Secretary of War Newton D. Baker considered his removal. Only the intervention of the avuncular and tactful American military representative to the Allied Supreme War Council, General (Retired) Tasker H. Bliss, smoothed the ruffled feathers on all sides and dispelled the controversy (Trask 1993, 156–158; Smythe 1986, 219–222).

After that, civil-military relations in the interwar years reverted to a condition of truce. Pershing returned to America to become General of the Armies, then Chief of Staff (July 1, 1921–September 13, 1924), the latter appointment naturally terminating his quarrel with the pretensions of that office. His prestige in fact carried over to invest the office with a higher stature than ever before; the Chief of Staff was at last indisputably the principal professional of the Army. Pershing's end-of-war dispute with President Wilson and Secretary Baker had no visible detrimental consequences. In the reorganization of the Army to adjust to the experiences of the war, Pershing actually adopted the anti-Uptonian policies of Colonel John McAuley Palmer, which (over the opposition of General March, while the latter was still Chief of Staff) called not for an Uptonian cadre conscript system but for a Regular Army, intended as a ready source of expeditionary forces for late-colonial interventions and as a training center. The bulk of any wartime army was to come from citizen-soldiers, as much as possible with their own officers. Palmer pondered how to create the most suitable army for a democracy, repudiating Upton's belief that, in military matters, democracy and civilian control ought to yield to military expediency. Victory over the German Army, against which Upton had suggested the American Army could never compete, surely nurtured a self-confidence that helped explain Pershing's support for Palmer. Their views prevailed in the National Defense Act of June 4, 1920 (Smythe 1986, 59–260; Vandiver 1977, 1035, 1038–1039; Holley 1982, 413–477, 736–748; Bernardo and Bacon 1957, 94–101, 469–470).

On the other hand, a militarily parsimonious Congress refused to vote enough funds to maintain the 280,000-strong Regular Army envisaged by the National Defense Act. With Army strength hovering around 125,000 officers and troops through the 1920s and 1930s, Palmer's idea of expeditionary forces ready for deployment gave way mainly to skeletal formations, and the same political parsimony restored a mood of Uptonian discontent with, and distrust of, the civil authorities. The naval limitations of the Washington Naval Treaty of February 6, 1922, made for a similar mood in the Navy, even though that service fared much better than the Army through the frugal interwar years (with, after 1926, the possible exception of the new Army Air Corps) (Bernardo and Bacon 1957, 385, 387; Baer 1994, 94–101, 469–470).

One perplexing strategic problem of the interwar years illustrates the prevailing combination of outward military acquiescence in civilian control and the actual failure of the two sides to communicate with candor: defending the Philippine Islands. Each new refinement of the principal strategic contingency plan for war with Japan, Joint War Plan Orange and its various subsidiary plans, made it plainer to American strategists that in the increasingly likely prospect of war, Japan would conquer the Philippines quickly. Congress simply would not provide the necessary funding to make the defense of the distant archipelago feasible. Therefore, Army planners considered seriously the advisability of abandoning any pretense of being able to hold the Philippines and of retreating to plans for the defense of the Alaska-Hawaii-Panama triangle, a much more realistic endeavor. Yet the military never felt confident enough of its capacity for forthright communication with the civilian government to present such a choice. Instead, military leaders felt obliged to fudge the issue of the indefensibility of the Philippines, prescribing instead in the Orange Plans a retreat of the defenders to the Bataan Peninsula of Luzon and the island of Corregidor in Manila Bay. There, supposedly, resistance to the Japanese would continue, denying the enemy the use of Manila Bay, until the Navy could fight its way westward across the Pacific from Pearl Harbor to the rescue. Almost nobody—the conspicuous exception came to be Field Marshal Douglas MacArthur of the Commonwealth of the Philippines Army—thought that any such scenario was realistic: almost everyone recognized that Bataan and Corregidor would fall before any relief from the Navy became possible.

Yet this point was not frankly discussed with the president. Even as late as December 7, 1941, General George C. Marshall—though he is rightly regarded as a model practitioner of sound civil-military relations—did not inform President Roosevelt fully that, notwithstanding that policymaking toward Japan was a presidential prerogative, the Chief Executive should realize that the consequences of inviting war meant Japanese conquest of the Philippines and the captivity of the American garrison. Such silent acquiescence in civilian policy might be interpreted as the true constitutional duty of General Marshall, but it is true also that in the final few months before Pearl Harbor, Marshall was somewhat persuaded by MacArthur, returned to the U.S. Army as a lieutenant general, that the Philippines could be defended after all. Even at that, the absence of full communication remains an example of the penalties imposed by incomplete trust.[7]

However, once the United States entered World War II, the constitutional system of civilian control functioned as well as it ever has in the history of the Republic. It seems probable that the pressure created by the war for all the country's leaders to work in harness helped bring about this result. But whatever the reasons, wartime civil-military relations were indeed a model of quiet, uncomplaining military acceptance of civilian supremacy. It was not that there were no disagreements: General Marshall in particular opposed President Roosevelt's long postponement, for two and a half years after American entry into the war, of the Army's principal strategic endeavor, the cross-Channel invasion of northwest Europe. All of the Joint Chiefs of Staff disliked the divided command in the Pacific, with the Pacific Ocean Areas under Admiral Chester W. Nimitz and the Southwest Pacific Area under General MacArthur. While this was largely the product of inter-service rivalry, neither service enjoyed violating the principle of unity of command. Still, any suffering went unspoken: there was no public military disagreement with the civilian leadership during the course of World War II.

The Cold War, the Problems of Today, and the Future

Harmonious conditions changed almost immediately once wartime pressures for harmony were removed, and the five years between World War II and the Korean War witnessed contentious and open inter-service squabbling over unification, missions (particularly the delivery of atomic weapons), and allocation of limited budgets. These soon appeared as mild disturbances, however, compared to the spectacular Truman-MacArthur controversy. All such contention was doubly disturbing after the tranquility of 1941–45, but it uncovered the lack of trust and candor

---

7.   These judgments regarding motives in the matter of the defense of the Philippines are those of the author. For the issues, see (Morton 1962, 34–44, 97–101); (Watson 1950, 412–452); (Morton 1953, 11–13, 48, 50). Presenting more problems for civilian control than Marshall was Admiral Ernest J. King (Fleet Admiral from December 17, 1944), Chief of Naval Operations and Commander-in-Chief of the United States Fleet. King was a difficult subordinate, impatient with democracy and civilian control, continually straining at the leash that the principle imposed, but he created no public crisis (Hoopes and Brinkley 1993, 169–184; Larrabee 1987, 194–199, 631; Who's Who 1975, 307).

that had always lain beneath the surface of American civil-military relations.

The Korean War enhanced the intensity of the Cold War, which probably accounts for the essential concealment of disharmonies again after 1951 under a renewed need for unity in the common interest. By the late 1960s and early 1970s, however, the discontents of the Vietnam War and its aftermath again brought tensions and distrust dangerously close to the surface, notwithstanding Cold War motives for unity. Then the close of the Cold War released them with remarkable rapidity to shape current civil-military friction.

As tensions and distrust emerged, at their heart have lain the very issues of differing values and limited communication that have always been the legacy of the Whig antimilitary tradition, and of Uptonian contempt on the part of the military for civilians' judgments on military affairs. During the Vietnam War, the American military grew increasingly convinced that it was trapped in an unwinnable military predicament by the civilian leadership's inability to comprehend the requirements of military victory. In part this military perception took root in the unwillingness of Presidents John F. Kennedy and Lyndon B. Johnson to make available the overwhelming resources and force needed for the near-absolute kind of triumph associated with the enemy's unconditional surrender that the armed forces of the United States had enjoyed in the Civil War and World War II. After Vietnam more than before, overwhelming force became for the American military a *sine qua non* for their support of military action. From the perception that uncomprehending civilians denied it adequate means for victory in Vietnam, the military progressed to the conception that the civilian leadership had never properly defined the objective of intervention in Vietnam, and that henceforth a precise definition of objectives must precede American military action.

It is understandable that the American military should have emerged from the Vietnam War determined not to allow itself to be entangled in a similar predicament again: that never again should the armed forces be mired in war without reasonable assurance of a satisfactory outcome; never again should the armed forces be thrust into a war in which they are denied the means to such an outcome, yet for whose loss the American public may blame them; never again should American soldiers, sailors, marines, and airmen fight a war without overwhelming public support, nor should they return home from war to jeers and contempt instead of welcoming parades.

As understandable as the Vietnam syndrome may be, the military's diagnosis of what went wrong has flaws, and has imposed new, unnecessary strains on civil-military relations. These strains are all the worse where they are based upon a misreading of history: these are among the most difficult to refute, because they are based not on facts but on faith and misperception to begin with.

The charge that Vietnam was lost because of failure to apply overwhelming force evades the question of whom the force was to be applied against: against the North, the Democratic Republic of Vietnam? Presumably the United States had the power to conquer North Vietnam if the full strength of America had been employed against it, but what then? Surely the American conquerors would then have confronted hostile insurgency in both North and South, and sooner or later the Americans would have had to depart. The charge that Vietnam was lost because of the lack of a clear objective does not fit reality either. The American objective in Vietnam was clear enough and specifically stated, in National Security Action Memorandum (NSAM) 288 of March 17, 1964: maintaining an independent, non-Communist South Vietnam (Herring 1986, 116–117). The trouble was not in lack of clarity but in the impossibility of achieving the objective by military means, given the weak indigenous foundation of the South, the Republic of Vietnam.

Nevertheless, overwhelming force and clear definition of objectives henceforth became obsessions. The Reagan administration's intervention in Lebanon in 1982–84 allegedly failed because of the absence of both desiderata. But in fact the objective was again clear enough, if only the political possibility of achieving it had existed: an independent Lebanon free of foreign interference and occupation. Because the circumstances of Lebanon did not, however, lend themselves to deploying the measure of overwhelming force that the American military preferred—especially because to do so would have undermined the objective—the military commanders themselves diluted the intervention in ways that assured its failure would be worse than it would have had to be, culminating in outright disaster.

In the summer of 1982, the Department of State and the National Security Council sought to interpose a sixty-day deployment of Marines between the Israeli Defense Force (IDF) on the one hand and, on the other, the forces of the Palestine Liberation Organization (PLO), Syria, and their Lebanese allies. The purpose was to bring about withdrawal of all the foreign occupiers, particularly the IDF and the PLO, and to strengthen the Lebanese Armed Forces. Under the pleas of the military chieftains, Secretary of Defense Caspar Weinberger secured a reduction to a thirty-day commitment and limited Marine occupation to a narrow area of the port of Beirut, which was not in any sense a real interposition. The total intervention force consisted of 800 Marines in the 32nd Marine Amphibious Unit who landed on August 25, plus 800 French and 400 Italian troops.

With the Marines armed only with personal weapons and light crew-served machine guns, the American military leaders were naturally nervous, and when all PLO and Syrian forces were reportedly evacuated, they persuaded Weinberger to insist on their own immediate evacuation, which was promptly ordered September 3.

This half-hearted intervention and precipitate departure, unsurprisingly, encouraged further disorders; the PLO was especially indignant because the United States had promised a full thirty-day American presence and a full Israeli withdrawal that did not occur. A reversion to civil war among rival Lebanese factions brought the Marines back on September 29. Again the American military leadership insisted on constricting their location, this time to the Beirut International Airport and its vicinity, although they eventually extended patrols into primarily Christian East Beirut. But the Marines insisted that their function was to maintain an admonitory presence and that such a role precluded any extensive fortifying of their positions. This approach did little to deter terrorists, who parked a van containing a 2,000-pound gas-enhanced bomb outside the U.S. Embassy and exploded it on April 18, 1983, killing sixty-three occupants of the building, including seventeen Americans. Yet further deterioration of law and order in October provoked the Marines to more aggressive patrolling against snipers, but even then defense fortification was largely ignored, as were intelligence warnings. On October 23, another bomb went off at Marine headquarters at the airport, killing 241, 239 of them Americans, and 220 of the total Marine force of 800. The second bombing virtually ended all sense of U.S. purpose in Lebanon, and the Marines were withdrawn by the end of February 1984. This second intervention, also half-hearted, with the American military refusing to do what was necessary even to protect its own troops, thus set up a self-fulfilling prophecy that without massive, overwhelming military intervention nothing useful could be accomplished (Hoffman 1996, 39–60; Millett and Maslowski 1994, 620; Tanter 1990).

The point of this episode for the history of the civil-military cultural gap is that, with the imperatives of Cold War national unity already moderating in the early 1980s, the Joint Chiefs of Staff resisted the efforts of civilian authority, even of the friendly Reagan administration, to breathe life into its policy of creating an independent Lebanon because the military would not take even a slight risk of "another Vietnam" under an administration more than willing to grant every assurance against that outcome.

Because the Panama intervention of December 20–29, 1989, Operation Just Cause, the Persian Gulf War of August 2, 1990–February 28,

1991, Operation Desert Shield, and Operation Desert Storm produced apparent military victories, the conventional military wisdom about them is that they met the criteria of overwhelming force and clear objectives. For the first criterion, this judgment is essentially correct. The second judgment, however, comes out of circular reasoning, that because there was apparent success the objectives must have been clear; in fact, the objectives were not well defined, and the successes were short-term rather than long-term.

The United States easily overwhelmed little Panama, and consequently the initial objective was relatively promptly achieved: the overthrow and capture of the dictator President Manuel Antonio Noriega Morena. The larger objective of establishing a democratic and friendly Panama was more subtle and less well thought out. While the course of Panamanian events since 1989 has not been unsatisfactory to the United States, the fact that Operation Just Cause installed a new government of Panama under blatantly Yankee auspices, in the presence of the U.S. military and the U.S. flag, hardly demonstrated desirable foundations for permanent Panamanian democracy (Hoffman 1996, 61–76; Donnelly, Roth and Baker 1991; Watson and Tsouras 1991).

Another reason that American military leaders found Operation Just Cause gratifying was that the administration of President George H.W. Bush allowed the military essentially a free hand. With the Gulf War, the hand was not quite so free, and in spite of the initially satisfying outcome, there were civil-military tensions unlike those of World War II. The situation at least hints at the notion that under the Vietnam paradigm, only if the military has virtually complete autonomy from civilian control in wartime will conflict be averted.

The Chairman of the Joint Chiefs during the Persian Gulf War, General Colin L. Powell, was a practiced Washington military politician of immense self-assurance in his dealings with civilian leaders. An articulate expounder of the Vietnam syndrome, extremely vigilant against subjecting the armed forces to an action they might be denied the means to win, General Powell would by 1992 codify his thinking in the Powell Doctrine, in which he added to the demand for overwhelming, decisive force the stipulations that force should be employed only with an important and clearly defined objective, when all nonviolent means have failed, when force is able to achieve the desired political objective, when the costs and risks are acceptable in proportion to expected gains—including assurance of sustained public support—and when the consequences of using force have been thought out. Powell's influence was the greater because beyond his personal characteristics, the Goldwater-Nichols Department of Defense Reorganization Act of September 20, 1986, had concentrated the influence and prestige of the Joint Chiefs of Staff in the Chairman (Powell 1992a, 32–34; Perry 1989, 338–340).

All these circumstances made General Powell a military spokesman restrained by little reluctance to challenge civilian leaders with whom he disagreed, but also that perhaps paradoxical figure, a soldier reluctant to employ military force. The assurances of rapid victory that he sought through quick deployment of overwhelming force, with a strategy so clear that it left no possibility of unforeseen consequences, and a guarantee of a prompt exit, were unfortunately almost never to be met amid the friction of the real world. When Iraq overran Kuwait on August 2, 1990, Powell apparently opposed President Bush's decision to intervene against that aggression. On this issue, nevertheless, Powell complied with constitutional principle and refrained from public dissent, as he did when he was similarly overruled in his opposition to following up aerial bombardment of the enemy with a ground war. At the point when the ground campaign quickly crushed Iraqi defenses, however, Powell successfully insisted that an immediate truce should end the fighting before any unforeseen developments might spoil the pleasing short-run outcome, even though he himself had earlier proposed to destroy the enemy's elite Republican Guard, and even though so prompt a truce had the effect of pre-empting presidential policy decisions about the future of Iraq that were still decidedly in flux.

Notwithstanding the military, and often the popular, belief that because the war ended in battlefield triumph its objectives must have been clear, in fact the policy objectives beyond freeing Kuwait were still being defined when Powell's urging, and the president's hasty acquiescence in it, cut the process short. The Bush administration and the Joint Chiefs both hesitated to invade Iraq further for fears of a Vietnam-style quagmire or aggravating Middle Eastern stability. But there were other options that might better have been pondered with a few days or even hours more time, such as the possibility of encouraging the Iraqi military to overthrow Saddam Hussein if dissidents' hands had been strengthened by eliminating the Republican Guard. Fear of another Vietnam, among military and civilians alike but especially among the military, prevented a successful military campaign from producing commensurate policy success (Hoffman 1996, 77–98; Gordon and Trainor 1995, 33–34, 36, 129–131, 396, 415, 422–423, 426; Freedman and Karsh 1992, 7, 403–405).[8]

Still, the rapid liberation of Kuwait made the Persian Gulf War so ap-

---

8. Hoffman's 1996 book constitutes an important critique of current national security policy and civil-military relations, and has much influenced this essay.

parently dramatic a victory, allegedly erasing the Vietnam syndrome, that General Powell emerged from it a national hero as the soldier who had presided over the triumph. He became more assertive than ever in arguing that military considerations must shape civilian policymaking. When the Bush administration began to agonize over military intervention in Bosnia and Herzegovina to halt the mass murders of Bosnian Muslims by the Yugoslav government's policy of ethnic cleansing, Powell again engaged in pre-emptive action, this time through public statements in *The New York Times* and *Foreign Affairs*, opposing intervention in Bosnia as unable to meet the criteria of overwhelming force and clear objectives, stated in the public announcement of his Powell Doctrine in the *Foreign Affairs* article. Thus, on allegedly technical military grounds Powell again interfered with the administration's policy deliberations (Powell 1992a, 32–42; 1992b; Gordon 1992).

Whether or not Powell had private assurances that President Bush and his administration did not object to these public pronouncements, and it is probable that he did, for a military officer on active duty to venture into public debate on foreign policy nevertheless —particularly in an election year—under the pretense that the issues were narrowly military constituted a serious breach of the constitutional principle of civilian control. The latter statement is a grave accusation of improper conduct by the country's ranking professional officer, and it is intended to be.

Powell's statements attempting to pre-empt the question of Bosnian intervention were not the end of the matter. President Bush enjoyed a considerable measure of respect from the military, both because he had a creditable combat record in World War II, and because the sponsorship of the Vietnam War by the Democratic administrations of Presidents Kennedy and Johnson, followed by largely Democratic opposition to the military's conduct of the war, had reinforced the already strong tendency of conservative military professionals to share President Bush's Republican Party political affiliation. When on January 20, 1993, the presidency was transferred to William Jefferson Clinton, the new commander-in-chief enjoyed as little favor from the military as any in American history.

Not only was Clinton a Democrat, but he was a Democrat of 1960s anti–Vietnam War vintage who had been a war protestor. He had never served in the military, and his record of avoiding military service could readily be construed by the hostile as draft-dodging. General Powell, with the enthusiastic support of almost all military commanders, undercut the new civilian chieftain's authority almost immediately. After preventing Clinton from lifting the ban on military service by open homosexuals, the Joint Chiefs under Powell's leadership agreed to what evolved during 1993 as Clinton's "don't ask, don't tell" policy of supposedly not seeking out offenders. The intent of the policy—to curb harassment—was sabotaged by the military so effectively that the practical effect became at least as persecutorial as anything before. Periodic efforts by civilian Department of Defense officials, especially Secretary William S. Cohen—long after the particular influence of General Powell had waned—to rein in restrictive zeal through educational programs and administrative review, collided with the reality that such palliatives "will not improve a policy that at its core tolerates and promotes bigotry" (editorial, *The New York Times* 1999). That statement captures succinctly the culture gap as it exists today, the legacy of a long history of differing values aggravated by the conditioning of the 1960s, which pushed civilian moral judgments in one direction and military judgments in another.

After the assertive General Powell stepped down as Chairman of the Joint Chiefs on September 30, 1993, relations between the military and the civilian leadership became less overtly confrontational. Nevertheless, long-standing sources of tension remained, and newer problems emerged. President Clinton's lack of military service represents an increasingly common phenomenon among civilian leaders, assured by the end of actively enforced selective service in the spring of 1973. As fewer members of the executive branch and Congress have had military experience, the opportunities for civil-military misunderstandings grow. We are returning to the uninformed civilian forays into military policy and strategy that Emory Upton and his followers so despised. The moral shambles of the Clinton administration further widened the gap between civilian and military perceptions, encouraging Americans in uniform to feel all the more ethically superior to civilians (notwithstanding a plenitude of sexual harassment problems in the military).

Most importantly, the Vietnam syndrome by no means died with the Persian Gulf War. The United States is the principal world power, bearing corresponding responsibilities for the maintenance of a humane world order; but the country is deeply reluctant to use military force as an instrument of its responsibility, particularly should using force endanger American lives. The Persian Gulf War actually reinforced at least one aspect of the Vietnam syndrome, because its nearly casualty-free ground campaign has dictated a policy that there shall be no employment of American military force to combat unless the situation assures similar freedom from casualties.[9]

---

9. The Army and Marine Corps suffered 122 battle deaths, thirty-five by friendly fire, and 131 noncombatant fatalities. The Air Force lost twenty dead in battle and six to other causes, including training. The Navy lost six dead in battle, eight to other

Under such circumstances, it is remarkable that American military interventions in Bosnia beginning April 10, 1994, and in the Yugoslav province of Kosovo beginning March 24, 1999, succeeded as well as they did. A fragile but real ethnic truce came to be imposed upon Bosnia by the United States, its North Atlantic Treaty Organization partners, and their Russian partners. Yugoslav removal of Kosovars from their home province was halted by June 11, 1999, and the province reopened to most of its inhabitants. In both places, however, the only American means of active combat was air power, which made the achievements precarious. Air power as the only American and NATO weapon for forcing the Yugoslav Serb ethnic cleansers out of Kosovo, used in such a way as to minimize casualties among the airmen (in the event, there were none), meant that there were bound to be numerous civilian casualties among all ethnic groups in the area, including the Kosovars who were ostensibly being protected. Moreover, air power became effective in Bosnia with the aid of Croatian ground forces; between them and their Serb opponents there was not much to choose from when it came to ruthless treatment of ethnic enemies. In Kosovo the triumph of air power came in conjunction with a ground offensive by the irregulars of the Kosovo Liberation Army (KLA) that made the Yugoslav Army more vulnerable to aerial attack, especially when the KLA functioned as forward observers to find targets for NATO aircraft.

Air power is not doomed to be ineffective, but neither does it offer assurance of effectiveness without accompanying action on the ground; thus the effectiveness of American military power surely demands a willingness to employ ground troops. This is all the more true because air power remains, even in an age of relatively precise missiles and bombs, a blunt instrument, not always well suited to the kind of small wars—low intensity conflicts, in the current military lexicon—in which the American armed forces are actually likely to be engaged in the post–Cold War era. The Powell Doctrine does not offer much guidance as to how to conduct such conflicts either; its main effect is to paralyze American power and policy by warning against all interventions. Thus we return to our original theme: the military leadership's insistence that it must employ overwhelming force, if force is to be used at all, tends toward becoming a prescription for no use of armed force whatever in a period of small wars

---

causes. Other Allied Coalition forces lost ninety-two dead in combat and 318 wounded. The total United States deployment to the Middle East was almost 500,000, with Allied forces numbering 254,000 (Millett and Maslowski 1994, 634; for the number of Americans deployed see p. 639).

and no superpower enemies. Because policy and diplomacy are bound sometimes to require force, here lies perhaps the most dangerous of all areas for civil-military tension, disagreement, and distrust.

Another prescription for no use of force is the post-Vietnam military insistence on clearly defined objectives before force is employed—on what has come to be called the end game or end strategy. This insistence is perhaps the most unrealistic of the mistaken conceptions to which the Vietnam syndrome has led. The consequences of armed force can never be certain, because the very injection of force into any political situation alters the initial equation and adds uncertainty and instability. Military force can never be the simple extension of policy, because its use always alters policy. If the American military leaders of 1775, 1861, 1917, or 1941 had insisted upon the kind of clear definition of objectives and consequences and the assurance of overwhelming military superiority that the military leaders of today have in mind, then there would have been no United States to begin with because there would have been no War of American Independence, no defeat of the Confederacy in the Civil War, no defeat of Germany in the World Wars. In every conflict, objectives were altered as the wars went on, and the consequences could not have been foreseen in the beginning. Insistence on foreseeing with clarity all the results of military action is another insistence on impossibility, paralyzing to effective civil-military relations.

Conclusion

Civilian suspicions of the military drawn ultimately from the English Whig tradition have undergone dilution and taken new forms, but have never altogether died in America. Neither have military suspicions of civilian understanding and intentions that were brought to a peak in the nineteenth century in the thought of Emory Upton and his disciples. Misunderstanding and distrust have underlain American civil-military relations from the beginning, and have been aggravated after the close of the Cold War. The great redemptive feature of this history has been the outward faithfulness of both sides, nonetheless, to the constitutional principle of civilian control. During the 1990s that principle has been subjected to greater strain than at any time in the past. Therefore the future of civil-military relations in the United States is uncertain.

Chapter 6

The Military's Presence in American Society, 1950–2000

James Burk

Supporting a large standing military force in peacetime is no longer a novel practice in American history. It has been done now for over fifty years, long enough to seem a hallowed tradition in many quarters and outlasting the forty-year Cold War security crisis that spawned it. Moreover, the military is a highly respected institution, as measured by public opinion polls, and has been for some time. Nevertheless, over the last decade, journalists, policymakers, and scholars have raised serious questions about the quality of the relationship between the military and American society. Their questions are not shallow-rooted in the flow of daily events, destined to dry up when a particular scandal is forgotten or one president succeeds another. They ask whether there is a fundamental difference between the military and civilian society, and reflect concern about the difficulty of establishing an effective working relationship between the two so both may flourish. This is not to say there is agreement about what makes the relationship a difficult one. Some are concerned that the civilian society has exercised too much influence over the military, and that influence is wearing away at the "warrior culture" that underpins military effectiveness (Moore 1998; Roberts 1998; Power 1996). Some are concerned that the military and civilian cultures are too little in touch with one another: that the values taught and supported by the military, are contrary to those taught and supported by civilian society (Ricks 1997c; Dionne 1998). Some worry that military leaders have become too

Thanks to Melissa Scheier for her help in collecting and analyzing the data and for her comments on an earlier version of the paper.

politicized, trying to exert influence over policy decisions that are right-fully reserved for civilian leaders to make (Kohn 1997; Dunlap 1994; Weigley 1993). That the range of concerns is so wide suggests that the un-derlying reality they seek to describe is more complex than any one of them allows.

My purpose in this chapter is to identify, describe, and explain this complexity from an institutional perspective. I assume that there is a gap—or, more simply, important differences—that separates the military from the larger society (Cohn 1999). But that fact in itself is not surpris-ing. Every social institution maintains a distinct culture, supporting val-ues that are to some degree different from those of the encompassing so-ciety. The military is no exception (Burk 1999b). The problem is to say how wide the gap is that separates the military and civilian realms, how it has changed over time and, most importantly, how it affects the quality of civil-military relations. Broad as it is, the task is limited. I do not here examine the values and attitudes held by individual members of society, military and civilian, or assess whether they are compatible or in conflict with one another. Nor do I examine directly how military and political elites work together to make policy. These are both important and rele-vant topics, but I leave them to others. My concern lies rather with the military as an institution; I seek to identify the kinds of connections it has forged with civilian society and to describe the ways these connections have changed since the Cold War ended in 1989.

My working hypothesis is simply stated. While the end of the Cold War diminished the military's presence in society, the military has not by any means become an isolated—and certainly not a peripheral or a pred-atory—institution, estranged from American society. On the contrary, it remains highly salient, as a central institution affecting our material well-being and active in contemporary projects to constitute what we think is a good and secure society. Indeed, in some respects, it is more central today than it was at the dawn of the Cold War. Never-theless, there are reasons to wonder whether it will remain so into the future.

To investigate these claims, I first introduce the concept of institu-tional presence as a tool for analyzing the military's relationship with so-ciety. "Institutional presence" refers to the material and moral integration of an institution with the larger society. Prior work in this area has bogged down in endless debate about the military's organizational con-vergence with or divergence from civilian society. That debate has too of-ten mistakenly assumed that the relationship between the military and society is dominated either by the military's "functional" imperatives or by "social" imperatives reflecting civilian values and concerns.[1] The concept of institutional presence establishes an analytical framework that does not require us to suppose that these imperatives are always in opposition; it permits us to consider whether there may be times when they are mutually reinforcing. No less importantly, it helps us to identify four analytically distinct types of relationship that the military may have with civilian society, which I describe below.

Next, I apply the concept to describe the military's changing connection with society, paying closest attention to the last half-century. The analysis draws on standard secondary sources to examine major trends relating to the military's material presence in the nation at large and in major regions of the country. This analysis is followed by a historical sketch of the military's moral integration with society. These descriptive analyses support the relatively optimistic portion of my claim about the military's current contribution to American society. To conclude, I consider what may explain the observed trends, especially with respect to moral integration, and on the basis of that explanation predict that the future course of civil-military relations may not simply reproduce the past, but could become potentially troubling.

The Concept of Institutional Presence

To my knowledge, "institutional presence" is a novel concept that has no prior history of use in institutional analysis or sociological theory. It is nevertheless a concept that implicitly underlies a number of sociological hypotheses, such as hypotheses about the role of significant others in socializing children, "tipping" hypotheses to explain the changing ethnic composition of neighborhoods, and secularization hypotheses that seem to suggest that religion is a declining presence in modern society.

When I talk about "institutional presence" I refer to the social significance of an institution in society. Institutional presence has two major dimensions, material and moral. Material presence refers to the degree to which social contact with an institution is likely, so that the insti-

---

1.   The seminal works in this debate are Samuel P. Huntington, *The Soldier and the State* (1957) and Morris Janowitz, *The Professional Soldier* (1960). Many other studies developed hypotheses that these works put forward. For an overview of that literature, see Gwyn Harries-Jenkins and Charles C. Moskos (1981). On Janowitz's importance as a founder of sociological studies of the military, see Burk (1993). The most pertinent work on the topic can be found in Biderman (1967); Biderman and Sharp (1968); Moskos (1973; 1977); Larson (1974); Segal, Blair, Newport and Stephens (1974); Janowitz (1977); Segal (1986); Moskos and Wood (1988); Boëne (1990); Moskos and Burk (1994); Feaver (1996).

tution has to be taken into account as an actor in society. But material presence alone does not indicate whether any accounting we make of the institution will be positive or negative. More importantly, it does not tell us along what substantive dimensions a positive or negative judgment might be made. What it does tell us is how salient the institution is, not only for those who are members of it, but also for other institutions and ordinary citizens, whether their contact with it is frequent and direct or intermittent and indirect. Moral presence refers to the degree to which an institution has to be considered an important actor in the normative order, that is, in our understanding of what constitutes a good society. It is the moral presence of an institution that gives us some ability (always imperfect) to reach a substantive judgment about whether and how a particular institution contributes to the construction of a good society. It is important to be clear from whose point of view such judgments are made. For present purposes, I care most about the judgments made from the standpoint of a member of society. As Edward Shils (1975) has argued, societies have a central value system that informs expectations about how institutions should conduct themselves if they are acting properly or legitimately. When institutions conduct their business and maintain relations with society that accord with these expectations, then we can say that the institution is morally integrated with society. To the degree these expectations go unmet, the institution is less well integrated and, at the extreme, held to be illegitimate. It is probably true—all things being equal—that an institution's moral presence is limited as its material presence is diminished, and vice versa.

These two dimensions of institutional presence allow us to develop an elementary typology of institutions based on the character of their presence in society (see Table 6.1). We may say that institutions are *central* to society when they rank high along the dimensions of material salience and moral integration, as did the church in Europe 500 years ago and as the judicial system does today. When institutions rank high along the dimension of moral integration, but are not materially salient—as we might say for instance about the carnival, long-distance train travel, and the small family farm in the present-day United States—these institutions are *peripheral* to the society. They are legitimate, but they do not define life in society as markedly as central institutions do. It is possible, of course, for institutions to rank high in terms of material salience but low in terms of moral integration. These are illegitimate institutions from the standpoint of the society but are nevertheless institutions whose conduct and influence has to be taken into account. An example would be the Mafia or other large-scale criminal organizations. But it is not only criminal organizations that fit this description: American colonists on the eve of the

Table 6.1. Types of Institutional Presence.

		Moral Integration	
		High	Low
Material	High	Central	Predatory
Salience	Low	Peripheral	Alienated

revolution certainly thought the British military was an illegitimate institution of this kind, and many in East Timor came to think the same about the Indonesian militia after it killed hundreds of East Timorese following a vote for independence in August 1999. Such institutions may be called *predatory*. If institutions are not morally integrated with or materially salient to society, they are *alienated* or isolated from the society. They are largely unheard of and without influence, as has been true throughout most of last century for traditional institutions of Native Americans on reservations in the United States. In the extreme, alienated institutions are simply absent from society. Poor houses and open slavery are no longer found in advanced industrial countries.

This typology is a useful tool for describing the military's relations with civilian society. Depending on the period of history we examine, the military has often been a central institution in the life of American society. It certainly was during the Civil War, both World Wars and, I argue, during the Cold War. When it is a central institution, the "gap" or difference between the military and society is at its lowest point. At other times, the gap has widened and in different directions. At least in relative terms, the military has sometimes been a peripheral institution, as it arguably was for most of the period between 1815 and 1860 (with a possible exception during the war with Mexico) and the two decades between the World Wars. Some might say that the frontier military following the Civil War was so small and culturally isolated that it was alienated from society until the Spanish-American War.[2] Critics of the Cold War military—and more generally of the "national security state"—have worried that during this period the military became a predatory institution: a large material presence in society that consumed many social resources, for purposes that endangered the values and way of life characteristic of a liberal democracy (Gottlieb 1997; Boies 1994; Mills 1957; Lasswell 1941; 1962).

If we ask why the military's presence in society has been so various,

---

2. See also Chapter 5 by Russell F. Weigley in this volume.

it is reasonable as a first step to suggest that the variation is explained by the seriousness of the threat the country has faced. That certainly helps to explain the military's material salience in society.[3] Historically, in response to war and to the experience of prolonged threat during the Cold War, both the size and budget of the military increased dramatically and remained high until the threat was overcome. More difficult to explain is variation in the military's moral integration with society. Unless one embraces a critical theory that American society has undergone militarization as a result of mobilizing for the World Wars and the Cold War, there are no dramatic incidents—such as a coup d'état—in which the U.S. military has acted to prey on society, using its power illegitimately to redirect social resources in pursuit of its own purposes (but see Dunlap 1994). Instead, we see more subtle movements along a continuum on which the military's moral integration with society is measured in terms of "more" or "less," rather than extremes.

To say what drives these subtle movements, we have to think through how judgments about the correlation of moral expectations and institutions are made. The critical point for our purpose is that judgments are made both by those who represent the institution and by the society at large. They may not agree. It is always possible that the normative expectations for military conduct held by the military elite will not match those held by civilian elites or ordinary citizens. If not, then their respective judgments about the military's contribution to a good society may be quite different; at least, they will differ in terms of that moral dimension along which their expectations diverge. Then the gap between the military and society will widen. Obviously, moral integration is highest when expectations are shared and highly correlated with institutional conduct, and it declines to the degree that conduct does not measure up to expectations, or expectations are not shared.

The next task is to use this conceptualization as a guide for describing the relationship between the military and American society over the last half-century. The goal is to consider whether the military and the democracy it protects are supportive of the same normative order. More concretely, we want to know: Is the military's place in American society as central now as it was during the Cold War? Has it retained its material salience in American life? Does it have the same weight in our calculations about what is required to maintain a good society? What kind of presence does it have and how has its presence changed over time? (If the word "militarization" were not so freighted with meaning, I might ask

---

3. This is not a complete explanation. Domestic factors may also determine the amount of defense spending. For an overview of the process see Mintz (1988).

whether the Cold War's end unleashed a de-militarization of American society and, if so, what consequences this might have for our national security. But "militarization" is often used as a pejorative term and using it here would subtract more than it would add to the argument.)

The Military's Institutional Presence

The concept of institutional presence suggests a framework for examining the military's relations with the larger society. It does not offer specific propositions about what particular relations to examine or why. It is a concept, not a full theory. Yet no other stronger theory is available that would provide a better guide to institutional analysis.

Institutional analyses of the military's presence in American society have been guided for over forty years by two contending and deservedly famous theories posed by Samuel P. Huntington (1957) and Morris Janowitz (1960). Both struggled with the classic dilemma of democratic civil-military relations: how to ensure both military effectiveness and the values of liberal democracy. They disagreed about how this might be done. Huntington believed that the military was a unique social organization and should remain so. Its capacity to be effective over the long run depended not only on its relative uniqueness and social distance from other institutions, but also on a movement in civilian society away from anti-military liberalism toward a more pro-military conservative realism. In short, the values of liberal democracy were to be subordinated to the requirements of military effectiveness. Janowitz, in contrast, believed there was an inevitable—though not total—convergence between the military and society. He argued for programs of political education to enhance the military professional's ability to grasp and respond effectively to socio-political demands. In short, he subordinated the technical pursuit of military effectiveness to the values of liberal democracy. While there is much to say in favor of both theories, in recent years scholars have noted that there are logical flaws in both and that neither is adequately supported by empirical evidence (Feaver 1996; Boëne 1990). The criticisms cast serious doubt on both theories, especially on their common belief that one could not maintain a strong military and strong democracy at the same time, but must ensure the maintenance of one good in order to get the other. Under these circumstances, it may be time to back away from strong theories that commit us to doubtful conclusions and try instead to re-examine the empirical data with fresh eyes through the conceptual lens of institutional presence.

It remains to say what data should be examined. Here I think the obvious answers are most appropriate. When examining the military's material salience, we should examine the military's claims on social resources by inspecting trends in defense spending and in the size of the military establishment. When examining the military's moral integration, we should examine those themes of moral debate over the last fifty years that have shaped expectations about what kind of society we want to be, and then consider whether and how the military altered its conduct in light of these debates, meeting (or failing to meet) changing ideas in society about what constitutes legitimate institutional conduct.

CHANGING MATERIAL SALIENCE

Speaking generally, we want to know whether the military's material presence in society is high or low. Whether it is one or the other flows from policy decisions typically related to perceptions of the degree of threat being faced. On Huntington's account, historically, the country pursued a policy of "extirpation" of the military during peacetime, withholding resources to ensure its low material presence and low salience in American society when its services were least needed. In contrast, during war, when resources could not be withheld, a policy of "transmutation" was adopted to ensure as much as possible a closer moral integration between the military and society. A more subtle view of the matter is required when we look at the last fifty years, because the Cold War and the years since have been a period of neither war nor peace. During this period, the military has maintained a highly visible material presence.

The indicators of material presence are various but not surprising. For present purposes, we examine national trends in defense spending and force size and structure, and regional distributions of military contract awards, payroll, veterans' expenditures and base closures.[4] The critical issue is how much the end of the Cold War diminished the military's material presence. Significant downsizing has occurred since 1990 and has been a source of turmoil and adjustment within the armed forces (McCormick 1998; Markusen and Yudken 1992). But are we free to conclude that, as a result, the military is no longer a salient material force in society: that it is no longer central, but has moved to the periphery of society or perhaps become alienated from society? The question is important. If material presence is diminished past a certain (indefinite) point, the military may lose its ability to attract national resources in sufficient quantity and quality to maintain institutional effectiveness (Goldich 1994). No mechanical formula permits us to calculate an exact answer to

---

4. Other indicators of presence would include variations in media attention to the military, whether as news or entertainment in such forms as films, songs, and books.

Figure 6.1. Defense and Federal Spending Trends, 1900–1995.

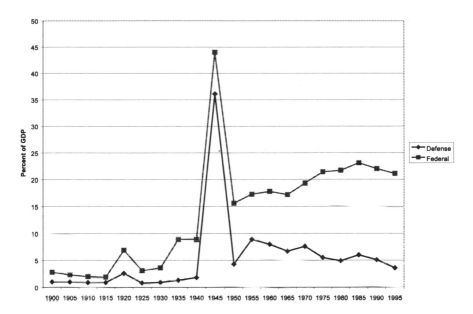

SOURCES: *Historical Statistics of the United States Colonial Times to 1970*, Tables F1–5 and Y457–465; *National Income and Product Accounts of the United States, 1929–94*, Table 1.1; and *Statistical Abstract for 1998*, Table 715. Note: For years from 1900–20, percentages are of Gross National Product rather than Gross Domestic Product.

the question; we must examine data covering long enough periods of time to have some confidence in our judgment.

The first step is to look at long-term economic trends. An overview of trends in defense spending is provided in Figure 6.1. The figure plots defense and total federal spending as a percent of Gross National Product (GNP) or Gross Domestic Product (GDP) from 1900 to 1995. The figure reveals how huge a claim World War II placed on the national economy, and shows that the state's claim on the economy for military and civilian purposes was much higher after World War II than at any time before. From 1955 to 1990, defense spending never dropped below 5 percent of GDP, whereas its highest peacetime level before World War II was 2.6 percent of GNP in 1920; this was a sharp drop from 13.1 percent of GNP reached in 1919, an effect of mobilization for World War I. But we can also observe that defense spending, after rising steeply from 1950 to 1955, has declined over the last forty years.

Federal spending rose from just under 16 percent of GDP in 1950 to over 20 percent in 1975, a level it has roughly maintained since then. Defense spending is a major component of that spending. In the mid-1990s it consumed a significant portion—17.2 percent—of federal outlays and 10.8 percent of net public spending. Yet its share of public spending has declined markedly and steadily since the height of the Cold War in 1955, when it was 51.4 percent of the federal expense. So, while federal outlays as a percentage of GDP are now higher than they were on average in the 1950s, defense spending as a percentage of GDP has dropped from a high of 8.9 percent in 1955 to a low of 3.6 percent in 1995. (Note that this low figure is much closer to the share of GDP that was devoted to defense spending in 1950.)

We get a somewhat different picture if we look at trends in defense employment. The portion of the national labor force employed by the Department of Defense, military and civilian, has fallen by over 60 percent between 1970 and 1995. A large part of this decline, however, reflects growth in private-sector employment more than a decline in the military's share of public-sector employment. Underlying these economic data, of course, are decisions about how large the armed forces should be. When we look at changes in the size of the uniformed force from 1986 to 1996, we observe a decline in strength of about one-third, with most of the change occurring after the Persian Gulf War in 1991. Yet there are interesting factors that mitigate the effects of these cuts in the size of the active-duty force from the point of view of military presence. Reserve force strength has been cut to a lesser degree over the period (only 18.6 percent as compared with 32.2 percent for active-duty forces), and fewer forces are stationed abroad. When we look at changes in total force size and only at forces maintained in the states, the decline in the number of military personnel is just about 22 percent, still a sharp decline over a short period, but significantly less than a reduction of one-third.

We might ask whether military downsizing since the end of the Cold War has affected all regions of the country equally. It is possible that the military's material salience is greater in some parts of the country than others. In 1996, for instance, 31.5 percent of all military personnel were stationed in the South, which had only 15.4 percent of the population. In contrast, only 11.4 percent of military personnel were stationed in the Midwest, which had 26.7 percent of the population. The military's material salience, in other words, may be high on average, but it is still limited in important respects and could be a source of political conflict if the military's presence is concentrated in some regions at the expense of others. To see whether this is the case and to see whether the military's patterns of material presence have changed over time, we examine regional trends

Figure 6.2. Defense Contracts, Payroll, and Veterans' Expenditures as a percentage of GDP, 1955–96.

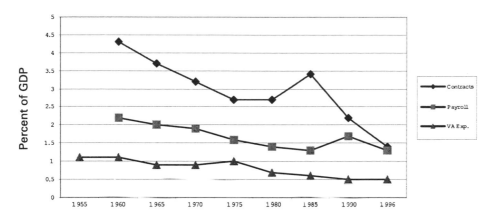

SOURCE: U.S. Department of Commerce, *Statistical Abstract of the United States* (various years).

in the award of military contracts, payment of payroll, and veterans' expenditures.[5]

Figure 6.2 plots national trends for the three categories of spending from 1955 to 1996 expressed as a percent of GDP. This figure provides an overview against which regional trends might be measured. As would be expected, the trends reflect the general pattern of total defense spending, a general decline from the height of the Cold War in the 1950s through the present. Looking at the data on military contracts, one might be tempted to say that the much steeper descent in military contracts compared with earlier periods is due to the end of the Cold War. No doubt, that is true to some extent. The level of military contracts dropped almost 22 percent from 1985 to 1996 in nominal dollars. But the slope of the decline is exaggerated because the starting period is a high point in the extraordinary defense buildup during the Reagan administration. If we extrapolated the trend from 1960 through 1975 to predict the level of military contracts for 1996, we would estimate that their worth would reach only 1 percent of GDP, a figure lower than we observe. Also, one must take the rate of economic growth into account. The economy in 1996 was

5.   Regions were defined by conventions adopted in the TISS elite survey. For a description of the survey, see Newcity (1999).

over 82 percent larger than the economy in 1985, an unusual growth spurt that exaggerates the relative downward trend in military spending. Given these qualifications, the most balanced interpretation would seem to be that while these measures of defense spending mirror the overall trend of decline over the last four decades, they do not clearly reveal any sharp departure from the decades-long trend that could be attributed to policy shifts made possible by the end of the Cold War.

Table 6.2 shows how regional shares of defense spending on contracts, payroll, and veterans' expenditures have changed from 1960 to 1996. These data should be compared to the national trends. Between 1975 and 1980, for instance, the national trend in military contracts as a percent of GDP was flat with levels remaining at about 2.7 percent. But during this five-year period, New England increased its share of the national spending while the Pacific Coast lost ground. Of course, fluctuations at lower levels of aggregation are normal. The key question is whether the regional patterns of spending suggest that the military's material presence is high in some regions and low in others. To make such a judgment, I compared the distribution of spending across regions at each point in time with the distribution of population across regions. My hypothesis was that regional concentration of the military's material presence could be claimed only if the distribution of regional spending differed significantly from the distribution of the regional populations.

Although there are stories that veterans are more likely to settle in some parts of the country than others (to take advantage of tax breaks, to be near former military posts, or have access to veterans' hospitals), in fact regional variation in veterans' expenditures mirrored regional variation in population. There were no significant differences for any distribution from 1955 through 1996. The same was not the case for military payroll. Payroll trends are a proxy for the distribution of military personnel around the country.[6] Not surprisingly, given the concentration of military personnel in the South, the regional distribution of payroll was significantly different from the population distribution in every period. Nor was it only the South that was responsible for this result. The Pacific Coast and the Southwestern states were also over-represented by military personnel as measured by payroll. New England and, even more, the Midwest failed to have an equal share of military personnel. The Mid-Atlantic region consistently received over 20 percent of the military pay-

---

6.   It is, of course, an imperfect proxy because military personnel are not all paid at the same rate. Given the differential distribution of high-ranking officers, one would expect per-capita payroll in the Washington, D.C., area to be higher than it would be in, say, the area of Texas that is host to Fort Hood.

Table 6.2. Changing Shares of Defense Spending by Type and Region, 1960–1996 (in percentages).

Type/Region	1960	1965	1970	1975	1980	1985	1990	1996
Contracts								
Mid-Atlantic	26.7	23.5	26.7	22.7	23.2	21.6	21.0	23.1
Midwest	18.5	19.2	18.5	16.6	17.6	19.3	17.4	16.4
Mountain	2.6	2.3	2.6	1.3	1.3	1.9	3.0	2.5
New England	10.1	11.2	10.1	12.2	13.2	11.1	11.2	8.4
Pacific Coast	28.0	25.3	28.0	26.9	25.1	24.3	22.2	20.4
South	6.6	10.6	6.6	12.2	9.4	12.0	13.6	16.9
Southwest	7.5	7.9	7.5	8.2	10.3	9.8	11.6	12.3
Total	100.0	100.0	100.0	100.1	100.1	100.0	100.0	100.0
Payroll								
Mid-Atlantic	23.6	24.1	21.8	22.5	23.2	23.5	22.3	21.8
Midwest	14.1	14.5	14.9	14.6	13.4	12.6	13.2	13.0
Mountain	3.5	3.8	4.3	4.4	3.9	3.6	4.0	4.0
New England	5.1	4.5	3.7	2.8	3.2	3.2	3.2	2.8
Pacific Coast	21.3	20.6	21.7	21.5	22.9	23.8	21.4	19.9
South	18.1	19.1	19.3	20.1	20.7	21.2	23.1	24.2
Southwest	14.3	13.4	14.3	14.1	12.8	12.0	12.8	11.4
Total	100.0	100.0	100.0	100.0	100.1	99.9	100.0	100.1
VA Expenditures								
Mid-Atlantic	26.2	26.8	25.8	24.2	24.8	25.5	26.9	23.8
Midwest	29.1	28.1	26.6	24.6	23.0	23.2	21.8	22.2
Mountain	2.8	2.7	2.8	2.9	2.9	2.8	3.0	3.0
New England	6.4	6.4	6.2	5.9	6.0	5.8	5.6	5.7
Pacific Coast	11.8	11.6	13.3	14.9	13.3	12.8	12.6	13.3
South	15.1	15.8	16.0	17.1	18.9	19.2	18.7	19.8
Southwest	8.6	8.7	9.3	10.3	11.2	10.6	11.3	12.2
Total	100.0	100.1	100.0	99.9	100.1	99.9	99.9	100.0

SOURCE: U.S. Department of Commerce, *Statistical Abstract of the United States* (various years).

NOTE: Because of rounding, some totals do not add up to 100 percent.

roll, but that share was closely in line with its share of the population. There is a different pattern for military contracts. In this series, the regional distribution of military contracts departs from the expected distribution in every period during the Cold War, from 1960 through 1985. During these years, New England and Pacific Coast states were consistently over-represented, while states in the South and Midwest were consistently under-represented in their share of military contracts. Once again, the Mid-Atlantic region maintained a share of military contracts that, although large, was in line with its share of the population. Since the end of the Cold War, however, these differences have disappeared. While traces of the old pattern can be discerned, in fact military contracts in the 1990s have been awarded to regions as would be expected by their population shares.

In sum, during the Cold War, some regions were clearly over- or under-represented along the key dimensions of payroll and contract awards. Along both dimensions, the military was more obviously present on the Pacific Coast and less obviously present in the Midwest than their population shares would have led us to expect. Some regions were under-represented along one dimension and over-represented along another. The South was less likely to receive contracts, but more likely to receive military personnel. It was just the reverse for New England. In some regions the military was present just as their population share would lead us to expect. That was true for the Mid-Atlantic region and, to a lesser degree, for the Southwest and the Mountain States. By the end of the Cold War, only regional differences in payroll remained. One wonders whether these differences have been reinforced or eroded by closing bases. While the movement to close and realign military bases, begun in 1988, has resulted in 387 "actions," the Department of Defense reports that only 95 "major" bases were scheduled to close through the fourth round of recommendations made in 1995. Following the same comparative logic applied above, when we calculate the total proportion of bases scheduled to be closed by region and compare the resulting distribution with population shares, we find significant regional differences. While many regions are being cut as expected by their population share, the Pacific Coast is being cut to a far larger degree, and the Midwest and the Southwest to a much lesser degree, than one would expect. Counting all bases as equal is a risky assumption, but it suggests that base closures may bring the regional presence of military personnel more in line with the population distribution.

On balance, the military's presence over the Cold War era has diminished steadily since the mid-1950s. We have seen evidence of this at both the national and regional levels. But that evidence offers no warrant for concluding that the military's presence is no longer significant.

Quite apart from whether we believe its present size is too large or too small, the military remains a huge establishment within the federal government and society. When we examine trends in force size since 1900, it is readily seen that even the downsized, post–Cold War military is a gargantuan institution compared to what it was before World War II. At just over 1.4 million members in 1998, the active-duty force is nearly five times its average size during the interwar years from 1921 to 1940.

What was novel about American civil-military relations after World War II was that, for the first time, the country maintained a large standing armed force during peacetime. The end of the Cold War has not changed that fact, nor has it eliminated the need to wonder how this arrangement affects democratic society: it is likely that we have reached the end of trends in force reduction, and we may see movements to increase force size in the near future (Department of Defense 1999; Burns 1999). Equally important, when force size is measured as a ratio to the total population—the military participation ratio—we find that the post–Cold War military, though two-thirds smaller than at its height in the 1950s, remains nearly three times larger than the peacetime military before mid-century. The persistence of a large standing army after two world wars and a forty-year Cold War should not be surprising. As the historian Bruce Porter has shown in his study of European state formation since 1500, the size of the state, including military forces, historically increases markedly after the end of large-scale conflicts when compared to pre-war levels (Porter 1994).

Overall, the military remains a formidable material presence in American society, although much less than at the height of the Cold War. There is no reason based on this analysis to say the military is a peripheral or an alienated institution. It is a highly visible institution in society and most likely will continue to be so. The question is, for what end? We know that scholars have disagreed about the significance of a large military presence. Some believe it undermines a democratic society by "militarizing" it, creating a national security state or a warfare society. Others believe that a large military promotes democratization because the military necessarily becomes more representative of society as a whole. Conflicting judgments often rest more on substantive normative claims about the meaning of the material facts than on the facts alone. Put in terms of our typology of institutional presence, we have to decide whether we believe that the military, having a salient presence in society, is morally integrated with society. Is it a central or a predatory institution? Answering the question requires a more refined historical analysis of normative trends in the military and in American society.

CHANGING MORAL INTEGRATION

Charting the moral presence of institutions is daunting, but not an impossible task (Selznick 1992; Jackall 1988; Glendon 1987). We begin by identifying particular substantive dimensions along which we can assess the military's contribution to the constitution of a good society. In light of recent intense public conflicts over moral issues, characterized by some as "cultural wars," any choice of themes may seem arbitrary, random, or ad hoc (Lakoff 1996). But that is not necessarily so. Organizational theorists are keenly aware that an organization's survival depends on its ability to be perceived as legitimate, at least by those on whom it must depend for support. The legitimacy they are referring to is a matter of practical consent (Thompson 1967; Galaskiewicz 1985; Powell and DiMaggio 1991). At issue is whether the organization can obtain the goods and personnel it requires to carry on its activities. To be thought legitimate, an organization must conform to social expectations about what constitutes appropriate conduct for an organization of its kind. Expectations are often written into law. For example, large business firms today are required by law to disclose detailed and certified financial statements containing information that, in the Gilded Age, would have been regarded as private. But expectations may also be informal prescriptions that are matters of local social custom. They are still important to know and follow, as many businesses have learned when attempting to penetrate foreign markets. Of course, not every expectation applies equally to every institution: expectations of efficiency are higher for business than public bureaucracies, and higher for both than they are for voluntary organizations. Nor is every expectation necessarily grounded in a moral concern. Customs governing appropriate dress, for instance, are important determinants of one's place in the status order, but they can rarely be rationalized in moral terms.[7] Finally, expectations—like the one about financial disclosure—are subject to change over time. The critical point is that expectations are knowable; there is such sufficient consensus about them—even in a period of "cultural wars"—that no institution could ignore them without jeopardizing its standing as a legitimate organization in society. When the expectations grounded in moral judgments change, we can treat the degree to which an organization alters its conduct to conform to the changing standard as a measure of its moral integration with the larger society.

Moral integration with society is a key element of organizational legitimacy. It is not the only element: organizational legitimacy also depends on whether the organization is viewed as effective at what it does. Sometimes there seems to be a conflict between these social moral imperatives and functional imperatives—between, for example, turning a profit and protecting the environment—forcing organizational leaders to choose between the two. That, of course, is what students and members of the military have often contended about the military; its legitimacy is threatened when it is asked to meet social and functional imperatives that

---

7. Medical garb in an operating room may be an exception.

are, in essence, opposed to one another. Technical proficiency at fighting wars is sacrificed, they argue, when the military is forced to be a "social laboratory." But the opposition between social or moral and functional imperatives is a matter to be established empirically, not assumed a priori.

To assess the moral integration of the military with society over the last half-century, I examine changing expectations in three areas. The first two treat general expectations relevant to all institutions in a democratic society. They are the expansion of citizens' rights and the closely-related interest in building decent or non-humiliating relations between institutions and the people they serve, which we might call the movement toward greater inclusiveness. The third deals with an expectation more relevant specifically to the military: changing norms about the use of force in pursuit of public policy.

Each of these issues touches on a matter of importance for the constitution of a good society. As important for present purposes, they are matters about which there has been lively public debate concerning the military's legitimacy. Compulsory mobilizations of citizens to fight in wars and the movement to an all-volunteer professional force have raised questions about the rights of citizens in the military. The military's record in race and gender relations has raised questions about its "institutional decency." With the end of the Cold War, expectations rose that the military should be able to limit its use of force, performing a wide range of missions using, as much as possible, non-lethal means, while limiting the number of casualties taken on all sides. The question is whether the military has altered its modes of conduct within these three areas to conform to changing social expectations. Put more pointedly, has the military over the last half-century helped to ensure its legitimacy by contributing positively to normative projects that the country at large believes are important to constitute a good and secure society? Has it maintained its moral integration with society?

Without question, the United States since mid-century has seen an expansion in the rights of citizens and a rise in "rights consciousness" (Epp 1998; Marshall 1977; Dworkin 1977; but see Glendon 1991). What "rights" are is a matter of scholarly debate, the more so as rights gain importance in regulating social life (Waldron 1984). It is enough here to say that rights are grants (from whom is a matter I'll leave aside) that empower people to act or prevent others from acting toward them in certain ways. Rights consciousness refers to "the general awareness of rights to be claimed or asserted against others, particularly the government" (Wasby 1992, 398). The expansion of rights and the rise of rights consciousness go hand in hand, and have often been promoted as conflicts are decided in the courts. Supreme Court decisions by the Warren and Burger Courts extended protection of citizens' rights to free speech, voting, separation of church and state, privacy, against race and gender discrimination and, in the area of criminal procedure, to legal representation and higher standards of due process. Notwithstanding reactions against these trends in recent years under the more conservative Rehnquist Court, our understanding of what constitutes a good society now includes a larger portfolio of civil liberties and rights for citizens than it did in 1950 or at any time before. It is not entirely clear whether the military has participated in this movement, and if so, how. Upholding the constitutionality of the draft in World War I, the Court said citizens were obligated to render military service and that the government could rightly compel it.[8] Throughout the first half of this century, the government required that applicants for citizenship promise to bear arms in defense of the country before it would admit them into citizenship. Failure to promise was considered a sign of bad character and lack of attachment to the principles of the Constitution.[9] Yet citizens in the military did not and do not enjoy all of the rights of citizens in civilian society. The Constitution recognized that the military is, in Justice Rehnquist's words, a "specialized society separate from civilian society," and under the Constitution, members of the military have been subject to a separate law and trial by military courts.[10]

Nevertheless, as the rights revolution affected even the populations of prisons, it is perhaps not surprising that it affected the military as well. In the mid-1980s, James B. Jacobs (1986) identified three major trends of military legal change since the end of World War II: an extension to service personnel of procedural and substantive rights, a shift in emphasis from criminal to administrative law, and increased emphasis on the contractual nature of military service. I examine only the first of these trends related to rights.

An early step in the extension of rights was adoption of the Uniform Code of Military Justice in 1950. It was "an explicit objective [of the code] to civilianize and liberalize the military's criminal law and procedure, as well as to extend certain rights of citizenship to service personnel" (Jacobs 1986, 6). With the code, Congress established a Court of Military

---

8. *Arver v. United States* (1918, 378).

9. This requirement was overturned in *Girouard v. United States* (1946). See Burk (1995).

10. *Parker v. Levy* (1974, 743). For a review of the Supreme Court's deference to the military on the basis of its special status, see Jaeger (1997). For a history of the military legal system, see Lurie (1992; 1998).

Appeals, to serve as an independent civilian court in review over military courts. Over the years, this court imported "almost all the procedural protections available to civilian defendants" (Jacobs 1986, 7). The Supreme Court has also been involved, controversially, in determining whether cases involving military personnel are subject to civilian or military law. In 1969, the Court significantly limited the jurisdiction of military courts by holding that they could only hear criminal cases if the alleged offense was "connected" with military service.[11] Otherwise, members of the military were subject to civilian law like everyone else. This test of appropriate jurisdiction was difficult to apply and ran contrary to a conservative view of the military as a "separate" society. The Rehnquist Court overturned it in 1987.[12] Yet the reversal did not lead to a wholesale retrenchment of the legal rights of military personnel. The Court of Military Appeals continued its tradition of embracing civilian legal standards in its review of military cases, with the effect of incorporating these into military law (Fidell 1997). Moreover, in *Loving* v. *United States* (1996), the Rehnquist Court acknowledged that military sentences of capital punishment had to pass the same Eighth Amendment constitutional tests required of civilian courts in *Furman* v. *Georgia* (1972).[13] While military personnel still have a special status in the law, with fewer rights than civilians, military justice is nevertheless far more liberal and civilianized than at any previous time. Its development has contributed to the extension of civil liberties and civil rights in the United States.

We can speak more broadly about trends in military legitimacy by examining the decency with which the military treats the people with whom it comes in contact. Avishai Margalit (1996) has written thoughtfully about the importance of investigating the "decency" of institutions in our quest for a good society. A decent institution is one that does not humiliate people. At its core, the act of humiliation entails rejection; it rejects someone from society or from participation in the life of the institution, sometimes by outright exclusion, sometimes by denigrating a person's presence within the institution. In these terms, American institutions, the military not excluded, have not always measured up to the standard of decency and still frequently fall short, especially with respect to race and gender relations. Over the last century, in part as a result of the rights revolution, our understanding of what constitutes a good society in these respects has been reformed. We are more inclined to require

---

11. *O'Callahan* v. *Parker* (1969).

12. *Solorio* v. *United States* (1987).

13. For commentary on this issue, see Jaeger (1997).

institutions to treat a broader range of people with decency.[14] Nowhere is this more evident than in efforts made through law, affirmative action, and other means to mitigate the historical effects of discrimination based on race and gender. The military has played an important role in these developments.

Like most institutions in American society, through mid-century, the military openly and legally discriminated against citizens who were minorities and severely limited opportunities afforded women. Although military service during war is often a great equalizer, it was not until 1948 that President Truman ordered an end to racial segregation in the military. Even then, it was not until combat experience in Korea provided a spur that the military moved to implement the order; the morale and fighting effectiveness of African-Americans sharply improved after the "color line" of segregation was broken down (Weigley 1967, 555; Nalty 1986). Still, integration was imperfectly implemented, and racial conflict within the armed forces was especially evident during the Vietnam War. (Much the same, however, could be said for institutions throughout American society.) Since then, as Charles Moskos and John Sibley Butler (1996) have documented, the military—in particular, the Army—has become a model of decency in race relations.

Race relations are still not perfect, but they are good. Reform in this area was a product of deliberate efforts made by military leaders. Three steps were crucial. First, the Army instituted a strict policy of intolerance against any form of racial discrimination and allocated resources to give commanders the tools to assess and improve the quality of race relations. Second, the Army adopted a policy of maintaining performance standards for promotion while adopting the goal of promoting all minorities—including women—at the same rate as all others being considered. If the goal was not met and subsequent review showed that it could not be met without lowering standards, then it would not be met. This was not discrimination. Absent a policy of promoting unqualified people, military personnel were less likely to question the qualifications of minority leaders. Third, the Army made a significant commitment to help blacks and others acquire the tools they needed to compete for advancement. The aim was to increase the pool of qualified people. Each of these pro-

---

14.   This is not to deny counter-trends, especially in popular culture where it often seems that the object of social life is to treat people with as little decency as possible. Yet even in the case of popular culture, the people denigrated are often those who are supposed to have authority or power over others. It is as if, in the world of art, there is an effort to compensate for humiliations endured in real life by creating a symbolic world humiliating to those who humiliate.

grams made a positive contribution, virtually eliminating the rejection of minorities from military life and making the military one of the few institutions where blacks are routinely in positions of authority over whites.[15] I have argued that the military's success in this regard was due in part to special conditions unique to the military: the need of the all-volunteer force to rely on minority volunteers to meet recruiting goals, and substantial agreement among military leaders on the military's central purpose, which made it easier for them to agree on programs to achieve their goals. It is unlikely that the military's success in this endeavor could be repeated in civilian society (Burk 1997). But success it is, and in this regard one can say that the military has progressed further than civilian institutions to encourage decency in race relations.

Gender relations are another matter. There have been many highly publicized scandals in recent years involving incidents of sexual harassment or other forms of sexual misconduct. Military leaders often seemed to respond to these scandals with more concern to protect the reputation of their services and perhaps of their colleagues than to resolve the problems. Systematic data on sexual harassment complaints have only been collected by the Department of Defense since 1987. A review of the data from 1987 to 1997 show a surge in the number of complaints in 1992 and 1993, with some moderation since then. Since 1992, over half of these complaints have been officially substantiated, which attests to a serious problem (Department of Defense 1999, Table G-2). Yet better data are required to say whether increased complaints measure an increase in the number of incidents or an increase in the willingness of servicewomen to report incidents when they occur.[16] What can be said more certainly is that since the 1970s, as part of the creation of an all-volunteer force, the military has steadily removed traditional barriers that previously limited women's opportunities for military service. The number of women in the service has increased in the all-volunteer era from less than 5 percent to

---

15. I do not wish to imply that every vestige of racism has been abolished from the military. There is evidence for instance of potential race bias in the administration of courts-martial under the Uniform Code of Military Justice. See Landis, Dansby, and Hoyle (1997). It is not clear from this article whether the evidence for race bias in the military criminal justice system is greater or lesser than the evidence for race bias in the civilian criminal justice system. The Department of Defense has just begun to collect data on criminal offenses committed within the military in a manner comparable to reports about criminal incidents in civilian society. The system will facilitate such comparisons when it is fully implemented. See Department of Defense (1999, Appendix G).

16. There is evidence that poor unit leadership increases soldiers' assessments that sexual harassment is a problem in their unit. See Rosen and Martin (1997).

roughly 14 percent today.[17] The number of roles that women are allowed to fill has increased steadily as well. There is resistance in some quarters to carrying these trends any further. It is no longer contentious whether women should serve in the military. What remains controversial is whether women should have a choice or even should be required, if qualified, to fill combat roles. The controversy is difficult to settle, as it affects deep-seated connections between (and fears about) masculinity and warrior prowess. More practically, the new technology of war makes it difficult to draw sharp lines separating combat and non-combat roles that women are or are not permitted to fill. In the present difficult recruiting environment, the military is most likely to strengthen efforts to create a force that is welcoming and respectful of all volunteers regardless of gender.[18] It is impossible to say whether the military is moving forward more or less quickly than civilian institutions on this issue. But, despite the scandals, it is obvious over the long term that the military has curbed, if not eliminated, its most humiliating gender practices and that its moral presence and progress in this arena is a matter that draws a great deal of public attention and support.

The last matter affecting military legitimacy has to do with the use of force and efforts to limit resort to coercion as a means of pursuing public policy. Once more the pursuit of democratic values can be tied to the pursuit of decency. To the fullest extent possible, public authorities should pursue their policy objectives by means of persuasion and reason. Morris Janowitz argued that the changing technology of labor—away from manual labor to white-collar "brain work"—was responsible for a long-term shift in the form of authority within bureaucratic institutions. The trend was away from authority based on domination by command, toward authority based on manipulation. Military authority was affected as well (Janowitz 1978, 237–240). Speaking generally, institutions and societies that try to rule by coercive means lose their legitimacy. They are inherently weak regimes. They may last as long as they have a coercive advantage, but when that advantage is lost, as happened in Eastern Europe at

---

17.   The number of women serving in the military can be found in *Selected Manpower Statistics*, published annually by the Department of Defense. For more on this issue, see Chapter 10 in this volume by Laura L. Miller and John Allen Williams.

18.   The Department of Defense (1999, Appendix G) states: "In recent years, career opportunities for women in the Services have opened, and more women are enlisting. As men's propensity [to enlist] declined, women's propensity remained at approximately the same level. Thus women represent a growing portion of youth interested in and serving in military service."

the end of the Cold War or earlier to the Shah of Iran, their rule will collapse.

Efforts to institutionalize reliance on peaceful means to achieve public policy goals—such as economic sanctions, humanitarian relief and peacekeeping missions, and civic action programs—are especially important in international affairs. In an era when the need to deter large-scale conflict is well understood by political as well as military leaders, there have been efforts to limit resort to violence as a means of conflict resolution. Rather than assume that the use or threatened use of violence is the only means of influencing outcomes in world politics, political leaders have placed increasing emphasis on creating international institutions within which cooperative pursuits of common interests might flourish. These efforts have been spearheaded by and are most advanced among democratic nations, leading many to refer to the development of a "democratic peace" (Wendt 1994; Dixon 1994). They are evident also in efforts to link human rights law with the law of war, largely in revulsion at the global growth of intra-state violence since 1950. The hope is to provide some protection in international law for people whose government commits violent atrocities against them. The experience has been too common, and norms of international law are frequently too weak to prevent horrifying outcomes. But they have helped develop a rationale for multinational strategic peacekeeping missions, in which outsiders intervene in hopes of protecting human rights (Burk 1996; Dandeker and Gow 1997).

Since the end of the Cold War, the American military has been called on increasingly to play a role in such efforts, greatly expanding the range of missions for which it must prepare, at some strain on limited resources in an era of downsizing (Moskos, Williams, and Segal 2000). Success is hard to measure. The immediate objective of curbing human rights violations is difficult to achieve, as the Balkan conflicts of the 1990s have shown repeatedly. It is also difficult to know how much force is enough, yet not too much, so that viable international relations can be maintained, while also providing a credible military presence. Moreover, political and military leaders are reluctant to take casualties or to inflict them against enemy non-combatants for fear of losing public support for the mission (Burk 1999c; Larson 1996). Other difficulties arise from the need to coordinate military operations in peacekeeping missions with the operations of civilian relief agencies in the area (Pirnie 1998). The simultaneous presence and cooperation of military and civilian agencies within the peacekeeping theater is evidence in itself of how far the military has developed its capacity as a constabulary force. Efforts by the United States and its allies to substitute and extend the normative ideal of a more peaceful pursuit of international policy have depended on expanding the military's role to include strategic peacekeeping and humanitarian missions.

Without pretending to have exhausted any of these issues, this brief survey is sufficient to demonstrate a close link between the military's institutional development over the last fifty years and support for moral projects that the country believes are important to constitute a good and secure society. The military of course is an imperfect institution, but along the substantive dimensions surveyed here, its contributions to the normative order shared by American society are greater today than they were at the dawn of the Cold War. It is hard to say what effect if any the end of the Cold War has had on these trends. Only along the last dimension, in the area of peacekeeping, is it possible to say with certainty that the diminished threat of large-scale war after 1989 encouraged the military to pursue institutional change in support of moral aims. The key point, I believe, is to recognize that these dimensions of moral change—increasing citizens' rights, limiting race and gender discrimination, and expanding the benefits of a democratic peace—are not marginal developments, but reflect core U.S. values. In these endeavors, there is little evidence of a growing gap or isolation between the military and society. On the contrary, by adjusting to the changing expectations of society, the military has retained its moral integration with society and protected its status as a legitimate institution. Coupled with its continuing high material saliency, we are justified in concluding that, over ten years after the Cold War, the military remains what it was during the Cold War, a central institution in American life.

Assessing the Prospects for Civil-Military Relations

The question left unanswered by this descriptive analysis was why the military changed. What propelled it to alter its system of military justice to be more respectful of soldiers' rights? What moved it to become a more inclusive institution? Why did it embrace its role in operations other than war even though it frequently defines its mission in terms of fighting and winning the country's wars?

It is possible to argue that the military did not take the initiative in any of these movements. The development of its judicial system was imposed by reforms begun in Congress and carried out by a military appeals court whose judges were civilian. Racial integration of the military resulted from the promulgation of an executive order by President Truman in 1948, and gender integration was imposed in part by court decisions expanding equal rights protection (especially in the 1970s) and in part by necessity, to meet recruiting goals after Congress and the president ended the draft. Finally, it is arguable that the military accepted an expansion of its mission to include operations other than war only to bolster its claims for material resources and personnel, to maintain itself as a large institution after the end of the Cold War. If so, in each case, institutional change may have resulted more from external impositions on the military than from a moral conviction shared by military leaders and the American people. To argue this way suggests, as Huntington might, that the military has been distracted from its central mission, and that, given a large standing military, society responded by shackling it with a variety of social projects. Whatever the moral value of those projects for civilian society, he would say that the net effect lowers military effectiveness. But is it true that social and functional imperatives are necessarily in opposition? Based on the descriptions of military change offered above, it seems a subtler and more accurate claim that the military and society have been morally integrated to the degree that the functional and social imperatives reinforce one another.

Consider the case of race and gender integration. There was always a claim in American culture to establish integration as a moral norm, and practical support for that norm has grown stronger over the last fifty years. But it could hardly be said that society imposed this value on the military. While it is true that President Truman took the first step toward integrating the armed forces with his executive order, it is not true that integration of the forces occurred immediately thereafter. An expectation of integration was created, and one may guess that minority soldiers were anxious to see it instituted. But the military elite did not move decisively toward integration until after they realized that failure to integrate was hurting troop morale and fighting effectiveness in the Korean War.[19] That is, when integration was not simply a moral imperative but was also a functional imperative, institutional change occurred. Not every vestige of racism and prejudice was eliminated. But it is instructive to see that the next major transformation in military race relations occurred in the early 1970s and was again related to mutually reinforcing moral and functional imperatives. By the 1970s, proponents of racial segregation were marginalized. Though not a color-blind society, the United States embraced the ideal of racial equality. Still, this moral consensus was not enough to spur new reforms in the military. Further reforms sprang rather from the realization that failure to promote good race relations was a source of disruption within the military deployed in Vietnam, in Eu-

19. The military elite were not exceptional in this regard: compliance with the Supreme Court's order, in *Brown v. Board of Education of Topeka* (1954), to integrate the public schools was far from swift.

rope, on board ships, and elsewhere. It limited effectiveness. Moreover, with the end of the draft, it became apparent that the military would rely more heavily than in the past on minority personnel at all levels of the organization. In short, good race relations had become necessary to military effectiveness as well as justified on moral grounds.

The integration of women into the military has a similar history. It is well known that acceptance of the women in the military has oscillated historically with the severity of the need for trained personnel. Since the end of the draft, the military's ability to perform its mission required increasing opportunities for women who were willing to serve. This has placed a great strain on traditional military culture and led to scandals as already noted, nor can we say that gender integration has proceeded as far as race integration. Progress made, however, was not simply a result of a moral commitment to gender equality or to a growing appreciation that all citizens, male or female, should be equally accepted in their nation's service: it was because that moral commitment provided an opportunity—a new source of "manpower" in the all-volunteer force—to help meet the functional requirements for military effectiveness.

Similar accounts could be given about the expansion of soldiers' rights in the system of military justice or the expansion of the military's mission to place greater emphasis on operations other than war. But my aim was limited: to illustrate the substantive direction of a causal account and to clarify the main explanatory hypothesis: that the military's moral integration with society—and its legitimacy—increases when social and functional imperatives are mutually reinforcing. Elaborated within the framework deduced from our concept of institutional presence, this hypothesis suggests several important implications for assessing the present or future quality of civil-military relations.

First, we should abandon the conventional notion that the functional imperatives for military effectiveness are logically opposed to social imperatives underpinning the moral order of a liberal society. The descriptive analyses presented here show that presumption to be wrong in fact and seriously misleading. What we observed over the last half-century was a complex process through which the military adapted to and remained integrated with society's changing moral order as it came to recognize that effective performance of its role required accepting moral change. It is reasonable to contend that the relationship was reciprocal; enhanced organizational performance helped to legitimate the military as it instituted moral change and increased society's confidence in it.

Second, it is naïve to suppose that if the military is a central institution, morally integrated and materially salient, then civil-military relations will always be harmonious. There is no reason to suppose that elites representing various central institutions—the military included—will not compete for influence and power to promote the aims of the institutions they represent. On the contrary, we should expect stiff competition among them, which often shows up as policy conflict. Changing levels and regional allocations of military spending are indirect evidence of that competition. But we should also expect policy conflicts to be bounded by the practical consensus on which the institution's legitimacy rests. For the military and civilian elites, that means unwavering observance of the norm of civilian control within the political process. How that is accomplished may be debated (Kohn 1997). But it is clear that institutional restraint is required. More generally it means keeping a watchful eye on regional distributions of the military's material presence in society. Concentration of military spending and personnel in a few places at the expense of others could reduce the legitimacy of the military's claim to be a national institution and distort the national competition for social resources.

Third, the moral integration of the military with society does not mean that the military must (or can) incorporate every moral value held in civilian society. Institutions are specialized and for that reason the military's moral integration is always partial, which is a possible source of tension within society. Military elites naturally think the social values promoted by their institution are most important (just as journalists value "free speech" and professors the "life of the mind"). Civilians without military experience are more likely to deprecate (or fear) the military for the values it does not or cannot promote. This tension is probably unavoidable, but it should not be confused with a genuine opposition of values. The test for incorporating a moral value is whether it is compatible with effective role performance. If it is, then the military has every reason to adopt it, and doing so helps to maintain military legitimacy. But if not, adoption should not be required unless the value in question is essential to support of the norm of civilian control or otherwise necessary to keep policy conflicts in bounds.

Finally, it is difficult to assess whether conditions associated with the military's centrality will persist into the future. We cannot simply project past trends. There is a tendency for institutions to do again what has always been done. But in a competitive social context, there is a sense in which the place of institutions in society is always under negotiation, and this introduces the prospect of real change. If the military's claims on material resources were reduced to the levels reached before World War II, we would have to conclude that the military had become a peripheral institution in American life. If the military no longer adapted to society's changing moral order, we would have to conclude that it had become separated from society, and was either alienated from or predatory on it, depending on the level of social resources it controlled. The concept of institutional presence, however, cannot be stretched into an explanatory theory to tell us when or how shifts of such magnitude occur.

This much might be said. If society's moral imperatives and the military's functional imperatives were strongly opposed, the expectations of civilians and the military about the military's proper conduct in society would seriously diverge. They would disagree about what counts as military strength and what standards should be used to tell how much strength is needed to ensure military security. The problem of civilian control of the military would loom large. If the military's material presence was great, it is possible that its more predatory presence might crowd out concerns other than its own. This is a nightmare scenario, but I would argue that it is a scenario that has no present empirical support.

The critical task is to keep it that way. There are no guarantees about how that might be done. But it matters how we approach disputes about what makes an effective military and whether an effective military is positively related to the goods of a democratic society. To suppose the requirements for an effective military inevitably conflict with the goods of democracy unwittingly disrupts the moral integration of the military with society, widening the gap between them. Alternatively, to reject false oppositions and work to find, in the midst of apparent conflicts, underlying positions that are mutually reinforcing may narrow the gap. Success at this is needed if the military is to remain a central institution in American society.

Chapter 7

Vanishing Veterans: The Decline of Military Experience in the U.S. Congress

William T. Bianco
Jamie Markham

While many observers have noted that the number of veterans in the U.S. Congress has declined substantially since the early 1970s (e.g., Kreisher 1996, Ricks 1997d, Shepard 1994), few have spent much time identifying the source of the decline, or characterizing its implications. That there are fewer veterans in today's Congress compared to a generation ago is no surprise. Over the last thirty years, individuals who reached adulthood during and after the Vietnam War have replaced legislators who came of age during World War II and the Korean War. The question is, does Congress contain fewer veterans than would be expected, *after* controlling for generational replacement? What are the policy implications of this change?

This chapter specifies the long-term trends in military experience in the U.S. Congress over the entire history of the nation. The analysis captures factors that shape the number of congressional veterans, including changes in the number and age of veterans in the population and the increased election of female representatives. The analysis also examines trends within the Republican and Democratic caucuses.

The results are striking. Military experience in both the House and the Senate has indeed declined over the last generation. Even with these declines, current levels of military experience in Congress are not at an all-time minimum: the Congress of the early 1900s contained fewer veterans. The trend over the last two generations reflects the entry into politics

The authors would like to thank Erin Coughley, Sarah Griswold, Lanik Lowry, and Chris Housenick for research assistance.

of World War II and Korean War–era veterans during the 1950s and 1960s, followed by their retirement beginning in the late 1980s and replacement by individuals who came of age during the Vietnam War and thereafter.

The analysis shows that generational replacement does not completely explain the decline in congressional military experience. Comparison of the actual and expected percentage of veterans in the House and Senate shows that up until the 1990s, there were more veterans in Congress than would be expected, given the number and age distribution of veterans in the general population. This veterans' surplus ended in the mid-1990s in both the House and the Senate. Now, veterans are under-represented in both chambers. This change is due mostly to the behavior of Vietnam and post-Vietnam cohorts, but over-representation has declined significantly for World War II and Korean War–era cohorts as well. We discuss various explanations for this decline, arguing that it probably has more to do with the end of conscription than with veterans' disillusionment with the political process or with other changes in American society.

We also address the policy implications of the decline in congressional veterans by analyzing a number of congressional votes taken in the early 1990s on use-of-force questions (such as the Gulf War) as well as votes on other military matters (such as funding for draft registration). These analyses show that at the margin of other forces (constituency, party, personal ideology, etc.), the impact of veteran status on how a representative voted on these proposals is generally quite small, and has a relatively small impact on total support for any of the proposals.

Trends in Military Experience in the House: 1789–1999

This section presents historical data on the trend in military experience in the House and Senate from the first Congress to the present, and a comparison to the expected percentage for the period 1901–99.[1]

While technical details on the data are published elsewhere (Bianco 2000), three points bear emphasis. First, because of the nature of the pop-

---

1. The data on military experience in the House were complied from McKibbin (1997), ICPSR dataset 7803, augmented by the *Biographical Dictionary of the U. S. Congress*, available on <www.house.gov>. Data on the number of veterans in various age cohorts, along with the size of the total male population in these cohorts, was obtained from *The Statistical History of the United States from Colonial Times to the Present on CD-ROM*; the Department of Veterans Affairs web page: <www.va.gov:80/vetstats/index.htm>; and data in Sorensen and Field (1994).

ulation data, the analysis focuses exclusively on male members of Congress.[2] Thus, references to legislators or to the general population should be read with the understanding that that they refer to males only in Congress and to adult males in the population. Second, the analysis uses data from the Inter-University Consortium for Political and Social Research (ICPSR) to measure the number of veterans in Congress, and data from the Veterans Administration to measure the number of veterans in the population. The definitions of veteran status in the two datasets are not quite the same, although the differences do not appear to be salient.

A third issue in the analysis is the calculation of a baseline or expected percentage of veterans in Congress—that is, the number of veterans that would be elected to Congress, if Congress were a perfect mirror of society at large. This baseline is essential for determining whether veterans in Congress over- or under-represent their numbers in the general population, or, equivalently, whether the decline in congressional military experience is the result of changes in the supply of veterans who are in a position to run for political office.

The calculation of a baseline is not a simple task (as explained in Bianco 2000). For example, if the general population is 40 percent veteran, the expected percentage of congressional veterans might not be 40 percent. This is because in contemporary America, the probability of being a veteran is higher for older cohorts than for younger cohorts. Therefore, a Congress with a high percentage of older members would have a higher baseline than a Congress with a disproportionate number of younger members. The baseline measure used in this analysis controls for these effects.

TRENDS IN THE ACTUAL AND EXPECTED PERCENTAGE
Figure 7.1 shows the actual percentage of veterans in each session of the House and Senate since the Founding, along with the expected percentage since 1901.[3] Figure 7.1 reveals that the percentage of veterans in the House has sharply declined over the last generation, from over 75 percent

---

2. This exclusion controls for one possible explanation for the decline of military experience in Congress. Since very few female legislators were veterans, and since the number of female legislators has increased in recent years, one hypothesis is that congressional military experience is declining because female nonveterans are replacing male veterans. The exclusion of female legislators from the analysis controls for this possibility.

3. Because of limitations in available Census data, the expected percentage cannot be calculated before 1901.

Figure 7.1. Actual and Expected Percentage of Senate and House Veterans, 1789–1999.

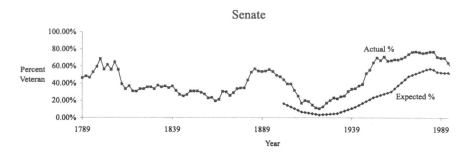

in 1971 to about 25 percent in 1999. A similar decline occurred in the Senate, although it began somewhat later and was somewhat smaller.[4]

However, Figure 7.1 also shows that both of these declines occurred from an unusually high base. The percentage of veterans in the 1970s-era House and Senate was the highest it has ever been in the history of the United States. From a historical perspective, the percentage of veterans in the contemporary Congress is not excessively low. Particularly in the Senate, the percentage is slightly above the long-run average.

Furthermore, the expected percentage lines suggest a partial explanation for the decline in congressional military experience. In both chambers, the actual percentage tracks closely with the expected measure: when there are a lot of veterans in the population, a lot of veterans are elected to the House and Senate. When the percentage of veterans in the population declines, so does the percentage in the House and the Senate. Thus, the observed decline in the number of congressional veterans is to some degree a reflection of larger trends in the population.

---

4.   Additional analysis, omitted here, shows that the decline is roughly the same across political parties, as well as on defense-related House and Senate committees.

The expected percentage lines also reveal a new and important facet of the decline in congressional military experience. Throughout almost all of the twentieth century, veterans in Congress have over-represented veterans in the general population: the actual percentage was greater than the expected percentage. This regularity ended in the mid-1990s. Now the number of veterans in the House and Senate is less than expected.

This analysis is the first to identify the under-representation of veterans in the contemporary Congress. Many sources have highlighted the decline of military experience in Congress. However, this decline is no surprise—fewer legislators are veterans because there are fewer veterans to elect. The real surprise is that the actual percentage of veterans has slipped below the expected percentage, suggesting that something more than demographic trends are at work. We return to this point later.

Generational Replacement and Congressional Military Experience

This section provides a deeper explanation of whether the decline in congressional veterans can be explained in terms of generational replacement. The analysis divides members of Congress into cohorts—groups with similar birth years. The aim is to capture trends in congressional military experience while controlling for the possibility that different cohorts have different probabilities of military service.

In particular, Figure 7.1 shows a decline in the absolute percentage of veterans in Congress, as well as a recent tendency for Congress to under-represent the percentage of veterans in the general population. These findings suggest two questions, both of which can be addressed by an analysis of cohorts. First, to what extent is the first trend a product of generational replacement—cohorts dominated by veterans of World War II and the Korean War being replaced by cohorts who came of age during Vietnam and thereafter? Second, insofar as there is under-representation of veterans in the contemporary Congress, does this trend exist for all cohorts, or just for younger ones?

The answers to these questions suggest that something more than demographics may be at work in shaping congressional military experience. Younger cohorts are less likely to be veterans compared to older cohorts. Thus, some of the decline in experience is an unavoidable product of generational replacement. However, the percentages of veterans in both younger and older cohorts in the contemporary Congress are lower than for their counterparts in the general population. Older cohorts, in particular, have moved from over-representation to under-representation.

DEFINING COHORTS

Our analysis divides members into four cohorts. The first cohort, "World War II/Korea," consists of members of Congress who were born between 1915 and 1934, and who reached adulthood (18 years old) between 1933 and 1953. These individuals were aged 35–44 in 1969, 45–54 in 1979, and so on. In substantive terms, this group is made up of people who were eligible for military service during World War II and the Korean War.

The second cohort, "1950s peacetime," captures members of Congress who were born between 1935 and 1944, and who came of age in 1953–62. While these individuals were subject to a limited peacetime draft, they did not face an all-out mobilization such as during earlier conflicts. The third "Vietnam" cohort comprises legislators who were born in 1945 to 1954, who came of age in 1963 to 1972, and who faced service during the height of the Vietnam War. The fourth "AVF" cohort includes legislators who were born in 1955 to 1964, and who came of age during 1973 to 1982, the era of the all-volunteer force.

HOW MANY VETERANS ARE IN EACH COHORT?

Data on the percentage of veterans in these cohorts (House and Senate combined) is shown in Figure 7.2.[5] We should expect the older cohorts to have a high percentage of veterans, and Figure 7.2 shows that indeed they do. In 1969, over 90 percent of the members of Congress who were eligible for service in World War II and Korea were veterans. The percentage declines somewhat over time, but even in 1999, the percentage of veterans from this group was over 70 percent.

The oldest cohort in Figure 7.2 is also the one with the highest percentage of veterans. Each subsequent cohort of legislators had a lower percentage of veterans in each year, culminating in the single datapoint for the AVF cohort in 1999, with less than 10 percent veterans. Moreover, the figure confirms that generational replacement is a critical part of the explanation for the decline in congressional veterans: younger cohorts in which veterans are a minority are replacing older cohorts dominated by veterans.

Are fewer veterans being elected to Congress because there are fewer veterans in the population, or are other forces at work reinforcing trends

---

5. The figure begins in 1969, or just before the peak of congressional military experience observed in Figure 7.1. Percentages for each cohort are plotted when their youngest member is 35 years or older. The reason for this restriction has to do with the organization of the VA data on veterans in the population: the youngest age bracket in the data is 35 and under. Eliminating these individuals from the analysis of cohorts has little impact, as there are only a few House members and virtually no Senators under 35 years of age.

Figure 7.2. Percentage of Veterans in Selected Congressional Cohorts.

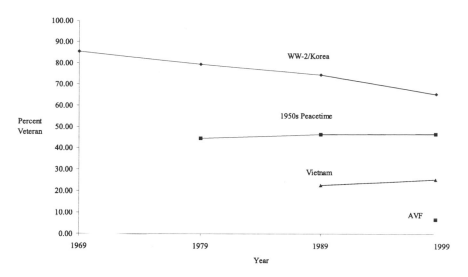

in the population? The answer is shown in Figure 7.3, which shows the extent to which the percentage of veterans in each congressional cohort over or underrepresents the corresponding population cohort.

For example, in 1969, Figure 7.3 shows that veterans in the World War II/Korea cohort substantially over-represented people of the same age cohort in the general population: the number of veterans in this cohort was more than 20 percent higher than the expected number. This cohort shifted to under-representation by 1999.

Figure 7.3 shows that in sharp contrast to the older cohorts, veterans in Congress who came of age during Vietnam or afterward substantially under-represent their population cohorts. Thus, the absolute decline in congressional veterans seen in Figure 7.1 is due to three factors. The members of younger cohorts in the general population are less likely to be veterans compared to older cohorts. Veterans in younger cohorts are less likely to become members of Congress, again compared to older cohorts. And veterans in some older cohorts, particularly those who served in World War II and the Korean War, have departed Congress at a disproportionately high rate.

What is driving this trend toward under-representation? The answer is not that there are fewer veterans in the younger cohorts, or the election of more female representatives, as the analysis here controls for these possibilities. One plausible explanation is an emerging divergence in attitudes between veterans and politicians, as veterans depart or refuse to

Figure 7.3. Over- and Under-representation By Congressional Veterans.

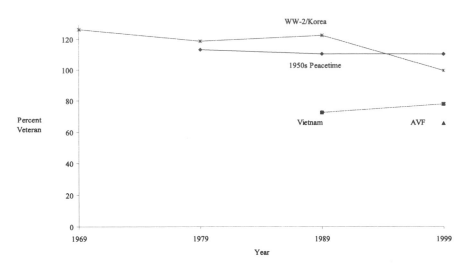

NOTE: 100 percent indicates the same percentage of veterans in Congressional cohort as in the same age cohort in U.S. population.

enter a profession that they see as marked by chaos and dishonesty. Such an explanation would be consistent with the comments of military officers in Ricks (1997c) and others.

However, the historical record suggests a second explanation for the patterns in Figure 7.3: a change in the nature of military service over the last few generations.[6] Consider the oldest cohort, legislators who came of age during World War II and Korea. A high percentage of this cohort served in one or both of these conflicts, either as enlistees or as draftees. For them, military service was a virtual certainty, not an option. Members of the later cohorts are a sharp contrast. Consider the Vietnam cohort. Some were drafted into service, others volunteered, but many others avoided military service, either through deferments or simply by having a high enough lottery number. The difference is even starker for the AVF cohort. The members of this cohort were never subject to conscription; the only way they could become veterans is by enlisting.

---

6.   There are at least two other possible explanations. One is that veteran status has become a less politically valuable characteristic for a would-be candidate, or that party leaders have become less likely to select veterans as candidates. A second possibility, which is related to the arguments about changes in the likelihood of military service, is that the move to an all-volunteer, careerist military made it harder for veterans to build the career in public life necessary to facilitate a later run for Congress.

These differences across cohorts in how individuals became veterans could explain much of the under-representation seen in Figure 7.3. Absent universal conscription, such as occurred in World War II and Korea, individuals with high educational levels and high socio-economic status, who are disproportionately more likely to serve as congressional candidates, are less likely to serve in the military compared to individuals who are less educated and of a lower socio-economic status. In an era marked by universal conscription, these behavioral differences wash out: essentially everyone becomes a veteran, because no one has a choice. But when military service becomes an option, as it increasingly did in the 1960s and thereafter, it would be no surprise to find that the kinds of people who typically serve in Congress are likely to remain civilians.

This argument suggests that while the probability of military service has been falling for everyone over the last two generations, it has been falling at a greater rate for the people who typically run for Congress compared to the rest of the population. As a result, there are fewer and fewer veterans in younger congressional cohorts. Moreover, in the absence of some form of universal conscription, this asymmetry is unlikely to change.

The Impact of the Decline: Veterans and Voting on Military Matters

This analysis has found two trends that can be identified as emerging political-military gaps: an absolute decline in the number of veterans in the House and Senate, and a relative decline in the number of veterans in congressional cohorts compared to the general population. This section considers the implications of these declines. What difference does it make to have fewer veterans in Congress?

The search for implications focuses on roll-call votes: whether veterans vote differently than nonveterans, and whether these differences translate into significantly different levels of voting on defense-related proposals.[7] The proposals used in this analysis, 15 House votes and 18 Senate votes, were cast during the 102nd, 103rd, and 104th Congresses.

---

7. Votes have the advantage that they are actual, measurable behavior. The alternative would be to determine whether veterans held different attitudes, preferences, or information compared to nonveterans. Aside from all the problems inherent to measuring these factors, focusing on them to the exclusion of behavior misses an essential point in the debate over the decline in congressional veterans. That is, does the decline make a difference in terms of policy outcomes?

The proposals were selected by searching through the Project Vote Smart database for all votes on defense spending, defense policy, and foreign policy in the 102nd–104th Congress where the losing side had at least 30 percent of votes cast.[8]

We use logistic regression to estimate the impact that being a veteran has on a representative's votes on each of these proposals. The analysis controls for other influences on vote decisions, such as a representative's party affiliation, personal ideology, gender, district or state partisan balance, the percentage of the constituent population working for the military, and the number of major military bases in the district or state.[9]

For each proposal, the logit parameters are used to estimate the total number of "yea" votes that would be observed if all of the members of Congress who voted on the proposal were veterans, rather than the third to a half that are actually veterans. This estimate is then compared to the actual number of yea votes. A large difference suggests that veteran status has a large impact on voting behavior after other factors are controlled for. A small difference implies that the impact of veteran status is small. For example, suppose that a proposal voted on in the Senate received 60 yea votes, while the analysis described above shows that if every Senator were a veteran, the number of yea votes would increase to 80. In that case, the percentage difference in the two coalitions, real and hypothetical, would be 33 percent: a substantial change.

If being a veteran had a significant impact on a legislator's voting behavior—and on the difference in the number of yea votes as measured above—then the decline in congressional veterans could have important policy consequences. If, however, the range between the actual and hypothetical number of yea votes is consistently small, then the decline has not made much difference in terms of votes on proposals.

The results of the comparison for the thirty-odd votes in the analysis are shown in Figure 7.4. Each column gives the number of votes that had a specific percentage-change estimate. These estimates are rounded to the nearest whole number; the 0 and 1 percent categories are combined. For example, one House vote and three Senate votes had percentage change

---

8.   For information on Project Vote Smart, see <www.vote-smart.org>. Details on each proposal are given in Bianco (2000).

9.   Details on this technique, model specification, and parameter estimates are in Bianco (2000). One question is whether veteran status might have an indirect impact on a representative's voting behavior. Specifically, veterans might differ from nonveterans in their personal ideology. Analysis of preference data available from the senior author shows that for the 1990s-era Congresses, there are no significant ideological differences between veterans and nonveterans.

estimates of 3 percent; seven House votes and three Senate votes had estimates of 1 percent or less.

As Figure 7.4 shows, the impact of veteran status on voting in the contemporary House and Senate appears in generally quite small: most of the percentage change estimates are 5 percent or less. For example, consider the 1990 House vote authorizing Desert Storm (House Joint Resolution 77): 249 representatives voted in favor of the proposal. The logistic analysis shows that if every representative had been a veteran—and all other factors were held constant—the number of yea votes would decrease only slightly to 248. Put another way, the two coalitions, real and hypothetical, differ in size by less than 1 percent. For the Senate vote on Desert Storm, there were 51 actual yea votes, while 48 would be predicted for an all-veteran Senate: this is a 5.9 percent difference in the size of the two majority coalitions. Thus, while the impact of veteran status was larger in the Senate for this vote, the differences do not appear to be substantial.

The impact of veteran status is larger for some proposals. For example, during the 1993 House vote on President Clinton's "don't ask, don't tell" compromise on homosexuals in the military (House Resolution 2401), 166 members voted for the compromise. If all representatives had been veterans, the coalition in favor would have shrunk to 138, a 16.9 percent reduction. Similarly, while 201 House members voted in 1993 to block the ending of draft registration (an amendment to House Resolution 2401, a defense appropriations bill), the analysis predicts that the coalition would increase to 241 representatives in the all-veteran scenario, a 19.9 percent difference.

The temptation from these three cases is to say that the impact of veteran status is potentially large in a narrow range of proposals, such as those that deal with issues of military lifestyle and culture. However, the analysis reveals no clear pattern. More specifically, while the percentage difference numbers are large for the two House votes, the corresponding percentages for Senate votes on these proposals are much smaller: 3 percent and 0 percent, respectively.

In sum, the analysis suggests that while veteran status can have a substantial impact on both member votes and overall outcomes, this effect will not be observed on all proposals, or even on a substantial percentage. Whatever information or perspective military experience conveys, this effect will often be washed out by the impact of other factors on the vote decision. This analysis does not imply that the decline in congressional veterans has had no impact on votes or outcomes. It suggests that this effect, if it exists, is primarily indirect. Having fewer veterans may change the kinds of proposals that are voted on in the House

Figure 7.4. Impact of Veteran Status in Voting, 102nd–104th House and Senate.

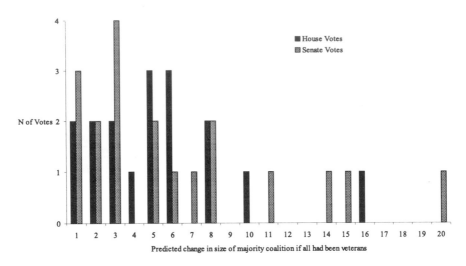

Predicted change in size of majority coalition if all had been veterans

and Senate, even if it does not have a direct impact when votes are actually cast.

Discussion

We have found that over the last generation, military experience in Congress has declined in both absolute and relative terms. Generational replacement explains much of this decline, but it is not the whole story. For the first time in this century, veterans are under-represented in Congress compared to their numbers in the general population. Simple replacement of high-percentage veteran cohorts by low-percentage veteran cohorts does not account for this trend.

Why is congressional military experience on the wane? One possibility is that the decline reflects a widening ideological or attitudinal split between the military personnel and political leaders. Lacking measures of attitude, this analysis has not attempted to test this explanation. However, the comparison of congressional cohorts with their population counterparts suggests a different explanation, one based in the elimination of conscription, and the resulting asymmetric decline in the probability of military service for high-education, high socio-economic status individuals who typically run for Congress.

Finally, the analysis of roll-call votes suggests a reorientation of the debate over the implications of the decline in congressional military experience. In the Congresses of the 1990s, being a veteran did not have a systematic impact on a legislator's voting behavior, at least not at the margin of other factors. Thus, if the decline in the number of congressional veterans is leading to significant changes in defense policy, its effects must be indirect, through changes in congressional agendas or in the quantity and kinds of the information available to legislators.

Chapter 8

**Explaining the Gap:
Vietnam, the Republicanization
of the South, and the End of
the Mass Army**

Michael C. Desch

Ole Holsti's Foreign Policy Leadership Project (FPLP) has conclusively established that there is a widening set of political, social, and cultural gaps between the officer corps of the United States military and the American civilian leadership. Holsti found that while civilian and military attitudes did not diverge across the board, there were significant differences on many different issues (Holsti 1997; 1998). His most dramatic finding was that the political attitudes of military officers had swung dramatically toward the Republican Party. As Figure 8.1 shows, in 1976, 33 percent of military officers identified themselves as Republicans, while by 1996, almost 70 percent did.

This stands in marked contrast with civilian political affiliations. In 1976 about 25 percent of civilians characterized themselves as Republicans. By 1996, that figure had grown to only 34 percent. Thus, there was a political "gap" between civilian and military officers in 1976 of 8 percentage points which by 1996 had grown to over 33 percentage points.[1] In a

I wish to thank for advice and comments on earlier drafts of the paper Alex Roland, Charlie Stevenson, Chris Gelpi, Ben Fordham, Richard Fording, Kavlev Sepp, Robert Angevine, Sean Lynn-Jones, Jacques Hymans, Talbot Imlay, Ronald Krebs, and participants in seminars at the John M. Olin Institute for Strategic Studies at Harvard University and the Security Studies Program at MIT.

1. Some critics worry that this political gap reflects not a gap between the military and the rest of society but rather a gap between the civilian elites (who are presumably more liberal) and the civilian non-elites (who are more conservative) and that the military is in fact representative of the latter. If true, this would refocus the gap debate

Figure 8.1. The Civil-Military Gap in Party Affiliation.

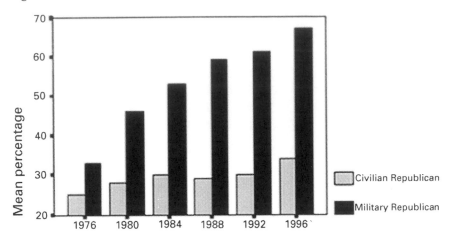

SOURCE: Holsti, FPLP Survey Data, 1997.

replication and extension of Holsti's FPLP survey, the Triangle Institute for Security Studies (TISS) survey confirmed Holsti's original findings and demonstrated that there were gaps on a host of additional organizational, political, and social cultural issues (see Chapter 1 by Ole Holsti in this volume). Since Holsti's study, the debate has shifted from whether there is a gap to two other questions: First, does the gap matter? (For arguments that it does, see Desch 1999c and Chapter 3 by Gronke and Feaver in this volume.) Second, what explains the gap? In this chapter, I will offer an answer to the second question.

Analysts have suggested that changes in the nature of the American military, changes in American society, or a combination of the two, explain this growing political gap. My argument is that some but not all of these factors account for the wide civil-military political gap identified by Holsti. This is particularly true for changes in the American military institution, largely the result of the decline of the mass army, combined with domestic political shifts, especially the Republicanization of the South. I also assess some of the policy recommendations offered to close or bridge

---

away from civil-military relations. However, if one looks at the National Opinion Research Center's annual General Social Survey data for political party affiliation (PARTYID) it becomes clear that the general population was slightly *less* Republican than Holsti's civilian elites during the sample period. This is also true of the TISS survey data (Q76). This fact makes Holsti's findings all the more striking because they contradict the conventional wisdom that the elite is less Republican than the masses.

the gap. My most important policy conclusion is that, contrary to popular belief, reinstituting the draft would do little to close or manage the gap. Solutions will have to found elsewhere, and I suggest a few possibilities.

This chapter begins with a brief discussion of the data available to ascertain the causes of this growing civil-military political gap. It then assesses some variables that might explain the gap: those that emphasize changes in the military and those that highlight changes in civilian society. Next, it suggests how changes in the nature of the military institution and changes in American domestic politics have combined to produce the gap. It then tries to account for other gaps Holsti identified in his FPLP data set. It also offers some conjectures based on this model to explain some of the various civil-military gaps identified by the TISS project. It concludes with an assessment of the policy recommendations available to close or manage the gap.

The Data

The data with which I assess the various explanations and construct my own argument about the causes of the gap come from a wide variety of sources. The dependent variable the level of Republican affiliation of military officers—is measured by a variable called MODMILRE derived from Holsti's data. I have also used Holsti's data to construct a measure of civilian political attachment to the Republican party called MODCIVRE.[2] Data for the percentage of officers from service academies (ACADEMY), percentage of officers from ROTC (ROTC), total size of the officer corps (TOOFF), mean age of the officer corps (AGE), average length of service (MOSERV), total enlisted force (TOENLIST), and quality of new accessions (QUALITY) come from the Department of Defense (Assistant Secretary of Defense 1997). The data on the total size (TOSIZE) of the military was a combination of TOOFF and TOENLIST, also from the Department of Defense. The data on presidential votes in the South (SOUPRES), party identification (PARTYID), age (AGE), feelings about conservatism (CONTEMP), and confidence in government (CONFED)

---

2. In order to generate enough data points to make MODMILRE and MODCIVREP compatible with other variables, it was necessary to estimate some missing data. I did so by drawing a line between the six data points in the original Holsti data and estimating missing values based on that line. This produced an additional 15 data points. I tested the robustness of this estimation by dropping some of the original data points and then checking how close this method put me. It worked very well. I acknowledge that by adding points this way I have artificially improved "fit" in the models in which I use this variable. I thank Richard Fording for suggesting this approach to me.

came from the "General Social Surveys, 1972–1998" (Davis and Smith 1999). The data on the military participation ratio (MILPART), which I use to measure the decline of the mass army, came from the U.S. Bureau of the Census (U.S. Bureau of the Census 1975; 1998). The data on southern votes in congressional and gubernatorial elections (SOUREP) came from *The Almanac of American Politics* (Barone, et al. 1972–2000). Data on southern officer accessions (OFFSOUTH) was provided by the Defense Manpower Data Center.[3] Finally, the data on the growth of military wages (PAYGROW) comes from RAND (Hosek, Peterson and Heilbrun 1994, 7, Figure 1, "ECI-Based Relative Pay Growth [in percentage]").[4]

Assessing Alternative Explanations of the Growing Political Gap

There have been many important changes in the U.S. military and American society that alone or in combination might explain the growing political gap between the military and civilian society. Changes in the military include the end of the draft and the transition to an all-volunteer force; changes in the location and character of the nation's Reserve Officer Training Corps (ROTC); changes in the regional origins of military officers; an increase in percentage of officers who are sons and daughters of career soldiers; an increase in the percentage of military academy graduates in the officer corps; an increase in the average length of service of officers; an increase in their mean age; the end of the mass army; and the Vietnam War. Changes in American society include a dramatic shift in the political complexion of the Democratic Party; a change in the political affiliation of the south; a general erosion in faith in American governmental institutions; and a secular decline in civilian experience with, and interest in, the military. In this section I lay out and assess the logic of these arguments and then examine the empirical evidence that might support or undermine their role as causes of the gap.

Understanding how the transition to an all-volunteer force contributes to the gap requires some analysis of why people enlist in the mili-

---

3.   Data supplied by Defense Manpower Data Center, Seaside, California. According to *Population Representation in the Military Services: Fiscal Year 1996* (Assistant Secretary of Defense 1997), the South includes Delaware, Maryland, the District of Columbia, Virginia, West Virginia, North Carolina, South Carolina, Georgia, Florida, Kentucky, Tennessee, Alabama, Mississippi, Arkansas, Louisiana, Oklahoma, and Texas.

4.   Aside from TOSIZE and SOUREP, these variables consist of interval-level data with normal distributions and so I can estimate relationships using parametric statistics such as Pearson's Correlations and Linear Regressions. A complete copy of this data-set is available from the author.

tary in the first place. There are two competing models. Rationalist or economic theories maintain that the decision to enlist is essentially an economic one: potential enlistees weigh the costs and the benefits of military service and decide on that basis whether or not to enlist. In addition to salary, such economic incentives include the level of unemployment in the economy as a whole, and the other benefits such as education or work experience that one might get in the military.[5] Such an economic model would predict that as pay goes down, unemployment decreases, or other benefits decline, fewer numbers of high-quality enlistees will join the military.

In contrast, normative/ascriptive models of enlistment stress such motives as patriotism and an affinity for the military lifestyle. John Farris argues that:

The processes of retention of junior officers and the formation of career decisions are relatively unaffected by the economic factors of pay, benefits, and marketability (as measured by current education), though no doubt for many officers these are key considerations. In fact, it appears that most career-oriented officers make their decision to remain in the military despite perceptions of economic loss. Much more significant in determining career plans are the satisfactions of the military work role, and the relationships with co-workers and supervisors (as seen in the reenlistment intentions of junior enlisted personnel). (Farris 1984, 270. Also see Shields 1980, 134–135; and in general see McKown, Udis, and Ash 1980, 113–132.)

The truth is that both economic and non-economic factors affect how many and what sorts of people join the military voluntarily. Let me illustrate how economic and non-economic factors might interact to change the political complexion of the military. Assume that for the economically motivated potential military enlistee, his or her decision to volunteer is represented by the following formula:[6]

$$P_1 > P - (1 + \delta) C$$

Assuming that aversion to military service is constant across the population, the likelihood that an individual will enlist rises with increases in

---

5. Perry, Griffith, and White 1991, 128; Fredland and Little 1984, 226; Bachman 1983, 86–104; Hosek, Antel, and Peterson 1989, 398–399. Gilroy, Phillips, and Blair (1990, 344) show that using money for college as an enlistment incentive attracts high-quality recruits. Also see Dale and Gilroy 1984, 207. On enlistment motivations in general see Gorman and Thomas 1991, 589–599.

6. In the equation C = civilian income potential, P_1 = level of pay necessary to get an individual to volunteer, P = military pay, δ = aversion to military service (Oi 1967, 242).

military pay. The problem with this economic approach is that it focuses excessively on how the difference between civilian and military pay might affect the number of potential enlistees (Farris 1984, 251). The puzzle is to explain the increase in the quality of military accessions at a time in which, by most measures, military pay is well below that of the civilian sector.[7]

One solution to the puzzle is the possibility that δ (aversion to military service) might vary among individuals in the general population and that some might actually be insensitive to variations in pay. If that is the case, then military wages well below those of the civilian economy may not just reduce the size of the applicant pool, but might change the political and social complexion of it. If one makes the reasonable assumption that low aversion to the military life-style coincides with other characteristics that are not common to the average individual in civilian society, then it is easy to see how an all-volunteer military, paying wages below those of the civilian job market, would attract individuals very different from the norm. (For further discussion of the differences between volunteers and conscripts, see Shils and Janowitz 1948, 280–315.) Individuals with a low aversion to military life are likely to be less sensitive to the gap between civilian and military wages. Therefore, as military pay decreases relative to civilian pay, such individuals are more likely to be over-represented among recruits.

The argument that the transition from a conscript to an all-volunteer force should produce a military that is not socially and politically representative makes logical sense. There are two caveats, however: first, even with conscription, some people still volunteer for military service, and those people are more than twice as likely as draftees to make the military their career (Sinaiko 1990, 244). Thus, the career part of a conscript military is still likely to be unrepresentative of the general population. Second, the largest career group in the military is officers. While some officers may originally have enlisted to avoid the draft (Oi 1967, 224), the vast majority were true volunteers. It is the officer corps that really matters in terms of the military's political role (Quester and Thomason 1984, 86; Friedman 1967, 205; Finer 1988, 227; and Van Doorn 1975, 155). There is little doubt, however, that the transition from a conscript to an all-volunteer force makes some difference in terms of its political and social composition. Indeed, the data suggest that lower military wage growth

---

7. Hosek, Antel and Peterson (1989, 7) provide data about the pay gap but argue that if calculated somewhat differently, the gap is much smaller.

and the increasingly Republican make-up of the military are significantly correlated.[8]

Another significant change in the military since the early 1970s has been in the location and character of the Reserve Officer Training Corps (ROTC) programs (W. Snyder 1984, 422; Coumbe and Harford 1998, 13–14; on ROTC in general, see Peck 1994, 217–237). As Table 8.1 shows, ROTC programs have been discontinued at a number of elite schools, primarily in the Northeast, but many new programs have been established in other schools, primarily in the South, where 49 percent of Army, 41 percent of Air Force, and 41 percent of Navy ROTC programs are currently located (Desch 1999b, Appendix I). Since many are located at state schools, it is more likely that participants in these programs would come from those regions. In addition, the character of the ROTC curriculum changed at about the same time. These changes include a decrease in the numbers of candidates admitted; an increase in the number of scholarships awarded; a decrease in the liberal arts and an increase in the military science components of the curriculum; and an increase in the required term of service after graduation (W. Snyder 1984, 402). The net effect was to produce an ROTC cadet pool that was more Southern and more likely to produce career officers than before.

There is abundant evidence that graduates of ROTC programs are very different from the rest of civilian society. While 29.1 percent of the nation's college students come from the South, 41 percent of military officers do (W. Snyder 1984, 415, Table 5). Most of the latter are ROTC graduates. Cadets are also on average smarter than the general civilian college population; the average Scholastic Aptitude Test score for ROTC cadets was 1250 at a time when the civilian average was only 900 (W. Snyder 1984, 410–411). It may seem that changes in the location and complexion of the ROTC program should play some role in the growing gap, but the statistical association between changes in the percentage of the officer corps coming from ROTC and the increasingly Republican bent of the military is not all that strong.[9] (However, the ROTC variable may measure the effects of changes in numbers but not the impact of qualitative changes such as the location and nature of the ROTC programs.)

---

8. The Pearson Correlation for PAYGROW and MODMILRE is $r^2(15) = -.816, p \leq .001$ (two-tailed). The closer the r^2 is to 1 or -1, the better; p should be equal to, or lower than, .05.

9. The Pearson Correlation for ROTC and MODMILRE is $r2(21) = .368, p = .101$ (two-tailed).

Table 8.1. ROTC Units Opened and Units Closed and Never Reopened, 1968–72.

	OPENED	CLOSED

MIDWEST	Central Michigan State
	Central State
	Kearney State
	Northern Illinois
	Northern Michigan
	University of Wisconsin at:
	  LaCrosse
	  Oshkosh
	  Platteville
	  Stevens Point
	  Whitewater
	Western Illinois	

NORTHEAST	Long Island University Rider College Rochester Institute of Technology St. John's	C.W. Post City College of New York Dartmouth Harvard New York University Pratt Institute Yale
SOUTH	Alabama A&M Alcorn A&M Arkansas AM&N Austin-Peay Campell College East Central State Florida Institute of Technology Francis T. Nichols State Jackson State Missouri Western Morehead State Northeast Missouri State Old Dominion Southwestern State State College of Arkansas Stephen F. Austin University of Tampa Virginia Commonwealth	Virginia Commonwealth
WEST	Boise College Brigham Young Eastern New Mexico Southern Colorado State Weber State	Stanford

Figure 8.2. Percentage of Southern Officers.

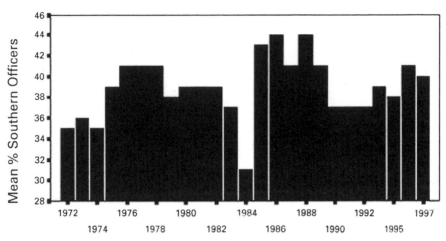

Year

SOURCE: Defense Manpower Data Center.

Another widely accepted argument is that the large percentage of military officers from the South explains the growing political and cultural gap. Huntington attributed this disproportionate number of Southern officers to the long tradition of warfare in the South, the romanticizing of violence in Southern culture, and the region's agrarian social and economic structures (Huntington 1957, 211–212). Figure 8.2 demonstrates that disproportionate numbers of officers do come from the South.[10] The main problem with this argument is that the disproportionate representation of southerners in the officer corps has been relatively constant, not variable. Thus if we try to correlate changes in the percentage of southern officers with changes in the number of officers who self-identify as Republicans, we do not find any association at all.[11] The high percentage of southern officers in the U.S. military is not, by itself, a factor in the growing political gap.

Another major change in the U.S. military since the early 1970s has

10. Defense Manpower Data Center data. In addition, there is corroborating evidence of the regional affiliations of officers from data on where they retire. For example, Snyder (1994, 587) shows that retirees tend to cluster in South and West; Hefner (1992, 410, Table 1) shows 48 percent of retirees settle in the South.

11. The Pearson Correlation for OFFSOUTH and MODMILRE is $r2(20) = -.078$, $p = .745$ (two-tailed).

Figure 8.3. Decreasing Size of the U.S. Military.

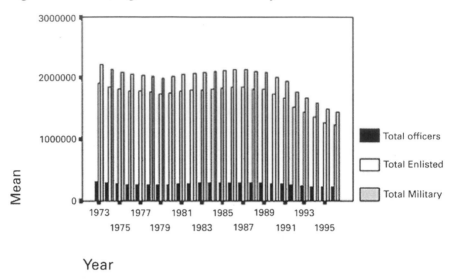

Year

SOURCE: Department of Defense, 1996.

been its decrease in size. Such a decrease might affect the political gap in one of two ways. First, the smaller the size of the force, the higher the statistical probability that individual soldiers will not be representative of civilian society (Phillips 1992, 15–16). Second, significant reductions in the size of the military may have increased their hostility to civilian society (Wong and McNully 1994, 199–216).

As Figure 8.3 shows, the size of the military has declined markedly since 1973. The association between the size of the military and its increasing identification with the Republican Party is unclear. The signs are in that direction but the findings are not significant except for the association between the decreasing size of the enlisted ranks and the Republicanization of the military.[12] This may help reconcile the finding of David Segal, et al. (Chapter 4 in this volume) that the enlisted ranks remain broadly representative of American society, with Holsti's data that show that the military seems to be growing more politically distinct. As

12. The Kendall's Tau-b Correlation between TOSIZE and MODMILRE is (21) = -.295, p = .061 (two-tailed). The Pearson Correlation between TOOFF and MODMILRE is $r^2(21)$ = -.236, p = .303 (two-tailed). The Pearson Correlation between TOENLIST and MODMILRE is $r^2(21)$ = -.591, p= .005 (two-tailed).

the size of the enlisted ranks—the most politically representative part of the military—shrinks, the unrepresentativeness of the rest of the force is likely to increase.

Another change has been the increasing numbers of sons and daughters of career military people who themselves make the military their career. The logic of this argument is that the more children of military professionals enlist, the more homogeneous the military is likely to become. John Farris concludes that sons and daughters of career military officers and non-commissioned officers (NCOs) are six times more likely to enlist and then make the military their career (Farris 1981, 550–554). This has been a more general phenomenon; 45 percent of officers in the French Army since World War II and one-third of U.S. Air Force cadets since 1976 come from military families (Martin 1981, 562; DeFleur and Warner 1987, 519). There is also some evidence that certain religions—especially Catholicism and other hierarchical/ritualistic religions—are more compatible than others with a successful military career (Karsten 1983, 427–440). This may also be an homogenizing factor. Unfortunately, we do not have longitudinal data with which to test these propositions.[13]

Yet another change in the U.S. military since the early 1970s has been the increasing percentage of service academy graduates in the officer corps. The logic of this argument is straightforward: service academy graduates develop a great sense of loyalty to the military service (like most members of other professions); they are smaller than the general population; and they probably are unrepresentative of the rest of society on a host of issues including political attitudes.

Figure 8.4 shows that the percentage of service academy graduates in the officer corps has almost tripled since 1972. Volker Franke has convincingly demonstrated that attendance at a service academy produces a significant increase in corporate identification with the service (Franke 1997). Robert Priest and his colleagues have documented the very different political and cultural attitudes of military academy and civilian undergraduates (Priest, Fullerton and Bridges 1982, 638). Janowitz demonstrated some time ago that West Point graduates dominated the top ranks of the Army, and thus have disproportionate influence (Janowitz 1971, 57). My data suggest that there is a substantial

---

13.   I could get data on religious affiliations of officers only for 1996 through 1999 from the Defense Manpower Data Center. Roman Catholics, for example, comprise 34 percent of all officers whose religious affiliation was known in 1996. The next highest percentage was Protestant–No Denominational Preference, which comprised 11 percent of all officers whose religious affiliation was known.

Figure 8.4. Percentage of Academy Graduates in the Military.

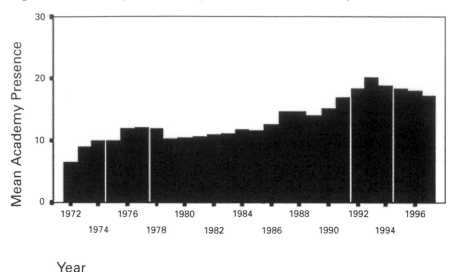

SOURCE: Department of Defense, 1996.

correlation between increasing percentage of academy graduates and the increasing level of Republican Party affiliation in the military.[14]

Another explanation of the growing gap might be that it is the result of the lengthening average term of service of enlistees. The logic of this argument is that the longer one is with the colors, the more culturally distinct one's attitudes are likely to be (Schreiber 1979, 122–131). As Figure 8.5 shows, the average term of service has risen from 116 months in 1973 to 129 months in 1996. The correlation with increasing Republican affiliation of the military is strong.[15]

Still another institutional explanation of the growing political gap is that with the increasing average age of the military since 1973, the political attitudes of the military should become more conservative. The logic of this argument is that people become more conservative with age.[16]

As Figure 8.6 shows, the average age of an officer has increased from

14. The Pearson Correlation for ACADEMY and MODMILRE is $r^2(21) = .775$, p ≤ .001.

15. The Pearson Correlation between MOSERV and MODMILRE is $r^2(21) = .650$, p = .001.

16. AGE and CONTEMP have a Pearson Correlation of $r^2(3589) = .095$, p ≤ .001.

Figure 8.5. Increasing Average Term of Service.

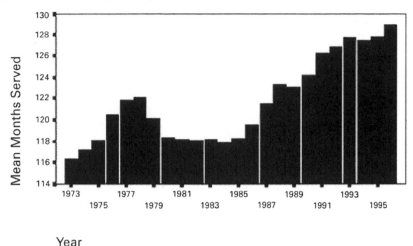

SOURCE: Department of Defense, 1996.

32 to 34 years. While this might seem like a small increase, it is strongly associated with the growing Republicanization of the officer corps.[17]

Another argument is that the decline of the mass army is in part responsible for the growing political gap. Major changes in the nature of warfare since World War II have altered the type of military structure necessary for great powers (Janowitz 1972, 10–16; Kelleher 1978, 3–29; Martin 1977, 355–406). From the French Revolution until World War II, the great powers relied upon mass armies that were almost by definition representative of broader society (Posen 1993, 80–124). A mass army is defined by the manner of accession (conscription, so everyone is liable for military service), size (large, so there is a high military participation ratio), and term of service (relatively short, so there is a large turn-over). After World War II, a number of developments contributed to the demise of the mass army. The most obvious of these was the "nuclear revolution," which dramatically reduced the likelihood of direct great power confrontation and therefore reduced the importance of large conventional military forces (Brodie 1946; Jervis 1989). Another major change was the rise of unconventional wars (Burk 1989, 438). Finally, increasingly complex conventional military technology made it necessary for soldiers to develop skills that could only be taught to a long-service, professional military. It is likely that the much anticipated "revolution in military af-

17.   The Pearson Correlation between AGE and MODMILRE is $r^2(21) = .840$, $p \leq .001$.

Figure 8.6. Increasing Average Age of Officer Corps.

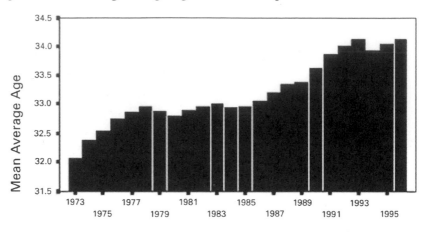

Year

SOURCE: Department of Defense, 1996.

fairs," the result of advances in information and precision-strike technology, will add more momentum to this trend (Krepinevich 1994, 30; Jablonsky 1994, 18–36). The mass army was not optimal for nuclear, high-technology conventional or unconventional conflicts and so it has gradually been replaced with smaller professional armies.

As Figure 8.7 shows, the MPR (military participation ratio, or the percentage of the population involved in military service at any given time) has dropped dramatically.[18] As many writers have suggested, the decline in the MPR was bound to produce militaries that were far less socially representative (Van Doorn 1975, 154; Martin 1981, 56; Haltiner 1998, 7–36). Some scholars such as Samuel Finer thought that this trend had already begun in the nineteenth century, when the European countries' leaders were no longer the same people who fought its wars (Finer 1988, 188–189). But Janowitz and Moskos more convincingly argue that the key transition point was 1945, when the United States went from a "mobilization force" to a "force in being" (Janowitz and Moskos 1979, 172–173). The nuclear revolution, the Vietnam War, and especially the end of the

---

18. The seminal discussion of the military participation ratio [MPR] is Andreski 1968. For a somewhat different take on the consequences of the declining MPR, see Chapter 6 by James Burk in this volume. Our figures differ because mine includes every year since 1820 while Burk's starts in 1910 and provides data in 10-year increments, thus excluding much of World Wars I and II.

Figure 8.7. Percent of U.S. Population in Military.

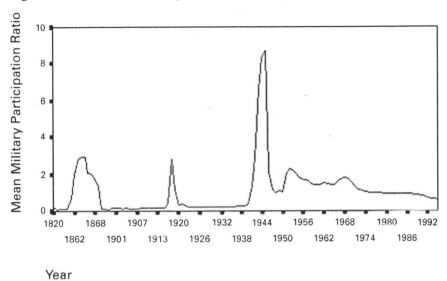

Year

SOURCE: U.S. Bureau of Census, 1975; 1998.

Cold War have accelerated this trend. Indeed, a professional "force in being" facing a prolonged period of peace increases the likelihood of political and cultural divergence between the military and society (Desch 1999a). As Jonathan Alford observes, "The limited experience of volunteer forces during long periods of peace inclines one to believe that such forces tend to become largely irrelevant and self-serving organizations which grow increasingly away from the society that is called upon to sustain and support them" (Alford 1980, 255–256, 250).

Historically, the American experience seems to fit this pattern. In periods of high threat, the gap between the military and civilian society shrank; in periods of lower threat, it grew. As one of the standard military histories of the United States notes, this pattern was evident early in American history:

An acute threat could result in an expeditionary force that more nearly represented a colony's social composition. For example, at a time when Virginia was raising its army almost exclusively from among the poorest elements of its populace, Massachusetts was acting quite differently. Far more immediately threatened by the French in Canada than was Virginia, Massachusetts fielded military forces during the 1750s that were not permanently weighted toward the permanently poor and vagrants but instead reflected the colony's overall social composition (Millett and Maslowski 1994, 9).

This pattern continues today. The Reagan administration, for example, was in office during a fairly acute period in Cold War tensions and it was only then, Colin Powell has suggested, that the civil-military gap caused by the Vietnam War was closed: "Possibly the greatest contribution the Reagan-Weinberger team made was to end the estrangement between the American people and their defenders. During this time, the rupture was healed and America once more embraced its armed forces" (Powell and Persico 1995, 313).

With the end of the Cold War, there is a growing recognition that this gap is growing again. "There's less of a [military] presence in the daily lives of most Americans," notes former Secretary of Defense William Cohen, "and to the extent that [the public] are not reminded of the role the military plays day in and day out, there's a danger they will not be as supportive" (quoted in Myers 1999c). Throughout American history, a threatening international security environment seems to have narrowed the civil-military gap, while peace has widened it.

Finally, the Vietnam War played an important, if unquantifiable, role in changing military attitudes on both organizational and political and social issues. The experience of the Vietnam war led the U.S. military to refocus largely on waging high-technology conventional warfare. (An excellent journalistic account is Kitfield 1997.) This institutional change produced one of the twentieth century's finest military machines, but also caused problems for civilian control of the military, especially when civilian leaders sought to get the military to undertake operations other than high-intensity conventional warfare. (On how the Powell Doctrine's limits on the use of military force are complicating civilian control, see Desch 1999a, 36–37.) Vietnam also caused less tangible, but potentially momentous, changes in attitudes among military officers toward political and social issues in society more generally. As David Petraeus notes, the "widespread acceptance of the lessons of Vietnam has produced a military leadership that today conforms more closely to Huntington's concept of military conservativism than it did in any other period since World War II" (Petraeus 1989, 499). This is one of the most striking conclusions in Thomas Ricks' *Making the Corps* and a theme that emerges strikingly from the Holsti FPLP and TISS survey data. The fact that the civil-military gap grew so markedly after the mid-1970s suggests that the Vietnam experience must have played a major role.

Four changes in American civilian society may also help explain the growing gap. These include a leftward shift in the political center of gravity of the Democratic party; a dramatic reorientation of the political landscape of the South; a general erosion in faith and confidence in government institutions; and a secular decline in civilian experience with, and interest in, military affairs.

One might argue that the source of the growing political gap is not so much the increasing Republican tilt of the military, but rather changes in the domestic political complexion of civilian society. The key change emphasized by many analysts is the leftward shift in the democratic party in the late 1960s and early 1970s. The thrust of this argument is that the military did not change; rather, the country's political complexion did and so the Republicanization of the military merely reflects the Republicanization of the country. As one former Democrat put it, "'We did not leave the Democratic Party, it left us'" (Radosh 1996, 181). There is some evidence, shown in Figure 8.8, that the country became more Republican between the early 1970s and the mid-1990s.

The statistical correlation between this and the growing Republican bent of the military appears quite strong.[19] This does not explain the great difference in magnitude between civilian and military allegiance to the Republican Party, however.[20]

A related argument is that the key change in the nation's political system was the end of Democratic hegemony and beginning of Republican dominance of the South. The primary cause of this was the Democratic Party's embrace of the civil rights movement (Glaser 1996, 4; Radosh 1996, x–xi, 2). "The 'betrayal' of the whole South on Civil-Rights," argues Alexander Lamis, "starting gradually with Harry Truman and ending momentously with Lyndon Johnson—precipitated the death of the one-party system" (Lamis 1990, 4). Of course civil rights was not the only issue that drove southern conservatives from the Democratic Party. Other issues such as fighting crime, reducing the role of the federal government, restraining judicial activism, and balancing the federal budget also played important roles in changing the political allegiance of the once "solid South." (Radosh 1996, 145–146; Lamis 1990, 21, 25 26). The logic of this argument is straightforward: since the South is over-represented in the officer corps, a decline in the fortunes of the Democratic Party in the South should be reflected in a major change in the political affiliation of the officer corps.

Figure 8.9 shows the growing political support for Republican candidates in presidential races (SOUPRES), and even more in congressional

---

19. The Pearson Correlation between MODCIVRE and MODMILRE is $r^2(21) = .914$, $p \leq .001$ (two-tailed).

20. The civilian mean (MILREPUB) was 29.33 while the military (MILREPUB) was 53.167.

Figure 8.8. Percentage of Republicans in the United States.

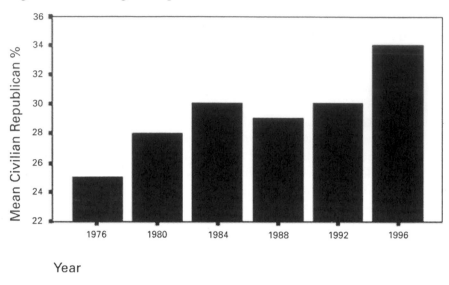

Year

SOURCE: Holsti, FPLP Survey Data, 1997.

and gubernatorial races (SOUREP). Data analysis suggests some evidence of a link between the increasing Republican dominance of the South and the Republicanization of the military.[21]

A third argument is that the widespread erosion in faith and confidence in governmental institutions might be a cause of the gap. The logic of this argument is that both military officers and civilians lost faith in the government after the debacle in Vietnam and the disgrace of Watergate. While military loss of confidence was less dramatic than among civilians, there is evidence that the military blamed civilians for the defeat (Bachman and Jennings 1975, 141–155). There is compelling evidence that people's faith in government eroded substantially in the early 1970s compared with earlier periods (Arterton 1974, 269–288). General Social Survey data suggest an association between party affiliation and confidence in government, with Republicans benefiting from a decrease in confidence in government.[22]

A final argument is that the source of the political gap is the decline

---

21.   SOUPRES and MILREPUB have an unimpressive Pearson Correlation of $r^2(5) = .562$, $p = .324$ (two-tailed). SOUREP and MILREPUB have a higher and significant Kendall's Tau-b of $(6) = .867$, $p= .015$ (two-tailed).

22.   PARTYID and CONFED have a $\chi^2(14) = 661.038$, $p \leq .001$.

Figure 8.9. Percentage of Republicans in the South.

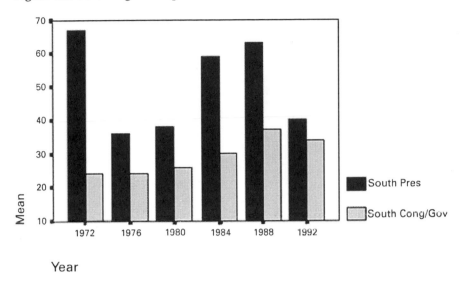

SOURCE: General Social Survey, various years; Barone, various years.

of civilian experience with and interest in military affairs. Figure 8–10 makes clear the large civil-military gap in interest in military affairs.

The logic of the argument is that the Vietnam war affected civilians in two ways. First, the war caused the nation's elite to eschew military service (Waldman 1997, 67; Converse 1987, 53–75; Bachman and Jennings 1975, 142–143). Second, in addition to driving ROTC off the campuses of the nation's elite universities, the Vietnam War also discouraged academic work on national security issues in the nation's leading universities (Davis 1987, 189; Pinch 1981, 580; Janowitz 1975, vii; Nailor 1978, 180). This has manifested itself particularly in the growing trend in history departments not to hire and tenure military and diplomatic historians and among political science departments not to hire and tenure national security specialists. (Haber, Kennedy and Krasner 1997, 34–43; Sharlet 1999; on military history, Coffman 1997, 761–776; on the problem in political science, see Walt 1991, 211–240.) Given the decreasing size of the U.S. military, there are few ways for civilians to gain much direct exposure to and knowledge about the military.

The evidence for the declining level of experience in the military is quite clear in Figure 8.11: after 1972, less than 10 percent of the nation's 18-year-old men and women were required for military service. Contrast this with the situation in 1954 when 27 percent of 18-year-old men and women (54 percent of males) were needed for military service (Assistant

Figure 8.10. Gap In Interest in National Security.

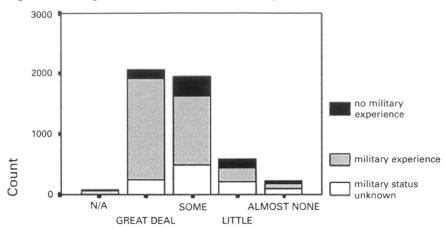

q23 FOLLOW MILITARY ISSUES

SOURCE: TISS, 1999.

Secretary of Defense 1997, Table D-1). Thus, far fewer people today are likely to have direct experience with the military. The correlation between this factor and the growing Republican tilt of the officer corps is strong.[23]

While a number of variables are clearly associated with the Republicanization of the military and the growing political cultural gap, two questions remain: how might these variables fit together and what, in turn, explains changes in them? In the next section, I suggest that the decline of the mass army and changes in the domestic political complexion of the South are largely responsible for the growing civil-military political gap.

How the End of the Mass Army and the Republicanization of the South Cause the Gap

Regression results reported in Table 8.2 suggest that the two most important variables explaining the growing political gap are the decline of the mass army (measured by the military participation ratio) and the Republican Party's dominance of the south. Together, these two vari-

---

23. The Pearson Correlation between MILPOP and MODMILRE is $r^2(21) = -.579$, p = .006 (two-tailed).

Figure 8.11. Percentage of 18-Year-Olds Required to Meet Annual Recruitment Goals.

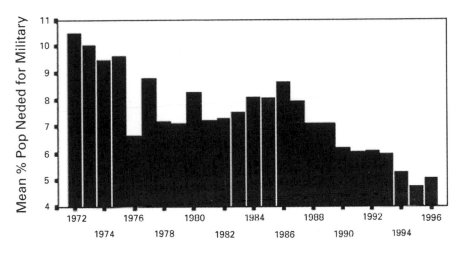

Year

SOURCE: Department of Defense, 1996.

ables seem to account for about 83 percent of the variance in the political gap.[24]

The decline of the mass army affects three important aspects of the military institution: the mean age of the officer corps, the quality of new accessions, and the pay gap. The Republicanization of the South tips the balance in favor of the Republican Party in the country as a whole, which in turn tilts the balance among military officers toward the Republican Party. Equation 1 in Table 8.2 estimates the general model, suggesting how changes in the military participation ratio and the Republicanization of the South may have caused the Republicanization of the military. Equation 2 in Table 8.2 suggests that the military participation ratio by it-

---

24. Some important caveats: since this model employs annual data with a relatively small N, the standard errors are probably understated and the fit statistics are apt to be exaggerated. I am less concerned about a time-series problem because the annual data is drawn from random samples at each point. The small-N is a more serious problem but cannot be overcome since the Holsti FPLP surveys did not ask many of the demographic questions we are interested in considering as possible explanations of the gap. All this is to say that the data analysis in this chapter can only be considered as suggestive and illustrative support for an explanation that seems logically and empirically plausible.

Table 8–2. Illustrative Data Analysis of the Causes of the Gap.

	Equation 1: MILPART → MODREMIL SOUREP ↗		
	β	S.E.	t
MILPART	−40.553	15.246	−2.660*
SOUREP	1.030	.287	3.591**
Constant	53.985	19.684	2.743*
adj. r2	.827*	N=9	

	Equation 2: MILPART → MODREMIL		
	β	S.E.	t
MILPART	−62.785	12.665	−4.957***
Constant	106.072	10.777	9.8842***
adj. r2	.554**	N=19	

	Equation 3: MILPART → AGE → MODREMIL		
	β	S.E.	t
MILPART	1.641	30.895	.053
AGE	16.899	7.527	2.245*
Constant	−510.589	274.844	1.858
adj. r2	.636***	N=19	

	Equation 4: MILPART → QUALITY → MODREMIL		
	β	S.E.	t
MILPART	−24.796	13.161	−1.889#
QUALITY	.455	.109	4.069***
Constant	50.788	15.713	3.232**
adj. r2	.761***	N=19	

	Equation 5: MILPART → PAYGROW → MODREMIL		
	β	S.E.	t
MILPART	−14.696	34.966	−.420
	1.862	.727	−2.561
Constant	51.275	35.249	1.455
adj. r2	.615***	N=19	

Table 8–2. *Continued.*

↗ QUALITY ↘

Equation 6: MILPART → PAYGROW → MODREMIL

↘ AGE ↗

	β	S.E.	t
MILPART	−8.088	23.381	−.346
AGE	−9.227	4.645	−1.987#
QUALITY	.587	.071	8.213***
PAYGROW	−.742	.314	−2.362*
Constant	330.632	169.042	1.956
adj. r2	.944***	N=14	

Equation 7: SOUREP → MODREMIL

	β	S.E.	t
SOUREP	.832	.218	3.810*
Constant	25.036	7.761	3.226*
adj. r2	.575*	N=10	

Equation 8: SOUREP → MODCIVRE → MODMILREP

	β	S.E.	t
SOUREP	−6.468E 02	.296	−.218
MODCIVRE	4.214	1.210	3.482*
Constant	−67.777	27.158	−2.496*
adj. r2	.810***	N=10	

***p ≤ .001
**p ≤ .01
*p ≤ .05
#p ≤ .10

self does not explain as much as the two combined. Equations 3, 4, and 5 in Table 8.2 suggest that age, quality, and the pay gap are intervening variables between the decline of the military participation ratio and the republicanization of the military. When these variables are added to the equation, the βs for the military participation ratio decrease in magnitude and lose significance. Equation 6 in Table 8.2 estimates the relationship of all three intervening variables together. Equation 7 in Table 8.2 estimates the direct relationship between the Republicanization of the South and the Republicanization of the military and, like Equation 2 in Table 8.2, suggests that the Republicanization of the South does not explain as much by itself. Equation 8 in Table 8.2 suggests that adding the intervening variable of the Republicanization of the country produces a more powerful model of the effect of the changing political complexion of the country on the political balance in the military. While other factors such as the lengthening term of service and the increasing percentage of academy graduates in the officer corps surely play some role, together the decline of the mass army and the Republicanization of the South seem to account for most of the growing political gap.

Explaining the Other Gaps

I have offered a plausible explanation of one of the most striking civil-military gaps: the Republicanization of the military. But as Table 8.3 makes clear, there are many other gaps identified by Holsti's original FPLP data.[25] These gaps involve attitudes on use of force, foreign policy, and domestic social issues. Because not all these gaps behave the same way over time, it is not clear that we can use precisely the same variables to explain them. In particular, Table 8.3 shows that there are a number of different trends in the data: there are gaps that are changing, either growing or shrinking; there are enduring gaps; and there are a few instances in which there is no civil-military gap at all.

The gaps that are growing and shrinking seem to be doing so roughly in synchronicity with the decline in the military participation ratio. Indeed, it is not especially surprising that, with the end of the Cold War, gaps between civilians and military leaders would shrink on some use-of-force issues. This is true of questions about the validity of the domino theory (Table 8.3.5, A1–2), the danger of a communist victory (Table 8.3.5, B), the usefulness of employing the Central Intelligence Agency (Table 8.3.5, D), and the need to contain aggression (Table 8.3.5, F). Pearson correlations for the domino theory, CIA, and containment of aggression seem to be particularly strong and significant.[26] The relatively constant gap on the question of the need to counter Russian expansion (Table 8.3.5, C1–2) and the supremacy of the offensive (Table 8.3.5, G) are no surprise to scholars who accept Huntington's argument about the military's conservative realism, and the "Cult of the Offensive" literature's argument about the military's bureaucratic preference for the offensive (J. Snyder 1984; Posen 1984; Van Evera 1986, 8–117).

General foreign policy issues present more mixed results. The fact that there is no gap in attitudes about the importance of the United

---

25. I am using data from the tables in Holsti (1997) in this section. All of these variables are normally distributed.

26. MILPART and DOMINO is $r^2(6) = .876$, $p \leq .05$ (two-tailed); MILPART and CIA is $r^2(6) = .895$, $p \leq .05$; and MILPART and CONAGG is $r^2(6) = .933$, $p \leq .01$.

Table 8.3. Trends in Other Gaps.

Holsti FPLP Question	Status of the Gap
from Holsti's Table 5:	
A1–2 (domino theory)	Gap/Shrinking
B (communist victory)	Gap/Shrinking
C1–2 (Russian expansion)	Gap/Constant (11%)
D (employ CIA)	Gap/Shrinking
E1–2 (contain aggression)	Gap/Shrinking
F (contain communism)	Gap/Shrinking
G (offense best)	Gap/Growing
from Holsti's Table 6:	
A (UN role)	No gap
B (foreign aid)	Gap/Growing
C (aid LDCs)	Gap/Shrinking
D (arms control)	Gap/Shrinking
E (hunger)	Gap/Constant (-26%)
F (strengthen UN)	Gap/Constant (-16%)
G (international cooperation)	Gap/Growing
from Holsti's Table 11:	
A (↓ taxes)	No gap
B (↑ environment)	No gap
C (private schools)	No gap
D (↓ ed. ↑ def. $)	Gap/Constant (-43%)
E (↑ nuke power)	No gap
F (redis. $)	Gap/Constant (-22%)
G. Busing	Gap/Constant (-18%)
H. (abortion)	Gap/Constant (-18%)
I (Equal Rights)	Gap/Growing
J (School prayer)	Gap/Constant (36%)
K (↓ gay teachers)	Gap/Constant (33%)
L. (↓ death penalty)	Gap/Constant (-28%)

SOURCE: Holsti, FPLP, Tables 5, 6, 11.

Nations in solving regional conflicts (Table 8.3.6, A) is striking, although the data cannot tell us if civilian and military officers have different rationales for this support. Civilians might support the UN on principle, for example, while military officers might support it as an alternative for the military having to deal with undesirable non-military missions. The growing civil-military gap on attitudes toward foreign aid (Table 8.3.6, B) and the prospects for international cooperation (Table 8.3.6, G) are to be expected from a bureaucratic politics standpoint, inasmuch as the federal budget is now a zero-sum game and so defense spending and foreign aid are in direct competition. Conversely, growing military pessimism about international cooperation is probably a function of both military realism and the unfortunate recent experiences with cooperative efforts at peace-keeping in the Balkans. The relatively constant gaps on combating hunger (Table 8.3.6, E) and strengthening the UN are largely a function of the military's more pessimistic mind-set about international politics. The most puzzling gaps are the shrinking gap on arms control (Table 8.3.6, D) and aid to less developed countries (Table 8.3.6, C). I suspect that what is going on here is that with the end of the Cold War, large numbers of nuclear weapons have become less critical for U.S. national defense, while many military officers may see non-military aid to less developed countries (LDCs) as a substitute for the use of the military in those countries.[27]

Explaining the TISS Gaps

The 1998–99 TISS survey expanded and added more nuance to the findings of Holsti's FPLP surveys.[28] It add yet another year of survey data and it also asked questions more explicitly focused on current policy concerns, such as the threat posed by China. In addition, it included a series of questions on the particular civil-military relations issues raised in the articles and book by Thomas Ricks that brought the "gap" into recent prominence. Finally, whereas the original FPLP surveys compared elite civilian views to those of the military leadership, the TISS survey distinguishes among eight different military statuses, from people on active duty to civilians with no service experience whatsoever. Given that the TISS survey asks nearly 250 substantive questions, with from two to over twenty possible answers for each, of eight categories of respondents, it is not possible in the confines of one chapter to explain the thousands of potential gaps in the same depth that I analyzed explanations for the growing military gap. What I do in this section is to suggest possible explanations for trends within eight different general clusters of issues.

Before doing so, I want to caution that some interesting cases in which military respondents fall between the civilian elites and civilian masses may in fact be an artifact of the particular demographic characteristics of the two samples. Briefly, the reason that the military sometimes looks a lot like civilian masses may be that they are demographically very similar to them. For example, in terms of regional origins (Q79), 21.4 per-

---

27.   MILPART and AC have an $r^2(6) = -.816$, $p \leq .05$.

28.   Data for this section came from the TISS data set and Holsti (1999).

cent of the mass sample and 20.1 percent of the military come from the TISS South region, while only 16.1 percent of the civilian elite sample list the South as their region of origin.[29] The median age (Q64) of the civilian elites is substantially higher than that of either the civilian mass or the military. Obviously these factors can be controlled in estimating the relationships between variables (Davis 1999). But since, as I have suggested, both variables are key causal factors in the increasing Republican tilt of the military, it is not surprising that cross-tabulations on various questions would find the military closer to the masses than to elites. The key question is whether that is because the military is more politically representative of the masses, or simply that this particular military sample looks more like the mass sample demographically. I am inclined to believe the latter is the case.

In addition to demographic variables, the first issues in the TISS survey data concern ideology and political attitudes. The TISS data clearly show the same gaps on party identification (Question 76: the military is 63.7 percent Republican, while the civilian non-veteran group is 30.1 percent) and political views (Question 75: the military is 53.5 percent "somewhat conservative" while civilian non-veteran is 24.1 percent). We can be confident that the Republican dominance of the South and end of the mass army account for these continuing gaps fairly well.

The second group of issues concerns foreign policy. Gaps between the military and civilian non-veterans here are largely explainable in terms of the military's more pessimistic view about international cooperation and its bureaucratic interest in avoiding costly non-military entanglements. Issues include helping less-developed countries (LDCs) (Question 20f), combating world hunger (Question 01b), fostering international cooperation (Question 01e), promoting and defending human rights (Question 01h), maintaining superior military power (Question 01j), using the CIA to undermine hostile governments (Question 02d), using force to counter aggression (Question 02e), the use of quick and massive force rather than gradual escalation (Question 02j), the guiding role of political goals in deciding how to use force (Question 02k), and the importance of non-military factors in U.S. national security (Question 02m).

Interesting areas of consensus emerged in a few categories. For example, there was civil-military convergence on "world wide arms control" (Question 01b); "containing communism" (Question 01f); "preventing the spread of nuclear weapons" (Question 01g); the "validity of the dom-

---

29. This is different from the Defense Manpower Data Center (DMDC) and DoD definition I used, which counts much of the Mid-Atlantic and some of the Southwest as being in the South.

ino theory" (Question 02a); "Russian expansionism" (Question 02c); the consequences of a Chinese victory for the United States (Question 02g); and the unwillingness of the public to accept casualties (Question 02i). It is easy to explain this consensus with reference to the changing international security environment, however: Russia and China are the only potential U.S. adversaries and so it is not surprising that there would be civil-military agreement on issues concerning them. Likewise, the threat of nuclear proliferation in the post–Cold War international system is widely recognized as one of the most pressing security concerns for the United States. Since neither Russia nor China is presently a serious threat to U.S. vital interests, civil-military consensus on the desirability of arms control, the irrelevance of containing communism, the fallacy of the domino theory, and the unwillingness of the public to tolerate casualties is not surprising. In general, there is much consensus on the identity and seriousness of various threats to American national security (Question 03a-l) with one notable exception: the military is far more worried than civilian non-veterans about the impact of the decline of morals and standards in American society (Question 03f). This particular gap is probably explained by the military's bureaucratic interest: a complex and hierarchical organization like the military cannot function without depending heavily on the integrity of its personnel. This issue may provide a crucial link between military respondents' concern about their institution's well-being and their strong feelings on a number of controversial domestic issues.

On use-of-force issues there was consensus only on the general statement that the military's role is to fight and win the nation's wars (Question 07b), while there was a considerable lack of civil-military consensus on various operations other than war (OOTW), such as redressing discrimination (Question 07c) humanitarian intervention abroad (Question 07e), domestic disorder in the United States (Question 07f), and combating drug trafficking (Question 07h). Again, from a bureaucratic interest standpoint, it is not surprising that the military would be less enthusiastic than civilians about performing these roles (Betts 1991).

The third group deals with contentious domestic policy issues such as busing for school integration, reducing the national debt, relaxing environmental regulations, tuition tax credits, abortion choice, mothers staying home, prayer in school, reducing the defense budget to promote other objectives, barring gays from teaching, constructing nuclear power plants, redistributing wealth, banning the death penalty, and gun control (Questions 05a-m). The biggest gaps here involve relaxing environmental regulations, tuition tax credits, abortion, prayer in schools, reducing the defense budget, gay teachers, the death penalty, and gun control. Bureaucratic interest easily explains why the military is less supportive of reducing the defense budget. I also suspect that the bitter legacy of the controversy over gays in the military at the beginning of the Clinton administration probably affects military attitudes toward homosexual rights generally. What is most striking is how closely the gap between active-duty military and non-veteran civilians mirrors the Republican-Democrat gap on these same questions. Clearly, the fact that the military is now overwhelmingly Republican explains much of these gaps on domestic political issues. Thus, I think that the decline in the military participation ratio and Republican dominance of the South explain most of these gaps.[30]

The fourth group deals with assessment of American institutions. The military is more likely to perceive a fraying of the moral fabric of American society (Question 08a) and also more likely to see itself as the agent of its repair (Questions 08b-d, Question 08f). As I suggested above, I think that this gap is explicable by the high premium placed on integrity in military culture. One particularly wide civil-military gap concerns the media: the military are generally less reliant on the mass media for information (Question 20) and less satisfied with their depiction of the military (Question 21). My guess is that the legacy of the Vietnam War, in which the press played a significant role in undermining public support for the war, particularly by highlighting military failures, explains much of these gaps. Another big gap is the large difference between civilians and military in terms of how many follow military issues (Question 23). My hunch is that with the end of the Cold War, public interest in military affairs has dropped significantly.

The fifth group deals with the relationship of the military with civilian society. One of the most dramatic manifestations of the growing civil-military gap is the increasing isolation of the military from the rest of American society. The differences in contact between military and civilian in social groups (Question 28), contact at work (Question 29), and friends in the military (Question 30) are all significant. There is also a gap in respect for the military: civilians feel that the military gets more respect than it deserves, while the military feels under-appreciated (Question 31). This translates into a concrete difference in confidence in the military (Question 32n), with civilians having much less than the military. Civilians also feel that the military has less respect for civilian society that it deserves (Question 32o). Civilian respondents are also significantly less likely to be proud of those who serve (Question 33e) than are military respondents. One of the most telling gaps is that civilians are more likely to

30.   Of the 13 domestic issues covered in the TISS survey, the military mirrored the Republican position on 10 of them (77 percent).

express disappointment if a child joins the military than are military respondents (Question 33k). These feelings also seem to translate into a gap in confidence in the military (Questions 33f–h). In general, the decreasing military participation ratio probably explains much of this growing isolation. As fewer and fewer people serve, knowledge about, interest in, and support for the military decline.

The seventh group deals with questions of military effectiveness. In this section there is surprising consensus on questions of the importance of the chain of command (Question 42a), the importance of military symbols (Question 42b), the importance of masculine values in the military (Question 42c), the continuing importance of martial virtues (Question 42e), women in the workplace (Question 41b), the military becoming less male-dominated (Question 41c), the military being involved in non-military affairs (Question 41d), bans on certain behaviors (Question 41e), the impact of a bad promotions system (Question 41f), the military's lack of confidence in political leaders (Question 41k), and inaccurate media reporting (Question 41l). That active-duty military respondents are close to the civilian non-veterans in attitudes on women in the workplace and the male-dominated culture of the military may be due to the fact that, unlike civilian life, the military has successfully circumscribed the role of women in the military without sacrificing much of its masculine culture. In contrast, big gaps emerge on the question of whether the U.S. military has done a good job on eliminating racial discrimination (Question 42d), the importance of unit cohesion (Question 42f), the impact of lack of trust in the military (Question 41a), civilians involving themselves in military affairs (Question 41g), sexual harassment in the military (Question 41h), and the military clinging to old-fashioned morals. My sense is that civilians are apt to give the military the benefit of the doubt on most questions of military effectiveness except when they overlap with divisive domestic issues such as race, gender, and sexual orientation. In those cases, civilian non-veterans, who are as a group more liberal, are likely to be much more skeptical of the military effectiveness argument.

The final group examines the proper relationship between the military and civilian leadership. There are puzzling civil-military gaps on a number of civilian control issues, including the supremacy of civilian authority on decisions to use force (Question 48a), whether the military should be free to criticize civil government (Question 47a), whether the military should be free to criticize society (Question 47b), whether members of the military should be free to express political views (Question 47c), whether the military should be free to defend government policies (Question 47d), and whether the military should be free to advocate policy (Question 47e). On each of these civilian control issues, the active-duty military seems more supportive of military subordination to civilian control than are the non-veteran civilians. In addition, more non-veteran civilians than active-duty military officers think that it is appropriate for members of the military to "leak" sensitive material to the press when given what they consider an unethical or unwise order (Question 43h and Question 44h). This is all the more surprising given that many non-veteran civilians believe that the military will try to "shirk" civilian orders at least some of the time (Question 49). Fewer non-veteran civilians than active-duty military officers are confident that civilian control of the military is absolutely safe and secure in the United States (Question 48f). It is hard to reconcile these contradictory positions other than by concluding that civilians are not paying very much attention to civilian control issues today. To the extent that they are, they are pessimistic about the strength of civilian control of the military, but they have not thought through fully what role the military should play in the national policy discourse. My sense is that the public expects the military, much like any other government bureaucracy, to pursue its own interests. It is not clear, however, that the public is any more alarmed by this than it would be by evidence that other government bureaucracies were behaving the same way. At bottom, the public does not seem to be very attentive today to national defense issues, and this indifference may account for the inconsistencies in non-veteran civilian responses to these civilian control issues.

The factors I have identified in this chapter may also help us understand the findings of some of the other studies in the TISS project. For example, Paul Gronke and Peter Feaver (Chapter 3) reconcile a very intriguing paradox: the military remains one of the most respected institutions in American society, yet fewer and fewer Americans want their children to serve in it. The root cause of this seems to be the increasing isolation of the majority of civilian society from the military itself, a development I attribute to the end of the mass army. In addition, William Bianco and Jamie Markham (Chapter 7) document the declining importance of veteran status for members of Congress, a development that can also be attributed to the drop in the military participation ratio.[31] Finally, building on Bianco and Markham's findings, Feaver and Christopher Gelpi argue

---

31.   The military participation ratio unsurprisingly correlates quite well with the percentage of veterans in Congress $r^2(5) = .976$, $p \le .01$ (two-tailed). While the MPR does not do well at explaining the changes in the percentage of veterans in the House $r^2(6) = .686$, $p = .133$, it does a very good job at explaining the veteran status premium in the Senate $r^2(6) = .777$, $p \le .01$ (two-tailed). I thank Bill Bianco for sharing his data with me.

that as the number of veterans in Congress declines, the willingness of the United States to use force has gone up historically, and vice versa (Feaver and Gelpi 1999a, 1999b). Since the MPR explains the decline in percentage of veterans in Congress, it may explain Feaver and Gelpi's findings as well. In sum, the factors I used to explain the growing political gap between military officers and civilian elites seem to provide some leverage for understanding many of the other civil-military gaps identified in Holsti's FPLP data and the TISS data. However, our confidence in this claim should not be too great until we are able to subject these other gaps to the same in-depth assessment I was able to undertake with the political gap.

Conclusions and Policy Recommendations

I argue that major factors in the growing political gap between civilian elites and military officers in the United States since the mid-1970s are the decline of the mass army and the growing Republican dominance of the South. The effects of these two changes are not direct. Rather, they have operated indirectly, through a number of intermediary variables: civil-military pay gaps, regional homogeneity in the officer corps, an increase in the quality of recruits and officer candidates, changes in the nature and location of ROTC programs, an increase in the percentage of service academy graduates in the officer corps, and other indicators of a long-service military such as increasing average age. In addition, domestic political changes such as a growing anti-military bias in the Democratic party, a decrease in confidence in government, and an increasing public ignorance of, and indifference to, national security affairs have contributed to this political gap as well.

Given the existence of this and other civil-military gaps, it makes sense to consider the various policy recommendations that have been proposed to deal with them. In doing so, we must distinguish the particular types of gaps. While it makes sense to try to close the political and social civil-military gaps, we may have to accept significant organizational cultural gaps because they could be integral components of military effectiveness. Specifically, the fact that the military has, until recently, been able to recruit high-quality enlistees and officer candidates undoubtedly provides the country with such an effective military force that we should be willing to live with the fact that this contributes to a number of gaps. On the other hand, it makes sense to think about addressing the causes of some of the less beneficial gaps.

Many scholars and policymakers who are uncomfortable with these gaps advocate taking steps to increase the diversity and representativeness of the services. The main policy tool for this is to reinstate the draft in one form or another. Some admit that this is politically infeasible but assume that were it feasible, it would be the solution to the widening civil-military gaps (Ricks 1997d, 78; Myers 1999c; Kinsley 1989, 26–27; Weisberg 1991, 12–14). This is unpersuasive. To begin with, the draft did not produce a socially representative military either (Lochman and Quester 1985, 179–180). Milton Friedman, for example, attacked the draft as unfair and argued that it produced a force that was not representative of American society (Friedman 1967, 201). The root of the problem with the peacetime draft is demographic: short of all-out war on the scale of World War II, the 18-year-old population far exceeds the number of men and women needed (Janowitz 1967, 80). If the draft were reinstated in peacetime, it is very likely that deferments would again multiply and disproportionately favor certain social and economic groups. This is what undermined the legitimacy of the Selective Service System even prior to the Vietnam War. It is hard to see, short of a total mobilization on the scale of World War II, how that problem could be avoided in the future even with a reinstated draft (Griffith 1985, 115; Burk 1989, 444; Levi 1997 on the importance of legitimacy for compliance with conscription). Moreover, it is striking how little interest the Department of Defense and the uniform services have in a return to the draft. Former Chairman of the Joint Chiefs of Staff General John Vessey concluded that "universal service may have value to the country, but its value is not to the Department of Defense" (quoted in Horowitz 1986, 184). Reinstating the draft is not only politically infeasible, but also would not erase the civil-military gaps.

Other means of increasing the diversity of the U.S. military ought to be considered. For instance, since women and African-Americans in the service are less overwhelmingly Republican than white males, increasing their numbers might make the military more politically representative.[32] A major problem with this approach that the political gap has grown despite the increasing numbers of African-Americans and women in the armed forces. Moreover, African-Americans are already over-represented in the enlisted ranks in terms of their percentage of the total population, and in the officer corps when compared to the population of African-Americans who are college graduates (Assistant Secretary of Defense 1997, Tables D-4 and D-22). It is simply not feasible to increase the num-

---

32. Active-duty military women are one-third less likely than active-duty military men to self-identify as Republicans; African-Americans are even less likely to do so. Cross-tabulation on Gender (Q63)*MILSTAT2*PARTYID and Race (Q80)*MILSTAT2*PARTYID.

bers of African-Americans, who are significantly less Republican than other groups, in order to make the military more politically representative. Women, in contrast, are still significantly under-represented in both the enlisted and officer ranks, but since they are more likely than African-Americans to self-identify as Republicans, it would take a much higher percentage of women in the services to make the military reflective of the civilian political spectrum.[33] Given these facts, increasing racial and gender diversity may not be the most effective way to close the gaps.

But increasing other forms of diversity could make a significant difference. First, since service academy graduates tend to be less representative of society, limiting service academy graduates as a percentage of the officer corps might produce a more heterogeneous and representative force (Friedman 1967, 207).[34] Second, in order for such limits to make a difference, changes must also be made in the ROTC program. Since the majority of officers come from the South, and most ROTC programs are presently also in the South, it makes sense ensure that ROTC becomes equally distributed in all regions of the country and to insist that it has a presence at the nation's elite universities (Friedman 1967, 207). Attention should also be given to the character of the current ROTC curriculum, particularly reemphasizing the role of non-military science courses in prospective officers' education (Ricks 1997c, 78; W. Snyder 1984, 422). Third, some means of bringing civilians in at higher levels of the military ought to be found as a means of promoting diversity (Ricks 1997c, 78; Friedman 1967, 207; Waldman 1997, 100). This has been done routinely with doctors and lawyers, and while it would be hard to do in the combat arms, it might nevertheless be feasible in combat support and combat service support positions such as military intelligence, engineering, and information technology. Fourth, and following from this, re-

---

33. In the TISS survey sample, military men have a 74 percent likelihood of being Republican, while military women have a 45 percent chance of being so. This produces a military sample which is 71 percent Republican. In this sample, men constitute 90 percent and women 10 percent. Assume that likelihood of voting Republican stays the same for both genders, but we adjust the demography of the active-duty military sample so it is 49 percent men and 51 percent women. Even with that change, the military sample is still nearly 60 percent Republican. Since the non-veteran civilian sample was 30 percent Republican, even a 100-percent-female military would not be truly politically representative!

34. According to DoD data, the percentage of Academy graduates in the service in 1976, when the military still reflected the political views of civilian elites, was slightly over 10 percent. That figure would be a good target.

newed emphasis on the role of the National Guard and the Reserves as a vehicle for producing representative citizen-soldiers is warranted because they are more regionally diverse than the active force. Fifth, it makes sense to think about shortening the term of service for both enlisted and officers to make it more likely that a larger number of Americans will serve at least one term. (Van Doorn 1975, 155; Moskos 1999). Sixth, more civilians might enlist for at least one tour in uniform if military service were a prerequisite for federal student assistance and for government employment (Farris 1984, 272). This would increase the military's turnover rate but enhance its social representativeness. Finally, it would be wise to think about keeping military pay commensurate with the civilian sector to ensure that the military becomes a reasonable career alternative for a representative sample of the American public.

In reducing the growing social isolation of the military, the nation's universities have a key role to play. One way they can do this is through the further expansion of the opportunities for company-grade and field-grade officers to study at civilian graduate institutions. This is a useful way of intellectual bridge-building between the military and civilian realms (Slater 1977, 112–113; Waldman 1997, 100; Bell 1986, 419–430). Janowitz pointed this out long ago: "Intellectual isolation from the main current of American university life may be one of the main trends that needs to be avoided. Much of the initiative to off-set such isolation will have to be taken by civilian universities, if they are to remain centers of vigorous intellectual investigation and discourse" (Janowitz 1971, lii).

The nation's leading colleges and universities also have an obligation to teach basic courses and support research in the area of national security. This is the only way to ensure that large numbers of civilians have at least some familiarity with the military (Van Doorn 1975, 155). This is even more important with the end of the Cold War, since fewer and fewer civilians, even in Congress and the federal bureaucracy, are likely to have direct military experience.

Finally, it is important that defense and national security issues once again become bipartisan. This means that the Democratic Party needs to shed its anti-military image. Historically, Democratic presidents such as Jimmy Carter and members of Congress such as Senator Henry Jackson and Senator Sam Nunn have been instrumental in strengthening the armed forces. Perceptually and rhetorically, however, the Democratic Party is still too often perceived to be viscerally anti-military. This stands in marked contrast to many left-of-center European political parties that take national security issues seriously and devote much effort to making sure that their militaries do not become the exclusive preserve of right-of-center parties. For example, the French Left spent much political capital trying to ensure that the French military was broadly reflective of political currents in France (Martin 1977, 377–379).

Since some gaps between the military and civilian society are inevitable, and even essential for military effectiveness, we must find ways to live with them. One major change that needs to be made is to take steps to arrest the trend among military officers to regard the military as just another interest group in American politics. Rather, we should encourage them to embrace an older notion of military service as a vocation, with distinct prerogatives and self-imposed limitations (Janowitz and Moskos 1979, 211; Moskos 1977, 41–50). One controversial but fundamentally sound recommendation is that military officers dramatically demonstrate their apoliticism, perhaps by not voting while on active duty (Bacevich and Kohn 1997, 22–25). Another way to manage the gap is for civilians to embrace some of the military viewpoint about international relations that Huntington called "Neo-Hamiltonianism," or what scholars of international relations call "realism" (Morgenthau 1985; Waltz 1979). In addition, civilian leaders and the public need to understand that civilian control of the military remains an important obligation that civilians can only exercise if they are attentive to, and informed about, military affairs. Ironically, this has become an even more pressing issue with the end of the Cold War. Finally, since the military and civilian realms are likely to remain quite distinct, it makes sense to consider reducing the size of the peacetime military even further (Huntington 1957, 346).

As we try to eliminate the political and social gaps, and manage the organizational cultural gaps, it is essential that we address them both. Nothing could be more corrosive to civilian control of the military and military effectiveness than increasing gaps between our nation's civilian leaders and the military professionals who serve them and protect our country.

Part III
Implications for Military Effectiveness and
Civil-Military Cooperation

Chapter 9

Military Interests and Civilian Politics: The Influence of the Civil-Military "Gap" on Peacetime Military Policy

Benjamin O. Fordham

In recent years, many observers of contemporary civil-military relations have expressed concern about what they believe to be a growing gap between the military and civilian worlds (Kohn 1994; Ricks 1997d; Weigley 1993). The scholars associated with this project have sought to describe the dimensions of this potential gap and to assess its effects on national policy. This chapter is intended to assess the effects of this gap, if any, on two key matters of peacetime military policy: spending and accessions (the recruitment and retention of military personnel). It will first examine the effect of exposure to the military, through both prior service and ongoing social contact with military personnel, on elite opinion about these two issues. The chapter then turns to an examination of policy outcomes for trends that might be consistent with increasing military isolation from American society. Although the TISS survey described in previous chapters offers some evidence that a socially isolated military might receive less support from civilian policymakers, there is little evidence that this situation has thus far influenced military spending or recruitment. Finally, I will argue that the problems so many observers perceive in contemporary civil-military relations do not stem from a gap between the military and civilian society, but rather from the way the military is integrated into civilian politics. Changes in the positions that civilian political factions have taken during the last thirty years have aligned the military more consistently with Republicans and conservatives than was the case before the mid-1960s.

Elite Opinion about Defense Spending and Military Service

In assessing the potential effect of military isolation from society on military spending and accessions, it is important to know whether exposure to the military has any effect on attitudes toward these policy areas. Of course, it is hardly surprising that military officers are more supportive of military spending and military service than civilians are. A more interesting question—and a major premise of concerns like that expressed by Secretary of Defense William Cohen about the potential social isolation of the military—has to do with the effect of exposure to the military on the policy attitudes of civilians. Do civilians with more extensive exposure to the military differ from those with less contact and experience? Do these attitude differences persist when one controls for other potential influences? The survey conducted as part of the Triangle Institute for Security Studies (TISS) project offers some answers to these questions. (See previous chapters and the Technical Appendix at the end of this volume for details on conduct of the survey.) Since this chapter is concerned with policy impact, the attitudes of the elite group likely to influence policy are most relevant. This evidence indicates that prior military service and social contact with military people are associated with more support for defense spending and military service. However, these effects are not as strong as those of other factors such as political ideology.

   Table 9.1 presents the results of the TISS survey question about military spending, disaggregated by the military experience of the respondent.[1] Civilians who had never served in the military were substantially more likely than veterans to agree that reducing the military budget in order to spend more on education was a good idea. While 53.4 percent of non-veterans "agreed" or "agreed somewhat" with this proposal, only 37 percent of civilian veterans did.[2] As one would expect, only 12.9 percent of the elite military sample, whose responses are presented here as a baseline, agreed with the proposal. Veterans view military spending more favorably than non-veterans, but their opinions are not identical to

---

1.   This question was not asked in the mass telephone survey. Students at the service academies are not included among the military officers examined here.

2.   For at least two reasons, the answers to this question provide a better indicator of the gap between civilian veterans and non-veterans than of the absolute opinion about military and education spending. First, the question asks about the federal budget for education. Respondents who prefer that education be funded and controlled at a local level might have been responding to this word rather than to the military-education trade-off. Second, many of the respondents completed the survey while U.S. military forces were in action in Kosovo. The war might well have influenced the respondents' beliefs about the need for military spending in the short term.

Table 9.1. Reducing the Military Budget to Increase the Federal Budget for Education.

Response	Military Officer	Civilian Veteran	Civilian Non-Veteran
"Agree strongly"	2.1%	10.3%	21.0%
"Agree somewhat"	10.8	27.0	32.4
"Disagree somewhat"	34.7	28.0	24.3
"Disagree strongly"	50.9	33.3	19.8
"No Opinion"	1.5	1.3	2.5

NOTE: The question was: "This question asks you to indicate your position on certain domestic issues. [A series of issue positions follow.] Reducing the defense budget in order to increase the federal budget for education." Both civilian categories are "elites" selected because of their specialized knowledge, access to policymakers, or role as opinion leaders. The military officer category includes active-duty and active reserve and guard officers.

those of current military officers, who have a much more direct stake in this question.

Table 9.2 presents the results of two survey questions regarding military service. One asks whether the respondent favors some form of mandatory national service for males. The other asks whether the respondent would be disappointed if his or her child joined the military. As with military spending, the answers to these questions indicate that veterans are more supportive of military service. Differences between civilian veterans and non-veterans appear in the responses to both questions. While 73.1 percent of elite civilian veterans "somewhat" or "strongly" agreed with a requirement for national service, only 51.2 percent of elite non-veterans did. Among the elite military, support was an overwhelming 82.6 percent. The question concerning one's own child joining the military tests attitudes toward military service somewhat differently. Once again, there were differences between veterans and non-veterans among the elite respondents. While 22 percent of civilian non-veterans agreed at least somewhat that they would be disappointed if their child joined, only 6.4 percent of veterans responded this way. On questions of defense spending and military service, veterans are different from other civilians.

Of course, these differences do not necessarily mean that military service creates a tendency to favor defense spending or military service. Veterans are not a perfect cross-section of the American public. For example, they are disproportionately male and, because a higher proportion of the population served before the advent of the All-Volunteer Force, older as well. It is important to know whether the apparent effect of being a veteran is due to military service or to the other characteristics of veter-

Table 9.2. Attitudes toward Military Service.

Response	Mandatory Male National Service			Disappointed if My Child Joined		
	Military Officer	Civilian Veteran	Civilian Non-Veteran	Military Officer	Civilian Veteran	Civilian Non-Veteran
"Agree strongly"	50.8%	41.8%	22.3%	0.8%	2.4%	9.9%
"Agree somewhat"	31.8	31.3	28.8	4.8	4.0	12.1
"Disagree somewhat"	12.3	16.5	24.8	17.6	23.6	26.9
"Disagree strongly"	4.4	9.8	21.2	74.6	67.3	46.4
"No opinion"	0.7	0.7	2.9	2.2	2.7	4.7

NOTE: The two questions were as follows: "Here are some statements people have made about the U.S. military. For each one, please indicate whether you strongly agree, somewhat agree, somewhat disagree, or strongly disagree. [Eleven items follow, including these two.] All male citizens should be required to do some national service. . . . I would be disappointed if a child of mine joined the military." Both civilian categories are "elites" selected because of their specialized knowledge, access to policymakers, or role as opinion leaders. The military officer category includes active-duty and active reserve and guard officers.

ans as a group. Regression analysis allows us to determine the average effect of military service while controlling for the other relevant political and demographic characteristics of survey respondents.

Table 9.3 presents the results of a regression analysis of responses to the questions discussed in Tables 9.1 and 9.2. In addition to the effect of veteran status on opinions about defense spending and military service, it allows us to examine whether social contact with military people is associated with opinions about the trade-off between military and education spending. It also controls for several other potentially important facts about the respondents. Demographic characteristics such as gender, race, age, and income often influence political opinions. The regression includes indicators of each of these factors. Similarly, political ideology and party loyalty can have an effect. Because veterans as a group differ from the rest of the elite sample in each of these ways, it makes sense to control for their relationship to attitudes on defense spending and military service.

The regression analysis reveals that military experience affects attitudes toward military service, but not toward spending. Social contact with the military influences opinion on both policy issues. The results indicate that many other factors also influence opinions on these issues. In fact, every variable except race was related to at least one of the three survey responses in a statistically significant way.

The results of the regression analysis indicate that, while exposure to

Table 9.3. Regression of Analysis of Opinions on Defense Spending and Military Service.

Characteristic of respondent	Survey Item		
	Reduce military spending for education	Male national service	Disappointed if my child joined
Currently serving in military	−0.40*	0.54*	−0.22*
	(0.06)	(0.06)	(0.05)
Civilian veteran	−0.02	0.28*	−0.18*
	(0.06)	(0.08)	(0.06)
Reports social contact with	−0.07*	0.04	−0.06*
military people[a]	(0.02)	(0.03)	(0.02)
Female	0.07	−0.03	0.20*
	(0.05)	(0.06)	(0.05)
Black	0.15	−0.01	−0.11
	(0.11)	(0.13)	(0.10)
Age	0.00	0.01*	−0.00
	(0.00)	(0.00)	(0.00)
Business executive[b]	−0.26*	0.16*	−0.10
	(0.06)	(0.07)	(0.05)
Democrat	0.18*	0.12	0.10
	(0.06)	(0.06)	(0.05)
Ideology[c]	−0.33*	0.09*	−0.12*
	(0.02)	(0.03)	(0.02)
Adjusted R-squared	0.31	0.10	0.15

NOTES: The models were estimated using ordinary least squares regression. Standard errors are in parentheses beneath the coefficients. In order to facilitate interpretation, the dependent variables were coded so that negative coefficients indicate greater *disagreement* with the statement in question. A constant was estimated for each model but is not reported here. The asterisk indicates significance at the .05 level. No undergraduates were included in the sample used here.

[a]Respondents were to describe the social or community groups to which they belonged on a 5-point scale ranging from "all civilians" to "all military."

[b]Because the respondents were not asked about their incomes, those who reported being business executives in response to a question about their occupation is used as a proxy for this variable here. While it is not an ideal indicator of income, it is preferable to omitting this variable altogether.

[c]Repondents were asked to place their political views on a 7-point scale ranging from "far left" to "far right." Conservatives are thus coded with a higher number than liberals.

the military has a statistically significant effect on elite opinions about military spending and service, other factors are just as important. In order to illustrate the implications of the regression, Table 9.4 shows the extent to which several categories of respondents could be expected to differ from the most common type of elite respondent, a white male civilian non-veteran, based on the regression results. The survey asked people to place their opinion on a four-point scale ranging from "strongly disagree" to "strongly agree." Thus, negative scores indicate that a given type of respondent tended toward disagreement with that particular survey item by the indicated amount.

Current military service was one of the factors with the largest effects on all three opinions, but veteran status and social exposure to the military had smaller effects than other factors in most cases. Concerning military spending, veteran status had no statistically significant effect, while social exposure to the military had less of an impact than that of ideology or being a businessperson. Ideology and partisanship had especially large effects on attitudes toward military spending. Liberal Democrats in the sample were more likely to favor military spending cuts to fund education, while conservative Republicans tended to take the opposite position. These effects exceeded even the influence of being an active-duty military officer. (The fact that most of the military officers in the TISS survey also consider themselves conservative Republicans may have affected this outcome, an issue to which I return below.) Veteran status had a substantial effect on opinions about military service, but social contact with the military had little or no impact. Being female had just as much effect as exposure to the military, and ideology was once again even more important. Overall, many factors influence elite opinion about military spending and service: exposure to the military does not dominate other considerations.

The survey results support concerns about the potential effects of military social isolation. At the same time, they serve as a reminder that many other factors help shape opinion support for military spending and service. For this reason, and because of the complexity of the policymaking process, opinion differences do not necessarily produce policy effects. The ability of the military to achieve its personnel and budgetary goals and aspirations depends on many other domestic and international factors. Furthermore, the premise of most arguments about a cultural or political gap between civilians and the military is that the chasm is widening. The survey data presented here do not reveal whether the differences between civilians and the military have increased since the advent of the All-Volunteer Force or end of the Cold War. However, it is possible to examine indicators of military spending and acces-

Table 9.4. Expected Differences from Civilian Non-Veterans among Survey Respondents.

Type of respondent	Survey Item		
	Reduce military spending for education	Male national service	Disappointed if my child joined
Military officer	−0.40	+0.54	−0.22
Civilian veteran	0	+0.28	−0.18
Entirely civilian social group	+0.09	0	+0.08
Mostly military social group	−0.11	0	−0.11
Liberal Democrat	+0.98	−0.34	+0.29
Conservative Republican	−0.52	+0.14	−0.19
Business person	−0.26	+0.16	0
Female	0	0	+0.19
Black	0	0	0

NOTE: In each case, differences are measured from the expected responses of a white male civilian non-veteran, not assumed to be a Democrat or business person. All other variables are held at their mean values. Only the indicated characteristics were varied in each case. Survey responses ranged from 1 ("strongly disagree") to 4 ("strongly agree"), with "no opinion" coded as 2.5, so negative signs indicate greater disagreement with the item proposed in the survey.

sions in order to determine whether they are consistent with a growing cultural or political gap. This is the subject of the next section.

Evaluating the Policy Impact of the Civilian-Military Gap

Evidence that exposure to the military influences elite opinions about defense spending and military service raises the possibility that declining military experience in the American public since the end of conscription could influence peacetime military policy. Has military social isolation had a substantial effect on military recruitment and spending? If so, key statistics concerning these policy areas should display a corresponding pattern. In this section, I examine military spending and accessions over time. It is impossible to assess the substantive importance of recent changes in important policy indicators without knowing whether they differ from typical historical patterns. We need to know whether recent changes are larger or smaller than similar shifts in the past, and whether what appear to be small annual changes might add up to a more important long-term trend. If the military has indeed gradually become alienated from civilian society, its effects on policy might only be evident as a statistical tendency over a long period of time. For example, a trend that began with the establishment of the All-Volunteer Force might have substantially affected policy, but these effects could be invisible in an examination of just the last five years.

In spite of the fact that opinion data suggest that the gap could influence policy, the evidence in this section reveals little actual impact on spending or accessions. The effects of military social isolation might still be at work, but they appear to have been swamped by the other influences on military spending and accessions. The third section offers an alternative interpretation of recent problems attributed to the gap.

TRENDS IN MILITARY SPENDING

Increasing isolation of the military from civilian society could have several different effects on military spending. Each of these potential effects should produce a distinctive pattern in the military budget. First, as the opinion data presented in the preceding section suggest, decreasing exposure to the military might make civilians less supportive of military spending, leading to lower military budgets. This is particularly likely because the military budget must compete with other programs. As Huntington (1963, vii) noted, "the ups and downs of military spending reflect changes in the tax structure and the attitude of the Administration in power toward welfare programs and unbalanced budgets." Recent quantitative research on the federal budget also points to the interdependence of the defense budget and other policy issues. Decisions about military spending are closely intertwined with both fiscal policy choices and other areas of the budget (Kamlet and Mowery 1987; Lowery and Berry 1990; Su, Kamlet, and Mowery 1993). If civilian policymakers with no exposure to the military focus on other policy areas that they understand better, there should be a downward trend in military spending. This trend should be especially evident after the end of the Cold War removed the most serious threat to American national security.

Although a declining budget is the most obvious possible effect of a civil-military gap, recent research on civil-military relations suggests others. Several scholars have argued that the diminishing number of civilian policymakers with military experience could magnify the impact of professional military officers' special expertise in decisions about military policy (Avant 1998). This possibility is supported by the general consensus that control over information is a source of power for bureaucracies generally (Bendor and Hammond 1992; Lebovic 1994; 1996). This could lead to larger rather than smaller military budgets. If the military's control over its budget has grown over time, then an upward trend should be evident in military spending, once one controls for the other dynamics of the time series.[3]

Although a gradual change in the budget is one possible result of increasing military alienation from society, a more abrupt change is also conceivable. The policy effects of a civil-military gap might appear quickly after a major threat disappears, as with the end of the Cold War. For some in the military, the rapid demobilization after World War II followed by the rapid buildup after the beginning of the Korean War is a painful precedent. The hypothesis tests in Figure 9.1 evaluate this way of characterizing the post–Cold War era.

Still another possibility is that a breakdown in cooperation between civilians and the military could lead to increasing fluctuation in military spending over time. In this scenario, the budget in any given year would reflect not coherent planning—something ruled out by the declining civilian understanding of military policy—but rather the outcome of a political struggle between civilians and the military. In this case, the variance of the time series should increase over time. Each of these four possibilities—an upward or a downward trend, a sudden downward shift, or increasing variance—should be evident in military spending data.

Figure 9.1 presents U.S. military spending in 1992 dollars for fiscal years 1947 through 1998. The table beneath the graph presents several models of the series permitting statistical tests of several hypotheses about it.[4] There is no evidence consistent with any of the civil-military gap hypotheses discussed above. Most importantly, the series contains neither a statistically significant trend nor an abrupt shift after the introduction of the All-Volunteer Force or the end of the Cold War. Although military spending is indeed somewhat lower now than it was at the end of the Cold War, the drop fits within the range of variation over the last fifty years. The level of military spending since the end of the Cold War

---

3.   I examined the autocorrelation and partial autocorrelation functions of each of the series presented in this paper. When there was significant time dependence, which was true in almost every case, I selected the simplest model that would adequately represent the error process, leaving only white noise. For all the series examined here, an AR(1) model was appropriate. Substantively, this means that the value of the series observed in each year is related to what was observed in the preceding year.

4.   The hypothesis tests presented in Figure 9–1 concern the period between fiscal years 1951 and 1998. Fiscal year 1951 was the first budget to reflect the Cold War priority attached to military spending after NSC 68 and the beginning of the Korean War. Military spending between the 1947 and 1950 fiscal years was much lower; including it would obscure any trends that might be present during the rest of the postwar era. Estimates are currently available through 2004, but these reflect only planning within the Office of Management and Budget. The actual budgets will also depend on the Congress.

Figure 9.1. U.S. Defense Outlays, Fiscal Years 1947–98, in Billions of 1992 Dollars.

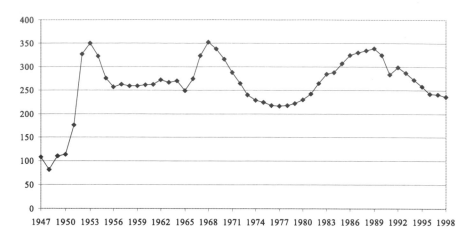

Hypothesis Tests

Variables	Model 1	Model 2	Model 3	Model 4
AR(1) (first-order	0.78*	0.78*	0.77*	0.80*
autoregression term)	(0.09)	(0.09)	(0.09)	(0.09)
Post-1951 trend	0.45			
	(1.10)			
Post-1969 trend		−0.10		
		(1.52)		
Post-1991 trend			−4.99	
			(6.44)	
Post-1991 shift				−31.61
				(25.43)
Log Likelihood	−227.22	−227.31	−227.00	−226.51
AIC	460.44	460.61	459.99	459.01

NOTE: Standard errors are in parentheses. The asterisk indicates statistical significance at the 0.05 level. A constant was estimated but is not reported. AIC is Akaike information criterion.

SOURCE: Office of Management and Budget, The Budget for the Fiscal Year 2000 (Washington, D.C.: U.S. Government Printing Office, 1999).

has not shifted in a statistically significant way from the level that prevailed between 1951 and 1991. Both visual inspection and statistical analysis indicate that military spending has risen and fallen within roughly the same range since the early 1950s.

The data also do not support the hypothesis that there has been greater instability in military spending in recent years, nor has there been any increase in the variability of military spending since Vietnam or the end of the Cold War. The standard deviation of the series does not increase after either of these events. Indeed, it is slightly smaller in both cases.[5] Military spending has become more stable over time, not less.

The attitudes of civilian politicians toward the military have certainly influenced variation in the defense budget since World War II. Some presidents, such as Ronald Reagan, have preferred to spend more, while others, such as Dwight Eisenhower, have sought to cut the budget. Whatever the inclinations of individual presidents, however, there is no evidence that a growing civil-military gap has influenced the budget. The analysis presented here does not indicate that there is no gap. However, its effects, if any, appear to have been overwhelmed by other considerations.

TRENDS IN MILITARY PERSONNEL ACCESSIONS

The prospect of a growing gap between the military and the rest of American society also has potentially important implications for the recruitment and retention of military personnel. The survey data discussed in the first section suggest that exposure to the military is associated with more positive attitudes toward military service. As fewer Americans have military experience or social contact with military personnel, it could become more difficult for the military to attract and retain adequate numbers of capable recruits. Recent military recruiting problems have led to some press discussion of this possibility (Graham 1999; Myers 1998a; Moniz 1999). Like the hypothesized patterns in military spending, these trends should be evident in military personnel statistics.

Since 1976, the Pentagon has collected data on the attitudes of potential recruits toward military service. Among other things, it has funded the Youth Attitude Tracking Study (YATS), a survey of high-school students intended mainly to determine whether they are likely to enlist in the military.[6] Figure 9.2 displays the proportion of 16-to-21-year-old men and women who said they would "definitely" or "probably" enlist for

---

5. The standard deviation for the 1951–68 period is 43.49. It falls to 39.96 for the 1969–98 period and 23.67 for the 1991–98 post–Cold War era.

6. Trends in the YATS data overstate fluctuations in the actual supply of potential military recruits. They are nevertheless highly correlated with actual enlistment rates (Asch and Orvis 1994). YATS data are not the only ones available on enlistment propensity. For an overview of recent trends in data provided by the Monitoring the Future Project, see Segal et al. (1999). Chapter 4 by Segal, et al. in this volume applies these data to the question of the civil-military gap.

Figure 9.2. Enlistment Propensity among 16-to-21-year-olds, 1976–98.

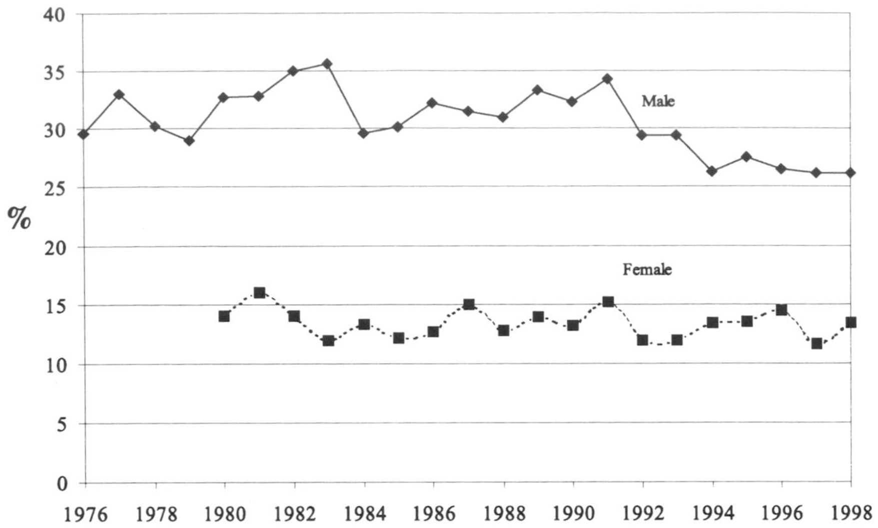

NOTE: Enlistment propensity is the percentage of respondents to Youth Attitude Tracking Survey (YATS) stating that they will "definitely" or "probably" enlist in the armed forces.

Hypothesis Testing

Variable	Male Enlistment Propensity	Female Enlistment Propensity
AR(1)	−0.03	−0.49
	(0.23	(0.28)
Unemployment	0.94*	−0.46
	(0.34)	(0.24)
College enrollment rate	0.30	0.40
among high school graduates	(0.32)	(0.20)
Trend through entire series	0.10	−0.60*
	(0.16)	(0.23)
Trend beginning in 1991	−0.95*	0.09
	(0.23)	(0.15)
Log-Likelihood	−39.25	−25.64
AIC	90.49	63.24

NOTE: Standard errors are in parentheses. The asterisk indicates statistical significance at the 0.05 level. A constant was estimated but is not reported. Gender-specific rates of college attendance were used in this analysis.
SOURCE: Office of the Secretary of Defense, Defense Manpower Data Center.

active-duty service in one of the military services. There has indeed been a downward trend in the proportion of high-propensity youth since the end of the Cold War, but it would be a mistake to attribute this trend entirely to the social isolation of the military since the establishment of the All-Volunteer Force.

First, other factors known to influence enlistment propensity explain much of the downward trend. Because potential recruits consider their alternatives in the civilian labor market or higher education, the civilian unemployment rate and trends in college attendance influence the percentage of high-propensity youth. The hypothesis tests shown beneath the graph confirm that increasing unemployment has been associated with increases in the proportion of young men strongly considering enlistment since 1976.[7] The recessions in 1982 and 1991 thus help explain the two peaks in the percentage of high-propensity males. Although college enrollment is not statistically significant here, qualitative studies strongly suggest that young people planning to attend college are less likely to enlist (Berkowitz et al. 1997). The rate of college enrollment among 18-to-24-year-old high school graduates has never been higher, having risen steadily from 39.1 percent in 1990 to 45.2 percent in 1997. At the same time, unemployment is at a thirty-year low. Falling unemployment and rising college attendance should certainly concern military recruiters, but they are not the result of a civil-military gap.

Second, an increasing gap between the military and civilian society is not the best explanation for the remainder of the downward trend since 1991. To the extent that the military has become increasingly socially isolated, the process has been a gradual one dating from the end of conscription. It is difficult to explain why the downward trend in the proportion of high-propensity young men begins only after 1991. The diminishing ideological appeal of military service after the Cold War is a better explanation because it can account for the beginning of the trend. An 18-year-old surveyed in 1998 would have been only 9 years old when the Berlin Wall came down in 1989, and would probably have little memory of the Cold War. This is not entirely bad news for military recruiters. To the extent that the experience of the Cold War increased the appeal of

---

7.   My analysis has focused on male propensity because the bulk of military recruits are men. As Figure 9.2 indicates, there is a slight downward trend in enlistment propensity among young women since the beginning of the series. If a civil-military gap is responsible for this decline in the proportion of high-propensity women since 1980, one would have to conclude that there is something gender-specific about it because the same trend does not appear among young men. Concerning the differences between male and female enlistment propensity, see Segal et al. (1998a). For an overview of the large literature on women in the military, see Segal (1999b).

military service, the fall in enlistment propensity produced by its end should be completed when the cohort surveyed no longer has any memory of this period. We may already have reached this point. Other factors must also be considered. Characteristics of the current youth cohort unrelated to the social isolation of the military, such as their attitudes toward peacekeeping missions or their reluctance to submit themselves to authority in general, could drive this pattern (Flacks 1999). Also, entry-level pay and educational benefits have not risen during the 1990s, and resources devoted to recruitment have fallen (Segal et al. 1999, 409). In light of all these considerations, the downward trend in the proportion of high-propensity men cannot be attributed exclusively to a growing civil-military gap. While this gap may have had some effect, there is at least as much evidence pointing to other explanations.

It is possible that a civil-military gap is not apparent before recruits actually begin their service. Indeed, one of the effects of such a gap might be to obscure the real nature of military life from potential recruits. If this is the case, there should be a decline in reenlistment or an increase in the proportion of new accessions leaving the military before the expiration of their term of service. Figure 9.3 presents data on attrition and reenlistment among first-term regulars. As was the case with the proportion of youth considering military service, there are some interesting trends in these data, but a growing civil-military gap is probably not the best explanation for them.

There is no evidence that the military is any more alienating to recent recruits now than it has been at any other time since the beginning of the All-Volunteer Force. Reenlistment rates vary in much the same way as the proportion of high-propensity young men. A higher proportion of first-term regulars reenlist when civilian unemployment rises, and fewer do so when a larger proportion of the 18-to-24-year-old population attends college. As with the proportion of high-propensity young men, there has been a downward trend since 1991. However, there has been a much larger upward trend since the beginning of the series. Clearly, the All-Volunteer Force has greatly improved its ability to retain the people it recruits. Even if the social isolation of the military has made it more difficult to retain new accessions, the services have handled this problem quite effectively.

Although it contains no statistically significant trends, the first-year attrition rate resembles the reenlistment rate in some respects. After reaching relatively high levels during the mid-1970s, it declined during the 1980s. Attrition has increased since 1992, but it has not exceeded its mid-1970s levels. Because military social isolation is a gradual process, while the upward shift in attrition has been abrupt, these two trends do

Figure 9.3. Attrition and Reenlistment Rates, FY 1972–96.

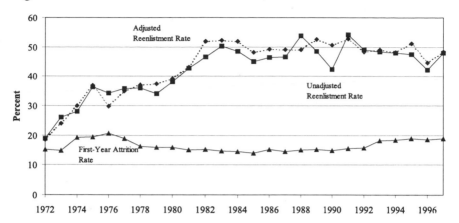

Hypothesis Testing

Variable	First-Year Attrition Rate	Unadjusted Reenlistment Rate	Aadjusted Reenlistment Rate
AR(1)	0.55*	–0.17	–0.37
	(0.17)	(0.23)	(0.22)
Unemployment	0.20	2.02*	2.18*
	(0.27)	(0.36)	(0.387)
College enrollment rate	0.22	–1.04*	–0.15
among high school graduates	(0.28)	(0.34)	(0.37)
Trend through entire series	–0.24	2.10	1.52*
	(0.15)	(0.17)	(0.18)
Trend beginning in 1991	0.53	1.49	–1.61
	(0.31)	(0.29)	(0.31)
Log-Likelihood	–40.58	–56.34	–60.98
AIC	93.16	124.69	133.96

NOTE: Standard errors are in parentheses. The asterisk indicates statistical significance at the 0.05 level. A constant was estimated, but is not reported. The first-year attrition rate is the percent of non-prior service accessions from the indicated fiscal year who separated before the expiration of their term of service during the first year after accession. The "unadjusted reenlistment rate" is the ratio of total reenlistments occurring in a given period to total separations of personnel eligible to reenlist during the same period, expressed as a percentage. The "adjusted reenlistment rate" is the unadjusted rate adjusted to exclude the effects of (1) early separation for immediate reenlistment, and (2) other early discharges of eligibles under early release programs for strength-control purposes.

SOURCE: On attrition, Defense Manpower Data Center; on reenlistment, Directorate of Information, Operations and Reports, *Selected Manpower Statistics* (Washington, D.C.: U.S. Department of Defense, annual).

not appear to be linked. Although the hypothesis tests do not support the argument that the shift was due to change in unemployment or college enrollment, a civil-military gap is no more attractive as an explanation. As was the case with aggregate propensity to enlist, one must also consider factors such as the end of the Cold War.

One thing all these series have in common is that they reveal increasing difficulties in recruiting and retaining military personnel since the early 1990s. The proportion of high-propensity youth and the reenlistment rate have fallen, and the attrition rate has increased. These trends are among the major sources of concern about the civil-military gap. While these trends merit attention, their long-term effects may not be as serious as recent alarm in the press has suggested. First, it is too early to tell if recent enlistment trends represent the effects of some new influence on individual decisions about military service. After all, they correspond to an unusually long period of economic prosperity and may not continue when this period ends. Even if these trends do continue, however, they will be at least partially offset by an increase in the number of potential recruits during the next ten years. Only 3.35 million Americans reached their eighteenth birthday in 1994, the lowest figure since 1964. By 2009, this number will rise by 14 percent, to 4.39 million (Assistant Secretary of Defense 1998, Appendix D-1). The reduction in the size of the military force during the 1990s greatly reduced the impact of the declining youth population on accessions (Eitelberg and Mehay 1994, 85). Although the services are now experiencing some of these problems as they increase their recruiting targets, the demographic trough is ending. Even if the propensity to enlist remains low, population growth should help alleviate current recruiting problems. Furthermore, previous research suggests that better pay, educational incentives, and other personnel polices can have a considerable impact on recruitment (Segal and Verdugo 1994).

Although exposure to the military influences attitudes toward military service, the data here indicate that declining exposure has not yet had much effect on military accessions. Military social isolation is not the only possible explanation for the declining proportion of high-propensity youth. Economic prosperity, high college enrollment, and the declining ideological appeal of the military service in the absence of a clear international adversary offer strong alternative explanations. Furthermore, whatever the reason for the recent decline in enlistment propensity, it has not seriously eroded the quality of the enlisted force. The military has proven quite resourceful in limiting the effects of these trends in accessions. Its problems are likely to lessen in the next ten years as the size of the youth population increases, particularly if the economy does not perform as well as it did in the 1990's. Overall, current concern in the press about shortfalls in military recruiting is probably exaggerated. There is little cause for alarm about the military's ability to recruit an adequate force.

Why Has the Gap in Elite Opinion Had so Little Policy Impact?

In spite of the evidence that exposure to the military influences elite opinion about military spending and service, and the fact that exposure to the military is declining, there is little evidence that a civil-military gap of this sort has had an impact on peacetime military policy. Our survey data indicate that concerns about the effects of military social isolation on public opinion are valid. However, both the survey data and the other evidence presented here underscore the fact that the path between the influences on elite opinion and actual policy outcomes is a complicated one. Many factors influence elite opinion, and these might well overwhelm the effect of declining exposure to the military. Above all, partisanship and ideology—two staples of American politics—have larger effects on attitudes toward military spending and service than does exposure to the military. The civil-military gap indeed influences public opinion, but it is not the most influential factor.

Furthermore, whatever its origins, public opinion is not the only factor shaping policy outcomes on these issues. The proportion of young people willing to enlist is influenced by environmental conditions such as unemployment, college attendance, military recruiting policies, and many other factors. Trends in the total size of the youth population can also reduce or magnify the effects of changes in the proportion of youth considering military service on the military's ability to meet its recruiting goals. The forces determining the level of military spending are also quite complex. Because policymakers are divided on these issues, peacetime military policy will reflect political conflict and bargaining as well as their opinions. The final outcome might be a complicated compromise rather than a reflection of the opinions of any one group. Furthermore, budgeting forces policymakers to balance their views on military spending with their priorities on many other issues, including funding for other programs, taxes, and fiscal policy. Even a policymaker who favors greater military spending in principle might oppose it in practice because he or she thinks tax cuts, domestic spending, or a balanced budget is more important. This could be true even of politicians with very extensive military experience. After all, Dwight Eisenhower's commitment to conservative fiscal policy led him to seek substantial cuts in military spending during one of the tensest periods of the Cold War. In sum, although the potential effect of the civil-military gap on peacetime military policy cannot be dismissed, it is not surprising that it has not yet had any discernible effects. There are simply too many other factors at work.

This does not mean that there is no civil-military gap, nor that it can have no effect on policy. There are at least two alternatives to this conclusion. First, the effects of military social isolation might be evident in other areas. This possibility is the subject of other chapters in this volume, particularly those by Bianco and Markham, Miller and Williams, Roman and Tarr, and Cohen. Second, the simple notion of a civil-military gap might not really capture the problems some observers perceive, as I argue next.

An Alternative Understanding of the Problem in Civil-Military Relations

Differences between the military and civilian segments of American society are not new. Perhaps because of its unique function, the military has always had traditions and practices that set it apart from civilian society. Considering its important role in the civilian economy and its high visibility in the news and entertainment media, the military was arguably never more integrated into American life in peacetime than it has been since the end of World War II. Something more than simply a gap between civilians and the military appears to be at work here. The problems many experienced observers of civil-military relations have noted cannot be dismissed. However, they are not necessarily consequences of a new or growing gap between the military and civilians.

The recent literature on growing tension in civil-military relations suggests an explanation of the essential problem that differs somewhat from the way in which it is usually framed. The most common and straightforward way of addressing the issue—the one that generated the hypotheses tested in the preceding two sections—is as a problem in the relationship between the military institution and civilian society as a whole. Peter Feaver (1998b, 596–7) has pointed out that treating "civilians" and "the military" as the principal actors is one of the identifying features of the literature on civil-military relations, even though not all scholars who adopt this approach do so explicitly. Indeed, the very term "civil-military relations" implies this conceptual apparatus. Although this approach is indeed helpful for understanding many issues, it does not adequately describe the recent changes in the political behavior of the military. The trouble with the civil-military gap hypothesis is that the military's culture, ideology, and policy preferences do not differ from those of all civilian society, but only from some parts of it. Many of the problems noted in recent civil-military relations do not stem from an increasing alienation of the military from civilian society, but rather from its increasingly close and exclusive identification with the Republican and conservative portions of it (Bacevich and Kohn 1997; Holsti 1998; Ricks 1997d). Understanding this situation as a "civil-military gap" is not the best way to approach it. Instead, it should be seen as a by-product of military efforts to link itself to civilian society.

The military must maintain ties to civilian society in order to get the resources it needs and have its policy expertise heeded. This need for societal linkages is not unique to the military. The argument that these linkages give state institutions greater autonomy and power has long been a staple of the literature on bureaucratic politics. For example, Roger Hilsman (1959, 371) pointed out forty years ago that even groups that were not especially powerful in their own right might force consideration of their views if they could influence some set of non-governmental opinion leaders. Even some critics of the bureaucratic politics approach recognize the importance of external allies in determining bureaucratic power. In pointing out that the bureaucratic politics perspective underestimates the power of the president, Robert Art (1973, 475) states that "it is presidential anticipation of Congressional and public response that causes him to heed those bureaucrats' demands he chooses to accede to."

Because, like any state institution, the military must rely on sympathetic political leaders and groups in the broader society, the necessities of building this support are bound to influence the dominant political outlook within the institution. For obvious reasons, military officers are likely to sympathize with political parties and interest groups that support more military spending and greater military freedom of action in the performance of its missions. Indeed, it would be surprising for any group of experts to behave otherwise when dealing with matters of great professional significance to them. At the same time, the bureaucratic interests of their organization are not the only force shaping officers' political attitudes. Military officers are a self-selected group with well-known conservative tendencies on issues that have little immediate connection to military service (Huntington 1957, 59–79; Janowitz 1971, 233–256). The research presented in the chapters by Holsti, Davis, and Segal, et al. in this volume generally confirm the military's conservative attitudes on many issues.

The changing identity of the military's civilian political allies can help explain the recent problems in civil-military relations often attributed to a growing civil-military gap. During the first two decades of the Cold War, civilian partisan and ideological cleavages cut across the institutional interests and ideological preferences of the officer corps, making open ideological and partisan commitments difficult. Changes in civilian politics during the last thirty years have aligned the interests and attitudes of the officer corps with those of conservative Republicans, making open partisanship much more attractive. This interpretation has somewhat different implications for peacetime military policy than the civil-military gap hypothesis reviewed in the first two sections of this chapter.

CIVIL-MILITARY RELATIONS AND THE POLITICS OF MILITARY SPENDING SINCE WORLD WAR II

During most of American history, the peacetime military's small size meant that political attitudes prevailing within the institution mattered much less for civilian politics than they do now. After World War II, however, the military acquired considerable resources with which to build a base of political support. As James Burk aptly expresses it in Chapter 6, the "institutional presence" of the military greatly increased after the war and has remained fairly high. Institutional presence implies considerable potential political influence. The arms industry, once a small and largely government-run enterprise, now constitutes an important part of the American economy. Military bases play a crucial role in the economic life of many towns and cities. These interests and their political representatives are potential political allies for the military in pursuing greater resources and autonomy. The high prestige of the institution, which Burk calls its "moral presence," is also a considerable asset (King and Karabell 1999a). When its representatives speak, the public is inclined to trust them.

In spite of its potential political clout, the military has not always translated its political resources into effective resistance to civilian authority during the last fifty years. At least two political considerations explain this. First, the policies adopted by the civilians have often divided the military services. If military leaders from different services cannot agree, then they cannot mobilize their political resources for any particular policy position. Second, even when military leaders from different services have had common interests on a particular policy matter, they have had to consider the dangers of making enemies among civilians who were their natural allies on other issues. If military leaders consistently agreed or disagreed with the same set of civilians across nearly all policy areas, they would not face this second barrier to political action. The fact that American civilian politics have removed both of these barriers to the effective exercise of political power by the military leadership helps explain the evidence that the elite military officers examined in the TISS survey and in Ole Holsti's Foreign Policy Leadership Project (Holsti 1998–99) have become more partisan and ideological. The positions generally taken by the Republican Party now match those of the military on nearly every issue.

This situation is relatively new. It is worth considering the different political circumstances American military leaders faced during much of the postwar era. Before the Vietnam War, the Democratic and Republican parties' positions on peacetime military policy often divided the military services. Even when the services were not divided, they did not consistently agree with the same political party. Several historical patterns contributed to this situation.

The different strategic emphases of Republican and Democratic administrations have tended to divide the services against one another. For several reasons, Democrats tended to stress conventional missions during much of the Cold War. Groups with the greatest interest in continuing economic access to Europe were more closely associated with the Democratic Party than with the Republican Party (Cumings 1990; Ferguson 1984; Fordham 1998; Frieden 1988; Hogan 1987; 1998). While neither party was prepared to abandon Europe, the Republicans were willing to run somewhat higher risks in order to reduce the financial burden of military spending. Democrats more strongly than Republicans supported maintaining a ground force on the continent both to deter the Soviets and to reassure the Europeans; Republicans worried more about the high costs of this commitment. The fiscal policy preferences of the two parties complemented their strategic tendencies. The Democrats' Keynesian orientation allowed them to spend more on both military and civilian policy goals, while Republicans adhered to a more conservative fiscal policy and pursued a balanced budget (Beck 1982; Hibbs 1987; Tufte 1978; Williams 1990).

As a consequence of these differences, Democrats allocated Pentagon funds in ways that emphasized general-purpose forces, while Republicans favored strategic nuclear forces. Some of the most visible military efforts to resist civilian authority can be traced to Democratic presidents' resistance to new strategic weapons and to Republican opposition to similar conventional force initiatives. In 1948, the Air Force went to Congress in defiance of the Secretary of Defense to resist the Truman administration's decision to limit its size and budget (Eden 1984). In the late 1950s, Army General Maxwell Taylor retired and wrote a book that was quite critical of the Eisenhower administration's reliance on nuclear weapons. John F. Kennedy, who undertook a major buildup of conventional forces, appointed Taylor Chairman of the Joint Chiefs of Staff. These partisan tendencies are evident in more than just anecdotes like these. Statistics on the allocation of the defense budget bear them out (Fordham 1999). Policies of this sort divided the military services against one another and made the effective exercise of the institution's potential political power difficult.

In addition to divisions along service lines due to the way the two parties allocated the budget during much of the Cold War, other considerations made a unified military alignment with either party unlikely. Both parties—and especially the leading ideological factions within them—took positions that matched the interests and attitudes of the military on some issues. It would have been difficult to make a compelling case within the military for aligning wholly with either one. Before the mid-1960s, liberal Democrats generally supported a larger budget and more institutional autonomy for the military than did conservative Republicans. These differences are evident in Congressional voting. Table 9.5 shows the average level of support for greater military spending and bureaucratic autonomy on key votes taken in the Senate and the House of Representatives between 1950 and 1998.[8] In the 1950s, the bureaucratic interests of the military were best served by the Democratic Party, a political fact that is unlikely to have escaped the attention of military leaders. Furthermore, until the mid-1960s, the Democratic Party also dominated the South, a region that has long produced a disproportionate share of military personnel. For Southerners, Democratic political loyalties did not imply a liberal ideology (Black and Black 1987; Butler and Johnson 1991; Carmines and Stimson 1989; Goertzel 1987).

Although the Democratic Party, particularly its liberal wing, generally offered more material support for the institution, many other policy positions typically taken by liberal Democrats clashed with political attitudes prevailing in the military. Interviewing military officers during the 1950s, Morris Janowitz (1961, 233–256; 388–392) found that most of them were suspicious of labor unions and the social reform efforts proposed by the liberal wing of the Democratic Party. The few high-ranking military leaders who became directly involved in partisan politics during the early part of the Cold War tended to do so as Republicans. On the other hand, Janowitz (1961, 244–248) also found that military conservatism included some distrust of business, which was generally hostile to military spending during most of the century. Throughout most of the 1950s, high levels of military spending required government controls on prices and the allocation of important raw materials in order to prevent inflation. Republicans and civilian business leaders generally opposed these controls (Friedberg 1992; Lo 1982; Russett and Hanson 1982). Military conser-

---

8. The "key votes" used here were selected by the editors of *Congressional Quarterly Almanac* to represent (1) matters of major controversy; (2) matters of presidential or political power; and (3) matters of potential great impact on the nation or the lives of Americans. The editors generally select one vote to represent each such issue.

Table 9.5. Democratic and Republican Congressional Support for Military Spending and Autonomy, 1950–98.

Time Period	House of Representatives			Senate		
	Democrats	Republicans	Number of Key Votes	Democrats	Republicans	Number of Key Votes
1950–54	0.710	0.200	8	0.867	0.254	6
1955–59	0.844	0.210	2	0.854	0.096	3
1960–64	n.a.	n.a.	0	n.a.	n.a.	0
1965–69	0.674	0.998	3	0.299	0.551	5
1970–74	0.343	0.752	6	0.299	0.705	13
1975–79	0.420	0.748	4	0.443	0.729	8
1980–84	0.322	0.758	12	0.391	0.740	10
1985–89	0.217	.0839	13	0.236	0.847	11
1990–94	0.354	0.940	5	0.279	0.841	7
1995–98	0.248	0.867	4	0.156	0.698	2

NOTE: The number shown is the average proportion of each party voting in favor of measures that would increase the funding or bureaucratic autonomy of the military, or against measures intended to reduce funding or autonomy. The key votes are taken from *Congressional Quarterly Almanac*.

vatism fit better with the Republican Party in the early part of the Cold War, but the fit was far from perfect.

Given the set of policies each party favored, unqualified allegiance to either of them would have been very difficult for military officers during much of the postwar period. Nonpartisanship was not just a professional norm during this period. It was also a practical response to the fact that neither party's core policy positions matched both the institutional interests and the prevailing political attitudes of the military.

This situation began to change in the 1960s. As Table 9.5 indicates, Democratic support for military spending and bureaucratic autonomy declined during the late 1960s. At the same time, Republicans were becoming increasingly supportive of military spending and many other aspects of Cold War foreign policy, abandoning the lingering suspicion of internationalism that Republican leaders had exhibited during the early Cold War era. Today, the fact that Republicans generally prefer higher military spending than Democrats is a well-established piece of conventional wisdom confirmed by the survey data presented in the first section.

Considering the political changes of the last thirty years, increasing military partisanship and hostility toward President Clinton is not surprising. The Democrats' preferences on major military policy issues, particularly defense spending, tend to unite the military in opposition. Furthermore, the costs to the military leadership of alienating the Democrats are low, since the Democrats are in any event unlikely to adopt positions supported by military leaders on most issues. The military can now serve both its bureaucratic interests and the ideological preferences of most of its members by aligning itself with the Republican Party. Bill Clinton had the misfortune of being the first Democrat to occupy the White House since the Reagan buildup, which consolidated this change.

These changes in the politics of military spending over the last thirty years suggest that the military could have become more partisan and ideological even without a growing gap with civilian society as a whole. The military has always been somewhat more conservative than most of American civilian society. Changes in civilian politics have created circumstances in which military leaders can publicly express these views without alienating potential civilian allies. Indeed, they probably help mobilize political support within some segment of civilian society. Comparable political conditions might have existed at other times in American history, but the military has never before had so many potential political resources at its disposal in peacetime. The changing significance of military conservatism in civilian politics has some important implications for military spending and recruitment. The remainder of this section will evaluate these possibilities.

A PARTISAN CYCLE IN MILITARY SPENDING?
Theoretically, the growing ties between the Republican Party and the elite military could create a political cycle in military spending linking it to partisan control of the White House and Congress. When Democrats control both institutions, military spending should decline. When Republicans control both institutions, military spending should increase. Although there has been no statistically significant partisan cycle in military spending in the past, the potential for such a cycle in the future is clear given the defense spending preferences of the two parties.[9] The potential danger of this pattern is that the military will be unable to warn Democratic civilian leaders effectively of cases when greater spending really is necessary to counter some international threat. Democrats might

---

9. In spite of the fact that visual inspection of the defense spending data in Figure 9.1 suggests that Democrats tended to spend more than Republicans before the mid-1970s, and that Republicans have tended to spend more since then, there is no statistically significant partisan cycle in the data. More fully specified statistical models of the federal budget have also found no evidence of a partisan trade-off, although none has examined the possibility of a change in the attitudes of the two parties over time. See, for example, Lowery and Berry (1990); and Su, Kamlet, and Mowery (1993).

dismiss these warnings as a parochial effort to gain a larger share of the federal budget. At the extreme, this could eventually endanger the United States, just as the failure to prepare for World War II endangered Britain and France during the 1930s.

Although a partisan cycle in military spending is possible, it is neither very dangerous nor very likely under present circumstances. Previous research on military doctrine suggests that civilians rather than the military are more likely to perceive international threats and force the military to respond appropriately (Posen 1984). Present international conditions also make the potential problem of a partisan cycle in military spending less serious. The United States does not face a serious threat to its political sovereignty or territorial integrity at present, and none is on the horizon. Under current circumstances, international "threats" will depend on broader U.S. policy goals and tolerance for risk, both of which are matters of political judgment that should arguably be left to civilians anyway. Moreover, voters might well respond to a serious international threat. The fact that the two parties now present voters with clearer choices on national security issues should enhance democratic control of defense policy. If voters feel threatened, they can turn to Republicans. When they believe military spending is too high, they can choose Democrats. While there are historical cases in which voters have failed to respond until it was too late, American public opinion proved quite responsive to variations in the Soviet threat during the Cold War (Holsti 1996, 40–45, 62–79; Russett 1990, 92–106; Jentleson 1992). There is no reason to assume that democracy will fail.

Furthermore, current political circumstances suggest that the Democrats may not attempt to cut the Pentagon budget substantially. Whatever its real preferences, the Clinton administration did not seek large cuts in the military budget. Indeed, the Clinton administration, toward the end of its second term, proposed spending increases and agreed to deploy a ballistic missile defense system, reversing the position Democrats have generally taken on the issue. Military spending appeared to be low on the administration's list of priorities, and it may have accepted Republican initiatives on this issue simply to avoid the political costs of fighting about it. If the Clinton administration is any indication, the Democratic attitude toward military spending is best characterized as indifference rather than hostility. As long as military spending does not threaten programs Democrats favor, they may be willing to let Republicans have their way on the matter.

Paradoxically, it is possible that conservative Republicans, not liberal Democrats, could initiate the largest cuts in military spending. The Republicans' commitment to fiscal conservatism and smaller government rests uneasily with their current advocacy of larger military budgets. It is worth remembering that conservatives in the party have been committed to small budgets much longer than they have been committed to high levels of military spending. The congressional struggle over funding for the F-22 fighter aircraft during the summer of 1999 illustrates this possibility. Conservative California Republican Jerry Lewis led the effort to cut funding for the plane, and the subsequent struggle mainly pitted conservative Republicans against one another (Towell 1999a). Because liberal efforts to cut the military budget routinely encounter strong conservative opposition, cuts proposed by conservatives like Lewis are more likely to be implemented. If a future Republican president decides to put his or her fiscal policy preferences ahead of the interests of the military, large cuts are possible because Democratic resistance in Congress is not likely. The fact that both the military leadership and many major figures in the Republican Party are skeptical of military intervention in cases such as Kosovo raises the possibility that a Republican president could cut funding for the capability to engage in them.

While a partisan cycle in military spending could be dangerous in the face of a serious international military threat, this danger is quite remote. There is no such threat at present and the political means for responding to one, should it arise, exist within our current system. In any event, the consequences of different levels of commitment to military spending in the two parties are not necessarily obvious. The budget process is complex, and these preferences have thus far not been translated into actual policy. Although the TISS survey data confirm that conservatives and Republicans prefer more military spending than do liberals and Democrats, the tension between conservative military and fiscal policies illustrated by the F-22 debate suggests that this situation could change. If "cheap hawks" come to dominate the Republican party, military officers who now consider themselves Republicans might once again begin to think of themselves as independents.

SELECTIVE APPEAL? MILITARY PARTISANSHIP AND ACCESSIONS

Although evidence presented earlier indicates that the military is not alienating an increasing proportion of potential recruits, an account of recent civil-military relations stressing increasing military alignment with the Republican Party and ideological conservatives suggests other possible trends. Military leaders like those in the TISS survey can strongly influence the character of the institution. Their political orientation might give military service an ideological tinge in the eyes of potential recruits. It might attract those who sympathize with the views prevailing in the institution and alienate those who do not. The survey data presented in the first section indicate that ideology and partisanship have large effects on attitudes toward military service. This evidence raises the possibility of changes in the composition of the force even if no trends appear in aggregate data on accessions. Although time-series data on the political attitudes of military personnel are difficult to find, demographic groups with characteristic political attitudes can serve as a rough proxy.

African-Americans, for example, overwhelmingly support the Democratic Party in elections and tend to take more liberal positions than whites on most issues (Tate 1994, 20–74; Goertzel 1987). An increasingly Republican and conservative military should be less appealing within this demographic group than in other segments of the population. Figure 9.4 shows the enlistment propensities of 16-to-21-year-old white and African-American men since 1984, the first year YATS data were disaggregated by race.

The fact that a higher proportion of African-American than white men have a high propensity to enlist might seem to rule out the possibility that the political orientation of the institution alienates more African-Americans than whites. However, the trends in these data tell a different story. In addition to responding to unemployment, the proportion of white males with a high enlistment propensity shows the same downward trend found in the data since 1991 on overall male enlistment propensity. By contrast, a downward trend in the proportion of those with a high enlistment propensity dominates the data on African-American men. There is no change at the end of the Cold War. Furthermore, the African-American enlistment propensity does not even respond in the expected way to unemployment. Although the evidence given here does not conclusively link these trends to the increasingly conservative and Republican image of the military, the proportion of African-American men with a high propensity to enlist has declined steadily in a way that is consistent with this hypothesis. Because the military relies on African-Americans for a disproportionate number of enlisted accessions, their declining propensity to enlist could become a problem if present trends continue.[10]

Although the declining proportion of high-propensity African-Americans is a cause for concern, it has not yet had any appreciable effect on African-American representation in the military services. Figure 9.5

---

10.   I have focused on male enlistment propensity here because they constitute the great majority of recruits. There is a downward trend in enlistment propensity among 16-to-21-year-old African-American women similar to the one found among young men of the same race. This downward trend has leveled off since the end of the Cold War. There is no trend in the data on white women.

Figure 9.4. Enlistment Propensity for 16–21 Year Old Males, By Race, 1984–98.

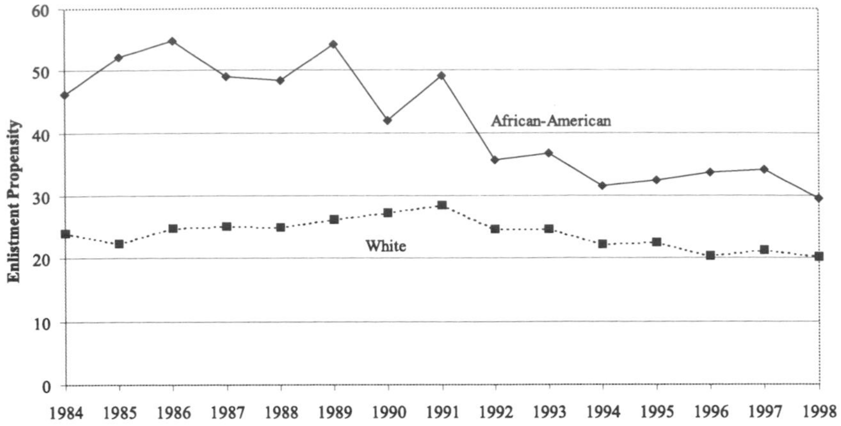

NOTE: Enlistment propensity is the percentage of YATS respondents stating that they will "definitely" or "probably" enlist in the armed forces.

Hypothesis Testing

Variable	White Male Enlistment Propensity	African-American Male Enlistment Propensity	
		Model 1	Model 2
AR(1)	−0.47	−0.40	−0.31
	(0.27)	(0.34)	(0.32)
Unemployment	1.04	−1.21	−1.90
	(0.29)	(0.99)	(0.89)
College enrollment rate	0.51	0.23	−0.46
among high school graduates	(0.40)	(0.54)	(0.53)
Trend beginning in 1984	−0.77	−1.16	−2.19
	(0.43)	(1.00)	(0.52)
Trend beginning in 1991	1.59	−1.23	—
	(0.26)	(1.02)	
Log-Likelihood	−14.77	−37.30	−38.12
AIC	41.53	86.60	86.25

NOTE: Standard errors are in parentheses. The asterisk indicates statistical significance at the 0.05 level. A constant was estimated, but is not reported. Race- and gender-specific unemployment and college attendance rates are used here.
SOURCE: Defense Manpower Data Center.

shows that the proportion of African-Americans among enlisted accessions has not changed significantly since the 1970s, while the proportion of African-Americans among new officers has steadily increased. In spite of the fact that African-Americans are well represented in the current force, it would be a mistake to dismiss the downward trend in enlistment propensity as an anomaly. It is strongly related to the decline in the proportion of African-American youth entering the military. The proportion of high-propensity African-American men and African-American non-prior service accessions as a proportion of the 18-year-old population are closely correlated (0.87). Reductions in the overall size of the force since the end of the Cold War and the relatively greater decline in the number of the white 18-to-24-year-olds currently have helped limit the impact of this trend on the racial composition of the military. If the trend continues, however, it could certainly have an effect.

Just as the African-American population is more liberal and less Republican than the population as a whole, a higher proportion of Southerners are conservative and, in recent years, Republican. Furthermore, the South is among the regions to benefit most from military spending on both weapons systems and bases, a tendency that may have been amplified by base closings since the end of the Cold War (Markusen et al. 1991; Trubowitz and Roberts 1992; Ricks 1997d). Figure 9–6 suggests that these factors have given the South an increasing tie to the military. Although Southerners have long been well represented in the military, their representation in it has grown steadily since the early 1980s. They have consistently joined the military at rates in excess of their proportion of the U.S. population ever since the mid-1980s. This has decreased the relative representation from the Northeast and North Central regions of the country, areas that benefited less from the Reagan buildup and that have produced some of the most important Congressional critics of military spending. While regional representation is a very crude indicator of political orientation, the fact that the enlisted military force is now drawn more from relatively conservative regions and less from relatively liberal areas is consistent with the argument that the political orientation of the military has affected accessions.

In spite of its limited impact on the composition of the military so far, there is some empirical support for the argument that the increasingly conservative and Republican orientation of the elite military could eventually affect the composition of the military force as a whole. Trends in aggregate enlistment propensity and the composition of the enlisted force indicate that the institution as a whole is increasingly drawing from more conservative and Republican elements of civilian society and less from

Figure 9.5. African-American Representation in Active Component Accessions, Fiscal Years 1973–97.

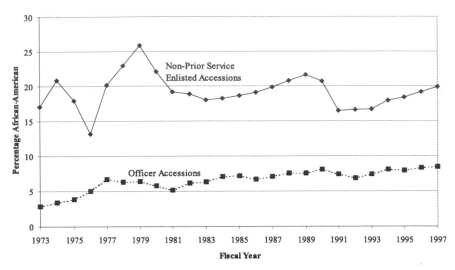

Hypothesis Testing

Variable	Non-Prior Service Enlisted Accessions	Officer Accessions
AR(1)	0.43*	0.61*
	(0.20)	(0.16)
Trend through entire series	0.06	0.26*
	(0.17)	(0.05)
Trend beginning in 1991	−0.22	−0.19
	(0.41)	(0.13)
Log Likelihood	−54.94	−20.00
AIC	117.89	48.00

NOTE: Standard errors are in parentheses. The asterisk indicates statistical significance at the 0.05 level. A constant was estimated, but is not reported. Race- and gender-specific unemployment and college attendance rates are used here.

SOURCE: Assistant Secretary of Defense for Force Management Policy (1998).

more liberal and Democratic segments. (Although the increase in African-American representation in the officer corps is an exception to this trend, military officers are still more likely to be white than the population as a whole.) These potential changes in its composition might not make the armed forces less effective, but they could have other undesirable effects.

Figure 9.6. Regional Over- and Under-Representation Fiscal Years 1973–97.

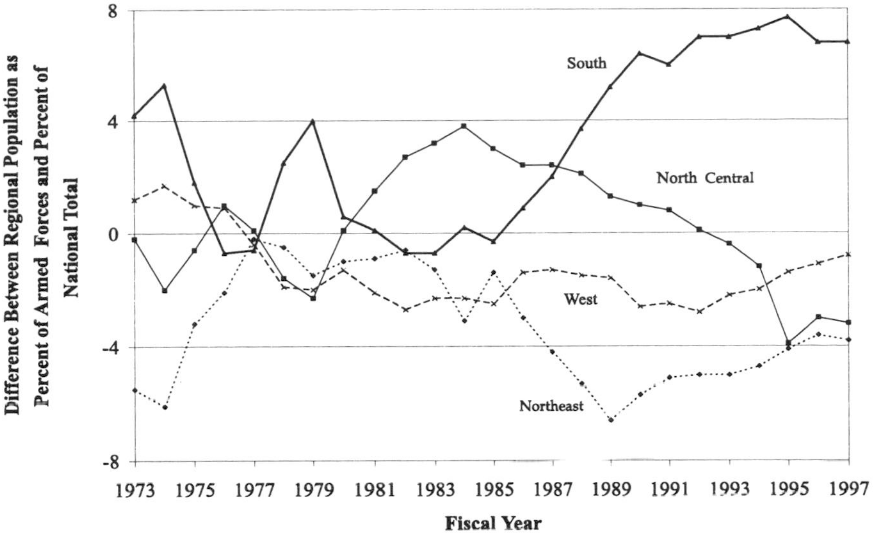

Hypothesis Testing

Variables	South	West	Northeast	North Central
AR(1)	0.59*	0.65*	0.81*	0.44*
	(0.18)	(0.16)	(0.11)	(0.19)
Trend through	−0.23	0.45*	0.22	0.40*
entire series	(0.18)	(0.14)	(0.21)	(0.10)
Trend beginning in	0.91*	0.32*	−0.45	−0.93*
1985	(0.31)	(0.08)	(0.36)	(0.18)
Constant	3.15*	1.10	−4.59*	−1.53
	(1.41)	(0.64)	(1.83)	(0.82)
Log Likelihood	−42.30	−19.95	−35.90	−34.06
AIC	92.60	47.89	79.80	76.13

NOTE: Standard errors are in parentheses. *$p < 0.05$
SOURCE: Assistant Secretary of Defense for Force Management Policy (1998).

Conclusion

What can be done to bridge the gap between the military and those elements of civilian society from which it is growing increasingly alienated? Must anything be done at all? The evidence presented here suggests that only modest policy actions in the areas of military spending and accessions would be appropriate. Some effort to correct demographic imbalances in the force makes sense and can probably be implemented by re-focusing current recruiting programs. More ambitious policies to address the recent problems in civil-military relations will have to be justified on other grounds.

The argument that exposure to the military influences elite attitudes toward defense spending and military service is generally supported by the TISS survey data. Veterans are more likely than non-veterans to hold favorable attitudes about military service, although not about military spending, once one controls for other influences on their opinions. People who have greater social contact with the military are more likely to support both military spending and military service. Because exposure to the military has been declining for some time, the concerns of Secretary Cohen and others are valid.

While military isolation from civilian society influences public opinion, trends in military spending and accessions indicate that the civil-military gap has not yet had much impact on actual outcomes in these areas of peacetime military policy. These findings should be reassuring to those worried about this issue. Neither the beginning of the All-Volunteer Force nor the end of the Cold War has brought about any statistically significant drop in military spending. Military spending has indeed fallen since 1990, but it has remained within the bounds of normal variation established during the Cold War, even though the major threat to U.S. national security has disappeared. Furthermore, military spending is actually somewhat less volatile now than it was during most of the Cold War. The evidence does not support comparisons to the rapid demobilizations that followed earlier wars.

Similarly, the data suggest that the linkage between the civil-military gap and recent recruiting problems has probably been overstated in the press. There has indeed been a drop since the end of the Cold War in the proportion of young people strongly considering military service. However, a strong economy, increasing college attendance, and other factors known to influence enlistment explain much of this trend. The possibility that military social isolation has also had some effect cannot be ruled out, but competing explanations fit the data better. Furthermore, although the military services have indeed had some difficulty meeting their recruiting goals recently, these problems are not nearly as serious as those the institution faced in the 1970s. The quality of new accessions has remained high, and an increase in the 18-to-24-year-old population should make it easier to meet recruiting targets in the next ten years. In short, the civil-military gap has not yet created serious problems in military accessions.

A consideration of changes in the way the military fits into civilian politics raises a different set of potential dangers, but does not demand sweeping policy action. The increasingly Republican political orientation of elite military officers raises the theoretical possibility of a partisan cycle in military spending: Democrats might cut military spending and Republicans might increase it, without regard to international conditions. Although this cycle carries the danger of wasteful spending or inadequate attention to military needs, depending on the party in control of the budget, the chances are at least as good that nothing serious will happen. There is no partisan cycle at present. Political circumstances also suggest that neither party will seek extreme changes in current levels of military spending in the future. The record of the Clinton administration offers no reason to expect a Democratic president to pursue aggressively deep cuts in military spending over Republican opposition. At the same time, the F-22 debate suggests that Republicans' commitment to limiting government spending will reduce their support for large increases in military spending.

One area in which policy action appears justified is the demographic composition of the force. Trends in this area are consistent with the argument that military service is becoming less appealing to those who do not share the conservative ideology and Republican party identification prevailing within the military. Military service has begun to attract fewer African-Americans, and the force now over-represents Southerners more than it has at any time since the end of the draft. If these trends are rooted in changing public perceptions about the political and ideological meaning of military service, then they probably cannot be entirely eliminated. Even in this case, however, their effects on the force can be limited (Segal and Verdugo 1994). Existing military recruitment efforts could be concentrated more heavily in under-represented regions. Similarly, additional educational and other incentives for enlistment might help arrest the decline in the appeal of military service to minority groups. These incentives would also help with recent problems in meeting recruiting targets generally.

Altering the political and ideological orientation of the military would be extremely difficult and is probably not necessary. While the consequences of the current problems in civil-military relations for peacetime military policy are not very great, the difficulties of curbing military partisanship would be enormous. The fact that the situation exists within the same political system that would have to repair it magnifies the difficulties of implementing an effective solution. Any potential policies would have immediate political costs and benefits for the politicians who would have to implement them, a fact that would greatly complicate the policymaking process. Military partisanship may be unseemly, but as long as it does not involve the use of the institution's coercive capabilities in domestic politics, it is probably best to manage its consequences rather than to attempt to eliminate it.

In view of the small impact of the civil-military gap on peacetime military policy, policies other than modest efforts to regulate the demographic composition of the force will have to be justified on other grounds. The potential problems caused by military partisanship can probably be handled within the framework of current policy. Military spending and accessions are only part of a larger set of policy problems. Major partisan and ideological differences between a predominantly Republican military and a more Democratic civilian policymakers might have more serious implications in other policy areas. The most that can be said here is that the risks and difficulties of closing the gap exceed the costs and risks of living with the present situation in peacetime military policy.

Chapter 10

Do Military Policies on Gender and Sexuality Undermine Combat Effectiveness?

Laura L. Miller
John Allen Williams

Military policies on women and homosexuals changed dramatically in the 1990s. Following the Persian Gulf War, Congress directed the armed forces to open most career opportunities previously closed to military women. Women may now fly combat aircraft and serve on most combat ships. The Department of Defense eliminated the "risk rule" prohibiting military women from entering areas deemed combat zones. Today restrictions remain on Special Forces and Sea, Air, and Land Forces (SEALS) teams, ground combat positions in the Army and Marines (such as infantry and armor), and from service on Navy vessels with very close quarters (submarines and patrol craft).

Meanwhile, several high-profile scandals ensured that the issue of women in the military remained in the public eye. The trouble began with the political fallout from the well-publicized sexually oriented activities of naval aviators and others at the 1991 Las Vegas convention of the

We are heavily indebted to Loyola University Chicago colleagues Shannon Jenkins and Angela Andersson for invaluable assistance in the data analysis for this paper. Substantive feedback was generously provided by Aaron Belkin, James Burk, Robert Goldich, Steven Michels, Mady Segal, and Patrick Van Inwegen, who also assisted with the data analysis. We are particularly grateful to Amy Denissen and Michael P. Noonan for substantive, bibliographic, and editorial contributions. Laura Miller would like to recognize the U.S. Army Research Institute for the Behavioral and Social Sciences for sponsoring her initial research on cohesion and unit performance.

private Tailhook Association.[1] This scandal effectively ended the careers of many naval aviators and weakened the ability of Navy leadership to oppose civilian initiatives to expand the roles of women.[2] In 1996, allegations of sexual relationships with recruits, sexual harassment, sexual assault, and rape by drill sergeants at the Army's Aberdeen Proving Ground training facility in Maryland rekindled public outrage. Tailhook, Aberdeen, and other such incidents brought considerable media attention to gender relations in the military, and convinced many that military leaders lag behind civilians in attitudes and workplace management. These scandals, in turn, led to commissioned studies, panels, and congressional hearings focused on how best to censure the top brass and improve the circumstances under which women serve in the military.

In 1992, then-Governor Clinton inflamed yet another division between civilian and military leaders when he declared his intention during his presidential campaign to lift the ban on open gay and lesbian service members by executive order. Once in office, and hardly beloved by the military for his efforts to avoid service in Vietnam, the new president advanced a proposal that drew strong disapproval from many veterans and active duty personnel. Even Colin Powell, Chairman of the Joint Chiefs of Staff, publicly criticized the intentions of his soon-to-be commander-in-chief. Before long it became clear that the Congress would pass even more restrictive legislation excluding gays than was already on the books if Clinton attempted to remove the ban completely.[3] The "don't ask, don't tell" compromise opened the door for homosexuals to enter and remain in the military as long as they keep their sexual orientation a secret. Sexual activity between members of the same sex, however, remains illegal, and gays who "tell" or are discovered are honorably discharged whether they wish to leave the service or not.[4]

---

1. For a balanced account of misbehavior of both men and women at this event, see Mitchell (1998).

2. Congressional scrutiny of Navy officer promotions was still required in 2000 to ensure that no one even remotely connected with the Tailhook scandal is advanced. Sexual harassment also continues across the services, although typically in a much less blatant manner than before.

3. Charles Moskos, preeminent military sociologist, frequent advisor to political leaders in Washington, and an insider in the process, has stated this publicly on numerous occasions and personally to the authors.

4. The details of current regulations with respect to this issue are beyond the scope of this chapter, as is the argument whether the military is upholding its part of the bargain by refraining from actively seeking out homosexuals for dismissal.

Much of the media focus on gender and sexuality in the military highlighted the positive contributions of women and gays, and framed the exclusionary policies as a prejudiced denial of civil rights. Support for civilian intervention in the area of military diversity and integration is predicated on the contention that the military leadership is sexist, homophobic, and unwilling to implement civilian directed personnel initiatives. Not everyone agrees with this depiction, however, and some of the most vocal opposition has come from men either currently or formerly serving in the armed forces.

Critics of permitting military women to serve in all roles, including ground combat, and of service of acknowledged gays and lesbians make three assertions: first, that there is a gap between civilians—especially civilian elites—and military leaders on appropriate policies concerning women and open homosexuals in the military; second, that this gap causes civilians to support policies that military leaders know to be unwise and detrimental, such as further integration; and third, that the proposed changes urged by civilians will hurt military cohesion, and the decrease in military cohesion as a consequence will reduce combat effectiveness to an unacceptable level. We explore these assertions in this chapter.

CLAIMS OF A GAP BETWEEN CIVILIAN AND MILITARY LEADERS

The critics of recent social reforms, whose claims we assess here, agree that diversity undermines the primary purpose of military forces: "The justification of the military remains—at least to date—national defense, not welfare or social engineering" (Moskos 1994, 59). A number of public commentators and authors, predominantly men with combat experience, have argued that military leaders witness first-hand the detriment of social diversity on military functioning, but that civilian activists and politicians tend to ignore these effects and instead prioritize individualism over national security. As a result, these critics assert, civilians suppress information about problems of gender integration and continue to push for personnel reforms, including accepting open homosexuals into the armed forces. They stress that most people with military experience believe that civil rights issues should not be the impetus for change when performance in combat is at stake.

Conservatives and liberal activists alike generally accept that gender integration is problematic, although they disagree on the nature of the problem and who should be held responsible. According to conservatives, military experience reveals the difficulties of implementing social reforms, and the problems which can be invisible to people who have never served. The majority of public figures who oppose women in combat and gays in the military are themselves veterans. Charles Moskos served as an enlisted man between the Korean and Vietnam Wars; critical authors and commentators David Hackworth, Darryl Henderson, Brian Mitchell, Ronald Ray, and James Webb are all former officers and combat veterans of the Vietnam War. John Hillen, who leads a new generation of critics, is a veteran of the Persian Gulf War. James Webb, who also served as Assistant Secretary of Defense and Secretary of the Navy under Ronald Reagan, articulated the commonly held belief among these veterans that the admission of women into ground combat roles would be an unwise social experiment:

While women make valuable contributions on a variety of levels, the military is and always has been a predominantly male profession. Its leaders should demand that any adjustment in sexual roles meet the historically appropriate criterion of improving performance, and should stop salving the egos of a group of never-satisfied social engineers (Webb 1997, 22).

Scholars have documented such sentiments from active-duty military men as well, who complain that civilians who are ignorant of how the military functions have implemented a form of gender integration which has produced what is commonly referred to as a "kinder, gentler military."[5] These soldiers believe that the current military environment is constrained by the rule of political correctness, which demoralizes and discriminates against heterosexual white men and produces units virtually unfit for combat (Bacevich 1997; Gutmann 2000; Harrell and Miller 1997; Miller 1997).

Some proponents of further integration note the opposition of many military leaders to the recent and proposed reforms of military policies on gender and sexuality, and argue that these officers' views are the cause of integration difficulties, not merely the revelation of them. These scholars criticize the masculine element of traditional military culture as institutionalized bigotry and a primary obstacle to the acceptance and success of any members who do not match a hypermasculine ideal (Enloe 2000; Katzenstein and Reppy 1999; Morris 1996).

Defenders of the status quo believe that civilians are attempting to change the military without regard for combat readiness. John Hillen criticized efforts to introduce women into combat and open homosexuals

---

5.   Indeed, this catch phrase is the title of a recent book on the subject (Gutmann 2000).

into the military, regarding these ideas as "agendas driven by political activists who see the military as a vehicle for social experimentation" (Hillen 1997, 35).[6] Brian Mitchell (1989; 1998) described the integration of women as the "feminization of the military," instigated by feminists who would be thrilled to witness the decline of the American military. He complains about the perpetuation of myths that serve ideological aims:

Library shelves groan under the weight of books praising the integration of women into the armed forces. *Women in the Military: Flirting with Disaster* [Mitchell's book] is the only in-depth treatment that offers an alternative view of the revolution that threatens to leave the American military no more disciplined, no more efficient, no more fearsome, no more military than the United States Postal Service (Mitchell 1998, xvii).[7]

Critics feel that political constraints paralyze even the most competent and experienced of our military leadership: "While many uniformed leaders showed great courage in their battlefield exploits to turn back the nation's enemies, they seem petrified before activists who might accuse them of 'turning back the clock'" (Hillen 1999, 51). They claim that some military officers even feel pressured to hide what they know about the failures of gender integration, which does not bode well for integration by sexual orientation:

The commander knows the political mantra for twenty years has been that sexual misconduct is simply one more cultural problem, and that, like racial insensitivity, it can be overcome by a few lectures and command supervision. He knows also that this is wrong. But to speak his mind or force the issue would most likely be his undoing (Webb 1997, 20).

As with gender, the arguments against a policy allowing open homosexuals to serve in the military are grounded on its supposed effect on unit effectiveness. In *Gays and Lesbians in the Military* (Moskos 1994), Moskos argued that despite its successes with racial integration, the military should not serve as a social laboratory for the society at large. An article in *Parameters*, the journal of the Army War College, illustrates military concern with how far a civil rights agenda could be taken:

---

6.   Hillen (1997; 1998b; 1999) discusses extensively the need to preserve a degree of separation.

7.   Gutmann (2000) is a more recent addition to this literature.

Would the Army protect the privacy of heterosexuals vis-à-vis homosexuals in the same way it now protects the privacy of gender, with separate sleeping quarters, showers, and latrines? Or would this simply be a one-way street, with homosexuality emerging as a newly recognized, constitutionally protected right which overrides privacy concerns by heterosexuals both male and female? (Adair and Myers 1993).

In this chapter, we assess the claims made by public figures defending the current policies limiting the participation of open homosexuals across the board and women from the remaining combat positions still closed to them. Our survey data confirm that military service is indeed correlated with more conservative policy agendas. These findings show that civilian leaders are less likely than members of the military to believe that further integration is at odds with military effectiveness, and thus are more likely to support changes to which military leaders would object. We do not find sufficient data in the literature to prove that lifting these bans would result in any significant level of immediate change: that either gays would reveal their sexual orientation en masse, or that many women would flock to or qualify for the combat arms. As to whether policy changes would lead to lowered cohesion in combat units, compelling evidence exists on both sides of the argument. The history of integration within and outside the military suggests that social change would not be easy or without cost. It would therefore have to be accompanied by advance planning and institutional support. Whether combat effectiveness would be harmed would depend to a great extent on how the institution implements the changes.

Is There a Gap Between Civilian and Military Views On Personnel Policies?

This section presents data on civilian and military leaders' attitudes toward gender, sexual orientation, and combat effectiveness, collected as part of the Triangle Institute for Security Studies' 1998–99 Surveys on the Military in the post–Cold War Era. The military leaders represented in our data are officers who, at the time of the survey, were on the verge of promotion and attending professional military education courses at staff and war colleges or the Capstone course for new flag officers.[8] Civilian

8.   Neither civilians nor military personnel, of course, are an undifferentiated mass in terms of their opinions. The survey permitted us to compare the views of several categories of respondents of practical or theoretical importance. Some potentially promis-

leaders were selected primarily from directories such as *Who's Who*, and include clergy, politicians, journalists, scholars, writers, labor leaders, and foreign policy professionals. Civilian mass responses were based on a random telephone survey conducted by Princeton Survey Research Associates.[9]

We use two types of statistics for our analysis. First are descriptive statistics that cross-tabulate the responses of various groups on the questions of interest and assess the likelihood that any differences observed are significant, that is, that they are unlikely to be due to chance. Except where noted, the relationships we discuss are significant at the .001 level.[10]

We then look more deeply into the findings of the descriptive statistics. For example, active-duty military leaders are much less willing than civilian leaders to agree that openly gay men and lesbians should be allowed to serve in the military. Is that because one group is military and another civilian, or are there other factors contributing to the result? The type of analysis we used (a logistic regression, or "logit" analysis) permits us to look at a number of variables, such as age, gender, education, past or present military status, and degree of religiosity, to assess the influence of each.[11] Although space does not permit the inclusion of each full logit analysis in this chapter, we report a summary of our findings for most survey results.[12] Our separate analyses of reservist populations and

ing distinctions, such as among the different branches of service and among different grades of officer, were not closely analyzed for the purposes of this chapter and are not reported here. Military reservists and academy and ROTC students not yet commissioned as officers were also surveyed. We report the relationship of their responses to other categories of respondents, but have not fully mined these data for the information they might provide.

9. For details on survey methods, including the survey instrument, selection of respondents, response rate, and so forth, see the Technical Appendix at the end of this volume.

10. We acknowledge professional debates on whether these conventional statistical significance tests are appropriate for the pooled nature of the elite samples. In any case, we do not rely solely on measures of statistical significance to determine substantive significance. On the primary issues of interest in this chapter, the differences between the relevant subgroups are of such great magnitude, and the sample N's are likewise so large, that considerations of statistical estimates are secondary.

11. Religiosity was measured by a variable (1 = strongly above average religiosity, 5 = strongly below) which aggregated responses to five questions on: opinions about the Bible, views on life after death, use of religious guidance in day-to-day living, prayer outside of services, and frequency of attending religious services.

12. Logit analyses and veteran/non-veteran and military student breakdowns are available from Williams upon request.

Table 10.1. Do you think women should be *allowed* to serve in all combat jobs?

	General Public (n = 1001)	Civilian Elite (n = 909)	Military Elite (n = 710)
Yes	53.1%	57.5%	37.6%
No	46.9%	42.5%	62.4%

N = 2600; Pearson's Chi-Square = 67.88; Significance = .000.

students in Reserve Officer Training Corps (ROTC) programs and the military academies revealed that the responses of these groups, which might be considered part civilian and part military, were in almost all responses more likely to resemble those of military leaders than those of civilians.'[13] We turn now to the survey results.

GENDER INTEGRATION

We first examine attitudes toward the progressive integration of women in more and more areas of military service, which are said to divide civilian and military elites. Civilians are generally believed to support these changes fully, while military leaders are said to view them as detrimental to military functioning.

The primary gender issues addressed by the survey were women's service in the combat arms of the military services, sexual discrimination, and sexual harassment. Tables 10.1 and 10.2 display the results of questions on whether women should serve in the combat arms, and whether that service should be on a voluntary or mandatory basis.

Table 10.1 shows that civilian and military respondents differed significantly on whether women should be *allowed* to serve in all combat jobs, which would by definition include ground combat. Civilian leaders were most likely to support permitting voluntary service, and were slightly more supportive of this policy change than the rest of society (57.5 percent compared to 53.1 percent). Civilians' support for changing policy was sizeable but hardly universal. The strongest support for the change came from non-veteran civilian leaders and members of the general public. Veterans were more likely to oppose voluntary combat serv-

---

13.   One notable exception was that reservists looked more like their civilian counterparts than their military ones in their assessment of the effectiveness of the civilian justice system for dealing with sexual harassment.

Table 10.2. Do you think women should be *required* to serve in all combat jobs?

	Civilian Elite (n = 906)	Military Elite (n = 710)
Yes	13.9%	12.7%
No	86.1%	87.3%

N = 1616; Pearson's Chi-Square = .521; Significance = .470.

ice for women. Of the military leaders surveyed, fully 37.6 percent agreed that women should be allowed to serve in all combat jobs. The multivariate analysis delved further into the differences by examining the effect of additional demographic characteristics on attitudes. Those most likely to support allowing women to serve in all combat jobs were women currently serving in the military and respondents who were more highly educated and less religious. Most strongly opposed were veterans and men currently serving in the military. Since our survey undersampled military women (8 percent, compared to 14 percent in the actual officer population at the time) and this variable was significant, actual military officer support for changing policy is probably a bit higher than our results represent.[14]

Although a significant gap was found between civilians and military leaders on whether women should be *allowed* into all combat jobs, there was general agreement that women should not be *required* to serve in all combat jobs. Civilian leaders and military leaders were statistically indistinguishable in their overwhelming rejection of this option, with around 86 percent opposed requiring women to serve in all combat jobs.[15] The multivariate analysis did not explain much variance in responses to the question, but two variables did emerge as significant: being a current member of the military made one more likely to oppose requiring women

14. Women made up 28 percent of our civilian elite sample and 51 percent of the general population sample.

15. Support for this option overall might have been slightly higher if it had been phrased differently. The wording may have been problematic given that the question was intended to propose a policy that would put women into jobs according to some combination of choice, availability, and military necessity, as men are assigned. Different wordings of the same concept on other surveys have found from slightly to markedly greater support for bringing the policy for women in line with that for men. See Harrell and Miller (1997); Miller (1997).

Table 10.3. If you oppose women serving in combat roles, which of the
following factors is most important in shaping your opinion? Please circle
the one reason that matters most to you.

	Civilian Elite (n = 388)	Military Elite (n = 427)	Pearson's Chi Square
Religious/moral convictions	9.5%	9.8%	.02
Will disrupt cohesion	21.4%	26.2%	2.61
Could be taken prisoner/abused	16.8%	5.9%	24.58***
Most not physically qualified	36.9%	34.0%	.75
Pregnancy limits deployability	4.9%	6.3%	.78
Little privacy	15.5%	10.5%	4.39*
Men not as effective when women present	13.9%	14.8%	.12
Deaths of women demoralizing	12.9%	17.6%	3.43
Other	7.0%	7.5%	.09

***$p < .001$
**$p < .01$
*$p < .05$
NOTE: Some respondents circled more than one reply.

to serve in combat, and low religiosity made one somewhat more likely
to support it. No other variables emerged as significant.

Some insight into the thinking of the respondents was provided by
questions asking them to name the most important factor in shaping their
opinions for or against women serving in combat roles. In keeping with
the critics of social policy reforms, people favoring women in combat
were concerned with the individual civil rights of women and did not see
those rights at odds with combat effectiveness; those opposed believed
that women's integration into combat would hurt morale and disrupt the
formation of cohesion among the men in combat units.

Table 10.3 shows that, for both civilian and military leaders, the main
objection to expanding women's roles was the belief that most women
are not physically qualified for the positions that are currently off-limits
to women. Over a third of both groups indicated that this factor was the
most important for determining their position on this restriction. Currently, although there are fitness qualifications for certain military positions such as in special forces units, most occupational specialties have no
physical ability or fitness standards used to determine the assignment of
recruits or officers. Although the implementation of such screening measures might alleviate concerns about women (and men) being placed in
jobs they are physically incapable of performing, almost two-thirds of

Table 10.4. If you support women serving in combat roles, which of the following factors is most important in shaping your opinion? Please circle the one reason that matters most to you.

	Civilian Elite (n = 597)	Military Elite (n = 338)	Pearson's Chi Square
Discrimination/wrong to exclude	23.1%	17.5%	4.16*
Some women more capable than men	50.6%	56.2%	2.74
Physical abilities less relevant now	17.4%	7.7%	17.06***
Should have same obligation as men	11.2%	15.1%	2.93
Will improve morale	.5%	.3%	.22
Recent performance an asset	9.1%	6.8%	1.43
Necessary to be first-class citizens	.8%	.6%	.18
Exclusion hurts women's promotion	6.0%	5.0%	.40
Other	1.7%	5.9%	12.51***

***p < .001
**p < .01
*p < .05
NOTE: Some respondents circled more than one.

people surveyed held other objections to integrating women into the currently closed combat arms jobs.

The second most common reason for supporting the status quo, reported by both military and civilian leaders, was the belief that women's presence would disrupt unit cohesion. In this survey, 26.2 percent of military elites and 21.4 of civilian elites expressed this concern.

Civilian and military leaders differed dramatically on what ranked as their third and fourth most important concerns. For civilians, 16.8 percent opposed women in combat because they could be taken prisoner and abused during times of war, and 15.5 percent thought that the lack of privacy was the most important factor shaping their opinion. For the military elites, however, the next most important factors were the beliefs that the deaths of women in combat would demoralize male troops (17.6 percent), and that men are not as effective fighters when women are present (14.8 percent). Thus, some civilian and military leaders who agreed that women should not serve in all combat jobs did so for different reasons. We found that civilians were more likely to be concerned with the dangers and conditions of women serving in combat jobs, while military elites were more likely to be concerned with the effect of women's presence on the group dynamics and effectiveness of combat units.

Table 10.4 reveals that for respondents who reported support for women in combat roles, the most important consideration by far was the idea that the most capable soldiers should be assigned to combat roles and that some women are more capable than some men. It again appears that a physical aptitude test for heavy labor occupations would eliminate a great deal of the controversy over this policy.

Other important factors for civilians were the beliefs that excluding women from combat is morally wrong (23.1 percent), and that technology and modern warfare have made physical abilities less relevant now than before (17.4). These arguments were less convincing for the military leaders. Only 17.5 percent of military respondents said that discrimination was the most important factor in their decision. Military elites were far less likely than civilians to believe that physical abilities are less relevant now: only 7.7 percent chose this answer, compared to 17.4 percent of civilian supporters. Military elites who support women in the combat arms were more likely than civilians, however, to express the view that women have the same obligation to serve and risk their lives as men do.

One survey question addressed people's perception of the costs associated with efforts to expand opportunities for women in the military, as well as whether these costs are worthwhile or not (see Table 10–5). According to public opponents of further gender integration, civilian leaders are unaware or unconcerned with these costs, whereas military leaders are said to find the costs too harmful to be justified. In our survey, however, respondents who indicated either that the costs were trivial or that they were justified (whether modest or sizeable) included 56.3 percent of the civilian leaders and 50.4 percent of the regular military leaders. In contrast, a fifth of civilian leaders (20.5 percent) and a third of military leaders (32.7 percent) registered the opinion that the costs do not outweigh the benefits. Notably, 15.2 percent of civilians and 10.0 percent of military leaders reported no opinion at all on this issue. Although there was a gap in civil-military perceptions on the costs and worth of further expanding combat opportunities to military women, the fact that over half of both groups view the costs as worth the benefits challenged the notion that civilian and military elites are polarized in their views on this issue.

For the multivariate analysis, the response categories were collapsed to sort respondents according to whether they said the costs are justified or not, regardless of the perceived size of those costs. Respondents most likely to believe that the efforts are worth the cost tended to be more educated, less religious, members of racial minorities, and/or women currently serving in the military. Those most likely to decide it is *not* worth the cost were military elites and veterans. No association with age or gender by itself was evident. Thus, the opinions of women outside the military did not set them apart from the general population, but, as one

Table 10.5. How would you characterize any costs associated with the effort to expand opportunities for women in the military?

	Civilian Elite (n = 909)	Military Elite (n = 710)
Trivial or non-existent	8.0%	6.9%
Modest but worth it	38.7%	31.1%
Sizeable but worth it	17.6%	19.3%
Sizeable and probably not worth it	14.0%	24.4%
Excessive and certainly not worth it	6.5%	8.3%
No opinion	15.2%	10.0%

N = 1619; Pearson's Chi-Square = 41.15; Significance = .000.

might expect, women in the military were significantly more likely to respond that expanding their own opportunities are worth the cost. Again, our under-sampling of women military elites means that the actual percentage of military elites believing the costs are justified is likely somewhat higher.

A great deal of public concern over gender in the military in the 1990s was based on a number of publicized scandals dealing with discrimination or abuse of women soldiers. Journalists, activists, and political leaders reacted to the incidents by contending that the armed forces were seriously lagging behind civilian workplace advances in gender integration and required closer civilian oversight and control of military leaders. To compare civilian and military perceptions on how the military measures up to civilian environments, Table 10.6 presents the data from a question asking our respondents to compare sexual discrimination in the military to that of society at large. This question produced one of the most dramatic differences in opinion. Of civilian leaders, about a third answered that there is more sexual discrimination in the military than in civilian society; almost half perceived the situation to be about the same in both areas; and only 13.4 percent said there is less discrimination in the military than in civilian society. In contrast, 72.7 percent of military leaders responded that there is *less* sexual discrimination in the military than elsewhere. Among civilians, veterans were split over which realm they believed to have more sexual discrimination, although almost half marked the answer that the two realms are roughly equal in this regard. More non-veterans believe sexual discrimination is greater in the military than believe it is greater in civilian society, but again, almost half said it is about the same in either place.

Analysis of this item by gender showed that civilian and military women were more likely than their male counterparts to believe the mili-

Table 10.6. Generally, do you think there is more, less, or about the same amount of sexual discrimination in the military as in civilian society at large?

	Civilian Elite (n = 909)	Military Elite (n = 711)
More	32.0%	3.0%
Same	47.3%	22.8%
Less	13.4%	72.7%
No opinion	7.3%	1.5%

N = 1620; Pearson's Chi-Square = 623.55; Significance = .000.

tary is more discriminatory. Most interesting was the revelation that elite civilian women were over four times more likely than elite military women to believe the military is worse than the civilian society, whereas military women were seven times more likely than civilian women to believe that civilian society is worse. Thus, military women thought the situation was better in the military, while civilian women thought it was better in the civilian realm.

Nowhere in the gender-related issues were the civilian elite and military elite differences greater than in their views of whether the military has done enough in dealing with the problem of sexual harassment (Table 10.7). While 57.4 percent of civilian leaders answered that the military has not done enough, 65.6 percent of military leaders responded that the military has already done what it should. In fact, 18.6 percent of the military leaders agreed that the military has gone too far, a statement chosen by only 5.7 percent of civilians. The most common response for both the veteran and non-veteran civilians was that the military has not done enough, although veterans were more likely than non-veterans to think the military has done what it should.

The multivariate analysis affirmed that military members and veterans were more likely to respond that the military has done enough or even gone too far in dealing with sexual harassment. Neither age nor education explained respondents' positions on this issue. In general, women, minorities, and less religious people were more likely to perceive that the military has not done enough. Oddly, although elite civilian women were significantly more likely than elite civilian men to think the military should do more to stop harassment, elite military women's answers more closely resembled those of elite military men. As with sexual discrimination, elite civilian women were more likely than elite military women to have a negative view of the military: over twice as many civilian women as military women said the military is not doing enough, but

Table 10.7. How do you think the military has done in dealing with the problem of sexual harassment?

	Civilian Elite (n = 906)	Military Elite (n = 710)
Not enough	57.4%	13.1%
What it should	25.3%	65.6%
Gone too far	5.7%	18.6%
No opinion	11.6%	2.7%

N = 1616; Pearson's Chi-Square = 455.61; Significance = .000.

over three times as many military women as civilian said the military has done what it should, and three times as many said it has gone too far in dealing with sexual harassment. At least at the higher echelon, the majority of high-ranking women officers appear to be satisfied with the military's recent progress in this area.

Civilian and military leaders were also asked to compare how the military and the civilian justice systems deal with sexual harassment. Table 10.8 shows that roughly 43 percent of civilians surveyed agreed that each system is doing the best it can. The remaining civilians were slightly more likely to agree that the military system (under the Uniform Code of Military Justice, or UCMJ) is allowing the guilty to get away with harassment (31.5 percent) than to agree that the civilian system is doing so (29.7 percent). More pronounced was the finding that only 14.2 percent of civilians worried that innocent people are being punished by the military system, compared to 22.2 percent who were concerned about this problem in the civilian system.

Military leaders overwhelmingly perceived the military justice system to be doing the best it can about harassment: roughly two-thirds marked this option. One quarter were more concerned that in the military system the innocent are being punished, while only 6 percent were more concerned that the guilty are going unpunished. This assessment contrasted not only with civilians' responses, but with officers' perceptions of the civilian system. Military elites expressed concern that the guilty go unpunished in the civilian system (40.5 percent). Less than a third thought the civilian system is doing the best it can, and even fewer believed that the innocent are being punished in the civilian system (16.4 percent).

Gender differences were significant on these items: both elite civilian and military women were more likely than their male counterparts to think the military system might be letting guilty people get away with harassment; however civilian women were nearly four times as likely to

Table 10.8. Sexual Harassment in the Military and Civilian Justice Systems.

	Consider how the *military* justice system deals with sexual harassment		Consider how the *civilian* justice system deals with sexual harassment	
	Civilian Elite (n = 895)	Military Elite (n = 712)	Civilian Elite (n = 900)	Military Elite (n = 709)
More concerned that it might be allowing too many people to get away with sexual harassment	31.5%	6.0%	29.7%	40.5%
More concerned that it is too often punishing the innocent	14.2%	24.3%	22.2%	16.4%
The system is doing the best it can in balancing these two concerns	42.0%	66.3%	42.6%	29.5%
No opinion	12.3%	3.4%	5.6%	13.7%
	N = 1607; Pearson's Chi-Square = 231.03; Significance = .000.		N = 1609; Pearson's Chi-Square = 67.50; Significance = .000.	

think this than military women. Military women were twice as likely as civilian women to say the military system is doing its best to deal with sexual harassment. With regard to the civilian justice system, military women were closer to civilian women in their assessment; however, military men were even more likely than either military women or civilian men to think the civilian system lets too many harassers go unpunished.

In sum, most of the military sample responded that the military system is doing the best it can or is, if anything, erring on the side of overenforcement. They were more likely to view the civilian system, however, as letting too many people get away with harassment. About 40 percent of the civilians agreed that the military system is doing the best it can, although nearly a third believe it errs on the side of letting too many people get away with harassment. These civilian leaders assessed their own system of justice in about the same way they did the military system.

MASCULINITY AND MILITARY CULTURE

Debates over gender integration in the armed forces have raised the issue of whether military culture should remain essentially "masculine" in its values and characteristics. Critics of integration argue that although

Table 10.9. Even though women can serve in the military, the military should remain basically masculine, dominated by male values and characteristics.

	General Public (n = 1001)	Civilian Elite (n = 907)	Military Elite (n = 705)
Agree strongly	28.2%	17.4%	14.6%
Agree somewhat	22.4%	23.7%	25.0%
Disagree somewhat	18.5%	29.1%	31.3%
Disagree strongly	28.4%	27.3%	25.1%
No opinion	2.6%	2.4%	4.0%

N = 2613; Pearson's Chi-Square = 84.02; Significance = .000.

women make valuable contributions to the military, the organizational culture must remain essentially masculine for optimal combat effectiveness. Military reformers, however, have criticized the masculine element of military culture as unnecessary and the source of sexism, harassment, and the abuse of women service members.[16]

Table 10.9 reflects reactions to the statement: "Even though women can serve in the military, the military should remain basically masculine, dominated by male values and characteristics." The civilian public respondents were more likely than the civilian elites or even the military elites to agree strongly with the idea that the military should remain basically masculine: 28.2 percent compared to only 17.4 percent of the civilian leaders and 14.6 percent of military elites. However, 28.4 percent of the general public respondents "strongly disagreed," and thus this group was more polarized on this subject than the elites.

The multivariate analysis revealed that veteran status was the only variable that made someone more likely to agree that the military should remain basically masculine. Women (overall and those currently in the military), racial minorities, those with higher education, and less religious people were more likely to agree that the military does not need to remain basically masculine. Current military membership and age were not significant variables in this analysis.

SEXUAL ORIENTATION

Defenders of traditional military culture argue that the civil-military gap over personnel policies widened recently because of civilian initiatives to permit the service of open gays in the military. Our data support this

16. A prominent critique of "masculinist" culture is made by Morris (1996).

Table 10.10. Do you think gay men and lesbians should be allowed to serve openly in the military?

	General Public (n = 1001)	Civilian Elite (n = 904)	Military Elite (n = 713)
Yes	56.4%	54.3%	18.1%
No	36.7%	35.6%	72.8%
No opinion	6.9%	10.1%	9.1%

N = 2618; Pearson's Chi-Square = 317.09; Significance = .000.

claim. The gap between the views of civilians (both mass and elite) and military leaders was widest on the issue of whether homosexuals should be allowed to serve in the military. Table 10.10 shows that slightly more than half of each civilian group (mass and elite) supported service by openly gay men and lesbians in the military, while some three-quarters of military leaders opposed it. These data suggest that the views of civilian leaders are not significantly more progressive than those of civilians at large, but that military leaders are substantially more conservative on this issue than either category of civilians.

The multivariate analysis contained no surprises, based on the above. Those most likely to oppose openly gay men and lesbians in the military were current or past members of the military. Those most likely to support the policy change included women (in general, and serving in the military), less religious individuals, and those with higher levels of education. The actual percentage of military elites who support changing the policy is likely to be slightly higher than in our results because we under-sampled military women.

Tables 10.11 and 10.12 affirm the presence of a gap between civilian and military leaders over sexual orientation and military service, and illustrate that military elites have a much stronger opposition to accepting openly gay soldiers than they do to accepting women commanders or women serving in ground combat units.

Table 10.11 conveys the percentage of respondents who reported that they would leave the military either if women were allowed to serve in ground combat units or if open homosexuals were allowed to serve in the military. For this question, civilians were asked to consider this hypothetical situation for themselves, whereas military elites expressed sentiments about their actual careers. Civilian leaders were twice as likely as military leaders to say that they would leave military service if combat units included women (13.9 percent compared to 6.5). In contrast, military elites were twice as likely as civilian leaders to say they would leave

Table 10.11. I would leave military service if . . .

	Civilian Elite (n = 166)	Military Elite (n = 644)	Pearson's Chi-Square
. . . women were allowed to serve in ground combat units	13.9%	6.5%	9.62**
. . . homosexuals were allowed to serve openly in the military	15.1%	27.5%	10.88**

N = 810 (for both questions); **p .01.

the armed forces if open gays were allowed to serve (27.5 percent compared to 15.1 percent). A roughly comparable number of civilians would want to leave the military over expanding women's roles as they would for allowing open gays to serve. In contrast, military leaders were four times more likely to want to leave over permitting service by open homosexuals than over permitting women to serve in ground combat.[17] These items varied by gender: men were more likely than women to say they would leave the military in response to the proposed changes, and elite civilian women were more likely than military women to say that they would leave the military (hypothetically) over either policy change.

Although Table 10.6 revealed that a third of civilian leaders believe there is greater discrimination in the military than in society at large, Table 10.12 suggests that military elites are more comfortable with women in military leadership roles than civilian leaders are. Some 68 percent of the military respondents reported that under present standards (excluding women from ground combat units) they would feel equally confident with a female commander as with a male commander, which is 9 percentage points higher than the level of civilian leaders considering the same type of situation. About 22 percent of military leaders and 25 percent of civilians surveyed would feel more comfortable with a male commander than a female commander. Among all respondents, the number who expressed more confidence in a female commander than a male was negligible. As one might expect, gender was a significant variable on this question: elite civilian women were four times more likely than elite military women to say they would be more confident with a male commander (16 percent compared to 4 percent), although both groups of

---

17.   These percentages cannot be taken as a precise assessment of how many would actually leave the service under a policy change. A number of factors would likely influence the degree to which people feel free or able to depart in protest of a policy change.

Table 10.12. If, under present standards, your commander was [female/gay], how would you feel?

	Civilian Elite (n = 903)	Military Elite (n = 707)		Civilian Elite (n = 903)	Military Elite (n = 704)
More confident with male commander	24.9%	22.3%	More confident with straight commander	34.6%	65.3%
Equally confident with male or female commander	58.7%	67.8%	Equally confident with straight or gay commander	49.9%	20.2%
More confident with female commander	1.8%	.6%	More confident with gay commander	.3%	0%
No opinion	14.6%	9.3%	No opinion	15.2%	14.5%

N = 1610; Pearson's Chi-Square = 19.93; Significance = .000.

N = 1607; Pearson's Chi-Square = 175.56; Significance = .000.

Table 10.13. Would you support removing a book in favor of homosexuality from your public library?

	Civilian Elite (n = 918)	Military Elite (n = 720)
Favor removing	10.2%	13.8%
Not favor removing	84.7%	81.7%
Don't know	5.0%	4.6%

N = 1638; Pearson's Chi-Square = 4.83; Significance = .089.

women were less likely than their male counterparts to say so. Military women were most likely to say they would be equally confident with either a male or female commander, followed by military men, who were slightly more likely than civilian women and men to say the same.

When a similar question compared a gay with a straight commander, however, civilians were the more progressive group, although both civilians and military leaders were much less comfortable with the idea of working under a gay commander than a female one. Approximately one-third of the civilian leaders and two-thirds of the military leaders would feel more confident with a straight commander than a gay one. Half of the civilian elite respondents indicated that they would feel equally confident with a straight or gay commander, compared to only a fifth of military elites. As was the case with female commanders, almost no one would prefer a gay commander over a straight one. On this issue, civilian and military women responded similarly: about a quarter would be more confident with a straight commander, and about half would be confident either way. In contrast, 38 percent of elite civilian men would prefer a straight commander, which is much lower than the 70 percent of elite military men who would.

In sum, Tables 10.11 and 10.12 revealed that although military leaders are often depicted as male chauvinists compared to civilians, and although they are less likely to support allowing women to volunteer for combat jobs (Table 10.1), they are in fact more accepting than civilians of women in command, and less likely to want to leave military service if the combat arms were to include women. In keeping with popular perceptions, however, military elites were indeed much more opposed to allowing open gays into the armed forces than either the general public or the civilian leaders.

Although civilian and military leaders held diametrically opposed opinions about sexual orientation and military service, Table 10.13 shows that they were similarly opposed to a hypothetical policy of removing

Table 10.14. Indicate your position on barring homosexuals from teaching in public schools.

	Civilian Elite (n = 914)	Military Elite (n = 722)
Agree strongly	10.5%	20.1%
Agree somewhat	10.7%	22.2%
Disagree somewhat	21.3%	29.4%
Disagree strongly	52.8%	21.1%
No opinion	4.6%	7.3%

N =1636; Pearson's Chi-Square = 179.32; Significance = .000.

books favoring homosexuality from their public library. Over 80 percent disagreed with censoring this kind of reading material. The multivariate analysis affirmed the lack of association between military service and censorship, when controlled for other factors. Highly educated and less religious individuals were even more likely to oppose removing books favoring homosexuality from public libraries. Other variables examined were not significant.

Both civilian and military respondents were less liberal in their views on barring homosexuals from teaching in public schools than they were on removing a book from a library (Table 10.14), and a dramatic gap in civilian and military attitudes reappeared on this item. Military leaders were twice as likely (42 percent) as civilians (22 percent) to support barring homosexuals from teaching. Among the civilians, non-veterans were most likely to disagree strongly with barring homosexuals from teaching in public schools. The multivariate analysis indicated that the characteristics most likely to predict support for banning gays from teaching in public schools were current or past military service. The characteristics that predict opposition to a teaching ban include higher levels of education, low religiosity, and being a woman in the military. Age, gender by itself, and race did not matter.

COMBAT EFFECTIVENESS

Objections to expanding the participation of women soldiers and gays are almost always linked to the perceived detriment of such changes to combat effectiveness. Table 10.15 presents the results of a questionnaire item asking respondents whether they believe certain conditions related to further integration might keep the military from being effective during times of war. Some of these items were present on the civilian public survey, providing another dimension of comparative data. Our findings contradict any notion that on these integration issues, civilian leaders would

Table 10.15. There are many different things that people say might keep the military from being effective during times of war. For each of the following, please indicate if it might greatly hurt military effectiveness, somewhat hurt military effectiveness, have no effect on military effectiveness, or it is not happening at all in the U.S. military.

A. The military trying to hold on to old-fashioned views of morality

	General Public (n = 1001)	Civilian Elite (n = 898)	Military Elite (n = 704)
Greatly hurts	13.3%	10.1%	2.6%
Somewhat hurts	29.5%	23.5%	13.1%
No effect	47.3%	45.8%	61.6%
Not happening	6.6%	12.7%	17.0%
No opinion	3.4%	7.9%	5.7%

N = 2603; Pearson's Chi-Square = 182.22; Significance = .000.

B. A ban on language and behavior that encourage comradery among soldiers

	General Public (n – 1001)	Civilian Elite (n = 900)	Military Elite (n = 709)
Greatly hurts	19.6%	10.9%	9.6%
Somewhat hurts	35.2%	33.9%	33.4%
No effect	32.1%	31.9%	39.4%
Not happening	4.6%	8.8%	10.4%
No opinion	8.6%	14.6%	7.2%

N = 2610; Pearson's Chi-Square = 93.69; Significance = .000.

C. Sexual harassment in the military

	Civilian Elite (n = 910)	Military Elite (n = 709)
Greatly hurts	35.5%	27.4%
Somewhat hurts	48.7%	51.1%
No effect	11.9%	15.9%
Not happening	1.3%	4.1%
No opinion	2.6%	1.6%

N =1619; Pearson's Chi-Square = 27.80; Significance = .000.

Table 10.15. *Continued.*

D. The military becoming less male-dominated

	General Public (n = 1001)	Civilian Elite (n = 903)	Military Elite (n = 713)
Greatly hurts	16.1%	7.0%	4.9%
Somewhat hurts	35.7%	25.4%	23.4%
No effect	42.8%	55.4%	59.7%
Not happening	3.1%	9.0%	8.0%
No opinion	2.4%	3.3%	3.9%

N = 2617; Pearson's Chi-Square = 150.65; Significance = .000.

E. Non-military people getting too involved in military affairs

	Civilian Elite (n = 900)	Military Elite (n = 708)
Greatly hurts	18.1%	23.0%
Somewhat hurts	43.6%	51.7%
No effect	20.7%	14.3%
Not happening	12.7%	7.8%
No opinion	5.0%	3.2%

N =1608; Pearson's Chi-Square = 31.30; Significance = .000.

be consistently on the liberal end of the spectrum, military leaders on the conservative end, and the civilian masses somewhere in the middle.

Table 10.15A shows opinions about the effect of the "military trying to hold on to old-fashioned views of morality."[18] Over 40 percent of the civilians queried through the mass telephone survey registered the belief that this phenomenon hurts effectiveness, while roughly a third of civilian leaders but only 15.7 percent of military elites did the same. About 62 percent of military leaders indicated that there was no impact on effectiveness, compared to about 46 percent of civilian leaders and 47 percent of the civilian population sample. This finding suggests that the general public is even more likely than civilian leaders to see traditional morality at odds with combat effectiveness. The gap between civilians in general and civilian leaders is modest when compared to the gap between either group and military leaders.

These three categories of respondents also varied significantly in their assessment of a "ban on language and behavior that encourage

18. The term "old-fashioned morality" was left up to respondents to interpret.

comradery among soldiers" (Table 10.15B).[19] More of the general population surveyed showed a belief that such bans hurt military effectiveness than did civilian and military leaders, whose responses were similar on this issue. Military elites surveyed were less likely than civilians to think that such prohibitions impede effectiveness.

Only the civilian elite and military elite were asked whether sexual harassment in the military has a negative impact on combat effectiveness (Table 10.15C). The majority of both groups agreed that harassment hurts effectiveness, but they varied significantly in the degree to which they believe it causes harm. Military leaders were less likely to believe that effectiveness is greatly hurt, and more likely than civilians to think there is no effect, or that sexual harassment is not happening in the military.

Table 10.15D addresses the trend of "the military becoming less male-dominated." Contradicting the portrayal of military officers as an old boys' club bent on excluding women whenever possible, the military respondents were the most likely of the three groups to say that becoming less male-dominated does not hurt effectiveness of their organization. Nearly 60 percent of military elites registered this opinion, while roughly 55 percent of civilian leaders and 43 percent of civilians in general did. Indeed, only around 28 percent of the military elite perceived any degree of harm, compared to around 32 percent of civilian leaders and 51.8 percent of the general population.

The final item we address measured people's perceptions about civilian leadership of the military, and whether "non-military people getting too involved in military affairs" is a detriment to combat effectiveness. Challenging assertions about the current state of civil-military affairs, the data do not show a polarization over this dynamic among leaders. In fact, 61.7 percent of civilian leaders and 74.7 percent of military elites viewed civilian over-involvement as harmful, with the military more likely to believe that it *greatly* hurts effectiveness (23 percent said so, compared to 18.1 percent of civilian leaders). These results suggest that both civilian and military leaders believe that high levels of civilian involvement translate into policies that are disruptive to the goals of the armed forces.[20]

---

19. "Comradery," an alternative spelling of camaraderie, was used in the survey. The interpretation of what language and behavior encourages comradery was open to respondents.

20. The survey included items on other issues, such as peacekeeping operations, and thus this item did not refer exclusively to civilian activities related to the roles of women and/or gays in the military.

Thus, many of the findings on attitudes regarding military effectiveness did not match the picture painted by critics of civilian-led initiatives for social change. The only findings that fit the general portrayal of recent civil-military conflict were those in Table 10–15A, showing civilians to be far more likely than military leaders to believe that "the military trying to hold on to old-fashioned views of morality" is harmful to combat effectiveness.

Civil-Military Gap Over Gender and Gays Confirmed

Overall, our data confirmed the claim that there is a gap between civilians and military elites on issues of gender and sexual orientation. Military leaders surveyed were less concerned with the effect of gender integration than they were about the possibility of known gay men and lesbians being allowed to serve among the troops. Civilian leaders and respondents from the general public demonstrated a greater concern about the impact of gender than did the military elite, but they were far less worried about the incorporation of homosexuals than were military elites. Given the similarity of responses among military elites, reservists, officer trainees, and veterans, it is clear that military service has an effect on attitudes on this issue.

Where did civilian and military leaders tend to agree? Although they varied at times in the intensity of their opinions, most civilian and military elites opposed requiring women to serve in the combat arms, opposed removing "pro-gay publications" from their public library, and were convinced that combat effectiveness is jeopardized by both sexual harassment and the over-involvement of civilians in military affairs. Yet the differences between civilian and military leaders on personnel policies were more numerous than the similarities.

Our data showed that the civilians surveyed were more likely than the military respondents to believe that women should be *allowed* to serve in all combat jobs, though both groups drew the line at *requiring* women to serve in these positions. Civilians who opposed permitting women to serve in all combat jobs reported concern that most women are not physically qualified for the work, that women's presence would disrupt cohesion, and that women combatants might be taken prisoner and abused. Civilians who supported opening combat jobs believed that some women are more capable than men of performing these duties and that exclusion across the board is inappropriate. The majority of civilians characterize any costs associated with the effort to expand opportunities for women in the military as worthwhile. Just under half said that sexual discrimination is about the same in both the military and civilian worlds, while a third perceived the military as more discriminatory.

Most military leaders surveyed opposed permitting women to serve in all combat arms, either on a voluntary or a mandatory basis. Their primary objections were that most women are not physically qualified, that women would disrupt cohesion in combat units, that combat deaths of women would demoralize their male counterparts, and that men would not fight as effectively if women were present. The minority segment of military leaders who supported opening all combat jobs to women preferred to have the most capable people in combat units regardless of their gender. Perhaps unexpected, given the strength of the opposition to opening all combat jobs, was the finding that half of the military elite surveyed agreed with a statement asserting that expanding women's opportunities are worth the cost. Yet a sizeable minority of military leaders (one-third) did not believe the effort is worth the cost. Finally, over 70 percent of military elites expressed the belief that there is less sexual discrimination in the military than in the civilian world, with most of the dissenters answering that it is not really that different from civilian society at large. Almost none of the military respondents expressed the belief that discrimination is worse in the military.

One of our most surprising findings was that civilians, especially those from the general population, were more likely than military leaders to think the military should remain basically masculine. Furthermore, they were more likely to believe that combat effectiveness is harmed both by the organization becoming less male-dominated and by bans on specific language and behavior. Also surprising was that more military than civilian leaders indicated they would be equally confident with a male or a female commander. Particularly illuminating was the finding that civilian women are more likely than military women to think the military's levels of discrimination and sexual harassment are unacceptable, yet more civilian women than military say they would prefer to work under a male commander or would leave the military if women were permitted to serve in the ground combat arms.

The most dramatic civil-military gap we found on any issue was on the attitudes toward allowing open homosexuals to serve in the armed forces. Although over half of civilians supported such a policy change, three-quarters of military leaders opposed it. Two-thirds of the military leaders reported that they would be more confident with a straight commander than a gay one, and nearly 28 percent projected that they would leave military service if known gays were permitted to serve. Only half as many civilian leaders expressed similar opinions on these issues and on whether gays should be barred from teaching in public schools.

Historically gays have been excluded from military service because of fears that they were mentally ill or that they could be more easily blackmailed than heterosexuals.[21] More recently, fears that gays would be promiscuous or would make sexual advances toward straight soldiers have taken on greater prominence. Current debates, however, focus almost exclusively on whether the presence of open gays would disrupt heterosexual male bonding and unit cohesion and thereby jeopardize combat readiness. Although secondary to physical ability, cohesion issues are also major concerns about the effect of integrating women into combat units. We now assess claims that diversity by gender and sexual orientation harm unit cohesion, thereby reducing combat effectiveness.

The Cohesion Debate: Arguments and Evidence

In the tolerance-oriented, multicultural political environment at the end of the twentieth century, arguments based solely on moral convictions or religious beliefs rarely determined social policy. Many opponents of the increasing diversity of military personnel believe that homosexuality is immoral and that traditional gender roles are preferable to gender-neutral ones. Indeed, our data found religiosity to be correlated with support for the current service prohibitions. Activists and scholars criticize these beliefs, however, as homophobic and sexist.

In the 1990s, the concept of "cohesion" moved to the foreground of public debate over personnel policies. One of the most prominent rationales for rejecting further integration of women and open gays in the military has been that these changes would disrupt unit cohesion and therefore harm combat effectiveness. This line of thinking reflects an effort to define and measure the potentially negative effect of integration and thus shift the debate from the grounds of belief to that of practical effects. In the 1990s, supporters of traditional American military culture charged that adding women and/or gays to combat units would create an atmosphere of distraction, mistrust, fear, resentment, sexual activity, and social conflict that would inhibit the maintenance of an effective fighting force. Whether this argument is correct or not is currently the focus of much research and debate, and the reason we now assess the available evidence in the literature. It is our conclusion that our current knowledge base does not allow us to make a clear judgment in either direction about the effect of diversity on cohesion, and that many factors influence the process of integrating previously excluded groups. Further-

---

21. For a comprehensive history of the evolution of views and policies on homosexuality and military service see Berube (1991).

more, we find the available data lacking concrete information about exactly how diversity and cohesion play out in combat situations.

Military leaders considered cohesion a central concept long before gender and sexual orientation became personnel issues. Guy Siebold (1999) has traced the earliest written reference to cohesion elements in military forces to descriptions of Spartan warriors in 480 B.C. The concept has evolved from its initial description, taking on particular relevance for military scholars in the twentieth century. Edward Shils and Morris Janowitz argued that primary group dynamics were crucial for successful German combat troop coordination and motivation in World War II (Shils and Janowitz 1948). In 1970, one of Morris Janowitz's students, Charles Moskos, challenged the centrality of primary group dynamics in combat motivation based on his field research in Vietnam. He argued instead that soldiers' belief in what they were fighting for and a Hobbesian strategy of cooperation for self-preservation held greater explanatory power for soldiers' behavior in war (Moskos 1970). In response, Janowitz countered that Moskos's work was complementary rather than contrary to the World War II study, because the Shils and Janowitz article was "never meant to suggest that the salience of the primary group should obscure the importance of other factors in combat motivation."[22] The 1948 article still stands as a classic in this debate, despite early critiques and qualification of the primary group argument, as well as recent challenges to specific conclusions from the data (Bartov 1991; Rush 1999). Research on military cohesion has accumulated in several social science disciplines ever since the publication of this influential study.

Academic studies of cohesion have developed some of the complexities necessary for defining the term. Investigations of experimental, athletic, and naturally-occurring work settings consistently identify a critical distinction between two types of cohesion:

Social cohesion refers to the nature and quality of the emotional bonds of friendship, liking, caring, and closeness among group members. A group is socially cohesive to the extent that its members like each other, prefer to spend their social time together, enjoy each other's company, and feel emotionally close to one another.

Task cohesion refers to the shared commitment among members to achieving a goal that requires the collective efforts of the group. A group with high task cohesion is composed of members who share a common goal and who are motivated to coordinate their efforts as a team to achieve their goal (MacCoun 1993, 291).

---

22. Charles Moskos has conveyed this view in numerous public speeches on military cohesion.

In general use, what most people refer to as cohesion is what the literature has identified as social cohesion. However, those who wish to improve cohesion in a given setting are often most interested in a group's ability to complete a task, meet a challenge, or resist disintegration as a working whole. This priority would seem to require a focus on task cohesion.

Because the military is interested in the functioning of units within the organization as a whole, cohesion research in this specific field identified multiple levels and types of cohesion: "(a) horizontal cohesion—peer bonding and teamwork; (b) vertical cohesion—leader caring and leader competence; and (c) organizational cohesion—pride and shared values, and attainment of needs and goals" (Siebold 1999, 19).

HOW DOES DIVERSITY AFFECT COHESION AND COMBAT EFFECTIVENESS?
Scholarship on combat and unit cohesion in 1980s argued that groups who share common attitudes and values are best able to form the close bonds needed for trust and motivation in combat, because they are able to communicate more easily from their shared cultural knowledge (Henderson 1985; Sarkesian 1980). In an oft-cited study, Darryl Henderson compared cohesion in the North Vietnamese, U.S., Soviet, and Israeli armies. He found that "major cultural factors enhancing cohesion are common social experiences based on soldiers' sharing a common religion, race, ethnic group, age, social-economic standing, or sex" (Henderson 1985, 26). Units drawn from racially and ethnically diverse populations are cohesive, he argued, only when the members share major cultural characteristics and are sufficiently integrated that no cliques form separately from the unit as a whole. A recent affirmation of this point is found in Anna Simons' ethnography (1997) of Special Forces units, which revealed that even in all-male (and usually all-white) teams, members often still work to obscure potentially divisive differences in politics, religion, or personal problems.

The literature on homogeneity and military cohesion among heterosexual men established the foundation for debates on the effect of further diversifying troops by gender and sexual orientation. Two schools of thought have since emerged. The first argues that diversity does not harm cohesion, and may even be good for the military. This side of the debate asserts that diversity—including gender and sexual orientation—helps rather than harms military effectiveness. This side also argues that even if cohesion were negatively affected by diversity, it is not relevant for combat units' performance in war.

Contrary to long-standing prior arguments, during the Persian Gulf War the American public did not express any greater outrage or demoralization over the deaths or capture of women soldiers than over men. Following the successes of the war in 1993 and 1994, Congress opened many combat specialties to women, including combat aviation and most combat ships. In 1997, Margaret Harrell and Laura Miller examined military units and occupations that had opened up to women in 1993 and 1994. When service members were asked the factors determining their unit's level of cohesion, only ten out of 619 written responses even mentioned gender, even though a survey cover and introduction announced that gender was an important component of the study (Harrell and Miller 1997, 57). "Gender was an issue only in units characterized as divided into conflicting groups, and then it took second place to divisions along the lines of work groups or, within work groups, along the lines of rank" (66). In the focus groups, some people commented that the presence of women "had raised the professional standards of conduct in the military workplace" (67).

Evidence that cohesion would not be harmed by integrating gays into the military comes from the experience of other nations that have done so. Dire predictions about the impact of gays on unit cohesion have not been realized. A mid-1990s study of eleven Western militaries revealed that "no violence has been reported in countries that have removed bans, even though surveys in those countries found that service personnel said that they would react violently to homosexuals in their units" (Gade, Segal, and Johnson 1996, 126). Recent investigations into the effect of lifting prohibitions against homosexuals in the Canadian, Israeli, and Australian armed forces were unable to locate any evidence of decline in cohesion, morale, or readiness (Belkin and Levitt 2000; Belkin and McNichol 2000a, 2000b). A collection of essays on the state of the "postmodern military" in a dozen Western countries reports a range of policies with regard to homosexuality and military service, but fails to identify any serious gay-related cohesion problems in even the most inclusive of militaries (Moskos, Williams, and Segal 2000). Each of these studies reported few if any problems, and few gay men or lesbians revealing their sexual orientation, after bans on their service were lifted.

Some gays serving in U.S. military units have already revealed their sexual orientation, which is offered as evidence that a ban does not keep everyone's sexuality a secret. It also suggests that lifting the ban would be a positive move to protect individuals from both personal and organizational prejudice and discrimination. In a survey conducted in December 1992 (prior to the implementation of the "don't ask, don't tell" policy), Laura Miller and Charles Moskos found that a significant minority of Army soldiers were aware of gays in their units. Asked "Do you personally know any men in your company who are gay?" 9 percent of the 474 men surveyed and 18 percent of the 472 women surveyed answered "yes." To the same question about lesbians, 14 percent of the men and 27 percent of the women responded affirmatively. When asked "Has a soldier of the same sex ever made a sexual advance toward you?" 6 percent of men and 17 percent of women said that such an advance had been made toward them, revealing that direct interaction rather than rumor is the source of knowledge for at least some of these troops (Miller and Moskos 1992). More recently, a questionnaire distributed by John Bicknell asked people to respond to the statement "I personally know a homosexual service member." Affirmative responses were given by 21 percent of 212 Naval officers, 4 percent of 74 Marine officers, 39 percent of 23 Navy enlisted and 29 percent of 59 enlisted Marines (Bicknell 2000). Clearly neither the strict ban on homosexuality nor the "don't ask, don't tell" compromise keeps service members from learning about gay men and lesbians among them.

Scholars who believe that the evidence supports an end to exclusionary policies note that although similar social backgrounds can make it easier for people to establish initial connections, those connections may lead to bonding on nothing more than a superficial level. Research demonstrates that only a moderate level of social cohesion is necessary for effective small group performance (MacCoun 1993). Moreover, a growing literature warns of the potential for significant negative effects on unit performance when members bond primarily because they are similar to one another socially.

An example of the problem of too much social cohesion is a work atmosphere that has become "clubby." In such settings, people can start to value their social relationships more than the work at hand, and may focus on socializing to the neglect of their duties. Chatting at work may slow down productivity levels. Leaders who become excessively close to their subordinates may have trouble exercising their authority when necessary, a principle at the foundation of fraternization prohibitions. Cliques can be a form of close bonding within the unit, but they undermine the unit's ability to work together as a whole. As a consequence, although the primary group may offer a social identity, it can become counterproductive when that social identity takes precedence over the job. Thus people who care about each other and are willing to fight together in combat may not develop the skills to do so effectively.

"Groupthink," a term introduced by Irving Janis in 1972, is a persistent problem of small, cohesive units, particularly when the level of social cohesion is high. When faced with making decisions, the group may not consider all alternatives and may prematurely reach a conclusion that turns out to be seriously wrong. This outcome can occur because of team-mates' desires to avoid conflict and preserve a friendly atmosphere. Members become so comfortable with the notion that they are "alike" that no one wants break this illusion by introducing a deviant opinion. The group may stick with their decision even when confronted with evidence that they are wrong (Janis 1982). Such behavior could have disastrous consequences on a battlefield.

Another hazard of too much social cohesion is what Donna Winslow has identified as "hyperinvestment" in the small unit over the larger organization. Small groups with high levels of social cohesion may come to think of themselves as superior to the larger organization, or exempt from some of its rules. This image is popular in television and movie portrayals of the military: "rogue units" and "black sheep" are presented as successful precisely because they violate military conventions or law. Yet this characteristic was in part responsible for the torture and murder of a Somali man by an elite Canadian unit serving in Somalia (Winslow 1997).

The potential for committing atrocities was recognized by Janis as well. He noted that groups that highly value in-group members are often hard-hearted toward people outside that group. They easily develop stereotypes about the "other" which may lead them to underestimate the abilities of enemies or to dehumanize them and commit atrocities, even against civilians. Where groupthink prevails, members believe in the inherent morality of their group, and are unlikely to raise ethical questions about their own behavior. They are also more likely to cover up ethical improprieties.

Arguments for changing the current exclusionary policies also tend to assert that the relevance of cohesion for combat effectiveness has never been proven. Among the numerous literature reviews and meta-analyses of cohesion were two reviews in the 1990s that addressed the issue of gays in the military and explored the possible causal link between social cohesion and work performance. Both of these reviews concluded that lifting the ban would not disrupt cohesion, and that even if it did, the kind of cohesion that would diminish is not relevant for combat effectiveness (Kier 1998; MacCoun 1993).

Studies of small primary groups have found that for work group outcomes across a spectrum of occupations (predominantly civilian), task cohesion is more relevant than social cohesion:

Task cohesion has a modest but reliable influence on performance; social cohesion does not have an independent effect after controlling for task cohesion. Under some conditions, high social cohesion is actually detrimental to unit performance; moderate social cohesion appears most beneficial. Research indicates that it is not necessary to like someone to work with them, so long as members share a commitment to the group's objective (MacCoun 1993, 330).

What this means is that regardless of the social composition of a group, members' commitment to the collective objective is the key to success. As teams overcome challenges together, they develop greater task cohesion and are motivated to continue their record of accomplishment. Thus, these literature reviews argue that social homogeneity is inconsequential for the work outcomes, and that achieving specific goals creates commonality among otherwise different people and forges productive social bonds.

Elizabeth Kier further questions whether military objections to integration are truly based on a concern for cohesion, or whether this debate is merely an attempt to justify otherwise indefensible prejudices:

Although the rationale for excluding open homosexuals from the U.S. armed forces is based on their purported negative effect on primary group cohesion, the U.S. military does not devote much attention to the development of unit cohesion. In fact, some of the fundamental components of its personnel policies are not designed to enhance unit cohesion. For example, unlike the British system in which soldiers remain in the same regiment for their entire career, the U.S. Army trains, assigns, and deploys its soldiers as individuals. Small units have high personnel turnover rates: indeed, some units have as much as 45 percent turnover annually (Kier 1998, 9–10).

This problem of unit instability has also been raised in research unrelated to integration by gender or sexual orientation. For example, Anna Simons found that a common complaint among U.S. Army's elite Special Forces units was that the constant deployment, transfer, and schooling of members on an individual basis disrupted team confidence and unity virtually as soon as they were established.

Aaron Belkin also challenges the military commanders' arguments about cohesion:

Gay discharges always go down in wartime. During the Korean and Vietnam Wars there were about half as many such discharges as in peacetime. In World War II the discharge rate was substantially lower than in the postwar period. In the Persian Gulf War, the military had a "stop-loss" order that suspended gay expulsions. What the Pentagon is saying is, when unit cohesion is most important and our survival is at stake, we'll keep them in. There is no intellectually honest case to be made that gays undermine cohesion in the military (Ireland 2000, 14).

A second school of thought argues that diversity threatens small-unit cohesion, and that cohesion is necessary for combat effectiveness. When considering the dynamics of front-line troops in the U.S. military, scholars have taken the straight white male as their starting point, as this is by far the most numerous type of soldier, especially in the combat arms. The reaction of the majority of soldiers to minorities is argued to be relevant because straight soldiers will not react well to gay ones, and men in combat units will not react well to women. Thus, these aversions will undermine team dynamics and combat effectiveness.

Claims about the negative effect of gender integration in combat units are often made on the basis of the dynamics in currently integrated settings. One study of military units found that women's participation tended to demoralize men in the unit (Rosen and Martin 1997). A 1999 comparison of five different military studies found that in most cases a high percentage of women in a unit was linked to lower cohesion (Rosen, Bliese, Wright and Gifford 1999). Dating and flirtation have been reported as disruptive, especially when couples allow the relationship to be apparent through their behavior while on duty or deployment (Harrell and Miller 1997). Furthermore, sexual harassment is obviously more likely in mixed gender than single gender settings, and the armed forces have certainly been plagued by sex scandals and sexual harassment in the 1990s.

Other research has documented gender harassment of Army women by male counterparts resentful of their presence (Miller 1997). This behavior is not limited to men and women in the armed forces, but exists in civilian settings as well, particularly in blue-collar occupations (Welsh 1999). Moreover, male ostracism and harassment were found to be a primary force driving out many of the Canadian women who joined the combat arms once that exclusionary policy was lifted (Davis and Thomas 1998). From 1989–96 women officers were about three times more likely to leave armor and artillery positions and about four times more likely to leave infantry units than their male counterparts. Enlisted women were about five times more likely to leave armor, three times more likely to leave artillery, and over six times more likely to leave the infantry than enlisted men (Davis and Thomas 1998, B1).

Claims about the potential negative impact of gays on military units tend to draw upon data reflecting the strength of negative attitudes toward gays among service members. Homosexuality is said to cause discomfort, mistrust, and fear of sexual advances in heterosexual men. Comparing findings presented in this chapter to earlier studies on troops' attitudes towards homosexuality reveals that negative attitudes persisted throughout the decade. In 1993, 75 percent of 1,943 men and 43 percent of 1,606 women in an Army survey supported the ban on gays in the military; 76 percent of men and 55 percent of women in a multi-service survey of 2,346 enlisted personnel supported the ban; and 67 percent of men and 43 percent of women in a survey of 800 Air Force personnel supported separating known or open homosexuals (Miller 1994, 70). A late 1990s survey of 72 active-duty male Marine reservists explored this issue at length and also found widespread negative attitudes. Of those surveyed, 72 percent support the ban, 85 percent believe lifting the ban would be very disruptive, 89 percent believe that lifting the ban would result in homosexuals being subjected to violence, 63 percent think "male homosexuals are disgusting," and 41 percent believe that "lesbians are sick." Curiously, however, 60 percent agree that "it is all right for gays and lesbians to be in the military as long as I don't know who they are," 43 percent that "allowing openly lesbian or gay men in the military would cause some problems but we could manage," and 31 percent that "allowing gay and lesbians in the military will increase soldiers' acceptance of gays and lesbians" (Estrada and Weiss 1999). Although there was an overwhelming rejection of homosexuality in this survey, Marines were less likely to agree with one another about the possible effects of integration on the service. However, the study supports the belief that there would be significant problems, most prominently in the form of violence against known gay soldiers.

A dangerous issue is that some people act upon their revulsion to homosexuality. The Servicemembers Legal Defense Network documented "400 incidents of anti-gay harassment, including death threats and verbal gay-bashing" in 1998 (1999, 1). This type of behavior is not limited to the military environment: in the broader U.S. society in 1998, 1,488 people were victims of reported hate crimes due to sexual orientation (FBI Uniform Crime Reports 1991–98). There is no doubt that homosexuals have long served in the military, many of them with distinction, but some have suffered abuse, harassment, or murder at the hands of their fellow service members. Given the strength of current attitudes among heterosexual military men, one might ask "how well the military cohesion so crucial in battle can withstand the stress of openly discussed homosexual orientations" (Williams 1999, 313).

Defenders of the status quo see themselves not as opponents of civil rights for minorities, but rather as opponents of anything that might lower military effectiveness and thus cost lives. Hostile reactions on the part of some male soldiers toward women and some straight soldiers toward gays indicate not merely an inability or unwillingness to bond across diversity, but that some will demonstrate this antipathy with violence.

The notion of justified military exclusion of certain groups of people did not emerge recently: the military has always been allowed to limit its uniformed members in a way that civilian employers are not. The civilian leadership has often deferred to military expertise on matters of national security, including decisions about who should serve in the armed forces. Although at times the courts have pressed the military to equalize some opportunities for men and women service members, they have also upheld policies enforcing unequal treatment due to consideration of costs, certain job requirements, and privacy between the sexes. Women are not required to register for the draft when they turn eighteen as men are. Children, the elderly, and people who do not meet specific physical and mental qualifications are not permitted to serve, and thus are "discriminated against" by the armed forces.

Those who do join the military are denied some of the legal and privacy rights of the general public, again with the justification that "the United States maintains a military for one purpose and one purpose only: to protect national security" (McDougall 1997, 45). Service members are not allowed to take part in public political demonstrations, for example, and discipline is managed by a military justice system separate from the civilian system. Even specific religious symbols and practices may be prohibited: in the 1980s the courts ruled that Orthodox Jews cannot invoke the First Amendment to secure the right to wear a yarmulke while in uniform (Katzenstein 1998, 88). Thus, civil rights of individuals have been curtailed legally under the premise that they conflict with the services' ability to enforce discipline, prepare for war in times of peace, or engage in combat.[23]

In addition to believing that diversity harms cohesion, the second school of thought also argues that cohesion matters for military combat effectiveness. Oliver et al. (1999) conducted a meta-analysis of 39 different studies aimed at assessing cohesion in actual (not experimental) military units. Adopting a loose working definition of cohesion as the amount of "stick-togetherness," or unity of a group in the pursuit of a goal, this synthesis revealed that "group cohesion was substantially related to soldier perceptions of job and military satisfaction." It also found that cohesion "was also solidly associated with performance, with group performance more strongly correlated with cohesion than was individual performance" (Oliver et al. 1999, 76). These findings suggested that "cohesion enhances well-being, increases retention and readiness, and works against indiscipline in military groups" (Oliver et al. 1999, 78). Other fac-

---

23. For an excellent yet succinct analysis of the law and court cases supporting and challenging the military's exemption from civil rights standards, see Chapter 4 in Katzenstein (1998).

tors affecting cohesion levels across time for deployed units include spending months at a time separated from family members and adjustments related to being stationed in a foreign country (Bartone and Adler 1999). These factors may be more significant for military units than for the typical civilian workplace.

Defenders of the current personnel policies place greater weight upon research conducted specifically with military units, and question whether the civilian settings drawn upon so heavily by scholars such as MacCoun and Kier are appropriate for generalization to the armed forces. It is unclear that the dynamics of experimental groups, sports teams, or 9-to-5 work environments replicate the dynamics in either a peacetime military or units engaged in waging war. Military personnel, in contrast, are often in contact with one another 24 hours a day, 7 days a week for extended periods. They not only share the work environment, but also eat, sleep, shop, exercise, and socialize with other troops. This structural difference may produce types of cohesion or conflict that are different than those arising among people with more limited interaction with one another; it may be impossible to separate social from task cohesion for members of groups whose lives are so intricately intertwined.

Another problem with drawing upon experiences in the civilian work force is that the populations typically included in cohesion research may not accurately represent the populations who tend to serve in the armed forces. Not only are military personnel are more likely to come from southern and rural areas (in 1997, 42 percent of new military enlistees came from the South; Weible 1998), they are also more likely to serve in southern or rural areas where most military bases are located. RAND research in 1993 exploring the potential impact of integrating homosexuals in the military (National Defense Research Institute 1993) took the successful integration of gays in police and fire departments located in large urban areas as a model for how military integration would proceed. These departments were in Chicago, Houston, Los Angeles, New York, San Diego, and Seattle. These organizations may successfully match the organizational structure of the military, however, their members may not accurately represent the values, beliefs, prejudices, experiences, or life stages of the common enlisted soldier.

Finally, we do not yet know for certain the degree to which combat uniquely bonds people in the face of an external enemy, making differences seem irrelevant in the face of human mortality. "Few studies examining group cohesion have used any measure of combat stress, and those studies that have employed such measures usually center on postcombat adjustment and clinical treatment" (Griffith and Vaitkus 1999: 29). Perhaps people put aside everyday differences to focus entirely on survival.

Conversely, however, it is plausible that the high demand for trust and cohesion called for when one's life is on the line may exacerbate the distance created by differences. This core issue will not be resolved in a library, but only by conducting first-hand research on the front lines.

DOES "COHESION" CAPTURE WHAT WE INTEND TO MEASURE?

A narrow focus on the particular concept of "cohesion" may cause us to lose sight of the original grounds of contention: whether diversifying troops by gender and sexuality will harm combat effectiveness. Cohesion is but one intermediate step in this link, and other indirect and direct causes of effectiveness must also be considered. A decline in cohesion could cause one unit to lose its ability to perform to standard, but another might be able to manage the change well based on the strength of leadership, stability of personnel, or focus on other, more pressing issues.

Social science research might be more beneficial to this inquiry if broadly mined for the experiences of integration, social conflict based on civil rights, and cultural change within institutions. For example, U.S. history teaches that the transition from segregation to integration has never run smoothly; conflict often escalates, at the very least initially as previously separated groups must newly face one another on a regular basis (Patterson 1997). Similarly, the results of a recent literature review of gender, race, and organizational dynamics found general agreement among researchers that people tend to be attracted to and identify with others who resemble them, and that numerical majorities often respond negatively to minorities. Diversity is repeatedly found to alter group functioning:

There is an impressive amount of high-quality laboratory and field research on diversity and demography in organizations. . . . Under ideal conditions, increased diversity may have positive effects predicted by information and decision theories. However . . . the preponderance of the empirical evidence suggests that diversity is most likely to impede group functioning. Unless steps are taken to actively counteract these effects, the evidence suggests that, by itself, diversity is more likely to have negative than positive effects on group performance. Simply having more diversity in a group is no guarantee that the group will make better decisions or function effectively. In our view, these conclusions suggest that diversity is a mixed blessing and requires careful and sustained attention to be a positive force in enhancing performance (Williams and O'Reilly 1998, 120).

Hence, casting the net more widely reveals that the magic word "cohesion" may overly constrain the data brought to bear on the question of integration on performance.

Conclusions

We conclude with a return to the claims of veterans such as James Webb, John Hillen, and Charles Moskos that a civil-military culture gap exists over military personnel policies, that civilian leaders support policies that affect unit cohesion adversely, and that diminished unit cohesion hurts military effectiveness.

Our survey results and assessment of the available evidence confirm a civil-military gap over personnel policies on homosexuals and women in the military. We confirm that, as the critics of military reform have argued, veterans and current military personnel are likely to oppose further integration of the armed forces in the areas of gender and of sexual orientation, arguing that these changes are harmful to combat effectiveness. Civilian leaders who have never served in the military are more likely to support removing exclusionary policies and less likely to view these changes as harming combat effectiveness. The gap is even more significant on the issue of military service for openly gay men and lesbians than it is on issues of gender integration.

We do find a consensus that expanding the role of women and open homosexuals will result in some degree of disruption to the units involved. There is considerable disagreement, however, on the cause and likely duration of this disruption, as well as the degree of its impact on overall combat readiness at the organizational level.

Some military reformers argue that negative changes in unit cohesion following further integration would be primarily the fault of a misogynist and homophobic military culture and the straight male leaders who perpetuate it. Advocates of changes in personnel policy acknowledge the likelihood of hostile and possibly violent reactions of male troops to their new comrades. They argue, however, that by changing the masculine military culture through training and close supervision by civilian leadership, such changes could be carried out successfully without diminishing military effectiveness. Task cohesion, the type of cohesion relevant for combat performance, does not, they argue, depend on team members having the same race, ethnicity, gender, or sexual orientation.

Veterans and military leaders, particularly the men among them, are more likely to believe that such changes would harm combat effectiveness, due to the perceived lesser capability of women to fulfill combat duties, the distraction that the presence of women would bring to male combat soldiers, and the effect of homosexuality on the non-sexual intimacy of military members. The critics of reform believe that expanding military service to women and open gays will produce more problems than military leaders can be expected to control, and be more detrimental to combat effectiveness than civil rights goals would warrant.

The arguments and evidence advanced by both sides of the debate suggest that the degree of impact on unit cohesion and combat readiness will depend on the context and implementation of the reforms. Thus, the likely impact cannot be assessed in the abstract because many factors will affect the pace and success of further integration of the armed forces, including:

- whether military leaders are committed to carrying out the new policies successfully;
- whether double standards by gender or sexuality are permitted;
- whether women are allowed to volunteer for ground combat units or are required to serve in them under the same conditions as men;
- whether realistic and uniform physical competence standards are properly developed and implemented to screen new entrants into ground combat units;
- if physical standards are enforced, how many women qualify for the new combat positions;
- how many women volunteer for or are required to serve in the ground combat arms;
- the degree of acceptance of homosexuality in American society at the time the ban on open gays is lifted;
- how many homosexuals reveal their sexual orientation;
- the degree to which the military will have overcome problems of harassment and sexual misconduct in the force at large at the time of integration;
- the degree to which other factors at the time, such as personnel, equipment, and training shortages, affect the dynamics of integration by gender or by sexuality; and
- whether integration takes place during wartime or when a draft is in place.

It is an oversimplification to say that military leaders and veterans are unconcerned with civil rights and civilian leaders are unconcerned with military effectiveness. Similarly, it is not correct to say that military leaders are convinced that diversity necessarily destroys cohesion or that civilians are blind to the problems of integration. Military leaders acknowledge that some changes are manageable and have been worth the struggle, and civilian leaders acknowledge that significant transformations will not occur rapidly or without incident.

Changing current exclusionary policies need not vitiate military readiness if done intelligently. There is no evidence that cohesion is so singularly influential that it overrides other factors, or so important that it should preclude considerations of civil rights. It would be unwise, however, to fail to plan for potential conflicts that may arise. In any case, we believe that the positions of the partisans on either extreme of these polarizing issues are a poor guide to policy.

Chapter 11

Military Professionalism and Policymaking: Is There a Civil-Military Gap at the Top? If So, Does It Matter?

Peter J. Roman
David W. Tarr

Civil-military relations in the United States are among the most success-ful and stable of any nation in the world. Nevertheless, American schol-ars and journalists remain vigilantly sensitive to perceived or potential dangers arising from a military improperly controlled by civilian authori-ties. In recent years there has been a resurgence of interest in and concern about the state of civil-military relations in the United States. A number of observers have asserted that civil-military relations have deteriorated in the last decade. A wide range of anecdotal evidence has been mar-shalled to support such observations. Illustrative expressions of concern include: allegations that an alleged "cultural gap" divides civil and mili-tary societies; an outcropping of contemptuous remarks made by military officers about President Bill Clinton; General Colin Powell's outspoken public opposition to reversing policy on gays in the military and on pro-posals for intervention in Bosnia; and the resignation of the Air Force Chief of Staff, General Ronald Fogleman, over the Khobar Towers contro-versy.

This chapter investigates the role of America's senior military leaders who are directly involved in the formulation of national security policies. Our purpose is to assess the state of relations between and among top U.S. civilian and military leaders. Our intent is to provide a leadership complement to the broader study of civil-military relations based on sur-vey data that was commissioned by Triangle Institute for Security Studies.

Our data are more sensitive and nuanced than can be gathered by survey techniques. Our information is drawn from a series of confidential interviews of military and civilian leaders undertaken between 1994 and

1999; almost all were conducted on a "not-for-attribution" basis. The kinds of questions posed by the TISS surveys—to large numbers of lower-level anonymous respondents—would not be appropriate to one-on-one interviews with high-level civilian and military leaders. Therefore, we have had to extrapolate from the information we have at hand; we have done so with great care not to go beyond our data. For this reason, a direct assessment of the value orientations of these leaders at the level of detail found in the TISS survey is not undertaken here.

Instead, we concentrate on findings that are relevant to the larger issues of the Gap Project; specifically, how effectively do civilian and military leaders come together to formulate national security policy? We give special attention to the military leadership cohort because so much less is known about them than about their civilian counterparts.

The Senior Military Leadership

A small but very influential group of military officers form the pinnacle of America's military leadership. This core group consists of the following top generals and admirals: the Chairman of the Joint Chiefs of Staff (CJCS); the Vice Chairman of the JCS; the chiefs of each of the four armed services (Army, Navy, Air Force, and Marine Corps); and the commanders-in-chief (CINCs) of the nine unified commands. These fifteen four-star officers are supported by a host of three-star and four-star officers, including the vice chiefs of each service, the deputy CINCs of the. unified commands, the Assistant to the JCS Chairman, and key members of the Joint Staff, in particular the Director of the Joint Staff, the J-3 (Operations), and J-5 (Strategic Plans and Policy). When we refer to the "senior military leadership," this is the group we have in mind. In short, our military leadership group consists of the counterparts to the civilian national security policy leadership group—the top Defense and State Department officials, the National Security Council (NSC) principals and deputies, and the major interagency committee members who deal with national security affairs. These are the people who interact with the senior military leaders, engaging them in the processes that lead to the formulation of national policy.

Professionals and the Policy Process

Civilian and military professionals are drawn into the policymaking arena by political appointees who need all the help they can get. As a result, traditional civil-military distinctions fail to capture the range of expertise and leadership that are brought together in national security policy deliberations. Civilian participants usually include political appointees and their subordinates, as well as high-level civil servants with national security credentials. These civilians are drawn from a number of institutions, including the White House, Defense Department, State Department, and other entities of the national security bureaucracy. Sitting alongside these civilians are professional officers of the military, foreign service, and intelligence communities. These professionals may be lawyers, economists, political scientists or trained in some other national security specialty. They come from highly-developed meritocracies whose most successful members arrive at the center of national security policymaking at the peak of their careers. As a result of this mix, a civil-military dichotomy hardly captures the complexity of the decision-making environment.

MILITARY PROFESSIONALISM

Military officers are schooled in a tradition that asserts as well as embraces the idea that the professional military officer is an expert in the management of violence for which there is no civilian peer. This is, in fact, a widely shared conception, both in military society and in the wider civilian community, of the professional credentials of the trained officer in our society. It is assumed that the higher the rank, the greater the professional expertise. This assumption of the special expertise of the military profession represents an important social myth: it is not that there is no truth to the idea, but the idea goes beyond the truth. As Eliot Cohen points out in his critique of military professionalism in Chapter 12 of this volume, military officers prepare to manage violence, anticipate its requirements, and study past uses of violence. However, they rarely engage in the central activity that defines their profession: "real war." In short, military professionals rarely practice their profession via actual combat. Mostly they just "practice." This fact distinguishes military professionals from other traditional professions such as physicians and lawyers, who not only studied medicine or law but who have gained experience daily through the actual application of their knowledge. In our view, this hardly discredits the claim that military professionals make, nor the credit society gives to them, for their expertise. Their specialized knowledge is substantial and involves much more than the management of violence. These senior officers have been consumed in activities involving the training and logistics that are necessary to the development and effective application of force. Civilian political leaders rely upon this claim of expertise. It is presumed that the Joint Chiefs bring unique expertise to the policy process. This is reflected is the special status accorded them: the Chairman serves as principal military advisor to the president and the NSC, while the service chiefs are military advisors. We do not deny their claim of professionalism.

We regard the distinctiveness of their competence as contingent on the activities in which they are actually engaged. At the beginning of their careers, almost all officers are trained in the techniques and mechanics of combat. As they rise through the ranks, their command responsibilities broaden. By the time that they reach the pinnacle of their professional careers, they have been transformed by training and experience into *generalists* (hence the term, for air and ground forces at least, "generals"). If selected to serve as members of the senior military leadership, they offer their civilian counterparts the generalized experiences and military wisdom of the military commander, more than the specialized technical skills of the warrior.

Military professionals may be trained in military science but as a practical matter their professional opinions are just that, opinions. Military advice is based upon the officer's experience and expertise and, as such, is valued by political leaders. However, military leaders' views are more fallible those of physicians or physicists. Social "scientists" should readily appreciate this observation. That is why our political leaders should not always accept, and so frequently will challenge, modify, or reject, the advice of their military advisors. By the same reasoning, is it justifiable for the military professional to go beyond his specialized military competence when developing policy with his civilian colleagues? We address this question later in this chapter.

To be perfectly fair to the military professional, Eliot Cohen's critique and our own—that few officers actually bring the experience of real wars to bear upon their jobs—is to some degree beside the point. Few political leaders actually end up leading the nation into war. The National Security Council system is designed for the coordination and orchestration of national security policy in times of peace as well as war. Top military leaders know more than their civilian counterparts about the military instruments of policy. They are experts in the same sense that economists know more about the substance of their professional domain. Even political scientists, few of whom ever engage in the practice of politics itself, presumably bring a special competence to the table that is valued by the others attending.

Therefore, we suggest bringing a sense of practical realism to the subject of civil-military relations, especially as it applies to the top civilian and military leaders. These are men and women drawn together by their particular political assignments and consequently by the problems posed by the country's security needs. They come to the policy tables of government with both the special claims of office and training and the more general talents that their experiences and personalities provide.

Like other governmental actors, military professionals reflect the organizational cultures from which they come. The literature on this subject is well established. James Q. Wilson, for example, points out that "every organization has a culture, that is, a persistent way of thinking about the central tasks of and human relationships within an organization. Culture is to an organization what personality is to the individual. Like human culture generally, it is passed on from one generation to the next" (Wilson 1989, 91).

Military professionals are products of a highly specialized military culture, yet they are complexly different among themselves, for each is also a product of more specialized organizational cultures, honed by their service branches, and within their services by their specializations (Builder 1989). Hence, every officer has a sense of identity and comradeship that is more specific than that of soldier, sailor, or marine. They are also infantry, airmen, and submariner; air cavalry, paratrooper, or bomber pilot. In short, military officers are hardly a homogeneous lot, any more than are civilians. They come from many professional "walks of life." To assume that military officers are otherwise is to engage is the simplifications of stereotypical categorization.

Professional Specialization at the Top of the Military

Our research has led us to make the following analytical distinctions among flag-ranked military professionals. Despite the "generalist" capabilities of the highest ranking officers, there are three types of professional military orientations operating within the policy process arena: *service* professionalism; *joint* professionalism; and *national security* professionalism. These arise because of the pattern of assignments and the experiences officers accumulate on their way to the top of the military hierarchy.

SERVICE PROFESSIONALISM

Service-based professionalism has been the dominant form of professionalism throughout American military history. Military officers climbed the ranks by proving their mettle within their respective services, often within a particular branch of that service. Today, the four service chiefs and their vice chiefs are the topmost service professionals. These officers have extensive flag-rank experience within their respective services. They possess a vision for their service's enduring mission. They use their leadership skills to rally their services and to be forceful advocates for their individual service's interests inside and outside the Pentagon. Former Chief of Naval Operations, the late Admiral Jeremy "Mike" Boorda, used to boast, "I am, modestly, the best ship handler in the Navy, still to this very day. There are some people who are very good. But nobody's close" (Vistica 1995, 385). This is a classic illustration of the powerful image of service-based professionalism for some flag officers.

JOINT PROFESSIONALISM

The second form of military professional specialization at the top is joint professionalism. Joint organizations and activities involve the integration of two or more services, as in joint task forces, joint operations, or joint commands. The term joint, as in Joint Chiefs of Staff, reflects the preference the services have had in the past for preserving their autonomy, while engendering inter-service cooperation. It is as close as the military normally allows itself to come to the ideal of service unification without the true unification once proposed. Even though joint institutions were first created over fifty years ago, joint professionalism has only gained significance in the last decade, largely due to the implementation of the Goldwater-Nichols Act of 1986. Before the act's passage, joint institutions, such as the Joint Staff, were kept subordinate to the four armed services and their separate staffs through a variety of formal and informal mechanisms. Unified commanders, on the whole, had minimal independent input into Washington policymaking, relying instead on the service chiefs to represent them. Duty on the Joint Staff and other joint assignments often signaled the end of an officer's career; joint military professionalism was neither cultivated nor rewarded. Career advancement was best accomplished within each service. The Goldwater-Nichols Act took a number of steps to correct these problems and to foster joint professionalism across all the services in order to promote inter-service cooperation and more military effective operations. Consequently, while not nearly as ingrained as service professionalism, jointness is now distinct, influential, and here to stay.

Joint experience builds upon an officer's service expertise to enable him or her to think and act across the services in terms of operations, doctrine, training, and other areas. Flag officers develop joint professionalism by serving on the Joint Staff, in a unified command, or in some other joint capacity. The Chairman, Vice Chairman, and the unified CINCs represent the pinnacle of joint professionalism in the senior military leadership (Roman and Tarr 1998).

NATIONAL SECURITY PROFESSIONALISM

The third type of professionalism prominent among the senior military leadership is what we call "national security" professionalism (Gibson and Snider 1999, 206–211). While joint military professionals develop the expertise and ability to think and act across the armed services, national security professionals undertake assignments that broaden their understanding of foreign and security policy across the entire national security policy apparatus of the U.S. government. Effective, intelligent advice in policymaking deliberations requires knowledge of how all national security institutions perform. This type of professionalism is unique to neither the military nor to civilians. It is, therefore, the most "civilianized" or "politicized" orientation of the three under discussion, and therefore, the most controversial. General Colin Powell's career epitomizes this type of flag officer specialization.

Military officers may begin to develop their national security expertise through coursework at civilian graduate programs and military schools like the National War College (although there is not much emphasis on this orientation in professional military education). However, the most important training comes via a developing pattern of assignments that require day-to-day involvement with civilian policymakers in various areas of the government. Today military officers regularly serve on the staffs of the Office of the Secretary of Defense, the White House, the NSC, the State Department, the Central Intelligence Agency (CIA), and Congress. Further, interagency participation is an on-going responsibility for some members of the senior military leadership, including the JCS Chairman, the Vice Chairman, the Assistant to the Chairman, and the J-5 (Strategic Plans and Policy).

The career orientation that we label "national security professionalism" has traditionally received less recognition as a form of military professionalism than service or even joint expertise. The reasons are fairly self-evident. National security professionals advise but do not command. They work too closely and too frequently with political leaders in the eyes of some military officers. Recognition of a formal national security professional among military officers might come too close to the dreaded "Prussian staff."

Political leaders and civilian strategists have lamented the absence of this broad policy-oriented expertise among the senior military leadership. Presidents and their political appointees wanted more capable military professionals who understood the political context of decisionmaking. President Kennedy issued a National Security Action Memorandum (NSAM) demanding that the Joint Chiefs think as national security professionals. The NSAM stated: "While I look to the Chiefs to present the military factor without reserve or hesitation, I regard them to be more than military men and expect their help in fitting military requirements into the overall context of any situation, recognizing that the most difficult problem in Government is to combine all assets in a unified, effective pattern" (Krulak 1987, 85–86). Military leaders began to recognize the importance of such skills within their own ranks. As Bernard Brodie observed in 1973:

the man who has risen to the top finds himself with new concerns, political and diplomatic. He is not simply directing the Army or Navy or Air Force. He is consulting with his colleagues and advising his civilian superiors, the Secretary of Defense and the President. . . . He is advising them on matters having to do with the goals and ends of peace and of war. For this he has certainly not been trained (Brodie 1973, 486).

After the Vietnam War, the armed services tried to remedy these deficiencies by improving and broadening officers' professional development. The Goldwater-Nichols Act reinforced and accelerated these trends. In their study of the backgrounds of civilian and military policymakers, Christopher Gibson and Don Snider concluded that "the military has dramatically improved the ability to operate at the higher political-military levels of government" (Gibson and Snider 1999, 206). This development makes senior officers more useful to civilian policymakers and, paradoxically, less distinctive. At the very time when civilian elites seem to have less interest in national security issues, military officers are increasingly able to offer their own national security expertise.

We regard service, joint, and national security professionals as closely related yet distinctive forms of military professionalism. As general officers move toward the top ranks, they are exposed to each avenue of assignment and final career specialization. Regardless of their broadening responsibilities as they reach the top echelons, some specialization occurs, as the pattern of their assignments is established. Some military positions, like those on the J-3 or J-5 of the Joint Staff, can further their development in several professional areas simultaneously. However, the limited number of assignments and years in rank means that flag officers end up specializing rather than establishing expertise in all three areas. In contrast to the pre–Goldwater-Nichols era, when professionalism was almost exclusively service-based, today's senior military leaders manifest greater professional diversity that these three sub-specializations imply. As a result, the political leadership has available not only the parochial advice of service-based professionals, but the integrative inter-service and national security oriented professionals who can give the civilian leadership the wider perspectives and skills that President Kennedy once demanded.

Selecting Senior Military Leaders

Political leaders have encouraged the development of these different forms of military professionalism among flag officers through the selection of the senior military leadership. Within the last decade, flag officers began to realize that joint or national security credentials would no longer prevent them from reaching the senior military leadership; indeed, it might enhance their chances. The selection and appointments process at the top places great emphasis on a senior officer's ability to contribute to policymaking, thus helping to bridge the gap between military profes sionals and political officials.

Military officers ascend to these highest positions through a process that is both professional and political. Political leaders do not enjoy unlimited freedom when selecting the Chairman and other senior officers; they must chose from the candidates that have been cultivated or "grown" by the armed forces. To become four-star officers, candidates must climb through two separate but overlapping promotion processes. First, they must climb the military hierarchy to reach the pinnacle of their service careers. Political leaders influence this process to only a limited degree; for the most part, the uniformed military evaluates candidates according to its own professional norms, standards, and expectations. Interference in promotion boards is a serious offense for civilian or military officials. In the 1980s, for example, Navy Secretary John Lehman was accused by some of exerting undue influence in Navy promotions by favoring officers close to him (Vistica 1995, 246–247). As officers move up the flag ranks, however, the control of the uniformed military over who gets promoted recedes and that of civilians grows.

Selecting the *senior* military leadership is the responsibility of the political leadership, usually falling to the Secretary of Defense and his staff, and sometimes directly to the president. Many other civilian and military officials have an opportunity to influence the promotion and appointment process. Administration leaders evaluate candidates according to what they believe constitutes the necessary combination of professional background, policymaking experience, personality, and political considerations that will make the candidate effective in a particular assignment. The special mix of desired qualities can vary according to the position. A very good unified commander might not be an effective service chief, and vice versa. Sometimes officials know what they do not want more than what they do want. For example, a senior defense department official told us that in seeking a successor to General Powell as Chairman of the JCS, the one thing they did not want was "another Powell." Further, the criteria as well as the process are not completely institutionalized. Each administration develops its own approach, rooted both in its perception of the military's role and the national security policy, or even the politics of the moment.

In selecting senior military leaders, political officials pay particular attention to an officer's knowledge of, and experience in, national security policymaking, as well to as his or her familiarity with the wider political world. Political leaders seem to value most those senior military leaders who can participate as national security professionals, not just as service or joint professionals. In short, today generals and admirals who possess national security experience have the advantage in the competition for the top posts. Not only can these officers speak the same language as civilian professionals, but often they will already know each other and even have some shared professional experiences. General Powell knew President Bush and other administration officials well before becoming Chairman of the JCS because of his service as Military Assistant to Secretary of Defense Caspar Weinberger and his tenure as National Security Advisor in the Reagan administration. Similarly, Admiral Dennis Blair, before serving as commander of the Pacific Command, gained national security experience in the Clinton administration by serving in the Central Intelligence Agency and as Director of the Joint Staff.

Political leaders have been able to take advantage of the developing cadre of national security professionals among the senior military leadership largely because of the changes brought about by the Goldwater-Nichols Act (Graves and Snider 1996, 53–57). That legislation mandated that flag officers serve in a joint assignment. Furthermore, it protected such officers by requiring promotion rates equal to officers on service staffs. Joint duty became more attractive as the unified commands and Joint Staff became more powerful and proactive. Thus, flag officers began to desire joint assignments rather than viewing them as merely tickets to be punched on the way to the top of their services. Joint assignments sometimes led to more "political" assignments because experience with joint posts, especially via the Joint Staff, often placed such officers in the interagency process, where they learned more about the political institutions that produce policy. Such knowledge became inherently valuable both to military leaders and their civilian counterparts. Hence, joint professionalism tended to spawn national security professionalism, as officers' national security expertise was fine-tuned through further additional assignments of that type.

By way of contrast, before Goldwater-Nichols, senior officers spent their flag years in service positions to prepare to become Chairman of the Joint Chiefs of Staff, instead of in joint assignments. In the process, they were promoted ahead of their cohorts on joint duty. Because the services controlled the path to the top of the military hierarchy, they insured that military professionalism kept a service, not joint, mind-set at the highest levels. Thus the autonomous service cultures maintained dominance. For example, the first ten JCS chairmen spent most of their careers balancing between service staff and service command positions. Of these ten, only General Lyman Lemnitzer and General Earle Wheeler served on a unified command staff or the Joint Staff as flag officers. More typical was Admiral Thomas Moorer who, in sixteen years of flag rank, did not serve on the Joint Staff. General David Jones held flag rank for seventeen years, during which time he never held a joint or unified assignment until he became Chairman (Webb and Cole 1995).

Political leaders use the selection process to identify those officers who are most capable of working within the constraints set by political leaders. It is increasingly unlikely that an officer could reach the senior military leadership without having developed at least a modicum of political acumen. Accordingly, several studies have found that there may be fewer policy differences between civilians and higher-ranking officers than between civilians and lower-ranking ones. Even before Goldwater-Nichols, such qualifications were sought, but were less obviously available. Almost four decades ago, Morris Janowitz found that "the mechanics of promotion and selection have operated to place in military power those who would conform and be in rapport with the system of civilian control." He continued: "Admirals and generals who have achieved personal success within the system are not very likely to challenge or tamper with the basic rules of the game. The sense of frustration falls heaviest on the rising generation of military leaders who have yet to achieve their mark" (Janowitz 1960, 368).

More recently, Ole Holsti wrote that "top-ranking officers . . . may be less likely to espouse very intense alienation from a system that has rewarded them" (Holsti 1998, 37). In our interviews with senior officers, many officers expressed a commitment not only to the "system" but to those civilian policy leaders who appointed them to the high ranks. Obviously, this sense of loyalty probably diminishes the potential for conflicts within the policy teams. It might also serve occasionally to compromise them in the eyes of their fellow officers.

Critics apply the derogatory label "political general" to those they believe to be ruthless self-promoting flag officers as well as to those who have developed a substantial national security professional background. The difference between the two may not seem evident, particularly to those outside the policy process. In the eyes of some, military officers—and their professionalism—become tainted by working too closely with political leaders.

There is also some concern within the military leadership that senior officers who concentrate their flag assignments in the joint or national security arenas are depriving their services of much-needed command leadership. A pattern of infrequent service assignments might engender a degree of animosity toward the senior officer from within his or her service. When Marine General John Sheehan became CINC of the Atlantic Command, some Marine officers complained that Sheehan "is not a real Marine." Worse still, careerist flag officers might be tempted to curry favor with political leaders in order to gain promotions and key assignments. There is never a shortage of military officers willing to bend their professional perspective for career advancement. It is not extraordinary for flag officers to campaign for top assignments, particularly for the JCS chairmanship, which some top officers call "the Chairman's sweepstakes." Unseemly campaigning is usually counterproductive. One unified commander remarked to us that you would not want someone to be Chairman who wanted the position.

The effects of the development of joint and national security specializations within the flag ranks are reinforced by the specific statutory responsibilities of the members of the senior military leadership. The JCS Chairman, the service chiefs, the unified commanders, and other top officers have duties, usually delineated in laws, that distinguish them from one another. The observation that viewpoints on policy issues are influenced by where the officer sits applies to the military just as it does to civilians. While the senior military leadership may be unified on some policy issues, many other issues cut across the top military leaders. We can illustrate this point by examining the differing perspectives of senior military leaders on two issues: force planning and use-of-force issues.

Force Planning

The dominant voice within the senior military leadership on issues of force planning, defense budgeting, and weapons development is that of the service chiefs. This has been the case for many decades. Service chiefs have a statutory responsibility for organizing, training, and equipping their respective services. All service chiefs work to protect their service's health for the near term as well as several decades into the future. Thus, service chiefs' concerns are service-centric. That is their job. These responsibilities can engender common perspectives among service chiefs on issues like gays in the military, the adequacy of the defense budget as a whole, or the effects of a high operations tempo. One service chief described his job for us as "looking to the future, and how do we organize for combat, so to speak. What do we buy? What don't we buy? What is the mission? Where are we really going? Not some pie in the sky vision that we all have already done at least ten times but translate that vision into programmatic reality and . . . the timelines to get there." Of course the competition for limited, scarce defense dollars has often pitted the services against each other in bitter inter-service rivalry. Divisions between the service chiefs over how to spend defense funds becomes readily apparent to policymakers in the executive and legislative branches as each service chief tries to promote his service's programs at the expense of those of the others. The realities of the budget process often mean that a service program can be expanded only at the expense of another program. As a result, inter-service rivalry has been a prominent and permanent feature of American defense policy.

The role of joint military institutions in force planning and budgets has grown over the past decade. This has helped to mitigate inter-service rivalries to a limited degree. The Joint Requirements Oversight Council (JROC), the Joint Staff's J-8 directorate (Force Structure, Resources, and Assessment), and documents like the Chairman's Program Assessment (CPA), Chairman's Program Recommendation (CPR), and the Integrated Priority Lists (IPLs) of the unified commanders were developed to provide civilian policymakers with joint evaluations of the defense budget and service priorities. Proponents believed that a joint perspective could help reduce redundancies between service programs and produce a force more closely tailored to the operational needs of the unified commanders.

These efforts have had erratic success at best, as illustrated by the JROC in the 1990s. In 1994, Vice Chairman Admiral William Owens enhanced the JROC process, which raised concerns among the services that a competing set of weapons-development programs would result. One four-star officer recalled for us that when this occurred, the services "felt a degree of discomfort" because "we had just put together our service plan and the JROC, in certain cases, might come in conflict in the interest of jointness or efficiency or effectiveness or whatever. It appeared that the chiefs were outside of the process." On the other hand, there have also been complaints that these joint assessments too frequently confirm service programs, instead of providing an alternative joint perspective. Admiral Owens writes that when unified commanders are "asked for recommendations on the size, structure, and character of future forces, they usually compile the separate recommendations furnished by service components assigned to their command which are often drafted back in Washington by service staffs" (Owens 1999, 93). One top Clinton administration official told us that "the quality of the JROC products was not very good. . . . The CPR and the CPA were unhelpful. They were only interested in defending the conventional service programs."

Use of Force Issues

The senior military leadership also approaches use of force decisions and issues from differing professional military perspectives. The burden of planning and conducting military operations falls most heavily on the unified commanders, particularly the geographic CINCs. The Goldwater-Nichols Act directed that the chain of command run from the president and secretary of defense directly to the unified commanders (Goldwater-Nichols Act 1986). The law placed neither the service chiefs nor the Chairman in the chain of command. Nevertheless, each president since Goldwater-Nichols has placed the Chairman in the chain for communications purposes. The service chiefs remain outside the chain of command.

In peacetime, unified commanders often compete with each other for resources. No unified commander ever has sufficient forces for the wars he imagines he may have to fight. One service chief explained a unified commander's perspective this way:

"A CINC's got one job and one job only: win his war. And if you think he's going to take into account the national or international picture, you're crazy. Binnie Peay [CINC of Central Command] is interested in winning southwest Asia. If he can get every single person, if he can get every single aircraft, every single ship, he's going to do it. Gary Luck [CINC, United Nations Forces, Korea] is interested in winning Korea. He's got a hundred thousand people along the border and slightly behind to insure that he doesn't. Ten thousand people will die the first day if he doesn't do his job right. You think he cares about Binnie Peay in southwest Asia? He doesn't. . . . He doesn't care about how much it costs. He doesn't care about how many forces he uses. He wants everything."

As a result, the unified commanders provide divergent professional perspectives by virtue of their particular geographic or functional responsibilities. For example, CINCs of the Special Operations Command have frequently conflicted with geographic CINCs over whether, or how, to employ special operations forces (Atkinson 1993, 140–144, 177–181). SACEUR General Wesley Clark advocated a ground option for the planned operations in Kosovo when the secretary of defense, the Chairman, and the Joint Chiefs were less than receptive (Priest 1999).

When force is employed, cleavages between unified commanders and other senior military leaders can be manifested in numerous ways. Each service chief is tempted to promote or protect his service's interests by trying to insure that the unified commander uses his service's forces in some significant way. On the other hand, the frequent military operations undertaken in the 1990s have placed the service chiefs in an awkward situation as they struggled to meet the operational demands of the unified commanders without burning out their troops. Not surprisingly, this has precipitated disagreements between unified commanders and service chiefs over operations. During the Gulf War, the Commandant of the Marine Corps, General Alfred Gray, worked to replace the top Marine general in Central Command and to alter the command's plans for using the Marines. Two Air Force chiefs, Generals Michael Dugan and Merrill "Tony" McPeak, undertook similar efforts to promote the use of air power in the Gulf War (Gordon and Trainor 1995, 100–101, 173–178; Kitfield 1995, 364–365). Such incursions into operations by service chiefs have been far less successful since 1989 due to the strengthening of the unified commanders by the Goldwater-Nichols Act, but they still can happen.

The JCS Chairman may also have views on use of force issues that differ from those of a unified commander. As the principal military advisor to the president and other top civilian leaders, the JCS Chairman must provide military advice that is tailored to fit into the larger context of national security policies and objectives. The Chairman and his deputy, the Vice Chairman, must grapple with political factors that unified commanders do not have to confront. Consequently, JCS chairmen and unified commanders do not always agree on use of force issues. In the late 1980s, JCS Chairman Admiral William Crowe and General Frederick Woerner, commander of the Southern Command, had long-running disagreements over planning for operations against Manuel Noriega (Cole 1995, 7–13). JCS Chairman Powell and General H. Norman Schwarzkopf (CINC of Central Command) clashed over when to begin the ground phase of the Gulf War in January 1991 (Powell 1995, 515–516). American military leaders were divided in 1993 over whether to send Delta Force to Somalia to kidnap the warlord Mohammed Aideed; they assessed the mission, risks, and probability of success differently.

JCS chairmen and unified commanders have also differed over tactics while conducting operations. During the Gulf War, Powell questioned Schwarzkopf over the hunt for Scud missiles, the use of cruise missiles, and air targets in Baghdad. Some senior officers in Central Command felt that Powell was "micro-managing," while others said that Powell provided "strong suggestions, not micro-management." General Schwarzkopf was so affected by the oversight from the Pentagon that, according to one of our interviewees, he once instructed Powell's operations deputy, Lt. General Thomas Kelly, not ever to call Central Command headquarters. Other unified commanders have found their tactics or plans questioned by the JCS chairman, as well as by the service chiefs.

As this brief discussion shows, the senior military leadership seldom speaks with one voice. Moreover, these leaders now manifest three forms of military professionalism, which are in turn reinforced by the specific organizational responsibilities to which they are assigned. The policy advice from senior military leaders reflects these all of these factors: organizational cultures, professional specializations, and specific duties, as well as personal political skills and other idiosyncratic factors. There are issues, such as gays in the military or the invasion of Panama, that have united the senior military leadership. But many policy issues cut across the senior military leadership orientations. Their professional expertise and their offices lead them to evaluate problems and options differently. While these differences are rarely acrimonious or even public, they are significant enough that political leaders are frequently confronted with a range of professional military perspectives.

These factors have contributed to an institutionalization of multiple advocacy which can enhance the quality of military advice as well as complicate it by its very diversity. The JCS Chairman's task is to unify the advice and channel it to the political leadership effectively. This is a demanding task, accomplished through the interagency process.

The Interagency Process

Political leaders, civilian bureaucrats, and national security professionals each lay claim to certain functional prerogatives by virtue of their specific offices. However, national security policy formulation is a shared domain that links the top political leaders and their national security professionals. Military and civilian political leaders need each other in order to make policies, fulfill responsibilities, and to accomplish goals (Gibson and Snider 1999, 194–197). The institutional setting that brings together the civilian and military policy leadership components includes the National Security Council, its subordinate interagency processes, and frequent meetings within the Defense Department and across the national security institutions.

The primary arena for resolving differences and formulating policy is the interagency process, which for national security decisions is centered around the National Security Council and its constituent bodies. Like other White House boards and processes, the National Security Council system has usually been shaped to fit each president's personality and decision-making style. However, the present NSC organizational structure has remained the same since 1989, an unusual occurrence in the history of the body. The Council is currently supported by two subordinate committees. The first, the Principals Committee, is made up of all of the statutory members of the NSC except for the president: the vice president, and the Secretaries of State and Defense, with the Director of Central Intelligence and JCS Chairman sitting as advisors. Principals Committee meetings are usually chaired by the president's National Security Advisor. The second committee, the Deputies Committee, consists of the policy deputies to each member of the Principals Committee, usually the immediate sub-cabinet officer, and is chaired by the Deputy National Security Advisor. The Deputies Committee supports the Principals Committee by sifting through policy issues and options. If the Deputies Committee reaches consensus on an issue, the Principals Committee will not normally discuss it further. Many other interagency committees feed into the NSC system through the Deputies Committee (Gates 1996, 458–459). The NSC system is thus the heart of national security policymaking.

Military participation in the NSC system and the interagency process emanates from the Chairman of the Joint Chiefs of Staff. The Goldwater-Nichols Act of 1986 named the JCS Chairman the Principal Military Advisor to the president and the NSC, and directed that he "attend and participate" in NSC meetings (Goldwater-Nichols Act 1986). It is noteworthy that the military is the only national security institution whose highest ranking *professional* officer, the Chairman of the Joint Chiefs of Staff, is guaranteed a seat in the highest policy deliberations, those of the NSC, by law. Because the Chairman is designated the Principal Military Advisor (rather than the corporate Joint Chiefs, as was the case before Goldwater-Nichols), the responsibility for representing the Chairman in the interagency process below the Principals Committee falls to his supporting staff. The JCS Vice Chairman attends the Deputies Committee and fills in on the NSC and on the Principals Committee when the Chairman is traveling. Key Joint Staff officers, primarily the Director, the J-3 (Operations), and the J-5 (Strategic Plans and Policy), participate in the interagency committees that support the Deputies Committee. On occasion, one of them will sit in for the Vice Chairman on the Deputies Committee. The Assistant to the Chairman, a three-star officer, represents the Chairman on traveling delegations led by the Secretary of State. He also sits on some issue-specific interagency committees.

Although there have been some slight variations from time to time, this has been the basic structure for the military's contribution to inter-agency deliberations at the top of the government. Importantly, military participation is driven by the Chairman and his staff; the other parts of the senior military leadership, including the chiefs, participate through the Chairman and his staff, or indirectly.

A sense of cohesion and teamwork is engendered within these NSC committees by the very frequency of their meetings and by the fact that the membership of these committees is stable. Civilian and military lead-ers who have served on these committees have consistently remarked on this in interviews with us. One Bush administration official explained to us that "you ended up not simply being the representative of your agency, you ended up being you—and your personality, your own views, and all that. I don't think anybody was any less of a participant than any-body else. Formal rank doesn't matter after a while. You either have good things to say or you don't." An Assistant to the Chairman told us, "I was a true team player" when traveling with the Secretary of State. Similarly, a JCS Vice Chairman remarked responded that "it's clear that in my view I am a member of the Committee. I am asked for my opinion, my advice, my recommendation." When the membership of these committees change, as during transition from one administration to the next, cohe-sion is diminished. As General Colin Powell wrote, "the waning hours of the Bush era were not particularly pleasant for me. Every day, more of my teammates over the past four years left, and I was starting to feel like the kid about to enter a new school full of strangers" (Powell 1995, 567). This remark not only illustrates the significance of group identity and affiliation, but also points to the problems that arise when a new "team" is being formed. Since the Chairman of the JCS is not a political ap-pointee, whoever is Chairman during the transition from one administra-tion to the next is likely to be under similar stress.

Once these committees are formed, group cohesion and effective par-ticipation are enhanced precisely because the same officials tend to meet in the same committees over time. According to a former Director of the Joint Staff, "these groups, the interagency groups, are very collegial. You develop influence based on your knowledge which is group-specific." Consequently, influence declines when a member routinely misses meet-ings and a substitute sits in for him or her. This became a significant prob-lem when Admiral William Owens served as JCS Vice Chairman. Accord-ing to one four-star general, Owens decided that he "didn't like the [interagency] process and therefore didn't" go to Deputies Committee meetings. Another four-star officer explained to us that, "when you get down to the Deputies . . . Owens had a heavy travel schedule and when he was gone we wouldn't send a service chief; we'd send a three-star. Now where you [should] have a four-star, you have a three-star . . . you're sending the substitute, so you're losing a lot of leverage. We lost a lot." When General Joseph Ralston replaced Owens as Vice Chairman, General John Shalikashvili, the JCS Chairman, made participation in the Deputies Committee a priority for Ralston.

In times of crisis or urgency the JCS Chairman, Vice Chairman, or even a unified commander might be called upon to deliver a formal recommendation to the NSC or to the Principals Committee. Far more frequently, however, senior officers on these interagency committees provide advice routinely to political leaders in the continuous policy dialogue across a range of issues that commonly fills their agendas. As one JCS Vice Chairman explained:

if you don't get the military view inserted into the interagency process and you wait until it reaches the Principals level, you're going to have more disconnects. You're going to have more times when you have to go to the President and say "Mr. President, I disagree with what the Principals have recommended." Hopefully, by my entering the process at the Deputies level and playing a strong role there, that will make things smoother for the Principals and the President.

Furthermore, as numerous civilian and military interviewees have pointed out, it would be problematic for senior officers to object to a consensus policy choice if they have already sat through the deliberations and not offered their advice. As one State Department official succinctly put it for us, "people should not participate on an 'if asked' basis." Nevertheless, senior officers participating in the interagency process often indicated to us that they usually tried to limit their participation to issues that fall within their purview as military professionals. "I try to restrict my substantive comments to those things that have an equity for the military," one top officer told us. But top-level committees deal with wide-ranging issues and in political-military affairs boundaries are not always obvious.

The participation of the Chairman, Vice Chairman, and other senior officers on interagency committees raises a number of important issues. First, the distinction between professional *advisor* and *policymaker* deteriorates for senior officers, particularly the Chairman and Vice Chairman. Senior officials, civilian or military, are unlikely to hold back simply because discussion turns to advocacy and the committee members begin to express and invite expression of the members' preferences. In this context, professional military advice is hardly ever offered on a "take-it-or-leave-it" basis; that might undermine cordial relations. When asked about the distinction between advisor and policymaker, General John Shalikashvili told us, "the lines get blurred . . . with the kind of discussions on Rwanda or Haiti or Somalia or whatever. . . . I think it is sometimes an issue. . . . It's a relationship that sometimes finds you getting very close to the line, so that would be the policy issue. I wish I could tell you it's always easier to avoid."

Countless other interviewees, both civilian and military, struggled with the idea that the roles of military advisor and policymaker could be readily discerned and used as a guide for limiting the military officer as a participant. In a typical answer, a Bush administration official stated, "I have trouble with trying to distinguish between advisor and decision-maker. I don't know if I could distinguish their [Chairman and Vice Chairman] advice from the other guys at the table." A Reagan administration official said, "I never bought the distinction between advisor and policy-maker." One Vice Chairman told us that the distinction had not occurred to him. In short, the boundaries between the professional advisory role and that of policymaker is difficult and often impossible for senior officers to sustain. The committee process draws them in, extracts their advice over time in increments, and keeps them on board as the policy is constructed and forwarded to the top—or, alternatively, deconstructed and sent back down for changes, or rejected outright.

Second, by according the JCS Chairman a place on the NSC (and, by extension, placing his representatives on other interagency committees), the Goldwater-Nichols Act mandated a relationship that has the potential for friction between the Defense Department's civilian and military leaders. The Defense Department is the only national security organization that has two seats at the interagency table, one for the uniformed military and one for the civilian side of the Pentagon. Consequently, while the Chairman is subordinate to the Secretary of Defense in all other aspects, they are nominal equals on the NSC and the Principals Committee. Senior Defense Department officials, chairmen, and vice chairmen have described for us how they work to coordinate their positions in preparation for interagency meetings or, conversely, claim they are collegial enough to disagree in interagency meetings. Still, the potential remains for a Secretary of Defense to feel that the JCS Chairman may be undermining his authority through his behavior in interagency meetings (Powell 1995, 464–466; Bush and Scowcroft 1998, 24). As one Defense Secretary told us, "the Chairman's role in the NSC invites trouble."

Some Defense Department officials fear that some officials could attempt "divide and conquer" strategies if they detected a difference of opinion between the Defense Secretary and Chairman. According to one senior defense official, Secretary William Perry thought "that if there were fissures between the Chairman and the Secretary that these would be exploited by others in the system, particularly the White House. The White House would start to go to the Secretary for one thing and to the Chairman for other things. Soon they would have one side of the building against the other." Such concerns were manifested early in the Clinton administration when National Security Advisor Anthony Lake tasked the JCS Chairman without informing the Defense Secretary. These problems were later corrected, but there is nothing preventing them from arising again in the future. When they do, the Chairman could become ensnared in an administration's political maneuverings.

Third, participation in the interagency process can have the effect of co-opting the military professionals, or at least create that appearance, when they end up embracing administration policy. A military professional who too readily and too often shapes his or her advice to political views may be accused of being "political" or co-opted. The consensus and incremental nature of the policymaking process leads civilian and military leaders to accept compromises throughout an extended process. On the eve of U.S. deployments to Bosnia in 1995, a service chief explained it this way for us: "You evolve with the process. In 1992, if you said we were sending 25,000 troops to Bosnia, we would stand up and say 'we need to see the President and engage the Secretary of State and the Secretary of Defense.' But now, you might say, 'well, okay.' The chiefs were not co-opted."

However, military and civilian officials who desire to be good team players cannot help but be co-opted at times. It may be inherent in the process. Certainly the Chairman and other senior officers are placed in extraordinarily difficult positions when the president selects a policy option that they may have argued against *in camera*, opposed in part but not on the whole, or might have advised against if asked. Signaling their opposition publicly would be a challenge to civilian authority, while maintaining their silence might be interpreted as co-optation or abject submission. Unless one is privy to the highest policy debates, it is impossible to determine whether a military officer was co-opted or simply that he argued his position and lost. In a 1996 interview, an Air Force four-star general accused General Shalikashvili of being co-opted: "When Colin Powell was giving advice on Bosnia to the NSC, the advice to him was coming from Shali, who was CINCEUR. Shali didn't change his mind on Bosnia, but he became a member of the administration." In short, he was accusing Shalikashvili of caving in. We presume, however, that most chairmen and vice chairmen would prefer to be wrongly accused of being co-opted than to try to prove otherwise.

By the time a JCS Chairman or Vice Chairman sits on the NSC or one of its committees, the gap between his professional military training and the political leadership has been bridged. These officers get there as a result of their increasingly "political" experience as they rise through the top ranks. The selection and appointments process for general officers enables political leaders to cultivate those top military leaders with whom they believe they can work. Further, the differences between civilians and military leaders are worked out daily in the interagency process as well as through informal meetings. One senior Defense Department official explained that Defense Secretary Perry and General Shalikashvili resolved their differing views "not by accident but by hard work." This is how gaps are bridged among top policymakers. As we have explained, senior military leaders encounter special problems by becoming part of the policymaking team. While these are acceptable costs when the system works, they also have troubling implications.

A Bridge Too Far?

In our view, the differences between the senior military leadership and top civilian policymakers are no more significant than the differences that mark other professional orientations. Professionals tend to come at problems with perspectives that are derived from their specialized training, organizational cultures, and experiences. In our interviews, we detected no disturbing "value gap" or "cultural gap" between the military and civilian leaders. We found, rather, that national security policymaking institutions and processes draw these people together in ways that engender mutual respect, enhance cohesion, and establish trust. There are many differences in views, but the cleavages that arise in the struggle over policy issues do not very often define themselves along civil-military lines. In short, civil-military relations appear to be, on the whole, cordial, and the policy process appears to work rather smoothly.

Certainly, the policy process cannot always bridge the gaps that develop between political leaders and their professional advisors. Angry debates, ill feelings, and unresolved issues will always be some part of any administration's policy deliberations. People have egos, and interests and values differ. More often than not, such hard feelings as might develop over a dispute are more accurately attributed to personality differences than to civil-military differences, world views, or cultural gaps.

Some proponents of the "gap" hypothesis have argued that the cultural differences between the military and civilian society are alarming. By implication, such differences can undermine good civil-military relations, especially by reducing the respect that the military should have for civilian authority and civil society. Our examination of the relationship between top civilian and military leaders fails to confirm this perspective. Civilian and military leaders regularly bridge gaps between one another in order ensure that the policy process is working and that the military is on board when controversial issues are addressed.

Any value differences that might exist between civilian and military authorities are less serious than the larger implications regarding the integration of senior military leaders into the politics of the policy process. Senior military leaders have, at times, been willing to become engaged in policy debates that occur outside the confines of an administration's interagency deliberations. This brings top officers into aspects of policy-making that are inherently political and, as such, should be left to political leaders. Unfortunately, too often senior military leaders have behaved like political leaders.

We have already described how many senior military leaders have developed their national security expertise, served in Washington in a policy capacity, and viewed themselves as members of the administration team. These flag officers are acutely aware of how forces external to the interagency process—Congress, the press, and public opinion—can influence an administration's decision-making. With the distinction between professional advisor and policymaker less than clear, senior officers who watch political officials using these avenues to influence policy debates may be tempted to do so as well. The end-run to Congress and the news leak have long been part of the senior military leadership's kit-bag. One four-star general explained his leaking strategy for us as follows: "If I was really angry and wanted to get something in the news, I would send a personal [message] to the Chairman and to both undersecretaries for policy [State and Defense]. . . . If you talk about personalities, which you don't like to do, you will be able to get your story out" (meaning that it is likely to leak). Obviously, such behavior is dramatically different from the public role we would expect for professional military officers. Rather than educating the public about military policies, here a senior officer is trying to shape those policies through the public arena.

The military leader most adept in recent times at operating outside the administration to promote his policy preferences has been General Colin Powell. He was well-known as a master of press relations when he was JCS Chairman. Three examples illustrate this. As he developed his Base Force proposal in the Spring of 1990, Powell gave a series of speeches, according to historian Lorna Jaffe, "hoping to set the terms of the debate with Congress." These speeches took place months before civilian and military leaders in the Defense Department reached consensus on Powell's proposal. Jaffe's analysis of Powell's speeches is insightful:

Before an audience composed of members of the foreign policy establishment who would be able to influence the course of the administration's debate with Congress over the defense budget, he challenged the contention that the Department was not recasting its thinking in response to the change in the threat. In answer to the Department's critics, he offered his views—still unendorsed by the Secretary—on the strategic approach and the configuration of forces needed to meet the new situation (Jaffe 1993, 28–30).

A second example involves Powell's tactics regarding the ban on gays in the military. A defense official in the Bush administration told us that, after the 1992 election, General Powell asked him to make a press statement opposing lifting the ban on gays because "I'm getting kicked around about the gay ban." Third, General Powell's October 1992 op-ed in the *New York Times* opposing U.S. intervention in Bosnia illustrates this issue as well. The JCS Chairman conformed to civilian control by clearing his statement with Defense Secretary Dick Cheney and the NSC (Powell 1995, 558–559). However, with an election a month away, the Chairman had taken his position to the public on an issue better left to the electoral process. General Powell's use of the public arena to advance his policy positions in these cases has been similarly employed by other generals and admirals at other times, although none as effectively.

Even if senior military leaders try to avoid being drawn into public dimensions of policymaking, presidents and other political leaders will pull them in to give credence to their particular positions. Pressure may be placed on flag officers to make statements endorsing the administration's policy, regardless of the officer's private views. Presidents find it politically valuable to cite the support of the Joint Chiefs of Staff or of the Chairman, and they like to have these officers appear behind them for a policy pronouncements and Rose Garden photo opportunities. Some senior officers view such actions as a necessary element of their job. According to one service chief, "I had no trouble standing up in the Rose Garden. It made no difference to me." Others find such use of military leaders distasteful. One four-star officer told us in 1995:

They have trotted John [Shalikashvili] out to nod when they are unveiling a politically unpopular policy. I'm not pleased with that. But the president is the commander-in-chief, so when ordered to do something, you do it. The current administration has no credibility militarily like the previous administration did so they have to use Shali in the background all the time like one of those toy dogs in the back of the car nodding his head up and down.

Members of Congress also seek to draw senior officers into public debates over national security policy, frequently in an effort to reveal divisions between an administration and its professional military advisors. Thus, senior military officers may have difficulty avoiding the political arena despite their best efforts to do so.

The distinction between professional military advisor and that of policymaker breaks down for many senior officers. This is not a problem if kept within the confines of an administration's interagency deliberations. However, personality, professional experiences, or encouragement from political leaders can draw military leaders into the public debate over policy issues. Prolonged activity of this type on the part of senior military leaders could have a detrimental effect on military professionalism. Regardless of whether top military officers are willing or unwilling participants in the public process of shaping policy, the result is that their military professionalism is compromised. If the civilian elite or the public considers the military leadership to be either co-opted or partisan-leaning, then military professionalism may too been seen as corrupted by politics.

It would be impossible for the senior military leadership to be insulated from these dangers and be able to operate effectively in the national security policy process, for the reasons we have described in this chapter. Still, some steps could be taken to reduce these problems while strengthening military professionalism. First, the uniformed military, especially the armed services, need to give greater formal recognition to national security professionalism as a form of military professionalism. This is needed in order establish professional norms, standards, and expectations for military officers who must participate with civilian political leaders to make national security policy. Absent a clearer notion of the military officer as a national security professional, officers will continue to rely on informal, *ad hoc* guidance. Second, the professional military education (PME) system needs to integrate national security professionalism into its curricula. PME is dominated by the service and joint perspectives; national security perspectives are far less prominent. A program of professional national security education could be developed that would be distinct and separate from PME. This program would include professionals from across the government with the aim of developing a better common understanding of national security policy and to improve policy coordination.

Third, the distinction between policy advisor and policymaker must be reinforced as much as is reasonable. Certainly, within the interagency arena, the JCS Chairman and other senior military leaders will find the line blurred. However, political and military leaders must not forget that the distinction must be maintained outside the interagency process. Political forces of the moment will create pressures for senior officers to become engaged in wider policy debates in the public realm. The ability of senior officers to resist them depends on an officer's integrity and his or her relations with civilian political leaders.

These three recommendations can help to develop national security professionalism amongst the senior military leadership. Without such changes, the inclusion of top officers in the policy process will periodically produce generals and admirals who behave too much like political leaders when they should not. This problem of military officers acting like political leaders is much more serious than military and civilian leaders thinking differently.

Chapter 12

The Unequal Dialogue: The Theory and Reality of Civil-Military Relations and the Use of Force

Eliot A. Cohen

In *The Edge of the Sword*, a short but profound work on civil-military relations written a bit more than a decade after World War I and reflecting its experiences, Charles de Gaulle captured some of the differences between the soldier and the statesman of his day:

The soldier often regards the man of politics as unreliable, inconstant, and greedy for the limelight. Bred on imperatives, the military temperament is astonished by the number of pretenses in which the statesman has to indulge. . . . The impassioned twists and turns, the dominant concern with the effect to be produced, the appearance of weighing others in terms not of their merit but of their influence—all inevitable characteristics in the civilian whose authority rests upon the popular will—cannot but worry the professional soldier, broken in, as he is, to a life of hard duties, self-effacement, and respect shown for services rendered. . . .

Inversely, the taste for system, the self-assurance and the rigidity which, as the result of prolonged constraint, are inbred in the soldier, seem to the politicians tiresome and unattractive. Everything in the military code which is absolute, peremptory and not to be questioned, is repugnant to those who live in a world of rough and ready solutions, endless intriguing and decisions which may be reversed at a moment's notice (De Gaulle 1960, 98–99; see also Hoy 1996; Spector 1999).

Half a century later, Ariel Sharon, an Israeli soldier turned politician, expressed an even greater sense of bafflement:

Like politics, military life is a constant struggle. But with all the difficulties and bitterness that may develop, at least there are certain rules. In politics there are no rules, no sense of proportion, no sensible hierarchy. An Israeli military man setting foot in this new world has most likely experienced great victories and also terrible defeats. He has had moments of exultation and moments of deepest grief. He knows what it is to be supremely confident, even inspired. But he has suffered the most abject fear and the deepest horror. He has made decisions about life and death, for himself as well as for others.

The same person enters the political world and finds that he has one mouth to speak with and one hand to vote with, exactly like the man sitting next to him. And that man perhaps has never witnessed or experienced anything profound or anything dramatic in his life. He does not know either the heights or the depths. He has never tested himself or made critical decisions or taken responsibility for his life or the lives of his fellows. And this man—it seems incredible—but this man too has one mouth and one hand (Sharon 1989).

Sharon had been a dashing paratrooper, hero of Israel's border conflicts in the early 1950s, as well as the 1956, 1967, and 1973 Arab-Israeli wars. As a civilian defense minister, he led his country into the ruinous Lebanon War of 1982. Nonetheless, there is something candid in the disdain that he expresses for politicians, and one suspects that many others in uniform have shared his views.

That a gap of personality, outlook, and personal background exists between civilian and military authority, particularly in wartime, is generally acknowledged to be the case. These two excerpts suggest that it can hardly be otherwise. The democratic statesman claws his way to the top in an unstructured environment characterized by shifting coalitions, unsparing and often unfair criticism from journalist, foe, and even friend, and the constant possibility of swift and humiliating defeat at the polls. "There is, in time of peace, organised opposition which with tireless industry assembles all the worst possible facts, draws from them the most alarming conclusions, and imputes the most unworthy motives," wrote Winston Churchill in the 1920s. The soldier, by contrast (at least as seen from Churchill's vantage point, different than that of de Gaulle and Sharon), "is in the main surrounded by smiling and respectful faces," a staff whose loyalty and "sense of discipline, lead them to try to win his favour, or at least to spare his feelings, on every occasion" (Churchill 1927, 195).

One might multiply such psychological sketches, but they are common from all wars. The modern military commander and the politician are, in most cases, very different kinds of ambitious people whose careers have taken them on very different paths; the one having risen, usually over decades, through gradually ascending ranks of responsibility, the other having struggled in the chaos of politics. One has learned to exercise command; the other to win favor and exert influence. The soldier has passed most of his life in a peaceful, structured, hierarchical environment dominated by the rhetoric, and often the reality, of duty, fidelity, and honor; the politician, ironically, has engaged in daily, swirling combat, albeit of a bloodless kind, in which seniority and experience may suddenly count for very little. The general or admiral may be expected, in modern times, to have mastered the technology and techniques of the peculiar craft of war; the politician is a generalist, whose interest in things military is, in most cases, intermittent but intense, and except in the rarest of circumstances, amateurish. It is to be expected that there would be a gap between individuals with such different experiences of life. Indeed, it would be astounding were anything else the case. It is at least as large as the gap between a doctor and patient, a lawyer and client, or architect and prospective mansion owner, although different from all of these and often greater.

To be sure, individuals have often bridged the gap in background and values between civilians and soldiers. The politician become soldier has been rare since the nineteenth century, although not entirely unknown: a Theodore Roosevelt, for example. There have long been politicians who crave the company and defer to the judgment of generals, which is not so much an obliteration of the gap as a unilateral bridging of it. But most often it is generals who have become politicians, like those mentioned above. In the American experience one thinks of Dwight D. Eisenhower as the most successful of these, leaving aside George Washington as a man *sui generis*. For the most part, American generals have made odd or awkward politicians, as in the case of Ulysses S. Grant, failing utterly (like William Westmoreland and before him Leonard Wood and Winfield Scott), or prudently withdrawing from the field (like Colin Powell and Norman Schwarzkopf), perhaps out of unwillingness to suffer the abuse that is normally the lot of an elected official. The general-as-politician flourishes in the aftermath of a great war, or at a time of great crisis, but even successes such as Charles de Gaulle or Yitzhak Rabin never really shed the aloofness and discomfort with routine democratic politics that characterized them as professional soldiers. The gap between khaki and mufti, "brass" and "frocks" persists, even after soldiers have doffed the uniform, or if civilians attempt to don it.

There is a second kind of gap, however, and one that is more problematic because it is normative, rather than positive—a description of how things should be, rather than how they are. This second gap is one of responsibilities, function, and expectation. It is the gap often declared desirable by soldier and statesman alike with respect to how wars should be fought. In this view—what we may term the normal theory of civil-military relations at the top—the politician and the soldier have very different functions. The politician sets goals and makes policy. He or she alone authorizes the use of force, setting broad boundaries for its use, establishing the objectives of war, and concluding it with peace negotiations. Providing the resources the military needs, the politician balances them with the other requirements of national life; he selects, and if necessary removes, the most senior commanders. He arranges alliances and pacts, and sets, in conference with his military advisors, the broad outlines of strategy. From the commander he has the right to expect candid advice, dedication to the mission at hand, and technical competence.

The soldier, within these limits, is the master of operations and tactics; his voice must be heard, if not entirely controlling, in the setting of strategy. He should be freed from scrutiny in matters of detail, such as the selection of weapons of war, the choice of subordinate commanders, the timing of military operations, the methods of attack or defense, and the arrangement of command relationships with other components of the armed forces. From the politician he has the right to expect unambiguous objectives, discretion, and public support. He must understand political constraints, but should have a free hand. Soldiers and political authorities should "divide the nation's war-making responsibilities, leaving each group to perform its own essential function in an optimal manner" (Matthews 1998, 3).

This theory of the normative gap reflects as well a view about the way in which countries should use force. Perhaps best articulated in the six rules devised by U.S. Secretary of Defense Caspar Weinberger, it calls for the use of force only for vital interests, with a clear commitment to winning, in support of simple and clear objectives, and the ensuring of public support before the actual conduct of military operations (Weinberger 1984, 21; Powell 1995; Cohen 1995, 102–110). If there is a clear gap between soldiers and politicians—between those who obediently but independently use force, and those who ordain its purposes—the objectives set for the use of force must be clear and simple. Thus, a theory of civil-military relations contains within it a theory of strategy.

The reality of wartime civil-military relations is far different. At its best—in the hands of a great statesman like Abraham Lincoln, Georges Clemenceau, Winston Churchill, or David Ben Gurion—it consists rather of an unequal dialogue between politician and soldier. In practice, as opposed to theory, the bounds of civilian and military authority seem far blurrier than either might like, or than scholars might expect. Rather than a comfortable division of labor, we observe in history a far more tense and exhausting interaction over matters of detail and not simply the broad outlines of strategy. The reasons for this difficult partnership, in which civil authority must hold the upper hand, lies not merely in the individual peculiarities of powerful leaders, but in the nature of war itself. Because strategy consists so often of seemingly detailed judgments that have broader implications, and because of limitations on the very nature of military professionalism itself, civilian authority must prepare itself to engage far more actively with its military subordinates than the normal theory would suggest.

The Normal Theory of Civil-Military Relations

The "normal theory" of civil-military relations rests, in the United States at any rate, on two pillars: a conception of professionalism most clearly described by Samuel P. Huntington in his classic work, *The Soldier and the State,* and on a reading of the experience of the Vietnam War. *The Soldier and the State* set the terms of debate about civil-military relations in this country. Huntington describes officership as a profession, much like medicine or the law. Like those vocations, officership was distinguished by *expertise* in a particular area of human affairs, a sense of *responsibility* that lends an importance transcending monetary rewards to one's activity, and *corporateness,* a social awareness and commitment to members of one's group (Huntington 1959, 8–11). For Huntington, the central skill of the soldier is the "management of violence," the arts of planning, organizing, and employing military force, but not applying it oneself. To be sure, this may mean that "not all officers are professional military officers" (Huntington 1963, 785–786). Those who specialize in career areas not directly related to the management of violence are not truly military professionals. Neither, by implication, are those whose specialty is the application of violence rather than its management and planning.

Huntington believes in the distinctiveness of the military mindset. It is, he says in a notable passage, "pessimistic, collectivist, historically inclined, power-oriented, nationalistic, militaristic, pacifist, and instrumentalist in its view of the military profession. It is, in brief, realistic and conservative" (Huntington 1959, 68). To be sure, this is an ideal type. But Huntington maintains that it is powerful nonetheless, and that this military ethos is a source of great strength, not merely for the military but for society more broadly. In the concluding pages of *The Soldier and the State,* he draws a striking contrast between the appearance and the inner reality of the U.S. Military Academy at West Point and the neighboring town of Highland Falls: appearances that reflect cultural differences. The dazzling heterogeneity and anarchy of democratic society have something to learn, he argues, from the austerity and purposefulness of the military order.

Huntington's recipe for ensuring civilian dominance over the armed forces requires a sharp division between civilian and military roles. "Objective control"—a form of civilian control based on efforts to increase the professionalism of the officer corps, carving off for it a sphere of action independent of politics—is, in his view, the preferable form of civil-military relations. He contrasts "objective control" with what he calls "subjective control," which aims to tame the military in various ways, chiefly by joining military and civilian elites, as in aristocratic armies, rendering it politically aware and possibly active, but also a self-conscious extension of the body politic. In the contemporary world those who support this latter means of control are "fusionists," who believe that the old categories of political and military matters have blurred (Huntington 1959, 80ff., 351–360). In a previous age they would have asserted civilian control by keeping officership the preserve of the ruling social class; in the current era they seek to blur the autonomous nature of military professionalism. "The essence of objective civilian control," by way of contrast, "is the recognition of autonomous military professionalism" (Huntington 1959, 83). Armies do best when military matters are left solely to officers, and when clear distinctions are drawn between their activities and those of politicians. Officers motivated by dedication to a politically sterile and neutral military ideal—"the Good Soldier," and "the Best Regiment"—will turn in a performance superior to those motivated by ideology or merely personal drives such as ambition or vainglory (Huntington 1959, 74).

For Huntington, then, the statesman is in the position of a patient under the care of a surgeon. He may freely decide whether or not to have an operation, he may choose one doctor over another, and he may even make a decision among different surgical options, although that is more rare and problematic. He may not, however, supervise a surgical procedure, select the doctor's scalpel, or rearrange the operating room to his liking. Even the patient who has medical training is well-advised not to attempt to do so, and indeed, his doctor will almost surely resent a colleague-patient's efforts along such lines. The result is, therefore, a limited degree of civilian control over military matters. Huntington quotes approvingly a 1936 Command and General Staff College publication:

Politics and strategy are radically and fundamentally things apart. Strategy begins where politics ends. All that soldiers ask is that once the policy is settled, strategy and command shall be regarded as being in a sphere apart from politics. . . . The line of demarcation must be drawn between politics and strategy, supply, and operations. Having found this line, all sides must abstain from trespassing (Huntington 1959, 308).

This sharp separation—the normative gap in civil-military relations—is possible because military expertise is, in Huntington's view, definable and capable of being isolated. "The criteria of military efficiency are limited, concrete, and relatively objective; the criteria of political wisdom are indefinite, ambiguous, and highly subjective" (Huntington 1959, 76). Political leaders enhance their control by making the military austerely professional, while reserving to themselves alone the passing of judgments on matters of policy, as opposed to technical military matters. Military expertise, in Huntington's view, is a constant:

The peculiar skill of the military officer is universal in the sense that its essence is not affected by changes in time or location. Just as the qualifications of a good surgeon are the same in Zurich as they are in New York, the same standards of professional military competence apply in Russia as in America and in the nineteenth century as in the twentieth (Huntington 1959, 13).

The Huntingtonian conception of military professionalism remains the dominant view within the U.S. defense establishment. As a practical matter, the Huntingtonian concept was most clearly vindicated in debate leading up to the Goldwater-Nichols Act of 1986, which substantially increased the power of the Joint Staff and the Chairman of the Joint Chiefs of Staff at the expense of the military services and even, to some extent, the Office of the Secretary of Defense (U.S. Congress 1985). Not only did the originators of that legislation explicitly endorse Huntington's reading of American military history; they saw their responsibility as one of providing more and better centralized autonomous military advice to civilian leaders (U.S. Congress 1985).

The Huntingtonian view of civil-military relations has been reinforced by the popular reading of the Vietnam and Gulf Wars, the one viewed as a conflict characterized by civilian interference in the details of warmaking, the other a model of benign operational and tactical neglect by an enlightened civilian leadership (Johnson 1997). The belief that the Vietnam debacle resulted primarily from civilian micro-management shaped the attitudes of, for example, President George H. W. Bush. In recounting the crisis leading up to the Gulf War, Bush recalled General Colin Powell's demand for "freedom of action to do the job once the political decision had been made. . . . I did not want to repeat the problems of the Vietnam War (or numerous wars throughout history), where the political leadership meddled with military operations. I would avoid micromanaging the military" (Bush and Scowcroft 1998, 354).

And, indeed, Bush is generally viewed as having refrained from doing just that. The chief of staff to General Norman Schwarzkopf, commander of U.S. forces in Southwest Asia, declared: "Schwarzkopf was never second-guessed by civilians, and that's the way it ought to work" (Gertz 1993). Bush declared, when he received the Association of the U.S. Army's George Catlett Marshall Medal, "I vowed that I would never send an American soldier into combat with one hand tied behind that soldier's back. We did the politics and you superbly did the fighting" (Masters 1993). Small wonder, then, that the editor of the U.S. Army War College's journal has recently written to his military colleagues:

there will be instances where civilian officials with Napoleon complexes and micromanaging mentalities are prompted to seize the reins of operational control. And having taken control, there will be times when they then begin to fumble toward disaster. When this threatens to happen, the nation's top soldier . . . must summon the courage to rise and say to his civilian masters, "You can't do that!" and then stride to the focal point of decision and tell them how it must be done (Matthews 1996, 36).

Such an understanding of the roles of civilian and soldier reflects popular understandings as well. The 1996 movie, "Independence Day," for example, features only one notable villain (aside, that is, from the aliens who are attempting to devastate and conquer the Earth)—an arrogant Secretary of Defense who attempts to direct the American military's counterattack against the invaders from outer space. Only after the interfering and deceitful civilian is out of the way can the president, a former Air Force combat pilot who gets back into the cockpit to lead the climactic aerial battle and, with his military assistants (aided by one civilian scientist in a purely technical role), get on with the job of defeating the foe.

In the modern American theory of civil-military relations—partly theory as understood by academics, but also theory as articulated by politicians and journalists—the failure of Vietnam resulted from civilian meddling and interference with the conduct of military operations; the Gulf War success resulted from a healthy constriction of the civilian role to ordering, launching, and then ending the war, and nothing in between. The shadow of the earlier war still loomed thirty years later, its gloom seemingly the darker for the bright example of the Gulf War. Thus, when American and European aircraft began bombing Serbia in March 1999, Air Force generals, unhappy about political restraints on targeting, "fretted privately about a 'new Vietnam'" (Harden 1999). A month into the campaign, Steven Lee Myers of *The New York Times* began a generally negative account with an ominous reference to President Lyndon B. Johnson, "who insisted on having almost absolute control over what to bomb and when to bomb it" (Myers 1999a). When reporters discussed civil-military relations at the top, it was to contrast, almost always unfavorably, the tense relationships between Secretary of Defense William Cohen, Chairman of the Joint Chiefs of Staff General Henry Shelton and General Wesley Clark, Supreme Allied Commander Europe, with the closer relationships between Secretary Dick Cheney and Generals Powell and Schwarzkopf (Myers and Schmitt 1999). Interestingly, and despite the critical account of civil-military relations in that war, the Kosovo conflict ended by evicting Serb forces from that unhappy province, as desired, without a single American combat casualty. The Serb dictator who had provoked American intervention fell from power, in contrast to his Iraqi counterpart who had, in the decade since the Gulf War, wriggled out from under the sanctions regime that was supposed to bring his rule to an end.

The Historical Record vs. the Normal Theory

Does military history really bear out the "normal" theory of civil-military relations, as President Bush believed? If the normal theory of civil-military relations were valid, one would expect the most successful war efforts to be characterized by the kind of civilian remoteness from military operational decision-making that it prescribes. This is not, in fact, the case. Indeed, it is precisely those cases in which the military has had the freest hand—Germany in World War I and Japan in World War II—that have produced the greatest ruin to a state. And ruin has stemmed not simply from political and hence strategic errors, but from egregious operational blunders as well. The catalogue of mistakes that emerge from military considerations untrammeled not only by political considerations, but by the sober scrutiny of mere common sense, is a large one. Thus, Germany's naval staff launched unrestricted submarine warfare against Great Britain in 1917 with a handful of submarines capable of operations in the North Atlantic, misjudging completely the ability of Great Britain to control losses by using of convoys, substituting for certain imports, and outbuilding the merchant-ship sinkings that it suffered, not to mention the calamitous effects, for Germany, of bringing the United States into the war (Herwig 1997). No less notorious was the Schlieffen Plan, by which Germany attempted to win the war in 1914 with a single throw of the dice. In World War II the Japanese military, obsessed with the big battle, ignored the importance of waging war against the tenuous American lines of communication to Australia and the South Pacific, and neglected, until too late, the imperative of fortifying the ring of islands it hoped to hold against American counterthrusts.

Nor have democratic militaries done much better when civilian leadership has failed to probe their technique, and test their assumptions. All of the militaries in World War I operated, to a remarkable degree, free of civilian constraints, yet, to a depressing degree, the generals of that war proved themselves incapable of changing their mental frameworks and patterns of command to adapt to the circumstances of trench warfare. Whether it was General John Pershing deprecating the need for even such essential tools of trench warfare as light machine guns, or British generals hoarding masses of cavalry for a breakthrough that never came, or French generals hurling masses of brightly clad men across open ground, the catalogue of general officer–induced errors—gross and even grotesque misjudgments about how to wage war—is no less impressive than that of politicians (Millett 1986, 235–256).

Nor were such errors peculiar to the first World War, for they recurred in the second. The U.S. Army Air Forces in World War II clung to a doctrine of unescorted precision bombing that dissolved in the slaughter over the skies of the Third Reich. The Army Ground Forces invested heavily in a technology and a concept—the tank destroyer—that failed miserably. The British army struggled for years to devise an organization suitable for armored warfare. In more recent times, the Israeli military in 1967 and afterwards has operated with remarkably little civilian oversight of its professional activities. Yet the dazzling campaigns of that war, shaped largely by a professional general staff, not only exceeded the goals set by civilian authority (who wished a halt at the Sinai passes, not along the Suez Canal); they paved the way, in some measure, for the disastrous war that followed only six years later. In that latter conflict the leaders of the Israel Defense Forces, clinging to an obsolete doctrine that scorned infantry and even, in some measure, artillery, in favor of tanks and jet aircraft, fell victim to their own arrogance as Egyptian and Syrian forces surprised the IDF and dealt it humiliating defeats in the first days of the 1973 War.

For Americans, much of the argument about "meddling" or "micromanagement" reflects the real or remembered experience of the Vietnam War. In that conflict, President Lyndon Johnson did indeed control the selection of targets in North Vietnam. However, as Mark Clodfelter has pointed out, the Joint Chiefs of Staff ultimately got most of the points they wished to hit (Clodfelter 1989, 203–210). What is often forgotten is how little scrutiny politicians gave the war in South Vietnam, which they left very largely in the hands of the American military, and in particular the commander of American forces there, General William Westmoreland. It was a military, not a civilian, decision to wage attritional warfare resting on the concept of search and destroy; indeed, the first critiques of the Vietnam War by military officers tacitly acknowledged just that point. Military operational concepts—especially Westmoreland's attritional strategy of killing more Communist guerrillas and soldiers than the other side could replace—were often proven wrong, particularly from the broadest strategic point of view. Beyond this, the record suggests that the Joint Chiefs of Staff had no alternative operational conception beyond increased bombing of North Vietnam, a course that risked widening the war, and whose payoffs were unclear. The extraordinarily rapid build-up of American forces in Vietnam from 1965 on—nearly 165,000 troops permanently stationed in a country with minimal infrastructure, nearly half a million within two years—bespeaks anything other than timid civilian incrementalism. Micro-management of the air war in the North—where the international political stakes were so much higher—certainly occurred, although its effects remain a matter of dispute; it is less accurate to say the same of the more complex struggle in the South.

Lincoln Finds a General

If the normal theory of civil-military relations is suspect, what have been the successful practices of the past? To begin with, effective war statesmen have acted well beyond the minimal roles assigned to them by the normal theory of civil-military relations, viz. the setting of purpose, the approval of action, and the termination of conflict. Success in the waging of war seems to have been accompanied by a great deal of crossing of the civil-military gap by politicians probing, testing, haranguing, and manipulating their military subordinates about technical matters as well as strategic ones. It has begun, however, with the selection and control of military leaders, a process far more complicated than one might think. A number of cases illustrate the point.

Abraham Lincoln's trials with his generals, beginning with his struggles with the self-pitying, operationally timorous, vainglorious commander of the Army of the Potomac from the summer of 1861 through the fall of 1862, Major General George McClellan, have assumed something of the status of parables. (Indeed, when a White House official in 1991 compared General Norman Schwarzkopf, the theater commander in the Persian Gulf, to McClellan, Schwarzkopf exploded in fury: he understood perfectly the implied aspersions on his competence and subordination to civilian authority.) The story of McClellan, and the corresponding rise of Ulysses S. Grant, who suffered from neither his predecessor's overweening ego nor his reluctance for battle, has led many authors to define Lincoln's achievement as a war president as a task chiefly, though not exclusively, of finding the man who could get the job done (Basler 1955, VII:324; Williams 1952, 7–8, 13). However, the closer one examines the record, the more difficult it becomes to sustain the thesis that the problem of high command in the Civil War boiled down to the problem of merely finding a general, rather than guiding and directing the one Lincoln found. Lincoln did not have a competent cadre of generals at his disposal; indeed competence itself was and is a slippery term. Some of these men, such as McClellan, were excellent drill masters, suitable for organizing an army and teaching it the fundamentals of its business, but no more. Others could provide outstanding service, but only in particular tasks (cavalry raiding, for example) or particular operational contexts (e.g., the defense). When the war came, none of them (with the possible exception of General Winfield Scott, the octogenarian commander of the Army in 1860) had the comprehensive military experience Lincoln required. Still others would show their talents only after a series of errors and mishaps that called their abilities into question. This is most notably true of Sherman and Grant. The former's mental instability, the latter's alcoholic bouts and failure on the first day at Shiloh, raised doubts about their military qualities that took some time to dispel. In considering his generals, Lincoln had to develop his own military judgment in order to know which personal traits and military failures to ignore, and which bespoke a fundamental lack of fitness for the job.

From the first Lincoln tended not to order, but to question, prod, and suggest. He did this, however, after soliciting military advice from various sources. He queried junior officers about the possibility of relieving Fort Sumter; he consulted General Scott after the latter's replacement by George McClellan; and he turned often to General Ethan Allen Hitchcock, grandson of the Revolutionary War hero Ethan Allen, and former inspector general of Scott's army in Mexico.

Lincoln also learned directly about the conduct of military operations from personal observation and interviews with senior military leaders. In July of 1862, for example, he visited the Army of the Potomac on the Peninsula, questioning McClellan and his chief subordinates on the army's health, morale, and operational prospects (Basler 1955, V:309–312). He repeated such visits to the front on a number of occasions, including in October of that year after the battle of Antietam and in April of 1863 before General Hooker's abortive Chancellorsville campaign as well as immediately thereafter. Although Lincoln often did not like what he heard—he warned Hooker of the cliques that had formed among the senior generals of the Army of the Potomac—the president thereby kept his finger on the army's pulse (Basler 1955, VI:217). On occasion he acted on the advice of subordinate generals, as when he imposed a corps-level organization on an unwilling George McClellan, who preferred not to see such an aggregation of divisional commands below him (Epstein 1991, 21–46).

Perhaps most interesting of all Lincoln's mechanisms of control was his reliance on Charles Dana, Assistant Secretary of War, as a personal observer of Union armies in the field. Dana, former assistant managing editor (and one-fifth owner) of the *New York Tribune* when the war broke out, was summoned in March 1863 by Stanton (who often acted at Lincoln's behest in such matters) and given a mission. The Secretary of War informed Dana that he and the president wanted such information "as would enable Mr. Lincoln and himself to settle their minds as to Grant, about whom at that time there were many doubts, and against whom there was some complaint" (Dana 1898, 20). Stanton would provide Dana with a cover assignment as "special commissioner of the War Department to investigate the pay service of the Western armies, but your real duty will be to report to me every day what you see," for which Dana used a private cipher. Dana went west to Grant, who wisely hid nothing from him, despite the misgivings of Grant's staff. In short order Dana became attached to Grant and, in fact, became one of his most articulate defenders in Washington.

Dana's training as a journalist made him a superb tool for the purposes that Lincoln and Stanton had in mind. A regular and faithful correspondent, he sent depictions of battle that were both accurate and evocative. Even more valuable, however, was his ability to read character. Thus he described Major General William S. Rosecrans at Chattanooga:

It is my duty to declare that while few persons exhibit more estimable social qualities, I have never seen a public man possessing talent with less administrative power, less clearness and steadiness in difficulty, and greater practical incapacity than General Rosecrans. He has inventive fertility and knowledge, but he has no strength of will and no concentration of purpose. His mind scatters; there is no system in the use of his busy days and restless nights, no courage against individuals in his composition, and, with great love of command, he is a feeble commander. He is conscientious and honest, just as he is imperious and disputatious; always with a stray vein of caprice and an overweening passion for the approbation of his personal friends and the public outside. Under the present circumstances I consider this army to be very unsafe in his hands; but do know of no man except Thomas who could now be safely put in his place. Weather pleasant but cloudy (Dana 1898, XXX:215).

Even after Grant had won Lincoln's and Stanton's trust, the president kept Dana attached to Grant's headquarters, reporting back on the Union general's movements. That Dana had become by this time a great backer of Grant did not diminish his usefulness. Not only did he remain an acute recorder of military operations, with a journalist's pen and a senior government official's access; as a sympathetic observer he provided Grant insight into the political environment in which the general had to operate. For example, Dana bluntly warned General Rawlins, Grant's chief of staff, of "the interior truth" of the political realities in the summer of 1864, following a bloody campaign that had cost 70,000 casualties, and that had left the capital undefended against a Confederate raid. Although the fault for many of the disasters that had befallen the army were the faults of Generals Benjamin Butler and George Meade, Grant, as general-in-chief, had received criticism for failing to relieve either: "That is true & there is no answer to it" (Simon 1967, 253).

As the end of the war approached, Lincoln maintained a close oversight of Grant's activities. On March 3, 1865, he gave Grant strict instructions, again through Stanton, that he was to "have no conference with General Lee, unless it be for the capitulation of Lee's army or on solely minor and purely military matters. . . . You are not to decide, discuss, or confer upon any political questions. Such questions the President holds in his own hands; and will submit them to no military conferences or conventions. Meanwhile you are to press to the utmost, your military advantages" (Basler 1955, VIII:330–331). The president's concern was far from theoretical. A few days after Lincoln's death, on April 18, 1865, Sherman agreed to extremely generous surrender terms for General Joseph Johnston's army, the last major Confederate force in existence. The terms of the agreement included such provisions as the recognition by the U.S. government of the Southern state governments, that conflicting claims to state power would be submitted to the Supreme Court, full political rights for all Southerners, and a general amnesty—all policies not countenanced by the administration (Sherman 1990, 842–866). Grant promptly instructed Sherman to revoke the armistice agreement, and Secretary of War Stanton administered a public repudiation that left Sherman so outraged that he publicly refused to shake Stanton's hand in Washington at the Grand Review of the Armies a month later (Dana 1898, 290).

Lincoln, then, did not merely "find" Grant and turn the war over to him. Rather, down to the last days of his life, Lincoln exercised a constant oversight and control, often using indirect means, and in particular working through the Secretary of War, Stanton, and chief of staff General Henry Halleck, while monitoring Grant's activities through Dana's reports. Lincoln did not shy from calling Grant's attention to operational and command problems, particularly during Jubal Early's march on Washington in 1864 (Basler 1955, VII:476). An extraordinarily subtle and sophisticated politician, the president did not engage in harangues or personal confrontation, and he exploited a seeming rusticity and simplicity with the guile that those who knew him best remarked on as a distinguishing characteristic.

Clemenceau Pays a Visit

Successful civilian war statesmen select leaders, and in so doing often probe deeply into the actual conduct of war. As the case of Lincoln suggests, their task is far from over even after they have "found their general." Georges Clemenceau, prime minister of France during World War I, had to handle two outstanding military leaders—Ferdinand Foch and Henri Pétain—who had risen through the rigors of more than three years of war. Foch, an audacious and indomitable commander, had contributed to the ruinous offense-mindedness of the French Army before the war, but had redeemed himself through a combination of tenacity and remarkable good sense in dealing with his British allies. Pétain—dour, pessimistic, mistrustful of Englishmen and Americans—was the better tactician, one of the inventors of the system of defense in depth that dominated the Western Front in 1917–18, the hero of Verdun, and a general who knew how restore order to an army racked by mutiny (Miquel 1996; Mordacq 1930).

Neither general alone could have brought France victory during the period from November of 1917, when Clemenceau became prime minister, until the war's end, almost exactly a year later. Foch and his disciples rejected Pétain's doctrine of defense-in-depth, believing that France should not cede one more hectare of French soil to the German invader. Pétain, for his part, deplored the resumption of the offensive in the summer of 1918, following the collapse of German offensives that spring. As it turned out, both men had a point, but on these and other matters their professional differences were deep and only partly reconcilable.

To arbitrate between the two, but above all to learn how the war was going, Clemenceau began a remarkable series of trips to the front lines, usually traveling to the trenches at least once a week, and often twice, often coming within several hundred meters of the enemy (Mordacq 1939, 128ff). Accompanied by his military chef de cabinet, General Jean Jules Henri Mordacq (himself a military intellectual and successful division commander), Clemenceau saw for himself, interviewed military leaders, and prodded the army to purge senior ranks still filled with an older and now very weary generation of general officers (Mordaq 1930, 72ff). Even when Clemenceau believed that he had finally found in Foch the right general to serve as supreme allied commander and bring the war to a successful conclusion, Clemenceau did not relax his attention. In very short order Clemenceau found himself confronted by a generalissimo who had his own views about how the war should conclude, and the terms on which peace with Germany should be made. Like Lincoln in this respect, but faced with a far less docile general than Grant, Clemenceau eventually prevented Foch from undermining the policies of the government in the name of military necessity (King 1960). For him, as for Lincoln, "finding a general" was not the end of the story, not least because of the way in which successful generals become political figures of enormous importance in their own right.

Churchill Asks a Question

If managing generals is one of the great tasks of civilian war leadership, so too is the management of risk. Winston Churchill's tenure as prime minister during World War II reveals this side of war statesmanship, and with it a very different technique of war leadership. Churchill, as his generals often complained, kept a close eye on many matters of military detail, including the scrutiny of exercises as well as actual operations. An illustrative case is that of VICTOR, an anti-invasion exercise conducted from January 22 to 25, 1941, under the auspices of the commander of Home Forces, General Alan Brooke. At that time, Britain had no major ally on the continent of Europe and, having staved off the Germans in the Battle of Britain the previous summer and early fall, was expecting a renewal of the onslaught come spring. Britain was, at the same time, mounting counteroffensives in Greece and the Middle East.

On March 30, 1941, Churchill sent a detailed query to General Hastings Ismay, secretary to the Chiefs of Staff:

I presume the details of this remarkable feat [the anti-invasion exercise] have been worked out by the Staff concerned. Let me see them. For instance, how many ships and transports carried these five Divisions? How many Armoured vehicles did they comprise? How many motor lorries, how many guns, how much ammunition, how many men, how many tons of stores, how far did they advance in the first 48 hours, how many men and vehicles were assumed to have landed in the first 12 hours, what percentage of loss were they debited with? What happened to the transports and store-ships while the first 48 hours of fighting was going on? Had they completed emptying their cargoes, or were they still lying in shore off the beaches? What naval escort did they have? Was the landing at this point protected by a superior enemy daylight Fighter formations? How many Fighter airplanes did the enemy have to employ, if so, to cover the landing places? (Prime Minister's Office 1941, 114.1)

Brooke replied on April 7, giving the figures demanded by Churchill, including estimates of relatively light enemy loss rates, plus the curious assumption that the Germans could sustain themselves with petrol and food captured on British soil. Churchill responded a few weeks later, noting that the exercise gave the Germans credit for far fewer logistical difficulties than the British had recently faced in conducting unopposed landings in Greece, and continued to press his inquiries (Prime Minister's Office 1941, 136.1). The exchange about the anti-invasion exercise continued until mid-May. This episode tells much about Churchill's manner of dealing with his subordinates: a relentless querying of their assumptions and arguments, not just once but in successive iterations of a debate. It is noteworthy that the commander in charge of the exercise, Brooke, responded to the prime minister's arguments and requests for information point by point: he provided the data but yielded stubbornly, if at all, on the assessment. Not only did Brook not suffer by standing up to Churchill, but he ultimately gained promotion to the post of Chief of the Imperial General Staff and chairman of the Chiefs of Staff Committee.

Churchill's central concern was not so much Exercise VICTOR itself, as how it would shape decision-making. "It is of course quite reasonable for assumptions of this character to be made as a foundation for a military exercise. It would be indeed a darkening counsel to make them the foundation of serious military thought" (Prime Minister's Office 1941, 136.1). At this very time, the Chiefs of Staff were debating the dispatch of armored vehicles to the Middle East. Churchill was arguing—against the position of several of his military advisors (including the Chief of the Imperial General Staff, Field Marshal Sir John Dill)—that the risks of invasion were sufficiently low to make the convoy worth the attempt.

The convoy went through, losing only one ship to a mine and delivering some 250 tanks to the hard-pressed forces in the Middle East. There was no "sound military judgment" that could be offered about whether the British could spare those tanks for the Middle East; it was, rather, a matter of risk, and as such, required a political decision. To know whether the risks were acceptable, Churchill had no choice but to delve into the details of military calculations, and to do that, he had to find out whether VICTOR was soundly rooted. Nor was he probing merely to establish the probabilities in his own mind. As in most war situations, a committee would deliberate although one man would decide; even those on the other side of the decision needed to believe that the risks, even if high, were not outrageous.

Ben Gurion Holds a Seminar

Yet another task of supreme command in war is assessing the health and effectiveness of military organizations: their aptitude for the tasks before them. Of this few better examples can be given—and with it, yet another technique of civilian control—than that of David Ben Gurion, Israel's first prime minister and defense minister, in the period shortly before the creation of the state of Israel. Ben Gurion, who assumed in December 1946 the "security portfolio" of the Israeli shadow government, had no particular background in military affairs; he had served as an unruly corporal in the British army at the end of World War I with the objective of furthering the Zionist project. He was, however, the leading figure not only in the largest labor party in Palestine, but the *de facto* head of the Jewish Agency, the shadow government of the Jews of Palestine. Since the 1920s the Jews of Palestine had constructed a remarkably elaborate defense organization, the *Haganah*, which included an effective intelligence service, an elite striking force, and a general staff.

From the end of March to the end of May 1947, Ben Gurion conducted what became known in the history of the *Haganah* as "the seminar." For two months he suspended his normal duties and instead undertook systematically to interview the high command of the *Haganah*, and many subordinate officers as well. Writing slowly in his diary, which he kept as a kind of ledger of his deliberations, he probed all the facets of the *Haganah*'s activities: the quality of commanders, the nature of training, the state of equipment, the position of the budget, the structure of the high command, the quality of intelligence collection. Underlying Ben Gurion's inquiry lay a simple, massive, and as it turned out, entirely correct political premise: that the upcoming confrontation between Jews and Arabs would not, as in the disturbances of 1921, 1929, and 1936–39, be a contest with gangs of Palestinian Arab villagers or clansmen, but instead with the Arab states (Ben-Gurion 1993, 150). Ben Gurion's judgment at the end of the seminar was typically harsh and direct: the *Haganah* was profoundly unsuited for the challenge looming ahead: "I know that I am saying very hard things. In my heart are even harder views, and I speak therefore the minimum. . . . We have to start everything virtually afresh, because the Arab front is becoming serious, and it is no longer a front of bandits."

The *Haganah* had been a generally successful adaptation to one problem: the threat posed by the Palestinian Arabs, in both organized units and as gangs of marauders, to the security of Jewish settlements. This very success, however, had in many ways rendered it unfit for the challenges of the future, and not least because its leadership refused to admit the fundamental differences in the nature of the future threat. Ben Gurion realized that the *Haganah*'s scale was all wrong: its leaders thought in terms of platoons, not brigades (Ben Gurion 1993, 159). Its support functions, such as static radio networks, were designed to support guerrilla warfare, not conventional mobile operations (Ben Gurion 1993, 176). Its prejudice against British trained officers, and its sheer bureaucratic incompetence, had caused it to fail to tap the experience of some 25,000 men who had served in the British military during World War II (Avidar 1977, 12–13).

By the summer of 1947 it was clear that the climactic struggle was at hand: Ben Gurion restructured the high command of the *Haganah*, dismissing some of its leaders and reaching out to veterans of the British army, whom he promoted to senior positions. He accelerated the programs for mobilization and acquisition upon which the military structure of a potential Jewish state would rest. Although hardly ready for the quasi-war that broke out in November 1947, by May 1948, when formal independence arrived, Israel was ready—if barely—to conduct war against neighboring Arab states.

The Problem of Military Professionalism

These tasks of civilian supreme command—selecting and monitoring generals, adjudicating their differences, managing risk, assessing organizational health and intervening to restore it—go far beyond what the normal theory of civil-military relations would seem to require. Statesman rarely discharge these tasks by means of fiat, but rather by the more indirect tactics described above. Direct orders are not unknown, of course, as when President Franklin D. Roosevelt simply ordered his military chiefs to undertake the North African campaign of 1942, despite their strenuous opposition to it as a diversion that could delay—fatally, perhaps—the ultimate liberation of continental Europe.

According to the normal theory, the practices described above should have led to disaster. To be sure, in all except exceptional cases, they did not involve the direct issuance of orders to soldiers to engage in particular tactical or operational activities, but they involved an intrusive scrutiny and set of interactions that ran counter to all that the normal theory would seem to require. One might, of course, say that the men involved were political exceptions, geniuses whose other virtues compensated for their vices of interference in military affairs, but we can be fairly certain that they, at least, viewed their interventions as central to their tasks of war leadership. A more extended argument than room permits here suggests that they were right (Cohen 2001, forthcoming).

It is more likely that there is a flaw in the concept of professionalism embedded in the normal theory of civil-military relations, a flaw that makes its prescriptions unworkable or dangerous. For although officership is a profession, it differs in many respects from all others: in some of the most important respects it does not at all resemble medicine or the law. Indeed, the Huntingtonian construct represents a concept of professionalism, prevalent in the 1950s, but since challenged in many spheres as unrealistically pristine: "incomprehensibility to laymen, rather than rationality, is the foundation of professionalism," in the acid words of a scholar writing in the more cynical 1970s (Layton 1971, 4; Parsons 1968, 536–557). Officership varies in a number of important ways from other professions. Unlike law, medicine, or engineering, it binds its members to only one employer, the state, and has only one fundamental form, the large service branch. But other differences are more important, particularly those bearing on the ends of the professional activity and the nature of expertise involved.

All professional activities present difficulties of moral choice and ultimate purpose to those who practice them. The wrenching choices facing a physician involved in the treatment of terminally ill patients are well known; so too are the ethical dilemmas of a lawyer who becomes privy to knowledge of a client's criminal activities. But by and large in the professions of law and medicine, on which the classical conception of professionalism is based, the ultimate goals are fairly straightforward. They are, for the doctor, to cure patients of their diseases, or at least to alleviate the pain they suffer. For the lawyer they are, at least within the American legal system, to achieve the best possible result, be it acquittal, maximum financial redress, or some other result for the client.

The soldier's ultimate purposes are altogether hazier: they are, as Clausewitz and others insist, the achievement of political ends designated by statesmen. But because political objectives are just that—political—they are often ambiguous, contradictory, and uncertain. It is one of the greatest sources of frustration for soldiers that their political masters find it difficult (or worse from the soldiers' point of view, merely inconvenient) to elaborate fully in advance the purposes for which they have invoked military action, or the conditions under which they intend to limit or terminate it. The "professional" concept of military activity, moreover, depicts political purpose in war as a matter of purely foreign policy; and yet in practice the "high" politics of war is suffused as well with "low" or domestic politics. A Lincoln wants a victory at Atlanta in the summer of 1864 in order to crush the Confederacy, but also to boost his own chances of re-election, which in turn is necessary for the ultimate victory of the Union. A Roosevelt, dismissing all professional advice, orders an invasion of North Africa in 1942 rather than a landing in France in 1943 in order to keep the public committed to a strategy of "Europe First" (although, in retrospect, the course recommended by his military advisors would most likely have proven tactically ruinous). A Johnson limits air attacks on Hanoi and Haiphong in 1965–68 in part to limit the chances that China will enter the war, but also to preserve his ability to launch the Great Society.

The traditional conception of military professionalism assumes that it is possible to separate an autonomous area of military science from political purpose (Huntington 1957, 56, 255). But this sharp separation breaks down in practice. Consider the question confronted by the Allies in the late summer and fall of 1944: whether to advance on a wide front in France and the Low Countries, or to concentrate scarce resources behind a northern thrust along the French, Belgian, and Dutch coast directed by a British general, or instead to devote them to a southern thrust into central Germany directed by an American general. One might say that there was a military "best answer," assuming that the ultimate objective was the quickest defeat of Germany. But in fact the political objectives were far more complex than that: they involved questions of cost in lives and treasure, minimization of damage to Allied civilian populations, including Londoners under threat from V-2 missile launchers in Holland, and matters of national prestige. These were not political modifications to a "military" objective of defeating Germany, but essential to it. "The distinction between politics and strategy diminishes as the point of view is raised," Churchill noted after World War I. "At the summit true politics and strategy are one" (Churchill 1923, 6).

That the good military officer requires a technical expertise no one would deny. But is it indeed true, as Huntington argues, that "the peculiar skill of the military officer is universal" across time, nationality, and place? The qualifications of a good North Vietnamese infantry officer in Indochina in 1965 would surely have differed in some important respects from those of a good American officer opposing him. The Vietnamese would have needed a ruthless disregard for his own men's suffering and casualties that would have rendered an American not merely morally unfit to command, but a likely candidate for assassination by his own men. He could easily have remained ignorant of large areas of technical knowledge (for example, the employment of close air support, or planning procedures for heliborne movements) that the American required.

More than one author has suggested that the American failure in Vietnam stemmed at least in part from the stubborn resistance of American officers to adjust their conception of professionalism to the peculiarities of the war before them (Krepinevich 1986). And American leaders have found themselves baffled by unconventional opponents like Somalia's Muhammed Farah Aideed who, in turn, have adroitly executed a style of warfare that exploits the American military's conception of what it is to be "a professional" (Bacevich 1995, 50–63).

The assumption that, in the last two centuries at any rate, apolitically professional armies are better armies requires, at the very least, some qualification. The more research that is done on one of the most formidable fighting machines of all time, the German *Wehrmacht*, the greater appears the role of ideology in motivating its soldiers in battle (Bartov 1991; Förster 1983, 413–447; Holmes 1985, 281–90). For a generation after World War II, scholars attributed the fighting abilities of the Germans in World War II to neutral professional characteristics, such as small-unit cohesion and careful selection and recruitment of officers and non-commissioned officers (Shils and Janowitz 1948; 1975; Van Creveld 1982). More prolonged and careful investigation, however, has revealed that the permeation of the German army by Nazi ideology made it a better fighting force. Not only did it instill in a large proportion of its men a fanatic determination to fight; it also contributed indirectly to the maintenance of tactical effectiveness. The ruthlessness of the Nazis allowed for the harshest possible repression of dissent or doubt, including the execution of 15,000 of their own soldiers during World War II (Bartov 1991, 96). The Hitler *Jugend* provided a reserve of junior officers and leaders, while Nazi ideology reinforced the central virtues of military leadership, including selflessness, physical courage, and initiative (Förster 1986, III:180–220). Perhaps the greatest proof of the contribution of ideology lies in the record of the units of the Waffen SS, which by war's end constituted no less than a quarter of Germany's army, and which repeatedly turned in an outstanding fighting performance. Of Theodor Eicke, the leader of the *Totenkopf* (Death's Head) Division, one of the most successful Waffen SS divisions, one historian notes: "Eicke's style of leadership differed little in practice from the methods he had used to administer the prewar concentration camp system. . . . What he lacked in formal training, imagination, and finesse, he attempted to overcome through diligence, energy, and a constant effort to master the baffling technical intricacies of mechanized war" (Sydnor 1977, 274). Eicke was a successful military leader not in spite of those characteristics that would have earned him trial for his numerous crimes against humanity had he survived the war, but *because* of them.

Nor is the German experience unique. Ideological armies—the Chinese People's Liberation Army, the international brigades in the Spanish Civil War, and the pre-independence Jewish Palestinian *Palmach* are all examples—have often turned in superior tactical performances against larger and better equipped regular forces. The ideologically motivated fighter may make a good junior officer: he often embodies the self-sacrifice, integrity, and drive that leaders of soldiers in battle require. More than a few higher-level commanders motivated by ideology have also demonstrated high orders of ability.[1]

If the content of military professionalism is, as Huntington contends, the "management of violence," it is a definition that excludes large areas of military activity (logistics, for example) that often have considerable civilian analogues and yet are indispensable to military operations (Huntington 1957, 11; 1963, 785). Many of these skills are readily transferable to or from the civilian world: it is no accident that the U.S. Army's chief logistician in the Persian Gulf became, immediately upon retirement, a successful executive at Sears, nor that the military rapidly promoted civilian executives to high military rank during the World Wars. Moreover, although all serious modern military organizations devote a great deal of effort to schooling and training, history is replete with examples of soldiers taken up from civilian life who very quickly master the essentials of military affairs. Even more common are great soldiers who spend only brief periods of their life in regular military organizations, and then flourish in times of actual war. General Sir John Monash, one of the best generals of World War I, was a civil engineer whose pre-war experience consisted solely of militia duty. Yet he rose to command perhaps the most formidable of all Allied units, the Australian Imperial Force (Falkus 1976, 134–143). There are hardly any accounts of self-taught or part-time doctors and engineers performing so well.

Military professionalism is contingent, much as business management is. The brilliant entrepreneur may prove utterly unable to cope with the problems of running the corporations their creative genius brought into the world. The skilled manager of a long-established, high-technology firm like IBM would probably find it difficult to assume equal responsibilities in an entertainment company like Disney. There is, to be sure, enough commonality in management experience to make it plausible to put a former manufacturer of repeating rifles in charge of a large ice cream company (Ben & Jerry's), but that does not guarantee success.

---

1. Examples are the outstanding Israeli commander of the 1948 War of independence, Yigal Allon, who had been commander of the *Palmach*, and Leon Trotsky, the Russian Revolution's "organizer of victory."

Indeed, the ruthless churning of higher management in many companies reflects what might be thought of as "wartime" conditions—a ceaseless turnover of executives who are unfit for their tasks or exhausted by their previous work. This should not surprise us, for in some sense businesses fight their "wars" every day, unlike military organizations.

This observation suggests a deeper problem with the notion that expertise in the management of violence is the essence of the military profession. While lawyers continually appear in court or draw up legal instruments, doctors routinely operate, diagnose, or prescribe medication, and engineers build bridges or computers, soldiers very rarely manage violence. They prepare to manage violence, they anticipate its requirements, they study past uses of violence, they practice in simulations, but they very rarely engage in the central activity that defines their profession (Hamilton 1921, 25). Many and perhaps most officers spend entire military careers without participating in a real war. Even those who do fight in wars do so for very small portions of their careers, and very rarely occupy the same job in more than one conflict. A lawyer may try hundreds of cases, or a doctor treat hundreds or even thousands of medical problems of an essentially similar type during the course of several decades; a soldier will usually have only one chance to serve in a particular position. There are few generals who have had the experience of being divisional or corps commanders—let alone theater commanders or chiefs of general staffs—in more than one war. As a result then, particularly at the beginning of a war, a country's most senior leaders—nominally, the most seasoned veterans—are in a professional position as close to that of the novice lawyer or doctor as to that of senior partner in a law firm or the chief surgeon in a hospital.

The lack of practice military people have in their profession at the highest level is but one factor that accounts for the astounding and by no means infrequent catastrophic errors made by competent military organizations (Cohen and Gooch 1990). These calamities stem not from incompetence as normally understood, but from the features that make the waging of war different from other professions: the distorting psychological effects of fear, hatred, and the desire of glory; the nature of a reacting opponent; and the absence of rules that bound the activity concerned. Moreover, as Clausewitz observed, "every war is rich in unique episodes. Each is an uncharted sea, full of reefs" (Clausewitz 1911, I:7, 120). Each age has its "own theory of war, even if the urge had always and universally existed to work things out on scientific principles" (Clausewitz 1911, 120, VIII:3, 593). Under these circumstances statesmen must work with their military subordinates in an unequal and uneasy partnership: unequal because free government requires it, and uneasy because political leaders will always trespass upon what the military conceives to be its prerogatives and area of expertise. Submitting to a thousand questions may prove more difficult for a general than accepting a single ill-conceived order. The unequal dialogue offers the promise of success, but the certainty of friction.

The Unequal Dialogue

One might still contend that the successful war statesmen described above, because they were geniuses, could meddle and interfere without damaging the forces under their command; but that the normal run of politicians would only breed disaster by so doing. Perhaps, although disaster may lurk on either side. When President Truman deferred to the advice of his military advisors in permitting an advance beyond the 38th parallel in Korea during the fall of 1950, he was largely accepting the implications of the normal theory of civil-military relations. When, in his sole conference with Douglas MacArthur about what would happen if the Chinese intervened in the war—"there will be the greatest slaughter" by American air power, MacArthur assured him—he was also heeding the dicta of the normal theory, accepting a technical military judgment. Disaster followed the next month because the military advisors themselves had systematically and thoroughly underestimated the fighting potential of the People's Liberation Army, notwithstanding the shock administered by earlier clashes with the leading units of the PLA operating in North Korea (Cohen and Gooch 1990, 165–196).

Truman had the right, indeed, the obligation to subject his military leaders to the kind of detailed scrutiny that American, French, British, and Israeli generals endured in the cases described above. In the same way, Lyndon Johnson and Robert McNamara failed as war leaders not so much because they micro-managed the war, but because they failed to manage it properly. They failed, in the words of Robert McNamara's remarkable, self-excoriating memoir, to create "what Churchill called a War Cabinet." It was this failure to "debate systematically the most fundamental issues," to review assumptions about military operations and their probabilities of success, that he identified as a critical failing of his and President Johnson's war leadership (McNamara 1995, 332; McMaster 1997). General Bruce Palmer, one of the senior Army commanders in Indochina, agreed that this lack of open debate was one of the critical failures in senior leadership—civilian as well as military—during the war (Palmer 1984, 35).

The Gulf War of 1991 has shaped much of contemporary American thinking about civil-military relations in wartime. The public face of the war was, as we have seen, one in which the military had a free hand in the formation of strategy, with a strong civilian leader making the difficult but relatively simple decisions: that there would be a war, what that war would be about, how to build the coalition and finance the effort, and when the war would end. Beyond this, according to the common narrative of the conflict, the civilian leadership of the Defense Department did little beyond mobilizing resources for the fight. The military, on the other hand, seems to have planned and executed its operations with near complete autonomy. It seems, in another words, like a war fought very much according to the tenets of the normal theory of civil-military relations.

The truth is considerably different. It is clear, for example, that the leadership of the military, rather than serving merely as loyal executors of a broader policy, had their own distinct views—strongly argued—about whether there should be a war at all. So much is at least to be inferred from a curious book by *Washington Post* editor Bob Woodward, who appears to have had privileged access to Chairman of the Joint Chiefs of Staff Colin Powell—and to his doubts—before the war (Woodward 1991; Gordon and Trainor 1995). Civilian leadership, in the form of Secretary of Defense Dick Cheney, made efforts to bypass the professional advice he was getting from General Powell, leading to at least one dramatic confrontation between Powell and Cheney's military aide, Rear Admiral William Owens. The supposedly simple political objectives laid out by President Bush—the protection of American citizens in the Gulf, the expulsion of Iraqi forces from Kuwait, the restoration of the legitimate government of that country, and the assurance of the security and stability of the Persian Gulf—turn out to have been far more complex than the normal theory of civil-military relations would allow. The objective of protection of Americans—a reflection of the initial Iraqi seizure of Western hostages—had become irrelevant by the time the war began; the objective of restoration of legitimate government to Kuwait depended upon an understanding of what "legitimate" meant in the Kuwaiti context; and the objective of security and stability in the Gulf was so nebulous as to be meaningless. Meanwhile, at least two unstated objectives—the overthrow of Saddam Hussein's regime and the destruction of its stockpiles and industrial base for the manufacture of weapons of mass destruction—loomed larger as the war unfolded.

Political pressure was indeed felt by operational commanders: local air commanders felt a strong Washington-originated urging to attack Iraqi surface-to-surface missile sites that threatened Israel. An American general's public dismissal of these targets as "militarily insignificant" added one more irritant to an already difficult U.S.-Israeli relationship.

Similarly, it would appear that political concerns led to a ratcheting down of U.S. attacks on Baghdad shortly after the destruction of the al-Firdos bunker on February 13, 1991, which killed hundreds of family members of the Iraqi regime's ruling elite. Where attacks on Iraqi governmental targets, defense installations, and communications infrastructure in Baghdad had occurred nightly to this point, such attacks ceased for several days, and then only resumed on a severely limited scale to the end of the war.

In those cases, as others, the relationship between politicians and generals was further blurred by the preemptive nature of much of the political control that was exerted. General Colin Powell, a man of extraordinary political sophistication, anticipated much of the civil-military discourse by his actions. In theory, General Schwarzkopf, the theater commander, reported directly to the Secretary of Defense. In practice, all communications went through Powell, and in fact Secretary Cheney appears not to have spoken with Schwarzkopf at all during the war. Powell's political sense undoubtedly averted much of the friction that accompanies normal warmaking. But Powell's preemptive sensitivity to the concerns of civilian control had its adverse consequences as well, and not least in the way the war ended. A hasty telephone conversation between Powell and Schwarzkopf led to the decision to terminate the war well before the core of the Iraqi regime, the Republican Guard, had been destroyed rather than merely evicted from Kuwait (Gordon and Trainor 1995, 400–432). General Schwarzkopf received, it would appear, no civilian guidance whatsoever in conducting the armistice negotiations, and thus ceded to the Iraqis the discretion to use combat aviation, with which they subsequently crushed revolts against the regime by forces in the south and north of the country. The story of civil-military relations in the Gulf War is one not of harmony resting on a wise distribution of roles, but one of blurring and muddle, culminating in a remarkable collapse of civilian oversight. If the war was largely successful, as indeed it was, it stems as much from American and allied advantages poorly understood before the conflict, but which loom ever larger in retrospect. These include massive superiority in every aspect of military strength, from alliances to technology, training to sheer numbers (*Gulf War Air Power Survey* 1991–1993).

The Gulf War, then, represented not a demonstration of the virtues of the normal theory of civil-military relations but in some aspects only its appearance, and in others, its weaknesses. Subsequent uses of American military power in Yugoslavia and Somalia followed a similar pattern. American civilian decision-makers hesitated before demanding much of their military subordinates. Thus in 1992, after having denounced the passivity of the Bush administration in Yugoslavia, the Clinton administration was paralyzed by military estimates that it would take 400,000 troops or more to intervene in Bosnia (Scarborough 1992). When the Clinton administration did use American forces, there was virtually no cooperation and communication—let alone subordination—to a broader political effort. Indeed, Richard Holbrooke, America's chief negotiator in the Balkans in 1995, recalls that his military counterpart, Admiral Leighton Smith, viewed himself as an independent force: "he told me that he was 'solely responsible' for the safety and well-being of his forces, and he would make his decision, under authority delegated to him by the NATO Council, based on his own judgment. In fact, he pointed out, he did not even work for the United States: as a NATO commander he took orders from Brussels" (Holbrooke 1998, 118).

The Somalia intervention of 1993 was little better. A commitment of American forces under the auspices of the United Nations allowed for the pursuit of parallel and conflicting policies, which culminated in a disastrous attempt to kidnap a Somali warlord whose cooperation would have been essential to any stable arrangement in Mogadishu. Here too, civilian abdication, not military arrogance, was to blame. Deferring to a zealous UN high commissioner—an American—neither the president nor the Secretary of Defense regarded American forces operating in Mogadishu as forces fighting a war, albeit a low-level one, in which some effort should be made by national authority to harmonize ends and means.

The decline in the quality of American civil-military relations at the top has coincided with the emergence of an American military edge—technological, organizational, and quantitative—that stems from the extraordinary U.S. economy and the overall quality of U.S. armed forces. Yet even in successes such as the 1999 NATO war with Serbia led by an American general, Wesley Clark, the failure of political leaders and commanders to come to terms with one another has had deleterious consequences. The early declaration by the president that no ground forces would be sent to Kosovo—an error that virtually guaranteed a prolonged air campaign during which Serb forces could massacre the Albanian Kosovars at leisure—seems to have preceded rather than followed any strategic discussions with military leaders. Similarly, the unthinking recitation of the requirement for "force protection" as the first mission for American soldiers, ahead of any objective for which they might be put in harm's way, reflects an unwillingness to come to terms with what the use of force means—the error of reckless dissipation of strength having given way to an only slightly less reckless conservation of it (Smith 1999).

At one level, contemporary civil-military relations are smooth and easy; senior military leaders mix far more easily with their civilian superiors than they did in Lincoln's or even Churchill's day. They attend the same meetings of the Council on Foreign Relations and converse with equal ease on political if not on military subjects. This superficial harmony has even led some scholars to talk of a theory of concordance as a more attractive paradigm for civil-military relations (Schiff 1995, 7–24; Roman and Tarr 1999 and Chapter 11 in this volume).

When it comes to the use of force, however, the heart of sound civil-military relations remains now, as in the past, an unequal dialogue. The imperatives of politics and of military professionalism invariably, and appropriately, tug in opposite directions; inevitably too, professional judgments require scrutiny rather than unthinking acceptance. The most successful war statesmen adopted, as we have seen, different techniques for interacting with their military subordinates: Churchill's questioning, Ben Gurion's deep study, Lincoln's indirect monitoring, Clemenceau's first-hand inspection. In no case was the relationship without tension and even hostility. For their military subordinates this attention was clearly maddening. In the memoirs and diaries of men as different as the grim Chief of the Imperial General Staff, Field Marshal Alan Brooke, the fiery Marshal of France, Ferdinand Foch, and the scholarly young archaeologist turned soldier, Yigal Yadin, one sees tremendous frustration and resentment flaring up at civilian chiefs who imposed yet another burden on men already strained by the burdens of high command. On more than one occasion the senior military leaders prepared to tender their resignations, although, interestingly enough, these crises have been averted in almost all cases, if barely, and the anger has not been publicly revealed until after the war. The unequal dialogue rests on the willingness of senior officers to court dismissal by obdurately making their case to their civilian superiors. The Grants, Brookes, Fochs, and Yadins on more than one occasion told their political superiors that their favored schemes would not work. In no case did they pay more than a psychic penalty for the ensuing conversation; in most cases an intermediary whose job consisted primarily of liaison prevented relations from breaking down. This was often a military man, such as Clemenceau's Jean Mordacq, or Churchill's Hastings Ismay, but sometimes it was a civilian, such as Roosevelt's Harry Hopkins. Each of these men intervened at critical moments to soothe the anger or temper the resentments that a brutally candid but unequal dialogue engendered.

The precedent of the Gulf War is a particularly dangerous one. In the absence of experience of real war—one in which the other side can inflict damage, and has options—civilian and military decision-makers alike will forget the lessons of serious conflict. Those are, above all, that political leaders must immerse themselves in the conduct of war no less than they do in great projects of domestic legislation; that they must master their military briefs as thoroughly as they do their civilian ones; that they must demand and expect from their military subordinates a candor as bruising as it is necessary; that both groups must expect a running conversation in which, although civilian opinion will not dictate, it must dominate; that that conversation will include not only ends and policies, but ways and means. "Our highest civilian and military heads [must] be in close, even if not cordial, contact with each other" (Palmer 1984, 201). Statesmen must possess, not genius, but common sense and a willingness to probe: qualities that the great war leaders of the past possessed in exceptional degree, but which are no different in kind from those of modern political leaders.

A famous fictional general once remarked: ". . . do you recall what Clemenceau said about war? He said war was too important to be left to the generals. When he said that, fifty years ago, he might have been right. But today, war is too important to be left to politicians. They have neither the time, the training, nor the inclination for strategic thought."

The words, one suspects, would win approval from more than a few practitioners and observers of contemporary civil-military relations, at least until they realized that these are the words of the half-crazed General Jack D. Ripper in Stanley Kubrick's dark-comedy film, "Dr. Strangelove." There are a few if any General Rippers in the American military, but the sentiment surely persists, and indeed is even shared by some politicians.

Altogether wiser are the words of Aleksandr A. Svechin, veteran of the Russo-Japanese War and World War I, and leading thinker in the general staff of the Red Army until his death in Stalin's purges on the eve of World War II. "A politics that would renounce the retention of its authority over the leadership of a war and acknowledge the primacy of military specialists and silently conform to their requirements would itself acknowledge its own bankruptcy" (Svechin 1991, 145). If such words held true for the titanic struggles of the first half of this century, all the more should they do so for the more ambiguous but, on a smaller scale, no less sinister conflicts of the second half, and indeed the next century. In the words of an important but neglected book by Bernard Brodie: "The civil hand must never relax, and it must without one hint of apology hold the control that has always belonged to it by right" (Brodie 1973, 496).

Chapter 13

Conclusion:
The Gap and What It Means for American National Security

Peter D. Feaver
Richard H. Kohn

The studies presented in this book—and those commissioned by the project but published elsewhere—answer many of the most important questions raised in the lively debate over the nature of the civil-military culture gap: Does a gap exist? If so, what is its nature? What shapes the gap? And what are its implications for national defense, particularly military effectiveness and civil-military cooperation? In this conclusion, we review the findings of the TISS project, discussing each of these questions in turn, and then address critiques that have been raised since the TISS findings were first released in September 1999. We close with a set of policy recommendations that follow from our analysis.

What is the Nature of the Gap?

As detailed in Chapter 1 by Ole Holsti, Chapter 2 by James Davis, and Chapter 4 by David Segal, et al., the views of the military officers we surveyed are much more conservative than those of the civilian elite, but not more so than those of the general public. However, "self identification" on a liberal-to-conservative scale indicates that military officers view themselves as more conservative than the general public considers itself to be. On social values, the military officers differ from both elite and mass civilians, but in doing so fit somewhere on a continuum between the two civilian publics: considerably more conservative than elite civilians but not quite as conservative as the general public. Likewise, there is now a consensus across the civilian and military samples on many defense policy issues that were contentious during the Cold War, such as the value of arms control and of cooperating with multilateral organizations such as the United Nations. On the issue of banning books, a frequently used indicator of attachment to freedom of thought, the military responses were unambiguously on the side of civil liberty; very strong majorities of the officers we surveyed said they opposed removing books from the public library that were anti-religion (89 percent), pro-Communist (94 percent), or pro-homosexuality (82 percent). Thus, elite officers are more supportive of free speech than a random sample of the American public. Intriguingly, one of the largest gaps between our military sample and the general public involves views of human nature. On the classic question of whether most people can be trusted, a strong majority in both our elite samples, civilian and military (65 percent), agreed, but an equally strong majority of our mass sample (63 percent) differed, agreeing instead with the statement that "you can't be too careful."

Military officers express great pessimism about the moral health of civilian society and strongly believe that the military could help society become more moral, and that civilian society would be better off if it adopted more of the military's values and behaviors. Elite civilians share this pessimism about civilian society, but strongly disagree that the military has an appropriate role in moral reform.

The military officers we surveyed appear to be more religious than civilian elites, but not as dramatically as some have claimed. If one measures how "religious" a respondent is by the frequency of attending religious services or the frequency of engaging in religious activity, the difference is slight. The difference is somewhat greater if it is measured by the degree of guidance respondents claim religion provides for their daily living and the specific content of those beliefs. For instance, roughly comparable percentages of officers and civilian elites report that they pray several times a day (18 percent vs. 22 percent), once a day (24 percent vs. 18 percent), a few times a week (24 percent vs. 18 percent), or once a week (23 percent vs. 20 percent), although only half as many officers say they never pray (12 percent vs. 22 percent). The military is more likely than civilian elites to agree that "the Bible is the inspired word of God, true, and to be taken word for word" (18 percent vs. 11 percent); more likely to agree that "the Bible is the inspired word of God, true, but not to be taken word for word" (48 percent vs. 34 percent) ; and less likely to agree that "the Bible is a book of myths and legends" (3 percent vs. 7 percent). In any case, the differences are not strikingly large. Except for a larger proportion of Roman Catholics and a smaller proportion of Jews, our officer sample's religious identification matched that of the U.S. population.

Many other findings are ambiguous. While each side, civilian and military, harbors strong negative stereotypes about the other beneath a surface expression of respect and confidence, civilian elites, while generally having little personal connection with the military, evince almost no hostility to warrior culture. Very few in either group (7 percent of elite civilians, 1 percent of the military sample) believe that the so-called "social engineering role"—redressing historical discrimination—is a "very important" role for the military, although somewhat more (23 percent of civilians, 14 percent of military) say it is at least "important." Elite civilians do not have a more optimistic view than the military of the military's ability to be effective in constabulary missions, although civilians are somewhat more eager to use the military for such roles as humanitarian rescue. The military officers we surveyed criticized the quality of civilian political leadership and expressed a pervasive hostility toward the media; at the same time, more members of the military (both up-and-coming officers and the rank and file) express trust and confidence in government institutions than do civilians, elite or mass.

As Chapter 10 by Laura Miller and John Allen Williams details, the officers we surveyed express little dissatisfaction with the current extent of gender integration in the military (about the same as the public and civilian elite). They do, however, oppose expanding combat roles for women, while civilian elites support such a move. Officers diverge sharply from civilians about allowing gays and lesbians to serve openly in the military. By a very large margin (76 percent), the military officers we surveyed oppose such a policy, while a majority of civilian elites (55 percent) and the mass public (57 percent) favor it.

While officers consider themselves neutral servants of the state, the officer corps has developed a distinctive partisan affinity; it is greater, in fact, than that of civilians in our samples. Over the last generation, the percentage of up-and-coming officers who identify themselves as Independent (or no party affiliation) has gone from a plurality (46 percent) to a minority (27 percent), and the percentage that reports itself as Republican has nearly doubled (33 percent to 64 percent) (see Holsti 1998 and Chapter 1 by Ole Holsti in this volume). Eight times as many officers identify themselves as Republicans than as Democrats, while elite civilians and the mass public are split about evenly between the two political parties.[1] The officers' political views, however, are not the "hard-right" Republican positions some observers expected to see.

These are brief highlights of the findings presented in the earlier

---

1. In our survey, the civilian self-identification of party preference was as follows: civilian elites, Republican (36 percent), Democrat (36 percent), and Independent, no preference, or other (28 percent); mass, Republican (31 percent), Democrat (33 percent), and Independent, no preference, or other (37 percent).

chapters, and even these chapters have only scratched the surface of the topic. Our project generated a rich treasure trove of data that can be mined for years and, we hope, will be followed up with subsequent surveys that will measure changes over time.[2] Our focus in this project was an overall comparison of the military to civilian society, elite and mass. It remains for further studies to make comparisons of the four armed services, officers at different ranks, and between civilian elite and mass public on a variety of issues.

What Factors Shape the Gap?

Observers have often seemed to agree on what factors have shaped the gap. Conventional wisdom asserts that the media dislike the military and portray it negatively, encouraging civilian hostility; that popular culture such as films and novels stereotype and caricature the military, exacerbating ignorance and misunderstanding; that the media disproportionately shape civilian views in the crucial area of the use of force, sometimes called the "CNN effect," in which visual images of human tragedy shock the public and pressure policymakers into hasty or unwise decisions; that the gap is widening, probably due to demography, specifically the decline in veterans as a percentage of civilian society, the downsizing of the armed forces since the Cold War, and the self-selection of the all-volunteer force; and that professional military education is a key place where the professional values and norms of the officer are shaped and thus where civil-military concerns can be addressed.

Some of our team's findings, published in the Winter 2001 issue of *Armed Forces & Society*, challenge these assumptions. Contrary to views widely held among elite military officers, the major daily newspapers do not emphasize negative stories about the military. In the last six months of 1998, content analysis showed that the ratios of positive to negative stories were in excess of 2:1 (Wiegand and Paletz 2001). Our researchers did find that popular fiction and film do stereotype both the military and civilian society. Some action films and thrillers (e.g., "Executive Orders," "Rules of Engagement") generally depict uniformed military as tough realists with higher moral standards and greater loyalty, responsibility, and competence than civilians, while disparaging politicians, political institutions, and soft, undisciplined, hedonistic, greedy civilian culture. The opposite stereotype of the rogue military officer is also prevalent (e.g.,

---

2. The website of the TISS Project on the Gap between the Military and Civilian Society, <www.poli.duke.edu/civmil>, will announce when the survey data will be generally available for secondary analyses.

"The Siege," "The Rock," "The General's Daughter," "Broken Arrow"). Highbrow fiction and film (for example, "Catch-22" or Stanley Kubrick's war films like "Dr. Strangelove" and "Full Metal Jacket") tend to present an especially critical view of the military (Harper 2001). The "CNN effect" may influence the U.S. public's willingness to endure the human costs of war, but this willingness is also affected by efforts of political and military leaders to provide a context for the images (Dauber 2001). Another factor is found in the curricula at military academies and war colleges, which fail to give officers a coherent understanding of American society, its culture, or the traditions of U.S. civil-military relations, and in some cases accentuate civil-military differences (Snider, Priest, and Lewis 2001; Stiehm 2001).

Our military and civilian samples did differ in background, suggesting that demographics may partly account for differences between the two groups. Compared to elite civilians and the general public, the up-and-coming officers in our sample were disproportionately male, white, Catholic, and very highly educated. Nevertheless, most differences remain even when one controls for these demographic factors, suggesting that the military may selectively attract and promote a certain profile of officer, those with more conservative values than the civilian elite and those with more education than the general public. Many opinion gaps between officers and the civilian elite are narrower at the lower military ranks than at the more senior levels. Such divergence is not merely a function of occupational selection (certain types of people entering the military) but in part the result of other factors, possibly selective attrition and the kind of professional socialization that occurs in a tightly bonded institution focused on a unique purpose. As argued by Michael Desch in Chapter 8, as well as by Segal, Freedman-Doan, Bachman, and O'Malley in Chapter 4 and Benjamin Fordham in Chapter 9, numerous factors have contributed to the "Republicanization" of the officers corps. These include the effects of the U.S. involvement in Vietnam; the Democrats' abandonment of the military and the Republicans' embrace of it (along with an increased enthusiasm for defense spending); an increase during the Reagan era in the proportion of young people who self-identify as Republican and express interest in joining the military; and the military build-up during the Reagan administration.

Do the Gaps Matter?

The differences between the military and civilians unquestionably affect national defense, but not always in the way observers of civil-military relations have believed.

The public respects the military and has confidence in it, but as Paul Gronke and Peter Feaver show in Chapter 3, this confidence is shallow, may be brittle, and may not last indefinitely. As Benjamin Fordham argues in Chapter 9, the defense budget has not yet been hurt by the gap, nor does the gap appear to be the principal factor affecting recent difficulties in recruiting and retaining people. However, personal connections to the military are declining, and because the gap in opinion does diminish with contact with the military (particularly service in uniform), support for national defense is likely to decrease in the future.

This experience gap is growing in the political elite, as William T. Bianco and Jamie Markham explain in Chapter 7. For the first seventy-five years of the twentieth century, there was always a higher percentage of veterans in Congress than in the comparable age cohort in the general population. This long preceded the introduction of the draft in 1940, but began to lessen with the end of the draft in 1973 and the changes in American politics following the end of the Vietnam War. Beginning in the mid-1990s, the percentage of veterans in Congress dropped below that in the comparable cohort of the population. Thus, not only are there fewer people with military experience in the political elite, but veterans are now under-represented rather than over-represented in the national political leadership. So far, this has not changed congressional voting patterns, but the change in veterans' representation may eventually affect agenda-setting in the Congress, the level of understanding of military affairs in that body, and ultimately, the quality of legislative policymaking for, and oversight of, the armed forces.

James Burk argues in Chapter 6 that the experience gap is partly offset by the military's institutional presence—its significance as an institution in society—which remains very high. The military is not isolated, although there are trends that suggest that this may change. The military has a significant material presence in American society: it consumes a large, if shrinking, portion of the gross domestic product; it is geographically distributed across the entire country, roughly in proportion to regional population distribution (although it is relatively sparser in the Midwest); and it is prominent on the public stage and especially in the media. However, the downsizing of the force is reducing social connections to the military, and these will inevitably reduce its institutional presence and thus its prominence in American public consciousness.

Emerging norms within the officer corps promise more friction in civil-military relationships. The principle of civilian control is well-entrenched in the United States, but the military officers we surveyed show some reluctance to accept one of its basic assumptions: that civilian leaders have a right to be wrong. Contrary to a traditional understanding of civilian control, elite military officers now believe that it is their role to insist rather than merely advise or advocate in private, on key decisions, particularly those involving the use of force. These include such issues as "setting rules of engagement" (50 percent), developing an "exit strategy" (52 percent), and "deciding what kinds of military units (air vs. naval, heavy vs. light, etc.) will be used to accomplish all tasks" (63 percent). Perhaps these views have come about as a result of the Vietnam debacle, which the military blames on civilian micro-management, failed strategies, and acquiescent military leaders. These beliefs have already caused real friction in policy- and decision-making, and could lead to real trouble. Many senior military officers with whom we discussed our research disagreed with our interpretation of this finding. Ironically, however, many of them mentioned a reading of *Dereliction of Duty*, H.R. McMaster's widely read and influential analysis of civil-military relations under President Johnson and Secretary of Defense Robert McNamara, to justify a norm that military officers ought to insist, and to resign in protest if unsuccessful, in cases where the senior civilian leadership is pursuing a reckless policy.[3]

The findings of our study on the political affiliations of officers have received considerable attention, and have in some cases been misinterpreted. While we discovered a remarkably high level of partisan self-identification, we did not ask other questions on our survey about partisanship and so have no systematic evidence one way or the other to know whether the high level of association has been accompanied by a high intensity of partisan activity. But there is anecdotal evidence that the old taboos against military partisanship are weakening, such as senior officers identifying their party affiliation in talks with junior subordinates, or writing letters to the editor critiquing one party over another. Future research should investigate whether the dramatic shift in officers'

---

3. H. R. McMaster, *Dereliction of Duty: Lyndon Johnson, Robert McNamara, the Joint Chiefs of Staff, and the Lies that Led to Vietnam* (New York: HarperCollins, 1997). In this book, McMaster argues that the civilians (and Chairman of the Joint Chiefs of Staff Maxwell Taylor) lied to the service chiefs and misrepresented their views to Congress and in public—and that the Chiefs went along with it—thus contributing to a misguided intervention and a disastrous strategy. Officers interpret the book to say that the Chiefs ought to have resisted the strategy, even publicly, and to have resigned over it. This interpretation is consistent with "received wisdom" in the officer corps for the last quarter-century. However, the author states that the book does not argue that the JCS should have insisted that the administration follow their advice; instead, it charges that the Joint Chiefs failed to give their best military advice to the national command authority. (One of the authors of this chapter—Kohn—was the advisor for the book in its prior form as a seminar paper, MA thesis, and Ph.D. dissertation at the University of North Carolina at Chapel Hill, 1992–96.)

partisan affiliation has been accompanied by other changes in political activity or consciousness, and what the implications are for civil-military relations and military professionalism.

Dismissals of this partisan gap grounded in explanations such as that "the military is simply identifying with the Republican Party out of self-interest" miss a crucial point: the development of any partisan identity, or behaving like "just another interest group," is dangerous for the U.S. military and national defense. If it were viewed as just another interest group, the military would lose the respect and support of the American people, money from Congress, and recruits from American society. Uniformed advice would be less trusted by the civilian leadership. Military professionalism would weaken. Officers who maintain (as many do) that they separate their personal views and voting behavior from their duties may underestimate the subtle and potentially corrosive effects of partisanship on their behavior, leadership, morale, and attitude towards the president. Soldiering is a "24/7" business, and such compartmentalizations are not normally accepted by military officers in other areas of their professional life. Officers have the right to vote, but those who go beyond the private exercise of that right need to be aware of the implications for civil-military relations.

These implications suddenly burst into public view during the 2000 presidential campaign, when the military was identified as part of the Republican electoral base. Accordingly, the Bush campaign went to great lengths to mobilize military voters, just as the Gore campaign sought to mobilize key parts of the Democratic base such as African-Americans. After election day, because of the closeness of the contest in Florida, the military absentee ballots emerged as a potential determinant of the outcome. As a consequence, during the crucial post-election vote-counting, Republicans charged that Democratic activists were attempting to minimize the military vote by challenging absentee ballots, including many from overseas military voters. The public outcry on both sides and from the military to these efforts was intense, and is likely to sour civil-military relations for the next Democratic president and to harden the view among the military and the public that the Democratic party is hostile to the military and to national defense.

Another of the findings of our study, published separately, is that the presence of veterans in the national political elite has a profound effect on the use of force in U.S. foreign policy (Feaver and Gelpi 1999a). At least as far back as 1816, the more veterans there are in the national political elite, the less likely the United States is to initiate the use of force in the international arena. This effect is statistically stronger than many other factors known to influence the use of force, including the "democratic peace" that has become a premise of U.S. foreign policy. The decline in the number of veterans in the national political elite suggests, all other things being equal, that we will see a high rate of military involvement in conflicts in the coming years.

We also found that the belief that the U.S. public is especially casualty-shy, widely accepted by policymakers, civilian elites, and military officers, is a myth (Feaver and Gelpi 1999b). All populations dislike casualties, and democratic societies are particularly able to express this dislike. However, our study found evidence that the American public will accept casualties if they are necessary to accomplish a declared mission, and the mission is being actively pushed by the nation's leadership. With regard to the constabulary interventions that have dominated the post–Cold War security landscape, the public is much more tolerant of casualties than the military officers we surveyed.[4]

Responding to Our Critics

Skeptics may still wonder whether the "gap issue" matters much. In our briefings to dozens of groups, from the students at staff and war colleges to some of the country's most senior civilian and military leadership, most of our audience has agreed at least in part that there is reason to be concerned about the state of American civil-military relations. Three main critiques have, however, been offered by those who think that the "gap flap" is much ado about nothing.

First, gaps of this sort have been around since the beginning of the Republic and we have survived, even flourished. What's the worry?

Second, the principal challenges facing national security today are recruiting, retention, modernization, organization, and the growing mismatch between military missions and the capabilities needed by the armed forces to meet these responsibilities; none of this is chiefly caused by any "gap."

Third, these divergences do not really matter because, as David Tarr and Peter Roman argue in Chapter 11, at the highest policy levels, the roles of civil and military leaders have become blurred, and they have suppressed their differences to cooperate and work together amicably.

Certainly many of the most extravagant claims about the existence

---

4. The military's casualty aversion is not merely an expression of self-preservation, but may well be grounded in a lack of confidence in the political leadership, concern for the troops, and a belief by senior officers that casualties will be interpreted as failure no matter what the outcome of the operation.

and dangers of a gap have proven untrue on closer investigation. Nevertheless, we conclude that danger may lie ahead.

First, while gaps have existed before, the post–Cold War era is the first in American history in which a large professional military central to foreign policy and national security is maintained in peacetime. For the first time in American history, mobilization of the citizenry *en masse* and of American industry is not central to national defense. Service in the military no longer constitutes a recognized or deliberate part of citizenship. As Russell Weigley argues so forcefully in Chapter 5, the lack of any real threat to the nation's existence, of the kind that, in the past, forced military and civilian to cooperate and reconcile their differences, may now permit a much higher level of civil-military conflict to develop. And if, as we foresee, public and political support for these forces and understanding of their needs wanes, they will be less capable and effective.

Second, while the gap may not be the principal cause of recruiting and retention problems, it is likely to exacerbate them in the future. The public's expressed respect and admiration for the military no longer translates into a propensity to join. The diminution of personal connections to the military means that recruiters today and in the future must persuade doubtful prospects with less help from "auxiliary recruiters" among family and friends who have themselves served in the military. Moreover, since expressions of support for the armed forces are partly a function of personal connection to the military, the reservoir of public confidence may shrink as the "war generations" die off.

Third, the civil-military fusion discernible at the most senior levels of policymaking cannot compensate for the distrust expressed at lower ranks of the military. In fact, the fusion contributes to a troubling gap *within* the officer corps. In endorsing a new civil-military norm—that the military has a responsibility not merely to advise but even to insist on certain courses of action—field-grade officers imply that while their leaders should not be openly insubordinate, they may, indeed sometimes should, resist civilian direction or even resign in protest of civilian policies. In our exchanges with hundreds of military officers, we have been offered a two-part rationale for this: that civilian leaders are increasingly ignorant about military matters and so cannot be trusted to make wise decisions, and that, in any case, the greatest disasters in U.S. history (Vietnam being the example usually cited) could have been averted had the senior military leadership voiced opposition, even publicly, to a misguided, even duplicitous, civilian leadership.

Mid-level officers who endorse this norm express frustration with their senior leaders for not standing up more vigorously to what they perceive as civilian mismanagement over such sources of discontent as readiness, gender integration, and perceived declines in standards of discipline and training. Nearly half of the officers we surveyed said they would leave the service if "senior uniformed leadership does not stand up for what is right in military policy."[5]

The implications for civil-military cooperation, for civilian control of the military, and even for American democracy, are profound. The senior military leaders we briefed expressed their understanding that civil-military relations in a democracy do not and cannot work that way. "The mid-level officers seem to think," one told us, "that we can 'insist' on things in the Oval Office. That is not how it works at that level." The military leaders advise and even advocate strongly in private, but once a decision is made, they must execute the policy or operation. The American military rejected individual and mass resignation—which can be indistinguishable from mutiny—at Newburgh in 1783 when dissident officers tried to sway the army to march on Congress or go on strike. They were dissuaded only by a dramatic confrontation with their commander, George Washington. The U.S. military has no tradition of resignation in protest of dubious or even unwise policies. In 1862, Union officers could not say, "we signed on to save the Union, not to free the slaves; we quit." General George C. Marshall did not threaten to resign in 1942 over the decision to invade North Africa, although he opposed it. A practice of resignation accompanied by protest would undermine civilian control, by giving the whip hand to the military: "do it our way or else." Paradoxically, it would increase the politicization of the force: if civilians feared protest resignations over policy disputes, they would vet the military leadership for pliability and compliance and promote only "yes-men."

What Is To Be Done?

No problem we identified is so acute or urgent as to require a drastic response. But troubling trends must be addressed both by some immediate, if modest, measures, and by serious consideration of more systemic changes. For now, we suggest the following steps: increase military presence in civilian society; improve civilian understanding of military affairs; and strengthen civil-military instruction in professional military education.

Unless we suffer a war or the draft is revived, fewer and fewer Amer-

---

5.   This is much higher than the intensity expressed on other hot-button issues about which the military has strong views: slightly more than a quarter said they would leave if "homosexuals were allowed to serve openly in the military" and only 6 percent said they would leave if "women were allowed to serve in ground combat units."

icans will have personal connections to the military. Our first set of recommendations, therefore, seeks to increase military presence in civilian society. One step that has already been taken is former Secretary of Defense William Cohen's recent "Public Outreach Initiative," a website devoted to public information about military affairs.[6] Public outreach should also be expanded beyond the Internet, perhaps by encouraging uniformed personnel at bases and in Reserve and Guard units to take a more visible role in their local community. Of course, the real need for such outreach is not in communities that already have military bases but in those regions and civilian sectors where there is no uniformed military presence whatsoever. The Marine Corps' recently announced "One Year Out" program places officers in civilian workplaces for a year to broaden their experience, and to give civilians some contact with the military. This is another positive step, especially when it places officers in settings outside the so-called military-industrial complex, and it should be expanded to include more officers and broadened to the other services. Geography should have greater weight in future base closures: economic efficiency should be balanced by the need to keep more local communities connected to the armed forces, particularly near large population centers.

The Reserve Officer Training Corps (ROTC) provides a singular opportunity to increase contacts between the military and future civilian leaders. It faces obstacles; for example, many professors on elite campuses want to ban the military, out of dislike for war and opposition to Department of Defense policies, while bean-counters and "culture-warriors" in the Pentagon and Congress want to shut down high-cost/low-yield ROTC programs, and punish schools for anti-military attitudes. We recommend instead that ROTC should be expanded without regard to "yield" until such time as the entire officer accession process can be revised to provide the presence ROTC affords in civilian society. It should be recognized that ROTC not only recruits high-quality young officers, but could also create relationships between elite youth and the military. It could provide the opportunity to expand courses in military history and national security for college students, which are popular courses that are also useful in teaching new generations of leaders about military affairs. The Department of Defense should support the fields of military history and strategic or security studies, not least because support in civilian academe is weak. Just as steps are taken to preserve vital defense industries despite the strains of the global market, so too should the Department of Defense act to preserves these basic scholarly subjects.

---

6.   The Defense Department public outreach website began in May 2000 and can be found at <http://www.defenselink.mil/specials/outreachpublic>.

It is crucial that the United States preserves the ability to think knowledgeably and critically about national security.

Finally, the importance of public education in military affairs cannot be overstated. Our most astounding survey results revealed mass ignorance in the civilian elite and the public about civil-military relations. Nearly a third of the civilian elite thinks that "if civilian leaders order the military to do something that it opposes, military leaders seek ways to avoid carrying out the order" all or most of the time. Nearly half of the general public does not agree with the statement that "civilian control of the military is absolutely safe and secure in the United States." At the same time, the military doubts the quality of civilian leadership: when asked whether the "political leaders share the values of the American people," only 41 percent of the officers we surveyed agreed, while as many as 35 percent disagreed. Nearly two-thirds of the officers believe that political leaders are "somewhat ignorant" or "very ignorant" about "the modern military." Thus, more short workshops and other opportunities are needed for government officials from the executive and legislative branches, elected officials, political appointees, and the civil service to learn about military affairs. The Department of Defense should expand, and Congress should fund, its outreach to the media and community leaders through such programs as the Joint Civilian Orientation Course, which takes reporters, local government officials, prominent business leaders, and other influential civilians on tours of U.S. military facilities round the world. In its cooperation with Hollywood, the armed services should emphasize explaining military culture more than the gee-whiz equipment "show-and-tell" designed to boost defense spending.

Tinkering with the civilian side will fail unless accompanied by change on the military side, and the place to begin is officer education. It is essential that the military continue to expose its most promising officers to the civilian world. This must include advanced degrees in residence at civilian universities, particularly for graduates of service academies. The topic of civil-military relations needs a thorough review and expansion at every level of professional military education, from military academies and ROTC through the Staff and War Colleges and flag-officer short courses. Each of the services needs to reconsider how the values of the profession are being shaped and how emerging norms are changing that service's historical relationship with civilian leaders and the broader society.

Important as they are, these recommendations are merely palliative. More systemic change should be considered to address at a more fundamental level the challenges facing civil-military relations. First, a zero-based review of the military personnel system is in order to assure the quantity and quality of people in national defense. The way we recruit enlistees and officers, promote personnel, and manage the precious human resources of the armed forces has changed remarkably little over the last half century. The existing system was created in response to World War and Cold War strategies and policies; it is an industrial-age system that we now depend upon to field an information-age force. The expensive up-or-out personnel system assumes that we can always fill vacancies with new top-quality people, which may no longer be true. There are many ideas to consider: short-term enlistments in exchange for a significant education benefit; sending all officers through civilian universities for undergraduate education followed by intensive professional training at the service academies; expanding lateral entry to bring more civilian-based skill-sets into the military at higher levels of responsibility; even dropping up-or-out promotions so that certain specialists (such as pilots and technology and communications specialists) remain for their entire careers in the jobs they enjoy. Merits must be weighed against costs, but nothing should be left unconsidered, not even so drastic a measure as some form of universal mandatory national service.

The quality of civilian leadership in national defense must also be addressed. The Goldwater-Nichols Act is nearly fifteen years old. It imposed jointness, improved military staff work, and strengthened the military formulation of strategy, but it neglected the civilian side. It may be time to consider similar reforms to ensure that the civilian officials with whom top joint staff officers interact, both civil service and political appointees, are equally knowledgeable and adept.

Finally, because national defense depends so heavily on the professional and personal relationships among the uniformed and civilian leadership, future administrations should institutionalize procedures for civil-military team-building between political appointees and their military counterparts and subordinates. Mandatory off-site meetings whenever the most senior leaders give way to replacements could lay the foundations for ongoing civil-military cooperation. Such efforts would also go some way to alleviating the experience gap and engendering trust and understanding; increasingly, the political leadership even in national security affairs will have little or no personal connection to or experience with the military.

These are practical proposals, but they depend on a level of cooperation between Congress and the executive branch that has been lacking in recent years. The next administration and the new Congress have an important opportunity, and a duty, to address these issues.

In response to our project's findings, one senior Pentagon political appointee pressed us twice to make sure he knew the bottom line: "there is no crisis now." We agreed because it would be a mistake to exaggerate the dangers of the civil-military gap. But it would be equally foolish—and we said so—to pretend that these problems are trivial and that nothing need be done.

Civil-military relations are an ongoing, reciprocal interaction. At the highest level, civilians have to exercise their responsibility, appoint strong military leaders, listen to them, query them closely, advocate national defense policies, and nurture the effectiveness of U.S. military institutions.[7] Military leaders must reciprocate with candid advice and loyal subordination. They must lead their institutions in adjusting to social change and civilian direction, and see that the proper professional values and traditions of democratic civil-military relations are transmitted to succeeding generations of officers. Like other professions, the military must shape its relationship with its clients.

Ultimately, however, responsibility for the relationship, as with everything else in military affairs, lies with the civilians: partly with Congress, but especially with the president. The performance of the new commander-in-chief should be measured in part by how well he carries out his duties to lead and manage the armed forces, his handling of foreign affairs, his use or abstention from using force, and his exercise of other aspects of the office of commander-in-chief. In the coming years, he should be held accountable for his stewardship of the nation's security.

The extraordinary 2000 election only serves to emphasize these concerns. Questions of civil-military relations lay behind much of the debate on defense policy during the campaign and were clearly a major component of Governor Bush's electoral strategy. These issues rushed to center stage once it became clear that the margin of victory in Florida would be so narrow that a few hundred absentee ballots from military personnel could swing the election one way or the other. For the first time since the Civil War, the votes of soldiers on active duty could have been the margin of victory in a presidential election, and as a consequence, civil-military relations became more politically divisive than ever before. The new president, and indeed all future presidents, must take seriously the responsibility of leading the military and managing civil-military relations if the nation's security is to be preserved.

---

7. Eliot Cohen notes in Chapter 12 that the success of democracies at war has involved effective questioning, oversight, supervision, and occasionally intervention by civilian leaders into the technical aspects of military affairs.

Technical Appendix

Triangle Institute for Security Studies
Survey on the Military in the Post–Cold War Era

(Questions in **boldface** were included in the telephone survey of a representative national sample.)

VARIABLE   QUESTION TEXT:
NAME:

1. Here is a list of possible foreign policy goals that the United States might have. Please indicate how much importance you think should be attached to each goal.

Q01A   A. Helping to improve the standard of living in less developed countries

Q01B   B. Worldwide arms control

Q01C   C. Combating world hunger

Q01D   D. Strengthening the United Nations

Q01E   E. Fostering international cooperation to solve common problems, such as food, inflation, and energy

Q01F   F. Containing communism

Q01G   G. Preventing the spread of nuclear weapons

Q01H   H. Promoting and defending human rights in other countries

Q01I   I. Helping to bring a democratic form of government to other nations

Q01J   J. Maintaining superior military power worldwide

———1=very important
———2=somewhat important
———3=not important
———4=no opinion

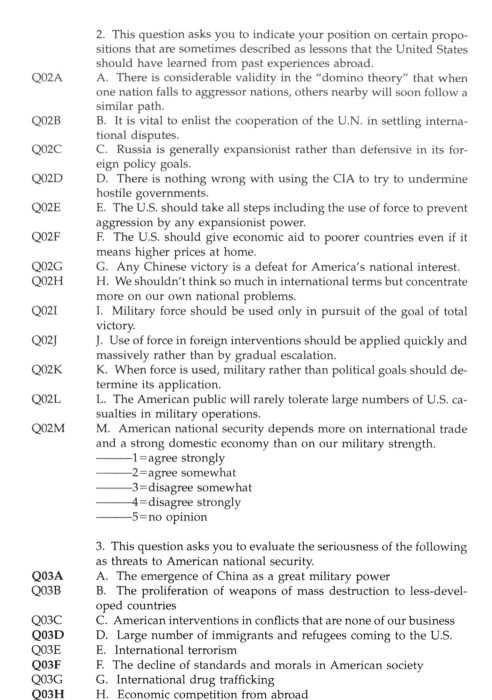

2. This question asks you to indicate your position on certain propositions that are sometimes described as lessons that the United States should have learned from past experiences abroad.

Q02A   A. There is considerable validity in the "domino theory" that when one nation falls to aggressor nations, others nearby will soon follow a similar path.

Q02B   B. It is vital to enlist the cooperation of the U.N. in settling international disputes.

Q02C   C. Russia is generally expansionist rather than defensive in its foreign policy goals.

Q02D   D. There is nothing wrong with using the CIA to try to undermine hostile governments.

Q02E   E. The U.S. should take all steps including the use of force to prevent aggression by any expansionist power.

Q02F   F. The U.S. should give economic aid to poorer countries even if it means higher prices at home.

Q02G   G. Any Chinese victory is a defeat for America's national interest.

Q02H   H. We shouldn't think so much in international terms but concentrate more on our own national problems.

Q02I   I. Military force should be used only in pursuit of the goal of total victory.

Q02J   J. Use of force in foreign interventions should be applied quickly and massively rather than by gradual escalation.

Q02K   K. When force is used, military rather than political goals should determine its application.

Q02L   L. The American public will rarely tolerate large numbers of U.S. casualties in military operations.

Q02M   M. American national security depends more on international trade and a strong domestic economy than on our military strength.

————1=agree strongly

————2=agree somewhat

————3=disagree somewhat

————4=disagree strongly

————5=no opinion

3. This question asks you to evaluate the seriousness of the following as threats to American national security.

Q03A   A. The emergence of China as a great military power

Q03B   B. The proliferation of weapons of mass destruction to less-developed countries

Q03C   C. American interventions in conflicts that are none of our business

Q03D   D. Large number of immigrants and refugees coming to the U.S.

Q03E   E. International terrorism

Q03F   F. The decline of standards and morals in American society

Q03G   G. International drug trafficking

Q03H   H. Economic competition from abroad

Q03I   I. Environmental problems like air pollution and water contamination

Q03J   J. Expansion of Islamic fundamentalism

Q03K   K. Terrorist attacks on the United States

Q03L   L. Attacks on American computer networks

————1=very serious

————2=moderately serious

————3=slightly serious

————4=not at all serious

————5=no opinion

4. Reviewing some of the earlier list of possible threats to national security, how effective is the use of military tools compared to non-military tools for coping with them?

Q04A   A. The emergence of China as a great military power

Q04B   B. The proliferation of weapons of mass destruction to less-developed countries

Q04C   C. Large number of immigrants and refugees coming to the U.S.

Q04D   D. International terrorism

Q04E   E. International drug trafficking

Q04F   F. Expansion of Islamic fundamentalism

Q04G   G. Attacks on American computer networks

————1=much more

————2=somewhat more

————3=equally

————4=somewhat less

————5=much less

————6=no opinion

5. This question asks you to indicate your position on certain domestic issues.

Q05A   A. Busing children in order to achieve school integration

Q05B   B. Using any budget surpluses to reduce the national debt rather than to reduce taxes

Q05C   C. Relaxing environmental regulations to stimulate economic growth

Q05D   D. Providing tuition tax credits to parents who send children to private or parochial schools

Q05E   E. Leaving abortion decisions to women and their doctors

Q05F   F. Encouraging mothers to stay at home with their children rather than working outside the home

Q05G   G. Permitting prayer in public schools

Q05H   H. Reducing the defense budget in order to increase the federal education budget

Q05I   I. Barring homosexuals from teaching in public schools

Q05J   J. Easing restrictions on the construction of nuclear power plants

Q05K   K. Redistributing income from the wealthy to the poor through taxation and subsidies

Q05L   L. Banning the death penalty

Q05M   M. Placing stringent controls on the sale of handguns

————1=agree strongly

————2=agree somewhat

————3=disagree somewhat
————4=disagree strongly
————5=no opinion

Q06   6. The American missile strikes against suspected terrorist sites in Afghanistan and Sudan were a legitimate response to the bombing of American Embassies in Kenya and Tanzania. *(This was the first question on the survey given at the Air Force Academy [AFA].)*
————1=agree strongly
————2=agree somewhat
————3=disagree somewhat
————4=disagree strongly
————5=no opinion

7. The following are some possible uses of the military. Please indicate how important you consider each potential role for the military.

Q07A   A. As an instrument of foreign policy, even if that means engaging in operations other than war

Q07B   B. To fight and win our country's wars

Q07C   C. To redress historical discrimination, for instance against African-Americans and women

Q07D   D. To provide disaster relief within the U.S.

Q07E   E. To address humanitarian needs abroad

Q07F   F. To deal with domestic disorder within the U.S.

Q07G   G. To intervene in civil wars abroad

Q07H   H. To combat drug trafficking
————1=very important
————2=somewhat important
————3=not important
————4=no opinion

8. This question asks you to indicate your position on a variety of social issues.

Q08A   A. The decline of traditional values is contributing to the breakdown of our society.

Q08B   B. Through leading by example, the military could help American society become more moral.

Q08C   C. The world is changing and we should adjust our view of what is moral and immoral behavior to fit these changes.

Q08D   D. Civilian society would be better off if it adopted more of the military's values and customs.

Q08E   E. American society would have fewer problems if people took God's will more seriously.

Q08F   F. All Americans should be willing to give up their lives to defend our country.
————1=agree strongly
————2=agree somewhat
————3=disagree somewhat

————4=disagree strongly
————5=no opinion

Q09   9. Generally speaking, would you say that most people can be trusted or that you can't be too careful in dealing with people?
————1 most people can be trusted
————2 you can't be too careful in dealing with people
————3 uncertain

Q10   10. Which of these would you say is more important in preparing children for life?
————1 to be obedient
————2 to think for themselves
————3 can't choose

Q11   11. There are always some people whose ideas are considered bad or dangerous by other people, for instance, somebody who is against all churches and religion. If some people in your community suggested that a book he wrote against churches and religion should be taken out of your public library, would you favor removing this book or not?
————1 favor removing
————2 not favor removing
————3 don't know

Q12   12. Consider a different case involving a person who admitted he is a Communist. Suppose he wrote a book which is in your public library. If some people in your community suggested that the book should be removed from the library, would you favor removing it, or not?
————1 favor removing
————2 not favor removing
————3 don't know

Q13   13. Consider a third case involving a person who admits that he is a homosexual. If some people in your community suggested that a book he wrote in favor of homosexuality should be taken out of your public library, would you favor removing this book or not?
————1 favor removing
———— 2 not favor removing
——— —3 don't know

Q14   14. Which of these statements comes closest to describing your feelings about the Bible?
————1 The Bible is the inspired word of God, true, and to be taken word for word.
————2 The Bible is the inspired word of God, true, but not to be taken word for word.
————3 The Bible is the inspired word of God, true for religion, but with some errors.

———4 The Bible is a great book of wisdom and history.
———5 The Bible is a book of myths and legends.
———6 No opinion.

Q15   15. Which of the following comes closest to your views on life after death?
———1 I am sure there is life after death.
———2 I believe in life after death but have some doubts.
———3 I am uncertain about life after death.
———4 I am certain there is no life after death.
———5 No opinion.

Q16   16. Would you say your religion provides some guidance in your day-to-day living, quite a bit of guidance, or a great deal of guidance in your day-to-day life?
———1 none
———2 some
———3 quite a bit
———4 a great deal

Q17   17. Outside of attending religious services, do you pray several times a day, once a day, a few times a week, once a week or less, or never?
———1 several times a day
———2 once a day
———3 a few times a week
———4 once a week or less
———5 never

Q18   18. Outside of weddings and funerals, do you go to religious services more than once a week, every week, almost every week, once or twice a month, a few times a year, or never?
——— 1 more than once a week
——— 2 every week
——— 3 almost every week
——— 4 once or twice a month
——— 5 a few times a year
——— 6 never

Q19   19. What is your religious affiliation? *Please be specific (e.g.,* "none," "Presbyterian Church, U.S.A.," "Southern Baptist," "Reform Judaism," etc.)

20. This question asks you about the information you obtain from the media about the military. Please circle your *top three* sources of information about the military.

Q20.1   1 newspapers
Q20.2   2 television network news
Q20.3   3 television local news

Q20.4	4 television talk shows
Q20.5	5 radio news
Q20.6	6 radio talk shows
Q20.7	7 general news magazines (e.g., *Time, U.S. News and World Report*)
Q20.8	8 special news magazines (e.g., *Congressional Quarterly*)
Q20.9	9 opinion magazines (e.g., *New Republic, National Review*)
Q20.10	10 movies
Q20.11	11 fiction books
Q20.12	12 nonfiction books
Q20.13	13 military trade/professional publications
Q20.14	14 *Army/Navy/Air Force Times (not on survey given at AFA)*
Q20.15	15 Internet newsgroups
Q20.16	16 other (please specify)

Q21

21. In general, mass media depictions of the military are:
———1 very supportive
———2 somewhat supportive
———3 neutral
———4 somewhat hostile
———5 very hostile
———6 no opinion

Q22

22. If you could recommend only one media source of information about the military, what would it be (please be specific, e.g., *Proceedings of the U. S. Naval Institute, The Weekly Standard, Army/Navy/Air Force Times, National Journal,* "The NewsHour with Jim Lehrer," *The New York Times, The Wall Street Journal,* etc.)? *(This question was blank in the survey at the Naval Academy.)*

Q23

23. Please indicate how closely you tend to follow issues involving the military, such as weapons systems, military deployments abroad, the capabilities of the armed forces, and so on. Would you say that you pay a great deal of attention to military issues, some attention, a little attention, or almost no attention?
———1 a great deal
———2 some
———3 little
———4 almost none

Q24

24. How knowledgeable do you think our political leaders are about the modern military?
———1 very knowledgeable
———2 somewhat knowledgeable
———3 somewhat ignorant
———4 very ignorant
———5 no opinion

Q25

25. Do you think our political leaders, in general, share the same values as the American people?

————1 yes
————2 no
————3 not sure
————4 no opinion

Q26

26. Do you think journalists, in general, share the same values as the American people?

————1 yes
————2 no
————3 not sure
————4 no opinion

Q27

27. Do you think military leaders, in general, share the same values as the American people?

————1 yes
————2 no
————3 not sure
————4 no opinion

Q28

28. Now consider the people you come in contact with in the *social or community* groups to which you belong. Are they all civilians, mostly civilians with some military, about equal civilians and military, mostly military with some civilians, or all military? For the purposes of this question, "civilian" here refers to civilians other than civil servants or contractors working for the military.

———— 1 all civilians
———— 2 mostly civilians with some military
———— 3 about equal
———— 4 mostly military with some civilians
———— 5 all military
———— 6 no opinion

Q29

29. Now consider the people you come in regular contact with at work. Are they all civilians, mostly civilians with some military, about equal civilians and military, mostly military with some civilians, or all military? For the purposes of this question, "civilian" here refers to civilians other than civil servants or contractors working for the military.

———— 1 all civilians
———— 2 mostly civilians with some military
———— 3 about equal
———— 4 mostly military with some civilians
———— 5 all military
———— 6 no opinion

Q30
30. Think of three adult friends you most enjoy spending time with. How many of these friends currently serve or have served previously in the military?

———1 zero
———2 one
———3 two
———4 three
———5 uncertain

Q31
31. Thinking about the way most Americans view the military, would you say the military gets more respect than it deserves, less respect than it deserves, or about as much respect as it deserves?

———1 more respect
———2 less respect
———3 about as much
———4 no opinion

32. The following is a list of some institutions in this country. As far as these institutions are concerned, would you say you have a great deal of confidence, only some confidence, or hardly any confidence in them?

Q32A	Organized religion
Q32B	Presidency
Q32C	The press
Q32D	U.S. Supreme Court
Q32E	Congress
Q32F	Major companies
Q32G	Primary and secondary education
Q32H	The executive branch of the federal government
Q32I	Universities
Q32J	Law enforcement agencies
Q32K	Labor unions
Q32L	The legal profession
Q32M	Organized political parties (such as the Republican and Democratic parties)
Q32N	The military
Q32O	The medical profession
Q32P	Voluntary organizations
Q32Q	Television

———1 = great deal
———2 = only some
———3 = hardly any
———4 = no opinion

33. Here are some statements people have made about the U.S. military. For each, please indicate whether you strongly agree, somewhat agree, somewhat disagree or strongly disagree.

Q33A   A. Most members of the military have a great deal of respect for civilian society.

Q33B   B. Most members of civilian society have a great deal of respect for the military.

Q33C   C. All *male* citizens should be required to do some national service.

Q33D   D. All *female* citizens should be required to do some national service.

Q33E   E. I am proud of the men and women who serve in the military.

Q33F   F. I have confidence in the ability of our military to perform well in wartime.

Q33G   G. The U.S. Armed Forces are attracting high-quality, motivated recruits.

Q33H   H. Even if civilian society did not always appreciate the essential military values of commitment and unselfishness, our armed forces could still maintain required traditional standards.

Q33I   I. The American people understand the sacrifices made by the people who serve in the U.S. military.

Q33J   J. I expect that ten years from now America will still have the best military in the world.

Q33K   K. I would be disappointed if a child of mine joined the military.
————1=agree strongly
————2=agree somewhat
————3=disagree somewhat
————4=disagree strongly
————5=no opinion

If you are not now serving in the military or have never served in the military, please skip to question 38. If you are serving in the military please continue.

Q34   34. How would you generally characterize your experience in the military?
————1 very positive
————2 somewhat positive
————3 mixed
————4 somewhat negative
————5 very negative
————6 no opinion

35. How would you characterize your *primary* motivation to join the military? Please circle the *one* closest to your primary motivation.

Q35.1   ————1 to avoid being drafted into another service

Q35.2   ————2 to gain skills valued in the civilian job market

Q35.3   ————3 to have a career in the military

Q35.4   ————4 to earn veteran's benefits

Q35.5   ————5 to serve my country

Q35.6   ————6 to obtain an education (*not on survey given at AFA*)

Q35.7   ————7 I was drafted

Q35.8   ————8 other (please specify)

36. I would leave military service if: (Please circle all that apply)

Q36.1 ———1 the senior uniformed leadership does not stand up for what is right in military policy

Q36.2 ———2 the country does not provide adequate facilities and weapons for the military to succeed

Q36.3 ———3 the pay and benefits further lagged behind compensation in civilian economy

Q36.4 ———4 there are reduced opportunities to train in my military specialty

Q36.5 ———5 deployment schedules keep me away from my family too much

Q36.6 ———6 women were allowed to serve in ground combat units

Q36.7 ———7 homosexuals were allowed to serve openly in the military

Q36.8 ———8 chances for promotion were less than they are now in my service

Q36.9 ———9 the challenge and sense of fulfillment I derive from my service were less (*not on AFA survey*)

Q36.10 ———10 other (please specify)

Q37 37. Morale in my service is (*different options on survey at AFA*)
———1 very low
———2 low
———3 moderate
———4 high
———5 very high
———6 no opinion

38. When American troops are sent overseas, there are almost always casualties. For instance, 43 Americans were killed in Somalia, 383 in the Gulf War, roughly 54,000 in Korea, roughly 58,000 in Vietnam and roughly 400,000 in World War II. Imagine for a moment that a President decided to send military troops on one of the following missions. In your opinion, what would be the *highest* number of American military deaths that would be acceptable to achieve this (*options given in different order for AFA survey*)

Q38A A. To stabilize a democratic government in Congo

Q38B B. To prevent widespread "ethnic cleansing" in Kosovo

Q38C C. To prevent Iraq from obtaining weapons of mass destruction

Q38D D. To combat the terrorist organization responsible for bombings at U.S. embassies

Q38E E. To defend South Korea against an invasion by North Korea

Q38F F. To defend Taiwan against invasion by China

39. This question asks you to make some judgments about civilian and military culture in this country. Please indicate all terms that you believe apply to civilian culture and then do the same for military culture.

Q39A.1 Civilian: Honest

Q39B.1 ———Intolerant

Q39C.1	———Materialistic
Q39D.1	———Corrupt
Q39E.1	———Generous
Q39F.1	———Self-indulgent
Q39G.1	———Hard-working
Q39H.1	———Rigid
Q39I.1	———Disciplined
Q39J.1	———Creative
Q39K.1	———Loyal
Q39L.1	———Overly cautious
Q39A.2	Military: Honest
Q39B.2	———Intolerant
Q39C.2	———Materialistic
Q39D.2	———Corrupt
Q39E.2	———Generous
Q39F.2	———Self-indulgent
Q39G.2	———Hard-working
Q39H.2	———Rigid
Q39I.2	———Disciplined
Q39J.2	———Creative
Q39K.2	———Loyal
Q39L.2	———Overlycautious

(Note: This series is blank for West Point [CLARIFY???].)

40. Please tell us how important the following issues are to you. Please rate them from 100 (most important) to 1 (least important).

Q40A	Financial stability of Social Security
Q40B	The illegal drug problem in the U.S.
Q40C	Protection of the environment
Q40D	The growing gap between rich and poor Americans
Q40E	The decline in integrity among public officials

41. There are many different things that people say might keep the military from being effective during times of war. For each of the following, please indicate if it might greatly hurt military effectiveness, somewhat hurt military effectiveness, has no effect on military effectiveness, or it is not happening at all in the U.S. military.

Q41A	A. Americans' lack of trust in the uniformed leaders of the military
Q41B	B. The tensions created when women enter a new workplace
Q41C	C. The military becoming less male-dominated
Q41D	D. The military getting too involved in non-military affairs
Q41E	E. A ban on language and behavior that encourage comradery among soldiers
Q41F	F. A system for promotions and advancement in the military that does not work well
Q41G	G. Non-military people getting too involved in military affairs
Q41H	H. Sexual harassment in the military *(different wording on AFA survey)*
Q41I	I. The military trying to hold on to old-fashioned views of morality

Q41J   J. A military culture and way of life that is very different from the culture and way of life of those who are not in the military

Q41K   K. The military's lack of confidence in our political leadership

Q41L   L. Inaccurate reporting about the military and military affairs by the news media

————1=greatly hurts

————2=somewhat hurts

————3=no effect

————4=isn't happening

————5=no opinion

42. Here are some statements people have made about the American military.

Q42A   A. An effective military depends on a very structured organization with a clear chain of command.

Q42B   B. Military symbols—like uniforms and medals—and military traditions—like ceremonies and parades—are necessary to build morale, loyalty, and comradery in the military.

Q42C   C. Even though women can serve in the military, the military should remain basically masculine, dominated by male values and characteristics.

Q42D   D. The U.S. military has done a much better job of eliminating racial discrimination within the military than American society in general.

Q42E   E. Even in a high-tech era, people in the military have to have characteristics like strength, toughness, physical courage, and the willingness to make sacrifices.

Q42F   F. The bonds and sense of loyalty that keep a military unit together under the stress of combat are fundamentally different than the bonds and loyalty that organizations try to develop in the business world.

Q42G   G. Since military life is a young person's profession, the chance to retire with a good pension at a young age is very important in the military.

Q42H   H. On most military bases there are company stores, childcare centers, and recreational facilities right on the base. It is very important to keep these things on military bases in order to keep a sense of identity in the military community.

Q42I   I. Military leaders care more about the people under their command than leaders in the non-military world care about people under them.

Q42J   J. The new emphasis on joint education, training, and doctrine across branches of the military has improved the effectiveness of the Armed Forces.

————1=agree strongly

————2=agree somewhat

————3=disagree somewhat

————4=disagree strongly

————5=no opinion

43. If a senior civilian Department of Defense leader asks a military officer to do something that the military officer believes is *unethical but legal*, would it be appropriate and acceptable for the officer to:

Q43A   A. carry out the order anyway

Q43B   B. attempt to persuade the civilian or military leader to change his/her mind but, failing that, carry out the order anyway

Q43C   C. attempt to change the civilian or military leader's mind by informing other civilian or military officials who might disagree with this policy

Q43D   D. retire or leave the service in protest

Q43E   E. refuse to carry out the order even if it means facing a court-martial

Q43F   F. appeal the matter to higher authority, even if it means leaping the chain of command

Q43G   G. report the matter to an Inspector General Judge or Advocate General office or officer

Q43H   H. leak the matter to the press to alert others to this problem

————1=appropriate

————2=not appropriate

————3=no opinion

44. If a senior civilian Department of Defense leader asks a military officer to do something that the military officer believes is *unwise*, would it be appropriate for the officer to:

Q44A   A. carry out the order anyway

Q44B   B. attempt to persuade the civilian or military leader to change his/her mind but, failing that, carry out the order anyway

Q44C   C. attempt to change the civilian or military leader's mind by informing other civilian or military officials who might disagree with this policy

Q44D   D. retire or leave the service in protest

Q44E   E. refuse to carry out the order even if it means facing a court-martial

Q44F   F. appeal the matter to higher authority, even if it means leaping the chain of command and/or going over the head of the leader making the request

Q44G   G. report the matter to an Inspector General or Judge Advocate General office or officer

Q44H   H. leak the matter to the press to alert others to this problem

————1=appropriate

————2=not appropriate

————3=no opinion

45. It is acceptable for a military member to leak unclassified information or documents to the press if he or she believes that:

Q45A   A. a crime has been committed and the chain of command is not acting on it

Q45B   B. doing so may prevent a policy that will lead to unnecessary casualties

Q45C   C. doing so discloses a course of action that is morally or ethically wrong

Q45D   D. he or she is ordered to by a superior

Q45E   E. doing so brings to light a military policy or course of action that may lead to a disaster for the country

Q45F   F. never

        ——1=agree
        ——2=disagree
        ——3=no opinion

46. This question asks you to specify the proper role of the senior military leadership in decisions to commit U.S. Armed Forces abroad. The following are typical elements of the decision the President must make. Please specify the proper role of the military for each element.

Q46A   A. deciding whether to intervene

Q46B   B. setting rules of engagement

Q46C   C. ensuring that clear political and military goals exist

Q46D   D. deciding what the goals or policy should be

Q46E   E. generating public support for the intervention

Q46F   F. developing an "exit strategy"

Q46G   G. deciding what kinds of military units (air vs. naval, heavy vs. light) will be used to accomplish all tasks

        ——1−be neutral
        ——2=advise
        ——3=advocate
        ——4=insist
        ——5=no opinion

47. This question asks for your opinion on a number of statements concerning the military's role in civilian society.

Q47A   A. Members of the military should not publicly criticize senior member of the civilian branch of the government.

Q47B   B. Members of the military should not publicly criticize American society.

Q47C   C. Members of the military should be allowed to publicly express their political views just like any other citizen.

Q47D   D. It is proper for the military to explain and defend in public the policies of the government.

Q47E   E. It is proper for the military to advocate publicly the military policies it believes are in the best interests of the United States.

        ——1=agree strongly
        ——2=agree somewhat
        ——3=disagree somewhat
        ——4=disagree strongly
        ——5=no opinion

48. This question asks for your opinion on a number of statements concerning relations between the military and senior civilian leaders.

Q48A   A. In general, high-ranking civilian officials rather than high-ranking military officers should have the final say *on whether or not* to use military force.

Q48B   B. In general, high-ranking civilian officials rather than high-ranking military officers should have the final say on *what type* of military force to use.

Q48C   C. When civilians tell the military what to do, domestic partisan politics rather than national security requirements are often the primary motivation.

Q48D   D. In wartime, civilian government leaders should let the military take over running the war.

Q48E   E. To be respected as Commander-in-Chief, the President should have served in uniform.

Q48F   F. Civilian control of the military is absolutely safe and secure in the United States.

Q48G   G. Military leaders do not have enough influence in deciding our policy with other countries.
 ———1 = agree strongly
 ———2 = agree somewhat
 ———3 = disagree somewhat
 ———4 = disagree strongly
 ———5 = no opinion

Q49   49. If civilian leaders order the military to do something that it opposes, military leaders will seek ways to avoid carrying out the order:
 ———1 all of the time
 ———2 most of the time
 ———3 some of the time
 ———4 rarely
 ———5 never
 ———6 no opinion

Q50   50. Do you think women should be *allowed* to serve in all combat jobs?
 ———1 yes
 ———2 no

Q51   51. Do you think women should be *required* to serve in all combat jobs?
 ———1 yes
 ———2 no

 52. If you oppose women serving in combat roles, which of the following factors is most important in shaping your opinion? Please circle the *one* reason that matters most to you. (*different wording of options on survey for AFA*)

Q52.1   ———1 religious/moral convictions
Q52.2   ———2. the presence of women will disrupt small unit cohesion
Q52.3   ———3 women could be taken prisoner and abused
Q52.4   ———4 most women are not physically qualified

Q52.5 ——5 women are not as readily deployable as men because of pregnancy

Q52.6 ——6 there is little privacy for men and women in combat specialties like the infantry or serving on subs *(not on survey at AFA)*

Q52.7 ——7 men will not fight as effectively with women present in combat units

Q52.8 ——8 the deaths of women soldiers will demoralize male soldiers and the American public *(not on survey at AFA)*

Q52.9 ——9 other (please specify)

Q52.10 ——10 I do not oppose women serving in combat roles

53. If you support opening combat roles to women, which of the following factors is most important in shaping your opinion? Please circle the one reason that matters most to you. *(Not on survey at AFA.)*

Q53.1 1 to exclude women is discrimination/morally wrong

Q53.2 2 the most capable soldiers should be assigned to combat roles, and some women are more capable than some men

Q53.3 3 technology/modern warfare have made physical abilities less relevant for combat

Q53.4 4 women should have the same obligation to serve and risk their lives as men do

Q53.5 5 having women in combat units will improve morale and motivate men to outperform them

Q53.6 6 women's performance in recent military operations has proven them to be an asset

Q53.7 7 the American public will not consider women first-class citizens until they serve in combat roles under the same circumstances as men do

Q53.8 8 excluding military women from combat roles hurts their promotion opportunities and prevents them from filling top leadership positions

Q53.9 9 other (please specify)

Q53.10 10 I do not support opening combat roles to women

Q54 54. If, under present standards, your commander was female, how would you feel?

——1 as confident with female commander as male commander

——2 more confident with male commander than female commander

——3 more confident with female commander than male commander

——4 no opinion

Q55 55. How do you think the military has done in dealing with the problem of sexual harassment? *(Different wording on survey for AFA.)*

——1 it has done what it should

——2 it has not done enough

——3 it has gone too far

——4 no opinion

Q56

56. How would you characterize any costs associated with the effort to expand opportunities for women in the military?
———1 trivial or non-existent
———2 modest but worth it for the benefits the effort generates
———3 sizable but worth it for the benefits the effort generates
———4 sizable and probably not worth it for the benefits the effort generates
———5 excessive and certainly not worth it
———6 no opinion

Q57

57. Generally, do you think there is more, less, or about the same amount of sexual discrimination in the military as in civilian society at large?
———1 more
———2 less
———3 about the same
———4 no opinion

Q58

58. Overall, are men and women held to the same standard in the military?
———1 yes
———2 no, easier for men
———3 no, easier for women
———4 no opinion

Q59

59. Do you think gay men and lesbians should be allowed to serve openly in the military? *(not on survey given at Naval Academy)*
———1 yes
———2 no
———3 no opinion

Q60

60. If, under present standards, your commander was gay, how would you feel? *(not on survey given at Naval Academy or Air Force Academy.)*
———1 as confident with a gay commander as a straight commander
———2 more confident with a gay commander than a straight commander
———3 more confident with a straight commander than a gay commander
———4 no opinion

Q61

61. Consider how the *military* justice system deals with sexual harassment. Are you more concerned that it might be allowing too many people to get away with sexual harassment, or more concerned that it is too often punishing the innocent, or do you think the system is doing the best it can in balancing these two concerns. *(Different wording on survey at AFA.)*
———1 more concerned the guilty are getting away with it
———2 more concerned the innocent are being punished

————3 think the system is doing the best it can in balancing these two concerns

————4 no opinion

Q62 62. Now consider how the *civilian* justice system deals with sexual harassment. Are you more concerned that it might be allowing too many people to get away with sexual harassment, or more concerned that it is too often punishing the innocent, or do you think the system is doing the best it can in balancing these two concerns? *(Different wording on survey given at AFA.)*

————1 more concerned the guilty are getting away with it

————2 more concerned the innocent are being punished

————3 think the system is doing the best it can in balancing these two concerns

————4 no opinion

Q63 63. Here are a few questions for background information:

————1 male

————2 female

Q64 64. Year of birth (last 2 digits)

Q65 65. What is the highest level of education that you have obtained?

————1 high school

————2 some college

————3 college graduate

————4 some graduate work

————5 graduate degree

Q66 66. What is/was your primary occupation? Please circle only one.

————1 business executive

————2 military officer

————3 State Department or Foreign Service

————4 labor official

————5 communications

————6 public official (other than State Department)

————7 health care

————8 lawyer

————9 educator

————10 clergy

————11 student

————12 other (please specify)

Q67 67. Are you currently enrolled at a service academy or in ROTC, and if so, which one?

————1 not in academy or ROTC

————2 Military Academy (West Point)

————3 Naval Academy

————4 Air Force Academy

————5 Naval Academy (Marine Corps)
————6 Army ROTC
————7 Navy ROTC
————8 Air Force ROTC
————9 Navy ROTC (Marine Corps)

Q68   68. Have you ever served, or are you currently serving in the U.S. military? (academies and ROTC defined as "no")
————1 Yes
————2 No - GO TO QUESTION 69

If so, during what years did you serve?
Q68FROM From
Q68TO   To (PRESENT=99)

If so, what was/is your primary service?
Q68PS.1   ————1 Army
Q68PS.2   ————2 Navy
Q68PS.3   ————3 Air Force
Q68PS.4   ————4 Marines
Q68PS.5   ————5 Coast Guard
Q68PS.6   ————6 Army National Guard
Q68PS.7   ————7 Air National Guard
Q68PS.8   ————8 Army Reserve
Q68PS.9   ————9 Navy Reserve
Q68PS.10 ————10 Air Force Reserve
Q68PS.11 ————11 Marine Reserve
Q68PS.12 ————12 Coast Guard Reserve

Q69   69. Have you ever served, or are you currently serving in the Reserves or National Guard without active duty time?
1 Yes
2 No - GO TO QUESTION 70

If so, what was/is your primary service?
Q69PS.1   ————1 Army Reserve
Q69PS.2   ————2 Navy Reserve
Q69PS.3   ————3 Air Force Reserve
Q69PS.4   ————4 Marine Reserve
Q69PS.5   ————5 Coast Guard Reserve
Q69PS.6   ————6 Army National Guard
Q69PS.7   ————7 Air National Guard

Q70   70. What is or was your primary arm or specialty?
————1 I never served
————2 logistics/supply/transport
————3 combat service support
————4 combat support

———5 combat arms or platform

———6 intelligence

———7 other support (please specify)

———8 precommissioned

Q71

71. What is the highest rank/rate you reached?

———1. never served

———2. highest rank/rate

Q71RANK

Q72

72. If you are or were an officer, what was the source of your commission?

———1 service academy

———2 OCS or OTS [Officer Candidate School; Officer Training School]

———3 ROTC

———4 direct

———5 commissioned after prior enlisted service

———6 never an officer

Q73

73. Have you deployed abroad for a military operation, including peacekeeping, as a member of the U.S. Armed Forces within the last five years?

———1 Yes

———2 No

Q74

74. Has a member of your immediate family (parent, spouse, sibling, or child) served, or do they currently serve, in the military?

———1 Yes

———2 No

———3 Not sure

Q75

75. How would you describe your views on political matters?

———1 far left

—— 2 very liberal

———3 somewhat liberal

——4 moderate

———5 somewhat conservative

———6 very conservative

———7 far right

———8 other

———9 no opinion

Q76

76. Generally speaking, do you think of yourself as a Republican, a Democrat, an Independent, or what?

———1 Republican

———2 Democrat

———3 Independent
———4 no preference
———5 other

Q77   77. What was the main kind of schooling before college that your
          children received?
          ———1 Do not have children
          ———2 public
          ———3 private, non-parochial
          ———4 private parochial
          ———5 home-school

          78. What is the highest level of education that your parents obtained?
Q78A   Father
Q78B   Mother
          ———1 less than high school
          ———2 high school
          ———3 some college
          ———4 college graduate
          ———5 some graduate work
          ———6 graduate degree

Q79   79. Where did you live most of the time when you were growing up?
          ———1 New England
          ———2 South
          ———3 Mountain States
          ———4 Pacific Coast
          ———5 Mid-Atlantic
          ———6 Midwest
          ———7 Southwest
          ———8 other (please specify)
          ———9 moved around

Q80   80. What is your racial/ethnic identity?
          ———1 White or Caucasian, not Hispanic
          ———2 Hispanic
          ———3 Asian-American
          ———4 Black or African-American, not Hispanic
          ———5 American Indian, Eskimo or Aleut
          ———6 other (please specify)
          ———9 refused

Q81   81. Are you a foreign officer?
           1 no
           2 yes

Bibliography

Abrahamsson, Bengt. 1970. "Some Elements of Military Conservatism." Paper read at the seventh World Congress of Sociology, Varna, Bulgaria (August).

Abrahamsson, Bengt. 1972. *Military Professionalization and Political Power.* London: Sage Publications.

Adair, R.D., and Joseph C. Myers. 1993. "Admission of Gays to the Military: A Singularly Intolerant Act." *Parameters* 23 (Spring): 10–19.

Alford, Jonathan. 1980. "Deterrence and Disuse: Some Thoughts on the Problem of Maintaining a Volunteer Force." *Armed Forces & Society* 6 (Winter): 247–256.

Allison, Graham T. 1971. *Essence of Decision.* Cambridge, Mass.: Harvard University Press.

Ambrose, Stephen E. 1964. *Upton and the Army.* Baton Rouge, La.: Louisiana State University Press.

Ambrose, Stephen E. 1966. *Duty, Honor, Country: A History of West Point.* Baltimore: Johns Hopkins University Press.

Ambrose, Stephen E., and James A. Barber, eds. 1972. *The Military and American Society.* New York: Free Press.

Andreski, Stanislav. 1968. *Military Organization and Society.* Berkeley, Calif.: University of California Press.

Arterton, F. Christopher. 1974. "The Impact of Watergate on Children's Attitudes toward Political Authority." *Political Science Quarterly* 89 (June): 269–288.

Art, Robert J. 1973. "Bureaucratic Politics and American Foreign Policy: A Critique." *Policy Sciences* 4 (December): 467–490.

Arver v. United States, 245 U.S. 366 (1918).

Asch, Beth J., and Bruce R. Orvis. 1994. *Recent Recruiting Trends and Their Implications.* Santa Monica, Calif.: RAND.

Assistant Secretary of Defense for Force Management Policy. 1997. *Population Representation in the Military Services: Fiscal Year 1996.* Arlington, Va.: Department of Defense (December).

Assistant Secretary of Defense for Force Management Policy. 1998. *Population Representation in the Military Services, Fiscal Year 1997*. Arlington, Va.: Department of Defense (November).

Atkinson, Rick. 1993. *Crusade: The Untold Story of the Persian Gulf War*. New York: Houghton Mifflin Company.

Avant, Deborah. 1998. "Conflicting Indicators of 'Crisis' in American Civil-Military Relations." *Armed Forces & Society* 24 (Spring): 375–388.

Avidar, Yosef. 1977. Oral history. Ben Gurion Archives—Oral Histories. Ben Gurion Research Center, Ben Gurion University (March 13).

Bacevich, Andrew J. 1995. "The Use of Force in Our Time." *Wilson Quarterly* 19 (Winter): 50–63.

Bacevich, Andrew J. 1997. "The De-Moralization of the Military: Why the Kelly Flinn Story Matters." *The Weekly Standard* (June 9): 25.

Bacevich, Andrew J., and Richard H. Kohn. 1997. "Grand Army of the Republicans: Has the U.S. Military Become a Partisan Force?" *The New Republic*. 217 (December 8): 22–25.

Bachman, Jerald G. 1983. "American High School Seniors View the Military: 1976–1982." *Armed Forces & Society* 10 (Fall): 86–104.

Bachman, Jerald G., and M. Kent Jennings. 1975. "The Impact of Vietnam on Trust in Government." *Journal of Social Issues* 31 (Fall): 141–156.

Bachman, Jerald G., John D. Blair, and David R. Segal. 1977. *The All-Volunteer Force: A Study of Ideology in the Military*. Ann Arbor, Mich.: University of Michigan Press.

Bachman, Jerald G., Lee Sigelman, and Greg Diamond. 1987. "Self-selection, Socialization, and Distinctive Military Values: Attitudes of High School Seniors." *Armed Forces & Society* 13 (Winter): 169–187.

Bachman, Jerald G., Lloyd D. Johnston, and Patrick M. O'Malley. 1996. *The Monitoring the Future Project After Twenty-Two Years: Design and Procedures*. MtF Occasional Paper 38. Ann Arbor, Mich.: The Institute for Social Research.

Bachman, Jerald G., David R. Segal, Peter Freedman-Doan, and Patrick M. O'Malley. 1998a. *Military Propensity and Enlistment: Cross-Sectional and Panel Analyses of Correlations and Predictors*. Ann Arbor, Mich.: Institute for Social Research, The University of Michigan.

Bachman, Jerald G., David R. Segal, Peter Freedman-Doan, and Patrick M. O'Malley. 1998b. "Does Enlistment Propensity Predict Accession? High School Seniors' Plans and Subsequent Behavior." *Armed Forces & Society* 25 (Fall): 59–80.

Bachman, Jerald G., David R. Segal, Peter Freedman-Doan and Patrick M. O'Malley. 2000a. "Who Chooses Military Service? Correlates of Propensity and Enlistment in the United States Armed Forces." *Military Psychology* 12 (Spring): 1–30.

Bachman, Jerald G., Peter Freedman-Doan, David R, Segal, and Patrick M. O'Malley. 2000b forthcoming. "Distinctive Military Values Among U.S. Enlistees, 1976–1997: Self-Selection Versus Socialization." *Armed Forces & Society*.

Baer, George W. 1994. *One Hundred Years of Sea Power: The U.S. Navy, 1890–1990*. Stanford, Calif.: Stanford University Press.

Barone, Michael, et al., eds. 1972–2000. *The Almanac of American Politics*. Washington, D.C.: National Journal.

Bartone, Paul T., and Amy B. Adler. 1999. "Cohesion Over Time in a Peacekeeping Medical Task Force." *Military Psychology* 11 (Spring): 85–107.

Bartov, Omer. 1991. *Hitler's Army: Soldiers, Nazis, and War in the Third Reich.* New York: Oxford University Press.

Basler, Roy P., ed. 1955. *The Collected Works of Abraham Lincoln.* New Brunswick, N.J.: Rutgers University Press.

Beck, Nathaniel. 1982. "Parties, Administrations, and Macroeconomic Policy Outcomes." *American Political Science Review* 76 (March): 83–93.

Belkin, Aaron, and Jason McNichol. 2000a. "Effects of 1992 Lifting of Restrictions on Gay and Lesbian Service in the Canadian Forces: Appraising the Evidence." Report prepared for The Center for the Study of Sexual Minorities in the Military, University of California at Santa Barbara (April). <http://www.gaymilitary.ucsb.edu>.

Belkin, Aaron, and Jason McNichol. 2000b. "Effects of Including Gay and Lesbian Soldiers in the Australian Defense Forces: Appraising the Evidence." Report prepared for The Center for the Study of Sexual Minorities in the Military, University of California at Santa Barbara. <http://www.gaymilitary.ucsb.edu>.

Belkin, Aaron, and Melissa Levit. 2000. "Effects of Lifting of Restrictions on Gay and Lesbian Service in the Israeli Forces: Appraising the Evidence." Report prepared for The Center for the Study of Sexual Minorities in the Military, University of California at Santa Barbara (June). <http://www.gaymilitary.ucsb.edu>.

Bell, John M. 1986. "Professional Military Education: Tasks, Topics, Needs." *Armed Forces & Society* 12 (Spring):419 430.

Bemis, Samuel Flagg. 1950. *John Quincy Adams and the Foundations of American Foreign Policy.* New York: Alfred A. Knopf.

Ben Gurion, David. 1993. *Chimes of Independence: Memoirs (March–November 1947)* (Hebrew), ed. Meir Avizohar. Tel Aviv: Am Oved.

Bendor, Jonathan, and Thomas H. Hammond. 1992. "Rethinking Allison's Models." *American Political Science Review* 86 (June):301–322.

Berkowitz, Susan G., Shelley Perry, Pamela Giambo, and Michael J. Wilson. 1997. *An In-Depth Study of Military Propensity: Follow-Up Interviews with 1995 Youth Attitude Tracking Study Respondents.* Arlington, Va.: Defense Manpower Data Center.

Bernardo, Charles Joseph, and Eugene H. Bacon. 1957. *American Military Policy: Its Development Since 1775.* Harrisburg, Penn.: The Military Service Division, The Stackpole Company.

Berube, Allan. 1991. *Coming Out Under Fire: The History of Gay Men and Women in World War Two.* New York: Free Press.

Betts, Richard K. 1991. *Soldiers, Statesmen, and Cold War Crises.* New York: Columbia University Press.

Bianco, William T. 2000. "A Change That Makes No Difference? The Decline in Congressional Military Experience." Unpublished paper.

Bianco, William T., and Jamie Markham. 1999. "Vanishing Veterans: The Decline in Military Experience in the U.S. House." Paper presented at a TISS conference on "Bridging the Gap." Chapel Hill, N.C.: Triangle Institute for Security Studies (July).

Bicknell, John W., Jr. 2000. "Study of Naval Officers' Attitudes Toward Homosexuals in the Military." M.S. Thesis. Monterey Calif.: Naval Postgraduate School.

Biderman, Albert D. 1967. "What is Military?" In *The Draft: A Handbook of Facts and Alternatives,* ed. Sol Tax. Chicago: University of Chicago Press.

Biderman, Albert D., and Laure M. Sharp. 1968. "The Convergence of Military and Civilian Occupational Structures." *American Journal of Sociology* 73 (January):381–399.

Black, Earl and Merle Black. 1987. *Politics and Society in the South.* Cambridge, Mass.: Harvard University Press.

Boatner, Mark Mayo III. 1974. "Continental Congress." In *Encyclopedia of the American Revolution,* Bicentennial Edition. New York: David McKay Company.

Boatner, Mark Mayo III. 1991. *The Civil War Dictionary,* Revised Edition. New York: Vintage Books.

Boëne, Bernard. 1990. "How 'unique' should the military be? A review of representative literature and outline of a synthetic formulation." *Archive Européenne de Sociologie* 31: 3–59.

Boies, John. 1994. *Buying for Armageddon.* New Brunswick, N.J.: Rutgers University Press.

Brehm, John, and Wendy M. Rahn. 1997. "Individual Level Evidence for the Causes and Consequences of Social Capital." *American Journal of Political Science* 41 (July):999–1023.

Broder, David. 1999. "Cheap Insurance; Selective Service, America, and Me." *The Washington Post* (September 22):A33.

Brodie, Bernard. 1946. *Absolute Weapon.* New York: Harcourt, Brace, and Co.

Brodie, Bernard. 1973. *War & Politics.* New York: Macmillan.

Brown v. Board of Education of Topeka, 347 U.S. 483 (1954).

Brunhouse, Robert L. 1971. *The Counter-Revolution in Pennsylvania 1776–1790.* Harrisburg, Penn.: Commonwealth of Pennsylvania, The Pennsylvania Historical and Museum Commission.

Builder, Carl H. 1989. *The Masks of War: American Military Styles in Strategy and Analysis.* Baltimore: Johns Hopkins University Press.

Burk, James. 1989. "Debating the Draft in America." *Armed Forces & Society* 15 (Spring):431–448.

Burk, James. 1993. "Morris Janowitz and the Origins of Sociological Research on Armed Forces and Society." *Armed Forces & Society* 19 (Winter):167–185.

Burk, James. 1995. "Citizenship Status and Military Service: The Quest for Inclusion." *Armed Forces & Society* 21 (Summer):503–529.

Burk, James. 1996. "Collective Violence and World Peace." *Futures Research Quarterly* 12 (Spring):41–55.

Burk, James. 1997. "A New Harmony?" *The Responsive Community* 7 (Summer):73–78.

Burk, James. 1999a. "Civil-Military Interaction." Paper prepared for the TISS project (August).

Burk, James. 1999b. "Military Culture." In *Encyclopedia of Violence, Peace and Conflict,* ed. Lester Kurtz. San Diego, Calif.: Academic Press.

Burk, James. 1999c. "Public Support for Peacekeeping Operations in Lebanon and Somalia." *Political Science Quarterly* 114 (Spring):53–78.

Burns, Robert. 1999. "Military Wants More Troops, Not Weapons." *Bryan/College Station Eagle* (July 10):A4.

Bush, George, and Brent Scowcroft. 1998. *A World Transformed*. New York: Random House.

Butler, John Sibley, and Margaret A. Johnson. 1991. "An Overview of the Relationship Between Demographic Characteristics of Americans and Their Attitudes Toward Military Issues." *Journal of Political and Military Sociology* 19 (Winter):273–291.

Buzzanco, Robert. 1997. *Masters of War: Military Dissent and Politics in the Vietnam Era*. New York: Cambridge University Press.

Campbell, Donald T., and Thelma H. McCormack. 1957. "Military Experience and Attitudes Toward Authority." *American Journal of Sociology* 62 (March):482–490.

Carmines, Edward G., and James A. Stimson. 1989. *Issue Evolution*. Princeton, N.J.: Princeton University Press.

Catton, Bruce. 1960. *Grant Moves South*. Boston: Little, Brown and Company.

Catton, Bruce. 1969. *Grant Takes Command*. Boston: Little, Brown and Company.

Chittick, William O., Keith R. Billingsley, and Rick Travis. 1995. "A Three-Dimensional Model of American Foreign Policy Beliefs." *International Studies Quarterly* 39 (September):313–331.

Chittick, William O., and Keith R. Billingsley. 1999. "Alpha and Gamma Changes in American Foreign Policy Beliefs." Paper presented at the annual meeting of the American Political Science Association, Atlanta, Ga. (September).

Christie, R. 1952. "Changes in Authoritarianism as Related to Situational Factors." *American Psychology* 7:307–308.

Churchill, Winston S. 1923. *The World Crisis, 1915*. New York: Charles Scribner's Sons.

Churchill, Winston S. 1927. *The World Crisis, 1916–1918*. New York: Charles Scribner's Sons.

Citrin, Jack. 1974. "Comment: The Political Relevance of Trust in Government." *American Political Science Review* 68 (September):973–988.

Clausewitz, Carl Von. 1911. *On War*, trans. Colonel J. J. Graham. London: K. Paul Trench, Trubner and Co.

Clodfelter, Mark. 1989. *The Limits of Air Power: The American Bombing of North Vietnam*. New York: Free Press.

Clotfelter, James. 1969. *The Garrison State and the American Military: Public Attitudes and Expectations*. Ph.D. Thesis, the University of North Carolina at Chapel Hill.

Clymer, Adam. 1999. "Sharp Divergence Found in Views of Military and Civilians." *The New York Times* (September 9):A15.

Coakley, Robert W. 1989. *The Role of Federal Military Forces in Domestic Disturbances, 1787–1878*. Washington, D.C.: U.S. Army Center of Military History.

Coffman, Edward M. 1966. *The Hilt of the Sword: The Career of Peyton C. March*. Madison, Wisc.: The University of Wisconsin Press.

Coffman, Edward M. 1997. "The Course of Military History in the United States Since World War II." *The Journal of Military History* 61 (October):761–776.

Cohen, Eliot A. 1985. *Citizens and Soldiers*. Ithaca: Cornell University Press.

Cohen, Eliot A. 1995. "Playing Powell Politics." *Foreign Affairs* 74 (November-December):102–10.

Cohen, Eliot A. 2001 forthcoming. "The Unequal Dialogue: Politicians and the Use of Force."

Cohen, Eliot A. Forthcoming. *Supreme Command*.

Cohen, Eliot A., and John Gooch. 1990. *Military Misfortunes: The Anatomy of Failure in War*. New York: Free Press.

Cohen, William S. 1997. *Remarks at Yale University (September 26)*. Available from the Assistant Secretary of Defense for Public Affairs.

Cohn, Lindsay. 1999. "The Evolution of the Civil-Military 'Gap' Debate." Paper prepared for the TISS project on the Gap between the Military and Civilian Society.

Cole, Ronald H. 1995. *Operation Just Cause: The Planning and Execution of Joint Operations in Panama, February 1988–January 1990*. Washington, D.C.: Joint History Office, Office of the Chairman of the Joint Chiefs of Staff.

Collins, Joseph. 1999. "Civil-Military Relations: How Wide is the Gap?" *International Security* 24 (Winter):199–203.

Converse, Philip E. 1987. "The Enduring Impact of the Vietnam War in American Public Opinion." In *After the Storm: American Society a Decade After the Vietnam War*. Taipei, Republic of China: Institute of American Culture, Academia Sinica.

Coumbe, Arthur T., and Lee S. Harford. 1998. "ROTC History (Unofficial)." Unpublished manuscript.

Crackel, Theodore. 1987. *Mr. Jefferson's Army: Political and Social Reform of the Military Establishment, 1801–1809*. New York: New York University Press.

Cress, Lawrence Delbert. 1979. "Radical Whiggery on the Role of the Military: Ideological Roots of the American Revolutionary Militia." *Journal of the History of Ideas* 40 (January):43–60.

Cress, Lawrence Delbert. 1982. *Citizens in Arms: The Army and the Militia in American Society to the War of 1812*. Chapel Hill, N.C.: The University of North Carolina Press.

Cumings, Bruce. 1990. *The Origins of the Korean War, Volume II*. Princeton, N.J.: Princeton University Press.

Cunliffe, Marcus. 1958. *George Washington: Man and Monument*. Boston, Toronto: Little, Brown and Company.

Dale, Charles, and Curtis Gilroy. 1984. "Determinants of Enlistments: A Macroeconomic Time-Series View." *Armed Forces & Society* 10 (Winter):192–210.

Dana, Charles A. 1898. *Recollections of the Civil War: With the Leaders in Washington and in the Field in the Sixties*. New York: D. Appleton and Company.

Dandeker, Christopher, and James Gow. 1997. "The Future of Peace Support Operations: Strategic Peacekeeping and Success." *Armed Forces & Society* 23 (Spring):327–348.

Danzig, Richard. 1999. *The Big Three: Our Greatest Security Risks and How to Address Them*. Washington, D.C.: Institute for National Strategic Studies.

Dauber, Cori. 2001. "Image as Argument: the Impact of Mogadishu on U.S. Military Intervention." *Armed Forces & Society* 27 (Winter):205–230.

Davis, James A. 1999. "The Brass and The Mass: Attitudes Among Senior Military Officers and a U.S. Cross-Section: 1998–99." Paper prepared for the TISS project (June).

Davis, James A., and Tom W. Smith. 1999. "General Social Surveys, 1972–1998." ICPSR No. 2685. Ann Arbor, Mich.: Inter-university Consortium for Political and Social Research. <http://www.icpsr.umich.edu/cgi-bin/archive.prl?path= ICPSR&num=2685>.

Davis, Lt. K. D., and Virginia Thomas. 1998. *The Experience of Women Who Have Served in the Combat Arms.* January. Ottawa, Canada: Personnel Research Team, National Defense Headquarters.

Davis, Otto A., Melvin J. Hinich, Peter C. Ordeshook. 1970. "An Expository Development of a Mathematical Model of the Electoral Process. *American Political Science Review* 64 (June):426–448.

Davis, Vincent. 1987. "The Vietnam War and Higher Education." In *Democracy, Strategy, and Vietnam: Implications for American Policymaking,* ed. George K. Osburn, et al. Lexington, Mass.: D.C. Heath.

Davis, Vincent. 1999. Comments at the TISS Conference on "Bridging the Gap: Assuring Military Effectiveness When Military Culture Diverges from Civilian Society." Chapel Hill, N.C. (July).

DeFleur, Lois B., and Rebecca L. Warner. 1987. "Air Force Academy Graduates and Nongraduates: Attitudes and Self-concepts." *Armed Forces & Society* 20 (Summer):517–533.

De Gaulle, Charles. 1960. *The Edge of the Sword,* trans. Gerard Hopkins. London: Faber and Faber.

Department of Defense. 1999. *Annual Report.* Washington, D.C.: Government Printing Office. <http://www.dtix.mil/execsec/adr1999/chap9.html>.

Derthick, Martha. 1965. *The National Guard in Politics.* Cambridge, Mass.: Harvard University Press.

Desch, Michael C. 1996. "Threat Environments and Military Missions." In *Civil-Military Relations and Democracy,* ed. Larry Jay Diamond and Marc F. Plattner. Baltimore: Johns Hopkins University Press.

Desch, Michael C. 1998. "Soldiers, States, and Structures: The End of the Cold War and Weakening U.S. Civilian Control." *Armed Forces & Society* 24 (Spring):389–405.

Desch, Michael C. 1999a. *Civilian Control of the Military: The Changing Security Environment.* Baltimore: Johns Hopkins University Press.

Desch, Michael C. 1999b. "What are the Determinants of Civil-Military Culture Gap." Paper presented at the annual meeting of the American Political Science Association. Atlanta, Ga. (September).

Desch, Michael C. 1999c. "Exploring the Gap: Assessing Alternative Theories of the Divergence of Civilian and Military Cultures." Paper prepared for the TISS project (June).

Deutrich, Mabel E. 1962. *Struggle for Supremacy: The Career of General Fred C. Ainsworth.* Washington, D.C.: Public Affairs Press.

Dionne, E.J. 1991. *Why Americans Hate Politics.* New York: Simon & Schuster.

Dionne, E.J. 1998. "Military Culture Grows More Foreign." *Denver Post* (May 26):B7.

Dixon, William J. 1994. "Democracy and the Peaceful Settlement of International Conflict." *American Political Science Review* 88 (March):14–32.

Donnelly, Thomas, Margaret Roth, and Caleb Baker. 1991. *Operation Just Cause: The Storming of Panama.* New York: Lexington Books.

Dunlap, Charles J. 1992. "Origins of the American Military Coup of 2012." *Parameters* 22 (Winter):2–20.

Dunlap, Charles J. 1994. "Welcome to the Junta: The Erosion of Civilian Control of the U.S. Military." *Wake Forest Law Review* 29 (Summer):341–392.

Dworkin, Ronald. 1977. *Taking Rights Seriously.* Cambridge, Mass.: Harvard University Press.

Eden, Lynn. 1984. "Capitalist Conflict and the State: The Making of United States Military Policy in 1948." In *Statemaking and Social Movements,* ed. Charles Bright and Susan Harding. Ann Arbor, Mich.: University of Michigan Press.

Editorial. 1999. "Bigotry in the Military." *The New York Times* (August 30):A18.

Eisenhower, Dwight David. 1961. "Farewell Radio and Television Address to the American People." In *Public Papers of the Presidents: Dwight D. Eisenhower, 1960–61.* Washington, D.C.: Government Printing Office (January 17):1035–1039.

Eisenhower, John S.D. 1997. *Agent of Destiny: The Life and Times of General Winfield Scott.* New York: Free Press.

Eitelberg, Mark J. 1988. *Manpower for Military Occupations.* Washington, D.C.: Office of the Assistant Secretary of Defense for Force Management and Personnel.

Eitelberg, Mark J., and Stephen L. Mehay. 1994. "Demographics and the American Military at the End of the Twentieth Century." In *U.S. Domestic and National Security Agendas,* ed. Sam C. Sarkesian and John Mead Flanagin. Westport, Conn.: Greenwood Press.

Ekirch, Arthur A., Jr. 1956. *The Civilian and the Military.* New York: Oxford University Press.

Elliott, Charles Winslow. 1937. *Winfield Scott: The Soldier and the Man.* New York: The Macmillan Company.

Enloe, Cynthia. 2000. *Maneuvers: The International Politics of Militarizing Women's Lives.* Berkeley, Calif.: University of California Press.

Epp, Charles R. 1998. *The Rights Revolution.* Chicago: University of Chicago Press.

Epstein, R.M. 1991. "The Creation and Evolution of the Army Corps in the American Civil War," *Journal of Military History* 55 (January):21–46.

Estrada, Armando X. and David J. Weiss. 1999. "Attitudes of Military Personnel Toward Homosexuals." *Journal of Homosexuality* 37, 4:83–97.

Everts, Philip. 2000. "Public Opinion in and After the Cold War: The Case of the Netherlands in Comparative Perspective." In *Decisionmaking in a Glass House: Mass Media, Public Opinion, and American and European Foreign Policy in the 21st Century,* ed. Robert Y. Shapiro, Pierangelo Isernia, and Brigitte Lebens Nacos. Lanham, Md.: Rowman & Littlefield Publishers.

Falkus, Malcolm. 1976. "Monash." In *The War Lords: Military Commanders of the Twentieth Century,* ed. Michael Carver. Boston: Little Brown.

Fallows, James. 1981. "The Civilization of the Army." *Atlantic Monthly* (April).

Farris, John H. 1981. "The All-Volunteer Force: Recruitment from Military Families." *Armed Forces & Society* 7 (Summer):550–554.

Farris, John H. 1984. "Economic and Non-economic Factors of Personnel Recruitment and Retention in the AVF." *Armed Forces & Society* 10 (Winter):251–275.

FBI Uniform Crime Reports. 1991–1998. <http://www.hrcusa.org/issues/hate/stats98.html>.

Feaver, Peter D. 1996. "The Civil-Military Problematique: Huntington, Janowitz, and the Question of Civilian Control." *Armed Forces & Society* 23 (Winter):149–178.

Feaver, Peter D. 1998a. "Crisis as Shirking: An Agency Theory Explanation of the Souring of American Civil-Military Relations." *Armed Forces & Society* 24 (Spring):407–434.

Feaver, Peter D. 1998b. "Modeling Civil-Military Relations: A Reply to Burk and Bacevich." *Armed Forces & Society* 24 (Summer):595–602.

Feaver, Peter D. Forthcoming. *Agency, Oversight, and Civil-Military Relations.*

Feaver, Peter D., and Christopher Gelpi. 1999a. "Civilian Hawks and Military Doves: The Civil-Military Gap and the American Use of Force, 1816–1989." Paper prepared for Triangle Institute for Security Studies project, "Bridging the Gap: Assuring Military Effectiveness When Military Culture Diverges from Civilian Society." (September).

Feaver, Peter D., and Christopher Gelpi. 1999b. "The Civil-Military Gap and Casualty Aversion." Paper prepared for the Triangle Institute for Security Studies project, "Bridging the Gap: Assuring Military Effectiveness When Military Culture Diverges from Civilian Society." (September)

Fehrenbach, T. R. 1963. *This Kind of War.* New York: Macmillan.

Ferguson, Thomas. 1984. "From Normalcy to New Deal: Industrial Structure, Party Competition, and American Public Policy in the Great Depression." *International Organization* 38 (Winter):41–94.

Fidell, Eugene R. 1997. "Going on Fifty: Evolution and Devolution in Military Justice." *Wake Forest Law Review* 32 (Winter):1213–1231.

Finer, Samuel E. 1988. *The Man on Horseback: The Role of the Military in Politics.* Boulder: Westview.

Fitzpatrick, David. 1997. "Emory Upton: The Misunderstood Reformer." Ph.D. dissertation. Ann Arbor, Mich.: University of Michigan.

Flacks, Marc. 1999. "Reluctant Patriots? Youth, Politics, and Declining Military Enlistment." Ph.D. Dissertation in progress, Department of Sociology, University of California at Santa Cruz.

Fordham, Benjamin O. 1998. "Economic Interests, Party, and Ideology in Early Cold War Era U.S. Foreign Policy." *International Organization* 52 (Spring):359–396.

Fordham, Benjamin O. 1999. "Partisan Politics and the Allocation of United States Military Spending during the Cold War." Paper presented at the Annual Meeting of the International Studies Association, Washington, D.C.

Förster, Jürgen. 1983. "Das Unternehmen 'Barbarossa' also Eroberungs—und Vernichtungskrieg." In *Das Deutsche Reich und der zweite Weltkrieg*, IV, *Der Angriff auf die Sowjetunion*, ed. Horst Boog, et al. Stuttgart: Deutsche Verlags-Anstalt.

Förster, Jürgen. 1986. "The Dynamics of *Volksgemeinschaft:* The Effectiveness of the German Military Establishment in the Second World War." In *On the Effectiveness of Military Institutions: Historical Case Studies from World War I, the Interwar Period, and World War II,* ed. Allan R. Millet and Williamson Murray. Columbus, Ohio: Mershon Center, Ohio State University.

Foster, Gregory D. 1997. "Confronting the Crisis in Civil-Military Relations." *Washington Quarterly* 20 (Fall):15–33.

Frank, Joseph Allen. 1991. "Profile of a Citizen Army: Shiloh's Soldiers." *Armed Forces & Society* 18 (Fall):97–110.

Franke, Volker C. 1997. "Learning Peace: Attitudes of Future Officers Toward the Security Requirements of the Post–Cold War World." Project on U.S. Post–Cold War Civil-Military Relations Working Paper No. 9. Cambridge, Mass.: John M. Olin Institute for Strategic Studies, Harvard University.

Fredland, J. Eric, and Roger D. Little. 1984. "Educational Levels, Aspirations and Expectations of Military and Civilian Males, Ages 18–22." *Armed Forces & Society* 10 (Winter):211–228.

Freedman, Lawrence, and Efraim Karsh. 1992. *The Gulf Conflict 1990–1991: Diplomacy and War in the New World Order.* Princeton, N.J.: Princeton University Press.

Freedman-Doan, Peter, Jerald G. Bachman, and Patrick M. O'Malley. 2000 forthcoming. *Is There a Gap Between Soldiers and Civilians? Comparing the Political Attitudes of Young Recruits with their Non-Service Peers, 1976–1997.* Ann Arbor, Mich.: Institute for Social Research.

French, E.G., and R.R. Ernest. 1955. "The Relationship Between Authoritarianism and Acceptance of Military Ideology." *Journal of Personality* 24 (December): 181–191.

Friedberg, Aaron L. 1992. "Why Didn't the United States Become a Garrison State?" *International Security* 16 (Spring):128–132.

Frieden, Jeffry. 1988. "Sectoral Conflict and Foreign Economic Policy, 1914–1940." *International Organization* 42 (Winter):59–90.

Friedman, Milton. 1967. "Why Not a Voluntary Army?" In *The Draft: A Handbook of Facts and Alternatives,* ed. Sol Tax. Chicago: University of Chicago Press.

Furman v. Georgia, 408 U.S. 238 (1972).

Gade, Paul, David R. Segal, and Edgar Johnson. 1996. "The Experience of Foreign Militaries." *Out in Force: Sexual Orientation and the Military,* ed. Gregory M. Herek, Jared B. Jobe, and Ralph M. Carney, pp. 106–130. University of Chicago.

Galaskiewicz, Joseph. 1985. "Interorganizational Relations." *Annual Review of Sociology* 11:281–304.

Ganoe, William Addleman. 1964. *The History of the United States Army.* Ashton, Md.: Eric Lundberg.

Gates, Robert M. 1996. *From the Shadows: The Ultimate Insider's Story of Five Presidents and How They Won the Cold War.* New York: Simon & Schuster.

Gertz, Bill. 1993. "Ex-commander in Somalia hits second guessing." *The Washington Times* (October 22):A8.

Gibson, Christopher P., and Don M. Snider. 1999. "Civil-Military Relations and the Potential to Influence: A Look at the National Security Decision-Making Process." *Armed Forces & Society* 25 (Winter):206–211.

Gilroy, Curtis, Robert L. Phillips, and John D. Blair. 1990. "The All-Volunteer Army: Fifteen Years Later." *Armed Forces & Society* 16 (Spring):329–350.

Girouard v. United States, 328 U.S. 61 (1946).

Glaser, James M. 1996. *Race, Campaign Politics, and Realignment in the South*. New Haven, Conn.: Yale University Press.

Glendon, Mary Ann. 1987. *Abortion and Divorce in Western Law*. Cambridge, Mass.: Harvard University Press.

Glendon, Mary Ann. 1991. *Rights Talk: The Impoverishment of Political Discourse*. New York: Free Press.

Goertzel, Ted. 1987. "Public Opinion Concerning Military Spending in the United States, 1937–1985." *International Journal of Sociology and Social Policy* 15 (Spring):61–72.

Goldich, Robert L. 1994. "American Society and the Military." In *Marching Toward the 21st Century*, ed. Mark J. Eitelberg and Stephen L. Mehay. Westport, Conn.: Greenwood Press.

Goldwater-Nichols Department of Defense Reorganization Act of 1986. U.S. Code. Volume 50.

Gordon, Michael R. 1992. "Powell Delivers a Resounding No on Using Limited Force in Bosnia." *The New York Times* (September 28):A1.

Gordon, Michael R., and General Bernard E. Trainor. 1995. *The Generals' War: The Inside Story of the Conflict in the Gulf*. Boston: Little, Brown & Company.

Gorman, Linda, and George W. Thomas. 1991. "Enlistment Motivations of Army Reservists: Money, Self-Improvement, or Patriotism?" *Armed Forces & Society* 17 (Summer):589–599.

Gottlieb, Sanford. 1997. *Defense Addiction: Can America Kick the Habit?* Boulder, Colo.: Westview Press.

Graham, Bradley. 1999. "The Bugle Sounds, But Fewer Answer." *The Washington Post* (March 13):A3.

Graves, Howard D., and Don M. Snider. 1996. "Emergence of the Joint Officer." *Joint Force Quarterly* 13 (Autumn):53–57.

Griffith, James, and Mark Vaitkus. 1999. "Relating Cohesion to Stress, Strain, Disintegration, and Performance: An Organizing Framework." *Military Psychology* 11 (Spring):27–55.

Griffith, Robert K. 1985. "About Face? The U.S. Army and the Draft." *Armed Forces & Society* 12 (Fall):122.

Gronke, Paul. 1999. "A Preliminary Assessment of the Civilian/Military Gap on Civilian and Military Roles." Paper prepared for the Triangle Institute for Security Studies project, "Bridging the Gap: Assuring Military Effectiveness When Military Culture Diverges from Civilian Society."

Gronke, Paul, and Peter D. Feaver. 1999a. "The Foundations of Institutional Trust: Reexamining Public confidence in the U.S. Military From a Civil-Military Perspective." Paper prepared for the TISS Project (September).

Gronke, Paul, and Peter D. Feaver. 1999b. "Uncertain Confidence: Civilian and Military Attitudes About Civil-Military Relations." Paper prepared for the TISS Project on the Gap Between the Military and Civilian Society.

Gronke, Paul, and Peter Feaver. 2000. "Further Analysis of the 'Uncertain Confidence' Thesis: The Civil-Military Gap and Public Confidence in the Military." Paper prepared for the Triangle Institute for Security Studies project, "Bridging the Gap: Assuring Military Effectiveness When Military Culture Diverges from Civilian Society."

Guttmann, Stephanie. 2000. *The Kinder, Gentler Military: Can America's Gender-Neutral Fighting Force Still Win Wars?* New York: Scribner.

Haber, Stephen H., David M. Kennedy, and Stephen D. Krasner. 1997. "Brothers Under the Skin: Diplomatic History and International Relations." *International Security* 22 (Summer):34–43.

Hagan, Kenneth J. 1991. *This People's Navy: The Making of American Sea Power.* New York: Free Press.

Halleck, H. Wager. 1846. *Elements of Military Art and Science, or, course of Instruction in Strategy, Fortification, Tactics of Battle & Embracing the Duties of Staff, Infantry, Cavalry, Artillery, and Engineers, Adapted to the Use of Volunteers and Militia,* First Edition. New York: D. Appleton.

Halleck, H. Wager. 1862. *Elements of Military Art and Science, or, course of Instruction in Strategy, Fortification, Tactics of Battle & Embracing the Duties of Staff, Infantry, Cavalry, Artillery, and Engineers, Adapted to the Use of Volunteers and Militia,* Third Edition. With *Critical Notes on the Mexican and Crimean Wars.* London: D. Appleton & Company.

Haltiner, Karl W. 1998. "The Definite End of the Mass Army in Western Europe?" *Armed Forces & Society* 25 (Fall):7–36.

Hamilton, Holman. 1941. *Zachary Taylor: Soldier of the Republic.* Indianapolis: The Bobbs-Merrill Company Publishers.

Hamilton, Holman. 1951. *Zachary Taylor: Soldier in the White House.* Indianapolis: The Bobbs-Merrill Company Publishers.

Hamilton, Ian. 1921. *The Soul and Body of an Army.* New York: George H. Doran.

Hammond, Paul Y. 1961. *Organizing for Defense: The American Military Establishment in the Twentieth Century.* Princeton, N.J.: Princeton University Press.

Harden, Blaine. 1999. "Waging War on the Serbs: Old Problem, New Lesson." *New York Times on the Web* (June 6):<http://www.nytimes.com/ library/world/ europe/060699kosovo -recon.html>.

Harper, Howard. 2001. "The Military and Society: Reaching and Reflecting Audiences in Fiction and Film." *Armed Forces & Society* 27 (Winter):231–248.

Harrell, Margaret C. and Laura L. Miller. 1997. *New Opportunities for Military Women: Effects on Readiness, Cohesion, and Morale.* Santa Monica, Calif.: RAND.

Harries-Jenkins, Gwyn, and Charles C. Moskos. 1981. "Trend Report: Armed Forces and Society." *Contemporary Sociology* 29: 1–164.

Hattaway, Herman, and Archer Jones. 1983. *How the North Won: A Military History of the Civil War.* Chicago: University of Illinois Press.

Hauser, William L. 1973. *America's Army In Crisis: A Study In Civil-Military Relations.* Baltimore: Johns Hopkins University Press.

Hefner, Frank L. 1992. "A Note on the Regional Impact of Military Retirees." *Armed Forces & Society* 18 (Spring):407–414.

Heitman, Francis B. 1903. "Commanders of the Army from 1775." and "Washington, George." In *Historical Register and Dictionary of the United States Army, From Its Organization, September 29, 1789, to March 1903.* Washington, D.C.: Government Printing Office.

Helmer, John. 1974. *Bringing the War Home.* New York: Free Press.

Henderson, Wm. Darryl. 1985. *Cohesion: The Human Element in Combat.* Washington, D.C.: National Defense University Press.

Herring, George C. 1986. *America's Longest War: The United States and Vietnam, 1950–1975.* New York: Alfred A. Knopf.

Herwig, Holger H. 1997. *The First World War: Germany and Austria-Hungary 1914–1918.* New York: St. Martin's.

Hibbing, John, and Elizabeth Theiss-Morse. 1995. *Congress as Public Enemy.* New York: Cambridge University Press.

Hibbs, Douglas. 1987. *The American Political Economy.* Cambridge, Mass.: Harvard University Press.

Higginbotham, Don. 1971. *The War of American Independence: Military Attitudes, Policies, and Practice, 1763–1789.* New York: The Macmillan Company.

Hillen, John. 1997. "The Military Ethos." *The World & I* (July):34–39.

Hillen, John. 1998a. "The Civilian-Military Gap: Keep It, Defend It, Manage It." *Proceedings of the U.S. Naval Institute* 124 (October):2–4.

Hillen, John. 1998b. "The Military Culture Wars." *The Weekly Standard* (January 12):10–13.

Hillen, John. 1999. "Must U.S. Military Culture Reform?" *Orbis* 43 (Winter):43–57.

Hilsman, Roger. 1959. "The Foreign Policy Consensus: An Interim Research Report." *Journal of Conflict Resolution* 3 (December):361–382.

Hinckley, Ronald. 1992. *People, Polls, and Policymakers: American Public Opinion and National Security.* New York: Lexington Books.

Hoffman, F. G. 1996. *Decisive Force: The New American Way of War.* Westport, Conn.: Praeger.

Hogan, Michael J. 1987. *The Marshall Plan.* New York: Cambridge University Press.

Hogan, Michael J. 1998. *Cross of Iron.* New York: Cambridge University Press.

Holbrooke, Richard. 1998. *To End A War.* New York: Random House.

Holley, Irving B., Jr. 1982. *General John M. Palmer, Citizens Soldiers, and the Army of a Democracy.* Contributions in Military History, Number 28. Westport, Conn.: Greenwood Press.

Holmes, Richard. 1985. *Acts of War: The Behavior of Men in Battle.* New York: Free Press.

Holsti, Ole R. 1996. *Public Opinion and American Foreign Policy.* Ann Arbor, Mich.: The University of Michigan Press.

Holsti, Ole R. 1997. "Continuity and Change in the Domestic and Foreign Policy Beliefs of American Opinion Leaders." Prepared for the Annual Meeting of the American Political Science Association, Washington, D.C. (September).

Holsti, Ole R. 1998. "A Widening Gap between the U.S. Military and Civilian Society? Some Evidence, 1976–96." *International Security* 23 (Winter):5–42.

Holsti, Ole R. 1999. "A Widening Gap Between the U.S. Military and Civilian Society? Some Further Evidence, 1998–99." Paper presented at a conference on "Bridging the Gap," Triangle Institute for Security Studies, Chapel Hill, N.C. (July).

Holsti, Ole R. 2000. "Promotion of Democracy as Popular Demand." In *American Democracy Promotion: Impulses, Strategies, and Impacts,* ed. Michael Cox. New York: Oxford University Press.

Holsti, Ole R., and James N. Rosenau. 1993. "The Structure of Foreign Policy Beliefs among American Opinion Leaders—After the Cold War." *Millennium* 22 (Summer):235–278.

Hoopes, Townsend, and Douglas Brinkley. 1993. *Driven Patriot: The Life and Times of James Forrestal.* New York: Vintage Books.

Horowitz, Irving Louis. 1986. "Human Resources and Military Manpower Requirements." *Armed Forces & Society* 12 (Winter):173–192.

Hosek, James R., John Antel, and Christine E. Peterson. 1989. "Who Stays, Who Leaves? Attrition Among First-Term Enlistees." *Armed Forces & Society* 15 (Spring):389–409.

Hosek, James R., Christine E. Peterson, and Joanna Zorn Heilbrun. 1994. *Military Pay Gaps and Caps.* Santa Monica, Calif.: RAND.

Hoy, Pat C. 1996. "Soldiers and Scholars." *Harvard Magazine* (May–June):64–70.

Huntington, Samuel P. 1957. *The Soldier and the State: The Theory and Politics of Civil-Military Relations.* Cambridge, Mass.: Harvard University Press.

Huntington, Samuel P. 1963. "Power, Expertise, and the Military Profession." *Daedalus* (Fall):785–786.

Hutcheson, Keith. 1996. "The Discipline Crisis." *Armed Forces Journal International* (March).

Ingraham, Larry H. 1984. *The Boys in the Barracks: Observations on American Military Life.* Philadelphia: Institute for the Study of Human Issues.

Ireland, Doug. 2000. "Search and Destroy: Gay-Baiting in the Military Under 'Don't Ask, Don't Tell.'" *The Nation* (July 10):11–16.

Jablonsky, David. 1994. "U.S. Military Doctrine and the Revolution in Military Affairs." *Parameters* 24 (Fall):18–36.

Jackall, Robert. 1988. *Moral Mazes: The World of Corporate Managers.* New York: Oxford University Press.

Jacobs, James B. 1986. *Socio-Legal Foundations of Civil-Military Relations.* New Brunswick, N.J.: Transaction.

Jacobs, James Ripley. 1947. *The Beginnings of the U.S. Army 1783–1812.* Princeton, N.J.: Princeton University Press.

Jaeger, Nicole E. 1997. "Maybe Soldiers Have Rights After All!" *Journal of Criminal Law and Criminology* 87 (Spring):pp. 906–910.

Jaffe, Lorna S. 1993. *The Development of the Base Force, 1989–1992.* Washington, D.C.: Joint History Office, Office of the Chairman of the Joint Chiefs of Staff.

Janis, I.L. 1982. *Groupthink.* Boston: Houghton Mifflin.

Janowitz, Morris. 1960. *The Professional Soldier: A Social and Political Portrait.* New York: Free Press.

Janowitz, Morris. 1964. *The New Military: Changing Patterns of Organization.* New York: W.W. Norton & Co.

Janowitz, Morris. 1967. "The Logic of National Service." In *The Draft: A Handbook of Facts and Alternatives,* ed. Sol Tax. Chicago: University of Chicago Press.

Janowitz, Morris. 1971. *The Professional Soldier: a Social and Political Portrait.* New York: Free Press.

Janowitz, Morris. 1972. "The Decline of the Mass Army." *Military Review* 52 (February):10–16.

Janowitz, Morris. 1975. *Military Conflict.* Beverly Hills, Calif.: Sage Publications.

Janowitz, Morris. 1977. "From Institutional to Occupational: The Need for Conceptual Clarity." *Armed Forces & Society* 4 (Fall):51–54.

Janowitz, Morris. 1978. *The Last Half-Century.* Chicago: University of Chicago Press.

Janowitz, Morris, and David R. Segal. 1967. "Social Cleavage and Party Affiliation." *American Journal of Sociology* 72 (May):601–618.

Janowitz, Morris, and Charles C. Moskos. 1979. "Five Years of the All-Volunteer Force: 1973–1978." *Armed Forces & Society* 5 (February):171–218.

Jennings, M. Kent, and Greg B. Markus. 1974a. "The Effects of Military Service on Political Attitudes: A Panel Study." Paper presented at the Annual Meeting of the American Political Science Association. Chicago.

Jennings, M. Kent, and Richard G. Niemi. 1974b. *The Political Character of Adolescence.* Princeton, N.J.: Princeton University Press.

Jentleson, Bruce W. 1992. "The Pretty Prudent Public: Post-Vietnam American Opinion on the Use of Military Force." *International Studies Quarterly* 36 (March):49–74.

Jentleson, Bruce W., and Rebecca L. Britton. 1998. "Still Pretty Prudent: Post–Cold War American Public Opinion on the Use of Military Force." *Journal of Conflict Resolution* 42 (August):395–417.

Jentleson, Bruce. W. 2000. *Coercive Prevention: Normative, Political, and Policy Dilemmas.* Washington: United States Institute of Peace.

Jervis, Robert. 1989. *The Meaning of the Nuclear Revolution: Statecraft and the Prospect of Armageddon.* Ithaca, N.Y.: Cornell University Press.

Johnson, David E. 1997. "Modern U.S. Civil-Military Relations: Wielding the Terrible Swift Sword." McNair Paper No. 57. Washington, D.C.: National Defense University, Institute for National Strategic Studies.

Johnson, Douglas, and Steven Metz. 1994. "Civil-Military Relations in the United States: The State of the Debate." *Washington Quarterly* 18 (Winter):197–213.

Kamlet, Mark S., and David Mowery. 1987. "Influences on Executive and Congressional Budget Priorities, 1953–1981." *American Political Science Review* 81 (March):155–178.

Karsten, Peter. 1972. *The Naval Aristocracy: The Golden Age of Annapolis and the Emergence of Modern American Navalism.* New York: Free Press.

Karsten, Peter. 1974. "Anti-ROTC: Response to Vietnam or 'Consciousness III?'" In *New Civil-Military Relations,* ed. John P. Lovell and Philip S. Kronenberg. New Brunswick: Transaction Books.

Karsten, Peter. 1983. "Ritual and Rank: Religious Affiliation, Father's 'Calling,' and Successful Advancement in the U.S. Officer Corps of the Twentieth Century." *Armed Forces & Society* 9 (Spring):427–440.

Katzenstein, Mary Fainsod. 1998. *Faithful and Fearless: Moving Feminist Protest Inside the Church and Military.* Princeton, N.J.: Princeton University Press.

Katzenstein, Mary Fainsod, and Judith Reppy, eds. 1999. *Beyond Zero Tolerance: Discrimination in Military Culture.* Lanham, Md.: Rowman and Littlefield Publishers.

Kelleher, Catherine McArdle. 1978. "Mass Armies in the 1970s." *Armed Forces & Society* 5 (November):3–29.

Kellestedt, Lyman A., John C. Green, James L. Guth, and Corwin E. Smidt. 1997. "Is There a Culture War?: Religion and the 1996 Election." Paper presented at the annual meeting of the American Political Science Association, Washington, D.C. (August).

Kennedy, William V. 1993. *The Military and Media: Why the Press Cannot be Trusted to Cover a War.* Westport, Conn.: Praeger.

Kier, Elizabeth. 1998. "Homosexuals in the U.S. Military: Open Integration and Combat Effectiveness." *International Security* 23 (Fall):5–39.

Kier, Elizabeth. 1999. "Discrimination and Military Cohesion: An Organizational Perspective." In *Beyond Zero Tolerance: Discrimination in Military Culture,* ed. Mary Fainsod Katzenstein and Judith Reppy. Lanham, Md.: Rowman and Littlefield.

Killian, Johnny H., and George A. Costello, eds. 1996. U.S. Constitution, 103rd Congress, 1st Session, Senate Document No. 103–6 (serial 14152), "The Constitution of the United States of America: Analysis and Interpretation: Annotations of Cases Decided in the Supreme Court of the United States to June 29, 1992." Prepared by the Congressional Research Service, Library of Congress. Washington, D.C.: U.S. Government Printing Office.

King, David C. 1997. "The Polarization of Parties and Mistrust of Government." In *Why People Don't Trust Government,* ed. Joseph S. Nye, Philip Zelikow, and David C. King. Cambridge, Mass.: Harvard University Press.

King, David C. 1999. "Yep, The Generation of Trust: Public Confidence in the U.S. Military Since Vietnam." Paper presented to the Defense Science Board. Arlington, Va. (July 22).

King, David C., and Zachary Karabell. 1999a. "An American Anomaly: The Evolution of Public Trust in the Military from Tet to Tailhook." Unpublished manuscript. Cambridge, Mass.: Kennedy School of Government, Harvard University.

King, David C., and Zachary Karabell. 1999b. "Yep, The Generation of Trust: Public Confidence in the U.S. Military." Unpublished manuscript. Cambridge, Mass.: Kennedy School of Government, Harvard University.

King, Jere Clemens. 1960. *Foch versus Clemenceau: France and German Dismemberment, 1918–1919.* Cambridge, Mass.: Harvard University Press.

Kinsley, Michael. 1989. "The Rich Don't Serve: So What?" *Washington Monthly* 21 (March):26–27.

Kitfield, James. 1995. *Prodigal Soldiers: How the Generation of Officers Born of Vietnam Revolutionized the American Style of War.* New York: Simon & Schuster.

Kitfield, James. 1997. *Prodigal Soldiers: How the Generation of Officers Born of Vietnam Revolutionized the American Style of War.* Washington, D.C.: Brassey's.

Kitfield, James. 1998. "Standing Apart." *National Journal* 30 (June 13):1350–1358.

Kitfield, James. 2000. "The Pen and the Sword." *Government Executive* 32 (April):18–28.

Kohn, Melvin L., and Carmi Schooler. 1983. *Work and Personality: An Inquiry into the Impact of Social Stratification.* Norwood, N.J.: Ablex.

Kohn, Richard H. 1970. "The Inside History of the Newburgh Conspiracy: America and the Coup d'Etat," *The William and Mary Quarterly.* Third Series, 27:2 (April 1970):187–220.

Kohn, Richard H. 1972a. "Rebuttal to 'Horatio Gates at Newburgh, 1783: A Misunderstood Role.'" *The William and Mary Quarterly* 29 (January):151–158.

Kohn, Richard H. 1972b. "Rebuttal to 'The Newburgh Conspiracy Reconsidered.'" *The William and Mary Quarterly* 31 (April):290–298.

Kohn, Richard H. 1974. "The All-Volunteer Army: Too High a Price?" *Proceedings of the U.S. Naval Institute* 100 (March):35–42.

Kohn, Richard H. 1975. *Eagle and Sword: The Federalists and the Creation of the Military Establishment in America, 1783–1802.* New York: Free Press.

Kohn, Richard H. 1994. "Out of Control: The Crisis in Civil-Military Relations." *The National Interest* 35 (Spring):3–17.

Kohn, Richard H. 1997. "How Democracies Control the Military." *Journal of Democracy* 8 (October):140–153.

Krehbiel, Keith. 1991. *Information and Legislative Organization.* Ann Arbor, Mich.: University of Michigan Press.

Kreisher, Otto. 1996. "Ranks of Veterans in Congress Have Begun to Fade Away." *San Diego Union-Tribune* (June 22):A22.

Krepinevich, Andrew F., Jr. 1986. *The Army and Vietnam.* Baltimore: Johns Hopkins University Press.

Krepinevich, Andrew F., Jr. 1994. "Cavalry to Computer: The Pattern of Military Revolutions." *National Interest* 37 (Fall):30–42.

Krulak, Lt. General Victor H., USMC (Ret.). 1987. *Organization for National Security: A Study.* Washington, D.C.: United States Strategic Institute.

Kull, Steven, and I.M. Destler. 1999. *Misreading the Public: The Myth of a New Isolationism.* Washington, D.C.: Brookings.

Kurtz, Stephen G. 1957. *The Presidency of John Adams: The Collapse of Federalism 1795–1800.* Philadelphia: University of Pennsylvania Press.

Lakoff, George. 1996. *Moral Politics.* Chicago: University of Chicago Press.

Lamis, Alexander P. 1990. *The Two Party South.* Oxford: Oxford University Press.

Landis, Dan, Mickey R. Dansby, and Michael Hoyle. 1997. "The Effects of Race on Procedural Justice: The Case of the Uniform Code of Military Justice." *Armed Forces & Society* 24 (Winter):183–220.

Lane, Jack C. 1978. *Armed Progressive: General Leonard Wood.* San Rafael, Calif.: Presidio Press.

Larrabee, Eric. 1987. *Commander in Chief: Franklin Delano Roosevelt, His Lieutenants, and Their War.* New York: Harper & Row.

Larson, Arthur D. 1974. "Military Professionalism and Civil Control: A Comparative Analysis of Two Interpretations." *Journal of Political and Military Sociology* 2 (Spring):57–72.

Larson, Eric V. 1996. *Casualties and Consensus*. Santa Monica, Calif.: RAND.

Lasswell, Harold. 1941. "The Garrison State." *American Journal of Sociology* 46 (January):455–468.

Lasswell, Harold. 1962. "The Garrison State Hypothesis Today." In *Changing Patterns of Military Politics*, ed. Samuel P. Huntington. New York: Free Press.

Laurie, Clayton D., and Ronald H. Cole. 1997. *The Role of Federal Military Forces in Domestic Disorders*. Washington, D.C.: U.S. Army Center of Military History.

Layton, Edward, Jr. 1971. *The Revolt of the Engineers*. Cleveland, Ohio: The Press of Case Western University.

Lebovic, James. 1994. "Riding Waves or Making Waves? The Services and the U.S. Defense Budget, 1981–1993." *American Political Science Review* 88 (December):839–852.

Lebovic, James. 1996. *Foregone Conclusions*. Boulder, Colo.: Westview Press.

Levi, Margaret. 1997. *Consent, Dissent, and Patriotism*. Cambridge, Mass.: Cambridge University Press.

Lewis, Lloyd. 1932. *Sherman: Fighting Prophet*. New York: Harcourt, Brace and Company.

Lifton, Robert Jay. 1973. *Home from the War*. New York: Simon and Schuster.

Link, Arthur S., and John Whiteclay Chambers II. 1991. "Woodrow Wilson as Commander in Chief." In *The United States Military under the Constitution of the United States, 1789–1989*, ed. Richard H. Kohn. New York: New York University Press.

Lipset, Seymour M. 1981. *Political Man*. Baltimore: Johns Hopkins University Press.

Lipset, Seymour M., and William Schneider. 1983. *The Confidence Gap: Business, Labor and Government in the Public Mind*. New York: Free Press.

Lipset, Seymour M., and William Schneider. 1987. *The Confidence Gap: Business, Labor and Government in the Public Mind*. New York: Free Press.

Lo, Clarence Y.H. 1982. "Theories of the State and Business Opposition to Increased Military Spending." *Social Problems* 29 (April):424–438.

Lochman, Robert F., and Aline O. Quester. 1985. "The AVF: Outlook for the Eighties and Nineties." *Armed Forces & Society* 11 (Winter):169–182.

Loving v. United States, 517 U.S. 748 (1996).

Lowery, David, and William D. Berry. 1990. "An Alternative Approach to Understanding Budgetary Trade-Offs." *American Journal of Political Science* 34 (August):671–705.

Lurie, Jonathan. 1992. *Arming Military Justice*. Princeton, N.J.: Princeton University Press.

Lurie, Jonathan. 1998. *Pursuing Military Justice*. Princeton, N.J.: Princeton University Press.

Luttwak, Edward N. 1994. "Washington's Biggest Scandal." *Commentary* 97 (May):29–33.

MacCoun, Robert. 1993. "What is Known About Unit Cohesion and Military Performance." In *Sexual Orientation and U.S. Military Personnel Policy: Options and Assessment*, National Defense Research Institute. Santa Monica, Calif.: RAND.

Mahon, John K. 1983. "History of the Militia and the National Guard." In *The Macmillan Wars of the United States*, ed. Louis Morton. New York: Macmillan Publishing Company.

Mandelbaum, Michael. 1996. "Foreign Policy as Social Work." *Foreign Affairs* 75 (January–February):16–32.

Margalit, Avishai. 1996. *The Decent Society*, trans. Naomi Goldblum. Cambridge, Mass.: Harvard University Press.

Markusen, Ann R., Scott Campbell, Peter Hall, and Sabina Dietrich. 1991. *The Rise of the Gunbelt*. New York: Oxford University Press.

Markusen, Ann R., and Joel Yudken. 1992. *Dismantling the Cold War Economy*. New York: Basic Books.

Marmion, Harry A. 1971. *The Case Against a Volunteer Army*. Chicago: Quadrangle Books.

Marshall, Patrick G. 1991. *Should the U.S. Reinstate the Draft?* Editorial Research Reports. Washington, D.C.: Congressional Quarterly.

Marshall, S.L.A. 1980. *The Soldier's Load and the Mobility of a Nation*. Quantico, Va.: Marine Corps Association.

Marshall, T.H. 1977. "Citizenship and Social Class." In *Class, Citizenship, and Social Development*. Chicago: University of Chicago Press.

Marszalek, John F. 1993. *Sherman: A Soldier's Passion for Order*. New York: Free Press.

Martin, Michel. 1977. "Conscription and the Decline of the Mass Army in France, 1960–1975." *Armed Forces & Society* 3 (May):355–406.

Martin, Michel. 1981. "Like Father, Like Son: Career Succession Among The Saint-Cyriens." *Armed Forces & Society* 7 (Summer):561–583.

Maslowski, Peter. 1990. "Army Values and American Values." *Military Review* 70 (April):10–23.

Masters, Kim. 1993. "Salute to the Old Chief; Army Association Warmly Greets George Bush." *The Washington Post* (October 21):B1.

Matthews, Lloyd J. 1996. "The Politician as Operational Commander." *Army* (March):36.

Matthews, Lloyd J. 1998. "The Political-Military Rivalry for Operational Control in U.S. Military Actions: A Soldier's Perspective." Carlisle, Pa.: U.S. Army War College, Strategic Studies Institute (June 22).

Maynes, Charles William. 1998. "The Perils Of (and For) an Imperial America." *Foreign Policy* 111 (Summer):36–47.

McClellan, George B. 1989. *The Civil War Papers of George B. McClellan: Selected Correspondence, 1860–1865*, ed. Stephen W. Sears. New York: Ticknor & Fields.

McCormick, David. 1998. *The Downsized Warrior: America's Army in Transition*. New York: New York University Press.

McDougall, Walter A. 1997. "Sex, Lies, and Infantry." *Commentary* 104 (September):43–47.

McFeely, William S. 1981. *Grant: A Biography*. New York: W. W. Norton.

McIsaac, James, and Naomi Verdugo. 1995. "Civil-Military Relations: a Domestic Perspective." *U.S. Civil-Military Relations*. ed. Don M. Snider and Miranda A. Carlton-Carew. Washington D.C.: Center for Strategic and International Studies.

McKee, Christopher. 1991. *A Gentlemanly and Honorable Profession: The Creation of the U.S. Naval Officer Corps, 1794–1815*. Annapolis, Md.: Naval Institute Press.

McKibbin, Carroll. 1997. "Biographical Characteristics of Members of the United States Congress." ICPSR No. 7803. Ann Arbor, Mich.: Inter-university Consortium for Political and Social Research. <http://www.icpsr.umich.edu/cgi-bin/archive.prl?path=ICPSR&num=7803>.

McKown, Robert F., Bernard Udis, and Colin Ash. 1980. "Economic Analysis of the All-Volunteer Force." *Armed Forces & Society* 7 (Fall):113–132.

McMaster, H. R. 1997. *Dereliction of Duty: Lyndon Johnson, Robert McNamara, the Joint Chiefs of Staff, and the Lies that led to Vietnam*. New York: Harper Collins.

McNamara, Robert S. 1995. *In Retrospect: The Tragedy and Lessons of Vietnam*. New York: Random House.

Melman, Seymour. 1970. *Pentagon Capitalism*. New York: McGraw-Hill.

Michie, Peter Smith. 1885. *The Life and Letters of Emory Upton, Colonel of the Fourth Regiment of Artillery and Brevet Major-General, U.S. Army*. New York: D. Appleton & Company.

Miller, Laura L. 1994. "Fighting for a Just Cause: Soldiers' Attitudes on Gays in the Military." In *Gays and Lesbians in the Military: Issues, Concerns, and Contrasts*, ed. Wilbur J. Scott and Sandra Carson Stanley. New York: Aldine de Gruyter.

Miller, Laura L. 1997. "Not Just Weapons of the Weak: Gender Harassment as a Form of Protest for Army Men." *Social Psychology Quarterly* 60 (March):32–51.

Miller, Laura L., and Charles Moskos. 1992. Unpublished survey data.

Millett, Allan R. 1986. "Over Where? The AEF and the American Strategy for Victory, 1917–1918." In *Against All Enemies: Interpretations of American Military History from Colonial Times to the Present*, ed. Kenneth J. Hagan and William R. Roberts. New York: Greenwood Press.

Millett, Allan R., and Peter Maslowski. 1994. *For the Common Defense: A Military History of the United States of America*. New York: Free Press.

Millis, Walter, Harvey Mansfield, and Harold Stein. 1958. *Arms and the State: Civil-Military Elements in National Policy*. New York: Twentieth Century Fund.

Mills, C. Wright. 1957. *The Power Elite*. New York: Oxford University Press.

Mintz, Alex. 1988. *The Politics of Resource Allocation in the U.S. Department of Defense*. Boulder, Colo.: Westview Press.

Miquel, Pierre. 1996. *Clemenceau: la Guerre et la Paix*. Paris: Tallandier.

Mitchell, Brian. 1989. *Weak Link: The Feminization of the American Military*. Washington, D.C.: Regnery Gateway.

Mitchell, Brian. 1998. *Women in the Military: Flirting with Disaster*. Washington, D.C.: Regnery.

Moniz, Dave. 1999. "Why Teens Balk at Joining Military." *Christian Science Monitor* (February 25):1.

Moore, William C. 1998. "The Military Must Revive its Warrior Spirit" *The Wall Street Journal* (October 27):A22.

Mordacq, General Jean Jules Henri. 1930. *Le Ministère Clemenceau: Journal d'un Témoin*. Paris: Librairie Plon.

Mordacq, General Jean Jules Henri. 1939. *Clemenceau*. Paris: Les Éditions de France.

Morgenthau, Hans J. 1985. *Politics Among Nations*. New York: Knopf.

Morris, Madeline. 1996. "By Force of Arms: Rape, War, and Military Culture." *Duke Law Journal* 45 (February):651–781.

Morton, Louis. 1953. *The Fall of the Philippines (United States Army in World War II: The War in the Pacific)*. Washington, D.C.: Office of the Chief of Military History Department of the Army.

Morton, Louis. 1962. *Strategy and Command: The First Two Years (United States Army in World War II: The War in the Pacific)*. Washington, D.C.: Office of the Chief of Military History Department of the Army.

Moskos, Charles C. 1970. *The American Enlisted Man*. New York: Russell Sage Foundation.

Moskos, Charles C. 1973. "The Emergent Military: Civil, Traditional, or Plural?" *Pacific Sociological Review* 16 (April):255–280.

Moskos, Charles C. 1977. "From Institution to Occupation: Trends in Military Organization." *Armed Forces & Society* 4 (November):41–50.

Moskos, Charles C. 1986. "Success Story: Blacks in the Military." *Atlantic Monthly* (May).

Moskos, Charles C. 1990. "Army Women." *Atlantic Monthly* (May).

Moskos, Charles C. 1994. "From Citizens' Army to Social Laboratory." In *Gays and Lesbians in the Military*, ed. Wilbur J. Scott and Sandra Carson Stanley. New York: Aldine De Gruyter.

Moskos, Charles C. 1999. "Short-Term Soldiers." *The Washington Post* (March 8):A19.

Moskos, Charles C., and Frank R. Wood, eds. 1988. *The Military: More Than Just a Job?* Washington, D.C.: Pergamon-Brassey's International Defense Publishers.

Moskos, Charles C., and James Burk. 1994. "The Postmodern Military." In *The Military in New Times*, ed. James Burk. Boulder, Colo.: Westview.

Moskos, Charles C., and John Sibley Butler. 1996. *All That We Can Be: Black Leadership and Racial Integration the Army Way*. New York: Basic Books.

Moskos, Charles C., John Allen Williams, and David R. Segal, eds. 2000. *The Postmodern Military: Armed Forces After the Cold War*. New York: Oxford University Press.

Murchison, William. 1999. "Boomer Ethic is Hostile to Military." *Dallas Morning News* (February 24).

Myers, Stephen Lee. 1998a. "Good Times Mean a Hard Sell for the Military." *The New York Times* (November 3):A16.

Myers, Stephen Lee. 1998b. "Young People Choosing Fun Over Being All They Can Be." *The New York Times* (November 3).

Myers, Stephen Lee. 1999a. "All in Favor of This Target, Say Yes, Si, Oui, Ja." *The New York Times* (April 25).

Myers, Stephen Lee. 1999b. "For Short-Handed Military, A Wisp of a Draft." *The New York Times* (February 7).

Myers, Stephen Lee. 1999c. "In Added Role, Pentagon Chief Is Traveling Salesman." *The New York Times* (February 19):A16.

Myers, Stephen Lee. 2000a. "Pentagon Taking Opportunity for Show." *The New York Times* (July 28): A1.

Myers, Steven Lee. 2000b. "Gore's Service Does Not Keep Vets From Bush." *The New York Times* (September 21): A1.

Myers, Stephen Lee, and Eric Schmitt. 1999. "Conduct of War Frays Commanders' Rapport." *The New York Times* (May 30):<http://www.nytimes.com/library/world/europe/053099kosovo-pentagon.html>.

Nailor, Peter. 1978. "Military Strategy." In *Approaches and Theory in International Relations*, ed. Trevor Taylor. London: Longman.

Nalty, Bernard C. 1986. *Strength for the Fight: A History of Black Americans in the Military*. New York: Free Press.

National Defense Research Institute. 1993. *Sexual Orientation and U.S. Military Personnel Policy: Options and Assessment*. Santa Monica, Calif.: RAND.

Nelson, Paul David. 1972. "Horatio Gates at Newburgh, 1783: A Misunderstood Role." *The William and Mary Quarterly* 29 (January):143–151.

Newcity, Janet. 1999. Description of the TISS Bridging the Gap Surveys, 1998–1999. Available from the Triangle Institute for Security Studies.

Nie, Norman H., J.R. Petrocik, and Sidney Verba. 1980. *The Changing American Voter*. Cambridge, Mass.: Harvard University Press.

Nye, Joseph S. 1997. "Introduction: The Decline of Confidence in Government." In *Why People Don't Trust Government*, ed. Joseph S. Nye, Philip Zelikow and David C. King. Cambridge, Mass.: Harvard University Press.

O'Callahan v. Parker, 395 U.S. 258 (1969).

Oi, Walter. 1967. "The Costs and Implications of An All-volunteer Force." In *The Draft: A Handbook of Facts and Alternatives*, ed. Sol Tax. Chicago: University of Chicago Press.

Oliver, Laurel W., Joan Harman, Elizabeth Hoover, Stephanie M. Hayes, and Nancy A. Pahndi. 1999. "A Quantitative Integration of the Military Cohesion Literature." *Military Psychology* 11 (Spring):57–83.

Olson, Daniel V. A. 1997. "Dimensions of Cultural Tension among the American Public." In *Cultural Wars in American Politics: Critical Reviews of a Popular Myth*, ed. Rhys H. Williams. New York: Aldine DeGruyter.

Owens, William A. 1999. "Making the Joint Journey." *Joint Force Quarterly* 21 (Spring):93.

Palmer, Bruce, Jr. 1984. *The 25-Year War: America's Military Role in Vietnam*. Lexington, Ky.: University Press of Kentucky.

Palmer, Michael A. 1987. *Stoddert's War: Naval Operations During the Quasi-War with France, 1798–1801*. Columbia, S.C.: University of South Carolina Press.

Parker v. Levy, 417 U.S. 733 (1974).

Parsons, Talcott. 1968. "Professions." In *International Encyclopedia of the Social Sciences*, ed. David L. Sills. New York: Macmillan.

Patterson, Kelly D., and David B. Magleby. 1992. "Poll Trends: Public Support for Congress." *Public Opinion Quarterly* 56 (Winter):539–551.

Patterson, Orlando. 1997. *The Ordeal of Integration*. Washington, D.C.: Counterpoint.

Peck, B. Mitchell. 1994. "Assessing the Career Mobility of U.S. Army Officers: 1950–1974." *Armed Forces & Society* 12 (Winter):217–237.

Perry, Mark. 1989. *Four Stars*. Boston: Houghton Mifflin Company.

Perry, Shelley, James Griffith, and Terry White. 1991. "Retention of Junior Enlisted in the All-Volunteer Army Reserves." *Armed Forces & Society* 18 (Fall):111–133.

Petraeus, David H. 1989. "Military Influence and the Post-Vietnam Use of Force." *Armed Forces & Society* 15 (Summer):489–505.

Phillips, John L., Jr. 1992. *How to Think About Statistics*. New York: W.H. Freeman and Co.

Phillips, Kevin. 1999. *The Cousins' Wars: Religion, Politics, and the Triumph of Anglo-America*. New York: Basic Books.

Pillsbury, Hobart B., Jr. 1987. "Raising the Armed Forces." *Armed Forces & Society* 14 (Fall):65–84.

Pinch, Franklin C. 1981. "Military Manpower and Social Change: Assessing The Institutional Fit." *Armed Forces & Society* 8 (Fall):575–600.

Pirnie, Bruce. 1998. *Civilians and Soldiers: Achieving Better Coordination*. Santa Monica, Calif.: RAND.

Pogue, Forrest C. 1880–1889. *Education of a General*, ed. Gordon Harrison. New York: The Viking Press.

Pogue, Forrest C. 1963. *George C. Marshall*. New York: The Viking Press.

Pogue, Forrest C. 1966. *George C. Marshall: Ordeal and Hope 1939–1942*. New York: The Viking Press.

Pogue, Forrest C. 1973. *George C. Marshall: Organizer of Victory 1943–1945*. New York: The Viking Press.

Pogue, Forrest C. 1987. *George C. Marshall: Statesman, 1945–1959*. New York: The Viking Press.

Popkin, Samuel L. 1991. *The Reasoning Voter*. Chicago: University of Chicago Press.

Porter, Bruce D. 1994. *War and the Rise of the State: The Military Foundations of Modern Politics*. New York: Free Press.

Posen, Barry R. 1984. *The Sources of Military Doctrine: France, Britain, and Germany Between the World Wars*. Ithaca: Cornell University Press.

Posen, Barry R. 1993. "Nationalism, the Mass Army, and Military Power." *International Security*. 18 (Fall):80–124.

Powell, Colin L. 1992a. "U.S. Forces: Challenges Ahead." *Foreign Affairs* 72 (Winter):32–45.

Powell, Colin L. 1992b. "Why Generals Get Nervous." *The New York Times* (October 8):A35.

Powell, Colin L., John Lehman, William Odom, Samuel P. Huntington, and Richard H. Kohn. 1994. "Exchange in Civil-Military Relations." *National Interest* 36 (Summer):23–31.

Powell, Colin L., with Joseph E. Persico. 1995. *My American Journey.* New York: Random House.

Powell, Walter W., and Paul J. DiMaggio, eds. 1991. *The New Institutionalism in Organizational Analysis.* Chicago: University of Chicago Press.

Power, Jonathan. 1996. "The Decline of Military Culture." *Toronto Star* (December 24):A29.

Priest, Dana. 1999. "A Decisive Battle That Never Was." *The Washington Post* (September 19):A1.

Priest, Robert, Terrence Fullerton, and Claude Bridges. 1982. "Personality and Value Changes in West Point Cadets." *Armed Forces & Society* 8 (Summer):629–642.

Prime Minister's Office. 1941. "Completion of and Conclusions from Exercise Victor." *Records of the Prime Minister's Office.* PREM 3/496/4.

Putnam, Robert. 1995a. "Bowling Alone: America's Declining Social Capital." *Journal of Democracy* 6: 65–78.

Putnam, Robert 1995b. "Tuning In, Tuning Out: The Strange Disappearance of Social Capital in America." *PS: Political Science and Politics* 28: 664–683.

Quester, Aline O., and James Thomason. 1984. "Keeping the Force: Retaining Military Careerists." *Armed Forces & Society* 11 (Fall): 85–95.

Rabil, Daniel J. 1998. "Please, Impeach my Commander in Chief." *The Washington Times* (November 9): 19–20.

Radatz, Martha. 1998. "Uniform Complaint." *The New Republic* (November 30):16–17.

Radosh, Ronald. 1996. *Divided They Fell: The Demise of the Democratic Party, 1964–1996.* New York: Free Press.

Remini, Robert V. 1977. *Andrew Jackson and the Course of American Empire, 1767–1821.* New York: Harper & Row.

Remini, Robert V. 1981. *Andrew Jackson and the Course of American Freedom, 1822–1832.* New York: Harper & Row.

Remini, Robert V. 1984. *Andrew Jackson and the Course of American Democracy, 1833–1845.* New York: Harper & Row.

Report of the President's Commission on an All-Volunteer Force. 1970. Washington, D.C.: Government Publishing Office.

Richman, Alvin, David B. Nolle, and Eloise Malone. 1999. "American Elites and the General Public: A Comparison of Attitude Structures and Priorities on Foreign Policy Issues During the 1990s." Paper presented at the annual meeting of the American Political Science Association, Atlanta, Ga. (September).

Ricks, Thomas E. 1996. "On American Soil: the Widening Gap Between the U.S. Military and U.S. Society." Project on the U.S. Post–Cold War Civil-Military Relations Working Paper No. 3. Cambridge, Mass.: John M. Olin Institute for Strategic Studies, Harvard University (May).

Ricks, Thomas E. 1997a. "Army Faces Recruiting Obstacle: A Less-Macho Image." *The Wall Street Journal* (July 15): A20.

Ricks, Thomas E. 1997b. "Duke Study Finds Sharp Rightward Shift in Military." *The Wall Street Journal* (November 11): A20.

Ricks, Thomas E. 1997c. *Making the Corps: Sixty-one Men Came to Parris Island to Become Marines, Not All of Them Made It.* New York: Scribner.

Ricks, Thomas E. 1997d. "The Widening Gap Between the Military and Society." *The Atlantic Monthly* 280 (July): 66–78.

Ricks, Thomas E. 1997e. "What We Can Learn From Them." *Parade Magazine* (November 9).

Rielly, John E. 1975–1999. *American Public Opinion and U.S. Foreign Policy.* Published every fourth year. Chicago: Chicago Council on Foreign Relations.

Robbins, Caroline. 1959. *The Eighteenth-Century Commonwealthman: Studies in the Transmission, Development and Circumstance of English Liberal Thought from the Restoration of Charles II until the War with the Thirteen Colonies.* Cambridge, Mass.: Harvard University Press.

Roberts, Paul Craig. 1998. "Cultural Demolition in the Military." *The Washington Times* (November 20): A20.

Robinson, John P. and John A. Fleishman. 1988. "Ideological Identification: Trends and Interpretations of the Liberal-Conservative Balance." *Public Opinion Quarterly* 52 (Spring): 134–145.

Roghmann, Klaus. 1966. *Dogmatismus und Authoritarianismus.* Meissenheim, Germany: Anton Hain.

Roghmann, Klaus, and Wolfgang Sodeur. 1972. "The Impact of Military Service on Authoritarian Attitudes." *American Journal of Sociology* 78 (September):418–433.

Roghmann, Klaus, and Wolfgang Sodeur. 1973. "Reply to Stinchcombe." *American Journal of Sociology* 79 (July): 159–164.

Roman, Peter J., and David W. Tarr. 1998. "The Joint Chiefs of Staff: From Service Parochialism to Jointness." *Political Science Quarterly* 113 (Spring): 91–111.

Roman, Peter J., and David W. Tarr. 1999. "Political-Military Relations at the Senior Policy Making Level: Conflict, Crisis, or Cooperation?" Paper prepared for the TISS Conference on Bridging the Gap: Assuring Military Effectiveness when Military Culture Diverges from Civilian Society. Chapel Hill, N.C. (July).

Rosen, Leora N., and Lee Martin. 1997. "Sexual Harassment, Cohesion, and Combat Readiness in U.S. Army Support Units." *Armed Forces & Society* 24 (Winter): 221–245.

Rosen, Leora N, Paul D. Bliese, Kathleen A. Wright, and Robert K. Gifford. 1999. "Gender Composition and Group Cohesion in U.S. Army Units: A Comparison Across Five Studies." *Armed Forces & Society* 25 (Spring): 365–386.

Rosenberg, Morris. 1957. *Occupations and Values.* Glencoe, Ill.: Free Press.

Rush, Robert S. 1999. "A Different Perspective: Cohesion, Morale, and Operational Effectiveness in the German Army, Fall 1944." *Armed Forces & Society* 25 (Spring): 477–508.

Russett, Bruce M. 1969. "Who Pays for Defense?" *American Political Science Review* 63 (June): 412–426.

Russett, Bruce M. 1974. "The Revolt of the Masses." In *New Civil-Military Relations,* ed. John P. Lovell and Philip S. Kronenberg. New Brunswick: Transaction Books.

Russett, Bruce M. 1990. *Controlling the Sword: The Democratic Governance of National Security*. Cambridge, Mass.: Harvard University Press.

Russett, Bruce M., and Elizabeth C. Hanson. 1982. *Interest and Ideology*. San Francisco, Calif.: W. H. Freeman and Company.

Sarkesian, Sam C., ed. 1980. *Combat Effectiveness: Cohesion, Stress, and the Volunteer Military*. Beverly Hills, Calif.: Sage.

Sarkesian, Sam C. 1998. "The U.S. Military Must Find Its Voice" Orbis 42 (Summer): 423–437.

Scarborough, Rowan. 1992. "Chiefs sound Bosnia alarm; Chaos seen for U.S. troops." *The Washington Times* (August 12): A1.

Schiff, Rebecca L. 1995. "Civil-Military Relations Reconsidered: A Theory of Concordance." *Armed Forces & Society* 22 (Fall): 7–24.

Schlesinger, Arthur M., Jr. 1995. "Back to the Womb?" *Foreign Affairs* 74 (July–August): 2–8.

Schreiber, E.M. 1979. "Authoritarian Attitudes in the United States Army." *Armed Forces & Society* 6 (Fall): 122–131.

Schwoerer, Lois G. 1974. *"No Standing Armies!" The Antimilitary Ideology in Seventeenth-Century England*. Baltimore: The Johns Hopkins University Press.

Sears, Stephen W. 1989. *George B. McClellan: The Young Napoleon*. New York: Ticknor & Fields.

Segal, David R. 1967. *The Socialization of Adolescent Politicians*. Ph.D. dissertation. Department of Sociology. University of Chicago.

Segal, David R. 1975. "Civil-Military Relations in the Mass Public." *Armed Forces & Society* 1 (Winter): 215–229.

Segal, David R. 1986. "Measuring the Institutional/Occupational Change Thesis." *Armed Forces & Society* 12 (Spring): 351–376.

Segal, David R. 1999. "The Influence of Accession and Personnel Policies on Changing Civilian and Military Opinion." Paper prepared for the TISS Conference on Bridging the Gap: Assuring Military Effectiveness when Military Culture Diverges from Civilian Society. Chapel Hill, N.C. (July).

Segal, David R., John D. Blair, Frank Newport, and Susan Stephens. 1974. "Convergence, Isomorphism, and Interdependence at the Civil-Military Interface." *Journal of Political and Military Sociology* 2 (Fall): 157–172.

Segal, David R. and John D. Blair. 1976. "Public Confidence in the U.S. Military." *Armed Forces & Society* 3, (Fall): 3–11.

Segal, David R., and Mady Wechsler Segal. 1976. "The Impact of Military Service on Trust in Government, International Attitudes, and Social Status." In *The Social Psychology of Military Service*, ed. Nancy L. Goldman and David R. Segal. Beverly Hills, Calif.: Sage Publications.

Segal, David R., and Joseph J. Lengermann. 1980. "Professional and Institutional Considerations." In *Combat Effectiveness: Cohesion, Stress, and the Volunteer Military*, ed. Sam C. Sarkesian. London: Sage Publications.

Segal, David R., and Naomi Verdugo. 1994. "Demographic Trends and Personnel Policies as Determinants of the Racial Composition of the Volunteer Army." *Armed Forces & Society* 20 (Summer): 619–632.

Segal, David R. 1995. "U.S. Civil-Military Relations in the Twenty-First Century: A Sociologist's View." *U.S. Civil-Military Relations,* eds. Snider and Carlton-Carew. Washington D.C.: Center for Strategic and International Studies.

Segal, David R., Peter Freedman-Doan, and Patrick O'Malley. 1998a. "Does Enlistment Propensity Predict Accession? High School Seniors' Plans and Subsequent Behavior." *Armed Forces & Society* 25 (Fall): 59–88.

Segal, David R., Thomas J. Burns, William W. Falk, Michael P. Silver, and Bam Dev Sharda. 1998b. "The All-Volunteer Force in the 1970s." *Social Science Quarterly* 79 (March): 390–411.

Segal, David R., Jerald G. Bachman, Peter Freedman-Doan, and Patrick M. O'Malley. 1999. "Propensity to Serve in the U.S. Military: Temporal Trends and Subgroup Differences." *Armed Forces & Society* 25 (Spring): 407–427.

Segal, Mady Wechsler. 1999b. "Gender and the Military." In *Handbook of the Sociology of Gender,* ed. Janet Saltzman Chafetz. New York: Kluwer Academy/Plenum Publishers.

Sellers, Shane. 1998. "Time to Send Clinton to the Showers." *Navy Times* (October 19): 70.

Selznick, Philip. 1992. *The Moral Commonwealth: Social Theory and the Promise of Community.* Berkeley, Calif. and Los Angeles: University of California Press.

Servicemembers Legal Defense Network. 1999. "Conduct Unbecoming: The Fifth Annual Report on 'Don't Ask, Don't Tell, Don't Pursue.'" (March 15). <http://www.sldn.org/reports/fifth/>.

Sharlet, Jeff. 1999. "Why Diplomatic Historians May Be the Victims of Triumphalism." *The Chronicle of Higher Education* (September 24): A19.

Sharon, Ariel, with David Chanoff. 1989. *Warrior: The Autobiography of Ariel Sharon.* New York: Simon & Schuster.

Shepard, Scott. 1994. "Number of ex-military in Congress does about-face." *Austin American-Statesman* (May 30): A3.

Sherman, William Tecumseh. 1990. *Memoirs of General William T. Sherman.* New York: Library of America.

Shields, Patricia M. 1980. "Enlistment During the Vietnam Era and the 'Representation' Issue of the All Volunteer Force." *Armed Forces & Society* 7 (Fall): 134–135.

Shils, Edward A. 1975. *Center and Periphery.* Chicago: University of Chicago Press.

Shils, Edward A., and Morris Janowitz. 1948. "Cohesion and Disintegration in the Wehrmacht in World War II." *Public Opinion Quarterly* 12 (Summer): 280–315.

Shils, Edward A., and Morris Janowitz. 1975. "Cohesion and Disintegration in the Wehrmacht in World War II." Reprinted in Morris Janowitz, *Military Conflict: Essays in the Institutional Analysis of War and Peace.* Beverly Hills, Calif.: Sage.

Shy, John. 1965. *Toward Lexington: The Role of the British Army in the Coming of the American Revolution.* Princeton, N.J.: Princeton University Press.

Siebold, Guy L. 1999. "The Evolution of the Measurement of Cohesion." *Military Psychology* 11 (Spring): 5–26.

Simon, John Y., ed. 1967. *The Papers of Ulysses S. Grant.* Carbondale, Ill.: Southern Illinois University Press.

Simons, Anna. 1997. *The Company They Keep: Life Inside the U.S. Army Special Forces*. New York: Free Press.

Sinaiko, H. Wallace. 1990. "The Last American Draftees." *Armed Forces & Society* 16 (Winter): 241–249.

Skeen, C. Edward. 1974. "The Newburgh Conspiracy Reconsidered." *The William and Mary Quarterly* 31 (April): 273–290.

Skelton, William B. 1992. *An American Profession of Arms: The Army Officer Corps, 1784–1861*. Lawrence, Kans.: University Press of Kansas.

Slater, Jerome. 1977. "Apolitical Warrior or Soldier-Statesman: the Military and the Foreign Policy Process in the Post-Vietnam Era." *Armed Forces & Society* 4 (November): 101–118.

Smith, Louis. 1951. *American Democracy and Military Power: A Study of Civil Control of the Military Power in the United States*. Chicago: University of Chicago Press.

Smith, R. Jeffrey. 1999. "A GI's Home is His Fortress: High-Security, High-Comfort U.S. Base in Kosovo Stirs Controversy." *The Washington Post* (October 5): A11.

Smythe, Donald. 1973. *Guerrilla Warrior: The Early Life of John J. Pershing*. New York: Charles Scribners Sons.

Smythe, Donald. 1986. *Pershing: General of the Armies*. Bloomington, Ind.: Indiana University Press.

Snider, Don M., Robert A. Priest and Felisa Lewis. 2001. "The Civilian-Military Gap and Professional Military Education at the Precommissioning Level." *Armed Forces & Society* 27 (Winter):249–272.

Sniderman, Paul M., Richard A. Brody, and Philip E. Tetlock. 1991. *Reasoning and Choice: Explorations in Political Psychology*. New York: Cambridge University Press.

Snyder, Jack. 1984. *The Ideology of the Offensive: Military Decisionmaking and the Disasters of 1914*. Ithaca, N.Y.: Cornell University Press.

Snyder, William P. 1984. "Officer Recruitment for the All-Volunteer Force: Trends and Prospects." *Armed Forces & Society* 10 (Spring): 401–425.

Snyder, William P. 1994. "Military Retirees: A Portrait of the Community." *Armed Forces & Society* 20 (Summer): 581–598.

Solorio v. United States, 483 U.S. 435 (1987).

Sorensen, Kathleen and Thomas Field. 1994. *Projections of the U.S. Veteran Populations 1990 to 2010*. Washington, D.C.: National Center for Veteran Analysis and Statistics.

Spector, Ronald H. 1999. "Operation Who Says: Tension Between Civilian and Military Leaders is Inevitable." *The Washington Post* (August 22): B02.

Stein, Maurice. 1960. *The Eclipse of Community*. Princeton, N.J.: Princeton University Press.

Stevenson, Richard W. 1999. "As G.O.P. Hopes for Tax Cuts Dim, Debt Reduction Gains in Appeal." *The New York Times* (September 11): A1.

Stiehm, Judith Hicks. 2001. "Civil-Military Relations in War College Curricula." *Armed Forces & Society* 27 (Winter):273–292.

Stinchcombe, Arthur. 1973. "Comment on 'The Impact of Military Service on Authoritarian Attitudes.'" *American Journal of Sociology* 79 (July): 157–159.

Su, Tsai-Tsu, Mark S. Kamlet, and David C. Mowery. 1993. "Modeling U.S. Budgetary and Fiscal Policy Outcomes: A Disaggregated, Systemwide Perspective." *American Journal of Political Science* 37 (August): 213–245.

Sullivan, John L., James Piereson, and George E. Marcus. 1982. *Political Tolerance and American Democracy.* Chicago: University of Chicago Press.

Svechin, Aleksandr A. 1991. *Strategy,* ed. Kent D. Lee, trans. unknown. Minneapolis, Minn.: East View Publications.

Sydnor, Charles W., Jr. 1977. *Soldiers of Destruction: The SS Death's Head Division, 1933–1945.* Princeton, N.J.: Princeton University Press.

Tanter, Raymond. 1990. *Who's at the Helm? Lessons of Lebanon.* Boulder, Colo.: Westview Press.

Tate, Katherine. 1994. *From Protest to Politics.* Cambridge, Mass.: Harvard University Press.

Thompson, James D. 1967. *Organizations in Action.* New York: McGraw-Hill.

Toffler, Alvin, and Heidi. 1993. *War and Anti-War.* New York: Warner Books.

Towell, Pat. 1999a. "Air War with the Pentagon: Jerry Lewis and the F-22." *Congressional Quarterly Weekly* (August 14): 1992–1996.

Towell, Pat. 1999b. "Is Military's 'Warrior' Culture in America's Best Interest?" *Congressional Quarterly Weekly* (January 2): 25–28.

Trask, David F. 1993. *The AEF and Coalition Warmaking, 1917–1918.* Lawrence, Kans.: University Press of Kansas.

Trubowitz, Peter. 1998. *Defining the National Interest.* Chicago: University of Chicago Press.

Trubowitz, Peter, and Brian E. Roberts. 1992. "Regional Interests and the Reagan Military Buildup." *Regional Studies* 26 (6): 555–567.

Tufte, Edward. 1978. *The Political Control of the Economy.* Princeton, N.J.: Princeton University Press.

U.S. Bureau of the Census. 1975. *Historical Statistics of the United States: Colonial Times to 1970,* Part 1. Washington, D.C.: U.S. Government Printing Office.

U.S. Bureau of the Census. 1998. *Statistical Abstract of the United States: 1998.* Washington, D.C.: U.S. Government Printing Office.

U.S. Congress, Senate, Committee on Armed Services. 1985. *Defense Organization: The Need for Change,* Senate Print 99-86, Staff Report to the Committee on Armed Services, 99th Cong., 1st sess. Washington, D.C.: Government Printing Office.

Upton, Emory. 1878. *The Armies of Asia and Europe.* New York: D. Appleton & Company.

Upton, Emory. 1904. *The Military Policy of the United States.* Washington, D.C.: Government Printing Office.

Van Creveld, Martin. 1982. *Combat Power: German and U.S. Army Performance, 1939–1945.* Westport, Conn.: Greenwood.

Van Doorn, Jacques. 1975. "The Decline of the Mass Army in the West." *Armed Forces & Society* 1 (February): 147–157.

Van Doren, Carl. 1943. *Muting in January: The Story of a Crisis in the Continental Army now for the first time fully told from many hitherto unknown or neglected sources both American and British.* New York: The Viking Press.

Van Evera, Stephen. 1986. "Why Cooperation Failed in 1914." In *Cooperation Under Anarchy*, ed. Kenneth Oye. Princeton, N.Y.: Princeton University Press.

Vandiver, Frank E. 1977. *Black Jack: The Life and Times of John J. Pershing*. College Station, Tex.: Texas A&M University Press.

Vistica, Gregory L. 1995. *Fall From Glory: The Men Who Sank the U.S. Navy*. New York: Simon and Schuster.

Waldman, Amy. 1997. "Strangers in Uniform." *Utne Reader* (March/April):64ff.

Waldron, Jeremy, ed. 1984. *Theories of Rights*. Oxford: Oxford University Press.

Walt, Stephen M. 1991. "The Renaissance of Security Studies." *International Studies Quarterly* 35 (June): 211–240.

Waltz, Kenneth J. 1979. *Theory of International Politics*. Reading, Mass.: Addison-Wesley.

Wasby, Stephen L. 1992. "History of the Court: Rights Consciousness in Contemporary Society." In *The Oxford Companion to the Supreme Court of the United States*, ed. Kermit L. Hall. New York: Oxford University Press.

Watson, Bruce W., and Peter G. Tsouras, eds. 1991. *Operation Just Cause: The U.S. Intervention in Panama*. Boulder, Colo.: Westview Press.

Watson, Mark Skinner. 1950. *Chief of Prewar Plans and Preparations (United States Army in World War II: The War Department)*. Washington, D.C.: Historical Division United States Army.

Webb, James H., Jr. 1997. "The War on Military Culture." *The Weekly Standard* (January 20): 17–22.

Webb, James H., Jr. 1998. "Military Leadership in a Changing Society." Naval War College Conference on Ethics (November 16).

Webb, James H., Jr. 1999. "The Silence of the Admirals." *Proceedings of the United States Naval Institute* 125 (January): 29–34.

Webb, James H., Jr. 2000. "Interview: James Webb." *Proceedings of the United States Naval Institute* 126 (April): 78–81.

Webb, Willard J., and Ronald H. Cole. 1995. *The Chairmen of the Joint Chiefs of Staff*. Washington, D.C.: Historical Division, Joint Chiefs of Staff.

Weible, Jack. 1998. "The New Military." *Army Times* (July 13): 12–14.

Weigley, Russell F. 1967. *History of the United States Army*. New York: Macmillan.

Weigley, Russell F. 1993. "The American Military and the Principle of Civilian Control from McClellan to Powell." *Journal of Military History* 57 (October): 27–58.

Weigley, Russell F. 1999. "The Soldier, the Statesman, and the Military Historian: The First Annual George C. Marshall Lecture in Military History." *The Journal of Military History*. 63 (October): 807–822.

Weinberger, Caspar. 1984. "Shultz vs. Weinberger—When to Use U.S. Power" From a speech to the National Press Club in Washington on November 28, 1984. *U.S. News & World Report* (December 24): 21.

Weisberg, Jacob. 1991. "A Slight Draft." *The New Republic* (March 11): 12–14.

Welsh, Sandy. 1999. "Gender and Sexual Harassment." *Annual Review of Sociology* 25: 169–190.

Wendt, Alexander. 1994. "Collective Identity Formation and the International State." *American Political Science Review* 88 (June):384–396.

Who's Who in American History. 1975. "King, Ernest Joseph." Chicago, Ill.: Marquis Who's Who.

Wiegand, Krista E., and David L. Paletz. 1999. "The Elite Media and the Military-Civilian Culture Gap." Paper presented at the annual meeting of the American Political Science Association. Atlanta, Ga. (September).

Wiegand, Krista E., and David L. Paletz. 2001. "The Elite Media and the Military-Civilian Culture Gap." *Armed Forces & Society* 27 (Winter):183–204.

Williams, John Allen. 1999. "The Military and Modern Society: Civil-Military Relations in Post–Cold War America." *The World & I* (September):307–317.

Williams, John T. 1990. "The Political Manipulation of Macroeconomic Policy." *American Political Science Review* 84 (September):1101–1123.

Williams, Katherine Y., and Charles A. O'Reilly, III. 1998. "Demography and Diversity in Organizations: A Review of 40 Years of Research." *Research in Organizational Behavior* 20:77–140.

Williams, Kenneth P. 1950–1959. *Lincoln Finds a General: A Military Study of the Civil War.* New York: The Macmillan Company.

Williams, T. Harry. 1952. *Lincoln and His Generals.* New York: Knopf.

Wilson, James Q. 1989. *Bureaucracy: What Government Agencies Do and Why They Do It.* New York: Basic Books.

Winslow, Donna. 1997. *The Canadian Airborne Regiment in Somalia: A Socio-cultural Inquiry.* Ottawa, Canada: Canadian Government Publishing.

Wittkopf, Eugene R. 1990. *Faces of Internationalism: Public Opinion and American Foreign Policy.* Durham, N.C.: Duke University Press.

Wong, Leonard, and Jeffrey McNully. 1994. "Downsizing the Army: Some Policy Implications Affecting Survivors." *Armed Forces & Society* 20 (Winter):199–216.

Woodward, Bob. 1991. *The Commanders.* New York: Simon & Schuster.

About the Authors

Jerald G. Bachman is a program director and distinguished research scientist at the Survey Research Center, Institute for Social Research, the University of Michigan. For more than three decades he has directed a program of social research on youth and social issues, beginning with the Youth in Transition project, and continuing with the Monitoring the Future project. His books include *The All-Volunteer Force*, and *Smoking, Drinking, and Drug Use in Young Adulthood*.

William T. Bianco is Associate Professor in the Department of Political Science at the Pennsylvania State University. He received his PhD. from the University of Rochester. His primary research focuses on American politics and the U.S. Congress. Among his article and other publications are the book *Trust: Representatives and Constituents*. He has also served as a consultant to political candidates and government agencies.

James Burk is Professor of Sociology at Texas A&M University and past editor of *Armed Forces & Society*. He has published numerous articles on civil-military relations in democratic societies and is currently studying U.S. Supreme Court rulings about the military obligation of citizens.

Eliot A. Cohen is Professor of Strategic Studies at the Paul H. Nitze School of Advanced International Studies. His books include *Military Misfortunes: The Anatomy of Failure in War* (with John Gooch, Free Press, 1990), and *Revolution in Warfare? Air Power in the Gulf War* (with Thomas Keaney, Naval Institute Press, 1995). He directed the United States Air Force's multi-volume *Gulf War Air Power Survey* and writes frequently for a variety of scholarly and policy journals. His next book, *Supreme Command*, is a study of civil-military relations in wartime.

Lindsay P. Cohn is a research associate of the Triangle Institute for Security Studies and a Ph.D. candidate in Political Science at Duke University. She specializes in international relations and national security.

James A. Davis is a research associate at the National Opinion Research Center (NORC) and Senior Lecturer in Sociology at the University of Chicago. He was previously Professor of Sociology at Harvard University and Dartmouth College. Since 1972, he has been a Principal Investigator for the NORC General Social Survey, an annual sampling of American social behavior and attitudes. His military experience culminated in appointment as a Cadet Captain in the West Rockford (Illinois) Senior High School Junior ROTC in 1945.

Michael C. Desch is Associate Professor and Associate Director of the Patterson School of Diplomacy and International Commerce at the University of Kentucky. He is the author, most recently, of *Civilian Control of the Military: The Changing Security Environment* (Baltimore: The Johns Hopkins University Press, 1999).

Peter D. Feaver is Associate Professor of Political Science at Duke University and Director of the Triangle Institute for Security Studies, a research consortium of Duke University, the University of North Carolina at Chapel Hill, and North Carolina State University. He is author of *Guarding the Guardians* (Cornell University Press, 1992) and a book-length manuscript on civil-military relations theory, *Armed Servants: Agency, Oversight, and Civil-Military Relations*, as well as dozens of articles and book chapters on civil-military relations, nuclear proliferation, and national security. He is a Lieutenant Commander in the U.S. Naval Reserve (IRR).

Benjamin O. Fordham is Assistant Professor of Political Science at the University at Albany, SUNY. He is the author of *Building the Cold War Consensus: The Political Economy of United States National Security Policy, 1949–51* (University of Michigan Press, 1998) as well as articles on American foreign policy in journals such as *International Organization, International Studies Quarterly, The Journal of Politics,* and *The Journal of Conflict Resolution.* He received his Ph.D. from the University of North Carolina.

Peter Freedman-Doan is a research associate with the Monitoring the Future program at the University of Michigan's Institute for Social Research. He is the author of articles on school and education related issues, and he has co-authored several articles on American youth and the military. He is currently involved in a research project that examines the linkages between changes in young adult roles and changes in alcohol, tobacco, and illicit drug use.

Paul Gronke is assistant professor of political science at Reed College. His scholarly interests include public opinion, elections, and American legislatures.

Ole R. Holsti, George V. Allen Professor Emeritus of International Affairs in the Political Science Department at Duke University since 1974, served as President of the International Studies Association in 1979–80. He has received lifetime achievement awards from the American Political Science Association and the International Society of Political Psychology, the Teacher-Scholar Award from the International Studies Association, and two undergraduate teaching awards from Duke. Holsti served on active duty in the 4th Infantry Division (1956–58) and in the active reserves (1954–56, 1958–62).

Richard H. Kohn is Professor of History and Chair of the Curriculum in Peace, War, and Defense at the University of North Carolina at Chapel Hill. A specialist in American military history and civil-military relations, he is the author, co-author, editor, or co-editor of many books, including *Eagle and Sword: The Federalists and the Creation of the Military Establishment in America, 1783–1802* (Free Press, 1975) and *The United States Military under the Constitution of the United States, 1789–1989* (New York University Press, 1991). His current work focuses on war as a human phenomenon, civilian control of the military, and presidential war leadership in the United States.

Jamie Markham is a Second Lieutenant in the United States Air Force, and a 1998 graduate of Harvard University.

Laura L. Miller is Assistant Professor of Sociology at UCLA. She received her Ph.D. from Northwestern University, and then spent two years as a postdoctoral fellow at the John M. Olin Institute for Strategic Studies at Harvard. From 1992–1998, Miller interviewed and surveyed soldiers at over a dozen stateside posts, bases in Germany, and during peacekeeping operations in Somalia, Macedonia, Haiti, and Bosnia. Miller is writing a book on gender relations in the US Army.

Patrick M. O'Malley is a senior research scientist at the Survey Research Center, Institute for Social Research, the University of Michigan. His principal research activity has been the Monitoring the Future project. He has published extensively on the epidemiology and etiology of use and abuse of psychoactive drugs, including the policy implications of this research. He has also co-authored a series of articles on youth and the military, including research on drug use patterns among military youth and their civilian contemporaries.

Peter J. Roman is Associate Professor and Chairman of the Department of Political Science at Duquesne University. He is author of *Eisenhower and the*

Missile Gap (Cornell University Press, 1995) as well as numerous articles. He is writing a book with David W. Tarr on the role on the U.S. military leadership in national security policymaking.

David R. Segal is Professor of Sociology and Affiliate Professor of Government and Politics and of Public Affairs at the University of Maryland, where he directs the Center for Research on Military Organization. He is also president of the Inter-University Seminar on Armed Forces and Society. His books include *The Social Psychology of Military Service* (Sage, 1976), *Recruiting for Uncle Sam* (University Press of Kansas, 1989), *Peacekeepers and their Wives* (Greenwood, 1993), and *The Postmodern Military* (Oxford University Press, 2000). He has published extensively on youth attitudes toward the military, and on the attitudes of military personnel.

David W. Tarr is Professor Emeritus in the Department of Political Science, University of Wisconsin-Madison. He is author of numerous books and articles on national security, including *Nuclear Deterrence and National Security* (Longman, 1991). He is writing a book with Peter Roman on the role of the U.S. military leadership in national security policymaking.

Russell F. Weigley is Distinguished University Professor Emeritus in the Center for the Study of Force and Diplomacy, Temple University, Philadelphia. He is a past president of the American Military Institute and the 1989 recipient of that organization's Samuel Eliot Morison Prize for his contributions to military history. Those contributions include *Towards an American Army: Military Thought from Washington to Marshall* (Columbia University Press, 1962); *History of the United States Army* (Macmillan, 1967; enlarged edition, Indiana University Press, 1984); *The American Way of War: A History of United States Strategy and Military Policy* (Indiana University Press, 1973); *Eisenhower's Lieutenants: The Campaign of France and Germany, 1944–1945* ((Indiana University Press, 1982); and, more recently, *The Age of Battles: The Quest for Decisive Warfare from Breitenfeld to Waterloo* ((Indiana University Press, 1991) and *A Great Civil War: A Military and Political History, 1861–1865* (Indiana University Press, 2000), winner of the Lincoln Prize.

John Allen Williams is Associate Professor of Political Science at Loyola University Chicago and executive director of the Inter-University Seminar on Armed Forces and Society. A retired captain in the naval reserve, he was a designated strategic plans officer with extensive Pentagon experience on service, joint, and civilian staffs. His most recent work is *The Postmodern Military: Armed Forces After the Cold War* (Oxford University Press, 2000), which he co-edited with Charles C. Moskos and David R. Segal.

Name Index

Subject Index

BCSIA Studies in International Security

Published by The MIT Press

Sean M. Lynn-Jones and Steven E. Miller, series editors
Karen Motley, executive editor
Belfer Center for Science and International Affairs (BCSIA)
John F. Kennedy School of Government, Harvard University

Allison, Graham T., Owen R. Coté, Jr., Richard A. Falkenrath, and Steven E. Miller, *Avoiding Nuclear Anarchy: Containing the Threat of Loose Russian Nuclear Weapons and Fissile Material* (1996)

Allison, Graham T., and Kalypso Nicolaïdis, eds., *The Greek Paradox: Promise vs. Performance* (1996)

Arbatov, Alexei, Abram Chayes, Antonia Handler Chayes, and Lara Olson, eds., *Managing Conflict in the Former Soviet Union: Russian and American Perspectives* (1997)

Bennett, Andrew, *Condemned to Repetition? The Rise, Fall, and Reprise of Soviet-Russian Military Interventionism, 1973–1996* (1999)

Blackwill, Robert D., and Michael Stürmer, eds., *Allies Divided: Transatlantic Policies for the Greater Middle East* (1997)

Blackwill, Robert D., and Paul Dibb, eds., *America's Asian Alliances* (2000)

Brom, Shlomo, and Yiftah Shapir, eds., *The Middle East Military Balance 1999–2000* (2000)

Brown, Michael E., ed., *The International Dimensions of Internal Conflict* (1996)

Brown, Michael E., and Šumit Ganguly, eds., *Government Policies and Ethnic Relations in Asia and the Pacific* (1997)

Carter, Ashton B., and John P. White, eds., *Keeping the Edge: Managing Defense for the Future* (2001)

Elman, Colin, and Miriam Fendius Elman, eds., *Bridges and Boundaries: Historians, Political Scientists, and the Study of International Relations* (2000)

Elman, Miriam Fendius, ed., *Paths to Peace: Is Democracy the Answer?* (1997)

Falkenrath, Richard A., *Shaping Europe's Military Order: The Origins and Consequences of the CFE Treaty* (1994)

Falkenrath, Richard A., Robert D. Newman, and Bradley A. Thayer, *America's Achilles' Heel: Nuclear, Biological, and Chemical Terrorism and Covert Attack* (1998)

Feaver, Peter D., and Richard H. Kohn, eds., *Soldiers and Civilians: The Civil-Military Gap and American National Security* (2001)

Feldman, Shai, *Nuclear Weapons and Arms Control in the Middle East* (1996)

Forsberg, Randall, ed., *The Arms Production Dilemma: Contraction and Restraint in the World Combat Aircraft Industry* (1994)

Hagerty, Devin T., *The Consequences of Nuclear Proliferation: Lessons from South Asia* (1998)

Heymann, Philip B., *Terrorism and America: A Commonsense Strategy for a Democratic Society* (1998)

Kokoshin, Andrei A., *Soviet Strategic Thought, 1917–91* (1998)

Lederberg, Joshua, *Biological Weapons: Limiting the Threat* (1999)

Shields, John M., and William C. Potter, eds., *Dismantling the Cold War: U.S. and NIS Perspectives on the Nunn-Lugar Cooperative Threat Reduction Program* (1997)

Tucker, Jonathan B., ed., *Toxic Terror: Assessing Terrorist Use of Chemical and Biological Weapons* (2000)

Utgoff, Victor A., ed., *The Coming Crisis: Nuclear Proliferation, U.S. Interests, and World Order* (2000)

Williams, Cindy, ed., *Holding the Line: U.S. Defense Alternatives for the Early 21st Century* (2001)

The Robert and Renée Belfer Center for Science and International Affairs

Graham T. Allison, Director
John F. Kennedy School of Government
Harvard University
79 JFK Street, Cambridge, MA 02138
(617) 495-1400

The Belfer Center for Science and International Affairs (BCSIA) is the hub of research, teaching, and training in international security affairs, environmental and resource issues, and science and technology policy at Harvard's John F. Kennedy School of Government. The Center's mission is to provide leadership in advancing policy-relevant knowledge about the most important challenges of international security and other critical issues where science, technology, and international affairs intersect.

BCSIA's leadership begins with the recognition of science and technology as driving forces transforming international affairs. The Center integrates insights of social scientists, natural scientists, technologists, and practitioners with experience in government, diplomacy, the military, and business to address these challenges. The Center pursues its mission in four complementary research programs:

- The International Security Program (ISP) addresses the most pressing threats to U.S. national interests and international security.

- The Environment and Natural Resources Program (ENRP) is the locus of Harvard's interdisciplinary research on resource and environmental problems and policy responses.

- The Science, Technology, and Public Policy (STPP) program analyzes ways in which science and technology policy influence international security, resources, environment, and development, and such cross-cutting issues as technological innovation and information infrastructure.

- The Strengthening Democratic Institutions (SDI) project catalyzes support for three great transformations in Russia, Ukraine, and the other republics of the former Soviet Union—to sustainable democracies, free market economies, and cooperative international relations.

The heart of the Center is its resident research community of more than one hundred scholars: Harvard faculty, analysts, practitioners, and each year a new, interdisciplinary group of research fellows. BCSIA sponsors frequent seminars, workshops, and conferences, many open to the public; maintains a substantial specialized library; and publishes books, monographs, and discussion papers. The Center's International Security Program, directed by Steven E. Miller, publishes the BCSIA Studies in International Security, and sponsors and edits the quarterly journal *International Security*.

The Center is supported by an endowment established with funds from Robert and Renée Belfer, the Ford Foundation, and Harvard University, by foundation grants, by individual gifts, and by occasional government contracts.